Wertheim Publications in Industrial Relations

Established in 1923 by the family of the late Jacob Wertheim "for the support of original research in the field of industrial cooperation. . . ."

Wertheim Publications in Industrial Relations

STUDIES IN LABOR–MANAGEMENT HISTORY

The CIO Challenge to the AFL

A History of the
American Labor Movement
1935–1941

Walter Galenson

HARVARD UNIVERSITY PRESS
CAMBRIDGE · 1960

© *1960 by the President and Fellows of Harvard College*

Distributed in Great Britain by
Oxford University Press
London

Library of Congress Catalog Card Number 60–5390

Printed in the United States of America

TO MARJORIE

FOREWORD

On November 2, 1954, announcement was made of a research project at Harvard University on the history of labor-management relations in the United States in recent decades. The anticipated merger of the AFL-CIO appeared to be a good vantage point from which to review and to interpret the epochal developments in the industrial relations system of the United States during the preceding quarter century.

The membership of labor organizations had increased fourfold from the levels of the late 1920's; the impact of government in labor-management relations had been altered and vastly expanded by the Wagner Act and the Taft-Hartley law in addition to wartime policies; collective bargaining had been extended to new industries and to new problems; the policies and internal organizations of industrial managements had been transformed to deal with industrial relations; the internal government of international unions was undergoing significant changes; and the labor movement had experienced a dramatic split which was to come to a formal close with the merger convention of December 1955.

Within this large range of interests, the project was begun with two general studies of the labor movement treating the period up to World War II and six studies of particular international unions, collective bargaining relationships, or industries. The histories of individual international unions and labor-management relations were designed to be of interest in themselves, to contribute to an understanding of collective bargaining institutions over a longer period, and to reinforce the two initial general studies of the labor movement. Additional volumes are planned which treat other topics and issues in further analysis of labor-management relations and labor organizations. The history of the experience of labor organizations in the South, for instance, is now in preparation; more theoretical and general interpretative work can be built upon these studies.

The project was planned jointly with professors Walter Galenson and Lloyd Ulman of the University of California, Berkeley. Both are former colleagues at Harvard University, and each spent a further year in research on this project in Cambridge undertaking responsibility for the two general studies of the labor movement. *The CIO Challenge to the AFL* by Professor Galenson treats the period 1935–1941. Professor Ulman's volume is concerned with the period up to the emergence of the CIO in 1935 and treats the origins and antecedents of industrial unionism as it developed in the 1930's. The first of the studies of particular industries or international unions appeared in 1958: *The Maritime Story: A Study in Labor-Management Relations* by Dr. Joseph P. Goldberg. Among others, the following volumes are in varying stages of preparation or in press: the New York hotel industry by Professor Morris A. Horowitz; the International Association of Machinists by Professor Mark Perlman; the Operating Engineers by Dr. Garth Mangum; the Butcher Workmen by Dr. David Brody; and the American Federation of State, County and Municipal Employees by Mr. Leo Kramer.

It is particularly appropriate that studies in the history of labor-management developments should be financed from a variety of sources: labor organizations, business enterprises, foundations, and the gifts of individuals. The following financial contributions to the general volumes and to the studies of particular industries, collective bargaining relationships, and labor organizations are gratefully acknowledged: the initial grant received from the Philip Murray Memorial Foundation by letter from its Director, Mr. Arthur J. Goldberg, dated May 24, 1954; financial support from the International Association of Bridge, Structural and Ornamental Iron Workers; International Association of Machinists; National Maritime Union of America; Amalgamated Meat Cutters and Butcher Workmen of North America; International Union of Operating Engineers; American Federation of State, County, and Municipal Employees; New York Hotel Trades Council; Hotel Association of New York City, and a number of individual hotels acknowledged in a separate volume; Ebasco Services Incorporated; Martin E. Segal and Company; Conrad N. Hilton Foundation; Mrs. Celia Frank Anderson.

In the instance of each financial contribution it was explicitly agreed that "the standards of scholarship and the interpretation of events would, of course, be the responsibility solely of those scholars working on the project." Moreover, full access to all records and files and magnanimous cooperation in answering questions was granted by every organization making a contribution. This cooperation, support, and interest in the history of labor-management relations and labor organizations is itself one index of the significant changes wrought in labor-management relations in the past generation.

A reassuring discovery of the past five years has been the generosity not only of organizations but also of individuals in making records and files available for research purposes. While the separate volumes make indi vidual acknowledgments, it is especially appropriate to cite here Mr. Benjamin F. Goldstein of Chicago and Mr. Raymond Tor of New York.

The Wertheim Publications in Industrial Relations has provided financial assistance for the publication of this present volume, which is Professor Walter Galenson's third book in the series.

There are two decisive and formative periods in the government of the American labor movement, particularly at the Federation level: the 1880's and the 1930's. These periods reflect some common features. Both followed prolonged periods of unemployment, the most severe in our history. They are probably the only two periods of extensive and spontaneous organizations of workers from below when workers literally sought out organization instead of the more usual traditional pattern of organizers enlisting members or signing collective bargaining agreements with employers. Membership expanded very rapidly. There was sharp and decisive conflict within the labor movement at the Federation level in the middle of both decades.

The struggle in the 1880's between the Knights of Labor and the national unions which comprised the Federation was significantly to shape the constitutional principles of autonomy and exclusive jurisdiction. These principles were not to be seriously questioned for fifty years. The challenge of the CIO in the 1930's, coupled with the governmental determination of "the unit appropriate for the purposes of collective bargaining" and the right of workers to ballot for the union of their choice, were to influence substantially the current constitutional principles of the merged federation as well as to modify significantly the Federation government established seventy years previously. The autonomy of international union affiliates was to a degree qualified, but the more drastic transformation was the replacement of the principle of exclusive jurisdiction by the no-raiding principle, the sanctity of "established collective bargaining relationships." The continuing debate over basic features of the government of the Federation, as evidenced in the action of the 1959 convention, still reflects the issues involved in the internal struggle of the 1930's and the implications of the governmental policies first adopted in the same period.

The critical decades of the 1880's and 1930's also saw the crystallization of attitudes toward industrial unionism. In the history of the American labor movement, industrial unionism has conveyed many different meanings. Often these distinct threads have not been separated.

1. Industrial unionism has been used, particularly by left-wing elements, as a symbol of the solidarity of the working class. It is an element of an

ideology. Many conservative advocates of craft unions have also sought to identify industrial unionism with a radical philosophy.

2. Industrial unionism has been used in an exclusive jurisdictional sense to define the scope of work, an industry rather than a craft or trade, within the province of the union. The exclusive jurisdiction of a union would define its craft, trade, or industrial structure. The Scranton declaration of 1901 in this sense states: "We believe that jurisdiction in such industries by the paramount organization would yield the best results to the workers therein. . . ."

3. Industrial unionism has since 1935 been used in the sense of the unit appropriate for the purposes of collective bargaining, the scope of the election district determined by the government. In this sense there is debate over integrated operations and craft severance.

4. Industrial unionism is sometimes extended to refer to the range of workers represented by the union side of a collective bargaining table. In this sense a council of crafts could represent the full range of workers employed in an enterprise or industry. This form of organization was regarded by some AFL leaders in the 1930's as a major reply to the industrial union challenge of the CIO.

5. Sometimes industrial unionism is used to characterize the technical and skill mix of an industry. For many purposes of union government and collective bargaining it is essential to know the occupational pattern of an industry. It may consist of a large group of semiskilled with a relatively small proportion of skilled trades as in the automobile industry, or it may involve a high proportion of skilled mechanics with only a few unskilled and semiskilled as in many laboratories or in a print shop, or there may be a relatively more even distribution of workers throughout a wide range of skills, as in basic steel, or one or two skilled groups may be dominant, as in a commercial foundry. The antecedents to industrial unionism in the 1930's is the concern of Professor Ulman's general volume.

One major consequence of the events of the 1930's was to turn much of the debate over industrial unionism from a contest over forms of exclusive jurisdiction and structure of international unions into a problem internal to most large international unions. The experience of the Machinists, Teamsters, and Electricians (IBEW) is illustrative. They contain both craft and industrial units in a number of different industries. They are not only in part industrial but multi-industrial. Similarly, in the period since the 1930's, many industrial unions have confronted special problems of wage setting, seniority, occupational jurisdiction, particularly in maintenance departments, and

demand for separate representation in bargaining from their skilled membership. This transformation of the debate over industrial unionism was decisively influenced by the events of the 1930's.

The period from the formation of the CIO to World War II is thus one
of the two most decisive and formative periods in the history of American
industrial relations and within the labor movement. It is the dramatic events
of this crucial period which constitute the exciting and significant narrative
in the present volume by Professor Galenson.

In *The CIO Challenge to the AFL* Professor Galenson brings to the interpretation of this period a career-long interest in the conflict between the
AFL and CIO. His first book was *Rival Unionism in the United States*
(New York, American Council on Public Affairs, 1940). His knowledge of
comparative labor movements gives perspective in appraising these American developments. In addition, the author has had access to a wide range of
basic documents not generally available. The significance of the events, the
access to new materials, and the distinction and industry of the author combine to make a notable volume which is likely to be a standard work for
many years.

November 30, 1959   John T. Dunlop

CONTENTS

TABLES

ILLUSTRATIONS

(*following page 620*)

Sitdown strikers in the Flint General Motors plant, 1936.

The riot at the Chicago Republic Steel Company plant, 1937.

Reuther and Frankensteen after the battle of the Ford overpass, 1937.

Lewis and Murray during the Little Steel strike, 1937.

The leaders of the Steel Workers' Organizing Committee, 1937.
  *Seated, left to right: Philip Murray; D. J. McDonald, Secretary-Treasurer of the
  SWOC. Standing, left to right: William Mitch, Birmingham area; Clinton S. Golden,
  Pittsburgh area; Van A. Bittner, Chicago area; and Lee Pressman, Counsel.*

The leadership of the CIO in 1937.
  *Left to right: John Brophy, Executive Director of the CIO; Charles P. Howard,
  President of the International Typographical Union; John L. Lewis, Chairman of the
  CIO; and Sidney Hillman, President of the Amalgamated Clothing Workers of
  America.*

Members of the Executive Council of the AFL, 1941.
  *Seated, left to right: George Meany, Secretary-Treasurer; William Green, President;
  William Hutcheson, First Vice-President of the AFL and President of the Brotherhood of Carpenters. Standing, left to right: Edward Flore, President of the Hotel
  and Restaurant Workers; Harry C. Bates, President of the Bricklayers Union.*

Tobin and Green study the expulsion of the CIO unions, 1937.

Roosevelt and Lewis during the 1936 Presidential campaign.

Roosevelt and Green on Roosevelt's birthday, 1941.

The AFL-CIO Unity Negotiating Committee, 1937.

AFL and CIO leaders with Secretary of Labor Perkins, 1941.

Lewis and Taylor concluding the captive mine strike, 1941.

AFL Executive Council members at the White House, 1939.
  *Left to right: George Q. Lynch, President of the Patternmakers League of North
  America; G. M. Bugniazet, Secretary of the International Branch of Electrical
  Workers; William Green, President; I. M. Ornburn, Secretary of the Union Label
  Trades Department, AFL; Harry C. Bates, President of the Bricklayers and Plasterers
  International Union; John P. Frey, Secretary of the Metal Trades Department, AFL.*

Author's Preface

The period covered by this study, from the formation of the CIO to the entrance of the United States into the second World War, was one of the most significant in the history of the American labor movement. Within the brief span of six years, American workers in the basic industrial sector of the nation witnessed the transformation of their bargaining organizations from relatively impotent bodies into equal partners in the industrial relations system. It is no exaggeration to say that there was a fundamental, almost revolutionary change in the power relationships of American society. Few episodes in our history have been as dramatic as the upward thrust of American labor, suddenly breaking the bonds of constraint which had checked it for half a century.

The plan of the work is simple. There is an introductory chapter which deals with the establishment of the CIO and the history of its tortuous peace negotiations with the AFL. There then follows a number of chapters on the development of unionism in particular industries. The final section is concerned with substantive issues common to the entire labor movement.

Slicing history into chronological segments is not without its difficulties. The stories of specific industries or unions do not always begin and end at just the right time. It was sometimes necessary to start in the middle of an episode, or to end on an inconclusive note. This problem proved less serious for the newly formed CIO unions than for the older AFL organizations. But even for the latter, I tried to focus on the central problems that faced the organizations, in order to keep the narrative from hanging in mid-air.

During the four years of accumulating the data that have gone into this volume, I incurred a heavy indebtedness to the many people who were generous enough to give me the benefit of their advice and assistance. Among those who read and commented upon portions of the manuscript were Arthur J. Goldberg of Goldberg, Feller and Bredhoff; Meyer Bernstein and Otis Brubaker of the United Steelworkers of America; Nat Weinberg and Frank Winn of the United Automobile, Aircraft and Agricultural Implement Workers; Professor Vernon H. Jensen of the New York State School of Industrial and Labor Relations; President L. S. Buckmaster of the United

Rubber, Cork, Linoleum and Plastic Workers of America; President Jacob S. Potofsky of the Amalgamated Clothing Workers of America; Solomon Barkin of the Textile Workers Union of America; President Ralph Helstein and Leslie Orear of the United Packinghouse Workers of America; Secretary-Treasurer Patrick E. Gorman and Hilton Hanna of the Amalgamated Meat Cutters and Butcher Workmen of North America; President O. A. Knight of the Oil, Chemical and Atomic Workers' International Union; Joseph P. Goldberg of the United States Department of Labor; Herman E. Cooper of the National Maritime Union; Professor Mark Perlman of Johns Hopkins University; Professor S. M. Lipset of the University of California, Berkeley; Matthew A. Kelly of the New York Employing Printers' Association, Inc.; Professor Morris A. Horowitz of Northeastern University; and Professor Philip Taft of Brown University. I am indebted to Professor Horowitz for research assistance on the electrical manufacturing industry and the railroads, and to Francis Gates, librarian of the Labor Collection at the University of California Library, for his unfailingly cheerful and prompt response to requests for publications that were often difficult to locate and secure.

This study is part of a project that was conceived jointly with Professors Lloyd Ulman of the University of California, Berkeley, and John T. Dunlop of Harvard University. Professor Ulman is preparing a similar volume covering the half dozen years immediately preceding 1936, and we spent many long hours in various parts of the country working together on materials of common interest. His sharp intelligence and never failing good humor helped turn what might have been a burdensome task into a genuinely pleasant one.

Professor Dunlop's contribution cannot be recorded adequately within the brief scope of this preface. He was indefatigable in tracking down important sources of documentary information, and helped open doors that might otherwise have remained tightly shut. He read the entire manuscript from the first word to the last, and his incisive line-by-line comment would make a small volume in itself. His great knowledge of the American labor movement, his keen insights into its history, structure, and practices, were unselfishly placed at my disposal. It is no exaggeration to say that without Professor Dunlop's assistance and encouragement, this study might never have seen the light of day.

My wife, to whom the volume is dedicated, also read the entire manuscript, and her suggestions did much to improve it both from the point of view of style and substance. Mrs. Ruth Whitman of the Harvard University

Press undertook the arduous editorial task, and it is a pleasure to record that our previously established amicable editor-author relationship has survived this latest obstacle unimpaired.

While working on this study, I was a Research Associate of the Institute of Industrial Relations at the University of California, Berkeley, and I would like to express my appreciation to the Institute and to its Director, Professor Arthur M. Ross, for the very considerable degree of help that was accorded me.

It goes without saying that I am solely responsible for any errors and shortcomings that remain. Had I accepted all the suggestions that were made to me, the end result would undoubtedly have been a better book, but it would not have been my own.

Walter Galenson

Berkeley, January 1959

The CIO Challenge to the AFL

1

Background of the Struggle

Formation of the Committee for Industrial Organization

The defeat of the industrial union forces at the 1935 convention of the American Federation of Labor marked a new epoch in American labor history. The establishment of the Committee for Industrial Organization heralded a split in the forces of labor deeper and more permanent than anything in the past. For two decades, the factories, the press, and the legislative halls of the nation were to resound with strife between the contesting groups, each attempting to secure the allegiance of workers and to enroll them within its ranks. Seldom, even where political ideological factors separated segments of a national labor movement, has interunion warfare been more bitter and more violent than that which characterized the American scene beginning in 1935.

During the closing days of the 1935 AFL convention, after the decision had been made against industrial unionism, a small group of trade union leaders representing the industrial union bloc in the AFL met informally to consider the next step. The group consisted of John L. Lewis, president of the United Mine Workers; Charles Howard, president of the International Typographical Union; Sidney Hillman, president of the Amalgamated Clothing Workers; and David Dubinsky, president of the International Ladies' Garment Workers' Union. The group discussed "the advisability of keeping the unions favoring the industrial union form of organization for the mass production industries in contact with each other and for cementing their forces for future AFL conventions." [1] It was generally believed that no formal action was taken at this meeting, and that there was merely agreement to meet again to discuss further action. [2] The minutes of the subsequent meeting of the group on November 9, 1935, however — the date usually given as the birthday of the CIO — state: "After extended discussion of organization problems in mass production and other corporate controlled industries, a motion was adopted by unanimous vote to make the temporary organization permanent. . . ." [3] The implication is clear: even before the AFL convention had come to a close, a temporary committee had been established to fight for the principle of industrial unionism.[4] In view of previous and subsequent events, it is difficult to escape the conclusion that John L. Lewis had come to the convention determined to act, and without delay, in the event that the convention took a turn unfavorable to his point of view.

It is interesting to recall the subsequent careers of the four participants of the Atlantic City conference which gave rise to the CIO. Howard died a few years later, having failed to bring his organization into the CIO with him. Dubinsky, the most cautious and hesitant of the group, steered his union out of the CIO after a few years of uneasy partnership. Lewis was of course the chief architect of the CIO, but he too was to repudiate it and withdraw. The Amalgamated Clothing Workers alone among the four unions stayed with the CIO until the final merger with the AFL, though even in this case a split was narrowly averted in 1940. The unions which came to comprise the bulk of the CIO were either in their infancy or not yet born in 1935.

Whatever the intentions of the participants in the Atlantic City conference, it was not long before more positive steps were taken. At a conference called by Lewis on November 9, 1935, the Committee for Industrial Organization was formally established. In addition to the original participants, four international union leaders were in attendance: Thomas F. McMahon of the United Textile Workers; Max Zaritsky of the Hatters, Cap and Millinery Workers' Union;[5] Harvey C. Fremming of the Oil Workers; and Thomas H. Brown of the Mine, Mill and Smelter Workers. The Oil Workers Union was in the throes of a bitter jurisdictional dispute with the Boilermakers and other building trades, while the Mine, Mill and Smelter Workers had clashed with the Metal Trades over jurisdictional rights in the Anaconda Copper Mining Company. Zaritsky appears to have been motivated primarily by a strong ideological commitment to the principle of industrial unionism, since his organization had but recently settled a long-standing quarrel with the Hatters' Union through amalgamation, and had no current jurisdictional difficulties. It is not entirely clear why McMahon, an old-line trade unionist who had once belonged to the Knights of Labor, decided to join, but his organization was strongly committed to the principle of industrial organization.[6] The six unions[7] initially comprising the CIO paid per capita tax on 828,000 members to the AFL at the end of 1935, compared with a total paid membership of 3,308,000 for the entire AFL.[8]

A number of other organizations which had voted with the industrial union bloc, or had displayed some sympathy, were invited to join with the dissidents. Formal invitations were sent to the Bakery Workers, the Brewery Workers, the Hotel and Restaurant Workers, the Flat Glass Workers, and the Brick and Clay Workers.[9] The Flat Glass Workers joined almost immediately, and the Brewery Workers eventually. The Bakery Workers replied that they "had refrained from affiliation with the Committee for Industrial Organization not because we were out of harmony with the apparent purpose of the Committee, but because we felt that the status of our organization in the general labor movement as well as our make-up, especially the importance of our label, could not afford to invite or bear the effect of any possible reprisal." [10] It may be surmised that similar reasons prevented other defections.

The Committee selected Lewis as president, Howard as secretary, and John Brophy as director. The latter, who had been a foe of Lewis in the 1920's, and had been expelled from the Miners' Union after a factional fight, had begun to work for Lewis in 1933. He was the first of the many miners who were despatched into the front lines of organization. Lewis' willingness thus to use a former leader of the left-wing Brookwood movement[11] attests to the fact that his conceptions of trade unionism had undergone a considerable shift, though the fact that Brophy had been a working coal miner for twenty-one years, and thus qualified as a member of the labor elite in Lewis' eyes, undoubtedly helped him to accept this former opponent. The Mine Workers, the Amalgamated Clothing Workers, and the ILGWU each pledged $5,000 to the CIO to enable it to start its activities.[12]

A program was formulated, which read in part:

The purpose of the Committee is to be encouragement and promotion of organization of the unorganized workers in mass production and other industries upon an industrial basis, as outlined in the minority report of the Resolutions Committee submitted to the convention of the American Federation of Labor at Atlantic City; to foster recognition and acceptance of collective bargaining in such industries; to counsel and advise unorganized and newly organized groups of workers; to bring them under the banner and in affiliation with the American Federation of Labor.

The attitude of members of the Committee as unanimously expressed was that its work would be to make organization efforts more effective, avoid injury to established National and International and Federal Labor Unions, and modernize the organization policies of the American Federation of Labor to meet the requirements of workers under modern industrial conditions.[13]

The conciliatory tone of this statement was soon offset by Lewis' curt resignation as a vice-president of the American Federation of Labor on November 23. Lewis took this step, which could not fail to cause a further deterioration of already strained relations, without consulting the other members of the CIO, and it was the first instance of the manner in which he was thenceforth to force the pace toward dualism. At the next meeting of the CIO, on December 9, Lewis offered his fellow members the following reasons for his resignation:

I realized that some would feel that my resignation was impetuous. It was a methodical attempt to dramatize what the committee is trying to do. My place on the Executive Council was worked out, and I couldn't attend a meeting until June. The Committee was not available to discuss the matter with. I had to pick a time when nothing else was on the front page. I resigned on Saturday A.M., figured that delay in explanation would make people draw on their imagination. . . . On Monday I met the press and gave them the background. We had five days of continuing publicity. Then I was asked to speak on the Columbia network. . . . I've been told that Green and the craft unionists think there's a deep dark reason back of all this of a political nature — that the Roosevelt administration encouraged our fight at Atlantic City.[14]

This artlessly frank explanation nevertheless contained the essential truth of the matter: Lewis was determined to break with the AFL, and used his resignation as a means of dramatizing the split and of driving a further wedge between the AFL and the CIO. He was obviously convinced that no action could be expected from the AFL, in view of the tenor of the debates at the 1935 AFL convention, and the reluctance of the Executive Council to move on the issue of industrial unionism. He was filled with a sense of urgency, believing that the time was ripe for extension of organization into the mass production industries, fired, no doubt, by the success with which the Miners' Union had used the favorable political climate swiftly to organize the coal mining industry in 1933. Lewis was disgusted with the preoccupation of the AFL craft unions with jurisdictional problems, and his experience as a member of the AFL Executive Council had not made him more sanguine. Thus, in May, 1935, he had expressed himself in the following vein with regard to the failure of the council to grant industrial union charters:

It still remains that some six months have gone by since we adopted that resolution in San Francisco and there still remains the fact that there has been no administration of that policy, no execution of the promissory note that the Federation held out to the millions of workers in the mass production industry and heralded on the pages of the newspapers and neither do I understand there is any immediate desire to carry out that policy . . . under the principles laid down by Vice-President Wharton there will be no execution of this policy because there is no industry in this country in which there is not employed workers who come under the jurisdiction of affiliated national unions.[15]

Relationships were not improved by a subsequent interchange of correspondence between Lewis and William Green, AFL president. On November 23, Green had sent to each member of the CIO a letter warning against the continuance of the Committee. He pointed out that the CIO could be regarded as dual in character; that it might eventually lead to separation, strife, and bitterness in the labor movement; and that all unions were bound to abide by the decisions of the convention.[16] Howard replied to this appeal in the name of the CIO, in a lengthy, polite letter in which he defended the right of the industrial union bloc to promote its views by educational activities. He stated firmly:

It is *not* the intent, aim or purpose of the Committee for Industrial Organization to "raid" the membership of any established national or international union.

It is *not* the intent, aim, or purpose to infringe upon the rightful jurisdiction of any chartered national or international union.

It is *not* the intent, aim or purpose to attempt to influence any national or international union to change its form of organization from craft to industrial.

It is *not* the intent, aim, or purpose to use any unethical or coercive method in conducting the educational campaign which has for its purpose organization upon an industrial basis the millions of workers in mass production industries who have not been and can not be organized upon a craft basis.

It is *not* the intent, aim or purpose to take any action that will invite or promote organization that in any way can be considered dual to the American Federation of Labor. Quite the contrary is true. We seek to alter a policy which now invites such dual organization.[17]

Lewis associated himself with this reply, and appended two paragraphs which for sheer felicity of expression and subtle insolence have few equals even among his own writings:

Now of other things: your official burdens are great. I would not increase them. I do not covet your office; in proof, I submit the record of years of support of your personal and official fortunes. It is bruited about, however, that your private sympathies and individual inclinations lie with the group espousing the industrial type of organization, while your official actions and public utterances will be in support of their adversaries. Such a policy is vulnerable to criticism and will hardly suffice to protect you against attacks that may feel rightfully that more is due them than perfunctory support.

Why not return to your father's house? You will be welcome. If you care to disassociate yourself from your present position, the Committee for Industrial Organization will be happy to make you its chairman in my stead. The honorarium will be equal to that you now receive. The position would be as permanent as the one you occupy. You would have the satisfaction of supporting a cause in which you believe inherently, and of contributing your fine abilities to the achievement of an enlarged opportunity for the nation's workers.[18]

Dubinsky testified soon after that this offer was made without consultation with him, at least; that it did not meet with the approval of the entire Committee; and that "we do not consider the letter that was sent to President Green, its tone and general attitude, as the purpose of the Committee." [19] Green, of course, sent an indignant reply in which he asserted that he was already in his "father's house" and intended to remain there.[20]

Actually, William Green was by no means unsympathetic to the industrial union point of view. As a former coal mine union official, he had little personal liking for the excessive preoccupation with exclusive jurisdiction characteristic of the old-line craft unions. During the internal AFL debates on the issue of union structure from 1932 to 1936, he expressed himself on many occasions in favor of the industrial form for the mass production industries. However, Green was the servant and not the master of the Executive Council. He had never been president of a national union, nor did he have any union base to fall back on in the event of his ouster as AFL president, except for the dubious largesse of John L. Lewis. Consequently, when the chips were down, he was completely responsive to the majority craft union sentiment on the AFL Executive Council, and there was never any doubt which way he would go. After the formation of the CIO, he attached himself firmly to the banner of antidual unionism which had first been held aloft by Samuel Gompers, his predecessor.

It might also be pointed out that William Green was never a member of an inner circle of the Executive Council which exercised a considerable degree of control over AFL policies. It is generally known that for many years evening poker sessions were held during the quarterly meetings of the Executive Council. This informal club was a going institution as early as 1919, and it continued actively until the second World War. Certain members of the Executive Council and general presidents of international unions were the regular players. Close associates of these officers from the same organizations were privileged to be in attendance in the room and to play when regular members were absent. William L. Hutcheson and Daniel Tobin were regular members. Neither William Green nor his successor, George Meany, was ever a member of the group.

The minutes of the December 9 meeting of the CIO reveal that the remaining members of the CIO were much more cautious and less certain of where they were going than Lewis. Hillman, who was closest to the Lewis position, nevertheless urged that the CIO confine its organizing efforts to the automobile and rubber industries, and stay out of steel and radios. He pointed out that "if we can show an increase in the AFL membership through such activity, we can get more votes at Tampa." (Tampa was to be the site of the 1936 AFL convention.) When Lewis warned of possible reprisals, however, Hillman stated: "When we had strikes, our members were told to join the [United Garment Workers] or lose their jobs. We have been raised under a policy of reprisals. There will be more reprisals if we do nothing at all. . . . If one of our organizations were put out of the AFL, I would feel obligated to join it."

Of all the CIO members, Dubinsky was the most disposed to move with extreme caution. Howard, like Dubinsky, was generally on the side of caution, but Lewis overrode them with this warning:

The Committee will . . . be under pretty heavy fire — Green has made up his mind. Maybe we can't create a formula now for the other industries. The suggestion on autos and rubber is the only practical thing as our first thrust. If we don't do anything we lose our prestige. . . . There will be reprisals. There has been talk around the Hamilton Hotel. The Teamsters will get the support of the Bakery Workers by letting them keep their men. They are threatening to boycott the typographical label.[21]

These discussions and other contemporary events reveal that even at the very birth of the CIO, the seeds of dissension were already present. But the founders of the CIO were held together in the initial stages by the conviction that the crying need of the time was organization of the mass production industries, and that this could be achieved only through industrial unionism. All considerations of tactics were subordinated to this central purpose, and even such strong men as Hillman and Dubinsky were willing to bow to Lewis' judgment because they regarded him as an ideal instrument for effectuating a basic trade union purpose which they well realized could not be accomplished on their own.

The AFL Reaction

The American Federation was not long in replying to the new threat to its hegemony. Answering Howard's letter, which was quoted above, Green, on December 12, 1935, renewed his appeal for the dissolution of the CIO, and concluded on a prescient note:

I deem it my duty to emphasize the note of warning, sounded in my letter dated November 23rd and as I repeat it now, against the formation of an organization within the American Federation of Labor. I am confident it will lead to serious consequences. It is bound to invite counter-action and reprisals from those who are uncompromising in their opposition to the purpose for which the organization with which you are associated is formed. We may attempt to reason otherwise or we may try to convince ourselves that cleavage and division will not occur, but experience, which after all is the best teacher, has shown that unity, solidarity and cooperation cannot be maintained where an organization, within an organization, is formed for the declared purpose of promoting a policy which is in conflict with the one adopted by a majority vote in a legally convened convention representative of the entire membership of the organization itself.[22]

When the Executive Council of the AFL convened for its January 1936 meeting, it was confronted with a going concern. Thirty-five thousand copies of a pamphlet extolling the virtues of industrial unionism had been distributed; another pamphlet answering Green's attacks was off the press; and groups of workers in the automobile, rubber, radio, gas and coke, and lumber industries, as well as several central trades and labor councils, had endorsed the CIO.[23] The problem was how best to deal with this menacing situation.

The council, as might be expected, was divided in its views. There was considerable sentiment for immediate suspension of the CIO unions, but Green replied in a statement which has considerable historical interest, in view of subsequent developments:

It would be very difficult for us to call upon organizations or individuals whom we believe are transgressing the law, setting it aside, to change their attitude as to law and procedure unless we are setting the example of conforming to the laws and procedure of the American Federation of Labor. . . .

I have searched the constitution of the American Federation of Labor, analyzed it, appreciated it. I cannot find in this constitution where this Council is clothed with authority to suspend an International Union affiliated with the American Federation of Labor. . . .

I am conscious of the fact that in some period of the development of the American Federation of Labor President Gompers ruled that there was a difference between suspension and revocation of a charter and he ruled that the charter of an affiliated organization could be suspended by a majority vote of the delegates at the convention. . . . Insofar as I have been able to find, no precedent has been established as a ruling that the Executive Council is authorized to suspend an organization from the American Federation of Labor.[24]

The significance of this statement lay in the fact that at the time the AFL Constitution required a two-thirds vote of the convention for revocation of a charter; nor was there any express power in the Executive Council to suspend an organization. In the light of the vote at the 1935 convention it seemed unlikely that the necessary two-thirds vote could be mustered in 1936. This was the dilemma faced by the Executive Council: there appeared to be no explicit constitutional power to act in the face of the threat to its authority.

When Howard appeared before the council to argue the case for the CIO, Green pointed out that the British labor movement was no further advanced than the American in organization, and argued that it was not industrial unionism, but the NRA, and the acquiescence of the operators, which brought about organization among the miners. In private, however, he counseled moderation.[25] Largely as a consequence of his efforts, the Executive Council confined itself to the issuance of a statement calling for immediate dissolution of the CIO, which was branded "a challenge to the supremacy of the American Federation of Labor and . . . ultimately . . . dual in purpose and character to the American Federation of Labor." [26] A committee consisting of George M. Harrison, Joseph N. Weber, and G. M. Bugniazet was appointed to meet with the CIO unions and to present to them the views of the Executive Council.

Dubinsky, who was a member of the Executive Council at this time, opposed the statement, and urged the council to restrict itself to the appointmeant of a committee to meet with the CIO as a better tactical move. He declared that there had been a close vote in the ILGWU Executive Board on the question of continued affiliation with the CIO, for which Lewis' offer of the presidency to Green had been responsible, and indicated that he was not happy with the way things were going in the CIO.[27] On the other hand, some members of the council, led by Hutcheson, appeared to favor stronger action. It is interesting to note that there had been a split vote on a slightly less belligerent version of the council statement, with Green, Woll, Coefield, Weber, Bugniazet, Harrison, Tobin, Gainor, Mahon, Knight, and Morrison voting in the affirmative, and Duffy, Rickert, Wharton, Hutcheson and Bates voting in the negative on the explicit ground that it was not sufficiently strong. The Executive Council also notified all state federations, city central bodies, and federal locals to refrain from supporting the CIO in any way.

The reply of the CIO was in the negative. At the convention of the United Mine Workers of America, which began just after the AFL Executive Council had adjourned, at the end of January 1936, Philip Murray, vice-president of the Miners, declared that if the AFL was not willing to cooper-ate in the organization of the mass production industries, "the sooner we get the hell away from them the better it will be for us." While there was no desire on the part of the CIO for a split, Murray continued, "so far as we know, there is no possible hope of changing the opinion of the American Federation of Labor upon this question. They are going to remain fixed in their course and they are going to continue the prosecution of their system of organization in this country of ours." Lewis, at his oratorical best, de-clared that unless the UMW convention ordered him to do so, "all the members of the Executive Council of the American Federation of Labor will be wearing asbestos suits in hell before that committee is dissolved." [28] The Miners were told by Lewis and Kennedy, the secretary-treasurer, that in the legislative fight on the Guffey Bill the Metal Trades Department of the American Federation of Labor had attempted to insert a provision guaran-teeing autonomous bargaining to craft workers employed in the mines, mak-ing the fight against the AFL in part a fight to preserve the jurisdiction of the United Mine Workers.

The climax of this convention came at the close of a speech by William Green, who appeared in person to argue the case against the CIO. Green stated that the skilled worker had a right to capitalize upon his key position in industry by getting the highest wage he could force from employers; that the 1934 convention of the AFL had moved substantially in the direc-tion of industrial unionism; that a dual organization could not be tolerated in the AFL any more than in the United Mine Workers; and he recalled that in the past the AFL had contributed substantial sums to the coal miners for strike relief. When he had finished, Lewis stated:

The President of the United Mine Workers of America will permit the dele-gates . . . to render their answer to President Green, of the American Federa-tion of Labor. Let me call upon all delegates in this convention who have changed their minds on this issue on account of the address of President Green to rise to their feet.

The Chair sees two delegates.

Again, the question recurs upon the fiat of the Executive Council of the Ameri-can Federation of Labor, read to this Convention as an ultimatum by President Green. It demands that the President of the United Mine Workers of America, with his associates on the Committee for Industrial Organization, like quarry slaves at night, scared to their dungeons, dissolve, disband, cease and desist with reference to the Committee for Industrial Organization. Let those dele-gates . . . who believe that the President of the United Mine Workers of America should comply with that request rise to their feet.

The Chair sees one delegate arise.

Again, let those delegates of this Convention who believe that the policies enunciated by this Convention should be carried out by the President of their organization and his associate officers rise to their feet.

(The delegates arose and applauded.)

President Green, you have received the answer of the United Mine Workers of America to your ultimatum.[29]

Lewis was clearly prepared to go much further than his CIO compatriots. Thus, Howard wrote to Hillman, after the adjournment of the Mine Workers' convention:

While I fully approve of the attitude and action of the convention of the United Mine Workers the press has taken advantage of the situation to play up the possibility of their withdrawal. I do not believe President Lewis and the other officers have any serious thought of withdrawing unless they should be forced to do so by some drastic action of the Executive Council. The difference is one over organization policy for the AFL and it is my opinion the better way to settle it is to win a majority, which I am confident can be done within reasonable time. To withdraw would play into the hands of those who have been crying "dual unionism." [30]

Hillman replied:

I am quite in agreement with the contents of your letter of February 3rd. I visited with the United Mine Workers at their Convention and found it to be a great convention. John certainly has hold over that crowd. The feeling of the crowd towards the AFL is very bitter, probably a bit too strained, in my judgment. I fully agree with you that the way to fight the industrial question is on the inside and that sooner or later we are bound to get on top.[31]

Thus, two of the top CIO leaders clearly expressed themselves against withdrawal from the AFL, and Hillman indicated a certain uneasiness at the strength of the anti-AFL line adopted by Lewis. When Dubinsky's attitude is taken into account, it is fair to say that during the early days of the CIO, Lewis alone in the CIO leadership was unconcerned at the prospect of a division in the labor movement.

At a meeting on February 21, 1936, the CIO leaders prepared a joint reply to the AFL, in which it was emphasized once again that the Committee did not intend to act as a dual body, and denied having solicited support from central bodies of the AFL. However, it was pointed out that central bodies of the AFL had the right to go on record in favor of industrial unionism, and to spread CIO literature among their constituents. The CIO also expressed willingness to meet with the committee appointed by the AFL, "to discuss these vital problems further." [32]

At the same meeting, however, the CIO took a drastic step which was to exacerbate relations further. In a letter to Green, the Committee pledged $500,000 and the services of organizers for the organization of the steel industry, provided the AFL raised an additional $1,000,000. This offer, and its consequences, are dealt with in detail below (p. 79).

The next few months passed with no direct negotiations between the AFL and the CIO. George Harrison, who had been designated as chairman of the AFL committee, left for Geneva immediately after the February meeting of the Executive Council, and upon his return was engaged in railroad wage negotiations. In the meantime, the CIO was far from passive. It gave assistance to the United Rubber Workers, who were then engaged in a long strike at Goodyear. The attempt of the AFL federal locals in the radio manufacturing field to force the issue of securing a national charter independent of the Electrical Workers, through the formation of a national union without specific AFL authorization, was strongly supported by the CIO. In April, the Federation of Flat Glass Workers formally affiliated with the CIO; this organization had been chartered by the AFL only two years before. The April 1936 convention of the United Automobile Workers adopted the program of the CIO and proposed to unite the various independent auto unions in existence at the time in one, large, industrial union. Votes favorable to the CIO were secured at meetings of the Pennsylvania, Tennessee, Virginia and Alabama State Federations of Labor. However, the CIO refrained from chartering any new unions, and in general, confined itself to educational work on a relatively small scale. Thus, up to April 14, 1936, the total direct expenditures of the CIO were only $13,900, as reported by Brophy to the Committee.

During this uneasy period, a few expressions of sympathy were forthcoming from within the AFL. Patrick E. Gorman, president of the Amalgamated Meat Cutters and Butcher Workmen, urged Green to secure a modification of the stand taken by the Executive Council on the dissolution of the CIO. "If you gentlemen remain steadfast in your decision," he wrote, "it would appear to me that the recognized leaders of the American labor movement will be responsible for a disastrous split in the ranks of organized labor to a greater extent than the CIO." [33] Joseph Obergfell, of the Brewery Workers, expressed the opinion that "the time is not far distant when the AFL will have to yield to the popular demand of the workers, granting them the right of freedom to determine for themselves the form of organization they desire as outlined in the Wagner-Connery labor disputes act." [34] But apart from the Flat Glass Workers, there were no additions to the CIO ranks.

When the Executive Council of the American Federation of Labor assembled in Washington on May 5, 1936, it was clear that a basic decision on how to deal with the CIO had been reached during the intervening months since the last council meeting. A long brief was submitted by Charlton Ogburn, acting as attorney for the AFL, in which it was argued that the AFL constitution empowered the Executive Council to make rules governing matters not in conflict with the constitution; and since the constitution was silent on suspension (as opposed to expulsion) of affiliated unions, it was within the authority of the council to adopt rules regarding suspension. The council immediately acted to this purpose, not only with respect to national union affiliates, but including all central bodies and other affiliates as well. A letter was sent to Lewis asking him and other CIO representatives to meet with the Harrison committee, and another letter was sent to the chief executive officers of every CIO union, which said, in part:

We regard the Committee for Industrial Organization as a rival and dual organization within the family of organized labor. Its activities justify such conclusion. It advocates the pursuit of organizing policies in opposition to those formulated and adopted at conventions of the American Federation of Labor. . . .

For this and other valid reasons we call upon the Committee for Industrial Organization to dissolve immediately and to recognize the convention of the American Federation of Labor as the sole authority within the American Federation of Labor to formulate and originate organization and administrative policies and to act on all fundamental policies of the American Federation of Labor.[35]

The recipients were given two weeks in which to reply.

On May 19, 1936, Harrison, Weber, and Bugniazet met with Lewis, Murray, A. D. Lewis (John L. Lewis' brother), Brophy, McMahon, and McCabe (the last named was president of the Flat Glass Workers) in what has been termed "an exchange of statements rather than a conference." Harrison reported McCabe as saying that he had little interest in the AFL, knew little about it, did not think his organization was getting much good out of it, and did not care whether he was in or out. McMahon and Murray reported that they were under mandates from their organizations to associate with the CIO. "Chairman Harrison stated that President Lewis wanted to discuss with the Committee of the Executive Council a basis of understanding between the American Federation of Labor and their Committee

(CIO). I indicated that we were not there for that purpose. We were there to urge him to accept the conclusions reached; they would have to abandon the Committee and get within the councils of the American Federation of Labor and talk out these problems." [36] It was thus clear that the AFL committee was in no sense a negotiating committee; its sole function was to convey formally to the CIO unions the demand that they dissolve that organization. As a footnote, Harrison reported that in a private conversation with Fremming of the Oil Workers, the latter had expressed his readiness to withdraw from the CIO if he could have his jurisdictional difficulties with the building trades adjusted.

At this meeting, Green, who theretofore had been conciliatory, expressed sentiments in favor of action. "The question of democracy is not involved, it is the question of rivalry, whether the American Federation of Labor is supreme or whether we can have a divided house and expect to live. . . . It is an unpleasant duty because it means a split. We can not shirk our duty. If it is to be a rival organization we will have to meet that." The Council agreed to reconvene shortly after the expiration of the time period allowed for a reply to its ultimatum.

Both in words and deeds, the CIO unions made clear their continued defiance of the AFL. On May 28, the convention of the Amalgamated Clothing Workers voted to continue support of the CIO.[37] The executive board of the United Mine Workers Union took similar action.[38] The executive board of the ILGWU replied that the Executive Council had not given the CIO unions an opportunity to present their case, and concluded: "Should it, at any time, be proved that the Committee for Industrial Organization engages in dual union activities, we assure you that there will be no need of any edict or ultimatum, but the Committee will either correct its policy or we will withdraw from it." [39] The United Textile Workers and Howard replied in similar vein.

More significantly, the CIO commenced to expand its organizational activities. An agreement was signed on June 4, 1936, with the Amalgamated Iron, Steel and Tin Workers, in which the CIO assumed complete control of a steel organizing campaign (see infra, p. 83). The newly formed United Electrical and Radio Workers Union, rebuffed in its effort to secure a charter from the AFL because of the opposition of the International Brotherhood of Electrical Workers, drew even closer to the CIO, and Lewis was reported to be assisting it in negotiations with the R.C.A. Manufacturing Co.[40] On July 2, the United Automobile Workers and the United Rubber Workers joined the CIO, though without severing their AFL ties.

After the receipt of negative replies from the CIO unions, Green invited each one individually to meet with the AFL Executive Council at its meetings beginning July 8. Again, the response was not promising. Brophy, replying for Lewis, asked for written, specific charges in advance of such a meeting, and questioned the authority of the Executive Council to take action.[41] Green refused to reply on the ground that Brophy was not an international officer of the United Mine Workers, to which the invitation had been addressed. The only break in an otherwise solid CIO front came from the Typographical and Hatters' unions. Howard replied that the International Typographical Union had never affiliated with the CIO, and that he was acting as its secretary in a purely personal capacity. The problem of the Hatters' Union was more complicated. In 1934, the United Hatters, an old craft organization, had merged with the Cap and Millinery Workers, which shared the general outlook of the New York needle trades. Under the terms of the merger, the Cap and Millinery Workers remained a virtually autonomous department, with Max Zaritsky as its president. It was this department, rather than the international union, that affiliated to the CIO, and supported its purposes to the extent of a five-thousand-dollar donation to the steel organizing drive.

Now that the hour of decision was at hand, latent differences of opinion within the AFL Executive Council began to come out into the open. George Harrison emerged as the chief spokesman for the conciliatory wing, a position he was to occupy consistently in the years ahead. Prefacing his remarks with the statement that he was not defending the conduct of the CIO, he continued:

I do not understand that this Council has any authority to suspend any union. I can not find it in the constitution. For that reason as a member of the Council I shall not vote to suspend any union notwithstanding any advice the counsel of the Federation may give because I can get as many opinions as I want to hire attorneys. I have consulted the three attorneys of the Brotherhood of Railway Clerks, all Judges of the Supreme Court of Ohio, . . . they tell me there is no such authority in the constitution of the American Federation of Labor for this Council to suspend a union except in a mandate of the convention. . . . I think organizations have the right to band together in furtherance of their interests. . . . If any of them transgress upon the jurisdiction of any other organizations, the constitution provides a guide to meet that situation. . . . This Committee which was set up to call upon the Lewis group, called upon them. We had no authority to develop any plan to adjust our difficulties. Some day there must be a settlement if this movement is to prosper. Why not try to confine our time and energy to solving the difficulty that confronts us rather than to find a way and means to create more difficulties.[42]

Green, on the other hand, came out strongly for suspension and, reversing his earlier doubts on the constitutional authority of the Executive Council, expressed his firm conviction that the council could legally take such action. Wharton observed that no international union "would tolerate a condition within its own ranks that the American Federation of Labor is now confronted with," while Tobin charged that "the honor, decency and character of every man connected with this Council has been dragged in the mire." It was proposed that formal charges against the CIO, prepared by John P. Frey, president of the Metal Trades Department of the AFL, be made the basis of a trial to be held the following month. Before this was voted upon, Harrison revealed that on the previous evening, he had met with John L. Lewis, who "said he would agree to dissolve the Committee for Industrial Organization providing the American Federation of Labor would agree to the organization of steel, rubber, automobile and one other mass production industry on an industrial basis." [43] Tobin, despite his previous militancy, expressed himself in favor of a conference with Lewis to see if an agreement could be worked out, but the council was in no mood for temporizing, and it adopted the proposal with only Harrison dissenting. (Dubinsky, who was still a member of the council, was not present at this meeting.)

In pursuance of this decision, the CIO unions were summoned to appear before the Executive Council on August 3, 1936, to answer a long bill of particulars drawn up by Frey, the essence of which was that the CIO was a dual organization, engaged in fomenting insurrection within the AFL, and that they were violating their charters of affiliation. [44] On behalf of all the CIO unions, Lewis submitted a detailed reply, in which, among other things, he questioned the constitutionality of the scheduled trial:

The AFL constitution provides that expulsion of an affiliated national or international labor union can only take place at a regular AFL convention and upon a two-thirds roll call vote of the delegates. Suspension would disqualify the unions affected from having any delegate representation in the convention, and in this case is intended to have the effect of an expulsion. . . .

The trial you threaten is plainly intended to forestall action of the convention and foreclose its judgment in the matter over which it alone has jurisdiction. . . .

The amendment requiring a two-thirds roll call vote of a convention to terminate the affiliation of a national or international union was adopted in 1907. Since then the convention has ordered many suspensions, but the Executive Council, through all these years, has never pretended to exercise the power until the present case. . . . [45]

There is no question that this was a telling point. If to the number of those voting against suspension of the CIO unions at the 1936 AFL convention were added the votes of the suspended organizations, there would have been slightly less than the two-thirds necessary to expel.[46] The chances are that if the CIO unions had appeared at the convention to fight the charges, they could have mustered additional votes. The Executive Council was undoubtedly mindful of this possibility, and was motivated by an urgent desire to retain full legal control of the Federation, and to forestall an impossible stalemate if the CIO had indeed been able to block action by the 1936 convention.

On August 3 none of the defendant unions appeared and the trial was held in their absence. Frey charged that the CIO, far from being a mere educational committee, had already become an organizing center in direct competition with the AFL, in terms of staffing, relations with affiliated national unions, and intent; that the jurisdictions of AFL unions were being transgressed; that AFL members were being coerced or induced to join CIO affiliates; that rudimentary local central bodies had been formed; and that this had been the purpose of the CIO from the beginning.[47]

While the final conclusion that the Executive Council would reach was foregone, there was by no means unanimity. Harrison, who did not attend the meeting, wrote to the council:

I have not changed my views in respect to the desirability of developing some mutually satisfactory basis of disposing of the pending controversy with the CIO, and I urge every possible effort be exerted in that direction. Further, I doubt the authority of the Executive Council to suspend an affiliated union without a direct mandate from the convention.[48]

Dubinsky, who attended the meeting, when asked by Green whether the CIO intended to organize an independent rival movement, replied: "In my judgment, no, rumors are there is such a thing. In my judgment no. On the other hand if there is a suspension of these unions, definitely yes." When Green persisted, he continued:

When twelve or fifteen unions are out of the American Federation of Labor I consider that a split. When two or three unions are suspended it could not be considered a split. When these unions should be suspended as it is contemplated here including our organization, if we should be suspended because we claim the Executive Council has not the right or authority because the Council was not patient enough, when it is a question of two or three months till the convention, you will probably find our union in the other camp.[49]

Tobin expressed some doubt about the legality of suspension, but said nonetheless that the council should go ahead in view of the fact that even if the convention upheld the position of the Executive Council, the CIO unions might refuse to abide by that decision. Whereupon Dubinsky inquired: "If I gave you assurance within half a day signed by five of these unions that they will comply with the decision, even to disbanding the CIO, would you consider referring it to the convention?" At this point, when there may have been some hesitation on the part of men like Green and Woll, the heavy guns of the anticompromise faction were brought into play. Wharton, president of the Machinists Union, demanded immediate action and questioned the right of Dubinsky to sit on the council. He was seconded by Hutcheson and Coefield, and this put an end to the debate. The next day, with Dubinsky recorded as not voting, the council adopted a resolution finding ten CIO unions guilty of dualism and in violation of their contractual obligation to the AFL, and ordered their withdrawal from the CIO by September 5, 1936, on pain of suspension from the AFL.[50] A letter was sent to the International Typographical Union requesting it to direct Howard to disassociate himself from the CIO, and to the Hatters, Cap and Millinery Workers, insisting that either the Cap and Millinery Department disassociate itself from the CIO, or that the Hatters' Department, which had never had any connection with the CIO, sever its ties with the Cap and Millinery Department.

In a public statement made soon after the Executive Council had adjourned, Dubinsky labeled the action "a deplorable subterfuge which will convince no fair-minded person of the justice or legality of these tragic proceedings."[51] Lewis declared the council resolution to be "an appalling blunder which Mr. Green and his confederates may continuously rue," and asserted flatly: "We will not disband the Committee for Industrial Organization. The decision of the executive council will not change the policy of the C.I.O. nor will it have any effect upon the organizing activities of the Committee."

When the CIO heads met on August 10, the AFL suspension ultimatum provided Lewis with all the ammunition he needed to overcome the hesitations of Dubinsky and others who previously had drawn back from the possibility of an outright break. Lewis stated that he was disposed to accept the decision of the Executive Council as the final decision of the convention, and argued in the following vein:

It is not desirable to enter an equity court and bring injunction proceedings, although counsel advise that we have a good case. The UMW has an inherent dislike to invoking an injunction writ in a labor controversy, and it would probably be appealed and take a year or more. Meanwhile the AFL would still be resisting with all its strength. It would be better to give the membership of the American Labor movement time to make up their own minds and demonstrate their position. There is apparently no chance of our getting admitted to the Tampa convention. It has been suggested that we ought to keep tendering the per capita tax, send in credentials, challenge the report of the credentials committee, and walk out after an adverse decision, but this seems futile. It would be preferable to carry on and not let suspension detract from our organizing activities.[52]

The CIO unions decided unanimously to stand firm by their previous declarations, and at the close of the meeting, "Mr. Lewis suggested that the unions pay their per capita to Mr. Brophy instead of Mr. Morrison." AFL records indicate that all the suspended unions, except the Oil Workers, ceased paying their per capita tax to the AFL by August 1936, the latter organization making a final payment in October.

During the next few months, the growing momentum of the steel campaign and the growth of CIO strength in other fields rendered it even less likely that the Tampa Convention of the AFL would see any reversal in the policy adopted by the Executive Council. Heywood Broun, president of the American Newspaper Guild, joined the CIO and announced that his union would hold a referendum to determine the question of its affiliation.[53] Conventions of the Hotel and Restaurant Workers Union, the American Federation of Teachers, and the Bakery Workers expressed sympathy and support for the CIO, though none of these organizations affiliated with the CIO at this time. The state federations of labor of Alabama, California, Georgia, Kentucky, Pennsylvania, Tennessee, Virginia, West Virginia, and Wisconsin, adopted resolutions in support of the CIO. Dubinsky resigned from the AFL Executive Council in protest against the suspensions, which he held to be a violation of the AFL constitution. At the same time, the General Executive Board of the ILGWU asked the AFL to reverse the suspensions and permit the entire matter to be discussed fully at the convention, promising: "Our international would regard a decision coming from the convention as a democratic solution of the critical controversy that is at present facing organized labor and would comply with its action." [54] When Green, in reply, expressed his doubt that a majority of the membership of the ILGWU favored "severance of a profitable relationship" with the AFL, Dubinsky denied that his union had withdrawn from the AFL, and reiterated that it stood unlawfully suspended.

On the CIO side, internal developments in two of the affiliates (or near-affiliates), the International Typographical Union and the Hatters, were causing some concern. In a letter of August 18, 1936, Howard had made clear that the ITU had taken no action on the question of affiliation with the CIO. He pointed out, however, that he had been reelected as president of the ITU in May 1936 in a referendum vote by a decisive majority, and argued further that the laws of the ITU did not require "that the President must seek approval or consent to take such action as he believes will advance the interests of this Union and the trade union movement." [55] Green attended the ITU convention in September 1936 and spoke at length on the CIO issue, urging the delegates to remain within the AFL.[56] At the end of considerable debate, a resolution was adopted pledging the ITU to moral and financial support of CIO organizing drives in steel and other industries, and giving the officers of the ITU the power "to take such action as in their judgment may be necessary to protect and preserve the autonomous rights, privileges and powers of the International Typographical Union as an affiliate of the American Federation of Labor." In the debate on the resolution, Howard and Secretary-Treasurer Woodruff Randolph made much of the fact that the ITU, as one of the founders of the AFL, had never received an AFL charter, and consequently could not be deprived of it. Randolph also charged that the AFL craft unions were afraid "that the rapid organization of millions of unorganized workers would make the AFL so big that all of those who are now in control as representing craft unions would be swept aside and untrained men from the larger mass production industries organized into unions of their own and voting the strength of their membership would take charge of the labor movement." [57]

Green regarded this outcome as a victory for the AFL. In reporting back to the Executive Council, he declared that the general expectation had been that the ITU convention would vote for direct affiliation with the CIO, instead of which mere support was authorized. Moreover, a referendum vote was required under the ITU constitution before financial aid could be given the CIO. Morrison, secretary-treasurer of the AFL, and a former official of the ITU, seconded Green's interpretation of the events and reported that he had found little support for affiliation with the CIO among the ITU convention delegates.[58]

There appears to be little doubt that the outcome of the ITU convention represented a defeat for Howard. After his death, his successor and political opponent, Claude M. Baker, produced a letter dated August 8, 1936, in which Howard is quoted as writing: "I am glad the payment of the per capita tax for the AFL has been withheld. It was my intention to suggest to the Secretary that no further payments be made, at least until after the convention, as I intend to recommend that action be taken to formally affiliate with the CIO." [59] Randolph, rising to the defense of Howard, did not question the authenticity of the letter. Long affiliation with the AFL and the necessity for close cooperation with the other printing-trades unions, none of which showed a disposition to join the CIO, made the Printers cautious, although not sufficiently so to prevent a worsening of relationships with the AFL in the years to come.

Max Zaritsky, secretary-treasurer of the United Hatters, faced an equally difficult situation at the October 1936 convention of his organization. The Cap and Millinery Department of the union clearly favored affiliation with the CIO, but the Hat Department, led by Michael Greene, an old-line AFL leader, was opposed. To force the issue might have disrupted the merger that had only recently been effected. A compromise resolution was adopted which, while expressing sympathy for the purposes of the CIO and for Zaritsky's participation in it, carefully refrained from advocating direct affiliation with the CIO and instead called upon the AFL and CIO to meet once again in an effort to work out their differences. Michael Greene assured the delegates that the resolution "does not in any sense commit you or place you in jeopardy in so far as your affiliation with the American Federation of Labor is concerned." [60]

William Green attended the Hatters' convention, and conferred there with Zaritsky and Dubinsky. He reported that both were strongly in favor of a settlement, but that he had repeated that a necessary pre-condition was the dissolution of the CIO. In response to an apparent intimation by Dubinsky that he might be willing to advocate such a step if the AFL supported the steel organizing campaign which was then getting under way, Green quoted himself as saying:

I cannot go into that with you now, I cannot discuss it because if I would tell you the truth as I know it you would probably charge me with sour grapes, pouring cold water on it, disparaging what you have done. But I am sure the Executive Council will never take that baby off your hands. You have a hold of it like you have a red hot poker and you will keep it, you are not going to unload it. . . .[61]

This is an interesting sidelight on the AFL evaluation of the chances of organizing the steel industry six months before the United States Steel Corporation signed a contract with the Steel Workers' Organizing Committee.

However, in response to the plea of the Hatters' Union, the Executive Council appointed a committee consisting of Harrison, Knight and Woll, "with authority to negotiate, offer and receive suggestions, offer this plan and refuse this plan subject to the approval of the Executive Council and after the negotiations are completed report back to the Executive Council." This action was taken on October 14, and since the AFL convention was scheduled to commence on November 16, Dubinsky wrote to Lewis requesting that the CIO meet "as early as possible for the purpose of considering the latest developments and our collective position towards the action of the Executive Council, particularly with regard to the selection of their committee and their letter as reported in the press." [62] In reply, he received a notice of a joint meeting of the CIO and the SWOC to be held on November 9. Dubinsky immediately requested Lewis to move up the date of the meeting in view of the imminence of the AFL convention, but Lewis wrote back that November 9 was the earliest feasible date. "Disappointed with this answer, President Dubinsky forwarded another letter to Lewis, suggesting a meeting of the CIO for November 5 or 6. Finally, the CIO meeting was scheduled to take place on November 7 and 8 in Pittsburgh."

Zaritsky had also been active as a go-between, and endeavored to schedule the negotiation as early as possible. After conferring with the AFL Executive Council, and having received a letter from the Harrison committee agreeing to meet "without commitments or stipulations, free to explore every possibility and avenue for reconciliation of all differences," he went to Lewis, who told him that the CIO would not take the matter up until after the impending presidential elections, for fear of injuring the chances of Roosevelt. Upon receiving a call for a CIO meeting on November 9, Zaritsky, on October 19, wrote to Lewis and urged him to hold an immediate meeting of the CIO, since he felt that the way was open for CIO representation at the forthcoming AFL convention. "It is extremely unlikely, however, that this result can be achieved if the meeting of the CIO is held on November 9 and 10, which is three weeks off and less than a week before the Convention. Should the CIO name a committee to confer with the committee of the Executive Council, there will be no time for the conferences and discussions to reach a point where, even if an understanding is reached, these organizations may be able to participate in the Convention." [63] The reply came in the form of a note from Kathryn Lewis to the effect that her father was away, could not be reached, and would not be back very soon. Lewis wrote on October 26 that November 9 was the earliest date on which a representative meeting could be arranged.

When the CIO convened on the appointed date to consider its final strategy, Lewis did not conceal his impatience at the pressure that had been brought upon him to enter into negotiations with the Harrison committee. "I don't think any peace will be worked out with that subcommittee," he declared.

Harrison the last time waited until May — and then was not prepared to discuss matters in controversy. I don't know that I care to confer with Woll. Knight is a new member. Any negotiation for peace should be participated in by the President of the AFL and the Chairman of the CIO. . . . The question of peace is secondary to organizing the unorganized. . . . Why continue on a course of action that means only embarrassment to the CIO? The conferences already held have done harm to the CIO's work. . . . Joseph Shaplen of the *New York Times* reports peace prospects. He has told other newspapermen that he intends to force peace down the throats of the CIO. He is well informed and in touch with Woll.

He was strongly supported by Philip Murray, at the time chairman of the Steel Workers' Organizing Committee, who observed: "Nothing has done more to injure the cause of organization than this constant bickering with people not prepared to yield anything." Howard also expressed himself in militant terms, declaring: "If there is peace, it must be on a CIO basis. It will be most ridiculous if they do not throw us out at the convention, and I think they will throw us out. Reversal of suspension should precede peace talks. If I were thrown out of the AFL, I would not talk to the man who threw me out unless he said he was wrong." [64]

Hillman also supported the Lewis position, but displayed greater interest in the political aspect of the split. He observed that two vice-presidents of the AFL had worked with the anti-New Deal Liberty League without censure, and that the AFL had blocked organizational progress during the NRA period. However, he favored the appointment of a committee to deal with the AFL, but declined to be a member of such a committee.

The only opposition to Lewis came from Dubinsky and Hochman, representing the ILGWU, and Zaritsky. Dubinsky argued that to refuse to meet the AFL committee would put the CIO in the position of opposing peace, and added:

To some unions the present condition is better than going back. Our union wants to be in the AFL if there is a possibility of adjustment, if it doesn't mean giving up our principles. . . . I want peace before this convention. If we can't get 90 per cent, we will see if we can get 80 per cent. . . . I am inclined to believe that they are the same bunch as ever, but I don't want to be placed in the position of opposing peace. I agree with Howard that the question of legality is the most serious phase. Some of the Executive Council know it and fear the consequences.

Zaritsky was the most forthright in advocating that it was incumbent upon the CIO to negotiate, and in criticizing Lewis for impugning the motives of the AFL negotiators. Lewis asked that he be empowered to wire Green requesting a meeting between the two of them, and Dubinsky inquired directly: "If Green asks that the committee meet, what will be your position?" Lewis replied: "That would depend on circumstances. If he just wires me that, my position will be that he should meet me." On this basis, Dubinsky voted for the motion.

On November 7, Howard, as secretary of the CIO, wired Green requesting a meeting between Green and Lewis. Green replied on the same day that the Executive Council had established a committee for the purposes of negotiating, but that while he lacked the authority to change the policy of the Executive Council, he would be glad to meet with Lewis at the convenience of the latter. On November 8, Lewis replied that since Green lacked the authority to change Executive Board policy, a conference would be futile. "When the American Federation of Labor decides to reverse and rectify its outrageous act of suspension and is ready to concede the right of complete industrial organizations to live and grow in the unorganized industries it will be time to discuss and arrange the details of a reestablished relationship. This statement has been approved by the Committee for Industrial Organization in session this date." [65]

In the light of the CIO discussions quoted above, Lewis' reply must be regarded as surprising. Not only had Green offered to meet, but there was still the question of the Harrison subcommittee. Lewis was obviously determined to make a clean break immediately, and utilized the pretext of Green's lack of authority, which must have been known to all the CIO members before the offer to meet was sent. In fact, it is highly unlikely that any such offer would have been made had it not been for Dubinsky's insistence.

Further action taken by the CIO on November 9 confirmed Lewis' intentions. The newly formed United Electrical and Radio Workers and the Industrial Union of Marine and Shipbuilding Workers, neither of which had AFL charters, applied for CIO affiliation. When Hochman objected that it would be better to wait "until we have set up a federation," Lewis replied: "I see no reason why not — I think it would strengthen the Committee somewhat if these unions were accepted." Hochman raised the point that "We have many friends in the AFL. Why take on additional burdens?" to which Howard replied, apparently with an eye on his own organization, "We have to play to keep such friends. A number of organizations are in sympathy with our plan of organization, but they are not here apparently because they believe that the AFL can give them more protection so far. If the CIO is to be a new federation we have to get as many organizations as possible to go along." [66] The admission to the CIO of these two unions marked the first overt step toward the creation of a rival federation, since all previous CIO affiliates had held AFL charters.[67]

The final matter that came up for discussion was whether the suspended unions should send delegates to the AFL convention and attempt to have them seated. Lewis maintained not only that such action would be futile, but that the undoubted rebuff that the CIO would suffer would be tactically disadvantageous, an argument which was supported by Murray, who said that if there were any prospect of peace with the AFL, the steel workers would not organize because of their detestation of the AFL. Howard suggested that the CIO call a meeting at St. Petersburg concurrently with the AFL Tampa convention for the purpose of attracting delegates away from the latter, but Charles Zimmerman of the ILGWU urged that first each union fight for reinstatement at Tampa, and in the event that no results were obtained, a CIO convention then be called. Hochman echoed this idea more specifically in the following terms:

How can we act so that when we are not taken in, we can retain Zaritsky's, Howard's and Brown's unions which have to go [to the AFL convention], and can win over maybe a number more. . . . I think we all ought to go and make a fight. I think all will be expelled. If any go out, all should go out and immediately have a convention.[68]

Randolph of the ITU thought that the best approach to his members "is by being thrown out," and advocated the immediate formation of a dual organization. Mindful of the strength of the ties that his organization had with the AFL, he apparently felt that this was the only way the issue could be resolved clearly for the ITU, an assessment amply justified by subsequent events. Zaritsky, in a surprising reversal of attitude, felt that it was futile for the suspended unions to send delegates to Tampa, and noted: "It is clear from what has been said today that we have to build another organization." However, it was agreed that each CIO union follow the policy it thought best, and that no unified policy be adopted, following a suggestion by Hillman that was calculated to mollify the ILGWU representatives. The precise status of the rival federation plan is indicated by the following colloquy:

Sherwood: Is the setting up of a federation left over to another time?
Lewis: No consideration of this matter has been given here.
Howard: We cannot act before the Tampa convention.

The Tampa Convention and Its Aftermath

The decision of most of the CIO unions not to attempt to seat delegates at the AFL convention which opened in Tampa on November 16, 1936, removed any element of uncertainty from the outcome of the debate on the handling of the CIO issue by the Executive Council. The council reported to the convention that it had adopted rules of procedure, in conformance with its interpretation of the constitution, empowering it to suspend affiliated unions in violation of AFL laws.[69] A resolution was introduced calling upon the convention to endorse the action of the Executive Council in suspending the CIO unions, to continue the Harrison committee in existence, and to empower the Executive Council to call a special convention to take such further steps against the CIO as might be necessary. The convention was not asked to empower expulsion because, in the words of the resolution, of "the sincere desire to avoid any possible future and permanent severance unless such permanent separation comes as the choice of those who would permanently divide and bring warfare instead of peace and unity into the ranks of labor."

The opposition to the resolution voiced from the floor was only token in character. The principal attack was made by Zaritsky, who was supported by Trotter of the Typographical Union, Davis of the Federation of Teachers, and a few delegates representing central bodies and federal labor unions. Woll and John P. Frey bore the main burden of defending the constitutionality of the suspension. It remained for Roy Horn of the Blacksmiths, however, to voice the sentiments of the dominant craft unionists:

the skilled craftsmen are not going to submit to the dictatorship of anyone. . . . I dispute the statement that the mass production industry or any other industries have to be organized only on industrial lines. As the Secretary of one crew that organized 56,000 men at one time and turned them over to their respective craft organizations and later on negotiated a national agreement with them, I say the thing can be done in any industry if you want to do it.[70]

The resolution was adopted by a vote of 21,679 to 2,043, the principal delegations voting in opposition being those of the Bakery Workers, the Hatters, the Brewery Workers, the Typographers, and the Teachers.

One of the first problems faced by the AFL in mounting a counteroffensive against the CIO, now that the battle lines were drawn, was to preserve the integrity of its state federations and city central bodies against CIO encroachment. On February 24, 1937, Green, by direction of the Executive Council, circularized all central bodies affiliated with the AFL and called upon them to remain loyal to the AFL and to repudiate the CIO. In areas where the CIO was strong, for example, Pennsylvania and New York City, no action was taken, but where AFL unions dominated the central bodies, such as Maryland and Cleveland, local unions affiliated with the CIO internationals were suspended from membership, with the result that the intensifying struggle at the national level gradually spread out locally. In Georgia, where the State Federation of Labor was headed by A. Steve Nance, who became Southern director for the Textile Workers' Organizing Committee, it became necessary to undertake extensive reorganization in the face of refusal of AFL local unions to disavow the popular Nance. Similar action subsequently proved necessary in West Virginia, where the Miners' Union was strong.

The CIO, in the meantime, was engrossed in the crucial drives to organize the automobile and steel industries. In February 1937, the General Motors Corporation agreed to bargain with the United Automobile Workers. On March 2, the secret Lewis-Taylor negotiations resulted in the unionization of the United States Steel Corporation. A week later, the CIO adopted the following resolution:

The executive officers of the Committee for Industrial Organization are authorized to issue certificates of affiliation to national, international, state, regional, city central bodies and local groups whenever it is deemed such action is advisable.[71]

The two great organizational victories, plus the informal assumption of the attributes of a federation of labor, left no doubt of the intention and the ability of the CIO to function as a rival central body. Green complained to the AFL Executive Council that "The country seems to be filled with CIO organizers. Every town and every city, small and great, seems to be filled with organizers employed, appointed and assigned to work for and by the CIO." [72] During the first six months of 1937, the CIO received $600,000 in donations from affiliated organizations,[73] and in addition, some of its affiliates, particularly the Steel and Textile Workers' Organizing Committees, borrowed organizers from the established unions.

To counter the CIO, the AFL resolved upon the following steps, in addition to the campaign to protect its central bodies:

Green was authorized to organize workers in textile, coal mining, and other industries directly competitive with existing CIO unions and to issue temporary certificates of affiliation.

The Carpenters' Union in April 1937, urged a special convention to expel the CIO unions, pursuant to the resolution adopted at the Tampa convention. The Executive Council was advised, however, that since the AFL constitution made no provision for revocation of charters by a special as distinguished from a regular convention, this step might lead to litigation. It was decided, instead, to call a special meeting of affiliated national unions to consider specific measures to counter the CIO drive. This meeting was held in Cincinnati on May 24. The following recommendations of the Executive Council were adopted unanimously:

(a). The affiliated national unions agreed to consider a resolution at the next AFL convention levying an assessment of one cent per member per month for the AFL, and pending formal ratification of the levy, to begin paying the assessment immediately.
(b). All AFL affiliates would immediately begin aggressive organizing campaigns within their respective jurisdictions.
(c). All affiliates would call upon their locals to join AFL central bodies in their respective localities.
(d). A recommendation was made that all local unions holding charters from CIO unions be disassociated from AFL central bodies.[74]

The Carpenters' Union pressed for suspension of the International Typographical Union for the moral support it was rendering the CIO. The ITU had refused to attend the Cincinnati meeting and to pay the assessment voted there. Green urged, however, that suspension at this juncture would impede the efforts of the pro-AFL group inside the ITU, and the Executive Council sustained him in his plea to defer action until after the next ITU convention, with only Frank Duffy of the Carpenters voting for immediate action.[75]

The step-up in AFL activities as a consequence of the new program and additional revenue was marked. During the last four months of 1936, the AFL payroll for organizers amounted to $82,000. The corresponding figure for the last four months of 1937 was $466,000.[76] In February 1937, there were 35 salaried organizers on the AFL payroll; by February 1938, the number had risen to 232. In October 1937, a contribution of $7500 a month for a period of six months from AFL funds was authorized to finance a campaign of organization on the Pacific Coast. For the first time, the AFL displayed a willingness to allocate resources for organization on a scale equivalent to that which characterized the great CIO drives of 1936 and 1937.[77] The impact of the CIO organizing drive and the Supreme Court decision upholding the validity of the Wagner Act upon the AFL can be appreciated from the following statement made by Green to the AFL Executive Council at the end of April, 1937:

At the present time it is almost impossible for me here, working 24 hours a day, to meet the requests that come in for organization. Many of these requests are coming from employers suggesting that they are ready to bow to the decision of the Supreme Court on the Wagner Act and they are ready to become organized. We are going forward in a wonderful way organizing, and I know most of our National and International Unions are meeting with the same situation, particularly those having jurisdiction in manufacturing and industry.

The new organizational drive more than anything else that was done at the time marked the beginning of an AFL resurgence from the defensive decline which had set in with the formation of the CIO, and the infusion of a new vitality which soon made it clear that the AFL was to remain the dominant force on the American labor scene.

The First National Conference of the CIO and the Unity Negotiations of 1937

By October 1937, when the first national conference of CIO national union officers was held at Atlantic City, the CIO was already past the apogee of its relative strength and influence in the American labor movement. Although a total membership of four million was claimed,[78] there is good reason to believe that it was considerably less than the claim. An economic recession had set in, adversely affecting employment and union membership. Beginning in August 1937, there was a severe decline in industrial production amounting to almost 30 per cent by January 1938. Manufacturing payrolls declined by 5 per cent from May 1937 to October 1937, and by 23 per cent between May and December. Manufacturing employment declined by 12 per cent between August and December 1937.[79] The momentum of organizational advance had been slowed by the loss of the Little Steel strikes in the summer of 1937.

At the time, however, the loss of momentum was hardly noticed by those at the helm of the CIO, for the record of the previous year was a brilliant one indeed. Between the AFL Tampa convention and the first national CIO conference, the Committee had become a central federation with 32 national union affiliates, numbering among them some of the largest in the country. There were in addition about 600 local industrial unions affiliated directly with the CIO, and 80 state and city central bodies. Some 198 field representatives were working under the direction of 48 regional offices, and an additional 286 field representatives on the CIO payroll were assigned to work with affiliated unions. The financial status of the CIO had been regularized by the institution of a 5¢ per capita tax effective June 1, 1937, although a balanced budget was not achieved until March 1938.[80] Philip Murray was able to tell the conference with pride: "We now occupy a position which we regard as without a peer in the field of labor in the United States of America. We are the dominant labor force in this nation. We are the powerful labor movement."[81] The CIO affiliates at the time are listed in Table 1.

The October Conference adopted resolutions on a number of issues,

Table 1.

CIO affiliates and claimed membership, October 1937

	Membership	Covered by contract
United Mine Workers	600,000	545,000
Amalgamated Clothing Workers	225,000	215,000
International Ladies' Garment Workers	250,000	250,000
Textile Workers' Organizing Committee	450,000	272,116
Steel Workers' Organizing Committee	525,000	498,000
Newspaper Guild	14,000	6,500
United Shoe Workers	50,000	47,500
American Communications Assn.	8,000	2,500
Packinghouse Organizing Committee	100,000	———
International Typographical Union	78,489	70,640
Oil Workers	98,000	65,000
Aluminum Workers	7,351	14,000
Transport Workers	80,000	———
Architects, Engineers, etc.	6,000	1,000
Flat Glass Workers	18,000	18,000
National Maritime Union	49,000	———
United Automobile Workers	375,000	300,000
Rubber Workers	75,000	50,000
Leather Workers	15,000	12,500
United Retail Employees	40,000	40,000
Fur Workers	35,000	35,000
Cannery Workers	66,350	11,000
Hatters, Cap and Millinery Workers	40,000	38,000
United Electrical Workers	137,000	165,000
Marine and Shipbuilding Workers	20,000	10,000
Office and Professional Workers	25,000	5,000
State, County and Municipal Workers	25,000	———
Woodworkers	100,000	60,000
Longshoremen's and Warehousemen's Union	25,000	———
Marine Engineers Beneficial Association	7,000	———
Federal Workers	10,000	———

Source: Typewritten report to Philip Murray from Ralph Hetzel, November 13, 1937, based upon a questionnaire filled out by affiliated unions at the October, 1937, conference.

including federal labor legislation, the need for observance of contracts, and farm policy, and authorized the executive officers to call a constitutional convention. A message was addressed to the AFL convention, which was then in session in Denver, asking that unity negotiations be resumed.

Following the Green-Lewis interchange of telegrams in November 1936, no formal contact had been maintained between the two organizations. Green reported to the AFL Executive Council that he had held conferences with Lewis on April 16 and 18, 1937, at which he had urged that the CIO unions dissolve their organization and reaffiliate with the AFL without stipulation, and that a special committee be appointed to deal with serious questions, to which Lewis had replied in characteristic fashion that the AFL should become part of the CIO.[82] Within the CIO, Dubinsky had continued to press for rapprochement with the AFL. When Matthew Woll appeared before the 1937 convention of the International Ladies' Garment Workers' Union and pleaded for peace in the labor movement, Dubinsky responded: ". . . when this controversy developed, Matthew Woll was one of the conciliatory members of the Council. (Applause). I am not on the Council now but I do know he has used his position to heal the situation. . . . On my own behalf and on behalf of this convention, I express my deep gratitude for your coming here, for your talk, for your friendship. We will look forward to continued friendship and co-operation for the general labor movement." However, the ILGWU delegates applauded Lewis just as loudly when he declared:

The simplest promise upon which peace conversations may be held is to give some indication that the Federation is willing to bargain on a basis of equality and on a basis of recognition of the principle which caused the cleavage in the first instance. If they do not do that thing, then I have no desire to waste any time or waste any energy in fruitless conversation with William Green and John Brown (sic) and Matthew Woll and Thomas Rickert and others of their ilk who created this situation. . . .[83]

Moreover, Dubinsky's ardor for peace was somewhat cooled by the fact that the AFL, in the summer of 1937, chartered six federal locals in the Cleveland knit goods industry after the ILGWU had made a considerable effort to organize the workers of that industry.[84] At the October 1937 CIO conference, Dubinsky seemed as solidly behind the CIO as at any time in the past. He told the delegates: "It is true that we favor unity, a unified labor movement, but at the same time it is true that there cannot be any successful labor movement unless the cardinal principle of industrial unionism for the mass-production industries will be recognized, otherwise no peace is of any value. . . . Here is a challenge to the AFL. Are they interested merely to perpetuate power on the part of a few individuals, or are they interested in helping form other policies for the general labor movement and organizing millions and millions which has been demonstrated to be possible through new methods?"

The CIO October conference proposal to the AFL convention, after reciting the achievements of the CIO and its desire for a unified labor movement, suggested that a conference be held, attended by one hundred representatives of each side, to "consider the methods and means whereby a unified labor movement can be brought about in America." [85] It was made clear, however, that there could be no compromise on the basic industrial union philosophy of the CIO. Lewis described the proposal in the following terms:

The Committee for Industrial Organization, like a certain great proconsul of Rome, advances today and offers to the American Federation of Labor either peace or war. They can take their choice. Candidly we prefer peace. The ways of peace are the best for all men at all times. If intelligence can predominate over passion and over selfishness and over the petty bickerings of a labor hierarchy, the time has come, and in the language of Mr. Green himself, "the hour has struck." He can fish or cut bait. But let the American Federation of Labor through its 100 champions in the forensic area assemble around the conference table facing an equal number of the representatives of the Committee for Industrial Organization and its affiliates and let us see whether in the American labor movement reason can prevail or whether after all the labor movement in this country has to resort to the law of the jungle, the tooth and the fang, in order to justify and ensure its existence. [86]

When this message was received by the AFL, considerable skepticism was expressed that there was any basis for a settlement. Green told his Executive Council that

the organizations affiliated with the American Federation of Labor will never allow those organizations chartered to come in with us as national unions, for instance, the International Brotherhood of Electrical Workers would not allow the Radio and Electrical Workers organization, chartered by the CIO, to come in as a national union, neither will the Carpenters allow the Wood Workers to come in as a national union. That means the CIO organizations if they returned would have to abandon these newly created unions and the only way it can be done is if some of the bona fide national unions broke away, then the door would be open to these other organizations. [87]

Nevertheless, it was decided to accept the CIO offer, though it was suggested that instead of the mass meeting proposed in the CIO message, small committees from each side be designated to conduct the negotiations. The AFL stated that its special committee "clothed with full authority stands ready and willing and anxious to meet a like committee" of the CIO, for the purpose of bringing the suspended unions and "all other labor unions and organizations of labor not now so affiliated" back into the AFL.[88] The CIO indicated its willingness to meet along the lines suggested by the AFL, and designated a smaller committee to represent it. October 25, 1937 was fixed as the date for the conference.

In view of subsequent controversy about what transpired at these negotiations, it is well to record in some detail such background facts as are available. The CIO was represented by Philip Murray, Sidney Hillman, Charles P. Howard, Homer Martin, David Dubinsky, James Carey, Harvey Fremming, Michael Quill, Joseph Curran, Abram Flaxer, Sherman Dalrymple, and Jacob Potofsky. Only Lewis among the top leadership of the CIO was not on the committee. The CIO committee was not bound by any formal limitations of authority, but the imposing figure of Mr. Lewis stood between it and complete power to commit the CIO. The AFL designated George Harrison, Matthew Woll, and G. M. Bugniazet as its representatives. The first two belonged to the conciliatory wing of the AFL, while Bugniazet, as an officer of the Electrical Workers, would have been expected to take a firmer position. When the AFL committee was appointed, Wharton expressed concern about its authority, and he was assured by Green that "there are certain things we cannot agree to. The carpenters will never agree to the wood workers being chartered, and Vice President Mahon would never agree to the transport workers being chartered. Vice President Bugniazet will not agree to the radio and electrical workers receiving a charter, and the marine organizations will never agree to the marine workers being chartered." [89] Harrison promised that his committee would not commit the Federation without the specific approval of the Executive Council. Realistically, then, neither committee was possessed of final authority to make a binding agreement.

At the initial meeting, the CIO made the following proposal:

1. The American Federation of Labor shall declare as one of its basic policies that the organization of the workers in the mass-production, marine, public utilities, service and basic fabricating industries be effectuated only on an industrial basis.

2. There shall be created within the American Federation of Labor a department to be known as the CIO. All of the national and international unions and local industrial unions now affiliated with the CIO shall be affiliated with such new department. This department shall be completely autonomous, operating under its own properly designated officers. This department shall have the complete and sole jurisdiction in regard to (a) the organization of the workers of the industries described in Point 1 above; and also (b) any matters affecting its affiliated organizations and their members.

3. There shall be called at such time and at such place as may be agreed upon between the American Federation of Labor and the Committee for Industrial Organization a national convention which shall be attended by all of the national and international unions and local industrial unions affiliated with the AFL and CIO. This convention shall be called for the purpose of approving the foregoing agreement and for working out the necessary rules and regulations to effectuate the same and to guarantee the fulfillment of the program.[90]

The AFL committee reported that an additional demand had been made: that the AFL agree to amend its constitution to prohibit the Executive Council from suspending national affiliates without direct authorization of the convention.[91] It made the following counter-proposal:

1. All national and international unions chartered by the American Federation of Labor now holding membership in the Committee for Industrial Organization are to return and resume active affiliation with the American Federation of Labor. Immediately upon resumption of such affiliation with the American Federation of Labor these organizations will be accorded all rights and privileges enjoyed by them prior to the formation of the Committee for Industrial Organization and as is provided in the Constitution and Laws of the American Federation of Labor.

2. In respect to other organizations affiliated with the Committee for Industrial Organization: Conferences shall be held immediately between representatives of organizations chartered by the American Federation of Labor and organizations chartered by the Committee for Industrial Organization and which may be in conflict with each other, for the purpose of bringing about an adjustment to bring the membership into the American Federation of Labor upon terms and conditions mutually agreeable.

3. Organization and administrative policies not mutually agreed to shall be referred to the next convention of the American Federation of Labor for final decision. In the meantime an aggressive organizing campaign shall be continued and carried forward among the unorganized workers along both *industrial* and *craft lines* as circumstances and conditions may warrant.

4. The foregoing contemplates the establishment of one unified, solidified labor movement in America and the termination of division and discord now existing within the ranks of labor. Therefore, the Committee for Industrial Organization shall be immediately dissolved.[92]

Beyond the fact that these two proposals were submitted, there is serious disagreement on what occurred at the meetings. The AFL negotiators maintained that there were no major difficulties over the twelve CIO unions which had once held AFL charters; the only problem centered around some twenty additional unions initially chartered by the CIO. To handle this, the following procedure was agreed upon, it is claimed:

a. The twelve original AFL unions would not apply nor be admitted to the AFL until all matters affecting the twenty new CIO unions were adjusted so that the interests of all would be cared for concurrently.

b. That a joint conference committee equally representative of the AFL and the CIO unions would be established for each of these twenty new CIO and dual or conflicting unions to resolve the conflict or to work out a mutually acceptable understanding.

c. That when these conflicts (b) were adjusted, then the membership of the CIO unions would be admitted into the AFL concurrently with the original AFL unions.

d. That if all other matters were adjusted the AFL Committee would consider recommending the amending of the Constitution of the AFL to provide that the Executive Council of the AFL could only suspend an affiliated International or National union or revoke its charter on direct authority of a convention of the AFL.

e. That a special convention of the AFL would be held within a reasonable time (sixty to ninety days) after all matters were adjusted and all affiliated organizations would be entitled to representation with all rights and privileges of other AFL unions.

f. That we would agree to specify certain industries where the industrial form of organization would apply.[93]

No minutes of the meeting were kept. Matthew Woll later asserted, however, that Charles Howard kept notes of the proceedings, and when he (Woll) asked Murray for a copy, "He tore off the first page and gave me the next two pages. I marked them as he gave them to me in order to prove their authenticity . . . they are the minutes as kept by Charlie Howard for the benefit of the CIO conference group and not for the benefit of the AFL.[94] The memorandum began:

This is a brief resume of results obtained in CIO–AFL conferences to date. It merely reflects the attitude of the AFL Committee. They have indicated their willingness to have the following organizations recognized by the AFL as industrial unions.

There followed a list of unions, some with qualification, some without. Among the latter group were the Mine Workers, Clothing Workers, Ladies' Garment Workers, Textile Workers, Glass Workers, National Maritime Workers (including the Inland), Automobile Workers, Cement Workers, Rubber Workers, Aluminum Workers, Steel Workers, Newspaper Guild. Notations appeared after other unions as follows:

United Shoe Workers — This might merge Boot and Shoe Workers of the AFL.

American Communications Association — This also to be merged with Commercial Telegraphers of the AFL.

Transport Unit — This to be merged with Amalgamated Association of Street Railway Employees affiliated with the AFL.

Federation of Architects, Engineers, Chemists and Technicians — This to be merged with the Draftsmen's Organization of the AFL.

National Leather Workers Organization — This to be merged with the AFL organization.

United Retail Employees of America — This to be merged with similar organizations in the AFL.

International Furniture Workers Union.[95]

United Cannery, Agricultural, Packinghouse and Allied Workers of America — This to be merged with organizations of similar nature in AFL.

Food processing industry to be organized along industrial lines.

The ITU to maintain existing status.

Oil Workers International Union — Conferences to be held concerning jurisdictional matters.

United Hatters, Cap and Millinery Workers — To continue present status.

Electrical Radio and Machine Workers of America — Conferences with International Brotherhood of Electrical Workers and AFL affiliates.

Industrial Marine and Building Workers — Bad situation in that craft, in conflict in almost every Navy Yard. Conferences necessary.

United Office and Professional Workers of America — Possibility of merging with the Bookkeepers and Stenographers on an industrial basis.

United Federal Workers of America — Conferences with American Federation of Government Employees of the AFL to establish industrial organization.

National Association of Die Casting Workers — very small unions — no determination of status.

State, County and Municipal Workers of America — Conferences may be had with organization of similar nature in AFL for purpose of perfecting industrial organization.

International Woodworkers of America — serious situation with Carpenters' Union, which needs conference for purpose of establishing status.

International Longshoremen and Warehousemen's Union — this will also necessitate conferences before agreement can be effected with the existing AFL unions.

National Marine Engineers' Organization — Conferences necessary with existing
    unions in AFL.
No discussion concerning local industrial unions or industrial councils.

The present writer has seen in the files of the CIO an undated typewritten memorandum titled "Report of Philip Murray" which read word
for word with the above except for a few abbreviations. This memorandum
contained, in addition to the material quoted above by Woll, the following:

The report here would indicate the willingness of the A.F.L. Committee to concede industrial organization in at least 21 of 32 C.I.O. national and international
unions . . . of the remaining 11 national and international unions, conferences
may result in recognition of industrial organizations in 4 or 5. The status of the
balance is doubtful. The Federation Committee has pointedly refused to grant
autonomous self-governing department CIO in Federation of Labor, but is willing to concede that industrial organization should have a department within
the Federation of Labor, like building and metal trades.

The memorandum also notes the willingness of the AFL committee to
recommend a constitutional change, as noted above, and to hold a special
joint convention following agreement.

The authenticity of the substance of the foregoing memorandum was
attested to by Dubinsky, one of the CIO negotiators, who said that the
industrial union issue had been met, that the AFL had agreed to concede
industrial unionism in all the basic mass production industries.[96] In view
of the previous attitude of the AFL Executive Council, the extent to which
the AFL committee was apparently willing to go is remarkable. One won-
ders whether the concession had the full approval of the Executive Council; there is nothing in the record to indicate otherwise, however, particularly since the AFL committee had been instructed by the council to report
back before making any commitments.

According to Woll, substantial agreement had been reached to proceed
on the basis of the points enumerated above. Woll declared that when an
agreement was reached one evening, the question remained of a press
statement. Howard then said: "Well, now, Phil Murray is not here this
afternoon. He is our chairman. In fairness to him, we request that no
announcement be made of our agreement or of our understanding of a
plan of adjustment until tomorrow when he will be with us." When the
AFL committee returned next morning, the CIO delegation was not
there and, Woll claimed, the agreement was repudiated soon after.[97]

In the official CIO version, the AFL refused to concede two points:

(a) There be set down in writing the specific industries which had been organized by unions affiliated with the CIO and which industries in the opinion of the CIO Committee could be organized only by industrial unions, and

(b) There be a [sic] agreement reached between the two negotiating committees that for such industries the industrial form of union be recognized in principle and in fact.[98]

According to the CIO, the AFL committee took the position that the jurisdictional rights of an AFL union could not be waived by it or any other AFL body; that, for example, the Steel Workers' Organizing Committee would have to meet with every craft union claiming some jurisdiction in steel in an effort to persuade it voluntarily to waive such jurisdiction; that even some of the original AFL unions in the CIO could come back in only on the basis of the restricted charters that had been given them, for example, the Automobile Workers would have had to recognize some craft jurisdictions. In a final effort to agree, the CIO asserted, Lewis and Murray met with Green and Harrison, and the latter two "admitted to the absence of any authority to agree upon the specific industries where industrial unionism would be granted." The breakdown of the negotiations was attributed to AFL insistence that its original counter proposal be accepted.

Conflicting statements on the issue of whether agreement had been reached continued to be issued long after the demise of the negotiations. Dubinsky, in general, supported the AFL viewpoint. On the question of putting in writing the specific industries in which industrial unionism was to be recognized, he had this to say:

The CIO had many demands. The AFL had only one demand — the dissolution of the CIO. Can you imagine the position of a conference committee committing itself in writing to an understanding involving one-sided concessions and not incorporating the concessions of the other side in the same memorandum? In other words, they told us: "If you are ready to put your position in writing, we stand ready to do the same." I could understand an argument of that sort.[99]

He denied emphatically that the issue of "22 outside" and "10 inside," that is, the immediate admission of the original AFL unions and the delayed admission of the rest, had been a stumbling block, since the AFL conceded that no union should return until the status of all had been determined. The issue to him was whether subcommittees should be designated to explore the individual points of difference. "Unfortunately, the CIO refused to make an effort to seek such a basis for adjustment in the industries affiliated with two unions. And the conflict at this hour is still on this same issue — whether there should be separate conferences to explore the possibility of accord in the dual-union sector of the conflict." He also expressed the belief that if Hillman, who could not attend the later conferences because of illness, had been present, the results would have been different.[100] It should be noted that at the time Dubinsky made the remarks quoted above, the ILGWU was still a member of the CIO; and that in the very same speech, he affirmed strongly the intention of his union to remain in the CIO.

Murray and Lewis, however, denied that the CIO had been responsible for the failure of the negotiations. They hammered away on the themes that the AFL committee had no authority to reach an agreement; and that the question of jurisdiction would have had to be negotiated with every individual craft. Murray put it this way:

Can you imagine, my friends, the kind of a task that might present itself to the leaders of the Steel Workers' Organizing Committee, for example, if the leaders of the Steel Workers' Organizing Committee were required to and did sit down with the leaders of these craft unions to agree upon questions of jurisdiction, the boundaries of the organization? How far do you suppose our committee would get with that great big hulk of a fellow known as Bill Hutcheson, of the Carpenters' Union? How many members do you suppose he would be willing to give us? . . . How far do you suppose we might get with Arthur Wharton of the Machinists Union, a man who has been constantly concentrating his efforts, his every effort upon raiding the Steel Workers' Organizing Committee . . . ? [101]

The essential point stressed here and elsewhere by Lewis and Murray is that whatever the stand of the AFL on the principle of industrial unionism, there would have been insurmountable difficulties in reaching agreement in specific cases.

Little purpose is served, if indeed it were at all possible, to assess the blame against one party or the other for the collapse of what was by all odds the most promising set of unity negotiations for many years to come. However, from the vantage point of almost two decades, the following observations may be made:

(1) The so-called "Howard memorandum" indicated that the AFL had substantially conceded the principle of industrial unionism, and was willing to go far beyond even Lewis' interpretation of the San Francisco resolution. The industries that remained in dispute were relatively minor in the entire picture. However, Lewis and Murray probably had a point in their contention that there would have been considerable difficulty in reconciling the divergent concepts of industrial boundaries held by the industrial and craft unionists.

(2) The evidence indicates that substantial agreement had been reached

on procedure, if not on all substantive issues. On the basis of the testimony of Dubinsky, who was the nearest to impartiality of all the negotiators in the sense that he had a foot in both camps, the AFL had indicated its willingness to move from the general to the specific on the crucial issue of conflicting jurisdictions. One can also understand the reluctance of the AFL to specify in writing industrial unionism in particular industries, in advance of a general settlement.

(3) In view of what is known of Lewis' attitude toward the AFL at the time, it may be surmised that he in effect torpedoed the *negotiations,* as distinct from an *agreement.* Lewis, it must be recalled, was not at all convinced that unity was a desirable objective. Speaking to his own convention shortly after the termination of the negotiations, he said on this score:

There are those abroad in the land who continue to say that this controversy in the house of labor is terrible, and they go about wringing their hands and calling upon all and sundry who observe their lamentations to see that it is weakening the labor movement. Let's see if it is. Who is hurt in this fight? Is the United Mine Workers of America any weaker because of this fight? . . . Well, are the steel workers any weaker? . . . But there is no union weaker. All of the Committee for Industrial Organization unions are stronger and gaining in membership every day, notwithstanding the industrial depression which affects our country at this time. Why, even the American Federation of Labor is no weaker. Every time we opened up areas in the steel industry or an area as in Logan County, West Virginia, or in 10,000 larger areas of this country where the Committee for Industrial Organization has gone in and organized a basic industry, it has made it perfectly safe for the American Federation of Labor to come along and gather up the butchers and the bakers and the candlestick makers. . . . Where is all the damage to the labor movement of this county from this controversy, a controversy that is a meritorious and a virtuous controversy over the question of the right of men to organize? . . .[102]

(4) While it is virtually certain that negotiations would have continued had it not been for Lewis, there is grave doubt that the final outcome would have been successful. The influential unions on the AFL side, such as the Carpenters and the Machinists, had given no real evidence of a willingness to compromise on their jurisdictional claims. In his report to the Carpenters' Union convention in December, 1936, Hutcheson gave it as his opinion that "if the American Federation of Labor should accept the plan of the Committee on Industrial Organization; namely, to organize all workers on an industrial basis, the only salvation for our organization would be to sever our affiliation with the American Federation of Labor." [103] The CIO, in the full flush of its organizational triumphs, was in no mood to compromise on the principle which it believed responsible for

its success. Lewis' position certainly had the support not only of his immediate cohorts among the ex-miners, but also of the left-wing heads of some
of the newer unions who might have lost their positions of prominence
in the event of a merger. All in all, the time was not propitious for labor
unity, as the record of the ensuing years shows.

The Formation of the Congress of Industrial Organizations

The collapse of the unity negotiations in December 1937 led the AFL
to swift action in severing its already tenuous ties with the CIO unions. By
a vote of 25,616 to 1,227, the Denver Convention of the AFL conferred
upon the Executive Council the authority to revoke the charters of CIO
affiliates. At this convention, John P. Frey charged that the Communist
Party had infiltrated the CIO, and was influential in determining its
policies. Specifically, he stated that 145 Communist Party members were
on the CIO payroll, and 200 others were serving as volunteer organizers,
and that the Communists, under the leadership of William Z. Foster, were
particularly active in the organization of steel. In a personal attack on
Lewis, he charged that the CIO president had been a frequent guest at the
Soviet Embassy, and that photographs of Lewis together with Soviet officials were being circulated widely in Russia.[104] This speech by one of the
most articulate spokesmen of the AFL, coming at the inception of the
1937 unity negotiations, was not calculated to promote friendly relations.

The Denver convention was marked by several other incidents indicative
of the heightening of AFL–CIO enmity. The Executive Council reported
that the Progressive Miners of America, a union up to that time functioning only in the Illinois coal fields as a rival to the United Mine Workers,
had been accepted into full membership in the AFL as an organization
with nationwide jurisdiction. The story of the Progressive Miners will be
told elsewhere; suffice it to say here that at the time of its chartering by the
AFL, this union promised very little in the way of becoming an effective
national organization, and its acceptance into the AFL must be attributed
primarily to the desire of the AFL leaders to annoy Lewis.

Also at the convention, the Carpenters' Union challenged the right of
Howard to be seated as a member of the Typographical Union delegation,
on the ground that he had fomented dual unionism. Howard was defended
vigorously by his codelegates, who argued that the AFL could not con-
stitutionally bar a delegate elected by an affiliated national union in good
standing. William J. Kelly of the Carpenters' Union made a particularly
bitter attack upon Howard:

I would say that John L. Lewis is almost a gentleman in comparison with Charles P. Howard. At least John L. Lewis is not here trying to tell us how to do our business. . . . Charles P. Howard attends every meeting of the American Federation of Labor. He is also seen whenever the Executive Council is meeting, or whenever there are conferences of any kind — you will always see Charles P. Howard very close by. He wants to find out what we are doing, I suppose, so that he can take it back to the other side and circumvent anything we may try to do to offset them.[105]

The convention sustained the debarring of Howard by an overwhelming vote. It also authorized the special assessment which had been agreed to at the May conference of national unions.

At its January 1938 meeting, the Executive Council of the AFL, in pursuance of the authority granted by the convention, formally revoked the charters of the United Mine Workers, the Mine, Mill and Smelter Workers, and the Federation of Flat Glass Workers. It followed this action by revoking the following charters at its April meeting: Amalgamated Clothing Workers, Amalgamated Association of Iron, Steel, and Tin Workers, United Textile Workers, United Automobile Workers, United Rubber Workers, and Oil Field Workers. The umbilical cord had finally been cut.

The year 1938 was not a good one for the trade unions. The deepening of the depression made organization difficult. Green reported to the Executive Council in January that he had laid off 70 organizers within the past six months, and in April reported cutting an additional 21 off the payroll. On the CIO side, Lewis stated publicly that "the CIO during this depression is not expending vast sums of money to effectuate organization among men and women who have no jobs, but the CIO is perfecting its organizations and rendering service to its unemployed, preserving the integrity of the union. . . . When we start organizing again we are starting from a base that represents a strength of nearly 4,000,000. When we have to slow up again, when the next depression comes along after this one, we will be just that much better prepared to do something about it." [106]

At a meeting on April 12 and 13, a conference of CIO presidents issued a call for a constitutional convention to take place later in the year. Brophy reported to the conference that while the number of affiliated national unions had grown to 39, adverse economic conditions required a reduction of staff.

This decision to formalize the existence of the CIO gave rise to the first schism within its ranks. Dubinsky and the ILGWU had from the beginning been unhappy at the speed and sureness with which Lewis was directing the CIO toward the goal of independence.

In December 1935, the General Executive Board of the ILGWU voted only by the close margin of 12 to 10 to join the CIO, and then only after Dubinsky assured the members "that we would be diligently on the lookout against the development of a dual movement." [107] Meeting on May 27, 1938 after receipt of the convention call, the ILGWU board adopted a resolution deferring action on the call until the final arrangements for a convention had been made.

The reasons for ILGWU hesitancy have been stated as follows:

the break with the AFL . . . was a painful step for the ILG. The women's garment workers' union's ties with the AFL dated from 1900 and its relations with the parent organization over the years were of inestimable value to it. The AFL and its presidents — Samuel Gompers and William Green — for decades were household names in the world of garment labor, participants in its woes and triumphs. To a much greater extent than the Amalgamated Clothing Workers' Union which joined the AFL only in 1934, the ILG . . . frankly was eager to remain within the AFL. But it would not knuckle down to an edict which it considered palpably unfair, one that might prove deadly to the unfolding organizing campaign in the basic industries.[108]

In the meantime, the ILGWU board appointed a committee consisting of Luigi Antonini, Isidore Nagler, and Julius Hochman to call upon the parties and bring about the resumption of the negotiations that had been terminated the previous December.[109]

On August 22, this committee called upon Green to inquire whether the AFL would be willing to meet with the CIO once more. Green informed them that "perhaps that could be done provided there would not be any impossible proposition presented . . . but if it was a matter of taking the matter up where it was broken off on the basis of what was proposed and what we understand was accepted that we would probably be willing to make another effort along that direction." [110] The following day, the committee called on Lewis, who informed them that he would not see them unless Dubinsky was present. The latter came to Washington immediately, and the meeting was held. Lewis stated that resumption of conferences would be futile unless all the existing CIO unions were chartered *en bloc* by the AFL, and that where jurisdictional disputes existed, they should be adjusted after the merger had been consummated. As an alternative, Lewis offered to admit all the AFL unions into the CIO. The ILGWU delegation endeavored to impress upon Lewis the impracticality of his proposals, without success, and concluded that "the position held by Chairman John L. Lewis, of the CIO, and the conditions outlined by him . . . as the basis for the resumption of peace negotiations, make our efforts for peace at this moment fruitless." [111] When the date for the CIO convention was fixed for November 14, the General Executive Board of the ILGWU issued a statement calling the formation of a permanent CIO a mistake, refusing to participate, and announcing that henceforth the ILGWU would remain independent.

Before the CIO convention met, another attempt to bring about new talks arose from an unexpected source. Daniel J. Tobin, president of the powerful Teamsters' Union, urged the AFL Executive Council, on the day before the opening of the AFL Houston convention, to recommend to the convention that a committee be appointed clothed with authority to reach final agreement with the CIO, and that all points in disagreement be referred to President Roosevelt for arbitration, his decisions to be final and binding upon the parties. In making this proposal, Tobin denied that he had seen or talked with Roosevelt since before the 1936 inauguration.[112] Coincidentally, Roosevelt sent a message to the convention, in which he said, among other things:

I venture to express the hope that the convention will leave open every possible door of access to peace and progress in the affairs of organized labor in the United States. If leaders of organized labor can make and keep the peace between various opinions and factions within the labor group itself it will vastly increase the prestige of labor with the country and prevent the reaction which otherwise is bound to injure the workers themselves.[113]

Tobin had never been a member of the extreme anti-CIO wing of the Executive Council, but neither had he been particularly friendly to the CIO. What motivated him to speak out so strongly at this juncture is therefore of some interest. He arose on the floor of the AFL convention, and in a long address declared that the interests of his organization demanded a settlement of the civil war in the labor movement. He pointed out that "it is all right for some of your trades that are 100 per cent organized and that live cloistered within your buildings where you are protected because of the skill of your trade, and because there is no access to your trade from the outside, to tell us this is a question of principle." But the Teamsters, Tobin stated, were subject to raiding by the CIO, and much of the energies of the trade union were devoted to fighting the CIO rather than to organization. Moreover, the existence of the CIO weakened union discipline, since aggrieved locals could switch their allegiance. Finally, he made a threat which had been even more pointed when addressed to the Executive Council: "Unless there is something done to establish peace, temporarily or otherwise, our international believes we ought to enter into an understanding with the CIO, that we would cease fighting them and they will cease bothering us or grabbing up our unions whenever we try to discipline them." [114]

Tobin's attack on AFL policies was replied to by Green, who asserted that the AFL remained willing to negotiate. There were no immediate repercussions at the convention, but the attitude of the Teamsters undoubtedly influenced the actions of the AFL in the ensuing months.

Lewis' reply to the overtures of the ILGWU peace committee, and to the events that took place at the AFL convention, was characteristic: he offered to resign from the presidency of the CIO if Green would simultaneously resign as president of the AFL, to permit the remaining leaders on both sides to conclude a peace pact. This offer was turned down indignantly by Green.

The CIO constitutional convention opened on November 14. It received a message from President Roosevelt similar in import to that which had been sent to the AFL. The proposed constitution submitted by the committee on the constitution was adopted with little discussion; only on the amount of the per capita tax payable by directly affiliated local industrial unions was there any objection. There was slight evidence of dissension in the discussion of a committee report on AFL–CIO relations, which contained the following policy recommendation:

The CIO states with finality that there can be no compromise with its fundamental purpose and aim of organizing workers into powerful industrial unions, nor with its obligation to fully protect the rights and interests of all its members and affiliated organizations. The CIO accepts the goal of unity in the labor movement and declares that any program for the attainment of such goal must embrace as an essential prelude these fundamental purposes and principles.[115]

Heywood Broun, president of the Newspaper Guild, thought that the door should be opened somewhat wider for peace negotiations, but with the ILGWU not in attendance, there was little support for his position. As unpromising as it seemed on its face, even the resolution as adopted apparently represented some softening of Lewis' position at the time. William Green later revealed that some time after the AFL Houston convention he had been approached by Frances Perkins, the secretary of labor, who told him that Roosevelt was interested in some plan for bringing about a discussion of AFL–CIO differences. When Green replied that there was no use in meeting so long as Lewis remained adamant in his position, she told him that she had been informed by Hillman and Murray that "at the Pittsburgh [CIO] convention Mr. Murray and others put in a number of hours with Mr. Lewis, attempting to prevail upon him to recede from the position he had assumed and that as a result of it the Pittsburgh convention had drafted a declaration and that declaration itself meant that the position was modified." [116]

In view of the role played by President Roosevelt in subsequent unity talks, it is instructive to see what Secretary Perkins had to say about his interest in the matter. She reported that internal union politics were not of great interest to him, and that he gave no special attention to the AFL–CIO split. However, difficulties were created with respect to labor legislation, and Roosevelt authorized Perkins to do what she could to heal the breach. Beginning in 1938, his annual messages to the CIO and the AFL contained pleas for peace, but they were drafted by Perkins, and did not reflect any personal interest on the part of the president. Only on the eve of the 1940 elections did Roosevelt evince any considerable interest in unity, and then for the purpose of consolidating his labor support. [117]

Largely at the instigation of Secretary Perkins and other labor advisors to the White House, Father Francis Haas in particular, a number of conversations were held between AFL and CIO leaders toward the end of 1938 and the beginning of 1939. Shortly after the close of the CIO convention, George Harrison met with Sidney Hillman in New York. Hillman disclosed that he had been on the committee which drafted the CIO resolution and that its intent had been to leave the door open for peace. Father Haas, who was present, asked whether the AFL would agree, while a truce was being arranged, to a no-raiding agreement and to the withdrawal of AFL-sponsored amendments to the Wagner Act then under consideration in Congress, but Harrison said that this was out of the question. "The conclusion, Vice-President Harrison stated, seemed to be that Mr. Hillman was worried as to how he could break the news to John Lewis that he was sitting down to talk the matter over. They had met secretly . . . Vice President Harrison stated that he got nothing out of the conference that in any way indicated there was any sentiment among the CIO to go into conference for the purpose of settling the matter." [118] It will be remembered that Harrison had consistently been the member of the Executive Council most disposed to work out a truce with the CIO.

In January 1939 Father Haas arranged a meeting between Woll and Murray, again in New York City. Woll asked whether the Pittsburgh resolution annulled Lewis' stand that all CIO organizations would have to be accepted into the AFL before negotiations could continue, and Murray replied that the Lewis statement still remained the position of the CIO. Haas then inquired whether the AFL might consider chartering the CIO *en bloc* as a separate unit for a year or two while negotiations on the status of individual unions were carried on, with the understanding that the arrangement would be terminated in the event of failure to agree. Murray expressed considerable interest in the proposal and said he thought it might be worth talking to Lewis about it.

A week before the Executive Council meeting of January 30, 1939, Green was called to the White House where Roosevelt told him that "the fight within the ranks of labor has gone too far and is creating a very disturbing situation economically, industrially, and politically." He informed Green that a letter had been drafted calling upon both partners to resume negotiations, and wanted to know what the reaction of the AFL would be, revealing that "he had talked with Mr. Hillman, for whom he has the highest regard, and Mr. Hillman is for peace." Green advised strongly against sending the letter out until he had a chance to consult with the Executive Council, and the president agreed. Hillman had thus taken Dubinsky's place as the principal exponent of peace within the CIO ranks.

Green advised the AFL Executive Council, when the facts had been placed before it, that the AFL could not refuse to meet with the CIO if the president made such a request, since "to refuse to do so would create a rising tide of condemnation by our own people because they do not understand all the complications that have arisen." Harrison suggested that Roosevelt be advised not to name the conferees, nor to insist that points of disagreement be referred to outside parties for adjustment. Harrison's last admonition was reinforced by a letter from Hutcheson which stated that there was nothing to arbitrate between the AFL and the CIO and concluded: "I might inform you that our Board definitely took action that if in endeavoring to settle the controversy between the two groups arbitration was agreed to it would mean the beginning of the disintegration of the AFL as our organization could no longer, under those circumstances, remain affiliated with the American Federation of Labor." [119]

On the basis of these preliminary preparations, President Roosevelt, on February 23, 1939, sent almost identical letters to Green and Lewis asking that committees be appointed to conduct negotiations. He declared in the letter: "The complicated economic and social problems of today require the cooperation of responsible groups of citizens in all walks of life and the effectiveness of labor in this type of council can only be realized by its fundamental unity of purpose and program." Unity talks were called

first, because it is right, *second,* because the responsible officers from both groups seem to me to be ready and capable of making a negotiated and just peace, *third,* because your membership ardently desire peace and unity for the better ordering of their responsible life in the trade unions and in their communities, and *fourth,* because the Government of the United States and the people of America believe it to be a wise and almost necessary step for the further development of the cooperation between free men in a democratic society such as ours. . . .[120]

Green, in nominating Bates, Woll, and Tobin as the AFL committee,[121] warned that "the preservation of the structure of the American Federation of Labor and the preservation of its democratic principles are of transcendent importance and cannot be compromised or made the subject matter of negotiation. . . . In addition, the economic and political philosophy evolved by the American Federation of Labor out of almost three-quarters of a century of experience cannot be compromised." Lewis, in a brief note, designated Murray, Hillman, and himself as the CIO committee.

The first meeting was held on March 7, 1939, at the White House. After a brief consultation with the president, as the conferees were about to leave, Lewis handed the president the following peace plan, which Secretary Perkins later described as "overambitious":

Between April 15 and April 30, 1939, the Congress of Industrial Organizations and the American Federation of Labor shall each hold a special national convention. These conventions shall be held separately and at any convenient place. The purpose of the conventions will be to pass upon and approve the following basic plan of procedure.

1. Not later than June 1, 1939, there shall assemble in the city of Washington, D. C., in the hall owned by the Daughters of the American Revolution, a convention of representatives of cooperation (a) the American Federation of Labor, (b) the Congress of Industrial Organizations and (c) the four brotherhoods in the railroad transportation field, heretofore independent.

2. This convention is to organize and dedicate the American Congress of Labor, designed to supersede and embrace the membership of the C.I.O. and the A.F.L., and to include the membership of the before-mentioned railroad organizations. The convention will outline its objectives, adopt a constitution and elect officers for a term of one year.

3. John L. Lewis and William Green shall not be eligible for election to any office in this convention. The A.C.L. will grant Mr. William Green a life tenure of his present salary for services rendered. The same arrangement will include Mr. Frank Morrison.

4. The executive board or governing body of the A.C.L. will be composed equally of representatives of the A.F.L. and the C.I.O., with proportionate representation for the four railroad brotherhoods.

The president of the A.C.L., to be elected by the convention, shall be selected from the membership of the brotherhoods, from such types of executives as A. F. Whitney, president of the Brotherhood of Railroad Trainmen, and D. B. Robertson, president of the Brotherhood of Locomotive Firemen and Enginemen.

5. During the year ensuing from the organization of the A.C.L., the services of the United States Department of Labor and its conciliation bureau shall be continuously available for cooperative mediation on all controversial questions affecting overlapping jurisdiction or other matters.

6. To insure the orderly, tranquil, and good-faith execution of the suggestions herein noted, the President of the United States is requested to preside at the sessions of the unified ranks of labor, when its constituent representatives assemble for the purpose of stating objectives, electing officers, and adopting a constitution.[122]

This plan, which had already been released to the press, took both the president and the AFL committee by surprise, since it had been anticipated that in this first meeting only a few pleasantries would be exchanged. The AFL committee immediately issued a statement regretting that Lewis had seen fit to use the White House as a sounding board for "fanciful statements for headline purposes," but agreed nevertheless to continue the negotiations. On the next day, at a meeting held in the Department of Labor, the AFL submitted a long reply to the Lewis plan, calling it impracticable, a dangerous move that would transfer direction of the labor movement to the hands of the government. It pointed out that railroad brotherhoods had not been consulted and might prefer to maintain their independent status; that the AFL convention could not bargain away its existence; that the plan "carries within it the germs of new dissensions, divisions, and conflicts." In turn, the AFL proposed an agreement similar to that alleged to have been reached in December 1937.[123] Harry Bates, chairman of the AFL committee, stated it as his opinion that Lewis' purpose in introducing the plan and insisting that it be discussed at the first negotiating session was to break up the conferences in such a manner as to put the onus on the AFL.[124] Lewis raised another issue at the same conference: he stated that "the representatives of the CIO . . . would not undertake to negotiate with the AFL on terms of peace while the hearings were on in Congress on the Wagner Labor Relations Act, on the grounds that there was no ground for talking peace with the Department of Labor, with war in the council chambers of the Capital at the same time." [125]

The next meeting was held on March 10 in New York, to accommodate Lewis, who was engaged in coal wage negotiations. At this meeting, the AFL proposal of the preceding year was taken up for discussion. Lewis asked whether the readmission of the original AFL unions was contemplated on the basis of the jurisdictions they exercised at the time of suspension from the AFL, or with the expanded jurisdictions subsequently acquired under the aegis of the CIO. For example, he pointed out that the United Mine Workers had recently organized chemical, coke, and by-product workers, an area over which they had no rights under their old AFL charter. To consider this question, a special meeting of the AFL Executive Council was held on March 22. The reply drafted by the council was not at all promising, from the CIO point of view. The AFL stated that all extensions of jurisdiction were subject to negotiation; that specifically, the extension of Mine Workers jurisdiction to the chemicals field was a direct transgress upon the territory of existing AFL organizations; that conferences would have to be held to reconcile the United Mine Workers with the newly-chartered AFL Progressive Miners, a particularly sore point with Lewis; and that any other of the original AFL unions which had extended their jurisdictions created problems, the solution to which "can be brought about through a transfer of members to the American Federation of Labor national and international unions having jurisdiction over them and to which they properly belong." [126] It was also suggested that as a preliminary to negotiations, each side should permit its books to be examined by an independent auditor so that membership claims could be verified. Lewis characterized this memorandum as "ambiguous and highly evasive in character"; the CIO representatives declared immediately that there was nothing further to discuss, "inasmuch as they construed the AFL memorandum as meaning the unions in question could not be admitted on terms the CIO would accept." [127] Nevertheless, at the urging of Secretary Perkins, it was agreed to continue the discussions.

Subsequent events are again the subject of conflicting testimony. According to the AFL story, the CIO representatives finally suggested that the originally affiliated unions be readmitted to the AFL on the basis of their existing membership, but without recognition of the extended jurisdiction involved. The AFL committee agreed to this, it claims, with the further condition that a satisfactory settlement would have to be reached with all organizations affiliated with the CIO, as well as with respect to such other questions as the status of the Amalgamated Clothing Workers vis-à-vis the United Garment Workers. Thereupon the CIO delegation is said to have repudiated its own proposal and to have urged instead that a charter be issued to the CIO as a department within the AFL, free of all AFL constitutional restrictions, and with full freedom and authority to act on its own. This proposal was rejected by the AFL.[128]

The CIO version is somewhat different. A few days before the Executive Council reply was delivered, Lewis set the stage for the CIO attitude in a public address in which he declared that the CIO unions "do not propose to dissolve themselves and cut themselves up into a multitude of pieces as the *quid pro quo* of becoming associated with the AFL"; and he warned that if peace talks failed, the CIO would change its "defensive" policy into one of aggression against the AFL.[129] Lewis and Murray admitted that the AFL, in the final meeting held on April 4, had agreed to admit the originally affiliated unions with their existing membership. But, said Murray,

after their readmission the question of jurisdiction would be one of major consideration by the American Federation of Labor. If we did not possess sufficient strength to protect our jurisdiction after we got in, the boys in a national convention of the American Federation of Labor could destroy that jurisdiction and leave it up to us either to get out of the A.F.L. again or stay in and yield portions of the membership that we had won over to these organizations during the period of the so-called split. So that the main and principal question, the one around which hovered the creation of the CIO in Atlantic City in 1935 has not been settled nor has there been any conscientious approach on the part of the American Federation of Labor toward a settlement of this question.[130]

It was the position of the CIO that it had never proposed readmission of the originally affiliated unions on the basis agreed to by the AFL, and that at no time was agreement even near. At any rate, on April 5, Lewis called Woll and said that the bargaining situation in coal made it impossible to meet that day as scheduled. He promised to communicate with Woll with regard to future meetings, a promise which was almost three years in the keeping.

It seems clear in retrospect that these negotiations had little chance of success from the start, less so than those that had been held in 1937–1938. Something of the atmosphere that prevailed at the conferences is conveyed by Murray's account of the first meeting in New York:

President Lewis pointed some very direct personal questions to members of the A.F.L. negotiating committee. He asked Matthew Woll how he could seriously and sincerely interest himself in the promotion of a legitimate, honorable, constructive peace. He said, "You are working as an appointed servant of the American Federation of Labor in the capacity of an insurance agent in the city of New York; you don't represent any members, you are not an official of even your own union, the strength of your International Union approximates 2500 people, your judgments in this situation are the judgments not of Matthew Woll, not of the American Federation of Labor, but the judgment of Hutcheson and Frey, and others in the Council of the American Federation of Labor, including Green."

He pointed a question then toward Tom Rickert, President of the United Garment Workers. He told Tom Rickert that he did not represent any substantial membership in the American Federation of Labor, that he was regarded in labor circles as an official entertainer for members of the Executive Council, that he furnished funds for certain occasions, that he was attached officially towards the promotion of an advertising enterprise from which he reaped substantial benefits. . . . The American Federationist, running the advertising, non-union advertising, Tom Rickert being a beneficiary of that advertising, a financial beneficiary. President Lewis had a copy of a will in his pocket that had been taken from the recorder's office in the city of New York, of deeds and wills, showing Tom had been left about one-third of John Morrison's estate, John Morrison being the fellow who promoted the advertising schemes for the American Federationist. . . .

. . . how in the name of all that is good, sound and reasonable could any sensible man . . . hope to attain decent, honorable, constructive peace with an organization that wants to bargain with you on the basis of effectuating peace in the city of New York, while down here on Capitol Hill they are officially slashing your throat from ear to ear? . . . I say . . . that President Lewis was blamed for breaking off the negotiations. He broke them off. He broke them off rather abruptly. That is an undeniable fact. But these are the circumstances that led to the breaking off.[131]

The CIO proposal which the AFL committee referred to the Executive Council had actually been drafted by Hillman, who apparently felt that the AFL reply constituted a recognition *de facto* of the expanded jurisdiction of the CIO unions.[132] However, this was not the understanding of Lewis and Murray nor, to judge from the reply, of the AFL.

The conclusion of the negotiations was followed by a heightening of ill-feeling between the two organizations. The CIO put on an intensive anti-AFL campaign in connection with the latter's sponsorship of amendments to the Wagner Act then pending in Congress. Lewis charged that the AFL amendments were prepared in secret conferences with representatives of the National Association of Manufacturers; as evidence the CIO produced some correspondence between Joseph A. Padway, the general counsel of the AFL, and Gilbert H. Montague, member of a New York legal firm that had represented a number of employers.[133] At its semi-annual meeting on June 13–15, 1939, the CIO Executive Board resolved upon an aggressive organizing campaign, with a warning to the AFL that the CIO was losing its patience. At this meeting, Lewis, Murray, Harry Bridges, Donald Henderson, Morris Muster, and Van Bittner argued that unity negotiations were weakening the morale of the CIO, and should not be continued. Lewis, for example, said:

While peace is desirable, do not forget that the philosophy of peace is opposed to the philosophy of war, and that your movement was born from the convulsions and the agony and despair between men on matters of profound and major policies. . . . It wasn't a very peaceful enterprise. The campaign of organization directed against the greatest combination of capital and employers in this nation, namely, the steel industry, was not a peaceful enterprise. . . .

So if peace was just as desirable in 1935 as it was in 1939 — and it must be in logic and in reason — then you made a mistake in creating the CIO . . . I don't ever expect to go back to the American Federation of Labor to repeat the experience that I had there from 1934 to 1935, when I was on the Executive Council, because I recognize the futility of it, the blind absurdity of it, the utter foolishness of it. Of course every man recognizes the tremendous increased scope of power of a unified labor movement, were one possible in this country.

Murray justified the continuance of the split partly on the basis of the "reactionary" leadership of the AFL, and pointed out that some members of the AFL Executive Council would probably support the Republican Party in the 1940 elections. "It may be argued that those fellows could not deliver the votes if they were given the leadership of a labor movement of some seven or eight million people, but I'll be damned if I am willing to give them that chance." [134] Of the Executive Board members, only Hillman and Powers Hapgood, then head of the Shoe Workers, argued in favor of the continuance of negotiations.

An interesting commentary on the attitude of the left-wing unions in the CIO toward the AFL at the time is provided by some remarks of Harry Bridges on the situation in the building trades. Observing that Public Works Administration work throughout the country was under the control of the AFL Building Trades, he remarked that "we would be better off if they were non-union than to follow the principle that any union is better than no union. We are looking at it from that realistic attitude in certain locations, and if we can make them non-union, so that we can move in and take over." Since the support of the building trades would be needed in his home base, San Francisco, during the forthcoming elections, he said that "up to next November naturally we will make no great attack on the building trades in San Francisco, but afterwards it is another story." [135]

From November to May 1939, average paid membership of the CIO was reported in the vicinity of 3 million, though affiliates were paying per capita on only 1.7 million members.[136] Average reported membership in the AFL for the eight-month period ending April 30, 1939, was 3.7 million,[137] so that by this token the balance of power had shifted somewhat toward the AFL in comparison with the situation prevailing during the previous round of negotiations.

In July 1939, the CIO launched the United Construction Workers Organizing Committee, under the chairmanship of A. D. Lewis, a brother of John L. Lewis. The AFL retaliated at its 1939 convention by chartering new unions in cement, shipping, textiles, and automobiles. The establishment of these unions was symptomatic of the developing pattern of complete dualism in the labor movement.

The 1939 Conventions and Further Presidential Intervention

The 1939 AFL and CIO conventions produced no surprises in terms of the relationships between the two organizations. On the eve of the AFL convention, President Roosevelt addressed a long letter to Green in which he called for continuation of the peace talks in order to further the national interest in the developing national emergency.[138] A resolution was adopted calling attention to the fact that "further appeals would be more fittingly directed to the CIO, for from the inception of the CIO the American Federation of Labor has been ready and most willing to confer with representatives of the CIO so that unity could be established, and your committee is of the conviction that this will continue to be the policy of the American Federation of Labor." [139] Tobin took the floor to urge against splitting hairs in negotiation, but his experience as a member of the AFL negotiating committee made him much less critical of the majority stand than he had been the year before.

A situation that came to a head during this convention involved the affiliation of the International Typographical Union. It will be recalled that while the ITU refused to follow Howard into the CIO, it remained rather cool to the AFL. The anti-AFL group within the union, led after Howard's death by Woodruff Randolph, the secretary-treasurer, managed to win a referendum vote on the issue of not paying the one-cent special assessment levied by the 1937 AFL convention. While the reason advanced for nonpayment of the levy was its alleged unconstitutionality, the real motive was actually a desire to withhold funds which were designed primarily to fight the CIO. The 1938 ITU convention, by a close vote, refused to submit the issue to another referendum. In consequence, pressure developed for the suspension of the ITU. The ITU delegation was none-theless seated at the 1938 convention, on the plea by Baker, the ITU president, that to do otherwise would cripple the forces in the union working for a regularization of relations with the AFL, and might drive the ITU into the CIO.

During 1939, Baker failed to make any headway in his quest to secure a new referendum on the issue. The issue was debated once more at the 1939 ITU convention, with the anti-AFL forces fighting the assessment on the popular question of national union sovereignty rather than on the narrower, legalistic question of the validity of the assessment. Notwithstanding the strong urging of President Baker, the convention once more refused to pay the assessment and, in consequence, the ITU delegation was not seated at the 1939 AFL convention. Shortly thereafter, the Executive Council notified AFL central bodies to suspend all ITU locals.

President Roosevelt sent to the CIO convention a letter similar in import to that which he had sent to the AFL. The question of unity was not debated; the convention merely adopting the following resolution:

As a substitute for the resolutions which have been submitted pertaining to labor unity this Committee wishes to point out that the CIO has created a Negotiating Committee with full authority, consisting of John L. Lewis, Philip Murray and Sidney Hillman. We recommend that this Negotiating Committee be continued and authorized to exercise its discretion in any future negotiations.[140]

At the close of the convention, Lewis wrote to Roosevelt indicating the intention of the CIO to continue negotiating, and soliciting specific recommendations. Lewis later claimed that he had received no answer to this letter.[141]

However, the White House had not yet given up in its efforts to mediate the controversy. On November 9, 1939, Green was called to the White House, where he was asked by Roosevelt what the chances were of negotiating an agreement with the CIO. He replied that a settlement could be reached by continuing along the lines of the previous conferences. On the same day, Lewis saw the president and, according to Green, had impressed the president with the feasibility of the "one big union" proposal which Lewis had advanced at the inception of the conferences. On December 6, Green visited Roosevelt once more for the specific purpose of preventing Roosevelt from making a public recommendation along those lines. He saw Roosevelt again on January 16, 1940, and this is his account of the meeting:

President Green stated that he had asked the President if Mr. Lewis had agreed that his committee meet with our A.F.L. committee. The President answered this in three words — "God only knows." President Green asked if Mr. Lewis had definitely rejected the President's request. The President replied "yes and no," that a month ago he indicated rather a favorable response and a willingness to meet but recently Mr. Lewis had changed.[142]

When these facts were reported, the AFL Executive Council wrote Roosevelt asking him to make the facts public so that the public could assess the blame for the continued division in the labor movement.[143]

These events must be read against the background of contemporary political developments. According to Secretary Perkins, John L. Lewis had vice-presidential ambitions in 1940, and intimated that AFL–CIO unity might be achieved if he received the nomination.[144] Whether because of Roosevelt's unreceptiveness to the idea, or because of other grievances against the administration, Lewis, at the January 1940 convention of the United Mine Workers delivered a strong attack on the administration. Accusing it of failing to give the CIO representation in the cabinet or in policy-making agencies of the government, or even seeking CIO advice on economic problems, and of failing to curb the antilabor propensities of the Democratic majority in Congress, Lewis prophesied that Roosevelt would not run for a third term, and "conceding that the Democratic National Convention could be coerced or dragooned into renominating him, I am convinced that, with the conditions now confronting the nation and the dissatisfaction now permeating the minds of the people, his candidacy would result in ignominious defeat. . . ."[145]

More than any previous issue in its history, the question of support for a third term split the CIO. Most of the CIO leaders were in disagreement with Lewis on political and unity matters, but few dared oppose him openly. One who did was Hillman, who of the prominent labor leaders was one of the closest to Roosevelt at the time. Speaking to the convention of his union in May, he said:

I believe that some progress was made during the course of the [AFL–CIO] conferences. By that I do not mean for one moment to imply that peace terms acceptable to the CIO were proposed by the AFL committee. Nevertheless, I am of the opinion that peace conferences should have been continued. . . . President Lewis has publicly stated that in his opinion unity is impossible on any basis acceptable to the CIO. I am not prepared to go so far. Because he believes that the prolongation of negotiations would be futile, he has failed to take steps for further conferences. I believe that this position is a mistake.[146]

Hillman's temerity did not go unchallenged. In a meeting of the CIO Executive Board on June 3, 1940, Lewis directed the following barbs toward Hillman:

I do not plan to call any meetings of the committee, in the absence of such knowledge, to wit, a sufficient change in the situation to warrant the opinion that conferences, if held, would be fruitful or permit of progress being made. . . .

One member of the Peace Committee desisted from that viewpoint, and carried the proposition to the convention of his own organization, and according to the public press rebuked the President of the C.I.O. and placed upon him the blame for the warfare between the C.I.O. and the A.F.L. Since that time the public press has indulged in an orgy of abuse of the President of this organization, which does not change the situation. I do not plan to call any meetings; I do not know when any meetings will be held. . . .

I think it is time for this Board to express itself in a vote on this question . . . I am holding in reserve plenty of observations I can make on this subject. Today I want to know where I am at, and I am asking you. I am either President of the C.I.O. or I am a busted flush. So tell me what it is.

Jacob Potofsky, who was there as the Amalgamated representative, attempted to smooth things over by arguing that "if the statement is read very carefully you will find it is a most laudatory statement of the work of the CIO, and all its intent and purpose was in line with the resolution that was passed at the San Francisco convention, to keep the door open so that if, as we surmise, there is no desire on the part of the AFL to make peace that the responsibility should be squarely placed upon them." [147] But Lewis' former subordinates in the Mine Workers, Murray, Bittner, and Kennedy rose to his defense with strong statements. Only R. J. Thomas[148] and Emil Rieve, after first pledging their allegiance to Lewis, ventured a few words in defense of Hillman's motives. On the unity issue, the question of continuing negotiations was left to the discretion of the negotiating committee.

But the estrangement among the top CIO leadership continued to grow. On July 2, Lewis, addressing a convention of the Townsend Plan organization, declared that only Senator Burton K. Wheeler could defeat Wendell Willkie in the coming presidential elections. The appointment of Hillman as the labor member of the National Defense Advisory Commission must have been galling to Lewis' pride. Finally, on October 25, Lewis took the plunge and in a dramatic radio address, came out in support of Willkie and promised to resign from the presidency of the CIO if Roosevelt were reelected.

Lewis' stand created consternation in the ranks of the CIO. He was formally repudiated by the general executive board of the Amalgamated Clothing Workers and by the United Automobile Workers, among others. Support of his position came mainly from such Communist-dominated organizations as the State, County, and Municipal Workers, the National Maritime Union, the Office and Professional Workers, the Mine, Mill and Smelter Workers, the Cannery and Agricultural Workers, and the Transport Workers.[149] Of the six vice-presidents of the CIO, only one — Reid Robinson of the Mine, Mill and Smelter Workers — came to Lewis' defense. Even Philip Murray, up to that time his most loyal supporter, came out publicly for Roosevelt.

The Executive Board meeting that was held three days before the opening of the CIO convention of November 1940, and after the Roosevelt electoral victory, was a tense affair. Controversy broke out almost immediately when Potofsky criticized the CIO for failing to have its books audited and to submit periodic financial statements to its affiliates. Lewis, after pointing out that the Amalgamated Clothing Workers had failed to pay their per capita tax since August, which resulted, according to Lewis, in the enforced layoff of 63 CIO organizers, continued:

Now, for a board member to come into this meeting and say this situation is created because we did not have a finance committee or because they did not know they were required to pay their tax, or because they were occupied in some campaign, is at least an insult to the intelligence of at least the President of the CIO. It is at least an insult to me, and I resent it, Board Member Potofsky, I resent the hypocrisy involved in the statement.[150]

This time Potofsky stood his ground:

Some people might have taken the last campaign lightly, or taken it in a way that was against the best interests of what some of us thought, of labor, but we didn't feel that way . . . the Amalgamated has contributed to the CIO close to a half a million dollars, in addition to having contributed more than a half a million dollars in the organization campaign of the Textile Workers. . . . Now, the problem is whether you are going to have a little more democracy in the handling of your finances.

To which Lewis replied:

I was perfectly aware of just how far the Amalgamated was sticking the knife into the CIO, and I don't expect any associate officer of mine to beg the Amalgamated to pay its tax according to the constitution. . . . It is not words we want from the Amalgamated, it is the per capita tax of the organization, if it is in truth and in fact a member of the CIO.[151]

Lewis, as usual, received the support of the left-wing group: Flaxer, Merrill, Emspak, Bridges, and Gold spoke in his support. Murray and Bittner, even at this late date, also remained loyal to him. When Emil Rieve ventured a few mild words in support of Potofsky's position, Lewis treated him to a dressing down that is remarkable when it is recalled that at the time, Rieve was one of the six vice-presidents of the CIO and president of one of its largest constituent organizations:

Brother Rieve is one of the critics of my administration, he says I am a betrayer of labor. I think he lies when he says it. . . . I see no purpose in advertising to the world that his organization was not able to pay its tax to the CIO, and that in order to keep the record straight and give him that adequate representation he wanted his organization to have while he fought the fight in the textile industry, we loaned him money so he could pay part of it back in tax and be credited as a dues-paying affiliate of the CIO. The United Mine Workers of America gave $200,000 in cash to carry on the textile organizing campaign, $33,333.33 a month for six months. This is the only great campaign that failed that the CIO conducted, the textile campaign. Do you want to advertise that fact? There are a million and a quarter employees in the textile industry, there is a handful of them organized, notwithstanding Mr. Rieve, as he sits here today, represents an investment of $338,000 of this organization so he can be president of the Textile Workers Union.[152]

The Change of CIO Leadership

The 1940 convention of the CIO marked the first leadership change in the history of that organization. Lewis declined to accept reelection, although the left wing and the Mine Workers' delegations were plumping for him. He nominated for the presidency his associate of many years, Philip Murray, who at the time held the dual positions of chairman of the Steel Workers' Organizing Committee and vice-president of the United Mine Workers. Perhaps with a premonition of what was ahead for him in his relations with Lewis, Murray was extremely reluctant to accept the presidency:

When I accepted the presidency of the Congress of Industrial Organization in 1940 in Atlantic City I did it after President Lewis had pleaded with me for ten long, weary days to take this job. I did it against my own good judgment, and certainly I did not ask President Lewis for any support then. He came to me and said, "Phil, whatever in hell it is, you get it. If you are right or if you are wrong, I am for you". . . . I accepted the Presidency with the distinct understanding that I would be President." [153]

Despite the events of the preceding months, no one dared attack Lewis directly at the convention. However, indirect attacks were made through criticism of the way the *CIO News,* edited by Len De Caux, had reported the presidential campaign, and Lewis was quick to seize this opportunity to defend his role in supporting Willkie. Hillman, now beginning to operate in the larger arena of national defense, pledged that the Amalgamated Clothing Workers would remain in the CIO; with Lewis out as president, full cordiality of relationships was restored with his organization.[154] For the first time at a CIO convention, the Communist Party was openly attacked when Hillman called the Communists "a menace to the labor movement" and congratulated the United Mine Workers upon their constitutional exclusion of Communists.

The labor unity question came in for more open debate than at any previous CIO convention. The Committee on Officers' Reports recommended to the convention that the negotiating committee consisting of Lewis, Murray, and Hillman be continued in existence and empowered with authority to participate in future negotiations in conformity with Lewis' last offer to the AFL.[155] Delegates of the Amalgamated Clothing Workers and the Textile Workers urged that a more affirmative position be taken, and that the CIO officers should be instructed to meet immediately with the AFL. Lewis put an end to debate and resolved the issue with the most slashing and vitriolic attack he had ever made on the AFL, as well as on his ex-associates and opponents in the CIO. Of Dubinsky and Zaritsky he said: "He [Dubinsky] has crept back into the American Federation of Labor. He abandoned his fellows and he abandoned what he claimed was his principle. And he has gone into that organization on his adversary's terms. He is crying out now and his voice laments like that of Rachel in the wilderness, against the racketeers and the panderers and the crooks in that organization. . . . And Zaritsky, he was the man representing the Millinery and Cap Workers. He said, 'Me too.' And now above all the clamor comes the piercing wail and the laments of the Amalgamated Clothing Workers." The choicest barbs, however, were saved for the AFL negotiators:

We have explored every proposition. What have we all been doing? I have been an explorer in the American Federation of Labor. Explore the mind of Bill Green? Why Bill and I had offices next door to each other in the same corridor for ten years. I was a member of the same Executive Council that he was for one year. I have done a lot of exploring in Bill's mind and I give you my word there is nothing there.

Explore Matthew Woll's mind? I did. It is the mind of an insurance agent, who used his position as an officer of the American Federation of Labor and a member of the Executive Council to promote his insurance business. . . .

Explore Tom Rickert's mind, of the United Garment Workers, who was on the Negotiating Committee? I did, and here is what was in his mind. He said he did not propose to let the Amalgamated Clothing Workers into the American Federation of Labor if he could help it. . . .

Explore the mind of Bill Hutcheson? I did. There wasn't anything there that would do you any good. So what? Waste more time on unprofitable explorations? [156]

The ILGWU Reaffiliates with the AFL

The AFL convention, which was held concurrently with that of the CIO, saw the reaffiliation of the ILGWU, the first of the original CIO unions to return to the AFL. The ILGWU had conditioned its reaffiliation upon three actions which it wished the AFL to take: (1) elimination of the one-cent per capita tax which had been levied to fight the CIO; (2) elimination of the constitutional provision giving the Executive Council the right to suspend affiliated international unions; and (3) the expelling of racketeers from the ranks of the labor movement.[157] The AFL convention took the following action on these three points: (1) The Executive Council recommended to the convention that the power to suspend should be vested only in the convention, with the proviso, however, that when two or more unions conspired to create a movement dual to the AFL, the Executive Council would retain the right of suspension.[158] Dubinsky took the floor to object that this recommendation constituted a violation of the explicit condition upon which the ILGWU had reaffiliated, and proposed instead that the Executive Council be permitted to suspend, but that in the subsequent appeal to the convention, the suspended unions retain their voting rights.[159] During the debate, Tobin revealed that he had opposed any restrictions on the authority of the Executive Council to suspend, but had been persuaded to go along with the recommendation of the council in order to bring about the reaffiliation of the ILGWU. The convention accepted the recommendation of the Executive Council, and thus in effect repudiated one of the conditions upon which the ILGWU had come back.[160]

(2) The second condition made by the ILGWU, the abolition of the special assessment, was met by converting the one-cent assessment into a temporary increase in the per capita tax, with a committee appointed to recommend to the next convention what the final per capita tax should be. We may anticipate a bit by saying that the committee recommended to the Executive Council that the per capita tax be set at $1\frac{1}{2}\cancel{c}$ per member per month, and that the Executive Council in turn passed this recommenda-

tion on to the 1941 convention.[161] However, just prior to the convention, at a meeting of the Executive Council, Tobin moved that the tax be set at 1¢ per member for unions with 300,000 or more members, and 1½¢ per member for unions with less than 300,000 members, citing the burden that would be placed upon the larger unions by a flat increase to 1½¢.[162] He received the support of Hutcheson, and the Executive Council revised its recommendation to this effect. Despite some objection from smaller unions, the revised recommendation of the Executive Council was adopted.

(3) With respect to racketeering, the delegates of the ILGWU to the 1940 convention introduced a resolution which would have empowered the Executive Council to order the removal of union officers convicted of offenses involving moral turpitude when international unions failed to act. The convention adopted a weaker resolution recommending that all affiliated unions be urged to amend their constitutions to require disciplinary action against dishonest officials, and authorizing the Executive Council to "apply all of its influence" to secure appropriate action if an affiliate failed to act.[163] Even in this form the resolution constituted a victory for the ILGWU point of view, though it should not be inferred that the stand of the ILGWU delegates was the only factor responsible for the action of the convention.

The Executive Council, in its report to the 1940 AFL convention on AFL–CIO relations, was particularly bitter in its denunciation of the CIO venture into the building construction field, as the following language indicates:

This action on the part of the C.I.O. is more than unethical. It violates every rule of trade union conduct and does violence to every moral obligation which members of unions have assumed toward each other. It has always been assumed that only strike-breakers and those who never belonged to a union would offer to work at rates of pay greatly below the union scale and union wage standards. It is bad enough to raid established unions, to persuade and beguile unsuspecting men to leave the bona fide labor movement which has functioned for three-quarters of a century and join with rebels in a dual movement, but it is infinitely and despicably worse for the leaders of such a rebel, dual movement to beg employers to utilize their men and to permit them to be used in lowering wage scales and in destroying working standards in a great industry such as the building and construction industry. This is a violation of the moral code established by trade unions and religiously observed by loyal union members. It is a crime which exceeds and transcends all others included in our trade union vocabulary.[164]

There were many in the ranks of the CIO who had similar qualms about the establishment in 1940 of the Construction Workers' Organizing Committee, with A. D. Lewis at the head. After Hillman's appointment to the National Defense Advisory Commission, he informed William Green that he had advised A. D. Lewis of his opposition to CIO entrance into that field, and he promised Green that the government would give no recognition to the Construction Workers' Organizing Committee.[165] This move on the part of Lewis was motivated by a desire to hit back at the most sensitive spot of the AFL in answer to the AFL's coal organizing efforts.

Labor Representation in National Defense Agencies

The appointment of Sidney Hillman in June 1940 as the only labor member of the National Defense Advisory Commission aroused the ire of both the AFL and John L. Lewis. The former labeled it a "grave injustice" that the "most representative organization of workers" in the country was not accorded representation on the Commission, and was not even asked to nominate representatives to the committee advisory to Hillman.[166] After Hillman's appointment, he had approached Green and asked that the AFL appoint a representative to work with him. Roosevelt subsequently called Green and advised him that he intended to appoint an AFL administrative assistant. The Executive Council decided not to respond to Hillman's invitation.[167] However, a number of AFL officials, when approached directly by Hillman, agreed to cooperate in the interests of their national organizations, among them Harry Bates of the Bricklayers, Dan W. Tracy of the Electrical Workers, and Harvey W. Brown of the Machinists. On the CIO side, Lewis complained that his advice had not been sought on defense questions, and made no effort to conceal his distaste for the Hillman appointment.[168]

Matters were not improved when Hillman became associate director of the Office of Production Management in December 1940. The AFL continued to resent its lack of direct representation, though this resentment was softened somewhat by a stabilization agreement between the Building Trades and the government procurement agencies which in effect gave the AFL preference in defense construction work and hindered the CIO construction union from entering this area.[169]

The events surrounding labor participation in the National Defense Mediation Board did not serve to bring the two organizations of labor closer together. The board was tripartite, with labor having two representatives, equally divided between the AFL and the CIO. After an existence of some ten months, the board finally broke down over a case involving the demand for a union shop in the captive mines by the United Mine Workers. A short strike by 53,000 coal miners, which threatened to halt the production of steel, was denounced vigorously by every sector of public opinion except the loyal Lewis cohorts in the CIO. The AFL *Weekly News Service* called Lewis' stand "a betrayal of America" and "a dastardly and indefensible betrayal of the best interests of all labor in America." [170] Although Murray defended the Miners, the attitude of the Hillman wing of the CIO may be surmised from Lewis' charge that Hillman, in his capacity as associate director general of the OPM, was motivated by "vengeful and malignant opposition to the interests of the United Mine Workers of America." [171] When the National Defense Mediation Board, with only the two CIO representatives, Philip Murray and Thomas Kennedy, dissenting, refused to recommend the union shop, the CIO representatives resigned. The CIO was particularly critical of the failure of the AFL board members to side with it, though matters were partly rectified when George Meany, the newly elected secretary-treasurer of the AFL, who had been represented by an alternate in this case, announced that he would have voted to give the Miners a union shop had he been in Washington.[172]

The 1941 Conventions and New Unity Efforts

The 1941 convention of the AFL opened in Seattle on October 6, that of the CIO in Detroit on November 17. In his message to the AFL, President Roosevelt declared that

In this hour when civilization is in the balance, organizational rivalries and jurisdictional conflicts should be discarded. Only by united action can we turn back the Nazi threat. The establishment of peace between labor organizations would be a patriotic step forward of incalculable value in the creation of true national unity.[173]

The Executive Council could only report to the convention that no peace negotiations had been held with the CIO during the preceding year, and reiterated its willingness to continue negotiations whenever the CIO was prepared to do so.

On one organizational issue, the status of the International Typographical Union, the Executive Council had disappointing news to impart. In February 1941, negotiations between AFL and ITU representatives had produced a memorandum of agreement whereby the Executive Council was prepared formally to advise the ITU as follows:

(1) that the AF of L constitution guaranteed the complete autonomy of all affiliated unions with respect to their internal affairs and government.

(2) that the AF of L did not define the jurisdiction of affiliated unions, but merely attempted to bring about adjustment in case of conflict between affiliates.

(3) that the only power to discipline possessed by the AF of L was that of revocation or suspension of charter by the convention, except that the Executive Council could suspend in the case of dual unionism.

(4) that AF of L funds were never to be used to destroy a trade union.

(5) that the AF of L was willing to recommend the reaffiliation of the ITU *de novo* insofar as financial obligations were involved.[174]

When the memorandum was submitted to the ITU membership for a referendum vote, Woodruff Randolph, the secretary-treasurer, and Vice-President Gill opposed it, and despite its strong endorsement by President Baker, the agreement was defeated by a sizable majority. By this time, there was no real reason for the refusal of the ITU to reaffiliate with the AFL, and credence must be given to the observation of the AFL Executive Council that the issue had become a political football in the internal struggle between the two parties within the ITU.[175]

The CIO convention was not very harmonious. The United Mine Workers' delegation was present — silent, contemptuous, and brooding. There were occasional fist fights around the lobby between UMW stalwarts and some of the CIO people, including one between Reid Robinson, president of the left-wing Mine Mill Union, and a UMW delegate.[176] The UMW was particularly resentful of the Communist faction, which was now solidly behind the national defense effort with the involvement of Russia in the war. Murray was reelected to the presidency by acclamation.

Events within the CIO, however, were shaping up to a major organizational crisis. Lewis was still smarting from his enforced retirement in 1940 and, in his pique, undertook to undermine the position of Philip Murray, who had faithfully supported the position of the United Mine Workers, of which he continued to be vice-president, during the difficult days of 1941. It was sometimes thought that Lewis was motivated by annoyance at Murray's independence in fulfilling the functions of CIO president, but there is nothing in the record to indicate that Murray differed with Lewis on any issue during his first year in office. Indeed, the two lunched together every day when both were in Washington, and gave the impression of retaining their close friendship.

Yet, Murray later charged, Lewis began to work against him early in 1941. In May, Ora Gasaway, head of District 50 of the UMW, took occasion in a veiled manner, in a public address, to suggest that Lewis be drafted for the presidency of the CIO at the next convention. Following the 1941 convention, "men were called into the offices of District 50, offered positions

with the United Mine Workers of America, with the distinct understanding
that upon their acceptance of those jobs they would immediately attempt
the destruction of the National CIO movement. There are gentlemen in
this hall who were called into the office of District 50 and told that there
was only one war going on in this country last January [1942], and that was
the war of Mr. Lewis against Philip Murray and the CIO." [177]

Murray also asserted that in September 1941, Lewis had entered into
secret negotiations with Hutcheson of the Carpenters' Union, and had
agreed to give up the Construction Workers' Union. A story appeared in
the *New York Times* on January 19, 1942, to the effect that in conferences
with Tobin, Lewis had agreed upon a merger plan whereby William Green
was to retire, George Meany was to become president and Murray secretary-
treasurer of a united labor movement. William Green, on behalf of the
AFL Executive Council, denied the veracity of the story, as did Thomas
Kennedy, who represented Lewis on the CIO Executive Board. In fact,
said Kennedy, "every citizen of this country knows, with respect to the
relative abilities of the men, that Murray should be the President in any
consolidated unity group that might eventually be organized." [178]

Lewis' version of the events of 1941 was quite different, as might be
expected. He told the convention of the United Mine Workers: "I retired
voluntarily [from the presidency of the CIO]; not because I had to. Those
of you who were there know that that convention would have re-elected
me unanimously had I chosen to run. I had put too much of myself into
the CIO, in combating its enemies, in preserving order in its own ranks, in
teaching inexperienced men how to organize, and how to bargain, and how
to administer the affairs of the Union." [179] He then went on to say that
during 1941 he had devoted himself exclusively to the affairs of the Mine
Workers, and had made no criticisms of the CIO leadership. But, he complained,

for more than a year the welkin has been filled with resounding cries of men in
this country who stated that John Lewis was a man of such overwhelming ambition that he would not cooperate with the present leadership in the CIO. . . .
I could have criticized the leadership in the CIO when they were attempting to
sell the United Mine Workers of America down the river in the captive mine
fight. I could name names and give dates and quote the text of these things, but
life is too short for me to answer the yapping of every cur that follows at my
heels. I hear the pack in my rear at times. I can turn my head and see the lap
dogs and the kept dogs and the yellow dogs in pursuit.

The climax of the growing estrangement between Murray and Lewis
came on January 17, 1942, when Lewis, without any prior consultation,

addressed identical letters to Murray and Green calling for an immediate resumption of unity negotiations between the standing committees of the two groups.[180] He took this step in his capacity as a member of the CIO negotiating committee that had been created to treat with the AFL in 1939, but which had since lain dormant and forgotten.

The AFL replied immediately that its committee, consisting of Bates, Tobin, and Hutcheson stood ready to meet with the CIO "anywhere, any time, any place." On the CIO side, however, the Lewis proposal met a cold rebuff. Murray informed Lewis that he would submit the latter's proposal to the Executive Board of the CIO, and noted in closing: "As you are well aware, all arrangements in behalf of the Congress of Industrial Organizations, with reference to unity with the American Federation of Labor, will necessarily have to be initiated through the office of the President of the Congress of Industrial Organizations." [181] Lewis replied as follows:

Your letter dated January 19 stated in effect that all future negotiations between the C.I.O. and the A.F. of L. will have to be initiated through you and you alone. Such an assumption on your part constitutes an astonishing error. No such delegation of power has been given you by the constitution of the C.I.O. . . . To the contrary, the Third Constitutional Convention of the C.I.O. specifically conveyed this authority to three of its representatives, designating them by name. . . . By agreement of the individual joint conferees, the negotiations of 1939 were adjourned, subject to being reconvoked upon the call of the undersigned. It is my opinion that the present is a propitious time to renew negotiations as contrasted with conditions in 1939. . . . I will not attend your board meeting. I am not a member of the Executive Board. The Board has no power to negate convention action.

In a meeting of the CIO Executive Board held on January 24, Murray openly lashed out at Lewis in a speech which showed how deeply hurt he had been at the action of his former chief. Addressing himself to Lewis' brother, who was present as a representative of the United Mine Workers, Murray declared:

All that I wanted here, Denny, was a little bit of conversation, a telephone call — that's all. I am entitled to that . . . the President of the United Mine Workers of America, who is a friend of mine, should call me and talk to me before he issues a letter of this description. John Lewis never experienced any difficulty in getting along with me. Hell, he never will, I hope. . . . All I have at stake here is the question of manhood. I don't challenge John Lewis' manhood. I have the greatest admiration for him, but by God, what he is entitled to I am entitled to. That is a question of common decency, that's all. . . . I thought that John ought to have come over here and talked these matters out with this Board, not to quarrel with me — damn it, I don't want to quarrel with him. . . . I have a grievance, and any other man who would be occupying my position would have one, and so far as I am concerned, when it comes to a question of manhood I will fight just as long as any other man who cares to defend the attitude of another man who won't call him up and talk to him about these things can go ahead and do it.[182]

There was no conspicuous enthusiasm for the undertaking of new negotiations with the AFL on the part of other members of the CIO Executive Board. Emspak of the Electrical Workers declared that "every damned craft in there would be after us the minute negotiations were opened up." On the other side of the political spectrum, John Green of the Shipbuilders cried: "You are asking me to sleep in the same bed with John Frey? You're crazy, because if there is this peace you can rest assured that the organization which I represent will be butchered up into twenty-six different craft unions. . . ." [183]

A few days after the publication of the original Lewis letter, President Roosevelt called Murray to the White House to inquire what, if anything, he could do to help promote labor unity. Murray urged him to convene an AFL–CIO committee for the immediate purpose of advising him on war and postwar problems, and eventually considering the problem of organic unity. This was done on January 22, 1942, when the president wrote to Murray and Green asking them to form a small Combined Labor War Board to consult with him periodically.[184] The acceptance of this invitation by the CIO Executive Board provided a convenient means of outflanking Lewis on the unity issue, a purpose that may in part have motivated the president's action at this juncture. This also enabled the CIO to abolish the standing peace committee of which Lewis was a member. Lewis said of the episode:

Why, the American Federation of Labor accepted the invitation, bad as their record is on that question. Foolish as is old Bill Green on a lot of subjects, give Bill credit, when his Executive Council ordered him to answer this he wrote me a letter saying, yes. Hand him that much anyhow! But the CIO — did it say yes? Oh, no! It said nothing in a meeting in New York, and its officers rushed down to Washington to ask the President to save them from that terrible man, John Lewis, and his peace plan. And they were saved! And they were given a joint Victory Committee. . . .[185]

The AFL, perhaps with the purpose in mind of deepening the split that had been opened in the ranks of the CIO, pressed the tactical advantage it had gained by repeating its invitation to the CIO to meet with its representatives, under date of May 23, 1942. In a letter to Murray, Green stressed the contribution that a united labor movement could make to furtherance of the war effort by eliminating "division, discord, disunity, jurisdictional strife, bitterness, hatred, from the ranks of Labor." [186] There was marked reluctance on the part of the CIO to have any dealings with the AFL on this issue; Murray told the Executive Board that "I see nothing on the horizon at the present moment — and this opinion is derived from conversations that I have had with officers of the American Federation of Labor — that would indicate any hope of an early organic unity between both the Federation of Labor and the CIO." [187] It was necessary, however, to avoid a negative stand and, in reply to the AFL, the CIO adopted a resolution proposing that the following steps be taken:

1. The executive councils of the AFL and CIO should meet to form a United National Labor Council to formulate a program covering all issues which might aid labor and the war effort.

2. This Council should make effective a program of cooperation and unity between the two organizations.

3. "Through this unity under the National Labor Council an increasing mutual confidence will be developed between the several national and international unions of the CIO and the AFL. On this firm basis, discussions can then be encouraged by the United National Labor Council between AFL and CIO unions having similar jurisdiction, looking toward organic unity."

In a long reply, the AFL pointed out that the Combined Labor War Board appointed by President Roosevelt was already fulfilling the liaison functions envisaged by the CIO resolution, and termed the CIO reply evasive. Green once more strongly urged the CIO to consent to a unity meeting between representatives of the two federations.[188] The AFL was not displeased with the way events had taken shape; Green reported to the Executive Council that "we are in the strongest position and have outmanoeuvred the CIO by the stand that we have taken." [189]

Murray launched a counterattack in a letter to Green on August 1, 1942. Observing that despite the no-strike pledge taken by the labor unions, jurisdictional disputes between AFL and CIO unions had led to work stoppages by AFL affiliates, he urged that the two organizations establish a joint committee, with an impartial chairman, to settle such disputes by arbitration, and noted that "with the usefulness and need of that committee having been established, I believe that we can initiate discussions regarding possible establishment of organic unity between our organizations." This was a shrewd move, since it touched upon a sore point that was very much in the public consciousness at the time. Several building trades disputes were involved, and the War Labor Board was at that moment threatening to appoint an arbitrator to settle the disputes. Therefore, the AFL was somewhat on the defensive when on August 4, Green replied that the issue raised by Murray was separate and distinct from that of organic unity.[190]

On this inconclusive note we may terminate our account of the series of attempts to eliminate dualism in the American labor movement that began almost with the formation of the CIO. More than a decade was to elapse before the goal of unity was finally achieved. As far as may be judged from the relevant documents, there was no serious possibility of achieving unity at any time up to the end of the period with which we are now concerned after the breakdown of the 1937 negotiations. The conversations that did take place were largely in response to public pressure and to the internal political requirements of the two organizations, rather than a consequence of any deep-seated conviction on either side that unity was possible, or even essential.

It remains only to consider an outcome of the events of January 1942, which was of considerable moment to the CIO. John L. Lewis, stung by what he regarded as insubordination on the part of Murray, caused the Mine Workers to withhold their per capita tax payment to the CIO beginning with the month of February, and intimated that future payments would be withheld until the CIO had liquidated an alleged indebtedness of $1,665,000 to the UMW. This maneuver stunned the CIO; Murray told the Executive Board that "It certainly created an unprecedented situation, because I have never known of any time in the history of the labor movement, to my knowledge at least, of one organization dunning another organization for per capita tax over debts for organizing purposes." [191] During Lewis' tenure as head of the CIO, he had handled its finances with the assistance of J. R. Bell, his brother-in-law, who carried the title of comptroller. It was therefore difficult for the Murray administration to challenge his assertions, but nevertheless the CIO resolved that "the United Mine Workers of America did not and does not consider the advances which it made to enable other and less fortunate workers to achieve economic freedom through union organization to be a debt to be repaid in dollars and cents." [192]

In May, 1942, District 50 of the United Mine Workers brought formal charges against Philip Murray to the effect that the latter was engaged in persecuting it. Murray appeared before the Policy Committee of the UMW to defend himself, but Lewis shortly thereafter convened a meeting of the International Executive Board and rendered a constitutional interpretation vacating the office of vice-president of the United Mine Workers, of which Murray was the incumbent up to that time. The removal was based upon the proposition that Murray was a dual job holder, since he was concurrently serving as CIO president, chairman of SWOC, and vice-president of the UMW. Murray pointed out that Lewis had for six years been president of both the UMW and the CIO, and that Thomas Kennedy had retained his position as an official of the UMW while serving as lieutenant-governor of Pennsylvania, but to no avail.

Lewis also removed Van A. Bittner, who was head of District 17, for refusing to break with Murray and the Steelworkers. According to Lewis, he simply called Bittner in and asked, "Would you like to resign now, or do you want the International Policy Committee to ask you to resign?" When Bittner challenged the veracity of this account, and said that Lewis had agreed that he could remain a member of the Miners Union and come back any time he desired, Lewis lashed out:

I regret that Mr. Bittner saw fit to mar his long career in the United Mine Workers of America by abandoning this organization and becoming an agent of another union whose policies are now antagonistic to our organization. . . . Mr. Bittner is engaged as assistant to the president of the United Steelworkers in carrying on a campaign against the best interests of the United Mine Workers. He is sending his organizers into our local unions to preach disruption and to preach division.[193]

The upshot of these events was that the 1942 convention of the United Mine Workers, by a vote of 2,867 to 5, resolved to withdraw from the CIO. Of the three major unions that had created the CIO seven years earlier, only one, the Amalgamated Clothing Workers, remained in the organization.

The conflict between the AFL and the CIO during the years preceding the war centered about a number of issues and took place at several levels:

Internal constitutional issues. The question was whether the AFL could "give away" the jurisdictional claims of its affiliates, with the dominant craft unions maintaining staunchly that it could not, and the industrial unions asserting that paper jurisdictions should not be permitted to stand in the way of organizing the mass production industries. A second major constitutional issue was the right of the AFL Executive Council to suspend an affiliated union, an issue which was resolved by the council itself under the spur of a threatened deadlock between the craft and industrial union forces.

Organizing strategy. Lewis and his associates insisted that industrial unions were required in the light of new technology and of great corporate power. The craft proponents preferred to rely instead on the method of the federal labor local, which could then be partitioned among the claimant crafts, or joined together with other federal locals in a new international union, as the circumstances required. The Lewis group was also more prone to use the government for its purposes, as against the traditional AFL view that "what the government gives, it can take away."

The struggle for leadership. John L. Lewis was undoubtedly desirous of becoming the acknowledged leader of American labor. The way to the top within the AFL was barred, for Lewis had long demonstrated his lack of regularity, for example, by running against Gompers for the AFL presidency in 1921 (William Green had nominated him for the office). A dual federation provided another road, one which might have proved more successful if Lewis had been able to curb his overweening ambition at crucial junctures.

The conflict of generations. The AFL in 1936 was controlled by men who were of advanced age, and who had been at the helm for a good many years. While the original CIO leaders were not young men, the new industrial unions were led largely by men in their twenties and thirties. Some of them had come from the AFL, but there was little sense among the new crop of leaders of the historical development of the AFL, of its slow growth in the face of intense employer opposition, or of its traditions, particularly with respect to jurisdiction. They could not understand the hesitation of the "old guard" to embrace the opportunities for organization that offered themselves, and they were impatient at the eternal quibbling over outmoded lines of demarcation. The AFL moguls, on the other hand, had little confidence in the staying power of the industrial workers and their young leadership. They had gone through the organizing boom of the period after the first World War, and had seen the complete collapse of efforts at industrial unionism. Lewis, for all his faults, had the genius to bridge the gap between the generations, and to put his experience as an AFL organizer and AFL international union president at the disposal of the forces which were thrusting the semiskilled industrial worker to a place in the sun alongside the craftsmen. It was not until a new generation had attained power within the AFL, a generation which was not only reconciled to the new status of the industrial worker, but eagerly embraced him as a member, that the long sought peace within the labor movement was finally achieved.

2

The Organization of Steel

If there is any single series of events in the labor history of this period which may be characterized as of momentous import, it is the organization of the steel industry. After a crushing defeat by the United States Steel Corporation in 1901, the Amalgamated Association of Iron, Steel, and Tin Workers of North America had eked out a precarious and meager existence. Unsuccessful organizing campaigns in 1919–1920 and 1933 left the Amalgamated, at the time of the organization of the CIO, a shell of an organization. Average membership in 1935 was only 9869. During that year, 84 local lodges were disbanded, and only four new ones established. Organizational work was at a standstill; not a single national organizer was in the field.[1] Yet by March 1937, the United States Steel Corporation, long a symbol of anti-unionism, had signed a collective contract with an outside union, an action that had repercussions throughout American industry. The first part of the present chapter will deal in some detail with the events that culminated in this agreement. Then we shall consider the refusal of Little Steel to follow the lead of the Steel Corporation, and the years of struggle which led finally to the organization of the entire industry.

The Capture of the Amalgamated by the CIO

The 1934 convention of the AFL had directed the Executive Council "at the earliest practical date [to] inaugurate, manage, promote and conduct a campaign of organization in the iron and steel industry."[2] When it came to implementation of this mandate, however, serious differences of opinion on appropriate procedure were manifest among the Executive Council members. In January 1935, William Green asked M. F. Tighe, president of the Amalgamated Association, to draw up a plan of organization for consideration by the Executive Council. In his reply, Tighe stated that a minimum of $200,000 would be required to start a new campaign, and added: "We are firmly convinced by the experience of the past 18 months that to make any headway, plants must be organized industrially."[3]

In the discussion of this report by the Executive Council of the AFL, William Green expressed the opinion that the 1934 convention resolution had authorized the AFL to proceed to organize steel workers into federal locals, and came out strongly for the industrial union point of view: "I do not believe at the moment we can organize these steel workers in the big plants of these powerful steel companies except on an industrial basis. Later on it might be we could transfer the men to the organizations to which they properly belong but at the moment the difficulties are too great, the state of mind is of such a character we cannot overcome it." [4] This position was strongly supported by John L. Lewis, who warned that it would be a waste of money to attempt to organize steel workers into more than a single industrial union. He urged that a new international union be created for organizing purposes, with complete jurisdiction over all workers in steel mills. Wharton of the Machinists observed, however, that

It is rather a complex situation to step in and ask us to contribute money to put our organization out of existence where we have a number of members employed. We think the craft organization is all right. We think an organizing campaign in the steel industry would have been quite successful if we had brought in the organizations that have jurisdiction, organize the men and form them into joint councils. With 109 international unions I feel you have just that many more representatives in the field to conduct an intelligent campaign. I do not feel disposed to obligate my organization in any way in a campaign that has for its purpose eliminating my organization from the jurisdiction belonging to it.

The craft point of view was echoed by Hutcheson, while Tobin expressed concern about setting aside the rights of the Amalgamated. The upshot of the discussion was the selection of a committee composed of Wharton, Lewis, and Tobin to confer with Tighe on the willingness of the Amalgamated to waive its jurisdictional rights.

At this meeting, which was held on the following day, Tighe refused to have the Amalgamated step aside and permit the establishment of a new international union. He and the secretary-treasurer of the Amalgamated, Louis Leonard, insisted that the Executive Council could only organize through the Amalgamated, and that it should confine itself to providing the Amalgamated with funds for organization. When the committee reported this back to the Executive Council, the same split that had manifested itself earlier continued. Green urged forcible action by the AFL, despite the objections of the Amalgamated. He declared: "I am satisfied in my own mind that the officers of the Amalgamated can not organize those workers with their own resources or with the set-up as it is, with the National organization based upon the philosophy upon which it rests or upon pursuing the policy which it was following." [5] Lewis, as might be expected, took the strongest position. He pointed out a fact which he was to cite many times again to justify his interest in the steel situation, namely, that an unorganized steel industry constituted a menace to the United Mine Workers' position in the captive mines:

Certainly the steel companies are going to push us around with a great deal more ferocity if they recognize they are free from organization in their own industry. It resolves itself down to the point that unless we carry the fight to the steel companies they are going to carry the fight to the organizations that are hanging on the fringe of the industry like the United Mine Workers.

Tobin was apparently won over to the Lewis point of view by his meeting with Tighe, and urged the Executive Council to proceed by organizing through federal local unions. Hutcheson and Wharton were opposed to any drastic action, however, and in the end a resolution was adopted authorizing Green to inaugurate a joint organizing campaign of all unions in the steel industry, with full authority to plan and direct the campaign. This resolution stopped far short of satisfying Lewis, who remained firm in his conviction that organization could be accomplished only by a single union, and not by a group of crafts.

During the following months, virtually nothing was done to implement this resolution. The Amalgamated was embroiled in an internal factional fight which engrossed whatever energies it still possessed. An attempt on the part of Green to mediate the controversy was rebuffed by Tighe and his associates with scant courtesy. But the quarrel was patched up, and the Executive Council reported to the 1935 AFL convention that "plans can now be formulated and organizing policies adopted so that an effective organizing campaign can be launched among the workers employed in the steel industries of the nation at the earliest possible date. The Executive Council is thoroughly alive to the situation. It is its purpose and determination to carry out the instructions of the San Francisco Convention to launch and conduct an organizing campaign in the iron and steel industry." [6]

John L. Lewis had made up his mind, however, that the AFL was not going to act. In a meeting with a few associates held at his home in May 1935, he reiterated the theme of the miners' exposed flank, and indicated that the Miners' Union was prepared to devote its resources to an organizational effort in steel. No definite plans were adopted, and one of those present gained the impression that Lewis was awaiting the outcome of the Atlantic City convention of the AFL before deciding what further steps were appropriate.[7]

The steel situation was very much in the minds of those who debated the issue of industrial unionism at the convention. Lewis asserted that he had been told by officers of U. S. Steel that they opposed collective agreements in the captive mines because they feared the consequent spread of unionism into the steel industry itself. He castigated the Executive Council for its inactivity in the following terms:

We are assured the way is now open for an aggressive campaign of organization in the steel industry. What kind of a campaign — a campaign to organize them in fifty-seven varieties of organizations? You ought to know without my telling you how effective that kind of campaign will be, and with several hundred thousands of members of the United Mine Workers of America who understand the position of interests of that character and who also understand the practical problems of organization in these big industries, they know that the officers of the American Federation of Labor might as well sit down in their easy chairs and twiddle their thumbs and take a nap as to conclude that any results will come from that kind of organization in the iron and steel industry.[8]

But the convention merely approved the report of the Executive Council and ordered that the resolution adopted the year before at San Francisco be effectuated. Concurrently, Leonard, the secretary-treasurer of the Amalgamated, was directed by the Executive Council to prepare a specific, precise plan of organization.

Such a plan was submitted to the Executive Council in January 1936. It stated in very general terms the necessity of an appropriate preliminary publicity campaign, and of concentrating upon United States Steel. The Executive Council would manage the campaign, but organization would be in local unions of the Amalgamated. There was very little of a practical nature in the proposal. The Amalgamated seemed to be mainly interested in the level of dues to be charged new members, and in the prevention of any dilution of its existing scheme of death benefits.[9] Nothing could have been more indicative of the bankruptcy of the Amalgamated than this plan, which was vague and platitudinous on the essentials and overly detailed on unimportant matters.

The AFL was finally convinced that nothing could be expected of the Amalgamated. The Executive Council bluntly rejected the plan as neither satisfactory nor practical, and directed Green to prepare and submit to the affiliated unions a specific plan for a one-year campaign, including an estimate of the monthly per capita cost to each union, and a structural scheme based on joint councils as a temporary organizing device with the ultimate recognition of the jurisdictions of all interested unions.[10]

This action, however, came too late. Immediately upon its organization, the CIO began to interest itself in steel as the first order of business. In January 1936, John Brophy urged the AFL Executive Council to take immediate action in steel, warning that "serious consequences may result if the council does not remove the present barriers to organization of these workers in the type of unions they desire. . . ."[11] This was followed by a widely publicized letter of February 22, 1936, from Lewis and Howard to Green, in which the CIO pledged $500,000 toward a steel organizing fund of $1,500,000 to be raised by the AFL under the following conditions:

(1) Organization must be along industrial lines. Past experience has shown that large numbers of steel workers can be brought into one organization by united and well-timed effort, but that organization breaks up and disappears when the workers are threatened with division into a multitude of craft unions. We therefore require assurance that all steel workers organized will be granted the permanent right to remain united in one industrial union.

(2) The leadership of the campaign must be such as to inspire confidence of success. There must be placed in charge a responsible, energetic person, with a genuine understanding of the steel workers' problems, who will work in conjunction with an advisory committee representative of the unions supporting the drive.

This letter provided the first intimation of a technique of labor organization of which John L. Lewis may fairly be designated as the originator, namely, the huge organizing campaign financed by millions rather than hundreds of dollars. AFL unions had contributed approximately $500,000 to the 1919 steel drive, but this was primarily for strike relief rather than for organizing work. Similarly large sums of money had been raised to assist coal miners in their strikes, but again for humanitarian rather than purely organizational purposes. The $200,000 that Tighe had estimated the Amalgamated would need in 1935 to start a new steel campaign seemed a considerable amount of money to the AFL Executive Council. Lewis had told his close associates that he was prepared to invest the entire treasury of the United Mine Workers in steel unionism, and this was the first overt expression of his intentions.

As a consequence of this offer, William Green, on March 2, 1936, addressed a circular letter to the heads of all AFL unions outlining a plan for organizing the steel industry. He urged the creation of a fund of $750,000 to be raised by contribution from the affiliated unions, to be placed at the disposal of the American Federation of Labor, which would direct the campaign in cooperation with the Amalgamated. Immediate replies were requested with indications of how much money would be forthcoming.[12] The CIO offer was not acted upon, since the conditions specified were obviously unacceptable to the AFL.

One of the first replies to the AFL appeal came from Wharton in his capacity as president of the powerful Machinists' Union. He told Green that there could be no reasonable hope of success so long as the CIO group remained in the AFL, and refused any financial support until such time as all affiliates of the AFL were behind the Green plan.[13] Other responses were equally discouraging. At the May meeting of the Executive Council, Tobin expressed the view that a steel drive would have little chance of success unless the Wagner Act were declared constitutional.[14] Among the members of the Executive Council, Green alone urged that the AFL undertake a campaign immediately, indicating it as his belief that not the form of organization, but rather the opposition of employers, was the main obstacle to unionism in steel.

When Wharton's refusal to contribute had been made public, Lewis addressed a letter to Tighe (April 15, 1936) in which he pointed out that the CIO supported fully the complete industrial jurisdiction of the Amalgamated, and offered unilateral CIO support on the following terms:

(1) We require assurance that all steel workers will have the right to remain united in one industrial union. As applied to the joint campaign now proposed, this means that the industrial jurisdiction of the Amalgamated Assocation must be respected and the members organized must be protected against future division because of jurisdiction claims of craft unions.

(2) Leadership of the campaign must be such as to inspire confidence of success, and unions contributing to the campaign should be represented in its direction. We propose that a joint committee be established, on which the Amalgamated Association will be represented, as well as the C.I.O. and other unions willing to contribute to a joint campaign. This joint committee would select a responsible and energetic person, in whom all members of the Committee would have confidence, to direct the actual organizing work.[15]

The Amalgamated convention, due to meet on April 28, was asked to consider this proposal, and was urged to clear the way for a campaign by giving the organizing committee "a reasonably free hand in regard to taking in independent and company unions as a body, keeping initiations and dues low enough to meet requirements of a mass campaign."

This offer placed the leaders of the Amalgamated in a quandry. The AFL had made no concrete countersuggestions and, moreover, there seemed to be no disposition on the part of the Executive Council to interpret the jurisdiction of the Amalgamated nearly as broadly as did the CIO. On the other hand, Tighe and his associates were basically loyal to the AFL, and somewhat fearful of John L. Lewis. In an attempt to solve their dilemma, the 1936 convention of the Amalgamated sent a delegation to the AFL Executive Council, which was in session at the time, with a request for positive action, and in particular, asked for a clarification of the jurisdictional rights of the Amalgamated.

The reply of the Executive Council came in the form of a letter from Green to the Amalgamated convention, on May 8. It reiterated the intention of the AFL to inaugurate and manage an organizing campaign, on the basis of "unconditional" contributions from affiliated organizations. With respect to jurisdiction, the letter stated: "While it is the purpose of the Executive Council to apply the broadest and most comprehensive industrial policy possible due regard and proper respect for the jurisdictional rights of all national and international unions will be observed in the execution of an organizing campaign." [16]

On the same day, John L. Lewis addressed a telegram to the Amalgamated convention, which read in part:

A. The statement is a rehash of the ancient and futile resolutions, adopted from time to time by the American Federation of Labor and the Executive Council, which have resulted in the frittering away of years of valuable time without contribution to the cause of collective bargaining in the iron and steel industry.

B. The statement of the Executive Council is obviously filled with venom and malice toward the nine major organizations of the American Federation of Labor which comprise the Committee for Industrial Organization and seeks to exclude those organizations from assisting or contributing to the cost of an organization campaign in your industry.

C. The policy of the Executive Council as expressed in the statement would immediately fill your industry with a horde of organizers attached to craft unions, fiercely competing with each other for the new members who might be organized and for the few dollars which might be taken in as initiation fees and dues collections. It would set aside your claim to industry jurisdiction.

D. The policy of the Executive Council would preserve the leadership of the organizing campaign in the hands of men who through the years demonstrated their utter incapacity to establish stable organization and modern collective bargaining in the mass production industries.

Lewis closed by renewing his previous offer of financial and organizational assistance.

The AFL made the following reply:

First. The charge made that "The statement of the Executive Council is obviously filled with venom and malice" is unwarranted by the facts. . . . Second. The charge that the Council attempted to exclude any organization from contributing to the cost of an organizing campaign in the iron and steel industry is untrue. Every national and international union including the nine organizations referred to in the telegram signed by John L. Lewis, Chairman, was officially invited and requested by the Executive Council to contribute to the fund to be used in organizing iron and steel workers. . . .[17]

Faced with these specific alternatives, there was little choice left to the Amalgamated. On the one hand there was a definite promise of $500,000, more money than had ever before been pledged for a single organizing campaign. On the other hand, there was merely a vague commitment for a campaign, tied in with the craft threat to the Amalgamated jurisdiction. Although the leadership managed to prevent the convention from accepting the CIO offer outright, a resolution was adopted calling for organization in cooperation with all unions affiliated with the AFL which conceded the jurisdictional rights of the Amalgamated and contributed organizers and funds.[18] But this provided only a short respite for the Amalgamated leadership, and in particular for Tighe, who was exceedingly reluctant to break with the AFL. On May 15, Murray, Brophy, and P. T. Fagan called upon Leonard and asserted that the CIO was in accord with the resolution of the Amalgamated convention, and was ready to act at a moment's notice, but warned that "the CIO would be forced to inaugurate a campaign to organize the steel workers on its own volition, if it became impossible to arrive at a cooperative understanding with the Amalgamated Association." [19] Pressure from the local lodges continued to mount, even from those lodges which had supported the compromise resolution at the convention.[20] Lewis wrote to Tighe once more on May 21, warning: "The CIO has stated its genuine desire to cooperate with your union in making good its chartered jurisdiction. But a right to jurisdiction ceases to have weight unless it is put into effect."

Even under this pressure, the Amalgamated leadership made one last effort to escape the clutches of Lewis. On May 29, an Amalgamated delegation headed by Leonard met with Green in Washington. The latter indicated that the AFL intended to place 35 of its own organizers in the field; but "the confusion created by the activities of the Committee for Industrial

Organization, and the offer of that Committee to contribute funds conditionally, has caused many of the affiliated unions to withhold the necessary support until the differences existing between the Executive Council and the CIO are adjusted . . . as the situation now stands it is President Green's opinion that the Executive Council will bide its time for the present." [21] The very next day, Leonard wired Lewis for an appointment, which was arranged for June 3. But the auspices were not too favorable for the Amalgamated, for Lewis wrote:

May I suggest that it will be a complete waste of time for all concerned for your committee to attend this meeting unless you are prepared to carry out the instructions imposed upon your officers by the recent Canonsburg convention. The policy of fluttering procrastination followed by your board is already responsible for the loss of some weeks of time and must be abandoned. . . .

Hundreds of thousands in the iron and steel industry are anxious to help in an honest effort to establish collective bargaining in the industry. These men are going to be given the opportunity to become organized, with or without the benefit of the Amalgamated Association of Iron, Steel, and Tin Workers.

Your executive board must decide whether it will cooperate or obstruct. If you do not yet know your own mind, please stay at home. . . .[22]

At the meeting, the CIO representatives made it plain that the CIO had decided to embark upon an independent campaign if the Amalgamated was not prepared to cooperate. After a day of discussion, the CIO submitted its proposition in writing. Leonard wired Tighe, who was ill and not at the meeting, that CIO aid was contingent upon formal affiliation with the CIO, and that a decision would have to be made immediately, whereupon Tighe authorized the Amalgamated delegation to use its own judgment. On June 4, the CIO proposal was accepted, with only a few minor changes.

This document provided for the creation of the Steel Workers' Organizing Committee, composed of members designated by the chairman of the CIO, two of whom were to be from the Amalgamated. The committee was to exercise policy functions, and to have exclusive authority to deal with employers. The Amalgamated pledged itself not to take any action affecting the organizing campaign without first consulting the chairman of the committee. The CIO agreed to provide funds up to $500,000, to be disbursed by the SWOC. Dues were fixed at $1 monthly per member, and the SWOC was empowered to dispense with initiation fees. The Amalgamated retained in effect only the right to issue charters. The termination of the campaign and the disbanding of the committee were to be within the joint province of the SWOC and the CIO — not the Amalgamated.[23]

Why, it may be asked, was the CIO so much concerned with the acquisition of a moribund organization of 10,000 members? The answer must be sought in the powerful concept of "legitimacy" that dominated the American labor movement. In the early months of 1936, the course of the CIO was not yet clear. The AFL remained the sole parent federation, and to set up a steel union *de novo* would have involved the commission of the cardinal sin of dual unionism. The Amalgamated, by virtue of its AFL charter, had the only legitimate right to organize those steel workers who did not fall within the jurisdiction of the craft unions. So long as it became part of the CIO, the Amalgamated could cause little trouble and represented a cheap investment. Within the AFL, it was a potential source of retaliatory power.

The Organization of the United States Steel Corporation

With the digestion of the Amalgamated, Lewis moved so surely as to leave little doubt that careful organizational plans had been in preparation for some time. Lewis named as chairman of the Steel Workers' Organizing Committee his long-time lieutenant, Philip Murray, vice-president of the United Mine Workers. David McDonald, Murray's assistant, was made secretary-treasurer of the committee. The other SWOC members were Julius Hochman of the ILGWU and Leo Krzycki of the Amalgamated Clothing Workers; M. F. Tighe and Joseph K. Gaither of the Amalgamated Association of Iron Workers; P. T. Fagan and Van A. Bittner of the United Mine Workers; and John Brophy, CIO director of organization.[24] Actually, the committee as such was never a functioning body; it met occasionally to approve the work of the chairman, but the latter exercised full executive and administrative power.[25] Clinton S. Golden, a former Amalgamated Clothing Workers organizer who had been affiliated with Brookwood Labor College, was appointed director of the important northeastern region, while the western and southern regions were headed by two Mine Workers' officials, Van A. Bittner and William Mitch. Twelve international representatives of the United Mine Workers were detailed to the SWOC staff, and these were to be supplemented by men working out of the UMWA districts.

At the first meeting of SWOC, held on June 17, 1936, Murray estimated that expenditures would run about $45,000 a week, since the hiring of 100 organizers was contemplated. Initiation fees were waived, since it was the experience of the CIO leaders that they were an obstacle to organization, and dues were fixed at $1 a month, payable in advance.[26] A statement was issued emphasizing that the SWOC was under the direction of representatives of established unions with successful collective bargaining records, and that its purpose was to avoid industrial strife if employers demonstrated a reasonable spirit of cooperation. On August 1, *Steel Labor,* the official newspaper of the SWOC, began publication.

The announcement of the organizing campaign met with an immediate response from the steel employers. The American Iron and Steel Institute took full-page advertisements in 375 metropolitan newspapers in an appeal to the public and the steel workers, which read:

A campaign to unionize the employees of the Steel Industry has been announced.

In order that the employees and the public may know the position of the Steel Industry in the face of the threatened drive, the Industry makes this statement through the American Iron and Steel Institute.

Persons and organizations not connected with the Industry have taken charge of the campaign.

There are many disturbing indications that the promoters of the campaign will employ coercion and intimidation of the employees in the Industry and foment strikes.

The objective of the campaign is the "closed shop," which prohibits the employment of anyone not a union member. The Steel Industry will oppose any attempt to compel its employees to join a union or to pay tribute for the right to work.

No employee in the steel industry has to join any organization to get or hold a job. Employment in the industry does not depend upon membership or non-membership in any organization. Advancement depends on individual effort and merit. These are fundamental American principles to which the industry will steadfastly adhere.

The Steel Industry believes in the principle of collective bargaining, and it is in effect throughout the Industry.

The overwhelming majority of the employees in the Steel Industry recently participated in annual elections under their own representation plans and elected their representatives for collective bargaining. The elections were conducted by the employees themselves by secret ballot. One of the purposes of the announced campaign is to overthrow those plans and the representatives so elected.

The Steel Industry is recovering from six years of depression and huge losses, and the employees are now beginning to receive the benefits of increased operations. Any interruption of the forward movement will seriously injure the employees and their families and all business dependent upon the Industry, and will endanger the welfare of the country.

The announced drive, with its accompanying agitation for industrial strife, threatens such interruption.

The Steel Industry will use its resources to the best of its ability to protect its employees and their families from intimidation, coercion and violence and to aid them in maintaining collective bargaining free from interference from any source.[27]

This statement made it very clear that the industry was prepared to resist the SWOC, and it sounded the tocsin for a repetition of the events of 1919.

Reporting to the second meeting of the SWOC in Pittsburgh, on September 29, 1936, Murray reviewed succinctly the various steps necessary to launch the committee as an effective organizing device:

There are three distinct stages through which this campaign must go before we reach the stage of negotiations. The first stage consisted of setting up the organizing machinery necessary to do the job. We recruited a staff of men who had to make contacts in the mills, become adjusted to a new situation and develop their organizing activities according to local conditions — but always under the strict and close supervision of the regional directors and the national office.

The second step consisted of using our organizing machinery to put our message across. . . .

. . . we begin — and we are just beginning — to enter the third stage. It is the job of organizing, signing up members, establishing lodges.[28]

Murray told the committee that 35 subregional offices had been established, with 158 full-time and 80 part-time employees. Disbursements up to that time totaled $186,000, while membership was 15,306, most of the members having been inherited from the Amalgamated. Some of the organizers were drawn from the staff of the Mine Workers' Union, but many came from other industries and owed their primary loyalty to Murray rather than to Lewis, which was to stand the former in good stead when the two men broke five years later.

It was soon made clear that the role of the Amalgamated was to be a minor one, and that the SWOC was by all odds a completely new organization. While charters were formally issued by the Amalgamated, this was a mere ministerial act, for they were issued in the name of SWOC. Where there was an Amalgamated lodge, but no collective agreement, the local was taken over by the SWOC, in return for which the SWOC agreed to continue per capita payments to the Amalgamated equal to the average per capita paid from July 1, 1935 to June 30, 1936. Five local lodges in Portsmouth, Ohio, and four in Cleveland were transferred in this way to the SWOC, the Amalgamated officers justifying this action on the ground that it was either a question of turning them over to SWOC whose resources permitted a proper approach to the task of organizing them, or losing what

organization they had maintained through bitter strife and company op-
osition. There was some bad feeling about these events. Edward W.
Miller, a vice-president of the Amalgamated, who had been fairly consistently pro-CIO in the earlier negotiations, complained to Murray that
the takeover of locals was destroying the Amalgamated.[29] And Tighe wrote
rather plaintively that "the taking over of the organization of the steel industry by the Committee for Industrial Organization and placing it in the
hands of what is known as the Steel Workers' Organizing Committee,
practically took all organizing of steel workers out of the jurisdiction of our
Association."[30]

In planning its campaign, the SWOC faced an industry with approximately 479,000 wage earners,[31] one with a long reputation as the stronghold
of the open shop in the United States. A high degree of concentration prevailed.[32] Employment, like output, tended to be concentrated in large steel
works and rolling mills. In 1937, 58.2 per cent of steel wage earners were
employed in 53 establishments, each of which employed in excess of 2500
persons. By far the largest concern in the industry was the United States
Steel Corporation, with some 222,000 employees. Next in order of size came
Bethlehem Steel, with 80,000 employees; Republic Steel, 49,000 employees;
Jones and Laughlin, 29,000 employees; and Youngstown Sheet and Tube.[33]

During and after World War I, a number of steel companies introduced
employee representation plans, or company unions, into their plants. Perhaps the most important of these was the Bethlehem Steel plan, which was
established in 1918, and served as the model for others. The United States
Steel Corporation, however, did not resort to the company union until the
enactment of the National Industrial Recovery Act in 1933, when this form
of employee representation was inaugurated at each of its plants.[34] Even
before the advent of the SWOC, some restlessness was manifested among
the company unions, particularly in the less well established organizations
of the United States Steel Corporation. In January 1936, a majority of the
employee representatives of the Carnegie-Illinois plant of U. S. Steel at
Gary, Indiana, secured a charter as a local lodge of the Amalgamated.[35]
In March, company union representatives of several Carnegie-Illinois plants
in the Pittsburgh-Youngstown area established a local council for the purpose of making the company unions more effective, in defiance of management.[36]

This activity in the company unions was by no means the creation of
the SWOC, although the union capitalized upon it. A veteran observer
wrote, four months before the formation of SWOC:

First . . . many individual steel workers have, just now, a sense of freedom that has been notably absent from the steel mills since the Homestead strike of 1892; second . . . this sense of freedom is resulting in certain steps in the direction of independent, collective action of a type that has been equally rare. And there is a third astounding fact: These steps toward independence are being taken where few had thought ever to see such a thing take place — in the company unions.

Arthur H. Young, vice-president of U. S. Steel, was quoted as saying of these developments:

7-a and the Wagner law have stiffened the backbone of the workers. At the same time, it would avail us nothing to buck prevailing sentiment. These movements in the direction of a wider area of collective action are absolutely inevitable and we don't propose to try to stop them. We intend to go along and by evidencing our sincerity of purpose keep matters from getting beyond the point of reasonable negotiation.[37]

Although Young was referring here to the growing independence of the company unions, his words foreshadowed U. S. Steel thinking when faced with outside unionism.

The initial strategy of the SWOC was to invade the company unions, for they were the only real centers of organization in the industry. Philip Murray explained the SWOC policy as follows:

It was apparent to us that to make any progress in steel we had first to "capture" these company unions. We realized that a great many of the employee representatives, perhaps the majority, were men honestly interested in doing a good job under the Plan which had been imposed upon them and their fellow employees. Our job was to show these men what real unionism meant. To denounce them all as company agents or stooges would be both untruthful and poor strategy.[38]

One of the first problems faced by the SWOC was to publicize its activities. Mass meetings were held in a number of steel towns, one of the most dramatic at Homestead, Pennsylvania, the scene of a memorable labor tragedy in 1892. To demonstrate the new political situation prevailing in the state, the principal speaker was Thomas Kennedy, lieutenant-governor of Pennsylvania and secretary-treasurer of the United Mine Workers, who was escorted to the platform by a guard of state police. Kennedy, on behalf of Governor Earle, promised that state relief would be forthcoming for distressed worker families in the event of a strike.

In its approach to the company union problem, the SWOC, as its first step, sought to enlist the support of influential leaders of these organizations.[39] With men in key places, the strategy adopted has been outlined as follows:[40]

1. The grievance procedure of the employee representation plan was used to push individual grievances as strongly as possible. If the cases were won, the "progressives" received the credit; if they were lost, the prestige of the plans suffered.

2. The SWOC supporters insisted upon verbatim reporting of employee representation council meetings. Portions of these records favorable to the SWOC side were later used for publicity purposes.

3. Enlargement of the committee system under the plans was pressed, with the pro-SWOC faction seeking to gain key positions on the committees.

4. Wage and hour demands were made persistently as a means of helping to raise the interest of workers in unionism.[41]

The focal point of the SWOC attack was in the relatively independent employee representation plans of U. S. Steel. Toward the end of August, the Pittsburgh-Youngstown council, representing 48,000 workers, pressed Carnegie-Illinois for a wage increase, followed shortly by similar demands raised by company union representatives in the Homestead plant of the same company. Representatives of 12 tin mills of Carnegie-Illinois met in Pittsburgh and resolved in favor of a $5 a day minimum, plus a general increase of $1 a day.[42] Benjamin F. Fairless, at the time president of Carnegie-Illinois, replied in a public letter dated September 8 that the financial position of the company did not permit of any general wage increase.[43] Philip Murray seized the opportunity to back the company union demands, arguing in a long public statement that the profit position of the corporation was adequate to meet the workers' demands.[44] For their part, the Pittsburgh company unions expressed dissatisfaction with Fairless' statement, and renewed their demand for a $5 a day minimum, the SWOC program. The Homestead employee representation plan threatened to throw the wage issue into arbitration, which was permitted under the plan.

The corporation, concerned with the continuing progress being made by SWOC, moved on two fronts: it attempted to bolster up the company unions, and at the same time initiated policy discussions with respect to wages. Plans were laid for the creation of a central joint committee, and on October 19–21, 1936, a conference was held for the purpose of establishing the Pittsburgh District General Council. Under this scheme, the council was to consist of two representatives of each steel plant, and would deal on an interplant level, something which management had theretofore refused to concede.[45] The plan was sent to the several plants for ratification.

On the wage front, Myron C. Taylor, chairman of the board of U. S.

Steel, was under pressure from company officials to negotiate a written agreement with employee representatives, and he appointed a committee to study the matter. In a report dated October 13, 1936, the committee recommended that the common labor rate be raised from 47 cents to 52½ cents per hour with corresponding increases in other categories; that one-year contracts be signed with employee representatives embodying the new wage scale; and that wages be tied to the cost-of-living index in the interim.[46] Announcement of the proposed changes were made on November 6, 1936.[47]

The first meeting of the newly established Pittsburgh General Council was held on November 9, with the tin mills, which had not been included in the original prospectus, brought in on the initiative of management. Much to the chagrin of the corporation, a CIO man was elected chairman of the employee group. Even worse, the council refused to accept the cost-of-living scale feature of the company's wage proposal, despite a personal appearance by Benjamin Fairless. As soon as the Council adjourned, Elmer J. Maloy, the newly elected chairman, left for Washington to confer with John L. Lewis.[48]

Although some individual plants accepted the proposed contract, the Pittsburgh Council and other plants refused to endorse it, and the company decided to put the wage increase in effect unilaterally in all plants, despite a previous threat to except those plants that had refused to sign. Failure of many employee representatives to sign the agreement was a serious defeat for company policy, as it later acknowledged.[49] The SWOC was able to point to the wage increase as a vindication of its earlier position that the corporation could afford higher wages.

While up to this time, November 1936, the organizing drive of the SWOC had made undoubted headway, the union was still far from the attainment of a commanding position. It claimed a total membership of 82,000 and the allegiance of 1,534 out of 2,500 company union representatives in the industry.[50] But the waiver of initiation fees made it cheap for workers to join the union, and the absence of collective agreements with any important producer rendered dubious the potential membership stability. In January 1937, moreover, the anti-CIO elements succeeded in ousting Maloy from the chairmanship of the Pittsburgh Council, after several months of intense effort.[51]

The SWOC altered its strategy at this juncture. Having exploited the employee representation plans to the limit, it moved swiftly in the direction of independent organization. In an effort to discredit the company unions, charges were filed with the National Labor Relations Board against

Carnegie-Illinois, alleging unlawful company domination. Hearings were held from December 1936 to February 1937, at which former employee representatives testified to the dominant role of the company in the affairs of the company unions. Concurrently, the SWOC launched a new organization of company union representatives at a conference of 250 delegates from 42 plants, with its avowed purpose the open enrollment of workers in the SWOC.[52] The stage of company union infiltration was ended, and the SWOC now began to press for the breakdown of these organizations. At the beginning of 1937, Murray claimed that SWOC membership had risen to 125,000.

In an effort to stem the tide, the loyal company unionists in the Carnegie-Illinois system established a Defense Committee, and solicited funds to fight the SWOC encroachments.[53] The management agreed to the establishment of an interplant grievance committee, known as the "little Supreme Court," with power to visit all Carnegie-Illinois plants for the purpose of investigating failures in the operation of the employee representation plan and suggesting improvements.[54] On February 16, 1937, the Pittsburgh District Council unanimously asked for another wage increase, borrowing the SWOC demand for a $5 a day minimum, plus an 80 cent per day raise.[55] But this late display of militancy by the now thoroughly anti-CIO Council proved of little avail; under the impact of unfavorable NLRB publicity and the organizational momentum of the SWOC, the company unions were losing strength.

In addition to the infiltration of the company unions, the SWOC had been carrying on an unremitting, intensive organizing campaign on many fronts. The nature of the campaign has been described by a leading participant in the following terms:

It was hard work, continual plugging away. It was a crusade without the Crusaders. It meant combing the towns which were completely dominated by the employer. It meant breaking down a resistance born of fear. It meant trying to convince people that they could be free. It took different forms in different places, but those differences did not result from the confluence of streams or geography, but from the history and strength of the individual employers.[56]

But organizing progress was slow, and no one was prepared, not even those privy to the inner secrets of the SWOC, for the peaceful capitulation of the United States Steel Corporation.

The decision of the corporation to recognize the SWOC rather than to fight, the reversal of a long established policy of resistance to outside unionism, was rationalized by the chairman of its board of directors, Myron C. Taylor, in the following terms:

It seemed to us that the situation was one in which our principles of representation exactly applied and that the grave danger was in allowing events to proceed to a point where the ordinary rules of reason would not govern. I felt that it was my duty as a trustee for our stockholders and as a citizen to make any honorable settlement that would ensure a continuance of work, wages and profits. I discovered that Mr. Lewis was similarly minded and we had an informal preliminary talk. We had the background of the captive coal mine agreements which preserved the principle of representatives in connection with union contracts. They had worked very well. . . .

The first talk with Mr. Lewis was on January 9th, 1937, in Washington, D.C. We went into the subject rather thoroughly, but on broad lines. At once on my return to New York, I discussed the whole situation with the available directors, and their unanimous opinion was that I should go ahead with the conversations to the end of reaching an agreement. Mr. Lewis and I continued our conversations on January 13th, but did not reach any conclusion that would conform with our policy.

On the 18th of February, in a meeting of the chief officers of our subsidiaries, I discussed the principles involved and asked each of those present whether, if the occasion arose, he would negotiate with the S.W.O.C., and they all answered in the affirmative. I also asked them whether, if an agreement were then reached, they would sign a contract in accord with the practice established with the employee representation groups in the steel plants in November, 1936. This they also answered in the affirmative.

Mr. Lewis was then in New York and expressed the desire further to explore matters with me, but we had no further meetings until February 25th, when at my house in New York, our conversations were resumed on the basis of this formula which, for the first time, I showed to him:

"The Company recognizes the right of its employees to bargain collectively through representatives freely chosen by them without dictation, coercion or intimidation in any form or from any source. It will negotiate and contract with the representatives of any group of its employees so chosen and with any organization as the representative of its members, subject to the recognition of the principle that the right to work is not dependent on membership or nonmembership in any organization and subject to the right of any employee freely to bargain in such manner and through such representatives, if any, as he chooses."

For a time the negotiations seemed to be off, but on Sunday morning, February 28th, Mr. Lewis and Mr. Murray came to my house with Mr. Moses and, after a short talk, Messrs. Lewis and Murray accepted the formula in principle.[57]

The Taylor-Lewis talks were held in the utmost secrecy,[58] and the public announcement of agreement was all the more sensational. The decision of the United States Steel Corporation to recognize the SWOC must surely rank as one of the critical junctures in American economic history. Not only did it ensure the existence of unionism in basic steel, but it provided inestimable assistance to the CIO in its drive to organize other industries. Even the recognition of the United Automobile Workers Union by General Motors a week earlier did not have the impact of the steel settlement, since the GM agreement had been reached after a long and bitter sit-down strike, and with the most severe form of pressure exercised by the federal and state governments. Here, on the contrary, there had been virtually no governmental intervention and no industrial strife. The agreement was worked out by the parties themselves on a voluntary basis.

In the agreement, which was signed on March 2, 1937, Carnegie-Illinois recognized the SWOC as the bargaining agent for its members, while the SWOC agreed not to intimidate or coerce nonunion employees into membership. Minimum daily wages were raised to $5, and a 40-hour week was established, with time-and-a-half pay for all hours in excess of 8 per day or 40 per week.[59] This was supplemented on March 17 with a series of collective agreements covering the several operating subsidiaries of U. S. Steel which contained, in addition to the wage and hour clauses, provisions for paid vacations, seniority, arbitration of grievances, and other standard clauses.[60]

Exactly what prompted the Steel Corporation to break so profoundly with its own past cannot be determined without full access to its policy papers and executive minutes. Among the factors that may have been determining, however, are the following:

(1) For the first time since 1930, the Steel Corporation was earning substantial profits. During the years 1931 to 1934 inclusive, net losses were sustained each year. Net income before taxes was $12 million in 1935, $67 million in 1936, and $130 million in 1937, compared with $220 million in 1929.[61] The corporation was certainly desirous of avoiding a strike, which would have interrupted these favorable business developments. Taylor remarked later that "the Corporation subsidiaries, during a very difficult period, have been entirely free of labor disturbance of any kind. The cost of a strike — to the Corporation, to the public and to the men — would have been incalculable." [62] Moreover, Lord Runciman, president of the British Board of Trade, was in the United States at the time of the Taylor-Lewis talks, arranging for the purchase of steel for Great Britain's rearmament

program, and it was rumored that he was insisting upon a guarantee of uninterrupted production before he would let contracts.[63]

(2) The costs of a strike, and the chances of success, had to be taken into consideration. It was by no means a foregone conclusion, as some contemporary observers implied, that victory for the union was inevitable or even likely.[64] Little Steel, after all, was able to battle SWOC to a standstill even after the latter had acquired the funds and prestige that went with recognition by U. S. Steel. Actual SWOC membership among U. S. Steel employees was neither large nor stable. Lee Pressman, then general counsel of the SWOC, has been quoted as follows on this point: "I don't know what we would have done without Lewis's brilliant move. There is no question that we [the steel workers] could not have filed a petition through the National Labor Relations Board or any other kind of machinery asking for an election. We could not have won an election for collective bargaining on the basis of our own membership or the results of the organizing campaign to date. This certainly applied not only to Little Steel but also to Big Steel." [65] The fact of the matter was that while unfair labor practice charges had been filed with the NLRB, the SWOC had never filed election petitions in U. S. Steel plants. Moreover, the important Pittsburgh District Council of the employee representation plans had purged itself of its SWOC leadership and was on the road to the achievement of an independent status in order to qualify as a bargaining agent under the National Labor Relations Act.[66] The recognition of the SWOC by Carnegie-Illinois did not entirely mark the demise of its company unions. Following the agreement, "the little supreme court" met with Fairless and negotiated a wage increase similar to that accorded the SWOC. The group was also told that the company was prepared to recognize it as the bargaining agent for employees who favored the company unions. This group appealed to William Green, president of the AFL, for assistance, but failing to get any encouragement from him, approached John P. Frey, head of the AFL Metal Trades Council. Frey met with the group and presented a plan for organization along craft lines, which was rejected, the group deciding instead to reorganize as a completely independent outside organization. A new organization was formed, called the American Union of Steel Workers, at the end of March. However, the fledgling organization was given a death blow when Carnegie-Illinois signed an NLRB stipulation agreeing to disestablish relationships with the existing employee representation plans, after the Supreme Court had upheld the constitutionality of the NLRA.

But if, as seemed not at all improbable, U. S. Steel would have been able to defeat the SWOC in open combat, the cost would undoubtedly have been high. The General Motors plants had just been shut down for six weeks as the consequence of a strike, and a stoppage of similar duration in steel was not at all impossible. Unlike the situation in 1919, the Pennsylvania state administration was, if anything, prounion, and the state police would not have been available for keeping the mills open. Lieutenant-Governor Kennedy had already served notice that state relief would not be withheld from the needy families of striking workers. The Steel Corporation thus had to balance immediate loss of production against the intangible future benefits of freedom from outside unionism, the magnitude of which was diminishing in proportion to the growing militancy of the company unions.[67]

(3) The current political atmosphere cannot be minimized as a factor in the steel settlement. The reelection of Roosevelt in November 1936, with the strong support of the CIO, was widely hailed as a victory for trade unionism. The National Labor Relations Board had opened hearings on alleged company domination of the Carnegie-Illinois employee representation plans, and the La Follette Committee of the United States Senate was threatening to look into labor espionage practices of the corporation. It was clear from the recent General Motors strike that public opinion would not support forcible suppression of trade unionism. To this may be added the fact that Myron Taylor was cut from quite a different stripe than his predecessor, Judge Elbert Gary, and was much more reconciled to the New Deal than his colleagues in Little Steel. How much his personal philosophy and ambitions had to do with the settlement is problematical, and should not be exaggerated; it is very doubtful that he could have swung his board without convincing arguments.

(4) It also seems likely that the corporation would have preferred dealing with a single industrial union rather than with a collection of craft unions, if outside unionism appeared inevitable. Moreover, John L. Lewis was a known quantity, and the corporation had learned to negotiate with him for its captive mines. Tom Moses, president of the H. C. Frick Coal Company, a U. S. Steel subsidiary, played an important role in advising Taylor on the more technical aspects of relations with the union based upon his coal experience, and he enjoyed a rather friendly relationship with Lewis.

The CIO was jubilant over the agreement. *Steel Labor,* the organ of the SWOC, wrote in an editorial: "And because of the fine attitude taken by management of Carnegie-Illinois in dealing with the union, the bugaboo of a strike in the industry seems to be put at rest . . . That was one of the most forward steps ever taken in the history of industrial America." [68] John L. Lewis declared: "The settlement is a fine example of an intelligent approach to a great economic problem. It has been made possible by the far-seeing vision of industrial statesmanship of Mr. Myron C. Taylor, chairman of the board of directors of United States Steel." [69] But the reaction of the remaining steel companies was quite different. Tom M. Girdler, president of Republic Steel, later wrote of the agreement:

Unquestionably many thousands of workmen interpreted this event as a wonderful victory for themselves. But I am sure that thousands of workers were shocked, even horrified by the news. Thereafter United States Steel Corporation abandoned its established policy of dealing with employees through an intra-corporation union. I was bitter about this. So were a vast majority of the steel men of the nation, including just about everybody from the rank of foreman up in the corporation itself. Why did we not all sign? Simply because we were convinced that a surrender to C.I.O. was a bad thing for our companies, for our employees; indeed for the United States of America. A majority of our employees did not belong to C.I.O. and we were not going to force them in against their wishes.[70]

Charles M. White, an executive officer of Republic Steel, told of having consulted officers of Pittsburgh Steel, Youngstown, Jones and Laughlin, and Inland Steel, and found their attitude to be that "their employees were more in favor of the methods they were then using in collective bargaining than they would be under the CIO, or under the SWOC." [71]

If the SWOC was under the delusion that its organizing campaign was finished, it was soon dispelled. Within a few months the intention of Little Steel to follow a line other than that adopted by U. S. Steel became unmistakably clear.

The Little Steel Strikes[72]

The first fruits of the U. S. Steel victory were not long in coming. During the following month, 51 companies, including five operating subsidiaries of U. S. Steel, signed with the SWOC on substantially the same terms. The SWOC, at the end of March 1937, claimed that it had 200,000 members in 492 local lodges. A month later the union claimed 88 companies under contract, and 280,000 members.[73] Beginning April 1, dues payments of $1 per month were resumed, and after May 1, an initiation fee of $3 was imposed for new members, signs that the union felt certain of its ability to attract and hold workers.

As in the case of U. S. Steel, the SWOC endeavored to infiltrate and capture the employee representation plans of the remaining steel companies. The evidence was conflicting on the progress that was made: the union claimed substantial membership among committeemen in Bethlehem,[74] and Jones and Laughlin,[75] but a contemporary observer expressed doubt over SWOC influence in the well established Bethlehem plan.[76] The SWOC also claimed substantial membership at Youngstown Sheet and Tube and Inland Steel, but Republic and Weirton were successful in preventing the spread of union influence among their employees.

At the end of March, the union requested bargaining conferences with the nonsigning steel companies. It was having some difficulty restraining its rank and file, as evidenced by the following circular letter of March 31, 1937:

We have been swamped both with demands on the part of Lodge officers and members and by steel companies that we begin negotiations for signing union agreements. Every effort is being made to get contracts signed up as rapidly as humanly possible. . . . To make matters still more difficult, new members of some of our recently formed Lodges have begun issuing ultimatums to their employers as well as to this Committee saying that unless the contract is signed by a certain date, the men will go on strike. This sort of action is equivalent to going to an employer with a gun in one hand and a pen in the other and demanding he sign the agreement. The effect of such action is extremely dangerous to the future of the Union. If our Lodge officers and members indulge in these methods, it will result in the destruction of the Union that has required the expenditure of so much money by other Union Workers and so much energy by our staff. . . . We promised the steel workers we would not call them out on strike. We have kept that promise. For the sake of the future welfare of the Union and its members we urge all to remain at work pending our efforts to get the contracts signed in good faith.

The first company with which the union came to grips was Jones and Laughlin, fourth largest producer in the industry. Its Aliquippa, Pa., plant had been dubbed "Little Siberia" in trade union circles because of a long record of anti-unionism. Tom Girdler, who managed the Aliquippa plant of J & L for many years until his departure to head the Republic Steel Company, acknowledged that "The reason Aliquippa was referred to as the 'Siberia of America' was because it was not a popular place for professional union men, and that was because of the men themselves who did not want professional union men there." [77] The National Labor Relations Board found that when the Amalgamated Association had attempted to organize the Aliquippa works in 1934, systematic terror was employed against it.

Officers of the union and organizers who came into Aliquippa were followed about by the private police of the respondent — the "J & L Police." The more important union officers were honored by the respondent with permanent shadows and were followed even into the neighboring town of Ambridge where they carried on their activities because of the difficult situation in Aliquippa. The house of Gerstner, the financial secretary, at which an organization meeting had been held, was surrounded day and night by the J & L Police. . . . Persons coming out of the house were questioned. Some were mysteriously beaten and hit on the head while walking in the streets.[78]

When the SWOC approached J & L with a request for an agreement, the initial response was negative. H. E. Lewis, chairman of the board of J & L, entered into negotiations directly with Philip Murray, but no agreement could be reached, whereupon the union called a strike for May 12.[79] The greater degree of organizing success attained among the employees of this company than in most of the other independents made it a logical union target. On the eve of the strike the company offered to sign a contract with the SWOC recognizing it as bargaining agent for its members, with the reservation that other employee groups could have similar contracts on request. In addition, the company stipulated that it would sign an exclusive bargaining contract with the organization obtaining a majority of votes at an NLRB-run election. Notwithstanding the fact that this offer was at least as good as the U. S. Steel contract, the union rejected it and the plant was shut down.

The company's attitude was undoubtedly greatly influenced by the April Supreme Court decision ordering it to reinstate a number of discharged workers with back pay. Its workers discovered that they had a right to join the union which would be protected by law, and union strength at J & L built up rapidly. The union was unwilling to accept a "members only" agreement, like that at U. S. Steel, under which the company could have continued to fight it, and it felt strong enough to hold out for a better settlement. However, the union was by no means sure of its ability to win an election,[80] and it may have wanted the strike as a demonstration of its power, to help convince workers who were on the fence.

The success of the strike far exceeded even union expectations. Very few men remained in the mills, and at Aliquippa there was virtually a civil upheaval. The workers were out only 36 hours before an agreement was reached providing for exclusive union recognition if a majority of the workers favored it. The stoppage was much more a declaration of political and economic independence on the part of the workers than a narrow labor dispute. A week later, the SWOC won a 2 to 1 victory in an NLRB election, carrying the Aliquippa and Pittsburgh plants of the company by about the same majorities.[81] In consequence, the SWOC became the exclusive bargaining representative for 27,000 employees of Jones & Laughlin, the first important company in which it attained that status. For the rest, the contract was substantially similar to the U. S. Steel agreement.

As an immediate consequence of the J & L victory, a number of additional mills signed with the union, among them Crucible Steel and Sharon Steel. At the beginning of June, the SWOC announced that it had contracts with 142 firms, and a membership of 375,000. It estimated that 70 per cent of the industry had come to terms with it,[82] a figure which was undoubtedly too high. Organization of the remaining portion of the industry proved much more difficult, and involved a far greater expenditure of resources.

Among the important steel companies which refused to follow the lead of U. S. Steel were Bethlehem Steel, under the chairmanship of Eugene Grace; Republic Steel, under Tom Girdler; Youngstown Sheet and Tube under Frank Purnell; National Steel under Ernest T. Weir; Inland Steel under L. E. Block; and American Rolling Mills under Charles R. Hook. This group of companies employed about 186,000 workers.[83] The La Follette Committee found that some of these companies were acting in concert in dealing with the request of the SWOC for recognition.[84]

At the end of March 1937, the SWOC had addressed a communication to each of these companies, requesting that a U. S. Steel-type agreement be executed. In the case of Republic Steel, no answer was received, and on May 3, the union again requested a meeting, this time threatening a strike. A meeting was finally held on May 11, following which Republic issued a statement accusing the CIO of attempting to secure a closed shop, and stating it to be company policy to refuse to execute written labor agreements.[85] On May 20, the company shut down its Massillon, Ohio, works. Six days later the union declared a strike against the plants of the company that remained open.

Negotiations with the other companies followed a similar course. In the case of Bethlehem, an ultimatum was issued on May 7 by the SWOC giving the company ten days to meet with the union. The period expired with no reply, and after a delay of a month, a strike began on June 11.[86] A meeting was held on April 28 between the top SWOC leadership and the executives of Youngstown Sheet and Tube, at which the company stated that while it would meet and negotiate with the union, it would not sign a contract. In the words of the company itself:

The point upon which the representatives of the SWOC and the company did not agree was that of signing an agreement. The company has no written employment agreements and its policy has been and is not to make written agreements of this character. . . .

A written agreement brings no advantages to employees which they do not now possess. It does create an artificial need for labor organization officials to negotiate annually a new agreement as each old one expires regardless of the necessity for any change in the provisions of the agreement. This creates the risk of periodical shutdown during annual negotiations for new agreements.[87]

Two additional conferences were held on a local level, but when they proved fruitless, a strike began on May 26, on the same day that Inland Steel was shut down. No strikes were called against the remaining holdouts.

Why did the Little Steel companies decide to fight the SWOC despite the example set by U. S. Steel? Were not the same economic and political considerations involved? What could these firms hope to achieve when the giant U. S. Steel Corporation had indicated the expedient policy?

At the beginning of May 1937, a sharp decline began in the volume of new business in the steel industry.[88] While there was no immediate decline in production, the business outlook was somewhat less favorable than it had been at the beginning of the year, when the U. S. Steel negotiations were taking place. As the strike progressed, what may have seemed at first like a seasonal decline in new orders began to look more serious.[89] It may be surmised that whatever effect immediate business prospects had upon the decision of the Little Steel companies to take strikes, their determination to resist once the strikes were underway was strengthened by current economic conditions.

Principled opposition to trade unionism appears to have been a major factor in the determination of Little Steel to fight. The personal animus of such men as Tom Girdler, who was the leader of the Little Steel group, against unionism was not to be doubted.[90] A few quotations from his autobiography serve to reveal something of the philosophy of this key figure in the Little Steel strikes:

An employer or a manager of a business can hire or fire, justly or unjustly. All of us would welcome the invention of an arrangement that would eliminate injustice from the relationship. However, even a tyrannical businessman's tyranny is limited to the enterprise he runs. But if the C.I.O. embraces all workers — and John L. Lewis was openly striving for that goal — then no American could work except by permission of this pompous ruler. Republic's workers knew that in 1937. We who run the company never fooled ourselves that these people on our payrolls were fighting chiefly for Republic Steel Corporation when they resisted Lewis and his mobs. They were fighting for themselves.

Tolerance for socialistic propaganda has increased in this country because Americans who know better have not sufficiently resisted the idea that a man with payroll responsibilities is necessarily less of a humanitarian than people of prominence without such responsibilities. . . . The mere fact that Eugene Grace, Frank Purnell and I were heads of big corporations put a tag on us. We were "bosses." It is impossible to be a boss and be popular with everybody. If Grace, Purnell and Girdler had been other than resolute men we would not have been running big industrial organizations. Because we were resolute men who understood not only our duty to our stockholders, but our duty to our workers and likewise to our country, we did not surrender. We did not sign.

A terribly *disorganizing* influence is at work at the base of all industry in America. The boss is no longer the boss. . . . Not greed but some perception of this must have been the thing that made so many employers the bitter opponents of the labor union movement in the old days. They foresaw what now eats at us.[91]

The Little Steel companies must have realized that they had a good chance of defeating the SWOC in pitched battle. The SWOC had been able to make less headway in such Little Steel towns as Johnstown, Pa. and the steel mills of Ohio than in Pittsburgh or Homestead, where there was at least a tradition of unionism. Moreover, the contemporary split in the labor movement deprived the SWOC of labor support that might have turned the scales. "My own observations . . . convince me," wrote one commentator, "that it was the absence of AFL support in strategic steel centers — notably Youngstown, Massillon, and Canton — that brought about the weakening of the strike and strengthened the back to work movement. The split at the top ran down to cleavages between the newer recruits to the CIO steel union and the older more experienced craft unionists in their localities. I find it difficult to believe that had the Ohio State Federation of Labor and the local union councils given the steel strike whole-hearted support, it could have failed." [92]

In short, Little Steel was convinced that the cost of winning a strike was outbalanced by the future gains that would accrue from the absence of trade unions in the mills. The ideological convictions of the Little Steel leaders served to augment the value of the expected flow of future benefits.

The actual events of the Little Steel strikes, which were among the most bitter that ever took place in the United States, fill several thousand pages of testimony before the La Follette Committee. We can do no more here than consider a few of the highlights.

The most notorious episode of the entire strike took place a few days after its inception, the so-called "Memorial Day incident." On May 30, 1937, near the plant of the Republic Steel Company in Chicago, 10 people were killed and 125 others, including 35 police, were injured. For several days prior to May 30 there had been some picketing of the plant by strikers who were endeavoring to induce nonstrikers to leave. A number of arrests had been made, but the police had enunciated no fixed policy on picketing.

On May 30, after a mass meeting at strike headquarters, it was decided by the strikers to march to the plant to establish a mass picket line. The police asserted later that the purpose of the marchers was to storm the police lines and assault the plant. The Senate Committee found, however, that "the evidence not only refutes the police charge that the parade assumed a military character, but establishes, on the contrary, that it lacked all of the elements which would indicate a preconceived plan to employ violence."

As the marching strikers approached the police line, violence broke out. On the basis of the evidence of scores of eyewitnesses, as well as moving pictures taken by a photographer on the spot, the committee concluded that "the first shots came from the police; that these were unprovoked, except, perhaps, by a tree branch thrown by the strikers, and that the second volley of police shots was simultaneous with the missiles thrown by the strikers." [93] After the first shots had been fired, the strikers broke and ran. The police pursued them with the following results:

Ten marchers were fatally shot. Seven received the fatal wound in the back, three in the side, none in front. Some of those fatally shot also received severe lacerations and contusions.

Thirty others, including one woman and three minors, received gunshot wounds. . . . Twenty-eight marchers received lacerations and contusions of the head, shoulders and back requiring hospitalization, and between 25 and 30 others received injuries requiring medical treatment. . . .

As against the injuries and fatalities suffered by the marchers, the police-accident and hospitalization records report 35 policemen injured, none shot. Nine of these received hospital treatment, although six of the nine were ambulatory, so that only three were actually hospitalized. . . .

The nature of the police injuries does not argue that the marchers put up marked resistance to the police; the medical testimony of the nature of the marchers' wounds indicates that they were shot in flight. . . .

The police were free with their use of clubs as well as guns. . . . Suffice it to say that the evidence, photographic and oral, is replete with instances of the use of clubs upon marchers doing their utmost to retreat, as well as upon those who were on the ground and in a position to offer no show of resistance. . . .

The uncontradicted photographic and oral evidence, corroborated by admissions of the police themselves, establish that their treatment of the injured was characterized by the most callous indifference to human life and suffering. Wounded prisoners of war might have expected and received greater solicitude . . . the police dragged seriously wounded, unconscious men along the ground with no more care than would be employed on a common drunkard.

By June 14, normal operation of the plant had resumed.[94]

Serious consequences also followed upon the strike against the Massillon, Ohio, plant of Republic Steel.[95] Shortly after the strike commenced, local business men organized the Law and Order League of Massillon, which worked in close cooperation with a back-to-work movement among employees and with officials of Republic Steel. When the company, with the help of these groups, decided to reopen the plant on July 2, the Ohio National Guard was sent in to preserve order. The strike remained effective, however, and no violence occurred, so that the troops were withdrawn on July 8 and 9. The Law and Order League demanded that special police be sworn in, and forty men were thus deputized on July 7, with Republic footing much of the bill for their wages. There were no untoward incidents until the night of July 11. On that night, a number of union people were gathered at union headquarters, preparatory to changing the pickets. Police gathered in the vicinity of the union hall, and after a series of incidents, raked the hall with gunfire. The La Follette Committee reached the following conclusions with respect to this episode:

In the absence of the chief of police on the night of July 11, Maj. Harry O. Curley and Republic Police Officer William Henderson led the special and regular police in an unprovoked and murderous attack on the headquarters of the Committee for Industrial Organization; an attack which destroyed the union and broke the strike. During the course of the riot three strikers were killed and many others injured. No members of the police were harmed in any manner except by the fumes from their own tear gas shells. Later that night and early morning, 165 persons living in the vicinity of the union headquarters were arrested without warrants and taken to jail. The riot resulted in the breaking of the morale of the strikers, followed shortly by the ending of the strike.

At Youngstown, Ohio, the strike affected plants of Republic Steel and Youngstown Sheet and Tube. During the first two weeks, the plants remained closed and the strike proceeded in a relatively peaceful manner. However, a riot occurred on June 9, and thereafter events took a different course. The county police force was augmented by 152 special deputies, of whom 94 were in the employ of the struck companies and thus had a personal interest in the outcome, while 144 special police were hired by the city of Youngstown, 59 of whom were in the employ of Republic and Youngstown Sheet and Tube. A back-to-work movement developed, the nucleus of which was three independent unions. On June 15, the two steel companies publicly urged workers to support this movement, and some of those who did were supplied with arms. The Mahoning Valley Citizens' Committee was organized for the purpose of supporting this movement; its initiator was a local banker who had close business affiliations with the steel companies. "This citizens' committee was in reality a small group with no significant membership, but it was amply supplied with funds which it expended for a series of newspaper ads designed to create public and official sympathy for the back-to-work movement." [96]

On June 19, amid deepening tensions caused by the development of the back-to-work movement, an altercation broke out on a picket line outside one of the entrances to the Republic plant. A large crowd of strikers gathered as rumors of violence spread, and 250 deputies were despatched to the scene. Rioting flared all night throughout the area, during the course of which two strikers were killed and 42 men and women were injured by bullets, birdshot, stones, or tear gas, all but eight of whom were strikers or sympathizers. Despite this, Republic and Youngstown Sheet & Tube announced their intention of reopening on June 22, and the latter delivered helmets to the headquarters of the back-to-work movement for the employees who intended to go through the picket lines. To avert violence, Governor Davey declared martial law and despatched National Guard detachments to Youngstown with orders to maintain the status quo until the conclusion of Federal mediation efforts then in progress.

With the advent of the troops, although the plants remained closed, picketing was sharply curtailed and numerous strikers were arrested. The homes of many union members were raided in a search for arms. The Citizens' Committee intensified its propaganda efforts on behalf of the back-to-work movement, and on June 24 when Federal mediation came to an end, Governor Davey directed the National Guard to permit the plants to reopen. Some strikers remained on the picket lines during the first weeks of July, but the strike had been effectively broken. The local Traffic Commissioner was quoted as making the following "typical comment" on the resumption of work: "We have broken the back of Bolshevism in America right here in the Mahoning Valley." [97]

The Iron Age noted in an appraisal of the strike that

from a practical point of view, steel manufacturers in the group opposed to signing contracts seem to have chosen a strategic battleground in selecting Youngstown, the capital of the independent steel industry. Union leaders found disadvantages. Railroads and the Mahoning River shut off many of the big Mahoning Valley plants from access to the streets. Lack of nearby members of the United Mine Workers Union . . . for picket purposes, as in some Pennsylvania mill areas, added to their difficulties. Other obstacles which exist in the Youngstown area, as compared with some steel areas in other states, include a lack of relief funds which might support an indefinite shutdown if substantial enough even to maintain soup and bread lines. There are no other industries of size in the Youngstown area to which the striking mill workers can turn as the shutdown of their own mills continues.[98]

The role of Governor Davey of Ohio in this dispute led to controversy. When on June 22 he prevented the reopening of the plants, Youngstown Sheet and Tube called his action a breakdown of law enforcement, and requested him to "inform the citizens of this valley when the state will resume its lawful functions, repel invaders and permit its citizens to take up their regular tasks of supporting themselves and their families." [99] The SWOC was equally bitter at the reopening of the plants under National Guard protection, and accused Davey of turning on labor and using the Guard for strikebreaking purposes.[100]

On June 11, some ten to twelve thousand of the 15,000 men employed at the Johnstown, Pa., plant of Bethlehem Steel left work.[101] This strike was even less successful than those against Republic and Youngstown Sheet and Tube. Union organization was weak among the Bethlehem workers, and the company union was an old and well established one. The chief feature of this situation was the close alliance between local officials and the company. Mayor Daniel J. Shields, in cooperation with business men and religious leaders of the community, was active in the back-to-work movement. Mayor Shields, who, it was later revealed, had received over $30,000 from Bethlehem Steel which he could not account for,[102] personally swore in hundreds of special deputies and took direct charge of their activities, despite the fact that very little violence occurred. A Johnstown Citizens' Committee, formed to combat the strike, received $63,000 in financial support to pay for radio broadcasting and newspaper advertisements, most of the money coming from outside Johnstown through a national fund-raising campaign handled by the John Price Jones Corporation of New York, a public relations firm.

On June 19, Governor Earle declared martial law at Johnstown because plans had been made for a mass meeting there on the following day. More than 20,000 steel workers and miners were expected to attend, this being a center of the bituminous coal industry. Despite the strenuous objections of the company, the plant was shut down by the state troops after Eugene Grace, president of Bethlehem, had earlier refused to close the plant during

Federal mediation efforts. Despite the pleas of local officials and the Citizens' Committee, martial law remained in effect and the plants closed until June 25. When the plant reopened on June 27, a strong back-to-work movement developed, and by July 7 it was reported that 11,000 men were at work in the plant.[103]

In this strike, the union had the assistance of the state administration, the company of the local authorities. The declaration of martial law was decidedly of advantage to the union. Governor Earle left no doubt about his sympathies when he addressed an SWOC rally on July 4, and attacked the steel companies for refusing to enter into written agreements.[104] The existence of a friendly state government was important to the union in preventing vigilante action of a type that occurred elsewhere during the Little Steel strike, but it was not sufficient to overcome initial organizational weaknesses.

We may summarize some of the other events of the strike more briefly. At Monroe, Michigan, the Republic Steel strike was admittedly a minority strike, since the SWOC had only about 150 of over 1,000 employees. The conclusions reached by the La Follette Committee were as follows:

The mayor of the town and the independent association of employees brought great pressure for the reopening of the plant. In an election conducted by the mayor, the majority of the employees of the plant signified their desire to return to work. . . . Pursuant to its plan to open the plant, the officials of the corporation paid for large quantities of tear gas equipment and clubs, which were furnished to the mayor. The mayor in turn recruited and deputized a large number of citizens to whom he supplied munitions purchased by the corporation.

In military array, this body of deputized armed men marched on a picket line which up to that time had conformed to a high standard of peaceful picketing. Under the threat of force the picket line blocked the road and armed itself with clubs. Tension in the little community was so great that a mob set upon and brutally beat the union organizer. In spite of the efforts of the Governor to find a peaceful issue, the deputized mob dispersed the picket line with tear gas. The obduracy of the company, the intemperate and biased action of the mayor, and the lavish purchase of munitions by the company, transformed what was a peaceful and relatively ineffective strike into an explosive situation.[105]

The strike against the Inland Steel plant at Indiana Harbor was ended on July 1 through the intermediation of Governor Townsend of Indiana. An agreement was reached in which the company recognized the SWOC as bargaining agent for its members and agreed to submit unsettled grievances to the Indiana Commissioner of Labor for arbitration. The question of a signed agreement, however, was left to the National Labor Relations

Board, so that the union failed to attain its principal demand,[106] although it did obtain a company memorandum on labor policy which approximated the Carnegie-Illinois agreement.

To summarize: the strike was relatively ineffective at Bethlehem Steel, the only period of complete shutdown having been a week when martial law was in effect. The strike proved fairly effective at the Ohio plants of Republic steel, while its South Chicago plant kept in partial operation. However, its Buffalo plant and two Alabama subsidiaries were completely unaffected. Youngstown Sheet and Tube's small Chicago plant, as well as its plant at Indiana Harbor, were completely closed, but the strike was ineffective at its Youngstown plants. The Chicago plant of Inland Steel was closed down.[107] By July 15, 1937, virtually all plants had resumed normal operation, though as late as March, 1938, the SWOC claimed that between 4500 and 5000 men were still out at the Canton and Massillon plants of Republic Steel.[108]

During the course of the strike, mediation efforts were made by the governors of Ohio, Pennsylvania, and Indiana, and by the federal government. Federal intervention was initiated on June 17, when the secretary of labor appointed a mediation board consisting of Charles P. Taft, Lloyd K. Garrison, and Edward F. McGrady, to meet with the parties. The board received an initial rebuff when the companies refused to delay reopening of struck plants until the conclusion of mediation efforts. Girdler informed the board "that he would not consent to a term contract because he believed it necessary for the proper operation of his company that they should be in a position to meet the fluctuating price of steel by wage variations if they became necessary." [109] The companies refused to meet with Lewis or Murray, but did agree to meet with local union officials on a plant-by-plant basis, although Bethlehem and Republic took the position that they would not even discuss the question of an oral or written agreement.

The board thereupon made the following settlement proposal to the companies: "The making and signing of an agreement with the union, to become effective only if the union wins an election; the calling off of the strike and the return of all the men to work, the holding of a secret ballot election in the company's plants by the National Labor Relations Board the agreement to go into effect if the union wins, and to be torn up if the union loses." [110] This proposal was rejected, and the board gave up its efforts on June 24.

The attitude of steel management toward the mediation board was made clear in an article in *The Iron Age,* which criticized the board members as biased in favor of written agreements.[111] Tom Girdler later wrote that "they were allowing themselves to be used shamefully" in mediating something where mediation was impossible. He continued bitterly: "If there had been labels on them they would have read 'liberal and progressive.' I dispute with anyone who holds that men such as Mr. Taft — or President Roosevelt — are necessarily more honorable men, more kindly men, less selfish men, because they were born under no obligation to make a living." [112]

It is impossible to estimate with any degree of accuracy the costs of the strike either to the companies or to the workers. Table 2 contains some sug-

Table 2.

A comparison of net income changes from 1936 to 1937 between steel companies affected by a strike in 1937 and those not affected

	Net income (thousands of dollars) [b]		Per cent increase
	1936	1937	1936 to 1937
A. *Companies on strike*			
Bethlehem Steel Corp.	$24,039	$45,654	90
Republic Steel Corp.	18,124	17,827	[−2]
Youngstown Sheet & Tube Co.	14,847	17,634	19
Inland Steel	16,804	18,187	8
B. *Companies not on strike*			
United States Steel Corp.	66,702	129,585	94
Jones & Laughlin Steel Corp.[a]	5,657	7,156	27
National Steel Corp.	18,164	26,055	43
Wheeling Steel Corp.	5,961	6,326	6
Armco Steel Corp.	9,717	10,733	10
Crucible Steel Co.	4,321	5,543	28

Source: Gertrude G. Schroeder, *The Growth of Major Steel Companies, 1900–1950* (Johns Hopkins University, 1952), pp. 216–227.
[a] This company had a strike lasting only 36 hours.
[b] Net income before interest and income taxes.

gestive data. Changes in net income from 1936 to 1937 are compared for the companies which were struck and those which were not. While the strike was by no means the only factor in the profit picture, the data suggest strongly that, except for Bethlehem Steel, at which the stoppage was shorter and relatively less effective than in the remaining companies, the strike was a costly affair. Republic Steel seems to have been the hardest hit. If it is compared, for example, with National Steel, a company of comparable size, its 1937 net income was some eight million dollars below the expected level.

Comparing it with Jones & Laughlin, which settled with the union, the deficit was about five million dollars. Both Youngstown Sheet & Tube and Inland Steel did worse than the large steel companies unaffected by the strike, although not as badly as Republic, on this basis. (Wheeling, Armco and Crucible were considerably smaller than the remaining seven, and comparisons with them are less valid.)

The strike costs did not end in 1937. As a consequence of National Labor Relations Board proceedings, Republic was eventually obliged to reinstate 7000 strikers who had been discriminated against, with back pay amounting to two million dollars, while Youngstown Sheet and Tube incurred a similar cost of $170,000. In addition, Republic in 1945 paid $350,000 to settle suits brought against it in behalf of strikers who had been killed or injured.[113]

Perhaps the best general commentary on the 1937 Little Steel strike was that made by the La Follette Committee:

To break the strikes of 1937, "Little Steel" resorted to the traditional practices of espionage, the "rough shadowing" of union organizers and men, the arming and deputizing of private persons, and coercion of law-enforcement officers. In pursuit of these practices, the "Little Steel" strike of 1937 was no less brutal and violent than previous strikes in the industry which have been the subject of other congressional investigations.

The strike of 1937, however, was more ominous than the others since in it the companies sought to incite a spirit of vigilantism in the citizens and to subvert the community to strikebreaking activities. . . .

The bloodshed, bitterness, and economic disorganization of communities resulting from the "Little Steel" strike might easily have been avoided had the companies conformed to the laws of the United States, instead of ranging their combined economic strength and the prestige and influence of their employer associations in opposition to collective bargaining. Their determination to flout the law, and their efforts, through a careful campaign of propaganda, to enlist local communities to assist them, must be condemned as dangerous to lawful government.[114]

The SWOC: From Organizing Committee to International Union

Since the SWOC collected no dues until April 1937, it was dependent upon outside sources to finance the initial organizing campaign and the Little Steel strike. As nearly as can be determined, the following funds were received by the SWOC in gifts and loans between 1936 and May 1, 1942:[115]

Loan from United Mine Workers	$601,000
Advances from CIO	997,648
Salaries and expenses of CIO organizers assigned to SWOC	20,965
Total	$1,619,613

In addition to these amounts, the SWOC received assistance, mainly from the United Mine Workers, in the form of the services of organizers and officials who were carried on the donors' payrolls. Lewis claimed that the Mine Workers provided the CIO with some $3,904,000 in this form,[116] although some of the money went to organizing campaigns other than steel. Philip Murray himself remained on the United Mine Workers' payroll as a vice-president until he became president of the CIO. It has been estimated that all in all, the SWOC spent some $2,500,000 up to the end of the Little Steel strike, the great bulk of which came from the United Mine Workers.[117] This may be compared with the $500,000 initially pledged by the CIO for an organizing drive in steel.

On top of its defeat in the Little Steel strike, the SWOC was faced with a major cyclical decline in business. A survey of 526 plants undertaken by the union in December 1937, revealed that of 547,000 steel workers normally employed when the plants were operating at 80 per cent of capacity, 153,000 (28 per cent) had been laid off completely, 309,000 (57 per cent) were on part time, and only 85,000 (15 per cent) were working full time.[118] During December 1937, the steel mills operated at only 25 per cent of capacity, compared with an average of 72 per cent for the year 1937.[119]

As an economy measure, expense accounts of all field representatives were eliminated, and they were cut down to 26 paid days a month, then 19 days, and in some areas, 14 days, although all were expected to continue at work full time.[120] The staff was reduced by December 1937 to 213 full-time field workers, 75 part-time field workers, and 66 administrative staff, from a high of 437 full-time employees in July, 1937.[121] However, the SWOC became self-sufficient after the Little Steel strike,[122] and by 1941 had managed to repay a loan of $601,000 that it had secured from the United Mine Workers.

During 1936, and until the close of 1937, the SWOC was directed completely by Philip Murray and the officers appointed by him. Professor Taft has written: "Funds for organizing the steel workers were supplied by other unions whose leaders could claim the right to appoint officers and administrators. Moreover, no objection of any consequence was made to 'outside' tutelage, for the outsiders had supplied the finances and the organizing talent which made the union a living reality." [123] When the SWOC began to be self-sustaining, the first steps in the direction of a permanent organization based upon democratic principles were taken, although the initial tutelage left a lasting imprint upon the character of the union.

A comparison with the United Automobile Workers' Union, which was self-supporting from the start, is instructive. In that organization, an active internal democracy, probably too active for the good of the union, prevailed during its early years, at a time when the SWOC was still a nonrepresentative organization. However, it should be pointed out that the high degree of concentration prevailing in the steel industry, and the proclivities of the steel employers for concerted action, made a centralized steel union inevitable.

The first convention of the SWOC was a so-called wage and policy convention, which was called for the limited purposes of adopting a wage policy to provide a basis for negotiating expiring agreements, and to adopt rules for the government of local lodges.[124] Murray summarily ruled out of order a resolution aimed at the establishment of an international union, on the ground that a properly authorized constitutional convention had not been called.[125] A set of rules was adopted for local lodges, under which, *inter alia*, all dues collected were to be sent directly to the SWOC, which was then to remit 25 per cent to the originating local.[126] This requirement ensured that the SWOC, rather than the local lodges, would have control of the bulk of the union's income.

The nearest approach to controversy at the first SWOC meeting came when a delegate attempted to amend a resolution condemning Fascist aggression by adding a condemnation of Communist aggression as well. Murray prevented the issue from coming to a vote by ruling the motion out of order,[127] but there was no doubt that this was a sore point. The steel companies, in fighting the SWOC, had been hammering away on the theme of Communist infiltration into the SWOC, and there seemed to be little question that a number of Communists or Communist sympathizers had managed to gain positions on the SWOC payroll. However, the Communist Party never got a strong foothold in the SWOC, and by 1939 the SWOC was openly fighting it, at a time when tolerance was the watchword in many other CIO unions. For example, David McDonald, secretary-treasurer of the SWOC, said in a public address in 1939: ". . . there are people who would like to use the steel workers union to build a classless society. Agents of the Communist Party quite naturally would like to turn the SWOC into an instrument for their own use. The steel workers do not want to join the Communist Party, nor to be guided by it. They will not subscribe to any political or economic theory which is anti-union or anti-American. They are not deceived by purveyors of false doctrines." [128] The fact that the SWOC drew a substantial percentage of its organizers from the Mine Workers Union, and that its officers until 1942 were possessed of supreme administrative authority, made it relatively easy to solve the Communist problem, which was the source of so much difficulty in other unions.

The major preoccupation of the convention was with the impending contract renewals, particularly with U. S. Steel. The convention confined itself to an expression of confidence in the leadership of the SWOC and an authorization to continue along the same lines in negotiating with the steel companies. Murray warned the delegates that "it is extremely difficult to move ahead in things such as we are interested in while the country is moving back. . . . I don't want our people to bubble with enthusiasm to the point where they might drive their officers to the development of a strategy that would lead to inevitable destruction." [129] The wage scale committee disclosed the objective of negotiating master agreements in each portion of the industry with trade associations representing the companies.

The renewal of the collective agreement with U. S. Steel in February 1938, in which additional conversations between Lewis and Taylor seemed to be an important factor,[130] gave the SWOC a breathing spell at a time when it was badly in need of one. At the time of the negotiations, the industry was operating at about 30 per cent of capacity, so that the maintenance of the existing wage level, which is what the contract provided, was a substantial achievement for the struggling union. The term of the contract was indefinite, with reopening at the option of either party. Contracts with the independent steel companies were renewed on much the same basis.

An important factor in the growth of the SWOC during the ensuing years was the assistance rendered by the National Labor Relations Board in a number of important decisions. As already noted, Republic Steel was obliged to reinstate a considerable number of SWOC strikers with back pay.[131] In a case involving the Inland Steel Co., the board held that refusal to enter into a written agreement with the duly authorized representative of the employees, after agreement had been reached, constituted an unfair labor practice, thus destroying the validity of one of the principles on which the companies had waged the Little Steel strike. The Bethlehem employee representation plans were found to be company-dominated, and their disestablishment was ordered; a similar decision was rendered in the case of the American Rolling Mills.

The case of Weirton Steel was an interesting one, for this company had been successful in resisting SWOC organization attempts and was not involved in the 1937 strike. The board found that management had spied upon the activities of the SWOC; that it had employed special watchmen who "roamed the streets, trailed the C.I.O. sympathizers, and assaulted S.W.O.C. organizers"; and that it had given considerable financial as well as moral support to an employee representation plan which was used to fight the SWOC. A number of CIO sympathizers among the workers were bodily evicted from the company's plants by fellow workers, under company inspiration.[132]

While NLRB orders permitted the SWOC to resume its organizational work, it was still necessary to gain majorities in order to attain the status of exclusive representative. Even the U. S. Steel agreement, it will be recalled, provided that the SWOC was to represent its members only. The process of accumulating majorities was a slow one. By May 1938, the SWOC had won 59 out of 77 elections in which it participated, and secured exclusive bargaining rights over 62,000 workers.[133] The gradual improvement in business conditions during 1938 and 1939 permitted the union to put itself on a firmer economic basis. However, actual dues-paying membership lagged far behind workers represented and membership in good standing. Although a membership of 525,000 was claimed late in 1937,[134] and 500,000 in 1940 (at the same time the union claimed to have collective agreements covering 600,000 workers),[135] Murray reported in November 1940, that the SWOC had 350,000 members in good standing and only 250,000 paying dues regularly.[136]

The SWOC held its second wage and policy convention in May 1940, a date which marked a transition from a period of quiescence to one of aggression against the unorganized sector of the industry. With several years of dues paying behind them, the steel workers were in a somewhat more belligerent mood regarding self-government. A delegate quoted the following passage from R. R. R. Brooks, *As Steel Goes:* "The Steel Workers Organizing Committee is a democracy. It is a democracy of steel workers and for steel workers, but not by steel workers." He continued: "I want to point out that in all the other mass production industries, rubber, automobile, electricity, those organizations which in many cases are less strong than our organization all have international unions." [137]

There had also been considerable grumbling among members of the old Amalgamated about their status. In his report to the 64th Annual Convention of this union, which still maintained an independent status, Secretary-Treasurer Leonard stated that no one had foreseen at the time the SWOC-Amalgamated agreement was signed that the period of organization for which the contract was valid might stretch over an unlimited number of years, and he suggested that the Amalgamated might well be justified in resuming its own organizing activities.[138] In February 1939 the president and vice-president of the Amalgamated conferred with Murray on the possibility of resuscitating their union, and were put off with polite suggestion that the proper role of the Amalgamated was to rehabilitate all its lodges which were not 100 per cent organized.[139] Another meeting was held with Murray in January 1940, at which the Amalgamated urged that the SWOC lodges be turned over to it in accordance with the 1936 agreement. Murray again put them off with the argument that if the SWOC became part of the Amalgamated, it would have to assume liability for the death benefit system of the latter, which he felt would be unfair to the SWOC membership.[140] Membership in the Amalgamated had dropped to less than 8000 by 1940, and since the organization no longer had even a symbolic value to the SWOC, this was a very peripheral issue.

Murray met the growing demand for formalizing the structure of the union by promising a constitutional convention in 1942. He pointed out that there were some difficult legal problems involved in absorbing the Amalgamated, and that the preparation of a constitution required a considerable amount of work. To the proponents of immediate action he replied:

I have a paper in my pocket that somebody gave to me this afternoon, a paper issued by some irresponsible individual, I suppose, and it is addressed to the 'Dear Brothers' in this convention. There is a whole program, all predicated upon the assumption that you are ready to take their advice. They indulge in some discussion about a class struggle and a policy. They insist that there should be an immediate constitution. . . . Now, I am wondering, I am just wondering, if it is the business of the Fascists or the Nazis or the Democrats or Republicans or the Communists to tell us what we are supposed to do in these conventions. . . . Anyone else outside who wants to help us, that's all right, as long as its constructive help, constructive help and cooperation — I welcome that, but I do not welcome and I do not want and I am not going to tolerate undue interference with the work of this organization.[141]

Put this way, there could be but one outcome: a resolution to postpone the constitution for two years was carried with but a scattering of dissenting votes. The episode was reminiscent in many ways of the perennial debate over district autonomy in the United Mine Workers, of which Murray had for many years been vice-president.

One of the principal preoccupations of the convention was with technological unemployment, which had become a pressing problem as a consequence of the introduction of the continuous strip-rolling mill. It was estimated that 85,000 workers had been permanently displaced due to this innovation, and a number of communities had become ghost towns with the closing of antiquated mills. The union adopted a program calling for six months' advance notice of displacement; and transfer to temporary jobs until permanent vacancies opened up, with a payment of 3 per cent of earnings for workers suffering a 10 per cent or more reduction in earnings due to technological displacement. Those who could not be reabsorbed in other jobs were to receive dismissal pay equal to 10 per cent of earnings for a ten-year period, with a minimum of $500 for workers with ten years of service.[142] On the wage front, the convention did little more than express confidence in the leadership, without making any definite wage pronouncements.

The first major expansion of formal collective bargaining relationships achieved by the SWOC in almost three years came in February 1940, when the Crucible Steel Co., which had refused to renew its original SWOC agreement in 1938, signed a new contract recognizing the SWOC as the representative of its members, and, in general, following the terms of standard SWOC agreements.[143] However, the fact that as late as 1940, the SWOC regarded a "members only" contract as a victory testifies eloquently to the union's status in the industry at the time.

One of the principal holdouts was Bethlehem Steel, the second largest producer in the industry. In August 1939, a campaign patterned on the 1937 drives was undertaken, aimed at the capture of the reorganized company unions. But the results were meager. In the words of a close student of the SWOC,

the methods used in early S.W.O.C. campaigns had become stale. The enthusiasm built up by the whirlwind successes of the 1937 campaign had been dissipated in the futile and unplanned strike against Bethlehem's Cambria plant. Disillusion and disinterest were the inevitable aftermath. Early in 1940 there were no signs of anything like the almost hysterical enthusiasm of 1937. Consequently, the organizing campaign against Bethlehem was settling down to a long-run educational program in which the primary emphasis was on the development of leaders from the bottom up, and detailed training in the elementary techniques of collective bargaining.[144]

The drive was renewed in October 1940, when Van A. Bittner was put in charge. Bittner was one of the outstanding organizational leaders of the CIO; coming from the Miners' Union, he had become Western director of the SWOC and director of the Packinghouse Workers Organizing Committee. Short, effective strike demonstrations at several mills of Bethlehem, those at Lackawanna, N. Y., Johnstown, Pa., and Los Angeles, attested to the growing power of the union. The issue which served as an excuse for the demonstrations was refusal of the company to discuss grievances with the SWOC. The first real breakthrough came when employees at Bethlehem's Lackawanna plant, on May 15, 1941, voted 8223 to 2961 in favor of the SWOC in an NLRB election. This was followed by similar results at the remaining Bethlehem mills during the next year. The big mill at Johnstown voted 8940 to 2108 for the SWOC. The largest adverse vote was at Bethlehem, Pa., where 5095 voters favored an independent union to 11,535 for the SWOC.[145] By the middle of 1941, the employees of Bethlehem Steel had demonstrated conclusively that they wanted the SWOC to represent them.

The momentum of the Bethlehem drive carried over into the remaining Little Steel companies. On July 25, 1941, Republic Steel, Inland Steel and Youngstown Sheet and Tube agreed to abide by the results of a NLRB cross check of SWOC membership cards against their payrolls, thus avoiding the necessity of elections. The tally revealed that at 17 Republic plants, the SWOC had 28,482 members in good standing out of total employment of 40,858; at Inland, 8700 out of 11,800; and at Youngstown Sheet and Tube, 14,800 out of 20,133.[146] The SWOC was thus entitled by law to become the exclusive collective bargaining agent of all the employees of these companies. In September 1941, the four Little Steel companies sat down to bargain with officials of the union which four years earlier had been defeated so decisively.

In the meantime, during January of the same year, the SWOC tackled U. S. Steel for the first substantial contract improvement since the original agreement of 1937. At the beginning of 1940, the industry was running at virtually full ingot capacity, thanks to domestic rearmament and the European war. While employment was below the peak 1937 level, this was a consequence of technological change rather than idle resources. For the first time in its dealings with U. S. Steel, the union was in a position to exert a considerable degree of economic power.

The demands of the SWOC were far-reaching, and included a wage increase of 10 cents per hour, an improvement in vacation rights and in the grievance system, a dues checkoff, and, most important from the union point of view, exclusive bargaining status on proof of majority through card cross check or by other means.[147] This was, of course, before the Little Steel companies had consented to a cross check of cards. The company countered with an offer of a $2\frac{1}{2}$-cent-an-hour wage increase, tied, however, to production, so that if production dropped below 85 per cent of capacity, the company would be privileged to withdraw the increase. On April 14, a settlement was reached, giving the workers a wage increase of 10 cents per hour, more liberal vacations, extra pay for holiday work, and additional subsidiary benefits. An elaborate mechanism for the processing of grievances was established. But on one important point, the union was unsuccessful — the members–only feature of the Taylor formula remained unchanged.[148] Within a few months, the wage pattern set by this agreement had spread to the entire industry.

The negotiations with the Little Steel companies proved to be long and arduous. Initially, the union demanded wage increases sufficient to bring the wage levels of these companies up to the levels prevailing in union plants, exclusive representation (to which the union was entitled by law), and other provisions similar to those contained in the U. S. Steel contract. In one major respect, the union demands went beyond that contract: they included the union shop and the checkoff.[149]

Before the negotiations had been consummated, the nation was thrown into war, and the dispute was referred to the newly created War Labor Board. The union now raised a specific wage demand of $12\frac{1}{2}$ cents an hour, basing its demand upon the fact that the wage increase of April 1941 had been offset by the rising price level. A three-man fact-finding panel consisting of Arthur Meyer, Cyrus Ching, and Richard Frankensteen, reported that the real weekly earnings of steel workers had declined by 13.3 per cent since the last general wage increase; that traditional differentials in earnings between steel workers and workers in all durable goods manufacturing in favor of the former had been impaired; and that the companies were financially able to pay the wage increases demanded by the union.[150] On the union security issue, the panel's findings were heavily weighted in favor of maintenance of membership combined with the checkoff.

In its award, the famous "Little Steel Formula," the War Labor Board granted the steel workers a wage increase of $5\frac{1}{2}$ cents per hour, the figure being based upon a decline in their real hourly wages since January 1, 1941 plus certain other equities arising out of the requirements of the national anti-inflationary program. The amount of the award was disappointing to the union, as evidenced by the dissent of the four labor members of the War Labor Board. However, with respect to the grant of maintenance of membership and the checkoff, the union newspaper editorialized: "We recognize the tremendous victory for the steel workers which is involved in this decision." [151]

In an earlier case, involving the Federal Shipbuilding and Drydock Company, a subsidiary of U. S. Steel, the National Defense Mediation Board had similarly ordered a maintenance of membership clause, and it had been received by the company as follows:

While this company has thus accepted the "directive order" of the National War Labor Board, we are bound to say that we have done so solely under the compulsion of war. We regard the so-called "maintenance of membership" directive as unwise and unsound and as tending without the sanction of Congress to set up a national war policy which will not be conducive to obtaining maximum production. . . .[152]

The reaction of the Little Steel companies was in much the same vein. The president of Bethlehem Steel characterized the decision as one which ignored "the basic principles upon which our government was founded and the result . . . will be harmful to our national economy and to the war effort." A statement by the president of Republic Steel said in part: "In normal times the company would exercise its right to appeal to the courts to test the legality of [the] directive orders." Frank Purnell of Youngstown Sheet and Tube also characterized the WLB decision as contrary to the national interest, but indicated acquiescence for patriotic reasons.[153]

Finally, in the first weeks of August 1942, the four Little Steel companies which had been involved in the 1937 strike entered into written agreements with the union embodying the terms of the War Labor Board directive. With the important assistance of the federal government, the union had in six years succeeded in forcing the powerful steel industry to revise its labor policy. Girdler wrote later of the new circumstances:

In our private discussions my associates and I find ourselves unreconciled. We can't help but feel that if the checkoff, which is now a fact in the steel industry, had been resisted by business generally as effectively as we and our employees resisted it in that so-called strike in Little Steel, everybody in the country would have been the gainer. . . . There is little comfort for me in the realization that my warnings of 1937 have been justified by subsequent events. When our plants were being besieged I was saying that C.I.O. leaders simply wanted to force workers to join their unions and pay dues. I said they wanted, not to help labor, but to gain for themselves tremendous political and economic power. Today, in

1943, when the nation is finally preparing to pitch its full might against enemies overseas, I do not believe there are many thoughtful people who would be disposed to challenge the accuracy of my observations made when we were fighting, not "labor," but wrong-headed and largely self-appointed "leaders" of labor. I do not believe a majority of workers in this country want such a system. But in the present circumstances, what are they going to do about it? [154]

While the SWOC was engaged on the War Labor Board front with Little Steel, it turned to the NLRB for the exclusive bargaining status with U. S. Steel that had been denied it in the 1941 contract revision. In March 1942, it filed NLRB election petitions for all U. S. Steel subsidiaries. The union won about 90 per cent of the votes at these elections;[155] on September 5, 1942, the U. S. Steel Corporation granted it exclusive bargaining rights, and, upon directive order of the War Labor Board, to which the union had appealed, maintenance of membership and the checkoff. Only two major steel producers remained outside the union fold: American Rolling Mills, with 15,000 employees, and Weirton Steel with 12,000 employees. Approximately 90 per cent of the industry had been organized on a basis that provided the union with a considerable degree of membership security.

The convention that transformed the SWOC into the United Steelworkers of America was held in Cleveland during May 19–22, 1942. "Enrolled" membership was reported to be 660,052. However, in June 1942, Murray disclosed to the CIO Executive Board that dues paying membership had fallen below 500,000.[156] It was disclosed that 903 steel firms were under contract with the union, 175 under union shop agreements, and 47 under maintenance of membership.[157]

As a preliminary to the foundation of the United Steelworkers, the 1940 convention of the Amalgamated Association of Iron, Steel, and Tin Workers had adopted a resolution, by a vote of 37 to 21, empowering the officers of the Amalgamated to negotiate with the SWOC for organizational consolidation. On July 20, 1940, the following agreement was reached between the two organizations:

1. The Amalgamated waives, surrenders, assigns, and yields to the S.W.O.C. all of the rights, powers, and privileges directly or indirectly conferred upon the Amalgamated by the aforesaid agreement of June 3, 1936.

2. All charters that have been issued to lodges of the S.W.O.C. by the Amalgamated shall be cancelled and the S.W.O.C. in its own name and authority shall issue new charters in their place and stead. Any charters which the S.W.O.C. may hereafter issue shall be in its own name and authority.[158]

The approaching demise of the Amalgamated aroused considerable bitterness among some of its members. William Grey, vice-president, reported to the membership:

Now we have the question as to whether we will go into a convention with the S.W.O.C. and there is even more confusion than we had before. I believe there was only one thing in the minds of the officials who were in office when the agreement with the CIO was signed, that is, that the CIO would organize the steel industry and that they would be turned over to the Amalgamated Association and that we would have a real organization in Steel. I have never been able to understand why men who have taken an obligation in our organization could pass it up and knock the A.A. In some cases we know they did this because they believed that they would be placed in positions with another organization if the A.A. passed out. . . . I see no sign of this move being of benefit to our members. It seems to fit in with the story, where the doctor said the operation was a success, but the patient died.[159]

Any lingering illusion that an organization of 500,000 members was going to turn itself over to an antiquated, creaky body of 10,000 men was finally dissipated when on April 3, 1942, the SWOC submitted the following proposals to the Amalgamated:

1. a. Immediately after the April 28 convention of the Amalgamated, all Amalgamated lodges shall dissolve and request SWOC charters.
    b. The SWOC will immediately comply with this request.

2. The Amalgamated will then dissolve and relinquish its charter to the CIO.

3. The SWOC will hold a convention on May 19, 1942, at which the former Amalgamated lodges will be entitled to representation.

4. Existing Amalgamated contracts will not be disturbed, and employers will be notified of the transfer.[160]

The Amalgamated made the following counterproposal:

a. Amalgamated and SWOC shall continue as separate organizations until the end of the national emergency.

b. Agreement shall be reached on an organizing campaign.

c. A tripartite committee shall be established to handle jurisdictional problems.

The counterproposal was unacceptable to the SWOC, and the Amalgamated was obliged to accept the SWOC terms, agreeing to its own dissolution. While the officers may have been willing to offer resistance, it was clear that the majority of the membership desired to join the new international union. Any other solution would have been certain to lead to serious friction.

When the proposed constitution of the United Steelworkers was submitted to the convention for approval, considerable dissatisfaction was expressed from the floor over the brief length of time which the delegates had to study the document. A minor tempest arose over a constitutional provision conferring upon the international president the authority to appoint and remove international organizers and representatives. A delegate stated:

When I was affiliated with the SWOC I came from the American Federation of Labor. I joined this organization wholeheartedly because I thought it would be an organization when we would have a little bit more to say than we did in the American Federation of Labor. I surely am surprised when I see this paragraph. Why, in most of the A.F. of L. locals the business representatives are elected by the rank and file.

An organizer complained:

I believe that this paragraph in our constitution does not protect the present staff members or those who may come later to the staff. . . . I do not know from one day to the next whether I am secure in my job, because I have no assurance of any constitutional measure which would protect me. I know our President realizes the men who are working for him are doing their very best, but this is a constitutional matter.

The chairman of the constitutional committee pointed out that in most large unions, field representatives were appointed rather than elected, and that this was a necessary arrangement in order to provide sufficient staff flexibility. The major arguments in favor of the proposal were made by Philip Murray in an address which merits lengthy quotation because of what it reveals of the organizational philosophy of the steel union leadership:

I should not like the delegates, in discussing this question, to discuss it from a base which might create the impression or at least some attempt to create the impression that we are an old union, that the functions of your organization have become so stabilized that we can run the gamut of every known kind of democratic procedure, even to the point of license in the operation of our affairs. I don't mind telling you in this convention that your interest still needs some safeguarding in this man's country. My personal judgment is that your situations are not sufficiently well stabilized to enable you to move into an election of all your representatives for this organization. I don't think that day has come as yet. . . .

I would not want to assume the hazards incident to directing the affairs of this mighty organization with a provision incorporated in the constitution requiring the election of all my field representatives under these circumstances. . . .

Your incoming President, whoever he may be, should be given the power to remove for justifiable cause any man who does not carry out the policies of this organization. If you have an elected field worker responsible only to the group that elects him in a given district, often times that individual does not feel responsible to the President of the Union or to the International Executive Board. He takes a certain kind of license unto himself, and he may very well, under certain conditions, defy even the President of the Union, creating internal strife and causing internal political friction.

Now, this Union is only six years old and is not old enough to survive internal political conflict. . . . If you would recommit this matter to your committee and ask for the election of all field representatives, I tell you that you will build a hornet's nest within your Union.

In the majority of unions, international representatives are appointed by national officers, rather than elected by local groups. The proposed constitution, moreover, provided for the election of district directors by referendum, and as Clinton Golden pointed out in the debate, staff proposals customarily originate in the districts. Of course, in a dispute between the international president and a district director, the former's appointive power provides him with an overwhelming advantage. But constitutional provisions are at best of secondary significance in curbing arbitrary actions on the part of union officials. In the present instance, both logic and numbers were on Murray's side, and the disputed constitutional provision was adopted by an overwhelming majority.

The only other constitutional provision that aroused controversy was one affirming previous practice regarding division of dues receipts between the international union and the local union. A number of local delegates objected that the 25 per cent allocated to them was inadequate to sustain local functions. Murray argued that the international needed a minimum of $300,000 a year for operating expenses, which was just the amount of its share under the current arrangement, and the proposed constitutional clause was adopted.

The rest of the convention was routine. All officers were elected unanimously: Philip Murray as president, David McDonald as secretary-treasurer, and Van Bittner and Clinton Golden as assistants to the president. District directors were elected by caucuses of the respective district delegates. The wage scale committee reported in favor of the demands which were currently being made on the steel companies: a wage increase of one dollar a day, a daily minimum guarantee, the union shop and the checkoff, industry wide agreements, elimination of the southern wage differential, union participation in the administration of wage incentive systems, and improvements in the vacation, holiday, and seniority provisions.[161]

3

The Automobile Industry

The history of organization in automobile manufacturing differs strikingly from that in steel. Many things have contributed to this: among them are differences in the character of the work force, technology, and industrial organization. But one thing was shared in common: the hostile attitude of management toward trade unionism.

There had been a long tradition of unionism in steel, before the suppression of the Amalgamated Association of Iron, Steel and Tin Workers around the turn of the century. The automobile industry, on the other hand, had begun to expand rapidly during World War I and in the postwar years, when trade unionism was already on the defensive. A plan on the part of the AFL Metal Trades Department to launch an auto organizing drive during this period never got beyond the verbal stage.[1]

The steel workers were largely immigrants or first generation Americans. While there were many immigrants among the auto workers as well, a large number of them were drawn from groups with previous industrial experience in the United States. Professor Taft records that the auto workers were more individualistic and self-reliant than the steel workers; that they had more confidence in their ability to organize, springing in part from the absence of the severe defeats that the steel workers had suffered.[2] The seasonal character of automobile operations resulted in greater mobility of the labor force, and in less reliance upon any individual employer. The auto industry was more vulnerable than the steel mills to stoppages in key plants because of the interdependent technological relationships. Indeed, this was one of the major factors in auto union strategy. Whatever the reasons, the unruly independence of the auto workers during the period of union upsurge, their insistence upon leadership drawn from their own ranks, stood in sharp contrast to the willingness of the steel worker to accept a much lesser degree of self-determination.

The First Constitutional Convention of the United Automobile Workers

From the very outset, the automobile workers made it clear that they were not going to permit outsiders to guide their destinies. In sharp distinction to the steel workers, the automobile workers displayed an independence of mind that was to continue to characterize their organization through a turbulent decade. The first target of their aggressiveness and impatience was the American Federation of Labor in general and William Green in particular.

The decision to grant a national charter to automobile workers organized in AFL federal locals had been forced through a reluctant AFL Executive Council primarily by John L. Lewis, supported by William Green. This action was based upon a resolution adopted at the 1934 AFL convention which called for industrial charters for the auto, cement, and aluminum industries, with the qualification that craft union rights were to be safeguarded.[3] In February 1935, Lewis urged the council to "set up an industrial union at once, by the issuance of a charter, by the selection of temporary officers by the President of the American Federation of Labor from the material you obviously have there. . . . A convention could be called in three months or six months or whenever in the judgment of this Council they are qualified. . . . Give them money to publish a paper. . . . If it is a question of money I would be willing to recommend to the Executive Board of the Mine Workers to contribute $5,000."[4] Wharton objected that his organization, the Machinists, had jurisdiction over 25,000 tool and die makers and other craftsmen in the industry which it had never agreed to relinquish. He was seconded by Bugniazet, Coefield and Bates, representing, respectively, the electricians, plumbers, and bricklayers, on behalf of maintenance men employed in automotive plants. Green replied:

it is impossible for us to attempt to organize along our old lines in the automobile industry. . . . I must confess to you that I am come, you will come, and all of us will always come face to face with the fact, not a theory but a situation actually existing, that if organization is to be established in the automobile industry it will be upon a basis that the workers employed in this mass production industry must join an organization en masse. We cannot separate them.

He also argued strongly that it would be poor judgment to attempt to separate the parts plants from the automobile manufacturing plants, citing the possibility of halting automobile production more easily by striking at the suppliers rather than directly at the manufacturers. Lewis moved that a broad international charter be issued at once, and that "all questions of overlapping jurisdiction in the automobile parts and special crafts organizations encountered in the administration of this policy be referred to the Executive Council for consideration at such time as the Council may elect to give these questions consideration." But he received little support on the council. Hutcheson observed: "I take it that you recognize the fact that the American Federation of Labor has been brought up to its present strength as a result of craft organizations. . . . I do not believe we should give them a charter so broad that they could go out and claim any employee that might be employed by these automobile manufacturers." Tobin agreed: "I am not at all in favor of industrial organization. It was tried in the early stages of this country and was found to be a complete failure with the exception of the Miners union." On a motion by Harrison, Lewis' motion was amended to grant the charter to include "all employees directly engaged in the manufacture of parts (not including tools, dies and machinery) and assembling of those parts into completed automobiles but not including job or contract shops manufacturing parts or any other employees engaged in said automobile plants." As thus amended, this motion was adopted by a vote of 12 to 2, with Lewis going on record in opposition, and Green warning prophetically: "If we lay down here a policy of organization and charge the President and his associates to organize these people I do not want you to blame us for failure but I know their state of mind. The moment you attempt to segregate them you will never get anywhere. . . . Whatever you do I will try to carry out but I will be the target of criticism and I know we will fail." [5]

This restriction in the charter was one of the principal targets at the constitutional convention of the United Automobile Workers. When the constitutional definition of jurisdiction was submitted to the convention, several attempts to amend it were ruled out of order by F. J. Dillon,[6] the chairman, who urged that the charter be accepted first and then questioned at the next AFL convention. After considerable debate, this course was followed, with the proviso that "unless these jurisdictional limitations are removed by the 55th National Convention of the American Federation of Labor, the International Officers of the United Automobile Workers be, and are hereby instructed to formulate such plans and take such action as in their opinion may seem advisable." [7]

Dissatisfaction with the policies of the AFL reached a peak when it came to election of officers. The Resolutions Committee came in with a request to William Green, who was very much in evidence at the convention as the representative of the AFL, to appoint Francis Dillon president of the newly established international. Green, who took over the chairmanship of the convention at this juncture, spoke strongly in favor of the resolution. The UAW, he said, lacked the financial resources to proceed independently, and he promised that the AFL would defray the salary of the president for the next year.

It will be several months, my dear boys, before you will have enough money in your treasury to pay the expenses of this International Union. It will take some time before you begin paying per capita tax into your International Union. It will take some time before you will be able to finance it, and if you run in debt to begin with you will be handicapped. And who is there among you that wants to be handicapped in that way. My God, is it possible that we cannot extend to you the help we are craving to give you while you are passing through this most important change in your national existence?

Green did not make clear why AFL help was necessarily contingent upon acceptance of Dillon as president, but he did promise the convention that it would have a free hand in selecting a secretary-treasurer and an executive board. Coming from the background of the Executive Council debate on the scope of the UAW charter, Green was concerned lest the infant union alienate the powerful AFL crafts and jeopardize its existence, and he felt that the firm, restraining hand of an experienced AFL organizer at the helm was the best guarantee of cordial relationships. But the angry delegates, despite his efforts, defeated the resolution asking for the appointment of Dillon by a vote of 164 to 113.

For the next three days Green worked feverishly behind the scenes in an effort to win support for Dillon, with little success. Finally, he returned to the convention and announced that in view of the deep divisions of opinion which prevailed, he deemed it wise to designate probationary officers. Dillon was named president, Homer Martin, vice-president, and Ed Hall, secretary-treasurer. Martin had backed Dillon, as had most of the men appointed to the executive board.[8] After making this announcement, Green told the delegates that his action was in line with the decision of the Executive Council, and that no vote of approval or disapproval on their part was necessary. Efforts from the floor to upset this action were ruled out of order. Dillon simply announced that "as the president of your union clothed with the authority to speak, I must now say that if there be those here who cannot conform to the terms and provisions of this document, then they must leave. . . . Now you are affiliated with the American Federation of Labor, and you all understand it, and it is done in a perfectly legal, orderly way."

This first convention was unique in that political ideological issues did not play an important role. At the outset of the convention, Green warned the delegates to have nothing to do with the communists, and Dillon took up the cudgels by assailing the left-wing followers of A. J. Muste for their role in the Chevrolet strike of April 1935. Virtually without debate a resolution was adopted "condemning the communistic centers of the world in meddling with the internal affairs of this country." [9] It was to be many years before an issue of this character could again be disposed of without entailing a major eruption.

The First Year

The organization which emerged from this founding convention was still a tiny group with very little influence. It represented a maximum of 20,000 workers in an industry which potentially employed about 445,000 workers.[10] Moreover, it was not the only contender for the allegiance of auto workers. The Mechanics Educational Society of America, the Associated Automobile Workers of America (based in the Hudson, General Motors Truck, and Lansing Oldsmobile plants), and the Automotive Industrial Workers Association (led by Richard T. Frankensteen, based in Chrysler, and under the influence of Father Charles Coughlin, the radio priest) had a combined membership which probably equalled that of the UAW. Nor did the latter enjoy any extensive collective bargaining rights. It had a total of sixteen written agreements with small parts manufacturers, but not even a verbal agreement with any major firm. Even the most optimistic trade union partisan would not have predicted a very rosy future for the UAW at this juncture.

Operating in its favor, however, the UAW, as well as its competitors, had one asset which was to prove more powerful than all the liabilities: the discontent and unrest that prevailed among the auto workers. This stemmed from a number of factors, which may be categorized as follows:

1. The automobile industry was just recovering from a major depression, which had witnessed a decline of average employment from 447,000 in 1929 to a low of 244,000 in 1933. Despite some degree of recovery, the memories of the depression days were still fresh, and these were to be revived when in 1938 employment again declined precipitously.

2. Aside from the fear of permanent unemployment, the irregular character of automobile production produced sharp variations in employment so that the worker was never certain from day to day whether he had a job. A National Recovery Act study in 1935 made the following pertinent observations:

One of the psychological problems faced by the automobile workers today is the gamble that he knows he is facing as he goes to work each day. He sees the men waiting at the gate for an interview for employment. If he is feeling badly on a particular day and slows down in his gait, his straw-boss or foreman tells him, "Step on it. If you don't want the job, there are thousands outside who do," or "Look out the window and see the men waiting in line for your job." [11]

Somewhat more vivid is the following account by a former worker on the assembly line:

The annual layoff during the model change was always a menace to the security of the workers. Along about June or July it started. The bosses would pick the men off a few at a time, telling them to stay home until they were notified to come back. There was no rhyme or reason in the selection of the fortunate ones chosen to continue working. The foreman had the say. If he happened to like you, or if you sucked around him and did him favors — or if you were one of the bastards who worked like hell and turned out more than production — you might be picked to work a few weeks longer than the next guy. . . . It was customary for auto workers to go broke during this layoff.[12]

3. Although the hourly earnings of automobile workers were relatively high, annual incomes were often low because of irregularity of employment. Annual income for 1936 was put variously at $1470 and $1270, depending upon the method of computation.[13] But such averages concealed tremendous variation. A study of four automobile plants in 1934 revealed that one-fifth of the workers earned less than $600 a year, and one-half, less than $1050. Those workers who were fortunate enough to work fairly steadily throughout the year, as in the Packard Motor Car Company, which had actively worked for the elimination of seasonality, were relatively well off,[14] but many were hard put to make ends meet.

It cannot be said, however, that automobile workers fared worse in this respect than the majority of American workers. An interindustry comparison for 1937 revealed that only 6 of 74 industries with an average employment of at least 25,000 a year paid higher average annual earnings than the automobile manufacturing industry, while auto bodies and parts ranked not far behind.[15]

4. One of the wage practices particularly resented by workers was described as follows by Harry Bennett, who was for many years one of the principal executives of the Ford Motor Company:

It was the custom in the industry, when changing models, to pay everyone off and close down the plant. Upon reopening, all the men would be rehired at the flat rate. Thus a man who might have worked his way up to $8.00 or even $10.00 a day, would be rehired at the wage of a beginner. This custom, practiced by the

Ford Motor Company as well as by all other automobile manufacturers, was the real motive power for the union movement.[16]

5. Perhaps of equal importance in explaining the dissatisfaction that prevailed among auto workers was the notorious "speed up," the significance of which has thus been described:

Rebellion against the industry hit the speed-up like a tidal wave at the point when the man in the shop was convinced that the machine had failed to live up to its promise insofar as it affected him . . . automobile labor was pushed to the breaking point. Prodigious new quotas of output were wrung from lines that had been fast and taxing in the 20's . . . the men who tended the lines at the time considered the pace more than their bodies could stand. They could feel the speed-up in their bones. They were convinced that standing up to such a pace was aging and debilitating.[17]

One of the consequences of the pace of production was premature superannuation of the workers. A 1935 study of the industry came up with the observation that men over 40 years of age found it very difficult to secure reemployment after layoffs.[18] With a large surplus of labor, constantly being augmented by immigration, the manufacturers could have their pick of the labor force. This was facilitated by the fact that most jobs required little training. It was estimated that in 1935, 26.9 per cent of all occupations in the industry required no experience, while only 9.8 per cent required more than one year of training or experience.[19]

6. Employer industrial relations policies acted, if anything, as a stimulus to unrest. Foremen were accorded considerable authority in hiring and firing, and they did not always exercise this authority wisely. "The petty whims of the foremen seem to be the controlling influences in the lives of many of the automobile workers. Favoritism and direct financial demands on the workers by the foreman seems to have been common. . . . There is evidence to indicate that if a foreman says 'do not rehire' on his lay-off slip, this snap judgment may be taken as final for that plant or that company and perhaps, through checking of references, final for the industry. If the foreman should write 'agitator' on the lay-off slip either as such or in code, the effect most certainly would be final insofar as that worker was concerned." [20] Seniority in layoff, rehiring, and promotion was not customary.

Espionage, both on an informal basis among workers and by contract with professional detective agencies, was common practice, particularly after 1933 when the manufacturers began to fear the incursions of trade unionism. From January 1934, through July 1936, General Motors paid

$994,855 for spy service, and at times had as many as 200 men reporting on employee activities. In 1935, Chrysler spent $72,000 for the espionage services of the Corporation Auxiliary Co. Even union officials, such as Arthur G. Dubuc, president of the Chevrolet local of the UAW in Flint and Leon Scott, secretary-treasurer of the Herron-Zimmer local in Detroit, were revealed to have been in the employ of detective agencies and engaged in reporting on the activities of their own organizations. In 1934, three of the thirteen members of the executive board of the AFL federal union in the Flint plants of GM were spies employed by the Corporation Auxiliary Co., and the La Follette Committee attributed the local's decline in membership from 26,000 to 120 by 1936 largely to the activities of the labor spies.[21] However, the labor espionage system reached its acme of perfection in the Ford Motor Company, as will be recounted below.

All these factors contributed to the tension and uneasiness that were prevalent in Detroit and other automobile cities in 1936, and that led eventually to one of the greatest outbursts of labor conflict in the history of the United States.

The UAW lost no time in protesting the actions of Green in appointing its officers. A delegation appeared before the AFL Executive Council in October 1935 with a petition signed by a majority of the delegates to the convention, requesting that a special convention be held not later than March 1, 1936 for the purpose of electing officers. But the council turned a deaf ear to these pleas, and merely authorized Green to use his judgment on the length of the probationary period.[22]

But the pressure of outside events, particularly the formation of the CIO at the end of 1935, forced the pace, and in January 1936, the council agreed to terminate its provisional control of the UAW by not later than April 30, 1936, despite the urging of President Dillon that election of new officers should not be permitted until August at the earliest. In consequence, a convention was called to meet in South Bend, Indiana, on April 27.[23] Prior to the convention, Martin and Hall, vice-president and secretary-treasurer, had attempted to dethrone Dillon by a *coup d'etat,* with the result that the latter was not on speaking terms with them.[24] To avoid further acrimony, Dillon relinquished the chair on the first day of the convention, and almost immediately Homer Martin was elected president by a unanimous vote, thus permanently severing Dillon's connection with the UAW.

This convention saw the commencement of the intense factionalism which was to be the hallmark of the UAW in the years to come. Almost every ideological group in the country was represented either among the delegates or by observers, including representatives of the Communist and Socialist parties. The left-wing groups were in firm control, as evidenced by the fact that a resolution in favor of the reelection of President Roosevelt was defeated. Adolph Germer, who was attending the convention on behalf of John L. Lewis, stated publicly that "Communists and Socialists have taken over the convention, and are voting not as auto workers but according to their political views." [25]

The newly elected officers reflected the predominantly left-wing orientation of the convention. Wyndham Mortimer and Ed Hall, elected vice-presidents, and George Addes, the new secretary-treasurer, were on the left, as were a majority of the executive board.

Walter Wells, another vice-president, was president of a small local union at the Gemmer Gear Company in Detroit, which had seven or eight delegates at the convention. This represented what the anti-AFL, anti-Dillon people thought might represent the margin of difference if Dillon ran for president. Wells was offered a vice-presidency for his votes. He figured very little in subsequent events, and faded from view after the 1939 split in the union.

A number of CIO organizers were in attendance, and exercised considerable influence in the proceedings, but since the CIO itself was still in the process of charting its own course vis-à-vis the AFL, the UAW was careful for the moment not to impair its relationships with the AFL. The first issue of the *United Automobile Worker* contained the following, in an editorial: "Let it be said here and now . . . that the auto union has no intention of leaving the AFL, either now or in the future, but that our intentions are to work in complete harmony with all sister organizations, as long as our rights and welfare are respected."

The elected officers of the UAW were mostly young men, and reflected in their backgrounds the heterogeneous character of the auto labor force — quite different, for example, from the men who worked in the mines and steel mills of the nation, and perhaps accounting in part for the continual ferment and agitation that made the UAW almost unique among American labor organizations. Homer Martin, the president, had been a Baptist minister in Missouri, and had gone to work at the Chevrolet plant in Kansas City in 1932 when his parish voted him out for his economic views. "He spoke with other-worldly fervor; his language was colored by Biblical phrases; no other man could pierce to the hearts of Southern-born workers as he could. A gifted agitator, he made men feel that in organizing a union

they were going forth to battle for righteousness and the word of God." [26]
Wyndham Mortimer had been raised in a coal mining town, had gone to
work in the mines at the age of twelve years, and had a good deal of organizing experience behind him. Ed Hall, a welder by trade, had been employed for most of his adult life in the automobile industry, while Walter
Wells had five years of employment at the Gemmer Gear Co. George Addes,
a metal finisher by trade, had worked since 1923 at Willys Overland in
Toledo.

A majority of the executive board members were under thirty-five years
of age. Russell Merrill had been a student at Marion College in Indiana,
and had been active in organizing the unemployed. Lloyd Jones was a Kentucky mountaineer and ex-evangelist. J. J. Kennedy, one of the older members at forty-three, had been an organizer for the United Brotherhood of
Carpenters until he went into the automobile industry in 1932, rising to
leadership in Chrysler. Frank Tucci had been employed at Fisher Body
since 1925. John Soltis, the oldest member of the Council at forty-eight, was
a former member of the Knights of Labor, and had held a number of district offices in the United Mine Workers before moving to Cleveland and
gaining employment with Hupp Motor Co. F. J. Michel had been active
in the Farmer-Labor party at Racine, Wis., while Willis Mauer and Delmond Garst were long-time employees of Fisher Body. Fred Pieper, though
only twenty-seven years old, already had a record of several discharges for
union activity. Lester Washburn was from the Reo plant in Lansing, while
Walter Reuther, at the time only twenty-eight years of age, already had
nine and a half years of experience as an automobile worker, although he had
gained some formal education by attending classes at Wayne University.[27]

One matter of note is that all the elected officials had been employed in
automobile plants prior to their election. Unlike the situation in other CIO
unions, which accepted professional CIO organizers from other trades as
leaders, the UAW insisted from the beginning that its leadership must
come from the auto industry.

Father Coughlin had appeared at a party given for UAW delegates at
the 1936 convention and had reportedly exclaimed, "Away with independent
unions." Whether because of his influence or for other reasons, the Automotive Industrial Workers Association voted in May to merge with the UAW,
as did the Associated Automobile Workers of America. But these organizations had declined in strength, and did not mean a great augmenta-
tion of membership for the UAW, although the strategic gains involved in

eliminating potential sources of rivalry were considerable. Only the Mechanics Educational Society of America, with about a thousand members, remained independent, though several of its Detroit locals which had been under communist influence broke away and affiliated with the UAW.[28]

Finally, on July 2, 1936, the UAW formalized its adherence to the principle of industrial unionism by affiliating with the CIO. It was shortly suspended and later expelled from the AFL, but these were mere formalities. William Green had been right in his assessment of the strength of industrial union sentiment among the automobile workers, and it was a foregone conclusion that the UAW should join forces with John L. Lewis in the latter's protest against restrictive craft jurisdictions.

The pattern of the relationship which developed between the CIO and the UAW was quite different from that which characterized CIO–Steel Worker relations. In steel, Lewis had created a new organization, with Philip Murray and other miners at the helm. These men remained on the payroll of the Miners' Union or the CIO for some years while serving as officials of the SWOC, and continued to rely heavily upon the CIO for financing organizing work. As already noted, Lewis' major concern at the start of the CIO drive was to organize steel in order to protect his captive mine flanks. Everything was to be concentrated on steel, with other industries coming later.

The UAW, however, was largely self-financing from the start, and received financial aid from other CIO unions only during the sit-down strikes and again later, when in the throes of sharp internal dissension. Even at the height of CIO influence in the internal affairs of the UAW, there was never any question of the imposition of outside leadership. The role of the CIO was restricted to working out compromises among the contending factions with respect to the choice among rival leaders within the UAW.

From the April 1936 convention to the end of the year, the UAW was engaged in putting its house in order in preparation for an invasion of the industry. It was reported in August that the international union had fifteen organizers on its staff, with five more to be added soon.[29] Not until November, however, did the organizing drive begin to gather momentum, when President Roosevelt was reelected and the steel drive contributed to increased interest in unionism among auto workers. On November 12, the UAW executive officers, after a meeting with Philip Murray and John Brophy, adopted the following program to serve as the basis of organization:[30]

1. An annual wage.
2. Elimination of the speedup.
3. Straight seniority rights.
4. Forty-hour week and eight-hour day.
5. Time and one-half for overtime work.
6. Reduction in hours worked until all displaced workers rehired.
7. Improved safety measures.
8. Collective bargaining.

This program is notable for the absence of a union shop demand and the prominent place accorded the annual wage, which was to remain a UAW demand until its partial fulfillment in 1955.

The General Motors Strike

The strike called by the UAW against General Motors at the end of 1936 ranks as the most critical labor conflict of the nineteen thirties. Up to this time, the UAW was a small, struggling organization, with great ambitions but few members. It emerged from the GM strike perhaps not yet a major power, but certainly a factor to be reckoned with in the industry. And it was able to capitalize upon its limited gains from the GM strike to consolidate its position into an impregnable one.

As a prelude to the General Motors strike, employees of the Bendix Corporation of South Bend, Indiana, manufacturers of automobile accessories, engaged in a sit-down strike on November 17, 1936. The sit-down strike was a relatively new device. It had been employed on a large scale by French metal workers in May, 1936, and while instances of sit-downs are to be found in the United States even prior to this date, it was the Rubber Workers who first used it as a regular instrument of union policy. Between March 27 and June 13, 1936, there were 19 known sit-down strikes in the Goodyear Akron plant alone,[31] and one rubber concern in Akron reported having had over 50 quickie sit-down strikes lasting from several minutes to several hours.[32] The Bendix local of the UAW had been rebuffed a number of times over a period of years in its attempt to be recognized as the bargaining agent for the workers in the plant. In none of the previous sit-downs had the workers remained in the plant overnight, but the Bendix employees decided to remain until the company agreed to recognize the union. After staying in for nine days, the union won a contract calling for recognition as representative of its members, a bilateral grievance board, two-hours call-in pay, and a day's notice of layoffs.[33]

On November 25, the day the Bendix strike was settled, workers in the Midland Steel Frame Company in Detroit sat down. This plant manufactured automobile frames for Chrysler and Lincoln, and within a few days, one Ford and five Chrysler assembly plants were shut down for lack of frames.[34] At the end of a week, the company settled for a ten-cent-an-hour wage increase, seniority in layoff and rehiring, and time and a half for overtime, the most notable union victory to that date.[35]

Another important preparatory strike occurred at the Kelsey-Hayes Wheel Company in Detroit during December. The workers remained in for five days, and the strike was called off sooner than it might otherwise have been to make way for General Motors. In this strike, Walter Reuther for the first time demonstrated his leadership capacities.

The General Motors strike was not the result of any strategic master plan. It began inauspiciously when, on November 18, workers at the Fisher Body plant in Atlanta sat down for a day in protest against the discharge of an employee for union activity. On December 15, employees of the Fisher Body plant in Kansas City sat down for the same reason, and forced the Chevrolet assembly plant in that city to close for lack of bodies. At Homer Martin's request, a conference was held between him and GM officials, which resulted in the following statement by William S. Knudsen, then executive vice-president of General Motors:

A personal interview was granted Homer Martin, president of the United Automobile Workers, at which Mr. Martin presented various alleged discrimination cases and grievances outlined in his published telegram and letter. Mr. Martin was advised to take the various matters up with the plant manager or, if necessary, the general manager having jurisdiction in the location involved, this being in conformity with a corporation operating policy.[36]

Following this rebuff to the union, the strike began in earnest. On December 28, a sit-down was commenced at the Fisher Body plant in Cleveland when the management postponed a conference with union representatives. The next day, the strike spread to the Fisher Body and Chevrolet plants in Flint, Michigan, which was to be the focus of events in the ensuing months. Actually, these strikes were premature. The top UAW leadership had planned no action until after January 1, 1937, when a Democratic administration under Governor Frank Murphy was installed in Lansing, the Michigan state capital. The workers at the Flint and Cleveland Fisher Body plants, key units in the General Motors system, jumped the gun in their impatience to have it out with the company. The importance of these plants has been described as follows:

These two plants were the major body manufacturing units of the corporation — "mother plants," according to GM terminology — being responsible for the fabrication of the greater portion of Chevrolet and other body parts which were then shipped in so-called "knock down" form to the assembly plants throughout the country. All the stampings for the national Chevy production were turned out in Cleveland. Fisher one [Flint] on the other hand manufactured irreplaceable parts for Buick, Oldsmobile, Pontiac and Cadillac. In particular the great dies and enormous presses needed to stamp out the mammoth simplified units of the new "turret top" bodies were concentrated in the Cleveland and Flint body plants. Possibly three-fourths or more of the corporation's production were consequently dependent on these two plants; an interlocking arrangement that was not unusual, moreover, in the highly specialized auto industry and especially among the leading corporations. There were perhaps a dozen other plants equally crucial to General Motors but in only the two designated was the union strong enough to halt production.[37]

During the following week, employees of the Guide Lamp Company in Anderson, Indiana, the Fisher Body and Chevrolet plants in Norwood, Ohio, the Chevrolet transmission plant, the Chevrolet and Fisher Body plants in Janesville, Wisconsin, and the Cadillac assembly plant in Detroit, were all struck. Slowly the tieup continued to spread through the vast General Motors system, and by early February almost all the 200,000 GM employees were idle, with the weekly production of cars down to 1,500 from the mid-December peak of 53,000.[38]

The first reaction of the GM management was one of shocked indignation. In reply to a letter from Homer Martin requesting a collective bargaining conference, Knudsen wrote:

Sit-down strikes are strikes. Such strikers are clearly trespassers and violators of the law of the land. We cannot have bona fide collective bargaining with sit-down strikers in illegal possession of plants. Collective bargaining cannot be justified if one party, having seized the plant, holds a gun at the other party's head.[39]

In a prior interview, Knudsen reiterated his previously expressed position that all problems should be settled on a local basis with plant managers. "I cannot have all these matters come here," he said, "because that would concentrate too much authority in this office and I would be swamped." Martin retorted to this: "General Motors is an operating company, not a holding company. That is why we want a national conference. Policies are made here and cannot be changed by local or divisional representatives." [40]

On January 2, 1937, upon the company's petition, Judge Edward Black of the Genesee County circuit court issued an injunction restraining the union from continuing to remain in the Flint plant, from picketing, and from interfering in any manner with those who wished to enter the plant to work. When the sheriff read the injunction to the Flint strikers and asked them to leave voluntarily, he was laughed out of the plant. A few days later it was discovered that Judge Black held a block of GM stock with a current market value of $219,900, which served to discredit his action and in effect rendered the injunction of no practical import.

On January 5, the company posted on all its bulletin boards a message from Alfred P. Sloan, Jr., its president, stating it to be the firm and unalterable position of General Motors "not [to] recognize any union as the sole bargaining agency for its workers, to the exclusion of all others. General Motors will continue to recognize, for the purpose of collective bargaining, the representatives of its workers, whether union or non-union." It may be recalled that the National Labor Relations Act, which gave exclusive bargaining rights to the majority union, was in effect at the time, but the Supreme Court had not yet ruled upon it and there was widespread belief that it would be held unconstitutional.

As a condition for meeting with union representatives, GM insisted that the plants be evacuated. The union offered to do so, provided the company in turn would agree that all plants would remain closed, without movement of equipment or resumption of activities, until a national settlement was effected.[41] This proviso was unacceptable to GM, and the first efforts at conciliation collapsed.

The corporation then turned to a frontal attack, and Flint, Michigan, became the center of the stage. More than 50,000 Flint workers were employed in GM plants, and a back-to-work movement was started under the sponsorship of the Flint Alliance, a new organization hastily formed in opposition to the UAW. The union claimed that the Alliance, the president of which was George Boysen, a former GM paymaster and at the time of the strike an independent business man, was company-sponsored, while industry pictured it as a spontaneous reaction on the part of loyal workers against a small minority of UAW strikers.[42] On January 11, the heat in Fisher Body Plant No. 2 was shut off and attempts were made by the company police to prevent food from being carried into the plant.[43] The sit-downers, faced with the possibility of being starved out, captured the plant gates from the company police to assure their source of food. At this point the city police attacked in an effort to recapture the plant gates. For hours the strikers battled the police, fighting clubs, tear gas, and riot guns with such improvised weapons as two-pound car door hinges and streams of water from fire hoses. The news of the riot spread, and the strikers were reinforced by thousands of supporters who poured into Flint. The battle ended with the strikers still in possession of the plant. Fourteen strikers suffered bullet wounds in this encounter, which became famous in union mythology as "The Battle of the Running Bulls." [44]

At this juncture there might well have been a prelude to the bloody events of the Little Steel Strike half a year later. The city was in a state of civil war, with the sit-downers determined to resist any further attempts at eviction. To prevent further bloodshed, Governor Frank Murphy of Michigan despatched 1500 National Guardsmen to Flint, with instructions to maintain the *status quo,* that is, to prevent attempts at forcible eviction of the strikers. He summoned union and company representatives to meet him in the state capital at Lansing, and on January 15, a truce was arranged: the strikers agreed to leave the plants on January 17, and negotiations were to begin the following day. Plants in Detroit and Anderson, Indiana, were evacuated, but shortly before the Flint strikers were scheduled to leave, the UAW learned that General Motors had sent telegrams to workers in the Cadillac and Fleetwood plants in Detroit directing them to report for work, and also had agreed to bargain with the Flint Alliance as well, and refused consequently to carry out any further plant evacuations. A few days later the company admitted that it had agreed to meet with representatives of the Flint Alliance, but asserted that since the UAW represented not more than 5 per cent of its employees, "it would be the height of absurdity for it to try to represent the whole body of company workers." Besides, said the company, meetings with the Alliance had been scheduled for 9 A.M., while the UAW conferences were not to begin until 11 A.M., so that no conflict of scheduling was involved.[45] The union learned about the intention of General Motors to bargain with the Flint Alliance through William Lawrence, then a reporter for the United Press, who had secured this information from Knudsen, and asked the union about its attitude toward the company's policy. It is likely that the evacuation of the plants would have been carried out on schedule if not for this piece of information.

General Motors declined to enter into negotiations, and the truce collapsed. Attempts at conciliation then shifted to Washington, where Sloan and Knudsen agreed to meet with Secretary of Labor Frances Perkins at her request, but refused to see John L. Lewis. The latter, angered, made the following statement to the press:

For six months during the presidential campaign the economic royalists represented by General Motors and the Du Ponts contributed their money and used their energy to drive this administration from power. The administration asked labor to help repel this attack and labor gave it. The same economic royalists now have their fangs in labor. The workers of this country expect the administration to help the strikers in every reasonable way.[46]

Sloan, in his turn annoyed at the turn of events, left Washington for New York, and upon receipt of a letter from the secretary of labor requesting him to return, replied: "we sincerely regret to have to say that we must decline to negotiate further with the union while its representatives continue to hold our plants unlawfully. We cannot see our way clear, therefore, to accept your invitation." [47]

At a press conference the next day, President Roosevelt expressed the view that Sloan's decision was a very unfortunate one, while Secretary Perkins went much further in her condemnation:

an episode like this must make it clear to the American people why the workers have lost confidence in General Motors. I still think that General Motors have made a great mistake, perhaps the greatest mistake in their lives. The American people do not expect them to sulk in their tents because they feel the sit-down strike is illegal. There was a time when picketing was considered illegal, and before that strikes of any kind were illegal. The legality of the sit-down strike has yet to be determined.[48]

Faced with this pressure, Sloan returned to Washington and met with the secretary of labor, but to no avail. The corporation then prepared to take the offensive once more on the industrial front.

The UAW, fearing that GM might succeed in reopening enough plants to commence production, decided to extend the area of the sit-down. Secret plans were laid to capture the strategic Chevrolet No. 4 plant in Flint, where motors were assembled. To draw police away, a detachment of men under Powers Hapgood and Roy Reuther made a feint at the nearby Chevrolet plant No. 9, thus permitting 400 workers to occupy Chevrolet No. 4 without difficulty.[49]

General Motors responded by securing an injunction from Judge Paul V. Gadola ordering the Fisher Body plants evacuated by February 3. Thousands of union supporters swarmed into Flint from other automobile centers, determined to prevent the forcible eviction of the strikers. All windows were barricaded with metal sheets, and defense squads were organized as the 2,000 men now within the plant prepared to resist. The sheriff, however, declined to attempt enforcement of the injunction without assistance from the state, and Governor Murphy, anxious to avoid bloodshed, wired the sheriff to take no action pending further negotiations. He also prevented state troops, which had surrounded the plant, from taking any violent action. Thus the deadline passed quietly, and the union had won a significant victory.

The situation still remained explosive, however. Flint city authorities were reported to be arming vigilante groups. The chief of police was quoted as saying: "Unless John L. Lewis wants a repetition of the Herrin, Ill., massacres he had better call off his union men. The good citizens of Flint are getting pretty nearly out of hand. We are organizing fast and will have between 500 and 1,000 men ready for any emergency." [50] At the direct request of President Roosevelt, Knudsen finally agreed to meet with Lewis. Following is Lewis' description of his reception upon his arrival in Detroit:

It is a matter of public knowledge now that the Governor of this State read me a formal letter in writing demanding that this action [evacuation of the plants] be taken by me, and my reply to the Governor of the State when he read that letter, with the knowledge of the President of the United States — and the approval — was this: "I do not doubt your ability to call out your soldiers and shoot the members of our union out of those plants, but let me say that when you issue that order I shall leave this conference and I shall enter one of those plants with my own people. And the militia will have the pleasure of shooting me out of the plants with them." The order was not executed. [51]

Although the negotiations came perilously close to rupture on several occasions, Governor Murphy succeeded in bringing about a truce on February 11, 1937.

Governor Murphy's role was a difficult one, and according to several observers, he was several times on the verge of a breakdown. "His state of mind sometimes bordered on the despondent and despite his efforts to preserve an atmosphere of hopefulness the situation — according to his own later description — had begun to take on for him the overwhelming impression of a nightmare in which hands were perpetually reaching for hats and overcoats, threats 'never to return' were being shouted and doors slammed for the last time." [52]

General Motors agreed to recognize the UAW as bargaining agent for its members only, a reduction of the original union demand of sole bargaining rights. Collective bargaining was to begin on February 16, and all court proceedings were to be withdrawn. To avoid a repetition of the incident which had ended the earlier truce, the corporation sent a letter to Murphy agreeing that for six months it would not bargain or enter into an agreement with any other union without securing his permission to do so. By this device,

GM was spared the embarrassment of agreeing directly to bargain only with the UAW, while the latter was virtually assured of sole bargaining rights for at least six months. For its part, the UAW agreed to evacuate all GM plants which it was holding.[53] The pertinent portion of the letter from Knudsen to Murphy read:

We have been told that the UAW in justifying its demand for bargaining privilege states that they fear that without protection of some kind we might deliberately proceed to bargain with other organizations for the purpose of undermining the position of this particular union. We have said that we have no such intention. . . . As evidence of our intention to do all we can to hasten the resumption of work in our plants and to promote peace, we hereby agree with you that within a period of six months from the resumption of work we will not bargain with or enter into agreements with any other union or representative of employees of plants on strike in respect to such matters of general corporate policy, without submitting to you the facts of the situation and gaining from you the sanction of any such contemplated procedure as being justified by law, equity or justice towards the groups of employes so represented.

Sloan paid handsome tribute to Murphy for his role in bringing about the settlement: "The corporation, its workers and the public are indebted to the Hon. Frank Murphy, assisted by Federal Conciliator James F. Dewey, for his untiring and conscientious efforts, as well as the fairness with which he has handled a most difficult situation. Only his efforts have made it possible to resume work at this time." [54] The union, of course, was jubilant. A retrospective union evaluation of the significance of the strike had this to say about it: "The heads of the corporation were compelled, for the first time, to bargain with the spokesman of their employes, the officers of the UAW and the CIO. The end of the strike came on February 11, 1937, in a brilliant victory for the workers. . . . This was the greatest and most historic victory of the UAW. It broke the back of anti-unionism in the most powerful industry in the world." [55] A *New York Times* correspondent who followed the events closely wrote a few months later that "By entirely stopping production of all General Motors cars in January and February and obtaining recognition in the first written and signed agreement on a national scale which that great citadel of the open shop had ever granted to a labor union, the CIO . . . opened the way for the remarkable upsurge in sentiment for union organization which is now going on in many sections of the country. . . . Since the General Motors settlement, the union has been spreading its organization rapidly in General Motors plants, which were weakly organized at the time of the strike." [56]

The only dissenting note came from the American Federation of Labor. On January 7, John P. Frey, in his capacity as head of the AFL Metal Trades Department, wrote to General Motors stating that no other organization had authority to represent the skilled craftsmen in the automotive industry, and received a reply to the effect that no agreement would be considered which interfered with the legitimate jurisdiction of AFL unions. On January 11, Frey met with Anderson, Knudsen, and John Thomas Smith of GM, and indicated that the Metal Trades were prepared at any time to sit down and bargain with them for the craftsmen, to which the conferees replied that the matter would be taken up with Sloan.[57]

Action was also taken with respect to the struck Fisher Body plant in Cleveland, where some AFL building tradesmen were employed. After consultation with Knudsen, four building trades unions sent a joint letter to the manager of the Cleveland plant in the following vein: "In behalf of our members who are employed in your plant, and who had no voice in this action on the part of an outlaw union in closing them, we request you to reopen the plants so they may return to their jobs, which they are out of through no fault of their own."[58] Frey went to Cleveland to consult with the plant manager, but nothing came of this effort.

When in late January and early February, the White House was putting pressure on GM to meet with Lewis, William Green twice met with President Roosevelt to protest the granting of exclusive bargaining rights to the UAW, but he received a noncommittal answer. Frey later described the AFL efforts as follows:

We wanted President Green to agree to a conference with the President [Roosevelt] so that President Green and the Presidents of the [metal trades and building trades] departments could tell the President that this was their interest [to preserve craft jurisdiction] and their only interest in any adjustment that would be reached. President Green informed us he had already seen the President twice on that same matter and the President had answered him that he was absolutely in agreement, that his only desire was to have the strike settled and that he was in no way interfering. However, the Presidents of the two departments and those who accompanied them, all National Presidents, wanted to have an additional effort made which would include representatives of the two departments to impress upon the President the vital character of that one feature of the strike and what it would mean if an agreement was reached with the known Presidential O.K., which would take away from us the people we had organized and turn them over to somebody else. President Green made an effort to secure the conference. Instead of being able to secure it, the President talked with him over the telephone and assured him his position was unchanged, that he was not interfering, had no intention to interfere and so, with that statement of the President, it was useless to meet him. However, so far as I am concerned . . . I knew that Governor Murphy was telling newspaper men in Detroit that he had just had two long-distance talks with the President of the United States. . . . I had reason to believe that entirely outside of anything the President of the United States might have been doing in the matter, that the effort to get a settlement which would give the Automobile Workers' Union exclusive jurisdiction was being made by Madam Secretary, was being made by Jim Dewey of the Conciliation Board.[59]

An effort by Frey and some building trades leaders to see Roosevelt on this issue proved unavailing, and the best that could be arranged was a telephone conversation in which the president again refused to commit himself. On February 6, a few days before the UAW-GM agreement was concluded, Green, Frey, and Williams, the president of the Building Trades, addressed a joint telegram to Governor Murphy, warning him against exclusive UAW representation. Frey expressed himself as being "reasonably certain that not long after Governor Murphy received that telegram, he showed it to Mr. Lewis." [60]

In the light of these efforts, the following interview given by William Green, the day after the signing of the UAW-GM pact, takes on a peculiar significance:

"The settlement represents a surrender in a very large way to the demands of General Motors management. We are not pleased at the defeat of any workers who have been engaged in a strike for forty days." . . . "You consider the settlement a defeat?" was the next query. "Well," said Mr. Green, "if you go on strike for one demand and press it for forty days and give up, what would you call it?" [61]

The demand to which Green was referring here was precisely that which the AFL was opposing so actively — exclusive bargaining rights. This episode served to exacerbate AFL-CIO relationships, and figured prominently in the fiasco attendant upon AFL entrance into the automobile industry several years later. It should be noted that the GM strike was supported by the Flint and Detroit central bodies of the AFL, as well as by John Reid, secretary of the Michigan State Federation of Labor.

The Sit-Down Strike in Retrospect

Scarcely any labor practice of the 1930's aroused as much animosity among employers, and public concern, as the sit-down strike, of which the General Motors strike was the most spectacular example. The sit-down strike trend, beginning late in 1936, rose to a peak in March 1937, when 170 such strikes, involving 167,000 workers, took place. In April, the month in which the Supreme Court upheld the constitutionality of the National Labor Relations Act, and in May, the number of strikes declined to 52 and 72 respectively. There was further tapering downward thereafter until by the end of the year the sit-down weapon had almost fallen into disuse.[62]

The principal argument in favor of the sit down, from the labor standpoint, was its effectiveness. With a minimum of organization, it proved possible for small groups of determined men to shut down indefinitely huge plants, and by concentrating upon strategic producing units from the standpoint of the flow of materials, to spread paralysis to plants with no organization. Some of the advantages of this form of action in distinction to a "normal" strike have been well summed up by a communist leader who was active in the automobile industry:

> Sit-down strikes give to the workers a greater feeling of strength and security because the strikers are inside the plants, in the solid confines of the factory, at the machines which are the sources of their livelihood, instead of away from the plant, moving around in "empty space," on the sidewalks surrounding the factories.
>
> Sit-down strikes give to the workers greater sureness that there are no scabs within the plants and no production is being carried on and makes it difficult to run in scabs. . . .
>
> The sit-down strike furthermore makes it difficult to resume operations even partially where scabs have gotten in because by holding down one section of the plant it is hard to begin operations.
>
> The sit-down strike affords strikers greater possibility of defending themselves against the violence of the police and company men. . . .
>
> The sit-down strike makes for a greater discipline, group consciousness and comradeship among the strikers because of the very position in which they find themselves and thereby enhances the militancy and fighting spirit of the workers.
>
> Finally, the sit-down strike arouses the widest sympathy and support among the working population because of the courage of the workers in taking "possession" of the factory and because of the self-sacrifice and hardship which such action entails.[63]

From a moral point of view, UAW and other CIO leaders argued that the sit-down strike was merely a logical extension of the growth of worker property rights in their jobs. "Is it wrong," asked Wyndham Mortimer, a UAW vice-president, "for a worker to stay at his job? The laws of the state and nation recognize, in a hundred ways, that the worker has a definite claim upon his job; more fundamentally, it is recognized that every workman has a moral right to continue on his job unless some definite misconduct justifies his discharge. These sit-down strikers are staying at their work places; no one has a better right to be there than have these men themselves." [64] Francis J. Gorman, then president of the United Textile Workers of America, was quoted in much the same vein: "A sit-down strike is clearly the most effective and least costly way for the worker to insure himself against encroachment on his 'property right' to his job by company-hired strikebreakers." [65]

The national CIO, while somewhat more cautious than its young, enthusiastic affiliates, was inclined to take a pragmatic view of the sit-down, as evidenced by the following statement made by John Brophy, at the time organizational director of the CIO:

We do not condemn sit-down strikes *per se*. We consider that various kinds of labor activity will be used to promote organization of workers and establish collective bargaining. Sit-down strikes, under some of these conditions, may be a very necessary and useful weapon. In the formative and promotional stage of unionism in a certain type of industry, the sit-down strike has real value.[66]

John L. Lewis took very much the same point of view: "The CIO stands for punctilious observance of contracts, but we are not losing any sleep about strikes where employers refuse to recognize the well-defined principles of collective bargaining. A CIO contract is adequate protection for any employer against sit-downs, lie-downs, or any other kind of strike." [67]

Despite the fact that AFL unions were involved in 100 of the 477 sit-down strikes that occurred in 1937,[68] the top AFL leadership disowned this strike technique from the first. In January 1937, the AFL Executive Council asked William Green to study the problem, and on March 28, he made public his findings, which read in part: "The sit-down strike has never been approved or supported by the American Federation of Labor because there is involved in its application grave implications detrimental to labor's interests. It must be disavowed by the thinking men and women of labor." He called the sit-down illegal and dangerous in the long run, and voiced the fear that its persistent use would result in the enactment of legislation inimical to the labor movement.

The press, business men, and legislators were with very few exceptions hostile to the sit-down strike. *The New York Times* condemned it as "a plain disregard of statutes forbidding the seizure of private property" and "essentially an act of lawlessness." [69] The *Christian Science Monitor* said that it placed "confiscation and seizure above law." [70] A group of Boston residents headed by A. Lawrence Lowell, president emeritus of Harvard University, wired Vice-President Garner on March 26, 1937, requesting that legislation be enacted to "establish the supremacy of constitutional government, law and order, national and state." Sit-down strikes were castigated in the following terms:

Armed insurrection — defiance of law, order, and duly elected authority — is spreading like wild-fire. It is rapidly growing beyond control. . . . The issue is vital; it dwarfs any other issue now agitating the public mind; it attacks and undermines the very foundation of our poltiical and social structure . . . freedom and liberty are at an end, government becomes a mockery, superseded by anarchy, mob rule and ruthless dictatorship.

The governors of Virginia, Texas, Mississippi, New Jersey, Illinois and California announced that they would not tolerate sit-down strikes in their states. The United States Senate, after considerable debate, passed on April 7, 1937, a resolution condemning the sit-down strike as illegal and against public policy, although it coupled with this a condemnation of industrial espionage and violations of the National Labor Relations Act.[71] Numerous anti-sit-down bills were introduced in state legislatures, and the State of Vermont enacted a law rendering a sit-down striker subject to imprisonment and heavy fine.

The courts were more directly involved than legislatures, and they almost uniformly declared sit downs illegal whenever called upon to enjoin strikers. On two separate occasions, as has already been noted, General Motors obtained equity injunctions, although in neither case was the order obeyed. The *coup de grâce* was eventually given the sit-down strike by the United States Supreme Court, which, in setting aside a National Labor Relations Board order that directed the Fansteel Metallurgical Corporation to reinstate sit-down strikers, declared: "It was an illegal seizure of the buildings in order to prevent their use by the employer in a lawful manner and thus, by acts of force and violence, to compel the employer to submit." [72] The Court also held in this case that sit-down strikers, by their lawless conduct, forfeited all rights under the National Labor Relations Act. However, the sit down as a union weapon for all practical purposes had been abandoned a year prior to the Supreme Court decision.

In retrospect, the following may be said of the sit-down strike epidemic that occurred in 1937:

The strikes were clearly illegal, and there was little disposition on the part of anyone to take an opposite point of view. Although they would be unthinkable today, they were tolerated in 1937, and even received substantial public support, mainly because large segments of American industry refused to accept collective bargaining. Trade unions were the underdogs, and they were widely represented as merely attempting to secure in practice the rights that Congress had bestowed upon them as a matter of law. Senator Robert F. Wagner made this point forcibly in defending the sit-down strike in a Senate speech:

The sit-down has been used only in protest against repeated violations of industrial liberties which Congress has recognized. The sit-down, even in the few cases where labor has used it effectively, has succeeded in winning for labor only such industrial liberties as both law and morals have long sanctioned. The sit-down has been provoked by the long-standing ruthless tactics of a few corporations who have hamstrung the National Labor Relations Board by invoking court actions . . . ; who have openly banded together to defy this law of Congress quite independently of any Court action . . . ; and who have systematically used spies and discharges and violence and terrorism to shatter the workers' liberties as defined by Congress.[73]

From an historical perspective, the sit-down era constituted an episode in the transition from one system of industrial relations to another; it hastened the replacement of untrammeled management prerogative in the disposition of labor by a system under which trade unions, as representatives of the workers, were to share in this function. It was perhaps inevitable that so violent a wrench with the past should have provoked management attitudes sharply antithetical to the new national labor policy. But by the same token, it is not surprising that industrial workers, having broken through on the legislative front, should seek to implement their hard won rights with whatever weapons were at hand, regardless of the law.

Despite all the public furor, the sit-down strike was actually a less costly weapon, in terms of human life and property, than, for example, the traditional form of labor strife as exemplified in the Little Steel strikes of 1937. No deaths were directly attributable to the sit-down strikes, despite their quasi-military character. One of the industry's trade journals had this to say of property damage, when the rash of strikes had run its course:

Damage at automobile plants caused by sitdown strikers appears to have been confined largely to non-essential materials with production machinery found unhurt after evacuation, a survey now shows. The losses were not insignificant, however. An insurance adjuster has made a guess that the physical damage done to plants during all automobile plant strikes in Michigan would approximate $200,000. This is apart from losses due to deterioration of materials left outside plants.[74]

There is no inherent reason for the sit-down strikes to have followed this relatively peaceful course. Most contemporary observers, however, credited Governor Frank Murphy with having averted what might have been a very unfortunate development in insisting upon negotiation rather than in employing force to evict the strikers.

The most important aspect of the sit-down strike was that it paved the way for rapid unionization of the automobile industry. John Brophy has testified to the fact that in November and December 1936, UAW attempts at mass meetings were generally failures; few workers stopped to listen to speeches that he and Philip Murray made at plant gates.[75] It is impossible to ascertain what UAW membership was at the outset of the strikes, but certainly not more than a small fraction of the employees of General Motors had enlisted under its banner. Within six months of the beginning of the sit-down strikes, the UAW claimed a dues paying membership of 520,000,[76] and the first stage of organization had been completed for the entire industry, with the exception of Ford. It is not at all unlikely that General Motors and other manufacturers could have resisted the UAW more successfully if the union had confined itself to more orthodox weapons.

The Aftermath of the General Motors Strike

The truce of February 11, 1937, was the prelude to hard bargaining between General Motors and the UAW, resulting in a signed agreement more than a month later. The UAW was obliged to content itself with recognition as representative of its members only, and a promise that the speed-up would be studied to eliminate injustices. The union's demand that its shop steward system be recognized as part of the grievance machinery was denied, and instead a shop committee system was installed. The practical difference was that the contract provided for a maximum of nine committeemen for each plant, whereas there was a union shop steward for about every 25 members. Thus, the shop stewards did not gain the prestige they would have enjoyed as grievancemen. Nor was the union successful in securing a reduced working week, the elimination of piecework, or a uniform minimum wage scale. Seniority in layoff and rehiring, an important union demand, was agreed to by the company, but with the proviso that married men were to be accorded preference when a permanent layoff was involved. There was no wage increase, the corporation having raised wages unilaterally while the strike was still on.[77]

Following upon the General Motors settlement, the UAW turned its attention to the Chrysler Corporation, which in 1936 was the second largest producer in the industry.[78] On March 8, after the corporation had refused to grant the union demand for sole bargaining rights, a strike was declared, and almost all the Chrysler plants were occupied. That sole bargaining was the principal issue involved was made clear by a corporation statement issued the following day:

We have offered not only to continue to recognize the U.A.W.A. as the bargaining agent for its members in our plants, but also to work out with them shop rules which would enable union officers and stewards to function effectively for the employees whom they may represent. The union has rejected this. We offered to discuss modification of the existing seniority rules. . . . This the union has also rejected.[79]

Nor did the union claim that Chrysler wages were below the general industrial level. The union strategy was simply to go a step beyond the General Motors degree of recognition; the sit down, it was felt, would quickly bring Chrysler to its knees.

But the union had failed to reckon with the mounting public clamor against the sit-down strike; the day when it could be used with impunity was already past. Governor Murphy lost no time getting Walter Chrysler and John L. Lewis together, and this time he made it clear to Lewis that he was prepared to use force to clear the plants. It was reported of the Lewis-Chrysler meetings that "the two men have been getting along famously at the conferences, amazing their colleagues by their amiability." [80] On March 24, Lewis agreed to the evacuation of the plants, and in return the company agreed not to resume operations or to move machinery from the plants while collective bargaining was continuing. In the agreement reached on April 6, the UAW was recognized as the bargaining agent for its members only, but the company promised that it would not "aid, promote or finance any labor group which purports to engage in collective bargaining or make any agreement with any such group or organization for the purpose of undermining the union." [81]

Although union officials attempted to interpret this language as a virtual grant of exclusive representation rights, it obviously was not. A union partisan later said this of the agreement:

The recognition for U.A.W. members and the death of the Chrysler Company union system could have been obtained without a strike. It was not surprising that the Chrysler sit-down strikers balked at leaving the plants when the settlement was brought to them. They had been told that the union would insist on obtaining sole recognition in a contract, as well as in practice.[82]

Again, Governor Murphy played a major role in effecting the settlement. Walter Chrysler described him as "tireless, patient and resourceful" and declared that "I have no hesitancy in saying he has done a great job." [83]

Other major agreements were shortly secured, either with or without strikes. Hudson, Packard, Studebaker, Briggs, Murray Body, Motor Products, Timken-Detroit Axle, L. A. Young Spring and Wire, Bohn Aluminum, and numerous smaller plants were brought under union contract. In some cases, for example, Packard and Studebaker, sole recognition was achieved after NLRB elections. The only holdout was the Ford Motor Company, and here the union came up against an organizational problem which it was not able to solve until 1941.[84]

The Growth of Internal Dissension

Now that the UAW had emerged as the sole labor union of any importance in the industry, and had achieved a certain measure of security against external attack through its collective agreements, organizational and internal political problems, which had been held in abeyance while the union was fighting for its life, came to the fore. There were numerous political factions, each one with a local base of operations which imparted stability. A strong Communist Party faction was led by Wyndham Mortimer, the first vice-president, and it had considerable strength in Flint, where Robert Travis had been the director of the sit-down strike and the leading spirit of Local 156, a large so-called amalgamated local which blanketed the entire city. The Socialist Party faction was led by Walter Reuther, who was based in Local 174, which covered a number of plants in the west side of Detroit.

An active participant in the socialist group has written of the socialist and communist factions in the UAW:

Walter Reuther at that time was not himself an active, functioning member of the Socialist Party, although he had been before he went to Europe and Asia in 1933. The Socialists who were active in the union, including myself and a number of others, looked upon him as a leader generally of our point of view. However, during that period of 1936 and 1937, I remember Walter's being present at only one Socialist Party meeting. That, as I recall, was not a business meeting of the Party, but a more or less educational, informative meeting to hear some speaker or other. . . . Walter himself was too thoroughly tied up and immersed in union activities to pay any attention to the activities of the Socialist Party. The union members who were Socialists and active in the Socialist Party actually operated in the union, not as representatives of the Socialist Party, but as trade unionists. In fact they were often and frequently criticized by the leadership of the Socialist Party outside of the union, because part of the leadership felt that they were working too closely with the Communists.

The Socialists in the union, however, were more concerned with the union itself and they felt that Martin was a danger and a threat to the stability and the effectiveness of the union. One has to realize the spirit of the times then as it existed among the union and the radical parties. While there were many sharp ideological differences between the Socialist and Communist Parties, the Communists were looked upon by a part of the Socialist Party with a great deal more tolerance than they are looked upon now and have been for many years since that time. And it must be recognized that, in those years, the Communists were, for the most part, functioning as good trade unionists. Occasionally, there would be times when the Party line imposed upon them activities or policies which were contrary to good trade unionism, but that was much more seldom than it came to be in later years. The Socialists, on the other hand, were functioning as trade unionists in the UAW and not as Socialists. They refused to be subjected to any outside discipline from the Socialist Party leadership, and when they could cooperate with the Communists on trade union matters, they did so. This did not mean that there were not any quarrels between Socialists on the one hand and Communists on the other within the UAW. In fact, the Socialists in the UAW looked upon the Communists with some suspicion and misgiving. . . .[85]

Richard Frankensteen, who had been in charge of the Chrysler strike, was a former partisan of Father Coughlin, but had broken with him and in 1937 was regarded as a conservative. George Addes, the secretary-treasurer, and R. J. Thomas, regarded as political neutrals, also had substantial personal followings. To complicate matters further, a small ideological group with no independent local base derived a certain amount of power by providing intellectual guidance to Homer Martin. This was the group headed by Jay Lovestone, who had been until 1929 the general-secretary of the American Communist Party, when he was expelled for "right wing deviationism," and had formed his own party which was eventually known as the Independent Labor League. Those who were alleged at one time or another to have been Lovestone adherents included William Munger, editor of the *United Automobile Worker;* Francis Henson, Martin's administrative assistant; Eve Stone, head of the women's auxiliary; John Tate, publicity chief of the union; and Irving Brown, an international organizer, who was beaten by Ford servicemen in one of the first UAW forays against the Ford Motor Company.[86]

The several groups coalesced into two principal "caucuses." The Unity Caucus, an alliance of socialists and communists, was made possible by the "United Front" tactics then being followed by the Communist Party. It was never a very firm alliance, however, and it fell apart when Martin, the common enemy, was eliminated. The Progressive Caucus was led by Martin and Frankensteen, and was strongly anticommunist in orientation. It, too, proved unstable in the face of intense factional warfare.

The UAW in 1937 resembled nothing so much as a feudal kingdom. Martin, the principal leader, sat on an uneasy throne, surrounded by semi-independent and self-sufficient lords whose allegiance to him was minimal, and whose efforts to unseat him were tempered only by the fear of splitting the organization and leaving it at the mercy of outside foes. The failure of one man, or a single group, to control the union, until Walter Reuther gained the ascendancy in 1947, assured continuous and lively struggles both at the national and local levels.

Homer Martin's principal stock in trade was a considerable oratorical ability, which made him very popular with the rank-and-file workers. But as a union administrator he left much to be desired. Benjamin Stolberg, a warm admirer, said of him: "He is a poor administrator, lacking all gift for detail. Though his aim is steady and his courage, especially in a tight situation, is magnificent, his daily tactics are often impulsive and his impromptu statements are likely to be injudicious." [87] The man was completely lacking in any ability to build up a bloc upon which he could count for support in a crisis. Eventually virtually all his followers deserted him as the consequence of a series of extraordinary political blunders through which he lost control of the organization, despite all the prestige that had fallen to him after the spectacular victories of the UAW.

Frank Winn, the union's publicity director during the Martin administration, and a Reuther adherent, has provided several examples of the erratic character of Martin's actions:

The premature strike . . . at the Atlanta plant that started in November [1936] was a matter of great concern to the union, because there was no way in which the union could come to the support of the strikers at that time, and the strike itself was bringing no kind of economic pressure of any significance against the General Motors Corporation. Every time Martin went to Atlanta to speak to the strikers, which was on numerous occasions between the time the strike started and the time the General Motors strike started around the first of the year, he would promise them in very belligerent and bellicose language that all of the General Motors workers were going to be called out in their support. One day early in this period, Martin called me into his office and directed me to draft a telegram to the presidents of all General Motors locals instructing them to call their workers out on strike at seven o'clock the next morning. I questioned the advisability of such a move, since we were not really well enough organized anywhere in General Motors, outside of Kansas City, to have a really effective strike. Martin assured me blandly that before seven o'clock the next morning, but only shortly before, he was going to telephone each of the presidents to whom the telegram was to be sent and call the strike off. The purpose of the telegram, he said, was to "scare" General Motors. This seemed to me to be obviously an extremely risky undertaking, but as a hired employee of the union, I was in no position to protest further. It so happened, however, that no other elected officers of the union were present in the office that day, and I had no way of reaching them. I took into my confidence Henry Kraus, who was alleged to be a member of the Communist Party and then editor of the *United Automobile Worker,* and William Munger, who was avowedly a Lovestoneite, and who was then Research Director of the UAW, and told them what Martin had instructed me to do. The only person in the CIO to whom we could appeal, because we knew him, and he knew us personally, that we could think of was Allan Haywood who at that time was in Akron, Ohio. We called Allan and told him what Martin planned to do. Allan in turn called John L. Lewis in Washington and Lewis in turn called Martin back in Detroit and told him not to do it. . . .

After the General Motors sitdown strike had started, Martin disappeared from his office one afternoon leaving no word as to where he was going or where he could be found. He was away for several hours. Sometime late in the afternoon, a federal labor conciliator came into my office with Mr. Martin in tow. From my office, Mr. Martin was able to get back into his office without walking through a number of antichambers which were thronged with newspaper reporters and photographers and other followers of the strike. We got him into his office unobserved. . . . The conciliator told us he had found him in a drugstore downstairs in the Hofmann Building where the UAW offices were located, that he was in a hysterical condition, was making a speech to all of those present claiming that the General Motors Corporation was determined to kill him. . . . It was another hour or more before Martin had calmed down enough so that he could again be spirited out of the building and taken over to his hotel room . . . where he could recover his equanimity and emotional balance.[88]

Martin was by no means unaware of the forces that were working against him within the union, and he struck back as soon as the smoke of the battle with the manufacturers had cleared. In April 1937, he began a purge of the opposition. The hold of the Unity group upon the powerful Flint local was weakened by the transfer of Roy Reuther, Ralph Daly, and William Cody to other cities, and the reduction in status of Robert Travis, who had led the General Motors strike there. Wyndham Mortimer was "exiled" to St. Louis; Victor Reuther, in charge of organization work at Anderson, Indiana, was demoted to a subordinate position elsewhere; and Henry Kraus, the editor of the *United Automobile Worker* who was closely associated with the communist faction, was displaced.[89] At the end of June, the first of a number of thinly veiled anticommunist editorials appeared in the *United Automobile Worker:*

There are instances even, of where groups . . . attempt to prevent the growth of the whole organization rather than risk loss of control. They follow a policy of their own and attempt to force others to abide by it. . . . It makes no difference what label this small group within a group gives itself. Whether it calls itself the left wing or anything else makes little difference. It is not the label which determines the kind of effect the group has. Its active opposition to the policy of the organization is of itself a menace to the continued effective functioning of the union.[90]

One of Martin's principal accusations against his opponents was that they were fomenting wildcat strikes in violation of contract for purposes of factional gain, hoping thereby to attract support by a show of militancy. There was a steady stream of complaints from General Motors on this score; on April 3, Knudsen sent a letter to Martin in which he listed 30 sit-down strikes that had occurred in GM plants since the agreement of March 12,[91] and by June 1937, the number had risen to 170.[92] The strikes were later attributed to "the cockiness of the victorious sit-down strikers and their need to let off steam accumulated during years of factory regimentation; management's unwillingness to accept the shop-steward system; and the inexperience of both in the daily process of collective bargaining."[93] While there is considerable truth in these observations, there seems to be little doubt that the left wing was capitalizing upon the dissatisfaction that prevailed among the workers.

The national administration of the UAW attempted by all means at its disposal to curb the wave of outlaw strikes, which were seriously jeopardizing its relations with employers. On May 22, the *United Automobile Worker* warned that "nothing is to be gained and everything is to be lost by bleeding a union to death through a constant stream of wild-cat strikes. . . . If the United Automobile Workers of America wishes to protect its right to strike it must strike when it is *right* to strike." In June, the Executive Board resolved that disciplinary action would be taken against members and officers responsible for unauthorized strikes. But Martin's dilemma was that he could not act firmly without laying himself open to the charge of knuckling under to the manufacturers. The UAW was still in its heroic stage, with the great sit-down strikes a living reality, not a dusty tradition. Therefore, when Knudsen wrote that General Motors would not negotiate with the UAW on new demands until the question of unauthorized strikes had been settled, Martin, after saying that the union was doing all it could in the matter, asserted that the refusal of GM to recognize union stewards as grievancemen, and the failure of the corporation to educate its supervisors in labor relations, were important factors contributing to the strikes.[94] This type of proviso, which accompanied all UAW admissions of guilt, served as grist to the mill of the opposition.

The 1937 UAW convention, which was held in Milwaukee, was one of the most disorderly conventions ever held by an American labor union.

Martin lacked the ability to maintain order, though it is doubtful that even John L. Lewis could have kept the delegates in check, so bitter was the feeling between the factions. One of the principal matters of dispute involved the seating of delegates from the Flint local, the Unity group charging that some of its adherents were being unfairly disenfranchised. The credentials committee did not make its report until the final day of the convention, when it decided against the Unity group. Amid pandemonium, Martin ruled that the action of the committee had been sustained by a voice vote of the convention, and when he attempted to proceed, the following ensued:

President Martin: The next order of business before this convention . . . (President Martin was interrupted by loud and continued shouts of protest.)

President Martin: The next order of business before this convention . . .

(The shouting continued.)

I will recognize this brother.

Delegate Steinhardt, 156: . . . I would like to ask, at this time, with your permission, that you call the house to order and take another vote.

President Martin: Just a moment. Now, let me say this to you. . . .

(Renewed shouting occurred, and there was a great deal of confusion.)

President Martin: I know you don't want me to speak. Where will the convention be next year?

(There were cries of "No, No," and the noise increased.)

President Martin: Where will the convention be next year?

(A number of delegates were standing on tables, and tables and floors were pounded with sticks, and there was a general condition of disorder.) . . .

President Martin: Where will the convention be next year?

(Disorder broke out again among the delegation.)

President Martin: Everybody take your seats, please. Just a moment. . . .

(The noise and disorder was resumed.)

President Martin: I think all of you realize. . . .

(President Martin was interrupted by cries of "Point of Order," and "We want Reuther. We want Reuther.")[95]

This incipient riot was quieted only when Addes and Walter Reuther appealed to the delegates to accept the ruling of the chair.

The principal issue at the convention was the question of centralization versus decentralization in the administration of the union. The Martin forces were desirous of strengthening the authority of the international at the expense of the locals, a move that was dictated by sound principles of organization as well as motivated by political considerations. By the same token, the obvious strategy of the Unity group was to keep power out of the hands of Martin, and as decentralized as possible. The convention refused to give the president the authority to remove international officers and representatives, lodging this authority in the executive board. An attempt to eliminate local newspapers, one of the most effective of which was Reuther's *West Side Conveyer,* was defeated. The Progressive group was also defeated on a plan to revise convention representation rules in favor of the smaller locals, from which Martin derived a good deal of his support.[96] In sum, Martin's strategy was thwarted not so much by the strength of the opposition, but rather by the fierce jealousy with which the locals, particularly the larger ones, guarded their autonomy.

The Progressive group, in a preconvention caucus, had decided to oppose the reelection of Mortimer and Hall as vice-presidents, and to support in their stead Frankensteen and R. J. Thomas. Fearing a split if this plan were effectuated, John L. Lewis took a personal hand in the convention and prevailed upon the Progressives to drop their plans for a clean sweep of the executive positions. Under the compromise which was adopted, the number of vice-presidents was increased to five, three of them, Frankensteen, Wells, and Thomas, being of Progressive persuasion, and two of them, Mortimer and Hall, adhering to the Unity group. On the new Executive Board, Martin had a majority of 16 to 8,[97] which seemingly afforded him a safe margin of control.

Although the issue of communism was not an explicit bone of contention, it was never far from the surface. A week before the convention assembled, the official newspaper of the UAW carried an editorial criticizing the "befuddled unionist" as a man "who believes that a left-wing political label is a protective cloak under which he may carry on destructive union policies without hindrance." [98] The issue was of such potential explosiveness that David Dubinsky, president of the International Ladies' Garment Workers' Union, who was at the convention as a fraternal delegate, and who had a record of militant anti-communism, pleaded with the delegates in this vein:

I have fought Communism perhaps more than anyone else in the labor movement. I fought not their philosophy. With this I was little concerned. And just as I disagree with their principles and with their philosophy, they have a right to disagree with my principles and with my conception of the trade union movement. But we have strenuously fought their tactics, though we are ready to admit that there are Communists in our union and that is because Communists are found working in our industries. This is not only true of CIO; the same condition exists in the AFL unions. And if Communists are employed in our industries, they are entitled to membership in the Union. And so long as they place the interests of their fellow members above the interests of a political party, they are entitled to participate in the Union's activities.[99]

John L. Lewis, whose own organization, the United Mine Workers, six months later adopted a constitutional amendment barring communists from membership, but who tolerated communists and their sympathizers among his close associates in the CIO family, was conspicuouly silent on the question.

Depression and Union Decline

The euphoria that had been created by the flood of convention oratory was soon dispelled by the harsh facts of economic life. It was reported in November 1937, that the production of automobiles was being trimmed because of declining demand, and by the beginning of December, production had fallen to two-thirds of the 1936 rate. At the end of the month, 30,000 General Motors workers were laid off, and all those remaining were reduced to a 24-hour week. Knudsen was quoted as saying of the month of December 1937: "The drop in sales in so short a period is the most severe experience in the history of General Motors. It was wholly unexpected and entirely beyond our control."[100] With the turn of the year, things grew worse rather than better. The UAW estimated that on January 29, 1938, out of a normal employment of 517,000 automobile production workers, 320,000 men were totally unemployed and 196,000 partially unemployed. The average number of hours worked by those partially employed was 12 to 16 hours for the week ending January 29, 1938. Some 200,000 out of 300,000 Detroit auto workers were unemployed, and only 35,000 were earning enough to render them ineligible for welfare assistance. The normal Spring pickup failed to materialize in March, and it was not until the end of the year that any improvement was noted. For the year 1938 as a whole, 2,000,985 passenger cars were produced in the United States, compared with 3,915,889 in 1937.[101]

It was against this background that the UAW approached its first real round of collective bargaining. On the advice of John L. Lewis, the UAW negotiated an agreement with General Motors which contained no gain for the union, but gave the company final authority to discipline or discharge union members guilty of instigating strikes in violation of contract.[102] The Unity faction denounced the agreement as a sell-out in so effective a fashion that Martin, who had been instrumental in negotiating the agreement, urged the ratification meeting of GM locals to reject it, which was promptly done.

The Unity group felt that despite the economic situation, a retreat would have been disastrous for union morale. Nevertheless, the Unity faction was somewhat shocked by the violence with which Martin denounced the agreement; not only did he urge that the Pontiac workers strike, but he practically advocated sabotage.[103] On the day this action was taken, November 17, 1937, UAW members occupied the Fisher Body plant at Pontiac, and refused to leave until November 22, when Martin personally went to the plant and pleaded for its evacuation. The executive board had issued a statement condemning the strike, although Mortimer and Reuther argued in favor of sanctioning it as a means of putting pressure on GM for better terms.[104] The *United Automobile Worker* reprinted verbatim, significantly, an article in *The New York Times* to the effect that the Pontiac sit-down had been the work of the Communist Party, and Martin declared that "there is every reason to believe that professional provocateurs were mixed up in the calling of the Pontiac strike and its continuation."

Negotiations were resumed with General Motors, and on March 12, 1938, the contract was renewed unchanged and with no termination date. In a supplementary agreement, the grievance mechanism was revised in the direction of reducing the number of shop committeemen as well as the number of hours' pay per day they could receive while engaged in handling grievances, a change which distinctly weakened the procedure from the union point of view. The agreement was defended on the ground that "the uncertain economic situation prevailing in the automobile industry must be recognized as an obstacle in the path of obtaining all that we might wish." [105] It was ratified by the Executive Board without referral to a GM delegate conference, which enabled the Unity opposition to use it for purposes of further harassment. An article in the *West Side Conveyer,* the Reuther paper, wrote of the "sharp criticism of the secrecy with which the negotiations were handled and of the undemocratic manner in which the agreement was signed," and continued:

The GM stewards vigorously disputed Pres. Martin's claim that the agreement was the best that could be had at this time. The depression conditions were admitted. But it was pointed out that the company took away things that would have cost it nothing to leave in the contract. In other words, the company was out to smash the union grievance procedure, not simply to economize.[106]

A few weeks later the Chrysler contract was also renewed without change. Until the last moment the union held out for a clause stipulating that there would be no wage reduction, but it was forced finally to accept an oral guarantee to this effect. R. J. Thomas made a realistic defense of the agreement which throws considerable light on the position of the union at the time:

The UAW negotiators felt that we had made very definite gains in that we had lost nothing in bad times that we had won after the strike a year ago, when the times were good. . . . There was unanimity of opinion among both the negotiators and the advisory board that we had not only obtained all that was possible under the circumstances but had made gains.

However necessary it may have been to sign new contracts on these terms, they did nothing to strengthen Martin's position. To make matters worse, the union's income declined drastically as a result of heavy unemployment, and staff curtailment was necessary. Martin took occasion, in trimming sails, to dismiss international organizers who were adherents of the Unity caucus, among them Victor Reuther, Stanley Novak, and Melvin Bishop, all of whom had played prominent roles in the 1937 strikes. A Progressive victory in the large Flint local, where Jack Little defeated Roy Reuther by a vote of 7540 to 4080, did much to bolster the administration,[107] but it was unsuccessful in its attempt to unseat Walter Reuther in Local 174, where the Reuther slate won by a vote of 2785 to 636.[108] Martin became increasingly frank in his public discussion of internal union affairs. In a press interview he charged the communists with endangering the life of the union in inciting strikes in violation of contract, and continued: "There is far too little being said about the influence of Stalinism and Stalinist propaganda in America. There is a hue and cry about Nazism and fascism, but if anyone mentions Stalinism they are immediately accused of 'red baiting.'"[109] The executive board voted to abolish all local papers in an attempt further to curtail the opposition activities.

There then occurred one of those strange tricks of history which no one, least of all Martin, could have foreseen. The Martin forces at the 1937 convention had wanted to elect Frankensteen as first vice-president, but under the compromise adopted, all vice-presidents were to be of equal rank. Shortly after the close of the convention, however, Martin designated Frankensteen as assistant president, which quite clearly meant an elevation to the second highest office in the union. Early in 1938, several prominent communists, among them William Z. Foster, William Weinstone, and B. K. Gebert, approached Frankensteen and urged him to head a movement for the elimination of factionalism in the union; the bait that was apparently held out to him was communist support for the UAW presidency. The communists had first approached Walter Reuther with the same offer, but he had rejected their approach. And Homer Martin later testified before the Dies Committee: "I was invited by Mr. Gebert, who came to my office, and I remember a certain Biblical illustration that reminds me of this: 'I was taken up on the mountain, and I was shown the promised land.' Mr. Gebert informed me that if I would just come down to Mr. Weinstone's office, or meet him, Mr. Foster, Browder, and others, and deal with them on the number of organizers to be appointed, the number of local unions that would be turned over, and I was to go out and see that they were given over to the Communist Party, that I, indeed, could be the greatest labor leader in America, even greater than John L. Lewis, greater than anybody." [110]

Frankensteen, out of a renewed sense of self-importance, made a public announcement of a plan to end factionalism which called for the abandonment of all caucuses in the union, much to the consternation of Martin, who reacted immediately by abolishing the post of assistant president, on the ground that there was no constitutional provision for it, and by removing Frankensteen from the directorship of the Ford organizing drive, to which he had been appointed six months earlier.[111]

The effect of Frankensteen's break with Martin was to reduce the latter's Executive Board majority to a 14 to 10 margin. If Martin had been a more astute politician, however, he might have been able to discern that in the Unity caucus a split was developing between Reuther and the communists, and that an alliance with Reuther against the newly formed Frankensteen-communist bloc was not out of the question.[112] But instead he attempted to use his slender board majority as a club against the opposition, without making any distinctions among them.

Martin presented to the Executive Board in May 1938, a twenty-point program which included, among other things, authority for the national administration to discipline irresponsible local leadership, and support of the Ludlow–La Follette resolution for a war referendum, to which the communists were violently opposed. The board accepted the proposal unanimously, and seemingly Martin's position was improved. But trouble developed at the very next board meeting, which was called to discuss a group insurance plan. When the plan was criticized, the meeting was adjourned to Washington, where the board met with John L. Lewis in an endeavor to resolve the differences. On June 8, the board reconvened in Detroit, and with Martin out of town, voted against the plan, whereupon

Frankensteen announced to the press that the anti-Martin forces were now in a majority in the board. Martin returned to Detroit by plane, and struck back at the opposition by suspending vice-presidents Frankensteen, Mortimer, Hall, and Wells, and secretary-treasurer Addes, leaving as the only functioning officers himself and R. J. Thomas. In protest, six members of the Executive Board — Reuther, Doll, Miley, Lamotte, Reisinger, and Cramer — walked out of the board and refused to attend any further meetings.[113] The split in the UAW, which had remained behind the scenes for several years, was now overt.

Martin charged the suspended officers with having publicly repudiated the twenty-point program adopted the previous month, and with illegal public discussion of private union affairs, and ordered them to stand trial, as provided in the constitution. The opposition retaliated by circularizing all local unions and asking them to remit their dues to the suspended secretary-treasurer, George Addes, rather than to Delmond Garst, who had been appointed to replace him.[114] The presidents of forty local unions in Detroit, under the leadership of Emil Mazey, met and formulated a peace proposal which called for support of Martin's twenty-point program, the reinstatement of the suspended officers, cessation of all personal attacks, and the arbitration of all internal differences by John L. Lewis.[115] Martin went ahead, however, and on July 8, George Addes, the first of the suspended officers to be tried, was expelled from the union. In a radio address, Martin justified his action as follows:

In the shadows, working its shameful hypocrisies upon a portion of our membership, stands the Communist Party, whose record for union-wrecking is a matter of history. Theirs has been the guilty hand in the creation of confusion and division that for months has brought reproach upon our union. . . .

There are those within the union who have been working hand in glove with the Communist Party in its nefarious activities within the union. . . . It is high time that those who profess not to be aligned with principles or motive with the Communist Party should quit their company. . . . There can be no "middle of the road," there can be no compromise in our efforts to maintain the UAWA as a labor organization. It shall not be a tail to the kite of the Communist Party.[116]

The trial of the remaining officers continued until August 6, amid mutual bitter public recrimination. The defendants were represented by Maurice Sugar, a former general counsel of the UAW, who was accused of filibustering the trial: "they [the defendants] proved there was no limit to their perfidy, no depth to which they would not descend in order to slander the union, its president and officers. They have abandoned every principle of trade-unionism in their wild attempt to sabotage the trial." [117] The defendants, in turn, charged that "the conspiracy that actually existed . . . was a conspiracy between Homer Martin and an irresponsible, disruptive political adventurer and meddler, Jay Lovestone." [118] In support of this charge, some private correspondence was produced. In a letter of March 27, 1937, Martin, addressing Lovestone as "Dear Jay," had assured the latter that Irving Brown, a Lovestone supporter, would be kept on the UAW payroll. Another letter had to do with an inquiry, made by Francis Henson, Martin's administrative assistant, on the advisability of Martin's signing an appeal relative to lifting the current arms embargo on Loyalist Spain. [119] Lovestone accused the defendants of using documents which had been stolen from his files by the Soviet secret police, [120] and it was never explained how they obtained possession of them. [121] However dubious the ethics of this situation — the *United Automobile Worker,* when Martin later lost control, printed some of this correspondence — it did serve to reveal that Martin at least was maintaining cordial relationships with a leftist-oriented ideological group.

On August 6, 1938, Frankensteen, Mortimer, and Hall were expelled from the union after the final sessions of the trial had been conducted *in absentia,* the defendants having refused to attend because "it is our understanding that we are to be brutally beaten and maimed, if not killed. [122] Wells received a three-month suspension. But this proved to be the beginning, not the end, of Martin's troubles, for the expelled officers possessed considerable strength within the union. On August 18, a meeting of the anti-Martin forces was held in Toledo, and it resolved to request John L. Lewis to appoint an administrator to supersede Martin. [123] Fearing a split in the UAW, Lewis formulated a peace plan under which the expelled officers would have been reinstated and all matters in dispute referred to the CIO for arbitration. Martin replied to the proposal in the following terms:

The entire membership of the United Automobile Workers of America was shocked last week when John L. Lewis . . . made a so-called "peace" proposal and told the International officers that they would either accept this so-called "peace" plan — or else. But the shock was turned to anger when John L. Lewis, going over the heads of the elected officers of the International Union . . . pushing aside the Constitution of the UAWA which he himself helped to write, communicated directly with local unions, urging them to put pressure upon the International Executive Board to adopt the so-called "peace" plan. . . . Mr. Lewis knows, as well as I know, that these people are either members of the Communist Party or are so-called "fellow travelers," and have for months consistently worked to place the Communist Party in charge of the International Union. [124]

With this show of resistance, Martin sealed his doom, for Lewis was not one to tolerate insubordination. Had Martin been at the helm of a strong, unified organization, as Murray was several years later when he broke with Lewis, he might have been able to weather the storm. But as it was, UAW membership was very low to begin with,[125] and its financial situation was worsened by the refusal of a number of locals to pay their *per capita* tax to the international. Urged by some of the remaining members of the Executive Board to compromise, Martin reluctantly entered into negotiations with the CIO, represented by Philip Murray and Sidney Hillman, and after nine days of continuous negotiation, the following agreement was reached:

1. The question of reinstating the expelled officers was to be submitted to Hillman and Murray, their decision to be final.
2. A joint committee composed of Hillman, Murray, Martin and R. J. Thomas was established "to determine matters of policy relating to cooperation between the UAW and the CIO, and to settle such disputes as may be referred to it."
3. The CIO recognized the full autonomy of the UAW, while the UAW pledged its loyalty to the CIO.
4. The UAW reaffirmed its 20-point program of May 1938.
5. The CIO pledged its support to the UAW in "any disciplinary action against any violation of the constitution or policies of the UAW." [126]

Soon thereafter, the expelled officers were reinstated by order of Murray and Hillman. Although Martin may have complimented himself on salvaging some vestige of control in accepting a bilateral supervisory committee in place of the receivership that the first CIO proposal implied, his days were numbered, for he had demonstrated his unreliability from the CIO point of view. Writing on October 19, Louis Stark, the veteran reporter of *The New York Times*, commented: "Today the union president is almost completely shorn of power because his majority deserted him during the recent peace conferences. One by one they were won over by Messrs. Murray and Hillman and finally the president had to capitulate to the proposal that the Murray-Hillman committee be authorized to reinstate the suspended officers. . . . Among some observers who are aware of the almost daily telephonic contact between the C.I.O. officials and the union, it is assumed that the union has relinquished its autonomy, in fact though not in name, to John L. Lewis's lieutenants." [127] The Executive Board forced Martin to replace William Munger, an alleged "Lovestoneite," as editor of the *United Automobile Worker*. Some inkling of the activities of the Murray-Hillman committee during this period may be garnered from the following statement which was later released:

Determined to perform a fair and painstaking investigation, the Coordinating Committee sent investigators into the field. They conferred with 134 officals of 26 local auto unions and with hundreds of rank and file members. They weighed the facts and drew up their findings. These findings were then discussed by the Coordinating Committee. Homer Martin agreed to each and every recommendation. . . . The keynote of the Coordinating Committee work was the *elimination of factionalism*. . . . It recommended in the Allis-Chalmers local, Milwaukee, the right of the International Union to *restrict and eliminate* those who would use the local for Communist Party purposes. In Lansing, it recommended against permitting the "Lovestoneite" Communists to manipulate the local for their sectarian purposes.[128]

At this juncture, there occurred a bizarre episode which became one of the principal charges against Martin. As we shall see, all UAW attempts up to this point to organize Ford had met with complete failure. However, according to Harry Bennett, the powerful head of the Ford Service Department, Martin's radio attacks on Ford induced Bennett to contact Martin,[129] and negotiations were begun, which were first revealed by the following laconic public statement by Martin: "Mr. Bennett and I discussed the various problems of the automobile industry, including the thirty-two hour week, equalization of wages, and proper working conditions for employees. The visit was cordial and friendly." [130] The Executive Board, fearing, perhaps, that successful negotiations would be interpreted as a great personal triumph for Martin, was reluctant to permit him to continue the talks, but Murray and Hillman urged that Martin be allowed to negotiate further.

What happened then is still not clear. Keith Sward claims that Bennett, through a representative, John Gillespie, a Detroit politician, offered to make paper concessions to Martin in the form of reinstatement of discharged Ford workers whom the NLRB had ordered reinstated, in return for which the UAW would drop all NLRB actions and personal damage suits against the Ford Motor Company and leave the CIO.[131] Bennett later said that Gillespie was operating entirely on his own: "Gillespie injected himself into that situation too, carrying on negotiations with Homer without my knowledge. All that Gillespie accomplished was a lot of confusion." [132] It was Martin's contention that by January 1939, he had worked out an agreement providing for Ford recognition of the UAW; reinstatement of all discharged workers; the open wearing of union buttons in the Ford plant; and the establishment of local grievance committees and of a national UAW committee to settle grievances that could not be handled on the local level.[133] But R. J. Thomas, who continued to collaborate with Martin until the end of 1938, charged that in meetings with Gillespie, "I didn't hear them talk about any contract.

The only thing I could ever hear them talking about was how Homer Martin could take the United Automobile Workers out of the CIO. . . . The statement was made in my presence that if the United Automobile Workers of America would withdraw from the CIO that Ford would then sign a contract. . . ." [134] The allegation was also made that the proposed agreement with Ford was to be an oral one; that it was to be made without witnesses; and that Martin alone was to be the sole UAW contact on grievance cases.[135]

It seems quite likely that Bennett, sensing that the day when the Ford Motor Company would have to engage in collective bargaining was not far off, was attempting to capitalize upon the internal strife within the UAW to secure the most favorable bargain possible, with the more conservative faction. There are indications that he had made earlier overtures to the AFL; J. N. Cummings, an AFL organizer, reported early in 1938 that there was some possibility of taking over the Ford Brotherhood, a company-sponsored union, and continued:

I am of the opinion that all of the skilled trades can be successfully organized in the Ford Motor plant, if it is handled in the right manner. I am pretty well acquainted with a number of the Ford officials and have had quite a lot of dealings with Mr. Harry Bennett, who is the personnel man of the Ford Motor Car Company. I have been told a number of times by Mr. Bennett that there would be no obstacle put in our way in organizing the Ford employees in the American Federation of Labor.[136]

Bennett himself has written that after the split in the UAW, "I got Bill Green and his attorney in my office: I told them that I'd sign an AFL contract covering the whole plant, providing they'd take Homer over. Green agreed to this, and Homer went to work trying to organize an automobile worker's union within the AFL. Homer worked on this about a year. His efforts were not particularly successful, and finally Green called me up and backed out on the whole thing." [137]

Civil War in Automobile Unionism

The long, bitter internal fight in the UAW entered its final phase on January 20, 1939, when Martin suspended 15 of the 24 members of the Executive Board, after its refusal to accept a program including dissolution of the CIO coordinating committee, and designated the remaining members as the acting board. Loren Houser was appointed to succeed George Addes — who was among those suspended — as secretary-treasurer. The suspended members in turn constituted themselves the official executive board, and in consultation with the CIO, R. J. Thomas was named acting president.

That Martin would act soon had been clearly foreshadowed in an open letter he had written to the membership at the beginning of January, which said, *inter alia:*

For the last several months we have been operating, to our great detriment, as an International Union without full autonomy. . . . It is well known that the special committee has not succeeded in ending factional activities within our international union; in fact, with the setting up of the coordinating committee, certain individuals and groups within the union have used the special agreement with the CIO as a cloak of immunity, under cover of which they have even intensified their destructive factional activities and propaganda. . . .

I call upon our membership to join with me in demanding the return of our Union to its members. . . . This can be accomplished by abolishing the so-called Coordinating Committee and the termination of the special agreement now in existence between the Executive Board of the UAWA and the CIO.[138]

Both factions moved swiftly in a race for control of the administrative apparatus of the union, as well as for allegiance of the larger locals. Just prior to the break, the Executive Board had created a special committee to supervise the publication of the *United Automobile Worker,* and the anti-Martinites secured a tremendous advantage in managing to publish the paper regularly by sending its own squads to secure the union mailing list at a printing company in Detroit. Martin did not succeed in getting out a rival paper until almost a month after the split. On the other hand, the Martin forces occupied the union headquarters and thereby gained control of all the records of the organization.

At the national level the controversy took on the form of an endless logomachy. In his letter of resignation as a member of the CIO Executive Board, Martin wrote to John L. Lewis:

In your actions you have adopted the methods of your Stalinist allies and you and your agents have resorted to downright misrepresentations and deliberate falsehoods. . . . Your actions have convinced me and multitudes who have followed you that you are unable to rise above your personal ambitions and dictator complex.[139]

The opposition charged Martin with irresponsibility in administration, slander of fellow officers, and the use of strong-arm tactics to maintain himself in office. To Martin's allegation that competent employees were being discharged for opposition to communism, the following reply was given: "The few that were removed were members or close associates of a small faction of communists who used to call themselves the Communist Party (opposition) or CPO, headed by Jay Lovestone. The CPO is not in opposition to communism, it maintains that the regular Communist Party is not communistic enough or revolutionary enough. . . . The removal of these Lovestone lieutenants was done by practically *unanimous* vote of the Board in an effort to end the misrule by a small factional clique that was going on in International headquarters." [140]

The deciding struggle was fought at the local level. Martin called a special convention for March 4, the CIO for March 27, and each group proceeded to round up delegates, by whatever means were available. Of the Plymouth local, which was controlled by Leo Lamotte, a CIO stalwart, the following was reported:

The Plymouth local of the union was thrown into an uproar during the past week following a special meeting at which Martin announced suspension of the local's officers following which a flying squadron raided the local's officers, seized its records and placed them in the hands of administrators appointed by Martin.[141]

Fountain has described vividly a meeting of the Chevrolet Gear and Axle local in Detroit, at which Martin was scheduled to speak. The anti-Martin forces, in control of the local, invited flying squads from two other locals "purely for the purpose of exchanging messages of 'fraternal solicitude,' of course." Adolph Germer and Ed Hall were invited from the CIO. When Martin arrived "escorted by a flying wedge of muscular henchmen," the meeting resolved to "let Martin in but instruct him to leave his goons outside. . . . Informed of this action, Martin's gang made one try at cracking the door, but the two gearcutters, backed up by the flying squads from other locals, laid the invaders out three deep on the sidewalk in front of the hall." When Martin finally got in and attempted to speak, he was heckled mercilessly, and finally called upon "good union men" to follow him out, which few did.[142]

Martin's chief strength lay in General Motors, particularly in Flint, Lansing, and Pontiac. In an effort to win over the important locals involved, the CIO despatched some organizers to help the anti-Martin forces. For example, three CIO men went to Flint, under the direction of William J. Carney, CIO regional director for Detroit. He reported after reviewing the situation that of the five main locals there — Fisher Body No. 1, Fisher Body No. 2, Chevrolet, Buick, and A.C., Martin controlled the first three and the CIO the last two. In an effort to recapture Fisher Body No. 1, the CIO began to distribute leaflets at the plant gate. According to Carney, "they were met by a squad of fifty or more 'goons' who took their papers from them, broke into their cars, took those papers in the cars — approximately 5000 copies — and burned them on the street. . . . We are faced with a police force which refuses to take any part. We feel that the famous battle of 'Bull's Run' is still in their mind and that they and General Motors would like nothing better than to have the auto workers beat each other to death as the auto workers had very nearly done to the police during that strike." [143] A week later, "our representatives and sympathizers were passing out the 'Flint Auto Worker' at the Fisher plant. The goons attacked our people with pool cue sticks, blackjacks, and ball bearings inserted in gloves. Several of our people were beaten up. Some very bad." After calling local rank-and-file meetings, policed by strong arm squads from loyal plants in the area, Carney was able to report that "we have definitely swung this local which was Martin's stronghold in Flint." Similar battles took place in all the disputed areas; meetings often broke up in disorder, and neither side was particularly scrupulous in the means employed. There have been few occasions in the annals of American labor on which fratricidal strife reached an equal pitch of bitterness and fury.

The first opportunity for evaluating Martin's success in holding the union came when Martin's convention assembled in Detroit. On the basis of the official number of votes at the convention, the maximum membership was put at 104,000.[144] Actual membership was much less, as subsequent events revealed. Martin's chief strength was in the smaller locals, his principal larger plant membership being in Flint. Shortly before the convention opened, Loren Houser, who had been named acting secretary-treasurer, went over to the opposition faction, another in the long list of Martin collaborators to desert him, and of the original members of the UAW Executive Board prior to the split, only Lester Washburn, Irving Cary, and Frank Tucci remained loyal to him.

Martin announced to the convention that since the UAW had never received a formal charter from the CIO, it had never actually been affiliated, and that there was therefore no need to withdraw. The main order of business was the question of affiliating with the AFL, and on this point the convention authorized the new executive board to exercise its discretion. Shortly after the split, Martin had conferred with the AFL, first through David Dubinsky and Matthew Woll, and then directly with William Green. Since the AFL was anxious to get a foothold in the automobile industry, affiliation was a foregone conclusion. Even at this stage, however, the old problem of craft versus industrial jurisdiction was by no means dead. Martin wrote to Green on April 21, 1939, agreeing to affiliate the UAW with the

AFL as "an autonomous, industrial union, which would retain all the plants then under its control," and emphasizing that "we are to have complete jurisdiction in the automobile and automobile parts plants." [145] Green, in reply, guaranteed the autonomy of the UAW, but made it clear that there were restrictions on the jurisdiction of the new affiliate:

Your charter of affiliation would provide for the exercise of the same jurisdiction over those employed in automobile manufacturing and automobile parts plants as was defined in the charter granted the International Union Automobile Workers of America on August 26, 1935. . . .

We will gladly arrange for conferences between committees representing your International Union and other International unions concerned where any dispute, great or small, relating to jurisdiction over those employed as tool makers, die sinkers, pattern makers and others in the event such disputes may arise anywhere or in any place. We will insist upon the autonomous jurisdiction and administrative rights of your International Union being respected and observed. In like manner we will insist that the jurisdiction of sister organizations affiliated with you in the American Federation of Labor be respected and observed.

The low state to which Martin's organization had fallen by May 1939, is indicated by the fact that its income was only $10,000 a month, and the AFL was obliged to lend it $25,000 to keep it going.

The subsequent decline of the UAW-AFL will be recounted below. It may be well at this point, however, to summarize the factors which made it possible to depose Martin, one of the few examples in recent years of a successful revolt against the leadership of a large trade union.

Certainly one of the major factors was the economic background against which the union was operating in 1938. Decline in membership, and consequently in revenue, made retrenchment in staff necessary, and hampered the building up of a machine loyal to the administration. The lack of progress, and even retrogression, on the collective bargaining front created dissatisfaction with the leadership among the members. Had production been maintained throughout 1938, and had the UAW continued to expand and gain improvements in employment conditions, Martin's position might have been stronger.

The support accorded by the CIO to the anti-administration group was probably the *sine qua non* of success. Despite some reversal of fortune in 1938, the CIO as a central body still enjoyed enormous prestige among industrial workers, and the name of John L. Lewis had a magic ring in those circles. In addition to these intangibles, the CIO assisted materially by providing organizers and funds at the crucial moment. Against this, Martin had little to offer. The AFL was not popular among the auto workers, and Martin himself had been instrumental in building up anti-AFL sentiment. For example, in telling the 1937 convention of the crucial negotiations with General Motors, he said:

I shall never forget the agonies of those questionable hours, when the fate of our union and the fate of the labor movement of this country and the fate of the welfare of the common people of this nation hung in the balance, that this so-called leader of labor [William Green], like a Judas Iscariot, gave us the kiss of death. . . . We shall never forget that William Green reached out his hand and took the hands of the exploiters of labor and gave them comfort in that hour of struggle. His action at that time, and the action of his confederates since, cause us to brand him and them as friends of the employer, enemies of labor, and to plant the brand of "company union" upon their efforts.[146]

Yet less than two years later, Martin was counseling the same workers to enter the AFL under the leadership of William Green, and, moreover, to accept a charter with the same jurisdictional limitations as those which had created friction between the UAW and the AFL when the former was first chartered.

Martin's personal limitations played a crucial role in his elimination from the main body of automobile unionism. Rising to the top on the basis of personal magnetism and great oratorical powers, he proved unequal to the tasks required of a leader. Even then, he might have been able to survive if he had adhered to a line of political neutrality, which was in accord with his personal philosophy. Instead, he permitted himself to become enmeshed in a desperately fought battle between rival ideological groups, and thus forfeited the possibility of appealing to the rank and file as a Simon-pure trade unionist, equally condemnatory of all the ideologies which were attempting to control or influence the UAW for their own purposes.

The quality of the opposition leadership was another cause of Martin's downfall. The men who were ultimately responsible for his ouster were in the main young, able, and ambitious. Like Martin, they had all risen to the top on the basis of organizational ability, but some of them, unlike him, showed considerable political acumen. This was particularly true of Walter Reuther, the most hard-hitting and singleminded of the young UAW leaders, who gathered beneath his banner, originally on an ideological basis but subsequently on the basis of ability in the work of running a union, some of the best brains in the UAW, including his brothers Victor and Roy, Emil Mazey, Leonard Woodcock and John Livingston. R. J. Thomas, who succeeded Martin to the presidency, has been well described as a "husky, tobacco-chewing auto worker," whose strength "stemmed from his earthiness, his simplicity, and his bigness of heart." [147] A nonsectarian politically, Thomas eventually lost out because of a lack of capacity as an administrator. Richard Frankensteen, whose main virtue was described as "great physical courage and the ability to take it on the picket line," [148] proved to be unstable politically, running the gamut from admiration of Father Coughlin to collaboration with the communists in the UAW, a victim finally of his own ambition to be president of the union. The fourth of the principal union leaders was George Addes, secretary-treasurer of the UAW almost from its formation until his defeat by the Reuther forces in 1947. Addes was not essentially an organizer, but rather an administrator, and developed a considerable personal following within the union. In all, there were few other unions so well endowed with capable leaders, a fact which redounded to the disadvantage of Martin.

Reorganization and Resumption of Economic Warfare

The anti-Martin faction, formally recognized by the CIO as the official United Automobile Workers, assembled in Cleveland on March 27 in a special convention. Although the convention was far more orderly and constructive than that of the previous year, any hope that the absence of Martin would eliminate factionalism was doomed to disappointment. Murray and Hillman, in the capacity of behind-the-scenes advisers, exercised a degree of CIO influence not matched before or since in UAW affairs.

A number of important constitutional changes were adopted, all in the direction of decentralizing authority within the UAW. The power to suspend or expel international officers and members of the executive board was vested in a jury of rank-and-file members chosen by lot from among the delegates to the previous convention, in an effort to prevent the recurrence of the frequent suspensions that had characterized the Martin regime. National councils of locals whose members were in the employ of the larger corporations were established as a body intermediate between the local and the international, namely, a General Motors Council and a Chrysler Council. The formal purpose of such councils was to "coordinate the demands of the separate members and to formulate policies in dealing with their common employer." [149] Actually, they assumed much of the authority previously exercised by the international union with respect both to the negotiation of new contracts and the administration of existing agreements, and served as a check upon the authority of the international president to negotiate national agreements. Numerous other constitutional amendments were adopted, all after vigorous debate, and for the most part designed to limit the authority of the executive officers.

The principal bone of contention at the convention was over the election of officers. Murray and Hillman advocated a slate of R. J. Thomas as president and George Addes as secretary-treasurer as a means of keeping the union free of control by ideological groups. Thomas in particular was a neutral in the struggle between the erstwhile allies in the Unity caucus, the communists and socialists, who were now at sword's point. Frankensteen, a Progressive at the 1937 convention, moved into an alliance with the communists against Walter Reuther, who now emerged as the principal spokesman of the socialist group. All the factions were induced to accept Thomas and Addes, though the Reutherites were reluctant because of Addes' leanings toward a Frankensteen alliance. The CIO representatives were also able to secure agreement on the elimination of all vice-presidencies, but the agreement was almost wrecked when the Frankensteen-communist group attempted to place Frankensteen, Mortimer, and Hall, all ex-vice-presidents, on the executive board as members at large. Largely because of the violent objections of Walter Reuther, this plan fell through. In the elections for members of the executive board, however, the Frankensteen-communist group won a clear majority, with the Reuther faction able to place only four members.[150]

The factional strife was by no means confined to hidden election maneuvers, but erupted occasionally to the floor of the convention. Reuther accused Frankensteen, who had been in charge of the unsuccessful Ford drive, of placing political ahead of organizational considerations in attempting to use Ford as a means of augmenting his power in the union. Frankensteen replied that Reuther's local had contributed very little to the Ford campaign, and at a later point stated: "I charge now that there is a group in this convention which is carrying on tactics which we certainly have learned in the past were not beneficial to this union and they are giving great comfort to Homer Martin and every soul opposed to us." [151] Nevertheless, the convention ended on a more friendly note after an appeal by Sidney Hillman for unity.

The UAW claimed to represent 355,000 workers at this time, but the dues-paying membership was only 90,000.[152] The union's treasury was empty, and it faced the challenge of the UAW-AFL. The principal danger of the latter lay in the refusal of some of the manufacturers, led by General Motors, to deal with either union until the question of representation had been clarified. On the credit side, however, the UAW-CIO had the gradual improvement in business conditions that took place during 1939. Despite major strikes, the industry produced 2.9 million passenger cars in 1939 as compared with 2 million in 1938, and average employment in the automobile, body and parts plants rose from 305,000 in 1938 (most of these on part time) to 394,000 in 1939.[153] Economic recovery increased the union's bargaining position and enabled it to take the offensive for the first time since early 1937.

Each of the rival organizations, by a show of force, attempted to demonstrate its right to represent the workers. The UAW-CIO struck first at the Briggs Body Corporation in Detroit over the alleged refusal of management to discuss grievances and negotiate a new contract. After a strike of two weeks, it was agreed to submit the dispute to arbitration, as the result of which the union won sole bargaining rights and improved grievance machinery.[154] Homer Martin, who had termed the strike unjustifiable, attempted to demonstrate his strength by striking General Motors plants in Flint and Saginaw. However, CIO workers refused to honor his picket lines, and enough workers remained on the job to maintain production. Martin was obliged to call the strike off on June 15, after General Motors had assured him that it would confer with his organization on problems concerning its members in the affected plants — an assurance that was also given to the UAW-CIO.[155] Because of financial stringency, Martin was obliged to discharge 35 organizers, and considerable dissatisfaction was reported within the UAW-AFL. Some of his associates complained to AFL officials

that Mr. Martin called the strike in General Motors plants last week without consulting his executive board, and that his strike order was sent out late at night without previous conferences with local officials, who were mystified by the command that they order their members to cease work. On calling the strike Mr. Martin chartered a plane and flew to Kansas City so that he did not direct the General Motors walkout from Detroit. . . . Although the union's executive board had requested Mr. Martin to cease his radio addresses or to cut down the number because of the expense, he insisted on buying additional time . . . at a time when his office employes and organizers were several weeks in arrears as to their salaries.[156]

The shift to the AFL had done nothing to improve Martin's administrative capacities.

The next move came from the UAW-CIO. A widespread strike against General Motors would have overtaxed the resources of the union, and besides, there was no guarantee that it could be made effective. Walter Reuther, as head of the General Motors department, devised the strategy of a national strike of tool and die makers at a time when the corporation was busily engaged in retooling for its 1940 models. When General Motors, as anticipated, refused to grant the UAW-CIO bargaining rights on a national basis, 7000 skilled workers in 12 tool and die shops were pulled off their jobs, effectively halting tooling operations. Production workers continued to report for work until they were laid off, whereupon they collected unemployment compensation. On August 5, after the strike had lasted almost five weeks, General Motors agreed to recognize the UAW as sole bargaining agent for tool and die makers in 42 plants and increased the minimum scale.[157] While the gains achieved were negligible, the agreement was important as a demonstration of the revival of CIO strength, particularly by comparison with the poor showing made by the AFL union.

In the summer of 1939, the UAW-CIO began to resort to a new weapon in its drive for bargaining rights — the NLRB election. Use of this device was contingent upon a sufficient degree of organization to secure majorities, and judging by the results, the UAW-CIO had made remarkable progress since its March convention. The first vote was held in Packard; the local there had remained with Martin after the split, but on July 18, it switched its allegiance to the CIO on the ground that "the AFL leadership was still interested in craft unionism and was supporting the Martin UAW faction only because of its nationwide fight with the CIO." [158] At an NLRB election held on August 17, the CIO won 6090 votes to 1547 for the AFL and 637 for neither. A week later, the count at the Motor Products Corp. was: CIO — 2033; AFL — 188; neither — 80. A third important vote among the minor producers was at Briggs, when the CIO triumphed with 13,301 votes to only 1052 for the AFL.[159]

The stage was set for an attempt to capture exclusive bargaining control of the first of the major producers, Chrysler. The CIO was unsuccessful in persuading the NLRB that all Chrysler plants constituted a single unit appropriate for collective bargaining, and balloting was held on a plant-by-plant basis, as the AFL had demanded. Nevertheless, the CIO carried 11 of 13 bargaining units, receiving 40,564 votes to 4673 for the AFL. The AFL carried a plant at Evansville, Indiana, while at the Kokomo, Indiana, plant, neither union was successful in winning a majority.[160]

Having thus won the legal right to exclusive representation, the UAW-CIO entered into collective bargaining with the Chrysler Corporation for revision of its old contract. One of the principal issues in controversy was the union demand for participation in setting production standards, a reflection of the desire on the part of the auto workers to control the speed of the assembly line. When the company refused to yield, a strike was called, which involved 55,000 workers and lasted 54 days, the longest continuous strike in the history of the automotive industry up to that time. While the union did not achieve its chief demand, it secured a 3 cent per hour wage increase, improved grievance machinery, and, as a consquence of its NLRB victory, exclusive bargaining rights in eleven plants.[161] In a joint press statement, R. J. Thomas and Philip Murray declared that "the new agreement, as a whole, represents the greatest gains for the Chrysler workers since the inception of unionism in the plants of the corporation."[162] By later standards, the gains seem meager indeed, but it must be remembered that in 1939, the UAW-CIO was still engaged in a touch-and-go battle for its very survival.

The next major target was General Motors, where the UAW-AFL had its principal strength. During the first months of 1940, intensive campaigning was undertaken. All the big guns of the CIO, Lewis, Murray, Hillman, spoke at mass rallies. An NLRB election took place on April 17, again on a plant-by-plant unit basis. Of 128,957 votes cast, 94 per cent of all eligible votes, the CIO won 84,024, the AFL, 25,911, and 13,919 were cast for neither union, the remainder being cast for other organizations or disqualified. The CIO carried 48 plants employing more than 120,000 workers, while the AFL carried five plants with 5600 workers.[163] Coming on top of the Chrysler defeat, this election marked the end of the UAW-AFL as a factor of any significance in the industry, although occasionally some violence erupted as a consequence of friction between the two unions. For example, in September 1940, fighting between the two groups at Fisher Body No. 1 in Flint, an old Martin stronghold, caused the plant to close down. Martin was forced out of the UAW-AFL at the end of 1940, and a bit of his subsequent career has been related by Harry Bennett of the Ford Motor Company as follows:

Homer was pretty hard up. Mr. Ford came to see me about Homer's plight, and said, "Harry, I guess this is our fault. Let's help Homer." So we gave Homer a couple of accounts, one with a chemical company. We also gave him a completely furnished home in Detroit. Later Homer traded this home for a farm near Ann Arbor, where he still lives. After 1933 this business of giving people homes became quite a thing with us. We built over sixty houses for people, after the Wagner Act was passed.[164]

The UAW-CIO clinched its superiority of status by concluding an agreement with the General Motors Corporation, which included the following provisions:

1. A lump sum equal to 40 hours pay was given to all workers with seniority of ten months or more.

2. Wage increases averaging 1½ cents per hour were to be distributed among workers to eliminate inequities in job classification.

3. The UAW was recognized as sole collective bargaining agent in the plants it had won.

4. An impartial umpire system was established for the final adjudication of all grievances.

5. There was to be one grievanceman for each 250 workers, instead of one for 400 workers as provided in the previous agreement.

6. The union won the right to question the timing of operations.

Despite these agreements, and equally favorable ones with Studebaker, Packard, Hudson, and other manufacturers, wildcat strikes of short duration continued to plague the industry, particularly in General Motors. The latter blamed the international union for failure to control its subordinates, and indeed the international, by its periodic educational campaigns, admitted implicitly that it was having difficulty in maintaining discipline.

A union official later wrote of the wildcat strike period: "The automobile companies more than any other industry in the United States had aroused among the workers a feeling of fear, hatred and mistrust. Once they had established themselves as a union and had gained some measure of independence from management discipline and reprisals, they lost no opportunity to flex their muscles, often to the embarrassment and concern of all of the UAW leadership of whatever faction." [165] On the other hand, the union was inclined to place the blame on management for its reluctance to handle grievances in a spirit of friendly cooperation. As a rank-and-filer put it:

General Motors people have been discriminated against, and if you members feel that they were discriminated against you have a job when you go back home. You can pass all the resolutions and motions you want on this floor, but if you haven't got the pressure back home then your motion is not worth a damn, because General Motors will tell you that they still don't want to talk to you. They were not going to talk to us, so we marched out in front of the plant and they were damned good and ready to talk.

It is probably fair to say that some of the fault lay with each of the parties. General Motors, before any of the other auto companies, adopted a strong position on discipline for which it was later praised by the UAW. At the same time, anti-union attitudes could not be eliminated overnight, particularly among the lower echelons of plant management. Another decade was required before General Motors and the UAW were able to achieve harmonious working relationships.

The UAW convention that began at the close of July 1940, found the union in a far different situation from that which it had occupied at its 1939 convention. It claimed a dues-paying membership of 294,000, and contracts with 647 plants employing 412,000 workers.[166] All the major producers in the automobile industry, with the exception of Ford, were under contract with it, for the most part on an exclusive representation basis. The officers and delegates had reason to be satisfied with the year's progress.

The principal issues debated at the convention were political rather than trade union issues. At this time, the communist political line was violently opposed to participation in the European war and to arming for national defense. The 1940 national election campaign was under way, and John L. Lewis had indicated unmistakably that he was not going to back President Roosevelt for a third term. Lewis had also embraced a violent isolationism very much to the liking of the communist faction, which attempted to capitalize on his prestige. For example, in arguing against a resolution to endorse Roosevelt, Wyndham Mortimer declaimed: ". . . to pass this resolution would be a direct kick in the face to the greatest labor leader that America or any other country has produced, and I for one, fellow workers, am not willing to do that. I would not give one hair of John L. Lewis' bushy eyebrows for all the politicians in both the Democratic and Republican Parties." [167]

The opposition was bolstered by Sidney Hillman, who spoke at the convention as a member of the National Defense Advisory Commission, and adopted a line on national defense and the reelection of Roosevelt completely at variance with that of Lewis. A resolution was introduced condemning the "brutal dictatorships, and wars of aggression of the totalitarian governments of Germany, Italy, Russia and Japan." Victor Reuther stated in favor of the resolution that "organizationally, from the standpoint of getting new workers into our Union, this convention has got to make its position clear. We cannot go to hundreds of thousands of aircraft workers actually engaged in national defense work and urge them to join our Union which is continually under attack by demagogues from without and within, because the Union has not seen fit itself, up to now, to clear the air on this issue." Nat Ganley, a communist stalwart, argued that the resolution was purely factional in its purpose and that Reuther knew "damned well that there are good members of our organization who have had the opportunity of consulting with people who have carried on impartial investigations of the Russian problem and have therefore come to the conclusion that Russia is not a totalitarian dictatorship similar to Germany, Italy, or the military dictatorship in Japan." Frankensteen, in a somewhat equivocal statement, supported the resolution, as did Thomas and Addes, and it was passed by a large majority. The resolution proved to be an effective device for isolating the communists on an issue in which there was no line of retreat for them. The anticommunist wing, again supported by Frankensteen, also succeeded in putting the convention firmly behind Roosevelt, after a forceful speech by Walter Reuther in which he recalled the "beautiful resolution" in behalf of Roosevelt which the communists had introduced at the previous convention.[168]

On one issue, the need for increasing the UAW income, Lewis and Hillman were in complete agreement. Yet a resolution raising the monthly dues from $1.00 to $1.25 was defeated without debate, as was a suggestion to levy a special assessment of $1.00 per member. No group was willing to take the responsibility for asking the membership for more money. It was agreed, however, to submit the $1.00 assessment to a referendum vote.[169] In elections to the Executive Board, the Reutherites made some gains, though alliances were subject to rapid and constant shift, so that no one group was in firm control. One fact clearly emerged from the convention, however: the Communist Party machine in the UAW had lost considerable ground due to its espousal of a political program which was considerably at variance with rank-and-file sentiment, the first time that had been true since the founding of the union. The Hitler-Stalin pact had many ramifications.

The Organization of Ford

The major task still confronting the UAW was the organization of the Ford Motor Co. The union had turned to this problem in 1937, after securing contracts with General Motors and Chrysler, but it was unsuccessful even in gaining a foothold at Ford. It was not until 1941, when most of the rest of the industry was under exclusive contract, that Ford was finally brought to heel.

A number of factors contributed to the ability of Ford to keep the union out, but by all odds the most important one was the use of sheer physical force by the somewhat misleadingly named Ford Service Department. This organization, under the leadership of Harry Bennett, was in fact a quasi-military force, recruited in part from among former athletes and convicts.[170]

Sward cites the following examples of the methods it employed inside the plant:

For years after Bennett came to power, it was the proud, undisguised aim of the Service Department to blot out every manifestation of personality or manliness inside a Ford plant. Striving for such an end, Bennett's mercenaries finally mastered every tactic from the swagger of the Prussian drill sergeant to outright sadism and physical assault. On the night shift they would jolt an incoming worker out of his wits and take the starch out of his system by flashing a light in his face and shouting at him, "Where did you get that badge?" or "Who's your boss?" Another intimidating practice that came into being under Bennett's rule was the act of "shaking 'em up in the aisles." In this case a workman summoned to the employment office for any reason at all, even one that was totally unrelated to his work, would be shoved and pushed along the aisle by a pair of officious Servicemen, like a felon in the custody of the police.

Beatings of employees and an elaborate system of espionage were among the other weapons in the arsenal of the Service Department. "Informers reported scraps of conversation overheard in the mill or on the approaches to the mill. While at their benches, workers had their overcoats ransacked and their lunch buckets pried into. They were shadowed on their way to the drinking fountain and the lavatory. They were plagued by spies during the break between shifts." [171]

Nor were these forcible methods of repression confined to employees. Early in May, 1937, three UAW organizers attempting to distribute leaflets near the Ford assembly plant in South Chicago were savagely beaten.[172] An episode that received wide publicity occurred on May 26, 1937, when five UAW organizers, led by Walter Reuther and Frankensteen, in the company of a large corps of newspaper men and photographers, approached the River Rouge plant in Dearborn with the intention of distributing handbills. They were met at a public overpass by a group of Ford Servicemen and beaten in the manner employed by professional gangsters. Roving bands accorded like treatment to other UAW men and women stationed in other parts of the city. The Dearborn police, who witnessed some of the beatings, did not intervene.[173]

When the UAW, by massing supporters near the plant, was able to provide protection to its handbill distributors, the Dearborn City Council enacted an ordinance which in effect made it illegal to distribute circulars within the city limits. It is claimed that from December 9, 1937, when the ordinance was passed, to January 23, 1938, 906 persons were arrested for violating it.

Any worker within the Ford plant who was remotely suspected of union sympathies was discharged without ceremony. Between 1937 and 1941, over 4000 employees were dismissed for this reason. The National Labor Relations Board upheld numerous discriminatory discharge complaints at virtually every Ford plant in the country. Henry Ford had announced at the commencement of the first UAW drive that "we'll never recognize the United Automobile Workers union or any other union," [174] and as Bennett has said, the Wagner Act did not exist for him.[175]

Union organization drives in 1937 and 1939, poorly financed and co-ordinated, foundered on the rock of company opposition. In the winter of 1940, the UAW initiated a new campaign which eventually brought success. The CIO contributed $50,000 to the drive, a sum matched by the UAW, and 54 trained organizers headed by Michael Widman, a close associate of John L. Lewis, were assigned exclusively to the task of organizing the Ford workers. Widman found only 900 union workers at River Rouge, but by the end of December, 1940, some 14,000 had been enrolled.[176] The task of reaching the workers was facilitated when in October 1940, Municipal Judge Lila Neuenfelt held the Dearborn antileaflet ordinance unconstitutional. One of the union's principal arguments was that Ford's much advertised "high wage policy" simply was contrary to fact; that actually, Ford wages were below those of General Motors and Chrysler. A Ford advertisement to the effect that it was paying a little over 90 cents an hour provided a string for the union's bow in that average hourly earnings in the industry were near $1.00 at the time.[177] Bennett's later admission that Ford was paying below-competitive wages is amusing, though it is difficult to judge how authentic the incident is:

Mr. Ford insisted to me that we were paying higher wages than any of the other automobile manufacturers.

"No, we're not," I'd say, but he'd go right on insisting.

Finally I sent to the accounting department for the figures, and showed him conclusively that our scales were below the others.

Mr. Ford then said to me, "By God, Harry, we ought to be able to pay more than General Motors or Chrysler. They've got stockholders to settle with, and we've only got the family." [178]

When Ford signed with the union, and agreed to meet the General Motors and Chrysler wage scales, the average annual wage increase received by each worker has been variously estimated at between $230 and $400.[179]

The organizing drive was given a powerful stimulus by a decision of the United States Supreme Court on February 10, 1941, refusing to review an NLRB order which directed the reinstatement of 22 River Rouge workers with back pay and the posting of notices of compliance with the National Labor Relations Act. The reinstated men reappeared at their jobs openly displaying their union buttons for the first time in a Ford plant. Gradually, organization spread throughout the huge plant, and an epidemic of sit downs occurred over grievances. For the first time, the company showed some indecision. There were clearly conflicting views in management on the proper measures to be taken. Once more an approach was made to the American Federation of Labor. William Green visited Bennett, and also talked with Henry Ford. "President Green stated that they did not give him any assurance that they would withdraw their opposition, but they did believe that most of their people felt that they would rather come with us." [180] The AFL opened an office in Dearborn, and set up a federal local as an organizing device. Bennett publicly endorsed these efforts. The AFL did manage to win considerable support at River Rouge, but fell far short of a majority.

The UAW petitioned for an NLRB election, which the company managed to stall by contesting the proposed NLRB election arrangements. Bennett was quoted as saying that if the government forced him to bargain, "we will bargain with the union because the law says so. We will bargain till Hell freezes over, but they won't get anything." [181]

The climax of the campaign came on April 1, 1941, when the eight-man UAW grievance committee of the River Rouge plant was discharged *en masse*. Without any order from the union, a strike spread rapidly through the gigantic plant, until by the end of the day it was shut down. The strike was endorsed by the union; pickets were massed around the plant, and all means of ingress were barricaded.

There remained within the plant members of the Ford Service Department and perhaps a thousand Negro workers who had been recruited by one of Ford's Negro agents as a bulwark against the CIO, many of them from the South and without previous industrial experience. Several hundred of them left the plant after an appeal by Walter White, president of the National Association for the Advancement of Colored People, and other Negro leaders, but the rest remained in.[182] Considerable violence ensued. "Iron bars were used freely in the rioting between workers and CIO pickets at the plant today. Bricks and other missiles flew as the police tried to stop the battles. Scores were hurt as the heavy forged iron shafts were thrown at pickets by nearly 200 Negroes who made sorties from Gate No. 4 on Miller

Road. Hand-to-hand encounters resulted in knifings and beatings to pickets and company supporters. In all, the union, which set up a field headquarters manned by eight doctors and six nurses, reported that 150 persons had been treated during the day." [183]

The company endeavored without success to secure the removal of the union barricades. According to Bennett, Henry Ford and he wanted to continue the fight by arming everyone in the plant and using tear gas, if necessary, to secure unrestricted access, but Edsel Ford became alarmed at these plans, and persuaded his father to adopt a more peaceful course of action.[184] Be that as it may, Governor Murray Van Wagoner of Michigan managed to keep discussions between Ford and the UAW going for ten days until an agreement was reached, providing: (a) reinstatement of 5 of the 8 discharged committeemen; (b) initiation of a grievance procedure; (c) referral of unresolved disputes to a mediation board; (d) suspension of newly initiated NLRB hearings against Ford; (e) Ford consent to an immediate NLRB election.[185]

What finally induced Ford to make its peace with the UAW? Among the explanations that may be adduced are the following:

1. The role of the Wagner Act was of overwhelming importance. The Ford Motor Company fought a long rearguard action in the courts, but by 1940 it was obvious that the company was risking contempt in its refusal to bargain collectively. Moreover, the NLRB was preparing, at the time of the settlement, hearings on unfair labor practice charges which would have dwarfed all previous hearings in the automobile industry and involved Ford in considerable unfavorable publicity.[186]

2. Ford's share of the automobile market had dropped from 22.9 per cent in 1939, a level which had prevailed for some years past, to 19.8 per cent in 1940.[187] The UAW had been carrying on an intensive boycott campaign against Ford, and this, combined with other unfavorable publicity that Henry Ford was getting at the time as a result of involvement with isolationist and both domestic and foreign fascist movements was undoubtedly a contributing factor to the Ford sales decline.[188]

3. Pressure was being exerted by the labor movement to prevent the United States Government from awarding defense orders to Ford on the ground that it was defying the national labor policy. Sidney Hillman, as labor's principal representative in the defense administration, was active in furtherance of this policy.[189] A large Army contract for trucks issued in January 1941, bypassed the Ford Motor Co.[190] Harry Bennett claimed that at the suggestion of Frank Knox, secretary of the Navy, he had persuaded

Henry Ford to make a nationwide radio broadcast supporting President Roosevelt's foreign policy in order to put the company in a better position, only to have Ford back out two days before the broadcast was scheduled.[191]

4. The Ford Motor Company was in 1940 the only unorganized producer of any importance in the industry. Its wages were below the competitive level, and working conditions were certainly no more favorable than elsewhere in the industry. The company could have attempted to offset the growing suspicion and hostility by competitors and workers alike through raising wages unilaterally, but this might have boomeranged by providing the UAW with the argument that only its pressure had induced Ford to improve conditions, and thus actually increased the tempo of union activity. Rationality clearly called for collective bargaining on this as well as other counts.

An NLRB election was held at the Detroit plants of Ford on May 21, 1941, one of the largest elections in NLRB history. The results at the River Rouge plant were: UAW-CIO, 51,866; UAW-AFL, 20,364; neither, 1958. At the Lincoln plant, the CIO margin was greater. The reaction of Ford officials to the election revealed that there had been no basic change in attitude toward the union. Harry Bennett declared that "It was a great victory for the Communist party, Governor Murray Van Wagoner and the NLRB," while I. A. Capizzi, the general counsel to the company, stated: "The Ford Motor Co. must now deal with a communist-influenced and led organization. . . . The Wagner Act is a most vicious law. . . . The NLRB is an exact replica of the so-called courts by which the Communist, Nazi, and Fascist partners purge the men who resist their tyrannies. It is a dictatorial concept imported from Europe."

Nevertheless, in the collective bargaining that followed the election, the UAW won better terms than it had been able to secure from any other manufacturer. Ford, as already noted, agreed to meet the competitive wage level in the industry. Grievance machinery was established, seniority was recognized as the guiding principle in layoff and rehiring, premium pay was given to night shift workers, two hours call in pay and time and a half for overtime were provided for. All members of the Service Department were to be uniformed. To cap the climax, the UAW was given a union shop and the checkoff of union dues, Ford being the first major manufacturer who was willing to grant this degree of union security.[192] Ford also agreed to stamp the union label on its cars.

There has been considerable speculation about the reasons for this abrupt about-face on the part of Ford. Sward has asserted that Ford was merely attempting to allay union suspicions to the end that the company could infiltrate and capture control of the local and even of the international union. "The trump card which Bennett played in the game of edging toward the UAW high command was the union shop and the check-off. Here was the prized concession, he was never tired of reminding his more important UAW callers. Under certain circumstances, he indicated time and again, this plan could be withdrawn as easily as it had been given. It was, in short, he let it be known, a gift horse; it was the instrument by which he meant to hold the UAW in captivity." [193]

Bennett's own explanation provides some corroboration for this hypothesis:

The union had not asked for either provision [the union shop and the checkoff]. They had won them nowhere else in the industry. Why did Mr. Ford offer them? Mr. Ford told me, "Give 'em everything — it won't work." He then explained that he felt if we gave the union just a little, then they'd be right back at us for more. But if we gave them "everything," he thought, then they would fall to fighting and bickering among themselves. The way he saw it, it was a case of "enough rope."

In addition, Mr. Ford rather liked the idea of the check-off. He said to me, "That will make us their bankers, won't it? Then they can't get along without us. They'll need us just as bad as we need them." [194]

The National Defense Period

Although it was preoccupied with the Ford drive, the UAW was by no means inactive on other fronts. It took advantage of the upturn in economic activity which accompanied the national defense effort to secure additional concessions from General Motors and Chrysler. On May 16, 1941, a new contract signed with General Motors contained a general wage increase of 10 cents per hour, the first such increase secured from GM, an additional 40-hour pay bonus in lieu of vacations, improved grievance and seniority provisions, and enlarged authority for the impartial umpire system which had been set up under the previous agreement. Chrysler, which had been paying slightly higher rates initially, gave its workers a general increase of 8 cents an hour.[195] Estimated average annual earnings in automobile, body and parts plants were $2084 in 1941 compared with $1574 in 1937, the prewar year of peak production (except for 1929).[196] This gain, of course, is attributable only in part to union activities, but coming as it did upon the heels of union organization, it provided to the automobile workers a convincing demonstration of the benefits of organization. The prestige and morale of the UAW attained new heights. Paid membership in October

1941 reached the imposing total of 640,000, with an average of 512,400 for the twelve-month period ending April 31, 1942.[197]

But the years 1940 and 1941, which preceded the entry of the United States into the war, were not without serious danger to the union, arising again from factionalism. The crisis came in the aircraft industry, in which the 1940 convention had authorized that an organizational drive be undertaken. The industry was located away from the traditional strongholds of the UAW, and here the UAW faced the competition of the International Association of Machinists, AFL, a much more formidable threat than the UAW-AFL. Richard Frankensteen was put in charge of the drive, and plants of Curtis-Wright, North American Aviation, Douglas Aircraft, and Vought-Sikorsky were brought under control.

In June 1941, the North American Aviation unit of the Los Angeles aircraft Local 683 called a strike at a time when its case for a wage increase was pending before the National Defense Mediation Board, in violation of an agreement by Frankensteen and regional and local officials of the UAW that in return for a retroactive pay agreement to May 1, no strike would be called until three days after the board had completed its findings.[198] The local was in the control of a communist-oriented group led by Wyndham Mortimer, former vice-president of the UAW and in 1941 an international representative; Elmer Freitag, who had admitted registration as a communist in the 1938 elections; and Henry Kraus, a former editor of the *United Automobile Worker*. Lew Michener, director of the West Coast Region 6 of the UAW, was at least sympathetic to the aims of this group, which prior to the German invasion of Russia in 1941, was following the communist policy of obstructing the national defense effort. The UAW had recently won an NLRB election from the Machinists by a narrow margin, so that noncommunist UAW activists within the local were impatient with the delay involved in negotiating a new agreement, and were thus induced to go along with the strike.

As soon as he received word of the strike, Frankensteen went to Los Angeles and prevailed upon the local officials to call a meeting of the negotiating committee. However, he was not permitted to address this meeting, which affirmed its support of the strike. The next day he attempted to address an open membership meeting which had also been called by the local officials, but he was prevented from doing so by a planted group of hecklers. He did manage, however, to read a telegram from R. J. Thomas, president of the UAW, urging the workers to return to work. "Lew Michener received a similar wire from Thomas urging him to support

Frankensteen's policies and uphold the International Constitution. Michener stated openly that he had received this wire and he disregarded the policy of the International Union. Later he excused himself to Thomas by stating he did not receive the wire." Frankensteen then dismissed five international representatives, including Mortimer, revoked the charter of Local 683, with the approval of Thomas, and appointed new provisional officers. He also charged publicly that the strike had been engineered by the Communist Party, and advocated an immediate return to work.

The failure of this appeal resulted in prompt and drastic action from another source. President Roosevelt, with the approval of Sidney Hillman, at the time codirector with William S. Knudsen of the Office of Production Management, ordered the Army to take over the plant and reopen it. On June 10, 1941, 2500 troops went into Inglewood, where the plant was located, and drove the pickets away from the plant. Shortly thereafter, with the encouragement of the UAW, 80 per cent of the employees returned to work, and the strike was called off. Negotiations were resumed in Washington, and a contract reached "embodying gains which, in instances, not only exceeded the original wage demands of the North American workers, but set a precedent for wage increases throughout the aircraft industry. . . ."

This strike was one of the chief topics of debate at the 1941 UAW convention. Three separate reports were submitted to the convention. One, the majority report of a special committee that had investigatd the strike, called for the suspension of Michener for one year. A minority report favored Michener's expulsion, the suspension of the five international representatives involved for five years, and the establishment of a trusteeship over all of Region 6. A one-man minority report advocated merely that Michener be barred from reelection to the UAW Executive Board and the directorship of Region 6 at the 1941 convention, with no further loss of membership rights. The majority report made no bones about what it considered to be the origin of the strike:

The interference of the Communists into the strike gave basis to the charge of Frankensteen that the wildcat strike was engineered by Communists, inside and outside the Union, who were interested in carrying out the policy they were then fostering in trade unions. They were interested in demonstrating their effectiveness in obstructing national defense. Communist leaflets were distributed on picket lines. The leaflets distributed by the strike committee were written by a well-known Communist writer and signed by one of the union strike leaders. This same individual was active in planning strike strategy and organizing the picket lines.

The minority report was even stronger: "Lew Michener, Mortimer, and other people since identified as being members of the Communist party, took over the North American situation and flaunted the wishes of the President of the United States, the President of the C.I.O., and the International President, along with that of Richard T. Frankensteen, the Aircraft Director." President Thomas also voiced the opinion that "the Communist Party did have abnormal influence over our Region in California."

Mortimer took the floor to defend himself, and accused Frankensteen of ultimate responsibility for the strike in stirring up the workers. "Brother Frankensteen, when he left the North American situation, was the most militant man you ever saw . . . and when he came back he was completely reversed. . . ." He branded charges of communism as nonsense, and asserted that Frankensteen had been on terms of close personal friendship with Henry and Dorothy Kraus, two of the strike leaders. Frankensteen retorted heatedly that "three members of your committee were registered members of the Communist Party. Another was a member of the Young Communist League, and another, if you please, was art editor of a Communist magazine. . . ." As for Mortimer: "If Mortimer is not a Communist — and I don't know that he is — but if he isn't he is sure as hell cheating them out of dues, because he certainly follows their line." Michener defended himself by taking the offensive, claiming the entire issue was a false one and raised for purely factional reasons:

We should put our finger on the people responsible for the situation in North American, and I refer specifically here to the North American Corporation and also to the Office of Production Management. So that we may make our position clear, we refer specifically to Sidney Hillman and his red-headed stooge in this convention, Walter Reuther. . . . If Walter Reuther, Sidney Hillman or any one else who subscribes to the principles of the OPM, the so-called friend of labor, think for a moment that Richard Frankensteen and I are going to engage in a death struggle on the floor of this convention and ignore the welfare of the workers while Walter Reuther sits back there gleefully as a spectator and laughs and smirks at what he apparently considers his high-handed maneuverings, I want to state here and now he is going to be mistaken.[199]

By a very close vote, the convention adopted the mildest of the three resolutions, barring Michener from membership on the International Executive Board but imposing no additional penalties. The attitude of Frankensteen, who urged clemency, as well as the dislike of the delegates for the manner in which the strike had been broken, were important factors in bringing about this result.

The North American strike was not the only national defense strike to plague the UAW. Some months earlier, in November 1940, a twelve-day strike had taken place at the Vultee Aircraft Co. at Downey, California. A wage dispute had been settled, but Wyndham Mortimer, who was conducting the negotiations, broke off relations on the issue of grievance procedure. Robert H. Jackson, U. S. Attorney General, charged that the strike was communist-inspired, and after considerable government pressure, it was settled personally by President R. J. Thomas. This strike, however, was not outlawed by the International, and no penalties were assessed against its leaders.

The longest and most serious of the UAW national defense strikes was a 76-day strike against the Allis-Chalmers Company in Milwaukee.[200] This company was manufacturing electrical engines and turbines, and the strike was estimated to have delayed the completion of numerous naval vessels for as long as six months.[201] Local 248 of the UAW and the management of this company had been at odds for some months prior to the strike, and there had been no less than 17 work stoppages during the preceding eight months. The president of Local 248 was Harold Christoffel, who had been associated with the communist faction in the union. It was alleged that he used fraudulent methods in getting a strike vote majority over the issue of a closed shop, which the union was insisting upon to forestall management efforts to introduce AFL men into some of the skilled tasks. After several months of negotiation, in which Sidney Hillman played a leading role, had produced no settlement, Secretary of the Navy Knox and OPM Director Knudsen wired the company that the plant would have to be reopened immediately. The next day, 1200 men out of 7800 returned to work, protected by the state militia. Rioting ensued for three days, at the end of which the plant was once more closed down. The National Defense Mediation Board thereupon took jurisdiction of the strike, and settled it on the basis of maintenance of membership.[202]

This strike came to the floor of the 1941 UAW convention in the form of a challenge to seating the Allis-Chalmers delegation, led by Christoffel. A majority of the credentials committee found that Christoffel had violated the UAW constitutional provisions for electing delegates to the convention, and it was later brought out that many workers had been disenfranchised for refusing to follow the orders of the strike leaders. However George Addes, who had not previously been an active factionalist, charged that the decision to challenge the delegates had been taken by a caucus "because a few individuals thought that those delegates represented the philosophies of

Stalin." Addes, himself a Catholic, accused the Association of Catholic Trade Unionists, a small group which was working together with the Reuther caucus, of attempting to make political capital out of the issue, and Reuther replied: "it is a simple question of whether or not this International Union convention, the highest tribunal of our organization, is going to put the stamp of approval on the worst kind of strong-arm political racketeering in this union which smacks of A.F. of L. machine control. . . ."

The convention voted to send a special committee to Milwaukee to investigate the situation, and upon its return, the committee reported: "It can be substantiated that the following expressions were uttered from Christoffel's lips. Those expressions follow: That Brothers R. J. Thomas, our International President, Richard T. Frankensteen, Walter Reuther, Dick Leonard, George Nordstrom, and the rest of their kind were nothing but a bunch of phoneys, rats and Hillmanites. On top of that he described this convention — I ask the ladies in this convention to pardon me and forgive the language — he described the delegates of this convention as a bunch of bastards." R. J. Thomas also attacked the leaders of Local 248, asserting that they did not represent the rank and file and were still in office only because he had no constitutional authority to displace them. The committee was ordered to return to Milwaukee and hold new elections, which it did, with the result that Christoffel and the remaining members of the original delegation were reelected and finally seated at the convention.

The failure of the convention to take firmer action in so flagrant a case of fraud and disrespect to international officers on the part of a local cannot be construed, however, as evidence that the Communist Party was in control of the convention. In the first place, there was still an uneasy alliance betwen the communists and the Frankensteen-Addes supporters, which the latter did not want to disrupt lest the Reuther faction gain control of the union. This explains Frankensteen's conciliatory gestures in the North American case and Addes' espousal of the cause of the Allis-Chalmers local. More important, however, was the unpopularity of the Allis-Chalmers Corporation among the auto workers. The president of the corporation, Max D. Babb, was a prominent member of the isolationist America First Committee, with a reputation as a foe of the labor movement. Even Walter Reuther, in attacking Christoffel, conceded that the workers of the plant "fought a glorious battle against one of the most vicious reactionary employers of the country. The President of that Company was tied up with the America First Committee, and I think he was playing Hitler's game, and wanted that plant tied up."

A conclusive demonstration of the true strength of the communists came when Victor Reuther, as chairman of the constitution committee, introduced the following proposed amendment to the union constitution:

No member or supporter of any organization whose loyalty to a foreign government or who supports organizations which approve of totalitarian forms of government, shall be eligible to hold elective or appointive office in the International Union or any subdivision thereof.

A minority of the committee attempted to set a backfire to this amendment by barring from office members of the Communist, Nazi, Fascist, *and Socialist* parties in an obvious attack upon the Reuthers, which was made explicit when a delegate declared that "the real question is whether or not the Socialist Party in the person and voice of Walter Reuther and Victor Reuther and the rest of the Reuther family is going to have a privileged minority position in this Union." Frankensteen and Addes split on the question, the former rising to declare briefly that he favored the majority resolution, while the latter supported the minority resolution in order to "eliminate the politics that are being played in this convention by one group or the other accusing one another of being a Communist, a Socialist, a Trotskyite, a Nazi, a Fascist, or what-have-you." President R. J. Thomas came out squarely for the majority report, advising against tolerance for subversives who "are the most intolerant people I have ever come in contact with."

The majority resolution was made more specific by an amendment which barred from union office any member "if he is a member of or subservient to any political organization, such as the Communist, Fascist or Nazi organizations, which owes its allegiance to any foreign government other than the United States or Canada, directly or indirectly." [203] In this form it was adopted by a roll call vote of 1968 to 1026. Thus, even with the support of Addes, the communists were able to muster only one-third of the convention votes on an issue which was of vital concern to them.

Thomas was reelected to the presidency without opposition, but the Reuther caucus decided to run Richard T. Leonard for secretary-treasurer in opposition to Addes, in retaliation for the latter's support of the communist position on the principal convention issues. Addes won by a vote of 1759 to 1307, a victory that was described by an observer as due entirely to the efforts of Allan Haywood, a CIO staff member who attended the convention as a representative of John L. Lewis.[204] Addes was reportedly an admirer and supporter of Lewis, who had been replaced the previous year by Philip Murray as president of the CIO, and was actively engaged at the time of the 1941 UAW convention in undermining his one-time lieutenant. The new executive board was about evenly divided between the two major caucuses.

One of the ironic aspects of the convention was that the communists, who were being pilloried for fomenting the national defense strikes, had changed their policy line abruptly when Russia was invaded in June 1941, and at the time of the convention were advocating all-out defense production. Thus, when Thomas declared in his opening address to the convention that he favored military aid to Great Britain, Russia, and China, he quickly added that this did not constitute an endorsement of the Communist Party. The communist about-face saved the UAW from any further repetition of the North American affair. Thenceforth, the communist faction, supported by Addes, favored such methods as incentive pay, which had long been opposed by the auto workers, and unconditional observance of the wartime no-strike pledge, in order to maximize the output of war goods.

During the months between the 1941 convention and the entrance of the United States into the war, the UAW leaders were concerned with an old problem — unemployment. As a consequence of a step up in the production of armaments, automobile output was curtailed sharply in the fall of 1941. This so-called "conversion" unemployment continued during the first months of 1942, until the industry was able to retool for the production of aircraft, tanks, and other war material. Walter Reuther, whose widely publicized plan for converting idle automobile manufacturing capacity to aircraft production had occasioned considerable controversy in 1940, emerged with augmented prestige from this last round of unemployment.[205]

At the outbreak of the war, the UAW was paying per capita tax to the CIO on a membership of 649,000,[206] and was one of the largest unions in the United States. Firmly entrenched in the nation's key manufacturing industry, its exploitation of this strategic position had to wait upon the renewal of peacetime production. But even in 1941, the union's achievements were impressive against the background of the traditional demands of the auto workers. Despite factional warfare as intense as any that has existed in the American labor movement, it managed to wrest from employers some degree of participation in what had always been areas of exclusive management prerogative. Production standards had been brought within the framework of collective bargaining; the union had the right to question the speed of the assembly line. Seniority provisions provided a method of distributing the burdens of unemployment in a manner that seemed equitable to the workers; the much-resented arbitrariness of foremen had been eliminated. A well-defined grievance procedure, heading up into an impartial umpire system, provided an effective means of securing redress on the minor complaints that constitute so important an aspect of working life. Espionage and discriminatory discharge were practices of the past. Wages and other conditions of employment had been improved to the extent that even on an annual basis, the auto workers were one of the most favored groups in the country.

This is not to say that automobile labor relations had reached a millennium. Collective bargaining relationships with the major manufacturers were far from cordial, and it was another decade before the UAW was finally accepted as a permanent institution in the industry. Nor were the union's internal difficulties at an end; that did not come until the Reuther forces finally captured absolute control six years later. But by comparison with August 1935, when the representatives of a few thousand men assembled in Detroit to adopt a constitution for the United Automobile Workers of America, the status of the union in December 1941, represented one of the most impressive achievements in the history of American labor.

4

Coal Mining

The Thirty-Fourth Constitutional Convention of the United Mine Workers of America, which convened from January 28 to February 7, 1936, found the Mine Workers Union in vastly different circumstances from those which had prevailed but a few years earlier. Opponents of John L. Lewis claimed that in 1930, only 84,000 out of 522,000 bituminous coal miners were in the UMW.[1] The union itself admitted to almost complete absence of organization in many parts of the country. District 5 in Western Pennsylvania, for example, was reduced to 293 members from 45,000 members a few years earlier. District 17 in West Virginia reported 512 members out of a potential 100,000.[2] Two years later, in 1932, total UMW membership has been estimated at between 100,000 and 150,000, with the greater portion of this membership in the anthracite industry. Between 1924 and 1928, the UMW had spent eight million dollars in assistance to striking members,[3] and the subsequent decline in membership made it impossible for the union to recoup its waning fortunes. On December 1, 1933, even after the membership curve had begun to rise sharply, the UMW had only $312,000 in its treasury.[4]

The great decline in the demand for coal and the resultant reduction in employment opportunities for coal miners, coupled with sharply differing views among officers and members on how best to handle the situation, had led to internal dissention within and fission of the once powerful coal miners' union.[5] The most serious split was in District 12, covering the state of Illinois, which had long been one of the best organized divisions of the union. There the miners refused to accept a wage cut which Lewis had negotiated in 1932, and formed a rival organization, the Progressive Miners of America, which was destined to achieve a measure of stability. Other less successful challenges to the UMW came from the communist-led National Miners' Union; the West Virginia Miners' Union, led by Frank Keeney, a former official of the UMW; the Western Miners' Union, confined to the state of Washington; and the Independent Miners' Union, a company-assisted organization in western Kentucky.[6] While none of these organizations, with the exception of the Progressive Miners, lasted more than a few years, their brief existence testified to the disorganized state of the United Mine Workers.

The transformation of the UMW between 1932 and 1935 from a weak, schismatic group into a powerful, well-disciplined organization was the result of one of the most rapid and successful organizing campaigns in American labor history. With the governmental encouragement to unionism afforded by Section 7(a) of the National Industrial Recovery Act, the coal miners flocked into the union in the wake of a campaign on which John L. Lewis staked the entire resources of his organization. "Through territory where, not long before, federal troops and government men had deployed against the marching unionists, into the Rockefeller domains of Consolidation and the Mellon-held strongholds of western Pennsylvania drove the organizers calling out: 'The President wants you to join. Your government says 'Join the United Mine Workers.' The instantaneous mass response to the organizers' appeals on the part of men who had never seen the inside of a union hall stunned the nonunion operators and must have come as a surprise to Lewis himself." [7] The culmination of the campaign came with the establishment of the Appalachian Joint Conference as a collective bargaining mechanism. First organized in 1933, the mining operators at the conference represented over 70 per cent of bituminous coal tonnage and employment, and included the coal fields of Pennsylvania, Ohio, Virginia, West Virginia, northern Tennessee and eastern Kentucky.[8] By the end of 1935, the UMW had secured for its members, as a result of master agreements with the operators, a seven-hour day, thirty-five-hour week; and a basic daily wage rate of $5.50 in the North and $5.10 in the South. The official organ of the United Mine Workers acknowledged:

Members of the United Mine Workers of America everywhere realize the great debt of gratitude which the miners owe to President Roosevelt for the very effective support he gave them in their fight for better conditions in their economic and home life. Had it not been for this sincere and selfless support by the President the miners never would have achieved the success that they did in their efforts to better their condition.[9]

By April 1935, the average paid membership of the UMW had reached 541,000,[10] which the union claimed represented 95 per cent organization of the bituminous and anthracite industries combined. The only important mines not yet organized, except for those controlled by the Progressive Miners, were the captive operations of the United States Steel Corporation in West Virginia and Kentucky; the Harlan, Kentucky fields; the miners of the Alabama Fuel and Iron Company and the West Kentucky Coal Company in Kentucky; and the mines of the Phelps-Dodge Company at Dawson, New Mexico. On December 1, 1935, the union's financial resources totalled $2,298,000, soon to be invested in the great steel organizing campaign. Well might Lewis tell his 1936 convention:

We are meeting here at a time when our industry is more completely organized than ever before, when collective bargaining is more universally accepted in the coal industry than at any time in the lives of any of us, when the membership of our Union is greater than ever before, when the financial resources of our Union are greater than ever before. . . .[11]

The 1936 Convention of the United Mine Workers

The 1936 convention of the UMW opened shortly after the formation of the CIO, just when John L. Lewis was beginning to move into the national arena after having successfully organized the coal industry. Although Lewis was clearly master of the situation, the convention did not proceed altogether smoothly from his point of view; the delegates still showed much of the independence of spirit that had long characterized mining unionism. The principal challenge to Lewis' stewardship came over the issue of district provisionalism. Under the union's constitution, the international president was empowered to revoke the charters of district organizations, the administrative branches of the UMW, to create provisional governments and appoint provisional officers. This action was subject to review by the international executive board, but since the president, upon declaring a receivership, could also appoint the district representative to the board, and thus control the board, this review was illusory. The decision of the executive board could be appealed, finally, to the convention, and it was this body to which the internal foes of Lewis carried their fight.

While the UMW was in its period of decline prior to 1933, Lewis had systematically deposed the elected officers of a majority of the districts and installed his own men in these key posts. Only Western Pennsylvania, Indiana, Iowa, Wyoming, Michigan, Nova Scotia, and Montana, plus the three anthracite districts, 10 out of 29 districts, still retained their autonomy in 1932,[12] which meant that Lewis appointed a majority of the international executive board. In January 1934, when the international convention met at Indianapolis, 19 of 30 districts represented were provisional. These provisional districts represented about two-thirds of the votes in the convention. Outside of the anthracite districts, only two districts of any importance,

Indiana and Pittsburgh, were even formally self-governing. One delegate to the 1936 Convention brought this fact out clearly:

They tell you to leave all questions pertaining to the autonomy of any district in the hands of the International Executive Board. How many men in this convention know how many members of the Board are elected officially? They are appointed men, all except three. . . . They have a majority, and on any question coming before that Board you know what the consequence has been.[13]

There were many similar expressions from the floor of the convention. A delegate from District 17 declared: "I want to see if you men have a backbone or if you are jelly. Most of us get nervous in the presence of men who have power over us." [14] Another, from District 2, argued: "Throughout my district the question of autonomy seems to be the most important subject. . . . We believe if we select our own representatives we should select better men than we are having now and we will accomplish more than we are accomplishing now." Delegate Houser, from District 21, said:

We feel if we are given the privilege to elect our officials the same men of the District will exercise discretion and will select officials that are good, honest union men, not politicians or political has-beens, but labor leaders from the heart, they will not elect a man who has been in office for twenty-five or thirty years and has become legal minded and politically inclined. . . . Our machinery has got to be a political machinery and we have lost the pulse beat of the workers, and it should be brought back close to the rank and file.

The principal speeches in defense of provisionalism were made by Philip Murray and John L. Lewis. Murray argued that since only 28 per cent of the miners had been organized in 1933, the union was in reality only three years old, and he warned that the security of the miners would be threatened by any internal dissention. Lewis, in a remarkably revealing statement of his basic trade union philosophy, presented his version of the dichotomy between democracy and efficiency in labor organizations:

It is not a fundamental principle that the Convention is discussing, it is a question of business expediency and administrative policy as affecting certain geographical areas of the organization. It is a question of whether you desire your organization to be the most effective instrumentality within the realm of possibility for a labor organization or whether you prefer to sacrifice the efficiency of your organization in some respect for a little more academic freedom in the selection of some local representatives in a number of districts.

He pointed to the experience of District 12, which had been the locus of a serious internal split leading to the formation of the Progressive Miners, of Districts 19, 2, 6, 5, and 17, all of which had gone into receivership after incurring large debts. (Lewis failed to point out, however, that virtually every branch of the UMW had suffered the same fate during the nineteen-twenties, for economic reasons quite apart from the efficiency of district management.) He continued:

After all, what is involved in this? Well, a chance for some of our energetic, spirited young men, active and vigorous, ambitious, which they properly should be and of which we are proud, to run for office in the organization. That is all that is involved in it. . . . But what do you want? Do you want an efficient organization or do you want merely a political instrumentality? That is all that is involved in this matter — business administration, effective internal policies, and no denial of the fundamental principles of democracy. But learn to walk before you run and learn to wait while you train some of these young men who come upon this platform today to be the successors of Van Bittner and President Mark and the men from these other districts.

Lewis had set out deliberately upon his ascendence to the presidency of the UMW to curb the district independence that had characterized the organization and to create in its place a strongly centralized body in which the international officers made policy on all major collective bargaining decisions. "The only way to do it was to develop a machine that would ensure control over the entire union. . . . Past experience was replete with proof that the union could not be mobilized into a single force on the basis of a working coalition of different, independently powerful districts. This passive compromise policy had failed in the past, and Lewis was determined that he was not going to repeat the error." [15] By 1936, the machine was already functioning in good working order, and the demand for local autonomy was beaten back by a roll call vote of 3169 to 1132.

The leadership of Lewis was challenged on one other issue. The committee on the constitution had recommended that the salaries of international officers be raised by about 100 per cent, with Lewis' new salary to be $25,000 per annum. Several speakers arose in protest. One delegate argued: "Isn't the present salary enough to sustain anyone in the standards of decency and health? Are the members of this organization able to sustain their families in health and decency? I am not, and I am confident many of you other brothers are not." Another declared: "I am willing for our International officers to have some raise, because they haven't had any raise while we have had three or four raises, but I am not willing to jump their salary one hundred per cent at one time. . . . I don't believe when you deduct his expenses off for shooting and blasting, and so forth, the average coal miner is making fifty dollars a month when he works five days a week. We have men that have slaved in mines for less than two dollars a day. . . ." Although the recommendation was carried, Lewis, declaring that "there is no man in this Convention that holds a lesser quantity of this world's goods than the executive officers of your International organization," announced that the officers would refuse to accept the salary increase voted.

The convention approved participation in the CIO without dissent, rejecting a personal appeal by William Green that the UMW withdraw. It also endorsed Roosevelt for reelection, although Lewis, a lifelong Republican, pointed out that this did not constitute identification with the Democratic Party, but merely an alliance "with a virtuous statesman who is giving to the fullest degree of his great strength, his marvelous ability, and his brilliant courage to protect the common people of this country from continued exploitation."

On the wage front, the report of the international officers emphasized that new problems were being created by mechanization of the mines and by a North-South wage differential of 40 cents per day established in 1933. A commission appointed by the 1934 Appalachian Conference to investigate the North-South differential had dissolved without any accomplishment, and a similar committee established in 1935 had thus far failed to produce any results. With respect to mechanization, the convention was warned that the introduction of new machinery by well-financed producers was jeopardizing the competitive position of many of the less well favored operators, and the employment opportunities of miners as well. "The fundamental objective of the United Mine Workers' Organization for the solution of these very distressing problems lies directly in a system of proper Federal regulation, which will encompass a synchronized system of price fixing and allocation of tonnages on a basis equitably fair to mine workers and operators alike." [16] This objective was achieved, at least on paper, by the Coal Conservation Act of 1935, the purpose of which was to establish such minimum prices for coal as would yield a return for each district within a minimum price area equal to the weighted average of total unit costs of the tonnage of the area. The act also provided for a Bituminous Coal Labor Board with power to adjudicate labor disputes, to supervise elections, and to order collective bargaining. However, this legislation was declared unconstitutional by the United States Supreme Court on May 18, 1936, before it became operative, on the basis of its labor provisions.[17]

The conclusion of the 1936 Convention found Lewis firmly in the saddle. With the bituminous contract having an additional year to run, the only specific problems on the immediate horizon were the forthcoming anthracite negotiations, the persistence of the Progressive Mine Workers of America as a dual organization in Illinois, and the inability of the UMW to organize the mines in Harlan County, Kentucky. Despite the progress made since 1933, however, there were still many unresolved general social problems facing the union. One of these was emphasized in a letter written by Mrs. Franklin D. Roosevelt to the *United Mine Workers Journal:*

It seems to me that the wives of the working men should do all within their power to do away with what is ordinarily known as the company town and the company store. They should come together in a group and consult as to what they can do to help the community as a whole by realizing that their value as human beings is to develop their own personalities and make their own special contribution to society, and that children and grown people should be allowed to plan their own lives and do the things which give them satisfaction.[18]

The Anthracite Contract of 1936 and the Formation of District 50

Shortly after the conclusion of the 1936 Convention, negotiations for renewal of the anthracite contract commenced. This section of the coal mining industry was suffering from a drastic decline in production which had begun in 1927, due in large measure to the substitution of other fuels for anthracite. One of the consequences of the severe unemployment resulting from the production decrease was widespread "bootlegging" of coal, that is, illegal mining of coal by hand and sale below the commercial price. The precarious economic situation of the industry produced a strong desire for peaceful consummation of the negotiations on both sides.

The union demands included the establishment of a six-hour day with a substantial increase in wages; overtime rates at time and one half; the check off; and seniority in discharge and rehiring. The employers countered with a request for a wage decrease; UMW help in ending the "bootlegging" of coal; a clause providing penalties for work stoppages in violation of agreements; and a five-year contract, with interim wage adjustments. An agreement was reached on May 7, 1936, and on the whole, it represented a victory for the union. Up to May 1, 1937, rates of pay and hours of work were to remain unchanged. From May 1, 1937, to April 30, 1938, when the contract expired, the work day was to be reduced from 8 to 7 hours, and the work week from 6 to 5 days, with the same daily wage to be paid for 7 hours as had previously been paid for 8 hours. A check off was installed, limited to dues of $1 per month and a maximum of $2 annually in assessments. The operators agreed to equalize working time among collieries within specified localities in order to spread employment equitably.[19] Although the contract was to expire in April 1938, it was subsequently extended to April 30, 1939.

Later in the year, the UMW broadened its jurisdiction to include gas and coke workers by the creation of a new unit, District 50, which was destined to play an important role in the events of the next decade. The first convention of District 50 was held in Boston in August 1936, attended by 23 AFL federal locals with a claimed membership of 4000. These locals, first established in 1933, had formed successively the Massachusetts Council of Utility Workers, the New England Council of Utility Workers, and the National Council of Gas and By-Product Coke Workers, and turned to John L. Lewis when the AFL refused to grant them a national charter. By February 1937, District 50 claimed 15,000 members in the coke departments of a number of large utility companies.[20]

Harlan County

The only coal mining area of any importance which the UMW had not organized by 1937 was that located in Harlan County, Kentucky, containing one of the richest bituminous coal deposits in the world. With a population of about 65,000 people, depending almost entirely upon coal mining for their livelihood, Harlan County, or "Bloody Harlan," as it was popularly called, was an incredible enclave within a nation which had legislated collective bargaining as the first principle of labor relations. The coal operators there had decided that unionism would be stopped at its borders, and they used every means, including murder, to ensure the success of their plans.

The situation at the end of 1935, when the UMW launched an organizing drive, was well summarized by the La Follette Committee as follows:

Collective bargaining prevailed in the coal fields of Harlan County under the protection of the Federal labor policy during the World War. Following the World War, the unions were disrupted. In substitution of collective bargaining, corporations ruled their workers in Harlan County through the ruthless use of armed guards. In order to prevent workers from organizing, the company towns were policed by large bodies of armed men, privately paid, many of them clothed with public authority as deputies. A large number of them were seasoned criminals who had been released from the State penitentiary where they had been serving sentences for crimes involving homicides. These conditions lasted through the period of N.R.A. and the National Labor Relations Act up to very recent times.

There were within Harlan County 30 company towns, and only five incorporated towns, with 45,000 people living in the company towns. In almost all the company towns, all the houses belonged to the companies, and the miners were obliged to lease, with immediate eviction facing them in the event of discharge. In one town, that of the Harlan Wallins Coal Corporation, which the La Follette Committee found to be typical, independent merchants were not permitted to open shops, and the miners even risked discharge if they went outside the company property to do their marketing. This company also provided medical service to the miners, financed by a compulsory monthly check off from their wages; it "employed two doctors at a monthly retainer to provide its employees with necessary medical treatment, but did not pay them all the money it collected from the miners for medical service." [21] The "yellow dog" contract was in common use, so that any miner who joined a union thereby gave the companies a cause for discharge.

While the daily wages paid in Harlan were equal to those generally paid in contiguous areas, the hours of work were longer. Even more serious from the point of view of the miners was the fact that they were denied the right to employ their own checkweighmen, so that they had no means of ascertaining whether their output was being weighed fairly. Nor were they paid for time spent in preparatory timbering and in cleaning up, as was the custom in union mines.

The system of law enforcement prevailing in Harlan was a major element in the mechanism of operator control. The principal executive officer of the county was the high sheriff. From 1930 to 1934, the incumbent of this office had been John H. Blair, who was ousted in 1934 by Theodore R. Middleton, running on a reform platform with the support of the miners. Middleton, however, proved to be as partial to the operators as his predecessor had been, and apparently not without personal advantage. The La Follette Committee found that when he took office he had assets of $10,000, and despite the fact that his salary as sheriff was only $5000 a year, he had amassed a net worth of $102,000 during the first three years of his incumbency.[22]

The sheriff was empowered to deputize the mine guards appointed by the companies to police company towns. These deputies were armed, and were vested with full police power. "Except for the sheriff himself, located in Harlan town, the county seat, far removed from many of the mining camps, the citizens of Harlan county had no police protection except that afforded by the deputy sheriffs who were paid by their employers, the coal operators." Between January 1, 1934, and March 1, 1937, at least 369 men had been deputized by Middleton, of whom only a few were on the public payroll. Among the deputies, 37 had served sentences in the state reformatory:

4 had been sentenced for murder, 14 for manslaughter, 3 for malicious shooting with intent to kill, and the rest for burglary and robbery. In addition, 3 deputies were convicted federal felons, while 64 had been under indictment one or more times. Sheriff Middleton himself had served five months in a federal penitentiary for illegal sale of liquor.

It was also discovered that Daniel B. Smith, the commonwealth attorney in Harlan, was receiving a monthly retainer from several companies, and that the county judge, who had to approve the sheriff's selection of deputies, had numerous lucrative business connections with the coal operators. To sum up, in the words of the La Follette Committee:

A situation was thus created which made possible the surrender of the authority of the sheriff's office to individuals selected by the coal companies, by means of the power of the sheriff to appoint deputies. The consent of the county judge was assured, and complaisance of the commonwealth attorney, who might have checked abuses by the deputies through vigorous enforcement of the laws, was not beyond expectation.

The anti-union activities of the operators were coordinated by the Harlan County Coal Operators' Association, to which some 26 companies in the area belonged. The "general" of the campaign was a man with the peculiarly appropriate name of Ben Unthank, the field man of the association. The UMW had managed to secure a contract with the association in 1933, at the height of the NRA drive, but its organizers were effectively kept from contact with the miners in true Western "posse" style, and when the contract expired in 1935 and was not renewed, no trace of organization remained in the county. The methods employed were brought out vividly in a colloquy between Senator La Follette and one Bill C. Johnson, a gunman imported from West Virginia:

> Senator La Follette.   What do you mean by "thugging"? I do not understand that term.
>
> Mr. Johnson.   Out hunting for union men, organizers, etc., in Harlan County.
>
> Senator La Follette.   You mean hunting for them, in what way? Not as you would hunt deer.
>
> Mr. Johnson.   Well, I never did kill nobody — in Harlan County.
>
> Senator La Follette.   What did you mean when you said that you had been out with Jim Matt Johnson thugging and you told me that was hunting union men. Tell us some of your experience in that kind of work.

Mr. Johnson. What they said we would do, we would catch them and take them out and bump them off.

The enactment of the National Labor Relations Act in 1935 gave a fresh impetus to union organizing efforts. In July of that year, the UMW succeeded in renting an office in the town of Harlan. However, when a group of organizers was proceeding by car to occupy the office, it was met by Unthank and a group of deputies, and forced to turn back at gunpoint. Despite the despatch of the national guard by a sympathetic state governor on several occasions during the summer of 1935, the union drive was crushed by a series of outrages against organizers. To cap the climax, Elmon Middleton, the county attorney, who had been engaged in secret conversations with several citizens looking toward a genuine law enforcement policy, was assassinated on September 5, 1935, by a bomb attached to the starting pedal of his automobile.

Frustrated on the local level, the Miners' Union turned to a campaign of publicity to bring conditions in Harlan to national attention. Several false arrest suits were brought in the federal courts, but favorable verdicts were difficult to obtain. A new organizing drive was undertaken in January 1937, and once again the Coal Operators' Association mobilized its forces for action. On January 23, a hotel at which two UMW organizers were staying in the town of Harlan was dynamited and tear gassed, and their automobile completely wrecked.[23] On February 8, a group of UMW organizers proceeding to Harlan by car was ambushed, and one of their number seriously wounded. Three boys who had witnessed the shooting were hidden by their parents in fear of retaliation, but when they were brought under subpeona by the La Follette Committee, their father was shot and killed.[24] A UMW organizer named Musick left the county on the advice of friends who feared for his life, but the day after he left a volley of shots was fired into his home, and his small son was killed. Although a grand jury was empaneled to investigate the murder, no indictment was returned, in part because witnesses were intimidated and refused to testify. As an aftermath of this series of events, Hugh Taylor, a deputy sheriff who expressed some concern about these excesses, was shot and left for dead by two fellow deputies. Once more, the UMW was beaten back.

The victory of the Coal Operators' Association proved to be a short-lived one. The full force of the federal authority was mobilized on the side of the union, and it proved too strong for the companies. From March 22 to May 5, 1937, the La Follette Committee held hearings in Harlan which were widely publicized, and more than any other single event called public attention to the situation there. The decision of the U. S. Supreme Court upholding the constitutionality of the Wagner Act also had a marked effect on the operators. On May 16, 1937, two mass meetings were held in Harlan:

The scenes were in sharp contrast to those a year ago. Such assemblies would have brought on pitched battles with coal company deputies. The leaders probably would have been arrested for "criminal syndicalism." There might have been kidnapings, bombings, house-raiding without warrants. But Sunday the throng cheered union organizers, signed membership cards by the hundreds, drank beer, ate sandwiches, laughed at memories of nights of terror. . . . Governor A. B. Chandler announced a few days before the meeting that state police would take the place of company-paid sheriffs as peace officers in Harlan from now on. And at the meetings a squad of thirty-five officers were on hand — and there was no trouble.[25]

On September 27, 1937, 47 company officials and deputy sheriffs were indicted by a Federal grand jury for conspiracy to deprive their employees of their rights under the Wagner Act. An eleven-week trial ended with a deadlocked jury on August 1, 1938; Welly Hopkins, who subsequently became John L. Lewis' attorney, was one of the Department of Justice attorneys assigned to assist the prosecution. When the government announced that it would retry the case, the coal operators, many of them Northerners who did not relish the prospect of another long trial in the company of somewhat disreputable codefendants among the indicted deputies, capitulated. On August 19, 1938, they signed a contract with District 19 of the United Mine Workers of America, covering about 13,500 men, which was basically the same in content as the standard Appalachian agreement. In return, the union agreed to withdraw all charges against the operators. However, the conspiracy indictments were not dismissed, and they proved useful to the union when a year later, the operators once more showed signs of recalcitrance toward the unionization of their men.

The 1937 Wage Agreements

Unlike the situation that was to prevail in later years, negotiations for renewal of the Appalachian Agreement in 1937 proceeded smoothly and were consummated peacefully. The principal union demands were for a six-hour day, thirty-hour week; an increase of 50 cents in the daily rate; time-and-one-half pay for overtime; a paid vacation; and the creation of a joint commission to study the problems arising out of mechanization. The operators countered with a proposal to continue the existing scale, but with the proviso that the prevailing seven-hour day be lengthened to eight hours without any increase in pay. The position of the operators was clearly taken for bargaining purposes only, but one can only wonder at the moderation displayed by Lewis, then in the full flush of his victories over General Motors and United States Steel. Moreover, the negotiations took place before the 1937 recession set in, at a time when the demand for coal was increasing.

The new agreement incorporated the union demand for a wage increase of 50 cents a day, as well as time and one half for overtime. The basic daily wage thus became $6.00 in the northern fields and $5.60 in the South, compared with 1933 rates of $4.60 and $4.20, respectively. A Mechanized Mining Commission was established "to make a joint study of the problems arising from mechanization of bituminous coal production by the use of conveyors and mobile loading machines in the area covered by the Appalachian Joint Wage Agreement, including the problem of displacement of employes." Although the commission met several times, the union alleged that the operators were not cooperative, and no report was ever issued.

The anthracite agreement was due to expire April 30, 1938. However, as the union explained in a general circular to its members, the industry was in poor economic circumstances toward the close of 1937 because of the general depression and the increasing inroads of substitute fuels. The circular continued:

to be quite frank with our members we realized that the negotiations faced obstacles that caused concern and apprehension. In many sections of the region our organization is fighting to secure for our people the full benefits of the present contract. It seemed to us that under present conditions it would be very difficult to enter negotiations with any degree of hope for improvement over and above the provisions of the present contract. . . . To disturb the situation with long-drawn-out negotiations without much hope for progress, in our judgment, would be a policy fraught with great danger to ourselves, the industry and the communities, and would invite propaganda and publicity which would not be conducive to the extension of the markets or to the stability of the industry.[26]

Under the circumstances, the anthracite agreement of 1936 was extended for an additional year without change. The union also pointed out to its members that it was cooperating with the anthracite operators in attempts to eliminate a Canadian tariff on anthracite, to secure downward revision of freight rates for anthracite, and to have a federal tax levied on fuel oil, the principal competitor of anthracite.[27]

Among the other important events of 1937 was the enactment of the National Bituminous Coal Act, replacing the 1935 Guffey Act, which had been declared unconstitutional. The new act, like the old one, provided for minimum price-setting by a commission, but omitted the labor provisions of the 1935 law, which the Supreme Court had found objectionable. Because of procedural problems, the first price schedule was not promulgated until 1940, when the onset of the defense boom rendered minimum pricing of academic interest.[28]

The Convention of 1938

As in the preceding convention, the 1938 Convention was highlighted by an acrimonious debate over the issue of regional autonomy. A week before the opening of the convention, the *United Mine Workers Journal* carried a long article charging that the coal operators had hired agents from the Baldwin-Felts detective agency to foment autonomy demands in District 17, covering part of West Virginia. "Autonomy in West Virginia at the present time," the article continued, "would turn the whole organization of the United Mine Workers of America into the hands of certain labor-hating coal companies and their Baldwin-Felts thugs. Such a change would mean a return to the long hours, poverty wages and frightful working conditions that scourged the industry before the United Mine Workers of America rescued the miners and their families from those awful conditions."[29] The *Journal* warned that some local officers who had been selected as convention delegates were in reality Baldwin-Felts agents, an ominous warning for the protagonists of autonomy.

In their report to the convention, the officers made some concessions to the advocates of autonomy. They proposed that the International Executive Board be authorized at its discretion to grant "substantial" autonomy to any district, which would consist of the right to elect all district officials with the exception of the president and secretary-treasurer, who would continue to be appointed by the Executive Board. This plan was designed to reserve for Lewis "that small measure of advisory supervision that is conducive to the proper discharge of the obligations resting upon the International Organization."

The attack on the report from the floor was bitter, but less effective than in 1936. One delegate pointed out: "You are going to leave it up to your Executive Board. It has been that way before. Have they granted autonomy to any district? No." As before, the burden of defending the status quo fell upon Murray and Lewis. The former based his argument primarily upon the need for a coordinated wage structure among the districts:

Do you know — and I know you must — that if in any one particular district definite weakness makes itself manifest and the International Union does not possess the power to control that situation in some way, wages may be broken down, and that has an immediate and direct effect upon the competitive structure of the entire bituminous industry, because in giving consideration to the negotiation of a policy to govern the conduct of a Union, we must also give consideration to the economic factors surrounding the industry, so that we will be able to maintain throughout our lives a closer knit relationship between the districts and the International Union for the maintenance of our economic strength, for the maintenance of our wage rates, our conditions of employment, and our improved standards.

While Lewis was probably motivated in part by the desire to retain control of the central machinery of the UMW, this economic argument was a powerful one. In order to prevent a repetition of the disastrous regional competition of the nineteen-twenties, a single-wage scale was imperative. It was also necessary to keep the weaker districts from contracting below the national scale. Lewis was certain that he knew what was best for the miners, and he was not going to permit his plans to be disrupted in the name of the old concept of democratic district autonomy.

Lewis also argued that many of the men who aspired to district office were not possessed of sufficient training, and that it was logical to require them to serve a period of apprenticeship in subordinate posts. He also warned: "There are certain interests in this country that have undertaken in a subtle way to stir up this question. . . . There are also some political influences in certain districts who are interested in this proposition. Some men act as their agents. Others go along with the proposition who know nothing about it and of whom advantage is being taken."[30] The recommendation of the officers was adopted by a rising vote, although a considerable number of delegates asked to be recorded in favor of autonomy.

UMW membership at the time of the convention was reported to be 606,000.[31] The members were informed that from June 1, 1937 to November 30, 1937, the following major disbursements were made to aid the CIO:

Loan to the CIO	$650,000
CIO per capita tax	180,000
Loan to the SWOC	475,000
Loan to the TWOC	99,000
Donation to Labor's Non- Partisan League	30,000
Total	$1,434,000

Notwithstanding these large disbursements, the union's net resources on December 1, 1937, amounted to $2,535,000.

The convention enthusiastically approved Lewis' policy with respect to the CIO. Lewis justified the continued expenditure of miners' funds for organizing other industries on the ground of self-interest. He argued that peaceful collective bargaining would not have prevailed in the 1937 coal negotiations had not the CIO carried on successful organizing campaigns in steel and automobiles: "the organization of these workers in America's basic industry has been an insurance policy for every man here and for every member of our organization." The Executive Board was directed to try William Green, who was still a member of the UMW, on charges of acting against the interests of the organization, after bitter personal attacks had been made upon him by Lewis and Van Bittner. Green avoided a trial by resigning from the Mine Workers Union.

A constitutional amendment, adopted almost without debate, barred members of the Communist Party from membership in the UAW, and provided for immediate expulsion from the union of any person who joined the Communist Party.[32] This action stood in marked contrast to Lewis' attitude toward the communists outside his own union. To charges that the CIO employed communist organizers, he replied: "I do not turn my organizers or CIO members upside down and shake them to see what kind of literature falls out of their pockets." And in regard to communist trade union members, he declared: "If they are good enough for industry to hire, they're good enough for us to organize." [33] Outside the UMW, particularly in staff CIO positions, the communists offered no real challenge to Lewis, but it would have been another matter had they been able to infiltrate the Miners' Union, the very seat of his power, and build upon the latent dissatisfaction with Lewis' leadership that existed in many districts.

The Progressive Mine Workers[34]

The only organization of coal miners that was able to survive beside the United Mine Workers during the latter half of the nineteen-thirties was the Progressive Mine Workers of America. This union was a thorn in Lewis' side, and its existence was in good measure responsible for Lewis' emphasis upon the goal of strong union security clauses for the UMW.

The PMWA arose as a consequence of dissidence among the members of District 12 of the UMW, covering the state of Illinois. The miners there were bitterly opposed to Lewis' acceptance of a wage cut in 1928, and when in 1932 Lewis forced upon them an additional wage cut, a considerable number seceded and formed the rival organization. Lewis, it may be added, set up a provisional government for District 12 in 1933.

Relations between the two unions were exceedingly bitter; indeed, it is doubtful whether one can find in the annals of American trade unionism an instance of rivalry in which hatreds were more intense and competition more ruthless.

The hostility between the two groups of miners became so great that neither the government nor the individual was able effectively to guard persons and property against harm, and the interunion conflict therefore took place in an environment of fatal shootings and frequent bombings. By 1932, carrying arms had become such a usual custom in some villages that at least one company had put up a so-called "gun board" where miners could place their guns before going below the surface. Being armed resulted in the unpremeditated killing of many persons in the mining communities during the years of the unions' most bitter hostility; to what extent it encouraged deliberate murder is almost impossible to assess. Very few of the deaths were followed by conviction of an alleged slayer.[35]

With the growing powers of the UMW, the operators of Illinois generally preferred to deal with that organization. The PMWA on numerous occasions resorted to intimidation of the operators by bombing their property. In 1937, 36 Progressives were convicted in a federal court of interfering with the mails, the prosecution having listed 45 instances of destruction of property. Each convicted man was sentenced to four years' imprisonment and fined $20,000, a sentence which added further to the embitterment of the PMWA men, who charged that UMW miners engaging in similar acts remained unmolested by the government.

Until 1937, the Progressive Mine Workers Union was confined to Illinois. At that time, however, the Progressives applied to the American Federation of Labor for a charter. The Executive Council of the AFL, which was anxious to retaliate against Lewis for his role in the CIO, voted to give the Progressives a certificate of affiliation over the objections of Victor Olander of the Illinois State Federation of Labor, who charged that the PMWA contained many radicals who had been engaged in systematic vilification of the AFL, and had caused trouble and bloodshed in the state. When the certificate of affiliation was granted, the UMW had not yet been expelled from the AFL. At the time of affiliation, the PMWA claimed 35,000 members.[36]

In 1938, after the expulsion of the UMW, the Progressive Mine Workers received an AFL charter as a full-fledged international union, with jurisdiction over all coal mine workers. However, the AFL assumed the authority to appoint temporary officers for its new affiliate, an authority which it never relinquished so long as the PMWA remained affiliated with it. A campaign of expansion was undertaken; the Executive Council, in August 1938, authorized the expenditure of $50,000 to assist the Progressive Miners in organizational work.[37] "The American Federation of Labor . . . was willing to help the Progressives extend their control because it saw in such a campaign a means of shaking Lewis's monopoly. To what extent the AFL looked upon the expansion of the PMWA to replace in part dues-paying members, recently lost to the CIO, is difficult to appraise. The fact that the Federation did not devote any effort to organizing miners who were employed in nonunion mines suggests that its primary interest was in reducing the power of the UMWA rather than in extending help to the unorganized."[38]

The Progressives moved first into West Virginia and Kansas. Organizational progress proved to be slow, in the face of fierce UMW resistance. Joe Ozanic, the president of the PMWA, complained to the AFL convention that his organizers had been severely beaten and his meetings broken up by UMW men. President Green of the AFL decried the "story of violence, of assault, of attack, not made by employed operators' thugs, gunmen and the authorities of a commonwealth, but by men employed by a labor union — thugs, assaulters, mob rule, beating up our men, causing us to pay hospital bills, attacking them nigh unto death. . . ."[39] In West Virginia, as in Kansas, the Progressives were able to establish a few locals, but they found themselves unable to secure collective bargaining rights. On June 11, 1938, they petitioned the NLRB for an election at the Alston Coal Company, of Pittsburgh, Kansas, as a test case. The company belonged to the Southwestern Inter-State Coal Operators Association, which was under contract with the UMW, and urged the NLRB not to separate out its Alston mines as a unit for purposes of collective bargaining. Thirteen months after the election petition was filed, the NLRB ruled that on the basis of past industrial practice, the operators' association was the appropriate bargaining unit.[40] This decision represented a crushing blow for the PMWA. According to Hudson:

In effect the Board's decision meant that a small union would have great difficulty in becoming strong enough to displace a well-established labor organization. Although all the men working for a company might wish to change their affiliation, they would be able to obtain the Board's approval for such a move only if they had won over to their side the majority of the men employed in the area controlled by the given operators' association. . . .

The Alston decision deprived the Progressive Mine Workers of America of protection through the representation election until such time as the new union would become the organization preferred by the majority of miners employed throughout an entire employers' association. This feat was unlikely in any district where the UMWA held a closed-shop contract.[41]

A similar fate befell the Progressives in their efforts to invade other areas. While the La Follette Committee was holding hearings in Harlan County, Progressive organizers were sent in to attempt to strike before the bargaining situation had crystallized. However, when the Harlan County Coal Operators Association signed a contract with the United Mine Workers and became a member of the Appalachian Wage Conference, the PMWA was once more frozen out under the Alston unit rule of the NLRB. In Western Kentucky, the Progressives took over the Independent Miners Union, a small organization of 3500 men, only to have the NLRB rule that the IMU had been a company-dominated union and therefore ineligible to bargain for the miners. In the anthracite fields of Pennsylvania, after a promising start, the PMWA again ran into the unit rule of the NLRB, although here the operators had not organized themselves into a formal association, but merely bargained as a group.[42]

Ozanic told the 1939 AFL Convention that during the first eight months of 1939, the PMWA had enlisted 85,000 mine workers into its ranks, 54,000 of them in the Appalachian fields, but had proved unable to make any headway in securing representation rights in the face of existing UMW contracts.[43] At every turn, the Progressives were frustrated by their rival, which had the advantage of vastly superior numbers and the support of government and operators. It was clear by 1941 that the Progressives were destined to remain at the most a small organization confined to its original stronghold of Illinois. Economically, its role was that of a follower rather than a leader; "There is no substantial evidence that the existence of the PMWA as a rival union has modified the wages or conditions of work provided in the contracts negotiated by the UMWA. . . . The PMWA has followed closely the standards set by the UMWA. It is not in a position to function independently in collective bargaining." Its reported membership at the end of 1941 was only 17,000.[44]

The 1939 Bituminous Strike

The 1939 Appalachian wage negotiations marked the beginning of a new epoch in Lewis' collective bargaining tactics. Prior to this year he had shown a considerable degree of circumspection in his dealings with the operators, either because of organizational weakness or unfavorable economic conditions. He had displayed sufficient flexibility in negotiation to avert the possibiltiy of all-out economic warfare.

But beginning in 1939, Lewis demonstrated that he had both the will and the means to attain whatever objectives he regarded as crucial. The National Industrial Recovery Act and the National Labor Relations Act had enabled him first to build and then to secure his union. By 1939, he was no longer dependent upon government, and was even prepared to defy it if it suited his purpose. Somewhere between 1935 and 1939, there was a basic change in the relationship between employer and union in coal mining, a change that was to produce a state of national alarm with the onset of the biennial negotiating period.

The union demands presented to the bituminous operators in March 1939, were characterized by the union itself as the most comprehensive document of its kind ever prepared by the organization. The basic points were: a standard six-hour day; an increase of 50 cents a day in wage rates; double time for Sundays and holidays; a guarantee of 200 working days a year; vacations with pay; establishment of seniority rights; an improved hospitalization plan, and additional miscellaneous provisions. The operators replied with an adamant refusal to raise wages, pointing to the net losses being sustained by the industry and the increasing competition from other fuels. The year 1938 had indeed been a bad one for the industry; bituminous coal output had declined to 348,500,000 tons, the lowest quantity since 1933, and a drop of 22 per cent from 1937. The union representatives later reported that "it soon became evident that it would be impossible to obtain any concessions which would add to the cost of production. Ever since the beginning of the year general business conditions had been slumping, which militated against any increases of prices."

Lewis then decided to salvage what he could out of the negotiations in the form of concessions which would not involve the operators in additional outlays. On the day the old agreement was to expire, March 31, he demanded either that the operators sign union shop agreements with the UMW, or that they consent to the elimination of the so-called penalty clauses in district agreements. The penalty clause was simply a stipulation whereby the employer was authorized by contract to fine, suspend, or discharge a worker for unauthorized strikes; elimination of this clause would enable the UMW workers at any mine to walk off the job with impunity in the event that nonunion men were hired, and was thus tantamount to the union shop. Demands for union security had been raised repeatedly during past negotiations, and the operators assumed that, as in the past, they would be dropped in the final analysis. Indeed, the original proposal of the UMW negotiating committee had been very vague with respect to this particular demand. Only after the contract had expired did the operators become aware of the fact that this time, Lewis was in earnest.

Lewis' motives are not difficult to appraise. In the first place, as already noted, economic concessions were out of the question, and he was determined not to go back empty-handed to his constituents. Secondly, the American Federation of Labor had but recently taken over the Progressive Mine Workers, and was attempting to build it into a rival to the UMW on a national basis. On this score, the 1940 UMW convention was told by its officers:

The American Federation of Labor, through the Progressive Miners and various craft organizations, was actively attempting to sabotage the United Mine Workers of America. Organizers had been sent into the mining fields, and in some places they were being aided and abetted by unfriendly operating interests. The Scale Committee came to the conclusion that the United Mine Workers of America had to be preserved at all costs, and that the union should resist to the utmost attempts to undermine and destroy it by either the American Federation of Labor or non-union interests. Elimination of the penalty clauses from district agreements would enable the members of the United Mine Workers to protect themselves against raiding expeditions, by the simple expedient of refusing to work with non-union or anti-union men.[45]

Upon refusal of the operators to agree to the union security clause, the Appalachian mines were shut down on April 3, the first working day after the expiration of the old agreement. The outlying districts, which were not party to the Appalachian Conference, were permitted to remain in operation at first.[46] The month of April passed with the parties remaining deadlocked; the operators declined "to act as recruiting sergeants to conscript for life all the mine workers of the Appalachian territory into Mr. Lewis's C.I.O. army for his war against Mr. Green of the A.F. of L." [47] In order to increase the pressure for a settlement, 130,000 miners in the outlying districts were called out, and by May 3, the entire bituminous coal industry was shut down.

As in most coal disputes, the initial impact of the strike was not great because of the available stockpiles of coal. But as the weeks wore on and stocks were consumed, manufacturing establishments were forced to close down and difficult situations prevailed in some of the large Eastern cities. John R. Steelman, director of the United States Conciliation Service, had met with the negotiators to no avail.[48] On May 5, President Roosevelt addressed a letter to the Joint Conference urging that negotiations be continued, and that a speedy settlement was vital to the public interest. A meeting was held the next day without result, and on May 7, Lewis addressed a letter to Roosevelt, in which he pointed out that the union had suggested that work be resumed pending a settlement (with retroactivity), but that the operators refused. He continued:

Failure of the Roosevelt Administration to approve or sustain the Mine Workers' offers to keep the industry in operation caused many coal operators to believe that they had carte blanche from the Government to disembowel the Mine Workers' Union if they could. In consequence, your Department must accept responsibility for its own administrative blunder.[49]

Lewis charged further that a majority of the operators were willing to sign a union shop contract, but that a minority representing from 20 to 30 per cent of the tonnage was blocking a settlement. Whatever the exact percentage, it seems clear that the northern operators were prepared to grant the union's demand, but that the southern operators were adamantly opposed.[50] Lewis informed Roosevelt that unemployment compensation payments were being withheld from the miners in Pennsylvania, Ohio, West Virginia, and Kentucky, "while Governmental authorities in Washington having to do with such matters are demonstrating a supine attitude or a lackadaisical interest. In the meantime, credit in the coal fields is being stopped, and women and children are deprived of dietary necessities. The implications of this situation are obvious when one considers the political control of the four states in question." [51]

This strike by no means marked the beginning of the break between Roosevelt and Lewis, but it served to widen an already existing rift. Lewis had supported Roosevelt wholeheartedly in the 1936 presidential election, and was nettled when the President refused to come out flatly for the union in the General Motors strike of 1937. Alinsky quotes Lewis as saying: "It was during the winter of 1937, when we were gripped in our fatal conflict with the Corporation of General Motors, that I discovered the depths of deceit, the rank dishonesty, and the doublecrossing character of Franklin Delano Roosevelt." [52] The differences between the two men were allayed temporarily in 1938, when the Mine Workers helped finance the attempted Roosevelt "purge" in the congressional elections, so that Lewis undoubtedly felt himself twice betrayed when the administration failed to come to his immediate support in the 1939 strike.

Nevertheless, the weight of the federal government was slowly but inexorably thrown in against the operators, and in the end proved decisive. On May 8, Secretary of Labor Perkins appeared in New York to urge resumption of negotiations, and the next day the conferees journeyed to Washington to meet with President Roosevelt, who told them that he wanted an agreement by May 10. On the evening of that day, when it was clear that neither side was prepared to yield, Steelman summoned the negotiating subcommittee, and in the name of the federal government, requested those operators who were in agreement with the union to sign contracts and begin operation immediately. What this meant, in effect, was that the government was urging a split in the ranks of the operators. There was considerable indignation among the latter; ". . . privately operators expressed resentment of what they characterized as 'the heat' put upon them by the government by coming forward with a proposal which, in substance, threatened the break-up of the Appalachian conference." [53] However, the statement had the desired effect. The next day sixteen operators' associations voted to grant the UMW a union shop, and their employees, as well as the miners in the outlying fields, returned to work. As one operator put it, "We might hold out against John L. Lewis . . . but we can't hold out against both Lewis and President Roosevelt." [54]

Six southern operators' associations refused to go along, and withdrew from the conference. However, they could not hold their ranks firm, and when individual Southern operators began to sign with the union, they bowed to the inevitable. The only holdout was the Harlan County Coal Operators' Association, which announced its intention of operating on a nonunion basis. Governor Chandler of Kentucky backed them up by calling out the state militia to protect men willing to go back to work under those conditions, an action for which he was bitterly denounced by the UMW. [55] The union claimed that only 20 per cent of the Harlan miners returned to work. Considerable violence ensued, this time between the National Guard and union supporters, and during the following months, 300 strikers were arrested for violations of law. Perhaps not altogether coincidentally, the Department of Justice sent special agents into Harlan to prepare for the retrial of the conspiracy indictments which had ended in a mistrial the previous year. On July 19, the Harlan operators finally made their peace with the union, although their agreement took the form of elimination of the penalty clause rather than outright grant of the union shop. Two months later, the indictments against them were dismissed. The United Mine Workers could now boast:

No longer will members of the United Mine Workers of America be required to work with scabs or with any other non-union miners. Those days are gone forever. From now on a union mine will be in fact a union mine. An employer may hire whomsoever he pleases to work in his mine, but if the new employe is not already a member he must join the United Mine Workers of America. The new agreement makes it impossible for any rival organization to obtain a foot-hold in the bituminous mining industry of the country. . . ."[56]

After the conclusion of the bituminous agreement, the anthracite nego-tiations, which had been postponed, were consummated on much the same basis: continuation of the existing agreement plus the union shop. The anthracite industry was engaged at the time in a devastating price war, which made it difficult for the union to obtain any economic concessions. The union took the lead in urging price stabilization upon the industry "to insure payment of wages provided under the agreement, to maintain work-ing conditions provided thereunder, and give the operating interests a reasonable return on their investments and management."[57] The alterna-tive to voluntary action, the union warned, was government regulation of the kind already provided for bituminous coal.

The 1940 Convention

As usual, the subject of district autonomy provided the occasion for the most ardent debate at the next biennial convention of the United Mine Workers. Between 1938 and 1940, provisional autonomy had been restored to Districts 2 and 6, that is, they were permitted to elect all officers except the president and secretary-treasurer. Delegates from Illinois, District 12, were particularly insistent that they be granted their autonomy as well. One of them complained:

Our membership feels we should have autonomy restored to the District. We were given to understand some time here last summer that a committee would come through Illinois investigating conditions in that state, as to whether or not we were to be given autonomy. That committee came through West Frankfort, Ill., one morning and there were fourteen local unions represented at the sub-district office, with fourteen men. The men called it the "Whirligig Committee"; the committee came in one door and out the other, and we were never given a chance to voice our opinion on autonomy in District 12. We are here today to fight for that end, for we believe it will be to the best interests of the United Mine Workers of America in District 12, and that will be the only way that the banner of the United Mine Workers of America will ever fly over all the mines in the state of Illinois.

Ray Edmundson, the appointed president of District 12, countered by charging that many of the advocates of autonomy were in the pay of the Progressive Mine Workers, and asserted that District 12 should not get its autonomy until the Progressives were eliminated. Lewis closed the debate with the argument, now familiar to all the delegates, that districts could have their autonomy only when they demonstrated their ability to support themselves financially. "That's all there is to it. It is a business proposition." The convention voted, by a large majority, to continue the policy adopted at the previous convention, namely, to leave to the discretion of the international executive board the extension of autonomy to additional districts.

During the course of the convention, a nationwide radio broadcast was arranged to celebrate the fiftieth anniversary of the United Mine Workers. While Lewis was speaking, someone in the balcony of the convention hall unfurled a communist flag. When the broadcast was over, Lewis delivered himself of the following remarks on communism:

You know there are no Communists in the United Mine Workers of America. There is a clause in the constitution of the United Mine Workers of America that is predicated upon the principle that no man can serve two flags or two masters, and if a man is a Communist and is a servant of a foreign power, he cannot be an American or a member of the United Mine Workers of America.

The interesting thing about this statement is that at the time, Lewis was working in close collaboration with communists or fellow travelers at the national CIO level. He was, like them, an ardent isolationist, and joined with them in opposing the growing interventionist wing of the CIO led by Sidney Hillman.

Membership in the UMW in January 1940, was put at 600,000, and its net resources at $2,500,000. While subsidies to the CIO had been reduced, the 1939 strike imposed heavy burdens on the UMW treasury. A special one-dollar assessment was levied in 1938, and again for the months of December 1939, and January 1940. This practice aroused some opposition among the membership, and a resolution was introduced which would have imposed the requirement of a referendum vote for assessments. Although defeated, it resulted, in conjunction with events of the ensuing year, in a change in the manner in which assessments could be levied.

Since 1940 was a presidential election year, politics were never far from the minds of the convention delegates. On January 24, Lewis startled them with an attack upon the Democratic Party which presaged his final break with Roosevelt. He accused the Administration of failing to give labor representation in the cabinet or in administrative agencies; of not seeking the advice of labor on domestic or international issues; and of permitting the Democratic leadership of Congress to defame labor without rebuke. He then made the following prediction:

I am one who believes that President Roosevelt will not be a candidate for reelection. Conceding that the Democratic National Convention could be coerced or dragooned into renominating him, I am convinced that, with the conditions now confronting the nation and the dissatisfaction now permeating the minds of the people, his candidacy would result in ignominious defeat.

A few days later, the committee on resolutions urged the convention to dispose of the question of UMW political support by referring it to the international executive board for such action as the board might deem appropriate, in the face of 72 local union resolutions favoring support of Roosevelt for a third term. It is doubtful whether Lewis had ever before espoused a policy so antithetical to the views of his rank and file, and strenuous objections were raised from the floor. A delegate said:

I am wholeheartedly in agreement with the resolution as read, providing, of course, that the inference as left by the newspapers throughout these United States is removed, that we have broken personally with President Roosevelt. I do not believe in my own heart that the resolution is aimed at Roosevelt himself. I believe it is aimed at the people who have gone into the legislative branches of office, who have been hanging on his coattails over a period of seven years and have been giving him the double cross and giving labor the double cross.

Delegate Hosey from District 17 declared simply: "For my personal part I would say that President Roosevelt is Ed Hosey's man and always will be." Delegate Murray, also from District 17 (not Philip Murray), also defied Lewis, stating: "American history shows that Mr. Roosevelt has been the greatest friend of organized labor and unorganized labor of any man who has ever sat in the White House. While he is not a member of our organization he has done as much for us as any man in the United States today." Delegate Reano, from District 12, commented: "The way my boys feel back home, to go down to defeat — and mind you, I say we won't have Roosevelt for a third term — but to go down to ignominious defeat with Roosevelt would be dying the death of a martyr for organized labor." Delegate Crawford from District 5 asked the convention to remember the attitude of the Republican administration of Pennsylvania toward striking miners in the strikes of 1927, 1930, and 1931, and warned: "I hate to make this statement, because I believe in this organization, but I say that if President Roosevelt runs and our Executive Board picks somebody else, then I have to make a split and our local union will go down the line for President Roosevelt." Delegate Davison, from District 11, put the dilemma of the union in a nutshell, when he said: "In our local union there are two things that we all stand for. One is John L. Lewis; the other is Franklin Delano Roosevelt." Despite what subsequent events proved to be the greatly predominant sentiment among the coal miners, the Lewis machine ensured adoption of the resolutions committee recommendation by what was described as an "overwhelming majority." [58] Philip Murray, who was still vice-president of the UMW, remained conspicuously silent during the debate.

The story of Lewis' break with Roosevelt and his advocacy of the election of Wendell Willkie is not properly part of the story of the miners, and is treated elsewhere in this volume.[59] Suffice it to say here that on October 25, 1940, Lewis urged his constituents to vote for Willkie, and promised to retire from the presidency of the CIO if Roosevelt were elected. He accused the Democratic Party not only of betraying labor, but also of leading the nation toward war.[60] However, on election day the miners cast their votes for Roosevelt. In the words of an experienced observer: "They would trust John Lewis's judgment in a wage negotiation or a strike situation. They would not follow his political vagaries." [61]

The Bituminous Coal Strike of 1941

The strike of 1939, and the ensuing settlement through the good offices of the federal government, proved but a pallid prelude to the events of 1941. In the course of the disputes which took place in that year, Lewis addressed correspondence to the president of the United States more vitriolic and disrespectful in tone than any labor leader before or since has used in addressing the nation's chief executive. He utilized effectively the national emergency, which created an urgent need for coal, but in the course of so doing, created a wave of public antipathy not only toward his own organization, but toward the entire labor movement, which canceled in large measure the sympathy that had been built up in consequence of a decade of employer excesses in dealing with trade unions.

The 1941 bituminous coal negotiations opened against a background of mounting world crisis. The United States was just beginning to arm itself in earnest against an ever more imminent German threat to its security, and could ill afford interruption in the supply of one of the most vital sinews of war, coal. This time, the principal real demand which Lewis brought to the bargaining table was economic, an increase of $1 a day in the basic rate. The prevailing day rate was $6, so that the increase requested was almost 17 per cent. Other demands included double time for Sundays and holidays; two weeks of vacation pay; seniority; the right to appoint a worker safety committee at each mine; and the installation of mourning periods throughout the entire industry after mine disasters during which no work would be performed, as a means of forcing the enactment of federal safety laws.[62]

There was one additional demand which was destined to become the principal obstacle to settlement: elimination of the existing wage differential of 40 cents per day in favor of the southern mines. This had long been an objective of UMW policy, but not until 1941 were conditions sufficiently favorable for the union to risk a fight for its achievement. The southern operators might be expected to offer fierce resistance, for 40 cents a day amounted to 3.6 cents per ton, and firms in the industry usually operated on profit margins of from 2 to 3 cents per ton.[63]

As the April 1 strike deadline approached with the parties deadlocked, the union proposed that work continue without interruption, provided that any future settlement be retroactive to April 1, but the operators refused on the ground that they could not do business with a contingent wage liability of unknown magnitude hanging over their heads. According to the union, agreement was near on March 28, but was forestalled by the receipt of a letter from William S. Knudsen, director of the Office of Production Management, which insisted that if no agreement were reached by March 31, production would have to continue nevertheless. Lewis charged that the letter made no mention of a retroactive wage clause, and thus stiffened the resistance of the operators, who felt that the government would prevent a strike even in the absence of such a clause.[64] On March 29, conciliation director John R. Steelman intervened on behalf of the government, but despite continuous day and night negotiations, no agreement could be reached, and on April 1 the strike began, on schedule.

This time, the government did not wait a month before putting pressure on the parties to settle. On April 5, Steelman publicly urged that work be resumed on the basis of a retroactive clause. The northern operators agreed, but the southern operators refused. The UMW demand for regional wage equalization had driven a wedge between the two groups, and thenceforth they operated at cross purposes. The northern operators offered the union a 10 per cent wage increase, on condition that the North-South differential be eliminated. The southern operators countered with an offer of 11 per cent, but with the condition that the differential be retained. They charged publicly:

The deal which the Northern operators seek to make with the United Mine Workers means that the wage of the Northern mines will be increased by 16⅔% and at the same time the wage in the Southern mines will be increased from 25 to 33⅓%. . . . This wage increase proposal is only another step in the effort of the Northern mine operators which has continued for twenty-five years to steadily restrict the markets of the Southern mines through progressive increases in the freight rate differentials against the Southern areas.[65]

The United Mine Workers, having started the fight between North and South, stepped to the side and encouraged the operators to battle it out. On April 11, the southern operators formally withdrew from the Appalachian Conference, formed their own Southern Coal Operators' Wage Conference, and requested that their case be certified to the National Defense Mediation Board. A few hours after the announcement of this action, Lewis and O'Neill held a joint press conference, at which the latter made the following statement, on behalf of the northern operators:

Despite assertions to the contrary and out of the knowledge of experience with conferences of this character, I charge that this conference is being sabotaged by several well-known Southern coal operators in order that they may retain in its whole great amount the differentials in wages and other considerations that they now have in their favor as against the Northern coal producers.

All that the proposal of the conference did to those differentials was to change a day's wage rate in the South to the same amount as that paid in the North. This differential amounted to 40 cents and on tonnage basis amounted to only 3.34 cents per ton.

We regret the withdrawal of the Southern operators at the behest of several gentlemen among their number who seek to destroy the Appalachian Wage Conference. These men, now as ever, have continued to make trouble for the industry and the country. . . .

The south refuses to recognize the principle in this small contribution to pay the same amount in wages as their competitors do. They also claim they were opposed to the elimination of the so-called "rejects" clause, a device by which men's weight of coal loaded each day is discounted by the so-called removal of impurities. In the north men are paid for the production they load. This ancient device to cheat workers of their earnings was abolished in the northern mines, in its last stand, twenty-seven years ago.

The Northern Coal Operators' position is that they will pay the same rates per day as their southern competitors, and not one cent more. They ask that the rejects clause be made universal in its application, or eliminated entirely from the industry. The Northern operators agree with the United Mine Workers that their plan was right; it was an evil practice that should be abolished from the mining industry, and that it is no more than a device to cheat.[66]

Lewis, for his part, complained that the union was caught between the upper and nether millstones, and said there could be no agreement "while these Northern economic carpetbaggers who call themselves Southern coal operators are holding up the coal industry and the nation by the thumbs." However, he was not willing to relieve the pressure on the nation's thumbs by permitting the northern mines to open, a step which was formally requested by the Secretary of Labor, for his trump card was precisely the developing shortage of coal. The southern operators retreated from New York, the scene of the Appalachian Conference, to Washington, where they induced a group of southern members of Congress to plead their case with the White House. In the North, an agreement was reached on April 17, but its effectuation was made contingent upon conclusion of an agreement with the southern operators as well.

On April 21, President Roosevelt, in the interests of the maintenance of defense production, publicly recommended the following solution:

1. The miners and operators already in agreement resume coal production under the terms of that agreement.

2. The operators and miners who have not yet reached an agreement enter into wage negotiations and at the same time reopen the mines, the agreement ultimately reached to be made retroactive to the date of resuming work.[67]

The next day, a committee of the southern operators returned to New York, and met with the union, after having attempted in vain to see President Roosevelt. Their stay proved to be a short-lived one, and upon learning that the northern operators and the union had agreed to the president's proposal, they returned to Washington.

The next step was certification of the dispute to the National Defense Mediation Board, which appointed a panel to hear the case. The members of the panel were William H. Davis, chairman; Walter C. Teagle, of the Standard Oil Company of New Jersey; and Clinton S. Golden, of the Steel Workers' Organizing Committee. After three days of meetings, the southern operators offered to raise wages by $1 a day, but refused to accede to elimination of the 40-cent differential or the controversial "rejects" clause.[68] The board panel then announced that it was recommending to the parties acceptance of the president's proposals of April 21, and in effect washed its hands of the matter.

Initiative toward a settlement now came from the Congress, a number of the members of which expressed themselves vigorously on the need for legislation in the event that the parties could not agree soon. A special Senate defense investigating committee, headed by Senator Harry Truman, called the parties to meet for a hearing on April 28. At the hearing, O'Neill again placed the blame for the stoppage on the southern operators, the spokesman for whom acknowledged that the dispute was fundamentally one between the northern and southern operators. Lewis, enjoying himself hugely, when asked to identify himself for the record, drawled: "The name is Lewis — J. L.," and continued:

This is a case where the tail of the industry is undertaking vigorously to wag the dog. The tail in this instance is those northern interests which call themselves southern operators. We have agreed with every suggestion made by every agency of government. We are not to blame for this situation. We have negotiated an agreement acceptable to 70 per cent of the coal operators of America.[69]

After the hearings had adjourned for the day, the southern operators were summoned to the office of Jesse Jones, secretary of commerce, and were urged to accept the president's formula, which they finally consented to do late the same night. Thus on April 29 and 30, temporary agreements were signed separately with the northern and southern operators and the miners returned to work, with the basic issue still remaining unsettled. After several weeks of further futile negotiation, the National Defense Mediation Board was obliged to intervene once more to prevent a new walkout. New hearings were held, in the course of which Lewis delivered the following warning:

when the southern districts departed from the Appalachian Joint Conference they placed themselves voluntarily in the category of being outlying districts and they forfeited their right to influence the conclusions of the decisions of the Appalachian conference. . . . Every outlying district outside of this Appalachian area, as our industry knows and understands, is obligated, in order to maintain the balance of competitive integrity of the industry in its relationships to apply the wage advances and improved conditions that are negotiated in this base conference. And so I say to this conference and to the public and to the southern operators if they be listening that if they expect to operate their mines in 1941 under an agreement of the United Mine Workers of America they are going to operate their mines under a contract that contains every one of those provisions reported to this conference by my distinguished friend, Mr. O'Neill.

Now the great drama is drawing to a close. The negotiating representatives of the southern operators are daily growing more and more weary. Their feet drag a little more each day as they come to the conference and their mental processes are a little slower each day, and they repeat the same thing in their unending persistence in their deadly monotone, and with a little less energy each day, and in the fullness of time and before very long the southern operators will execute a contract. . . .[70]

On June 5, 1941, the NDMB made public a proposed settlement between the UMW and the southern operators which essentially gave the union what it had asked. On June 19, the northern operators signed a formal contract with the union, and finally, on July 5, the southern operators fell in line and agreed to the same terms, except for a few minor points. Under the new agreement, the basic inside day labor rate became $7, for North and South alike; the "reject" clause was eliminated from southern contracts; and seniority reemployment rights were given to men displaced by technological change. The outcome represented a complete victory for Lewis and the Miners' Union; the basic original goals had been achieved.

While the bituminous negotiations were in session, Lewis took time out to negotiate a new contract with the anthracite producers. He presented to them the same demand for a $1-a-day wage increase, plus 23 additional demands, including vacation pay, time and one half for overtime, and double time for Sundays and holidays. The anthracite conference was in session for six weeks, during which the anthracite mines were operating only two days a week, despite the concurrent bituminous strike, for lack of orders. Despite the union's own admission of the poor economic circumstances of the industry, it persisted in its demands, arguing that the growing oil shortage would cause conversion of households from oil to anthracite. After a one-day strike, the operators agreed to an increase of 7½ per cent to September 30, 1941, and of 10 per cent from the latter date to the expiration of the contract, which meant about 60 cents a day more on a daily basis.[71] This represented the industry's first general wage increase in 18 years.

Before embarking upon his next dispute with coal operators, Lewis gave his attention to several internal union problems. One of them concerned District 50, which, after a promising start, had stabilized at 25,000 members. In August 1941, its officers were removed, and new ones installed: Ora Gasaway, a trusted Lewis lieutenant, became president; Kathryn Lewis, the daughter of John L., was made secretary-treasurer; and Michael Widman became director of organization. All UMW organizers who had been lent to the CIO or its affiliates were withdrawn and assigned to the staff of District 50. Amidst considerable fanfare, an organizing drive was undertaken. The phase of the drive which received the most publicity was that undertaken among dairy farmers, who were placed into a United Dairy Farmers' Division of District 50.

Lewis also faced, in the fall of 1941, an unusual event in the recent history of his organization, an outlaw strike. Early in September 1941, representatives of 38 of the 42 anthracite locals in the Hazleton, Pa., area (District 7), met and invited the 20,000 miners of the district to stop work in protest against an assessment of 50 cents per member per month levied beginning July 1941, for the purpose of building up a strike fund. This assessment had been submitted to a referendum, and carried by a vote of 152,000 to 87,000, but 7 districts recorded majorities against it, including the anthracite districts.[72] In all, the maximum number of workers out on strike at any one time appears to have been only 7000. Lewis appeared at a meeting of the insurgents at Hazleton, but was booed when he asked the men to return to work. Three representatives of the UMW who appeared at a public meeting at Coaldale, Pa., to propose a secret ballot on returning to work were met with cries of, "Who's going to count the ballots?" and required police protection to make their escape. The strike was finally ended on October 6 when an international union commission was established to consider the complaint against the assessment. Lewis also agreed to consider a demand that Hugh V. Brown, president of District 7, who was not popular with the rank and file, be removed.[73] Lewis eventually turned this episode to his advantage by revoking the charter of District 7 and appointing provisional officers of his own choosing.

The Captive Mines Dispute

The tumult of the Appalachian negotiations had hardly died down when Lewis began another campaign in comparison with which the battle between the North and the South faded into insignificance. His target this time was the so-called "captive" mines, which were coal mines owned by and producing for the large steel corporations. These mines employed some 50,000 out of the total employment of 450,000 bituminous coal miners and produced about 10 per cent of the annual coal output. Although about 95 per cent of the miners employed by the steel companies, which included the United States Steel Corporation, Bethlehem, Weirton, Republic, Crucible, and Youngstown, were members of the United Mine Workers of America, the companies refused to sign the Appalachian agreement because of its union shop provisions. This position was based upon the fear that to accord the UMW union shop status might set a precedent which the Steelworkers' Union would not be slow to utilize. The spirit of the Taylor-Lewis accord of 1937, it will be recalled, could not be reconciled with the union shop, and it became a matter of principle to steel management that this union security clause would not be conceded.

The position of the United States Steel Corporation was later summarized by Benjamin F. Fairless, its president, in the following terms: "My biggest dispute with John Lewis was over the issue of the closed shop in 1941. His United Mine Workers had won the closed shop elsewhere. Now they wanted to impose it on the 'captive-mines' owned and operated by the steel companies. Most of the miners belonged to the union anyway, but a matter of principle was involved. In our private conversations I would say, 'John, it's just as wrong to make a man join a union if he doesn't want to as it is to dictate what church he should belong to.' Lewis could not see it that way. He would say, 'It's wrong to have men getting the benefit of better hours and conditions won for them by the union without giving a penny to help support the union.' " [74]

Lewis, on the other hand, was determined that the captive mines should follow the rest of the industry in this respect. Lewis' attitude at the time is reported as follows:

He felt the administration had gone so far that war was inevitable, and that national policy during a war period had always been the fixing or freezing of the status quo. Lewis felt that he owed it to the mine workers union and to the entire labor movement to "batten down the hatches" and see to it that when the mine workers union was frozen, it would be with a union shop prevailing every place a man dug coal.[75]

After prolonged negotiations had failed to secure a resolution of this issue, a strike was called for September 15, 1941, and on the appointed day, 45,000 miners quit work. The Jones and Laughlin Steel Corporation granted the union shop, and was thus not involved in the strike. On the same day, the National Defense Mediation Board assumed jurisdiction over the dispute, and asked that work be resumed. Subsequent to hearings before a panel consisting of William H. Davis, Walter C. Teagle, and Hugh Lyons, Lewis agreed to a thirty-day truce, and the mines resumed operation. The NDMB panel then proceeded to consider the case, and on October 24 it recommended to the parties (with the labor member dissenting) either that the dispute be submitted to the full board for final adjudication, or that the parties create a joint board which, if it could not agree, would then select an impartial arbitrator to render a final decision. At the same time, the board issued a recommendation attributed to President Roosevelt, in which it was suggested that Lewis and Myron Taylor assume leading roles in any arbitration attempts, and asked that the two men make themselves available immediately.[76] Lewis agreed to meet with Taylor, but refused to extend the strike deadline beyond the 30-day truce limit. In his reply to President Roosevelt, Lewis wrote:

The attitude of the Board towards this problem during this period has been casual and lackadaisical to the point of indifference. Over the protest of the United Mine Workers, the Board has called before it only the inferior executives of the corporations involved. . . . The Board now emerges with a report devoid of conclusions as to merit, evasive as to the responsibilities of the Board, and dumps its own sorry mess into the already overburdened lap of the Chief Executive.

Mr. Hillman, of course, is responsible for the fantastic procedure which has been followed. His attitude of vengeful and malignant opposition to the interests of the United Mine Workers of America is only equalled by the fury of his actions against the United Construction Workers in the Currier Lumber case. It is unfortunate that he is able to use his great powers to intimidate governmental agencies to a point where they deprive legitimate organizations of labor of the right to a judicial determination of their grievances under the law.

I regret that the United Mine Workers of America had no opportunity to present you a statement in their own defense prior to your approval of the Hillman procedure yesterday. Under these circumstances, I do not feel warranted in recommending an additional extension of the temporary agreement. . . .[77]

The president's reply came the next day. He ignored the attacks upon Hillman, whom Lewis had never forgiven for his role in leading the opposition within the CIO during the 1940 presidential elections, and was now raising to the status of the central Machiavellian figure in the drama,[78] but urged strongly that Lewis reconsider his decision not to postpone the strike, on the following grounds:

In this crisis of our national life there must be uninterrupted production of coal for making steel, that basic material of our national defense. That is essential to the preservation of our freedoms, yours and mine; those freedoms upon which the very existence of the United Mine Workers of America depends. . . .

I am, therefore, as President of the United States, asking you and your associated officers of the United Mine Workers of America, as loyal citizens, to come now to the aid of your country. I ask that work continue at the captive coal mines pending the settlement of the dispute.

It must be remembered that this letter was written a month and a half before Pearl Harbor, at a time when it was obvious that the security of the nation was being jeopardized by pressures from abroad. Under the circumstances, there were probably few men in the United States who would have resisted this direct appeal from the president, as Lewis did in his reply to Roosevelt, under date of October 27:

Sir:

Your letter is at hand.

I have no wish to betray those whom I represent. There is yet no question of patriotism or national security involved in this dispute.

For four months, the steel companies have been whetting their knives and preparing for this struggle. They have increased coal storage and marshalled all their resources. Defense output is not impaired, and will not be impaired for an indefinite period. This fight is only between a labor union and a ruthless corporation — the United States Steel Corporation.

Lest we forget, I reassert the loyalty of the members of the United Mine Workers of America as citizens of our republic. This Union gave seventy thousand of its members to the armed forces of the United States in the last World War. The per capita purchases of war securities by its members during that period exceeded those of any other segment of our national population. They are willing, when required, to make equal or greater sacrifices in the future to preserve the nation and its fine institutions.

If you would use the power of the State to restrain me, as an agent of labor, then, Sir, I submit that you should use that same power to restrain my adversary in this issue, who is an agent of capital. My adversary is a rich man named Morgan, who lives in New York. . . .

There are sixteen members of the Board of Directors of the United States Steel Corporation. Mr. J. P. Morgan is a member of the Board. Mr. Morgan shall determine who else shall sit on the Board. Mr. Morgan will decide what Mr. Taylor will do when he meets me on Wednesday. Mr. Morgan's great wealth is increasing from his profits on defense orders. Mr. Morgan has a responsibility at least equal to my own. Mr. Morgan should be asked to make a contribution. I submit, Mr. President, that it is not unreasonable to ask Mr. Morgan's companies to accept the wage agreement approved by the National Defense Mediation Board, and accepted and signed by other captive and commercial coal companies in the nation. . . .

In the interest of settlement, I would be glad, Mr. President, if you concur, to meet with you and my adversary, Mr. J. P. Morgan, for a forthright discussion of the equities of this problem.

On the day the letter was written, the captive mines were once more shut down. Within two hours of its despatch, the following curt reply from the President was in Lewis' hands:

I am sorry that in your letter to me early this afternoon you have not replied to my request that, in the interest of the defense of our country, the captive coal mines be kept running.

Whatever may be the issues between you and Mr. Taylor or you and Mr. Morgan, the latter question of adequate fuel supply is of greater interest and import to the national welfare. There is every reason for the continuance of negotiations. There is no reason for stoppage of work.

It is, therefore, essential that the mining of coal should go on without interruption.

For the third time your Government, through me, asks you and the officers of the United Mine Workers to authorize an immediate resumption of mining.

Roosevelt's exasperation was undoubtedly heightened by the difficulty he was having in preventing antilabor groups in the Congress from using the captive mines dispute as a pretext for passing legislation that might affect adversely the entire labor movement. Lewis was castigated severely in both the House and the Senate, and even the president, in a public address, warned that defense production "cannot be hampered by the selfish destruction of a small but dangerous minority of labor leaders for a minute." [79] Philip Pearl, an official spokesman for the American Federation of Labor, termed the strike "not only a betrayal of America . . . but a dastardly and indefensible betrayal of the best interests of all labor in America," and said of Lewis:

Lewis today is the most cordially hated man in America. His scornful refusal to consider the best interests of the nation, his deliberate attempts to embarrass the national defense program, his bitter feud with President Roosevelt, his insulting arrogance are more than the American people can stomach.[80]

On October 29, Lewis met with Taylor, and was later joined by William Davis, chairman of the Mediation Board. They then visited the White House and met with the president for an hour and a half, after which it was announced that Lewis had agreed to reopen the mines until November 15 pending submission of the dispute to the full Mediation Board. It was made clear, however, that its decision was not to be binding on the parties; the steel companies were willing to permit final decision by the board, but Lewis was not.[81]

Lewis probably anticipated that the Mediation Board would decide in his favor, in which event acquiescence by the employers was a foregone conclusion. An official UMW document stated: "All intelligent sources of opinion indicated that the Mine Workers would receive favorable action from the Board. This was based on the fact that if the American Federation of Labor Members of the Board would support the Miners, as it was thought they would do, there would be four favorable votes at the beginning, and it would be necessary to receive only three more results from the seven of the employe and public members. This appeared probable because of the overwhelming membership of unionized workers in the captive mines — approximately 97 per cent of the total." [82] He must have been astounded when on November 10, the board decided by a vote of 9 to 2 against the union shop, on the ground that the security of the union was not jeopardized by a small number of nonunion miners, and that membership in a labor union should not be compelled by governmental edict. The board urged nonunion miners to join the UMW voluntarily, at least for the duration

of the national emergency, but refused to force them in.[83] The regular AFL
members of the Mediation Board, George Meany and George Harrison, had
not sat on this case, and it was their alternates, William A. Calvin of the
Boilermakers and George Q. Lynch of the Pattern Makers, both ardent
proponents of craft unionism, who cast the AFL votes against the UMW.
George Meany announced a few days later that he would have voted for
the union shop had he been present, but Calvin declared that he had advised
William Green of his intention to vote against it, and had received Green's
approval.[84] The UMW expressed disappointment at the adverse vote of
Frank Graham, a public member, who, it was conceded, "had given prolonged, sincere, and disinterested consideration to the matter, and apparently, because of his views as to what should be the democratic procedures in industry, could not conscientiously bring himself to support the
closed shop as an industrial standard." Chairman Davis' vote was called
illogical and contradictory, while that of the third public member, Charles
Wyzanski, was attributed to the machinations of Sidney Hillman.

This decision precipitated the breakup of the Mediation Board. On
November 11, Philip Murray and Thomas Kennedy, the vice-president and
secretary-treasurer, respectively, of the UMW, resigned from the board, and
were followed shortly by all other CIO representatives. In their letter of
resignation Murray and Kennedy averred that as a consequence of the
decision, "regardless of the merits of any case, labor unions shall be denied
the right of normal growth and legitimate aspiration, such as the union
shop, and the traditional open shop policy of the anti-labor employers shall
prevail." [85]

Lewis responded by calling a meeting of his policy committee which
was almost certain to endorse his proposal for a renewal of the work stoppage. On November 13, a controversial amendment to the Neutrality Act,
permitting the arming of American merchant ships, was up before the
House of Representatives, and Roosevelt promised the House in his message
urging passage of the bill:

I am holding a conference tomorrow in the hope that certain essential coal mines
can remain in continuous operation. This may prove successful. But if it is not
successful, it is obvious that this coal must be mined in order to keep the essential
steel mills at work. The Government of the United States has the backing of the
overwhelming majority of the people of the United States, including the workers.
The government proposes to see this thing through.[86]

The meeting held at the White House on November 14 included the
heads of the nation's major steel companies, as well as Lewis and his fellow

officers of the UMW, Murray and Kennedy. Roosevelt addressed the conferees, and, after citing the urgent need for continued steel production, told them:

Because it is essential to national defense that the necessary coal production be continued and not stopped, it is therefore the indisputable obligation of the President to see that this is done.

In spite of what some people say, I seek always to be a Constitutional President.

If legislation becomes necessary toward this end, the Congress of the United States will without any question pass such legislation. And, as some of you know, the pressure on me to ask for legislation during the past couple of months, for one reason or another, has been not only consistent, but it has been very heavy.

I am telling you this with absolutely no element of threat. To this conference I am stating a simple fact. . . .[87]

After calling for a continuance of collective bargaining, and the submission of the dispute to arbitration in the event of failure to agree, the president continued:

I tell you frankly that the Government of the United States will not order, nor will Congress pass legislation ordering, a so-called closed shop. It is true that by agreement between employers and employes in many plants of various industries the closed shop is now in operation. This is a result of legal collective bargaining, and not of Government compulsion on employers or employes. It is also true that 95 per cent or more of the employes in these particular mines belong to the United Mine Workers' Union.

The Government will never compel this 5 per cent to join the Union by a Government decree. That would be too much like the Hitler methods toward labor.

This conference proved to be as fruitless as had all those that had gone before. On such a matter of principle, there was no room for compromise. Lewis' next move was to order a work stoppage for November 17, and to warn the president that it might be necessary to call a strike throughout the entire Appalachian area in order to preserve the integrity of his agreement with the commercial bituminous producers.[88] This direct defiance of the president gave rise to a new wave of anti-Lewis demonstrations. Newspapers carried stories to the effect that the Army was prepared to break the strike.[89] General antistrike legislation was introduced in Congress. Only the CIO, which had convened for its fourth annual convention on November 17, offered any support for Lewis, though there were many in that organization, including the right-wing group led by Sidney Hillman, and the communists, who were now all out for war production at any cost, who would not have been averse to seeing Lewis beaten.

President Roosevelt, instead of meeting Lewis' challenge head on, as he so easily might have done, chose to adopt the less popular alternative of conciliation. On November 19, he wrote once more to Lewis and to the steel employers, indicating that he was doing two things: (1) informing all coal operators signatory to the Appalachian agreement that they would be expected to continue to operate under those agreements, which included the union shop, without change in the interest of national defense; (2) asking the operators of the captive mines to notify each of their employees that they did not wish to discourage membership in the UMW. He closed as follows:

I am therefore asking all of you, as patriotic Americans, to accept one or other of the following alternatives:

(a) Allow the matter of the closed shop in the captive mines to remain in status quo for the period of the national emergency, all other parts of the Appalachian agreement applying, or

(b) Submit this point to arbitration, agreeing in advance to accept the decision so made for the period of the national emergency without prejudice to your rights in the future.[90]

The operators accepted this proposal, but Lewis replied that the officers of the UMW had no authority to sign an open shop agreement. As to arbitration, he declared: ". . . it is obvious that a judicial decision based upon the logic and merit of our contention would be difficult under existing circumstances. Your recent statements on this question, as the Chief Executive of the nation, have been so prejudicial to the claim of the Mine Workers as to make uncertain that an umpire could be found whose decision would not reflect your interpretation of government policy, congressional attitude and public opinion.[91] Again there was an impasse, and the president seemingly had no alternative but to seize the mines and operate them under government aegis, as he was reported to be prepared to do.[92] Why he did not do so remains a matter of conjecture. It may have been that the captive mine operators feared government seizure more than the union shop; or that the president was not sanguine about the possibility of manning the mines without union cooperation, a not unreasonable expectation, as later events were to demonstrate; or simply that he hesitated to take so drastic a step and risk continued turmoil at a time when foreign affairs were rapidly approaching a crisis. Whatever the reason, he chose instead to surrender, in effect, to Lewis. This was done in the form of a letter advising Lewis of the establishment of a three-man board of arbitration, consisting of John R. Steelman, director of the U. S. Conciliation Service; Benjamin Fairless, president of U. S. Steel; and Lewis himself.[93] Steelman, it will be recalled, had been of great assistance to the UMW during the 1939 and 1941 bituminous coal negotiations, and his decision could be anticipated with some confidence. As Alinsky has said, "Lewis promptly accepted 'arbitration,' for he knew as well as the President that this was not arbitration. Steelman was a good friend of Lewis and markedly a proponent of the union shop." [94] The captive mine employees were ordered back to work immediately. Why the operators were willing to accept a board of arbitration is not clear. In principle, they had the support of President Roosevelt and the Congress, as well as of public opinion. Perhaps they felt that all these factors would make it impossible for a government employee to decide in favor of the union. Or Myron Taylor may have been prevailed upon to acquiesce in this face saving device as his contribution to the national interest. Lewis had chosen a simple bargaining strategy; he formulated a demand and stuck by it. Unless his opponent followed the same strategy, only one outcome was possible.

The final result was anticlimactic. The board of arbitration, with Fairless dissenting, directed the operators to execute union shop agreements covering the captive mines. Steelman, in a long opinion, argued that the grant of a union shop simply meant the maintenance of the status quo, in view of the large membership of the UMW among the captive mine employees, and he absolved the union of the charge that it was using the national emergency to further organization.[95] The decision was announced on December 7, 1941, the day of the Japanese attack on Pearl Harbor, and though it was still first-page news the following day, the repercussions that might have been expected failed to materialize as the nation was plunged into war.

The Break with the CIO

Throughout 1941, Lewis' relations with the CIO had been deteriorating steadily. According to Philip Murray, Lewis, beginning in May 1941, began systematically to attempt to undermine him in his position as president of the CIO. Lewis, Murray claimed, was piqued at the latter's support of Roosevelt's foreign policy instead of following him into isolationism.[96] Lewis' position was that he attempted to be as helpful and considerate as possible toward his former lieutenant, but that Murray was consumed by jealousy and was the recipient of bad advice, particularly from the communists, who turned on their former ally after the Nazi attack on the Soviet Union.[97] The initiative taken by Lewis in January, 1942, toward a renewal of AFL-CIO unity negotiations served further to exacerbate relationships between the two men.[98] The activities of District 50 of the UMW, which had been revitalized and showed ambitions of becoming "one big union," infringing upon the jurisdictions of other CIO unions, also became an issue. The CIO was told that from the time of its organization to 1941, District 50 had received $294,000 from the UMW for its organizing work, but that since its reorganization under Gasaway and Kathryn Lewis in August 1941, it had received an additional $264,000. The United Construction Workers, CIO, an organization headed by Denny Lewis, the brother of John L., caused further dissention within the CIO. A report was submitted to the CIO Executive Board to the effect that gangsters had infiltrated the organization, and a committee was established to investigate the charges.[99]

Beginning with the month of February 1942, the UMW withheld its per capita payments to the CIO, and requested that the amounts due be deducted from loans allegedly made to the CIO during its early days. Murray continued to occupy his office in the United Mine Workers building, but the atmosphere was not pleasant. "Everyone knew the break had come and that Murray would soon be a past memory in the organization. He was shunned by his colleagues as a moral leper, traitor, and Judas Iscariot. Those who still liked him were panicked with fear that fraternization with Murray would be interpreted as being anti-Lewis." [100] Finally, Lewis called a meeting of the International Policy Committee for May 25, at which he accused Murray of hostility toward both the organization and toward him personally. According to Alinsky, the following transpired:

Lewis paused and then struck, "But Vice-President Murray had already called me a Jap." Murray hastily scrambled to his feet. Bellows of rage came from the delegates, which changed into a barrage of boos interspersed with cries to Murray to sit down and shut up. Lewis continued, "And another Pearl Harbor." A murmur of angry whispers could be heard all over the hall. Murray seemed on the verge of collapse. While he had schooled himself to hostility from the mine workers officials, nevertheless the spectacle of all his old friends and every ranking official and delegate of the union now shouting their hatred and telling him, who for twenty-three years had been the second ranking official of the union, to sit down and shut up was just too much. Murray gripped the table in front of him; pale and shaking, he screamed, "You big, bold, brave courageous men. I will sit down. But I want to answer this record, see, when President Lewis sits down. You big, bold courageous men that you are, paid officers of the organization, booing an officer of your organization. God forgive you." [101]

The formal charge against Murray was that he had accepted a paid position as president of the Steelworkers Union, in violation of the UMW constitution. The office of vice-president was declared vacant, and John O'Leary was designated to fill the vacancy.[102] The events which flowed from this action showed how far the UMW had moved in the direction of central control:

For some days the basement of the United Mine Workers Building became a confessional chamber. Official after official arose beating his breast and publicly proclaimed his guilt of past association with Philip Murray and of having followed and been a friend of the now perfidious, leprous Murray. It was a mass orgy of self-abnegation and personal debasement that can only be rivaled by the spectacle of highly disciplined Communist leaders beating their breasts and confessing their sins when there is a change in their national leadership and policy.[103]

In addition to Murray, Lewis removed from his post Van A. Bittner, president of District 17, who elected to go with Murray. Lewis charged that Bittner was neglecting to enforce the contract in his district, and was stirring up autonomy sentiment among the miners. Bittner sent a telegram to the 1942 Convention defending his position, but Lewis disposed of the matter simply by challenging Bittner's veracity.

The final break with the CIO came at the 1942 UMW Convention, in October 1942. The motion to sever affiliation was adopted by a vote of 2867 to 5. Indeed, delegates vied with one another in recounting stories of how Murray and Bittner had long been attempting to undermine the UMW. Lewis himself dwelt on the financial assistance the UMW had rendered to the CIO. "Don't think I don't count the cost to the coal miners of this country when they are asked to give these dollars to help other unfortunate men. Don't think I don't know what it means to load coal in bad air, under bad trap, in water, amid the hazards of explosions and dust. . . ." He stated, probably quite correctly, that he could have been reelected as president of the CIO in 1940 had he chosen to run, but that he had withdrawn "because I had given too freely of my strength and I had put too much of myself into the CIO in combating its enemies, in preserving order in its own ranks, in teaching inexperienced men how to organize, and how to bargain, and how to administer the affairs of the union." He argued, with justification, that there would have been no CIO had it not been for the financial assistance and services provided by the United Mine Workers, and complained that for his pains the new CIO leadership had turned upon him without provocation. "Life is too short for me to answer the yapping of every cur that follows at my heels. I hear the pack in my rear at times. I can turn my head and see the lap dogs and the kept dogs and the yellow dogs in pursuit." Thus did Lewis characterize his former close associates.

The remainder of the 1942 convention followed a familiar pattern. Since the previous convention, one additional district had lost its autonomy (District 7), and a rank-and-file delegate complained that between 60 and 70 per cent of the membership were in provisional districts.[104] This and similar complaints proved of no avail. Proponents of autonomy were linked with the now execrated CIO and with the Communist Party. Lewis compared the district presidents with the members of the Federal Cabinet, and argued that in both cases it was necessary for the president to have a free hand in selecting his advisers. The convention voted overwhelmingly in favor of continuing the existing autonomy policy, with a dwindling number of delegates asking to be recorded in opposition.

On only one other question, that of increasing the monthly dues from $1 to $1.50, was there any real debate. Assent of the delegates was secured in part by removing from the international executive board the power to levy special assessments, and providing for a referendum instead if it became necessary to raise additional funds. The UMW had in its treasury as of June 1, 1942, the net sum of $6,340,000, and the new dues scale placed the international in a stronger financial position than it had ever had before.

McAlister Coleman, a close student of and participant in the affairs of the United Mine Workers, poses the following pertinent question:

How did it happen that a group as indigenously democratic as the American miners could so willingly accept the dictates of one man? Lewis had long been out of favor with the Roosevelt Administration. He was the object of contumely on the part of both the A.F. of L. and the C.I.O. Since 1937 the press as a whole had adopted an increasingly hostile attitude toward the mine leader, and because of his anti-interventionist war stand the liberal and more latterly the Communist journals had held him in dark suspicion.[105]

Coleman and others have ascribed the Lewis dictatorship, which by 1942 had already come to full maturity, to the improved economic conditions which he had secured for the miners. From 1935 to 1941, average hourly earnings in bituminous coal rose from $0.745 to $0.993, or 33 per cent. During the same period, average hourly earnings in all manufacturing increased 32.5 per cent; in iron and steel, by 36 per cent; in automobiles, by 41 per cent.[106] For this period, at least, it is difficult to see the force of the economic argument, unless it be maintained that the miners were more grateful to their leaders than other workers for achieving identical gains. Miners' wages began to outdistance those of other workers only after 1941. Nor can Lewis' power be ascribed to the introduction of nonwage gains, for travel-time pay, vacation pay, the welfare fund, and elimination of the abuses of the company town and company store came later. Indeed, the United Automobile Workers Union, which in 1941 was notable for its lack of domination by a single man or group, moved much more quickly than did the UMW to eliminate the industry practices which were disliked by the workers.

Moreover, the gains achieved by Lewis during this period were not without cost to the miners. Despite the great increase in bituminous coal output from 1935 to 1941, from 372 million tons to 514 million tons, employment declined from 462,000 to 457,000, due largely to the introduction of mechanical loading devices. In the words of a close student, "Without question the major factor underlying the heightened pace of mine mechanization was union wage policy." The possibility of interruption in the supply of coal, due to strikes, was an important factor in placing coal at a competitive disadvantage with competing fuels, and thus further restricted employment opportunities.[107] Another factor to be entered on the cost side is the considerable amount of wage and other losses sustained in the periodic strike waves,[108] though here it is difficult to assess the losses precisely due to what has been termed the "offset factor," that is, the ability of the industry to make up production losses due to work interruptions by anticipating the stoppage and by steadier work in subsequent periods.[109]

The United Mine Workers is not the only trade union in America to have fallen under the complete domination of a strong leader. But the UMW provides an outstanding example of the manner in which an ambitious man can establish himself in absolute power, despite a long tradition of union democracy and an exceedingly democratic constitution. The full story of how this was achieved remains to be written, although it is clear even from the cursory account in the foregoing pages that the chief factor involved was the clever manipulation of men and statute to the end of constructing an invulnerable political machine, which not even the highest officials could stand up against. Whatever the precise means, the results are clear. Alinsky, an admirer of Lewis, has written:

There is no question that Lewis runs the union with a strong, dictatorial hand. His union policy committee is a mere rubber stamp as is everyone else in the union . . . when Lewis makes a "recommendation," it is an order. And no one knows that better than those who surround him. Occasionally they will be given the thrill of a free debate and decision on an issue, but only when the issue is so minor and so unimportant that the democratically arrived at decision is also unimportant. Even so, they find themselves in a strange and terrifying situation, for their initiative is so atrophied through disuse they find it difficult to make any kind of a decision. Their servility is reflected in the unhealthy awe that permeates every cranny and every stone of the UMW building in Washington, from its outside step to the ceiling of its sixth floor, and to that great Holy of Holies, where the union God abides.[110]

The captive mines dispute was by no means the last or greatest alarm raised by the formidable figure of John L. Lewis; his subsequent adventures in collective bargaining were to gain him even greater notoriety. But he had already passed the zenith of his power in American life by 1941. His fateful decision to oppose Roosevelt in 1940, and his subsequent break with the CIO, placed him outside the mainstream of the American labor movement, notwithstanding a brief but unsuccessful flirtation with his old antagonist, William Green. His own wage policies, leading to what amounted to a technological revolution in the mining of coal, steadily reduced his union in size and importance until it has become one of the relatively lesser labor organizations of the country. Why Lewis was unsuccessful in building District 50 into a powerful general union, as he attempted to do, is an important problem for the labor historian of a later period. It would be a gross oversimplification to deny that Lewis had considerable influence on collective bargaining in the United States subsequent to 1941, but his real place in history had already been established by then.

5

The Electrical and Radio Manufacturing Industries

The history of labor relations in electrical machinery and equipment manufacturing from 1935 to 1941 offers some sharp contrasts with that in steel and automobiles. Although there were some serious strikes, there was no counterpart either of the spectacular sit downs that forced General Motors and Chrysler to capitulate to the United Automobile Workers, or of the bloody Little Steel riots. The leading manufacturers accepted collective bargaining as the law of the land, and attempted in the main to live within the Wagner Act. The union which came into existence with the formation of the CIO, the United Electrical, Radio and Machine Workers of America, had achieved a commanding status in the industry by the end of 1941, but it had also attained the dubious distinction of complete domination by the Communist Party. How this came to be is an important part of our story.

Formation of the United Electrical, Radio and Machine Workers Union

The origin of the United Electrical, Radio and Machine Workers (or UE, as it was known colloquially) may be traced back to the organization of the radio workers at the Philadelphia Storage Battery Company (Philco Radio) in July 1933. Philco had been the leading storage battery manufacturer, and by 1930 had also attained a position of leadership in radio production. When the NRA gave rise to talk of unionism in the plant, an employee representation plan was established. A company order requiring employees to work ten hours a day temporarily to make up for the July 4th holiday occasioned a spontaneous strike by some 350 assemblers, testers and repairmen, which tied up the work of over 2000 additional workers. Three days later, on July 15, 1933, the company signed an agreement with the newly formed American Federation of Radio Workers, which was headed by a twenty-one-year-old employee of the company, James Carey.

The contract granted the workers an eight-hour day, a forty-hour week, time and one half for overtime, the abolition of penalties for errors and bad work, grievance machinery, and a minimum scale of 45 cents per hour for men and 36 cents for women.

On the basis of this contract, the AFL chartered the union as Radio and Television Workers Federal Labor Union No. 18,386, on August 3, 1933. Several weeks later, Philco went the whole way in granting the local a union shop, in return for which the AFL, through William Green, guaranteed that no radio local affiliated with the AFL would accept wage rates lower than those in the Philco contract. The magnitude of the company concessions at so early a date has been attributed to "the desire of company officials not to be bothered by 'labor problems,' and, in part, at least, from ignorance of the significance of their concessions." [1]

Under the impetus of NRA, the Philco example spread to other firms, and on December 28 and 29, 1933, a group of AFL federal locals and independent unions met in New York to discuss mutual problems. Out of this meeting came the Radio and Allied Trades National Labor Council. It was decided that a national charter would be desirable, and a delegation headed by Carey, who had been elected president of the council, appeared before the Executive Council of the AFL with such a request during the following month. The delegation argued that craft organization could not solve the problems of the radio workers, to which various members of the Executive Council replied that the problems of the radio workers did not differ from those of other organized workers. At the conclusion of the meeting, President Green requested the committee to draft a statement outlining just what was wanted, and stated that every possible assistance would be extended to them. However, the request for a charter was denied on the ground that the petitioning group included independent unions as well as AFL affiliates. [2]

In December 1934, a conference was called in Buffalo of delegates from directly affiliated AFL unions. To meet the objections of the Executive Council, delegates from independent unions who appeared in Buffalo were not seated and were denied any voice in the proceedings. The name of the organization was changed to the National Radio and Allied Trades, and once more it was resolved to petition the AFL for a national charter. When he appeared before the Executive Council in January 1935, Carey stated:

We found we had to have more power that will be recognized so our wage scales can be maintained throughout. We have some companies that have their employees organized with wage scales far below other companies where the employees are organized. The [Philco] Company is getting our people to feel we are not doing our part in organizing these other companies. We have to have some form of organization to set the scales for these Federal Labor Unions. We have no power to adjust wage scales or set wage scales.

It was brought out during the hearing that there were twelve chartered federal locals of radio workers with a membership of 7407, of whom 5686 were in Philadelphia, mainly in Philco. John L. Lewis urged that the charter be granted, but Bugniazet, who represented the International Brotherhood of Electrical Workers, interposed the following objection:

The electrical workers to which the radio workers are allied agreed to yield jurisdiction temporarily until such time as their conditions would warrant them to pay tax and participate in the benefits of the Electrical Workers. We are considering providing for a separate membership in our organization where these men who are so low paid that they could not participate in the benefit features, can be organized under our guidance, and if our membership will agree to it that will be our policy. To be frank with these men, we will have objection to this charter because they are only in the Federation on our consent.[3]

The upshot of the discussion was that action on the charter request was deferred. However, the Radio Council received recognition as an official AFL body by the Executive Council.

The Radio Council met again on March 30, 1935, in Cincinnati, and this time several electrical worker locals from General Electric and Westinghouse plants were in attendance, thus bringing the council into direct jurisdictional conflict with both the Electrical Workers and the Machinists. Approximately 15,000 workers were represented at this meeting. In July, another meeting of seven radio locals, including Philco, was held at which it was decided to withhold further per capita tax payments to the AFL.[4] It should be noted that this action preceded the formation of the CIO.

With the formation of the CIO in November 1935, matters came to a head. The National Radio and Allied Trades held a convention in Pittsburgh on December 27–29, 1935, and claiming to speak for 30,000 organized workers, renewed the demand for a national charter. The delegates voted unanimously not to affiliate with or be a subdivision of any craft union then in existence in the AFL. John Brophy and Philip Murray of the CIO addressed the meeting, but urged against any break with the AFL.

The final appearance of the radio workers before the Executive Council took place on January 17, 1936. Carey presented a document in support of a charter application, which said in part:

I want to make it clear why the radio workers insist that they cannot function if divided into craft locals and why they therefore insist on an Industrial Union. We have had experiences in trying to arrange council forms of negotiations with employers without success. We have attempted to arrange joint agreements with craft organizations and Federal Labor Unions and the results have been detrimental to the interest of the workers. Time and again we have sacrificed opportunities to organize plants one hundred per cent (100%) by attempting to coordinate the activity of several representatives of different organizations and in many cases our efforts in this direction have entirely destroyed our opportunities for organization.

The document went on to state that the Machinists' Union had recently made overtures to several of the independent radio unions, offering to take them in as a group with full membership rights, and that the Electrical Workers were preparing to offer the radio workers restricted membership rights, and warned that any attempt at parceling the workers out among craft unions with "paper jurisdictional claims" would lead to the withdrawal of the radio locals from the AFL. When Green, attempting to lay the basis for a possible compromise, asked Carey whether a charter with the type of jurisdictional restriction contained in the charter issued to the Automobile Workers' Union would suffice, Carey replied: "I do not believe the organization would be satisfied with the demarcation as in the case of the Automobile Workers. They want a policy set up to organize these plants on a basis similar to that at the Philco plant."

Bugniazet, on behalf of the Electrical Workers, told the council that his organization had amended its constitution to provide for Class B membership for low-paid industrial workers. He offered the Radio Trades two proposals: if they were willing to pay the regular dues, they could come in as regular members, with concomitant rights to $1000 death benefits and old age pensions of $40 per month; or they could pay lower dues and come in as nonbeneficial Class B members with one vote per local in conventions and referenda as compared with one vote per member in the Class A group.[5] To the Brotherhood, which placed great emphasis upon its benefit system, this seemed a perfectly reasonable proposal. Dan W. Tracy, the IBEW president, urged the radio workers:

Affiliate with an organization built upon a half century of experience gained in successfully advancing and protecting the interests of electrical workers. Affiliate under the beneficial membership proposal if you can afford it. If your present earnings are insufficient to permit affiliation as beneficial members then join the I.B.E.W. as non-beneficial members and help that organization to help you to improve your wages and working conditions so that you can afford a decent death benefit and pension protection that wage earners are entitled to receive the benefit of.[6]

This argument fell upon deaf ears. The radio workers were overwhelmingly a young group, and had little interest in death benefits and old age pensions. They resented the proferred offer of second class status in the Brotherhood, and feared that the claims of other craft unions to portions of the radio industry would be recognized. The die was cast when the Executive Council of the AFL denied the request for a national charter and ordered all federal locals in the radio field transferred to the Electrical Workers.

A meeting of representatives of the radio workers was called for February 8–10, 1936, in Washington, D. C., to act upon the decision of the Executive Council. The day before the meeting convened, the United Mine Workers voted to support the radio workers in their effort "to establish a national industrial union for that industry." Dan Tracy of the IBEW appealed to the convention to abide by the decision of the Executive Council, but with only two dissenting votes, the radio workers rejected the invitation to join his organization.[7] "The chief objections raised to the IBEW proposal were that the radio locals would have no national department of their own; that there was no guarantee they would not later be divided among other craft unions, whose jurisdictional claims have not been waived; that they would have only one vote per local as Class B members, as against one vote per member for the skilled electricians who make up the bulk of the membership; and that the IBEW is primarily a building trades union, unadapted to organizing in manufacturing mass-production industries."[8] The delegates decided to launch a national union without AFL sanction, and to invite the independent Electrical and Radio Workers Union, which claimed some 25,000 members, to join with them.[9] The Committee for Industrial Organization, meeting on February 21, supported them by demanding that the AFL grant an industrial charter.

The new national union was launched at a convention held in Buffalo on March 21 and 22, 1936. Named the United Electrical and Radio Workers of America, it included the independent electrical locals as well as the former radio federal locals. James Carey was elected president, and Julius Emspak of the independent General Electric local at Schenectady, secretary-treasurer. The Schenectady local, which was to play an important role in UE affairs, first saw the light of day in 1932 as a semi-secret organization, but gradually gained influence in this important center of the electrical manufacturing industry. However, at the time of the February 1936 convention, it had not yet attained the status of collective bargaining representative. The influence of the Philco local, where Carey first made his name, was due to its early collective agreement.

The AFL retaliated by revoking the charters of all federal locals participating in the convention, and branded the new union as dual and unlawful. Green wrote to Tracy: "Mr. Carey is a young man, new in organization and glibly talks about unity of workers. He now finds himself at the head of an organization of about 8,000 members, when he could be functioning within a large organization of electrical workers, long established and a growing concern." [10] When Carey once more sent the AFL a *pro forma* request for a charter, Green noted that Carey's federal local had not paid its per capita tax since September 1935, and concluded:

How could you expect me, as the official representative of the American Federation of Labor, to accept any communication written by you now asking for a charter for a dual union? Surely you and the members of Federal Local Union No. 18368 ought to pay the per capita tax due the American Federation of Labor before you could assume to write me in either a personal or official capacity.

When Carey replied that the matter of the per capita tax could be settled when the question of affiliation had been arranged, Green simply did not reply.[11] This marked the final rupture of formal relations between the two organizations.

The first regular convention of UE was held in September 1936, in Fort Wayne, Indiana. While the convention was in session, the suspension of the CIO unions from the AFL went into effect, and almost immediately a resolution was adopted directing the officers to apply for affiliation with the CIO. Actually, a close relationship had existed between the two organizations since early 1936. In addition to moral support, the CIO had assisted UE in a strike against RCA; Powers Hapgood, a CIO organizer, had been sent to help direct the strike, and John L. Lewis had participated in the negotiations and signed the strike settlement. When the UE application was submitted to a meeting of the committee, Hochman of the ILGWU cautioned: "It will be better not to accept such affiliations until we have set up a federation," but Lewis overruled him brusquely with "I can see no reason why not — I think it would strengthen the Committee somewhat if these unions were accepted." [12] UE thus became the first new, industrial non-AFL union to be admitted to the CIO.

A further step in the establishment of UE jurisdiction was its expansion into the machinery industry in 1937. In the spring of that year a group of locals of the International Association of Machinists left the IAM and joined UE, adding approximately 15,000 to the UE membership rolls. These locals had previously been part of the communist-dominated Federation of Metal and Allied Unions, under the leadership of James Matles, and had subsequently been admitted to the Machinists Union early in 1936. They moved into the CIO in response to a change in the Communist Party line from boring within the AFL to cooperation with the CIO.

At the following convention, in recognition of this affiliation and of the possibility of making organizational inroads into this important industry, UE changed its name to United Electrical, Radio and Machine Workers of America. At the same time, the constitution was amended to include the new area of organization. "The jurisdiction of the United Electrical, Radio and Machine Workers of America shall consist of the employees of any manufacturer of electrical machinery and products, instruments, tools and dies, light and meter machinery, equipment, and employees of all electric light and power utilities." [13]

The First Organizational Successes

The growth of UE took place through accretion in three relatively unrelated fields. It began with the radio workers, the key group in the formation of the union. Early in 1937 jurisdiction was extended to electrical manufacturing and public utilities, though the latter was soon sloughed off. Finally, the union began to cater to workers in light machinery shops and machine tools.

There are no official membership statistics of the UE in its infancy. In January 1936, when Carey appeared before the AFL Executive Council to request a national union charter, he claimed a membership of 30,000 in the National Radio and Allied Trades.[14] When a national union was formed in February 1936, it was reported that 25,000 non-AFL workers were to be added to the ranks of the former AFL federal locals. However, when UE was admitted into the CIO in November 1936, the UE was described as having only 33,000 members in all.[15] An estimate of UE membership by a UE local placed the number at approximately 16,000 in March 1936,[16] which is as good a figure as it is possible to obtain under such circumstances.

The first task of UE was to secure recognition from the giant corporations in the radio and electrical industries. General Electric and Westinghouse jointly accounted for about 25 per cent of the annual sales in electrical manufacturing, while Philco and RCA stood in about the same relationship to radio manufacturing. The first target of the new union was RCA, which as Philco's principal competitor had to be brought up to the Philco wage standards if the union's favorable contract with the latter were to be protected.

Early in 1933, an independent union had been formed at the RCA plant in Camden, New Jersey, closely followed by the formation of a company union. For more than two years both organizations were of fairly equal strength. In the spring of 1936, the independent union affiliated with the UE as Local 103, and on May 20, 1936, it asked the corporation for a signed agreement. The refusal of the company led to the commencement of a strike on June 23.[17] On the first day, 8000 out of 10,000 men employed at the plant remained away from work, but by the end of the second week of the strike, 7000 employees were back at work. The CIO sent Powers Hapgood in to lead the strikers, and with the help of workers from the nearby Camden shipyards, mass picket lines were thrown around the plant. Considerable violence ensued, during the course of which Carey and other UE officials were arrested. In the meantime, John L. Lewis engaged in negotiations with the company in New York, and on July 21, an agreement was finally reached.[18] It has been estimated that the company spent at least $244,000 to fight the strike, plus $586,000 expended on getting its orders executed elsewhere. The union had been supported financially by the Philco local to the extent of over $50,000, and was as anxious as the company for a compromise.

Under the terms of the agreement, all employees were to be reemployed without discrimination. No new employees were to be hired before March 31, 1937, unless there were no persons on the payroll prior to the strike qualified to fill vacancies. The corporation agreed to "maintain the policy of paying as high wages under as favorable hours and working conditions as prevail in Camden-Philadelphia manufacturing establishments engaged in similar class of work," thus protecting the Philco standards. It was also agreed that an NLRB election should be held to determine majority representation, the sole bargaining agent to be the union securing a majority of the votes of all those eligible to vote.

A few days before the scheduled day of the election, August 16, the company union decided to boycott the election, and waged a campaign to keep the workers away from the polls. In consequence, only 3163 ballots were cast out of an eligibility list of 9752, of which UE received all but 147. The National Labor Relations Board certified UE as sole bargaining agent for the plant, on the theory that to recognize the election boycott might thwart employees in the exercise of their right to bargain collectively. On the advice of General Hugh Johnson, its labor adviser, RCA refused to grant exclusive bargaining rights to UE, and for some months there was considerable friction in the plant between UE and the company union. The matter dragged on into 1937, when Edward F. McGrady, former assistant secretary of labor, became vice-president in charge of industrial relations for RCA. McGrady, one of the nation's leading conciliators, soon worked out an agreement whereby UE became exclusive bargaining agent for all employees at RCA (the agreement was dated October 8, 1937).[19] Thus, it required a bitter strike and a year of negotiation for the union to attain its goal.

During 1936, the union made relatively slow progress. At the time of its second convention, in September 1936, it was reported to have increased its membership by about 40 per cent over the April level.[20] Seven new locals had been chartered, in addition to the 18 in existence in April, only one of which was a casualty. Local 603, at the Pittsburgh Equitable Meter Company, went on strike prematurely and was unable to recover.[21]

A period of rapid growth began in December 1936, and continued throughout the first half of 1937. The secretary-treasurer told the 1937 Convention: "If you will recall, the spring of this year witnessed organizational activity on an unprecedented scale. The great auto sitdown late in the winter dramatized labor's right to organize. These sitdowns aroused an enthusiasm among workers for the CIO that resulted in huge gains for all organizations affiliated with the CIO. Our own organization was not excluded from this whirl of activity. CIO became a magic word." [22]

On December 15, 1936, the UE won a surprise NLRB victory at the Schenectady plant of General Electric. At the time it filed the election petition, Local 301 had only a few hundred members in the plant, the largest of GE's 23 units and the seat of its home office. This was the first important NLRB election to be held with the consent of the employer, and it was generally expected that the company union, one of the oldest and strongest in the country, would win a majority.[23] However, although the company union was disbanded soon after the election, it required more than a year to negotiate an agreement with the General Electric Company, which was indicative of the weakness of the union, despite its majority.

Early in 1937, UE engaged in a series of strikes against the major electrical manufacturing concerns in St. Louis. The union took on Emerson, Century, Baldor, and Superior in rapid succession, in each case winning the strike. The strike at Emerson, in which about 2000 workers were involved, lasted for 68 days, and at its conclusion the union was recognized as bargaining agent for its members only, and secured a minimum wage scale of 35 cents per hour.[24]

The next major gain was made at the East Pittsburgh works of the Westinghouse Company. This plant and five smaller contiguous plants constituted the center of the Westinghouse system, employing a fifth of the corporation's 45,000 workers. Company unionism had been introduced in the early 1920's, and attempts at organization by outside unions in 1933 and 1934 ended in failure. Not until 1935 was a successful independent union, which eventually became Local 601 of UE, launched. Following the tactics in steel manufacturing, the independent pursued a policy of boring from within the company union, and managed to elect half the members of the executive committee of the company union in elections held in November 1936. In April 1937, the union filed a petition with the NLRB, and was certified as exclusive bargaining representative after hearings in June, when it was shown that more than 7000 of the 11,500 employees in the unit were members of UE.

But at this juncture, UE met with an obstacle to collective bargaining which it required four years to overcome. It was the position of the Westinghouse management that collective bargaining "was simply an opportunity for representatives of the employees to bring up and discuss problems affecting the working force, with the final decision reserved to the company. It rejected the notion of a signed agreement because business conditions were too uncertain. . . . It refused to permit joint signatures to any statement on a specific issue which was to be posted on the bulletin board." [25] When agreement was reached on any matter, the company simply posted the condition over the signature of the plant manager.

This was by no means to the liking of the union, but it was not strong enough to attempt the use of economic force immediately. Nevertheless, significant changes were made in wage and other labor practices. An incentive scheme disliked by the workers was modified, and grievance machinery gradually introduced. However, the failure to secure a signed agreement remained a constant irritant to the UE.

UE also entered the public utility field in 1937. A Utilities Division was established under the direction of Albert Storkus, a former IBEW official. By September 1937, 60 locals had been established, some of them former affiliates of the IBEW, others directly chartered by UE. However, only seven signed agreements had been gained, the most important of which covered the Michigan properties of Consumers Power, which had been obtained after a successful strike in which the automobile workers provided assistance.[26]

In this industry, UE ran into the active opposition of the IBEW. The first clash occurred at the Consolidated Edison Company in New York City. Faced with a CIO organizing drive, the Company, on April 21, 1937, entered into a "perpetual" agreement with IBEW, automatically renewable at the end of each year unless either party gave 30 days notice of termination. Upon complaint of UE, the National Labor Relations Board found that the company had permitted its department heads and foremen to recruit for the IBEW, and had made clear to its company union that it favored bargaining with IBEW. The board ordered the company to cease and desist from discouraging membership in UE, or encouraging workers to join the IBEW.[27] This order, which was eventually reversed by the United States Supreme Court,[28] occasioned a heated campaign waged against the NLRB by the IBEW, in conjunction with other AFL unions.

Another particularly bitter struggle between the IBEW and UE occurred at the National Electric Products Corporation of Ambridge, Pa. According to the National Labor Relations Board, UE commenced organizational activities among the employees in March 1936, and was immediately confronted with company hostility. The IBEW, on the other hand, was permitted to solicit members during working hours.[29] On May 22, 1937, the company recognized the IBEW as exclusive bargaining representative of its employees, whereupon UE called a strike. "We had not only our own strikers picketing but their friends and wives and children swelled the picket lines to over 5,000 milling around the plant gates, shutting it down, shutting off traffic on all streets leading to the plant. We kept that plant closed for nineteen days. No one got in, not even the owners of the plant." [30] The IBEW claimed that the "friends" of the UE were husky coal miners and steel workers from nearby towns.[31] The NLRB held the contract invalid, and ordered elections to determine the choice of the employees. These were held on September 11, the IBEW winning by a slender majority of 105 out of 1,445 votes cast.

The 1937 Convention and Subsequent Recession

The 1937 Convention of UE which was held in September, marked a first high point of organizational success, and preceded by only a few months the rapid decline in economic conditions which limited the possibilities of union progress for several years. The union claimed a membership of 125,000, organized into 275 locals.[32] In his report to the convention, President Carey took pride in the rapid growth of the union:

A skeleton international of 18 locals only a year and a half ago, we have been transformed into a powerful organization of approximately 275 affiliated local unions with contracts with many of the most important corporations of the industry. At our last convention in Fort Wayne we had 26 locals. Do you remember how proud we were of the eight new locals we had chartered during the first five months of our life as a union? Now, with a membership 300% greater than it was then, we are carrying on or preparing to enter into national negotiations with such firms as General Electric, Westinghouse and General Motors. We have won exclusive bargaining rights in many of the most important electrical and radio manufacturing shops in the country, as well as in scores of smaller plants.[33]

Unquestionably, UE had good reason to rejoice in its progress. Secretary-Treasurer Emspak reported month-to-month figures, representing actual paid per capita membership, as follows:[34]

August	1936	19,000	February	1937	27,200
September	1936	21,100	March	1937	30,800
October	1936	23,400	April	1937	41,000
November	1936	22,900	May	1937	47,000
December	1936	26,400	June	1937	62,400
January	1937	27,500	July	1937	70,900

Discrepancies between these data and higher membership claims do not necessarily invalidate either set. The July figure of 70,900, which was probably somewhat higher by September, represented members for whom locals actually sent in their per capita payments, whereas other estimates undoubtedly included persons who had signed membership cards but were not paying dues, because of unemployment or other causes.

The 1937 convention was a generally harmonious affair. The only controversial subject, presaging future controversies, was a resolution endorsing the American League Against War and Fascism, a communist front organization, and urging the union to participate in its forthcoming congress. Local 202 of Springfield and several smaller locals objected strongly. The resolution was introduced shortly before the convention was to adjourn, apparently in the hope that it would slip through unnoticed, but in the face of the considerable opposition that was expressed, its sponsors permitted it to be referred to the Executive Board.[35]

The latter half of 1937 and the year 1938 constituted a difficult period for UE. Writing in September 1938, the general officers reported:

For the past six months our union has been undergoing a severe test. It is our first experience in maintaining the organization in the face of adverse economic conditions. We not only have maintained our position as a Union but we have forged ahead.

The beginning of the present depression started shortly after our last convention one year ago. Business fell off remarkably fast beginning in October and within a few short months, it was down to almost the lowest ebb reached in the previous depression. Comparison of the past six months of this year with the same six-month period last year is enlightening. For the first six months this year, the total sales of all kinds of electrical equipment was approximately $750,000,000 compared with $1,150,000,000 in the corresponding period last year. This represents a decline of approximately 35 per cent.[36]

With an estimated 60,000 members unemployed, the union could do little but attempt to maintain its organization. Fortunately for it, the major manufacturers, with the exception of Philco, were not in a combatative frame of mind. Had they chosen to fight, they might well have broken the UE at this critical juncture.

After more than a year of negotiation, General Electric agreed, on February 20, 1938, to deal with UE on an interplant basis for all GE plants in which the union was designated as majority representative, a major union goal. The agreement was largely procedural in character, and the union gained no specific wage concessions. However, General Electric was operating on a so-called "community wage" pattern, whereby wages were adjusted to equal those paid for comparable work in nearby industries on the basis of surveys undertaken every three months. General Electric was regarded as offering good conditions of employment, so that this agreement, limited in scope though it was, represented a considerable achievement for the union.

The most severe test to which the union was put came from an unexpected quarter — Philco. Although there had been a wage strike against this company in 1937, union relations with it were of long standing and relatively good. In February 1938, however, with less than 2000 out of a normal force of 8000 workers employed, the company informed the union that it would have to acquiesce in concessions which would bring Philco standards in line with those being maintained in competitive firms. The company demanded a wage reduction of from 25 to 40 per cent, a forty-hour week in place of the prevailing thirty-six hour week, alteration of the seniority system, and other changes in the direction of increasing productivity. The union refused to accede, and on May 1, the plant was shut down.[37]

The strike was a severe one, since the UE believed that the company was endeavoring to break the union. In the words of the local strike leader:

The Company saw its advantage during this last Wall Street-made depression to bust our union. So they started laying off people, figuring by the time our agreement would run out, the morale of our people would be broken down and it would be an easy matter for us to offset any kind of an agreement. On March 1st, we were informed by the Company that they intended to terminate the agreement and would we please come up to their office and sit down and negotiate a new contract. We went up there and boy! did we get a set-back. It was perfect. It was not an agreement. It was disaster. It was disaster just to look at that paper they prepared. . . . For forty-five days we only had one more meeting. That was all. I often wished we had accepted the proposal by the company, just to see what they would have done. They would have died of shock and would never have stuck by it anyhow.

The strike lasted for more than four months. In the agreement that ended it, the company gained most of its objectives. Basic rates were reduced, the forty-hour week was installed, and the union shop clause was eliminated. However, the company agreed not to hire new workers until all former employees had been rehired, thus in effect continuing the union shop. Despite the length of the strike, there was considerable resistance against accepting the agreement:

We know that we have gotten all that it is possible to get from the Company. Everything that was possible to get was there. We then decided it was time to have a meeting of our members. A meeting was called. . . . I am proud to say that when I got upon that floor to recommend the acceptance of that agreement, I was very heartily booed. I am proud of that, because of this fact I am proud of the membership that had been out of work for a year. We had a soup kitchen running for eleven months and still there were about 20% of these people who did not want to go back to work.[38]

The union retained exclusive bargaining rights, so that if it had been part of the purpose of Philco to dispense with the union entirely, this aim was frustrated. However, the relative bargaining position of UE had certainly deteriorated.

Another strike that received considerable publicity during this period was against the Maytag Company of Newton, Iowa, a manufacturer of electrical appliances. Situated in a semirural community in which it was the dominant employer, the company was able to marshal the full force of community opinion, as well as the local and state police power, in a campaign to reduce wages and perhaps ultimately to destroy the union. The strike had one unusual feature, in that UE received the full support of the AFL Iowa State

Federation of Labor. A number of UE leaders, including Carey, were charged with criminal syndicalism and sedition in a manner reminiscent of an earlier era of labor history. Faced by several injunctions, the union was forced to return to work without a contract.[39]

Further contributing to a decline in UE strength was the decision of the CIO, in February 1938, to set up the Utility Workers Organizing Committee, to which all UE locals in the utility industry were transferred.[40] It was felt at CIO headquarters that an industry as diverse and widely scattered as utilities could best be administered separately. The fact that the organizers who had been working in the utility field had been on the payroll of the CIO rather than of UE [41] may help explain why the latter was willing to accede to the transfer of jurisdiction without overt protest.

The foregoing events led to a much less optimistic convention in 1938 than in the previous year. The general officers, in their report to the convention, admitted frankly: "Even if we only held our ground we could say that our Union has made progress. Maintaining wage levels and general working conditions in times such as these is a step forward. Maintaining the terms of existing agreements, and in some cases improving them, is an excellent manifestation of how well our Locals have been consolidated and strengthened in the past year." [42] The current membership figure was not given to the convention. The union subsequently revealed, however, that paid membership as of July 31, 1938, was 95 per cent of the previous year's figure,[43] which would mean about 67,000 members. At the constitutional convention of the CIO, held in November 1938, UE voted on 157,891 members.[44] Again, the difference may have been due in large measure to unemployment. Unemployed members could, upon request, receive an "unemployment stamp" free of charge for their dues book in lieu of a dues stamp. As long as an unemployed member continued to draw unemployment stamps, he was continued in the local as a member in good standing. Particularly in locals like those in Philco, where a union shop prevailed, the unemployed maintained their membership assiduously.

The impact of the recession of 1937–1938 may be seen clearly from the data in Table 3, which were compiled by the union for the electrical manufacturing and radio industries, on the basis of census and other statistics.

The employment figures do not adequately reflect part-time work in 1938, and overstate the actual average level of employment for the year. Unemployment was placed at 70,000 in 1937 and 172,000 in 1938,[46] but there is no indication of how these data were secured.

Table 3.

Employment, production, and wages in electrical manufacturing, 1935–1938

Year	Number of workers employed	Production (millions of dollars)	Average annual wage (dollars)
1935	225,000	1350	1430
1936	263,000	1668	1530
1937	306,000	1980	1660
1938	284,000	1417	1540

Source: *UE News,* June 17, 1939, p. 8.

Economic Revival and the Development of Factionalism

Despite an improvement in business conditions beginning late in 1938, and continuing throughout 1939, UE remained relatively stationary. This lag of organization behind the business cycle may have been due to recession-induced caution on the part of both labor and management. Unemployment continued at a high level, and in September 1939, the UE general officers, after pointing to the increase in electrical equipment sales during the three months ending June 1939, and to the large volume of orders currently being booked, warned the membership: "It would be very unwise . . . to see in this present upward direction any guarantee that the trend will continue in such a direction. The highly complicated external and internal economic situations in these times mean that the direction of these trends could alter overnight, and your general officers bear these possibilities constantly in mind." The organizational staff was continued at the 1938 level, with 28 field organizers in the employ of the international union in September 1939.

During the year, UE was faced with an aggressive campaign against it by the IBEW. The UE complained that the IBEW, instead of remaining within the building construction industry and trying to build up its organization there, was "dissipating its members' funds in trying to break up our organization by signing 'back door' collusive agreements and by attempting to institute a boycott through the building trades locals that it has organized." [47] UE resorted to the unusual step of instituting a suit in the federal courts charging IBEW with a conspiracy to deprive its members of their rights under the Wagner Act through boycotting their products. In a number of other cases, UE brought NLRB complaints against employers whom they charged with collusive action in favoring the IBEW; among them were the Jefferson Electric Company, the Electric Vacuum Cleaner Company, the Ansley Radio Company, the Pilot Radio Company, and the Cornell-

Dubilier Electric Corporation. At the Camden Plant of RCA, where a former company union had been chartered by the IBEW in 1937 and remained in active opposition to UE, the NLRB granted the request of the former for another representation election in October 1939. Indignant at having its bargaining status called into question, UE threw every resource into the election fight and won handily with 6294 votes to 1035 for the IBEW.[48] The IBEW, for its part, felt justified in using every weapon at its command in the internecine strife with UE. President Dan Tracy, who became United States assistant secretary of labor in 1940, characterized UE as "nothing more nor less than a branch of the secret service of Joseph Stalin, Russian dictator. One of the communist fronts signified to the Congress of the United States as deeply tinged with communism is the United Radio and Electrical Workers' Union, so-called. This puppet of the communist executive board is but a branch of the so-called Communist Party. . . ."[49]

The communist issue in UE first began to reach an acute state late in 1939. Prior to that year, the three general officers had worked in harmony, and ideological issues were not permitted to come to the floor of the annual conventions. President James Carey had said of his relationships with his fellow officers: "We got along well enough until the Nazi-Soviet pact in August, 1939. Then my leftist associates suddenly laid off Hitler and started ranting about the imperialist war . . . as the months passed I discovered that they were in complete control of the national office; they dominated the executive committee, ran the union paper, and were strongly entrenched in the locals and districts. All the organizers were party-liners."[50]

The men who performed this feat of organization under the unsuspecting nose of President Carey were Julius Emspak and James J. Matles, respectively secretary-treasurer and director of organization of UE. Both men had come into UE from the Steel and Metal Workers Industrial Union, an affiliate of the communist Trade Union Unity League.[51] Emspak had been a leader of the independent local union in the Schenectady plant of General Electric, and occupied the post of secretary-treasurer from the very beginning of the union. He was also editor of the union paper, the *UE News*, from the date of its establishment in January 1939. (Before that time, the official organ of the union was a special edition of the *People's Press*, a publication which was commonly known as a front for the Communist Party.[52]) Matles had started as a local lodge master in the International Association of Machinists, had led 10,000 members into the TUUL, and then back into the Machinists when the TUUL dissolved in 1935. He switched to UE in 1937 at the head of 15,000 machinists, and at the 1937 Convention became director of organization, a strategic post which gave him supervisory power over the field staff of the union and enabled him to colonize it with followers of the Communist Party line. Although Matles denied being a member of the Communist Party, the *Daily Worker* of November 6, 1933, quoted him as follows: "Only the Communist Party as the party of the working class represents the interests of the entire working population." Emspak and Matles were not the only left wing stalwarts in UE. Among the prominent early officials of UE who have been placed in this category were William Sentner, president of District 8; James Macleish, president of District 4; and James Lustig, Ruth Young, and Thomas F. Dwyer.[53]

As president, Carey undoubtedly had more power and authority than the other general officers. However, as the principal public representative of UE, as well as the secretary of the CIO beginning in 1938, he was called upon for numerous activities outside the union. A religious Catholic, Carey was interested in many social movements, and gradually relinquished the running of the union's daily affairs, including negotiations with employers, to his willing associates. When he awoke to the communist danger, it was too late; "for two years I fought back, but my improvisations were no match for the smooth running Communists' machine."[54]

There is some doubt, however, that "The UE, from the very beginning of its organization within the CIO, was dominated by an organized Communist minority."[55] At the 1936 Convention, for example, a resolution putting UE on record in support of the action of a so-called Trade Union Committee, which was raising $100,000 to aid the Spanish loyalist government, was defeated.[56] A 1938 Convention resolution in favor of lifting the arms embargo on Republican Spain was carried only by a close vote, while another resolution putting the convention on record "as being opposed to any efforts toward undermining or circumventing the democratic processes of our nation, and further [condemning] attempts by any minority to overthrow such government by force and violence" was adopted. Even more surprising, the following resolution was adopted unanimously:

Be it resolved that the members of the United Electrical, Radio and Machine Workers of America . . . hereby agree in principle with the Congressional investigations into un-American activities, but condemn the undignified and un-American conduct of the Dies Committee as unbecoming the dignity and tending to lower the prestige of the United States Congress.[57]

To the assertion that the communist faction accepted these resolutions for tactical reasons, to mask their real control, it may be replied that the later history of UE does not bear out such a theory of communist strategy.

The 1939 Convention took place shortly after the signing of the Russo-German pact, before the new communist line had trickled down. Germany was still the enemy, as the following quotation from the *UE News* indicates: "By this fact system it appears that the firmer the treaty that pledges Germany and Russia not to fight, the firmer will be the rest of Europe in resisting further aggrandizement of Germany, and the longer the treaty lasts, the longer will resistance to German aggression continue." [58] The convention voted in favor of a third term for President Roosevelt, and in favor of permitting all nations to purchase armaments from the United States. There was still no cause for political conflict between left and right. The officers' report, for example, contained the following passage:

The President's peace policy is, in our opinion, one of the outstanding contributions to national policy. On the one hand, it has avoided the direct entanglement of this nation with European quarrels; but on the other hand, it has reaffirmed our national intention never to renege on our moral obligations to those democracies most like our own.

The convention was a fairly routine affair, and again as in 1938, the emphasis was on holding the line rather than on new gains. It was stated that UE written contracts covered 140,000 workers, while 70,000 additional workers were covered by less formal agreements,[59] but no membership figures were given. From subsequent data, however, it appears that paid per capita membership as of July 31, 1939, was precisely at the level of the previous year.[60]

The following year was notable for two series of events: a resumption of organizational progress for the first time since the onset of the depression in 1937, and the intensification of ideological conflict within UE. The most significant gains were made at Westinghouse, which alone among the major producers had refused to enter into a written agreement with UE. On March 29, 1940, the NLRB ruled that refusal to reduce a contract to writing constituted a violation of the company's legal obligation to bargain collectively.[61] This decision was a great moral victory for the union, and spurred organizational work among Westinghouse employees, so that by September 1940, UE had gained sole bargaining rights at nineteen Westinghouse plants.[62] The company appealed the NLRB decision to the courts, and not until the U. S. Supreme Court in the Heinz case[63] upheld the board on the matter of a written agreement did Westinghouse finally agree to sign a contract with the union.

The union reported in December 1939, that membership had risen by 65 per cent over the same period the previous year. During the first three months of 1940 more than 10,000 new members joined UE, and 17 new companies were brought under contract.[64] In March, the Fort Wayne, Indiana, GE workers voted 3052 to 901 to make UE their collective bargaining agent. In May, Local B-1010 of the IBEW in New York City voted to abandon its Class B charter and affiliate with UE. In August, the Erie Works of GE became the 19th and last of the large GE plants to come under the national UE contract.[65]

In sum, the UE ended its fiscal year, July 31, 1940, with contracts covering (a) 19 GE plants, a gain of nine during the year, with 15,700 additional employees covered; (b) 19 Westinghouse plants, a gain of five, covering an additional 8200 employees; (c) four plants of the General Motors Corporation Electrical Division as against one at the beginning of the year, for a gain of 15,000 workers covered.[66] Paid up per capita membership was 130 per cent of the 1937 level, or about 92,000.[67] UE contracts covered 230,000 workers, but of course many of these were not union members.

Soon after the September 1939 Convention, the *UE News* began to mirror the Communist Party line on both foreign and domestic affairs. A full page article on September 30 was headed "Tories Use War Scare as Screen to Hide America's Real Problems," [68] initiating a theme that was hammered again and again during the ensuing months. In February 1940, a full page of favorable comment was devoted to a pamphlet entitled "The Yanks Are Not Coming," which had originated with Harry Bridges' longshoremen's union, and was one of the principal communist propaganda slogans while it was pursuing its "neutralist" line.[69] President Roosevelt was mentioned in an increasingly critical tone, notwithstanding the fact that the 1939 convention had endorsed his re-election.

President James Carey did not react very quickly to the new communist line, perhaps because it coincided in part with what was then a strong anti-war sentiment not only in the CIO as a whole, but among the American people generally. There were few labor leaders in 1940 who were willing to advocate policies that might lead the United States into war. In response to a charge by the Dies Committee that the UE was communist-dominated, Carey wrote:

Our union is managed and administered by leaders who receive their mandate directly from the membership. We have frequent and democratically conducted conventions. The will of the membership was expressed freely and clearly. There is no control by Communist leaders in our national union, and there won't be.

In July, however, he came out flatly for the reelection of Roosevelt, at a time when the communists were preparing to follow John L. Lewis into the opposition, thus straining relations among the general officers.

At the September 1940 Convention, the main battle took place over the issue of conscription. The resolutions committee presented a report condemning peacetime conscription, whereupon Vice-President Campbell introduced a substitute minority motion opposing the Burke-Wadsworth Bill, the specific conscription measure which was before Congress at the time, but favoring conscription in principle as essential to the defense of the United States. Matles made the key speech in defense of the majority (anticonscription) position, which was adopted by a vote of 423–197. There were undoubtedly many anticommunists who were opposed to conscription, so that this vote cannot be taken to indicate the true relative strength of the communists. But against the background of the debate that took place, it does indicate that they were in firm control of the convention.

Another indication of their strength, and of its limitations, came on the question of endorsing Roosevelt for a third term. The resolutions committee submitted a resolution instructing the general officers to investigate the question, and authorizing the executive board to make a final decision. A substitute motion from the floor favored outright endorsement. The antiendorsement speakers argued that withholding the endorsement would strengthen John L. Lewis in bargaining with the administration on labor matters, and there is no doubt that many delegates were swayed by this appeal for support to the CIO president. The other group based its case on the plea that of the three candidates, Roosevelt, Willkie, and Browder, Roosevelt was the only possible choice. Finally, a compromise resolution was adopted authorizing the general officers "in consultation with John L. Lewis . . . and Chairman Philip Murray . . . to represent the interests of the UER & MWA relative to the endorsement of President Franklin D. Roosevelt for a third term and to transmit their joint recommendation for action to all UE locals." [70]

Communist Capture of the UE

The year 1941 witnessed a phenomenal rise in UE organizational activity. The tempo of defense production was increasing rapidly, and the electrical manufacturing industry, particularly heavy machinery, was in the forefront of the defense drive. During the twelve-month period ended July 31,

1941, UE signed up and received initiation fees from 116,000 new members. Paid membership on July 31, 1941, was put at 255 per cent of the 1937 level,[71] about 180,000 members. The spread between paid and total membership had undoubtedly declined, due to favorable employment conditions.

In their report to the 1941 Convention, the general officers listed the following items as the outstanding events of the preceding year:

1. The conclusion of a written agreement with Westinghouse. This agreement, which was similar in content to a new agreement negotiated at about the same time with General Electric, provided for a wage increase of ten cents per hour; an increase in the night bonus of 5 to 10 per cent; double time for work on Sundays and holidays; vacations of one week after one year of service and two weeks after five years; and in the case of General Electric, abolition of the community survey method of establishing wage rates.[72]

2. The signing of the first national agreement for the General Electric Division of the General Motors Corporation, covering 26,000 employees. Here, too, the union won a ten cent per hour wage increase.

3. The conclusion of a national agreement with the Phelps Dodge Copper Products Corporation, covering 3500 employees.

4. The conclusion of an agreement with the Electric Storage Battery Company, covering 3000 employees.

5. The successful close of a four-year battle with the Westinghouse Airbrake and Union Switch and Signal companies for written agreements.

In line with communist policy, "UE set in motion a general strike campaign throughout the industry, in October 1940. . . . A few of the strikes did take place. . . ."[73] However, no major strikes were called, indicating either that the communist leaders were uncertain of their hold on the rank and file or that they were unwilling to risk hard-earned collective agreements in political adventures. Perhaps obligations to the Communist Party were considered fulfilled merely by cheering the aircraft workers who were engaged in serious defense strikes.[74]

The general officers presented to the 1941 convention a five-year record of UE successes in NLRB elections, as shown in Table 4.[75]

These figures emphasize the spurt in organizing activity that occurred in 1941. It is noteworthy, however, that the size of the average bargaining unit declined significantly in comparison with earlier years, indicating that membership gains were being achieved by pushing out to smaller plants. The role of the NLRB in union organization emerges as well, for over the five-year period some 125,000 workers voted in elections in which UE par-

Table 4.

Results of NLRB elections involving UE, 1937–1941

Year	Plants won or lost		Ballots	
	Won	Lost	UE	Other
1937	21	12	19,454	11,712
1938	34	10	13,171	6,981
1939	28	3	2,370	2,148
1940	45	10	23,911	11,910
1941	121	19	28,067	15,022

ticipated. The percentage of votes won by UE for the period as a whole was 70.

It is an interesting and curious fact that the considerable membership gains of 1941 were achieved in the face of an increasingly overt espousal of communist policies by leading union officials, and by the union's newspaper. Shortly before the 1940 elections, the general officers announced that after meeting with Lewis and Murray, they had reached the following conclusion: ". . . we recommend that our locals take such action that will best express the desires and aspirations of their local membership." [76] Thus the national union failed to endorse Roosevelt despite overwhelmingly pro-Roosevelt sentiment among the members. Editorial after editorial attacked Lend Lease, characterizing it as tantamount to a declaration of war.[77] It may be objected that there were many people in the United States apart from communists who opposed Lend Lease and other aid to the embattled democracies. However, the editorials in *UE News* bear the unmistakable stamp of communist authorship in their phraseology. A few samples will make this clear:

The only way that Wall Street can make a profit out of the jobless is to invest them in a war of conquest. War, which cripples the power of labor; war, which brings juicy arms contracts in its train; war, from which the profiteers may reap rich colonial empire.

The Lend-Lease Bill is badly named. It should be called the Give-Away Bill, for surely it is giving away the war aims of Washington. The politicians see the bill as a barometer of the people's resistance to war. If it goes through without much difficulty Washington will take it as a green light for war. Nothing that could happen today would slow up the pro-war, anti-labor campaign as much as defeat of the Lend-Lease Bill.[78]

On the very eve of the German attack on Russia, the *UE News* reprinted in bold type the following editorial from the *Dayton Union News:*

Is Nazism frightful and hateful? of course. Every American believes so — and rightly. But how about the millions of coolie laborers in England's India, where thousands of union leaders are now in jail, and how about the fine Irishmen, whom England would now starve out . . . ? The NMU suggested to CIO President Philip Murray that he call a national congress for peace. We must support such a call. We must start an organizing drive for peace.[79]

This was the very last issue of the *UE News* which contained peace talk. A month later the editor asserted that "with a new and greater emergency facing the country, the time is ripe for a wholesale overhauling of the entire defense structure," [80] while in September, the following account was given of the passage of a UE convention resolution: "Some 400 cheering delegates rising almost to a man in an impressive defiance to the forces that seek to conquer and enslave the working people of the world, voted approval of the anti-Hitler foreign policy of the United States. . . ." There was no mention of Indian coolies or the starving Irish.

At the beginning of 1941, Carey finally mounted an offensive against the communists, but in the parlance of the times, it was too little and too late. The first inkling that an assiduous reader of the *UE News* would have gained that something was amiss with the administration of the union came in an article appearing in Carey's personal column, which was not subject to editorial censorship, in which he said in part:

I am confident that our principle of equality of membership to all workers in our industry will not be disturbed unless one group seeks position of leadership out of proportion to the group's way of thinking among the membership. Should any group do so, particularly an undemocratic and intolerant political party, the UE rank and file will certainly take positive steps to restrict or eliminate such aggression on the natural and equal rights of others.[81]

The issue which precipitated an open split between the left and right wing forces in the union arose in March 1941. A local union inquired of Carey whether it could adopt a local constitutional provision barring a proven communist, nazi or fascist from a position of responsibility and trust. Carey discussed the problem in his *UE News* column and replied in essence that the proposal was not in conflict with the constitution or bylaws of the international union. Emspak, as editor, appended a note at the foot of Carey's column, stating that he had asked Carey to postpone its insertion in the newspaper until after a meeting of the general executive board, but that Carey had refused.

Shortly after the outbreak of war between Germany and Russia, and the consequent reversal of the Communist Party line, Carey wrote openly on the communist issue for the first time:

A back flip with a full twist and presto — Great Britain is purged of all her sins. Hitler is to be hated even more than Roosevelt. The "imperialistic blood bath" becomes a people's war for freedom; Summer Welles becomes a progressive and Wheeler an enemy of the people. The performance of a trapeze artist in a circus is entertainment, but political acrobats in pink tights posing as labor leaders are a disgrace to the union and insult the intelligence of the membership.[82]

The political issues were kept alive in the letters-to-the-editor columns of *UE News* for the remainder of the summer. Carey referred to his having been told that he would be reelected to the presidency of the union if he changed his position on the right of local unions to bar communist officers; he nevertheless reasserted his contention that local membership had the right to determine the qualifications of their officers. A month before the convention, several locals banded together in the Inter-Local Committee for Progressive Trade Unionism in support of Carey's reelection, and openly criticized other leaders of the union for following the communist line.

The 1941 Convention of the United Electrical Workers was easily the most controversial and bitterly fought in the union's history, though by comparison, for example, with conventions of the United Automobile Workers, it was a relatively orderly and restrained affair. Disingenuously, the international officers reported to the delegates:

Those who thought that the British Government was a reliable source of the will and power to defeat Fascism — they may continue to think so if they wish; and those who thought the Soviet Union with its Army was the reliable force to do the job — they, too, may continue to think it was they who were right, if they wish. For certainly, both groups now agree that the united might of *both* the British and the Soviet Governments, *backed by the United States and supported most of all by that hatred for Fascism that is bred in the bone of every worker* — such a combination can hardly fail to rid humanity once and for all of the very fountain-head of world Fascism, the Nazi Government of Germany.

The principal battle of the convention was over the issue of local union rights. The resolutions committee proposed that any person guilty of hostile acts toward the United States or the UE could "have no place whatever either as member or officer in this union . . . [and] that any good-standing member of the Union is entitled to all rights and privileges without discrimination, unless such member be proved guilty of acts against the nation or against the Union in accord with the procedure set forth in our Constitution. . . ." This was a substitute for four resolutions submitted to the committee, one of which would have prevented communists, fascists and nazis from holding union office.

Carey, who was in the chair, stated that the issue was being considered by the committee on constitution and was therefore out of order. Albert J. Fitzgerald, chairman of the resolutions committee, immediately appealed the decision of the chair, and on a roll-call vote, Carey was overruled, 714–450. A long and acrimonious debate on the resolution itself then ensued. One delegate declaimed: "The report of the Resolutions Committee makes no mention of Communism, Fascism or Nazism. What is going on? Are we afraid to mention these words around here? I have been to three conventions, and this is the first time I ever heard it mentioned, and we are not going to cover up any more. We are going to bring it out." Another delegate noted that decisions of the UE executive board were published in the *Daily Worker* before they were reported to the membership, despite the fact that the union constitution provided that the content of executive board meetings was not to be divulged to any outside interest. Nevertheless, the resolution was carried by a voice vote.

The same issue arose once more when the constitution committee, by a vote of 17 to 1, recommended the following constitutional interpretation:

That a local union has the right to set up qualifications for its local officers, provided such qualifications are not in conflict with the policy that any good standing member of the Union is entitled to all rights and privileges without discrimination, unless such member be found guilty of acts against the nation or against the Union in accord with the procedure set forth in our Constitution.

The minority report held that there was nothing in the international constitution denying locals the right to establish qualifications for their elective officials. Carey argued on behalf of the minority position, while Emspak and Fitzgerald carried the brunt of the argument for the majority. Fitzgerald prefaced his remarks with the statement: "I am not a Communist. I am not dominated by Communists. And as a citizen of the United States of America, I despise the philosophy of the Communist Party. But as a member and present officer and coming officer of this union, I will not let that issue tear this union apart." [83] On a roll call vote, the majority recommendation was carried by 792 to 373.

In the election of officers, Albert J. Fitzgerald was nominated to oppose Carey, the first time the latter had faced any opposition for the post since the founding of the union. Fitzgerald was from the General Electric local in Lynn, Mass. He was elected by the close vote of 635 to 539, attesting to Carey's personal popularity among the rank and file delegates. Carey has asserted that "I twice had to reject Communist offers of support in my re-election campaign, in return for future good behavior. The party wanted me as president because I was good window dressing." [84] In Fitzgerald, the

Communist Party secured a respectable Catholic who was nevertheless willing to provide "window dressing."

In view of Carey's awareness of the communist threat to the union, his subsequent behavior at the convention was remarkable. He seconded the nomination of Emspak for the position of secretary-treasurer, saying: "I think I know Jules better than any delegate in this convention. I have had the pleasure of living with him and working with him, and I sincerely hope that he receives the unanimous vote of this convention to assure the good continuation of the splendid organization we have all played a part in building." Later on, he asserted: "When somebody says, you have a difference of opinion to Jim Matles, I say that I have many differences of opinion with Jim Matles — but I can sit down with him any day and we can work out an agreement. The same thing is true of Julius Emspak and the other members of the General Executive Board." [85] In return, Matles warmly praised Carey and suggested that the convention endorse him for reelection as CIO secretary. Carey's motives in acquiescing quietly in his removal from the presidency may have been mixed; he may have feared expulsion from the union, remembering the fate of Homer Martin of the Automobile Workers, and felt, possibly, that only in this way could he continue to work within the union; or, believing that his defeat was inevitable, he may have wanted to do nothing to impair his position as CIO secretary. On the other hand, not being versed in sectarian politics as, for example, the Reuther brothers were, Carey may have genuinely misinterpreted the true nature of communist purposes in gaining control of the union, and considered that their victory was simply an incident of union politics which had to be accepted in a sportsmanlike manner.

Thus, in 1941, the communists gained unchallenged control of a trade union organization of about a quarter of a million members, employed in some of the most critical of the nation's industries. "It has been estimated that three-fourths of its membership was employed in defense industries, manufacturing aircraft and marine equipment, gauges, aerial cameras, motors, and cartridges." [86] It had no effective competition from the International Brotherhood of Electrical Workers, which had been unable to make any substantial inroads into the manufacturing end of the electrical industry. Almost a decade was to elapse before the electrical workers were afforded an organizational alternative to UE, once more under the banner of the CIO, and led by James B. Carey.

6

The Rubber Industry

Rubber manufacturing was the first of the mass production industries into which the CIO moved following upon its formation. This was not the result of any plan, but was due to the activities of the rubber workers themselves. It was the rubber workers who pioneered the potentialities of the sit-down strike technique which was later used with telling effect by the auto workers, and there is considerable justice to the boast of the United Rubber Workers that the Goodyear strike of February-March 1936, was the "first CIO strike." [1]

As in automobiles, steel, electrical manufacturing, and other mass production industries, the enactment of Section 7a of the National Industrial Recovery Act set off a wave of organization in rubber. The workers were first organized in federal labor unions by the American Federation of Labor, and by the end of 1933, membership in these organizations may have been as high as 50,000. Yielding to the demand of the workers, the AFL permitted the federal locals to form the United Rubber Workers' Council in June 1934, "but the craft workers were given separate representation so that although they formed only a small proportion of the total membership they could outvote the production locals." [2] Even in 1955, more than twenty years later, the official organ of the Rubber Workers' Union wrote of these events with some bitterness:

The FLU's were ordered to surrender their skilled tradesmen and maintenance men to the various AFL craft unions and to surrender funds which had been collected from such craftsmen for initiations and dues despite the fact that 35 cents had been paid to the AFL in per capita for each of them.

The little which was left in FLU treasuries from the dues dollars had been used up already in efforts to get recognition from the rubber companies, which had been won in only a few cases. This bloodletting by the Rubber Workers' Council . . . almost obliterated the rubber workers' organizations. [3]

A general strike of rubber workers in Akron was narrowly averted in early 1935 through the intermediation of Secretary of Labor Perkins, but the settlement, which failed to provide for union recognition, broke the morale of the workers and led to disintegration of the federal labor unions. Under the prodding of John L. Lewis, the Executive Council of the AFL in May 1935, agreed to charter the federal locals as an international union. But the charter excepted from the jurisdiction of the new union workers employed in rubber plants who were engaged in building, manufacturing or installing machinery, or maintenance work.[4] When Lewis raised the objection that this limitation of jurisdiction repudiated the 1934 AFL convention resolution on industrial unionism, Hutcheson replied: "There is a vast difference between the Mine Workers in the manner they are employed and the rubber workers. The rubber workers and automobile workers work in factories and buildings and these buildings have to be kept in condition. There is a big difference between these buildings and the mine buildings and I think there is a vast difference between the two groups of workers." [5]

The constitutional convention of the United Rubber Workers convened in Akron, Ohio, on September 12, 1935. It was called to order by Coleman Claherty, a veteran AFL organizer who had directed the activities of the AFL in the rubber industry since 1933. Only 26 federal labor unions were represented, and these had a total membership not much in excess of 3000,[6] a far cry from the membership that had been built up in 1933. The first order of business was the presentation of the AFL charter, for which purpose William Green had come to Akron. Sensing the rebellious mood of the delegates, Green opened the convention with a long address in which he intimated that the AFL would have to retain a degree of control over the new organization, justifying this in the following terms:

the American Federation of Labor must be convinced beyond peradventure of a doubt that when a new International Union is launched that it is soundly and permanently established, that it will live to serve the workers in the industry over which the International Union has jurisdiction, that it will not fail, that it will not pass out of existence. . . .

He then went on to warn the delegates that they would have to respect the jurisdictions of other unions, as defined by the AFL Executive Council. At the conclusion of his speech, Salvatore Camelio, who was to play an important role in the organization, arose and queried: "I would like to ask if we the delegates assembled accept this charter, does this give the President [Green] the right to appoint its officers?" Green replied that it was not for the delegates to decide whether to accept or reject the charter. "It cannot be amended and it cannot be accepted and it cannot be rejected. The parent body is creating a new International Union and it cannot barter with the

Union that it is creating. . . . This confers upon me the right to designate or appoint your officers for a probationary period providing I think, and in my judgment it seems necessary, to do that to protect your International Union. . . ."

On the very next day, the conflict between Green and the more militant rubber workers came to a head. A minority of the committee on resolutions presented a resolution calling upon Green to appoint Coleman Claherty the first president of the union, to pay his salary and expenses, and to finance the international headquarters while the union was getting started. Delegates rose to urge that the leaders of the new union should be rubber workers (Claherty was a boilermaker by trade), and protested that they were being deprived of the right to choose their own representatives. Green warned that the AFL would withhold financial assistance unless Claherty was accepted, but Sherman Dalrymple and other delegates argued that leadership which enjoyed rank-and-file confidence would soon bring in sufficient members to make the union self-sustaining. By a vote of 45 5/6 to 9 1/6, the minority resolution was rejected, and a substitute resolution conferring upon the convention full authority to elect officers adopted in its stead. Green accepted this decision, although with some reluctance. In taking leave of the convention, he said:

you have decided to refuse to request me and the Executive Council to establish and finance your International headquarters. You have said that you don't want that from the American Federation of Labor. So I accept your word as final. . . . Now the convention is turned over to you. You may elect your officers now from top to bottom and you may arrange to finance your convention and your organization work and carry on.

As a parting shot, he warned: "Do not, under any circumstances, transgress upon the jurisdiction of other International Unions. . . ."[7]

The delegates then proceeded to elect their own officers, all of whom were rubber workers. Sherman Dalrymple, president of the Goodrich local, was elected president, Thomas F. Burns was elected vice-president, and Frank Grillo, secretary-treasurer. These men continued as general officers until 1941, when Burns withdrew from his post to accept government employment. All were trade unionists without ideological motivation, and during their tenure the union largely escaped the factionalism which plagued the Automobile Workers' Union. This is not to say that the union was not militant; the following quotation from a lead article by Dalrymple in the first issue of the *United Rubber Worker* attests to the temper of the time: "We, as rubber workers, believing that by united action we could best improve the conditions of the workers employed in the rubber industry and being class conscious, we realize the necessity of organization, based upon the class struggle, in order to bring about a more equal distribution of labor and the products of labor." [8]

Shortly after the close of the constitutional convention, rubber worker delegates to the 1935 AFL convention introduced a resolution calling for URW jurisdiction over all employees in rubber factories, in protest against the jurisdictional limitation contained in its charter. It was the point of order raised by Hutcheson against discussion of this resolution, and Lewis' angry retort, which caused the dramatic encounter between the two men and signaled the formation of the CIO. The point of order was sustained by a close vote, and the resolution died. [9]

The new union started out in a precarious financial situation. The AFL turned over to it the furniture and equipment of the Rubber Workers' Council, a balance of $1800 remaining in the treasury of that organization, and donated $1000 in cash. [10] Efforts were made to induce all the AFL federal locals to affiliate, and by the end of 1935, 38 federal locals had done so.

The First Organizing Efforts

Early in 1936, spontaneous sit-down strikes developed as a manifestation of the drive to organize the rubber workers. The first one occurred at the Firestone plant in Akron, where workers stayed in for four days beginning January 28 to protest a discriminatory penalty against a union man. A few days later, 100 men at Goodyear struck against a 10 per cent wage cut, and on February 8, 1500 men sat down at Goodrich over the appropriate wage rates to be paid to persons transferred from one job to another. [11] This method of demonstration became so troublesome that the union was soon obliged to take a firm stand against it. Dalrymple wrote in the May 1936 issue of the union newspaper: "It is not the policy of our International Union or any of its affiliated locals to encourage unnecessary cessations of work or sit-downs. We believe in the settlement of disputes by proper negotiation with Management. Sit-downs do not occur in plants where true collective bargaining exists." [12] Nevertheless, the sit downs continued; in August, the Goodrich plant at Akron was closed for three days as a result of such a strike. Dalrymple wrote of this episode:

Local Union No. 5, employees of the B. F. Goodrich Company, did, in our opinion, stage an unjust sit down, which caused the entire main plant to cease operations for a period of three days. The members admitted their wrong and corrected the mistake and hundreds of new members were taken in within the next few days.[13]

A heated debate on the justifiability of the sit down as a weapon in industrial disputes occurred at the 1936 Convention. A resolution which would have required authorization of all strikes by responsible union bodies, aimed directly at the sit down, was opposed by some of the more radical elements in the union, who argued that the workers should not be deprived of this means of protest. Although the resolution was not adopted on the ground that it might unnecessarily stigmatize previous union actions, the international officers indicated their firm opposition to the sit down as disruptive of collective bargaining relationships.[14] Although there were occasional sit downs subsequently, the rubber workers had virtually abandoned this weapon by the time the automobile workers first put it to such effective use.

The first major pitched battle in which the URW engaged was with the Goodyear Tire and Rubber Company. Before describing this event, it is necessary to say a few words about the rubber tire industry and Goodyear's position in it. As of July 1, 1936, daily tire capacity was estimated as follows:[15]

Goodyear Tire and Rubber Company	85,000
Firestone Tire and Rubber Company	45,000
United States Rubber Company	38,000
B. F. Goodrich Company	35,000
Rest of industry	75,000
Total	278,000

In 1937, more than 60 per cent of the workers employed in tire and tube plants were located in Ohio, the great bulk of them in Akron.[16] Of the "big four," only United States Rubber did not have its main producing units located in the Akron area. Thus, in striking at Goodyear, the union was facing the dominant producer in the very center of the tire industry. The URW was attempting what the Automobile Workers undertook almost a year later in the General Motors strike, but the outcome proved to be quite different.

In the background of the strike was a series of wage cuts which Goodyear had instituted in 1935 in an effort to reduce costs, and an increase in the basic working day from 6 to 8 hours.[17] The immediate cause was the layoff of 70 older workers without the customary three-day notification. The strike spread rapidly, and by February 18 the entire plant, which normally employed 14,000 workers, was shut down. In a roaring blizzard, a picket line eleven miles long was established. Four days later an injunction was issued limiting picketing to ten men at each entrance to the plant, but according to contemporary observers, it was not honored in the absence of any effective enforcement machinery. The local Akron community was generally sympathetic to the strikers, while Governor Davey of Ohio refused to send in the state militia on the ground that no violence had occurred.[18]

The CIO, from its very beginning, had looked upon the rubber industry as a likely area of operations. At a meeting of the Committee in December 1936, Hillman urged that immediate attention be given to the automobile and rubber industries, and Lewis agreed that "the suggestion on autos and rubber is the only practical thing as our first thrust."[19] No time was lost in moving into rubber. In January 1936, Lewis addressed a mass meeting in Akron, and when the Goodyear strike broke out, he furnished organizational and financial assistance. Adolph Germer and Powers Hapgood of the Miners' Union, Leo Krzycki of the Amalgamated Clothing Workers, Rose Pesotta of the ILGWU, and Ben Schaffer of the Oil Workers were sent in to help organize the strike. The CIO contributed $3000, the AFL, $1000, the United Garment Workers, $1000, and the Brewery Workers, $500. Cash donations of $34,500 were received by the Goodyear strikers from all sources.

The strike was peaceful and completely effective. There was an abortive attempt at the creation of an anti-union movement when C. Nelson Sparks, a former mayor of Akron, organized a "Law and Order League," but his appeal to violence solidified public opinion behind the strikers, and the League was denounced as provocative and inflammatory by both the local newspapers. Edward McGrady, assistant secretary of labor, was despatched to Akron to attempt a settlement, but the company refused to deal with the union. President Litchfield of Goodyear was quoted as saying: "The company will not sign any agreement with the United Rubber Workers even if a vote of employees shows that a majority wish to be represented by the union. There are two reasons: first, the law does not require it. The second we won't discuss."[20] However, after the strike had continued for five weeks, an agreement was finally reached. The company agreed in writing to reinstate all employees without discrimination; to deal with its employees individually or through duly chosen representatives for purposes of negotiation on all questions of mutual interest; to notify employee representatives of wage changes before they were put in force; to observe a 36-hour week and

6-hour day, and to take a vote of employees before weekly hours were re-duced below 30 or raised above 36; and to make lists of contemplated layoffs available for inspection by representatives of affected employees.[21]

Roberts has termed this agreement a "major victory" for the union, despite the failure of the union to obtain collective bargaining rights, and despite the fact that the company continued to extend financial assistance to the Goodyear Industrial Assembly, a company union which had been established in 1919.[22] But in the light of the subsequent relationships be-tween the URW and Goodyear, it is difficult to agree with this judgment. When the outcome of this strike is compared with the United Automobile Workers' strike against General Motors a year later, it takes on rather the aspect of a defeat. It was not complete defeat, for the union managed to survive, although until 1941 Goodyear Local 2 remained weak and with little influence in the Akron plant.

That the attitude of Goodyear toward the union had undergone no change was made clear in June 1936, when President Dalrymple of the URW was savagely beaten when attempting to organize workers at the Gadsden, Alabama, plant of Goodyear. Following this episode, six organ-izers were sent to Gadsden, but they were withdrawn after several had been beaten and the union offices sacked.[23] At the Akron plant, guerilla warfare continued, with President Litchfield of Goodyear emphasizing on a number of occasions that the company had not conceded the union any bargaining rights.[24] This phase continued until the summer of 1937, when victory in an NLRB election provided the union with a new representative status.

Short strikes occurred at the Goodrich and Firestone Akron plants dur-ing 1936, when these companies followed the lead of Goodyear in refusing to deal with the union. Only U. S. Rubber, among the big four, was willing to bargain with the URW, and consequently avoided the turmoil which characterized industrial relations at the plants of its competitors.

Cyrus S. Ching, who later became a nationally known figure in American labor relations, was director of industrial relations for United States Rubber at the time. He wrote of this period: "The U. S. Rubber Company started dealing with unions in the latter part of 1934 and early 1935. It was a gradual movement which spread from plant to plant. In dealing with the union, I placed great confidence in Sherman Dalrymple, then International Presi-dent of the Rubber Workers, and the other officers, and I believe they had confidence in me. Mr. Dalrymple was informed at the outset that when he told us he had a majority of employees in a plant, we would bargain with him. We took his word without challenge, and I am sure he never claimed a majority when he didn't actually have it." [25] Ching had joined U. S. Rubber in 1919, and it is in large measure due to him, and to the willingness of top management to back his policies, that this corporation went without a single strike from 1920 to 1942.

Despite the inconclusive nature of these early battles, the URW claimed some 30,000 members at the time of its first annual convention in September 1936.[26] Dalrymple told the convention that the union had been self sustaining since its establishment, which placed it in the same category as the Automobile Workers' Union and distinguished it from many other new CIO unions, which were subsidized for some time after their formation. During this convention, the union came nearer to factional strife of an ideological nature than at any other period of its early history, though nothing like the disciplined caucuses of the UAW plagued it. A motion to permit Norman Thomas, the presidential candidate of the Socialist Party, to address the convention was carried over some strenuous objections. Acrimonious debate developed over proposed endorsement of a local Farmer-Labor Party, which some delegates charged was communist-inspired. Dalrymple took the floor in opposition to the resolution, arguing:

We are a young International Union. Our Local Unions are young Local Unions in the Labor Movement, and when we begin to confuse the mind of new-born babes in the great Labor Movement with Townsendism, with Coughlinism, with Farmer-Labor Parties; with Utopian and about every other form of heavens on earth that we can think of for the working class of people, I am of the opinion that we are going to create dissention among ranks and we are going to retard our progress." [27]

The resolution was defeated by a vote of 61 to 39. However, although another resolution which linked communism with other "progressive" forces that were fighting fascism was challenged, it was carried after defense of the Communist Party from the floor. And a suggested amendment which would have deleted the words "founded upon the class struggle" from the preamble to the union's constitution was defeated, again after considerable debate. Although there were undoubtedly communists within the union, as well as among the convention delegates, Dalrymple was remarkably successful in preventing their infiltration into key positions. It was not until he resigned from the presidency in 1945 that a factional fight of great virulence, with one side strongly influenced by communists, burst into the open and threatened to wreck the union.[28]

The First Collective Agreements

The breakthrough of the URW to the status of a permanent factor in the rubber industry came during 1937. It began on March 3, 1937, when union workers of the Akron Firestone plants went on strike to secure sole collective bargaining rights for the union, and to eliminate the Employee Conference Plan, a company union. Some 10,500 workers were involved in the strike, which lasted 59 days. During this time Firestone made no effort to operate the plants. On April 4, 75,000 workers paraded in Akron to demonstate their sympathy with the strikers, showing how much support the union had gained in the local community. Perhaps the most important event that occurred during the strike was the decision of the U. S. Supreme Court on April 12, upholding the constitutionality of the National Labor Relations Act. In an agreement reached on April 28, the company agreed to bargain collectively with the URW (though not exclusively) and to refrain from interference with the right of employees to become members of the union. The union agreed, for its part, not to cause or tolerate any sitdown strike or work stoppage. The standard workweek was fixed at 36 hours, and the workers were granted three hours call-in pay, time-and-one-half pay for hours over 8 per day or 40 per week, vacations with pay, a seniority plan, and a promise of three days' notice before layoffs.[29]

During the following months, the union appealed to the NLRB machinery for assistance in organizing, rather than resorting to strikes. Elections in the Akron plant of Goodrich resulted in 8212 votes for the URW and only 834 opposed. At Goodyear, the vote was much the same: 8464 for the union to 3193 against. Membership at this time (August 1937) stood at 75,000, a peak from which the union was soon to retreat. In October, the union was recognized as bargaining agent for all employees in seven plants of the U. S. Rubber Company, without a strike.

By the end of 1937, the union had signed agreements with two of the four major tire producers, and had won the legal right to exclusive bargaining in the major plants of the remaining two. But before it could solidify its position, the recession of 1937–1938 struck the rubber industry and greatly weakened its bargaining power. By November 1937, 5000 men in Akron had been laid off, and two months later, 25 per cent of the labor force in rubber was unemployed.[30] Plans to organize an estimated 50,000 nonunion rubber workers through an augmented staff of organizers, including three assigned by the CIO,[31] went by the board. The only concern of the union now was to protect itself against the counterattacks of the employers.

In March 1938, the union invited Firestone, Goodyear, Goodrich, General Tire and Sieberling, all of which operated in Akron, to a joint conference "to adjust matters between labor and management in Akron and Barberton to the end that amicable cooperation shall take the place of the friction that now exists." [32] The reply of Goodrich was to issue an ultimatum to the union: permit a wage reduction of 17½ per cent, and cooperate with the company to raise the efficiency of operations, or the company would move 5000 jobs out of Akron. To put pressure upon the workers, a "Keep Goodrich in Akron" campaign was organized. According to Dalrymple:

Wives of workers were told that if their husbands did not take wage cuts they would lose their jobs. Workers were threatened with losing credit if they did not take a cut. Salesmen were pressed into service to propagandize workers. The newspapers joined in a daily chorus denouncing the union, painting it as damaging the city and insinuating that union officials were sacrificing the community to their own ends. Various groups, like the Chamber of Commerce and the neighborhood Boards of Trade, carried on unremitting propaganda against the workers.[33]

After some negotiation, Goodrich offered to freeze wages for a six-month period if the wage cut were permitted. A government economist, brought into Akron at the request of the union to study the situation, reported that in view of substantial increases in productivity, no wage cut was justified.[34] By a vote of 778 to 55, the employees of Goodrich refused to accept the company's offer, and the union proposed instead that wages be reduced by 6 cents an hour (the company insisted upon a reduction of 10 to 20 cents) in return for a pledge against moving operations out of Akron. After a week-long strike beginning on May 20, Goodrich signed its first agreement with the union, providing for maintenance of the existing wage scale, retention of the six-hour day, seniority, and a grievance mechanism.[35] The union had succeeded in staving off the first counterattack.

Although Firestone had entered into an agreement with the union, it had not conceded exclusive bargaining rights, and trouble developed in December 1937, when the Firestone Employees Protective Association challenged the URW. This organization petitioned for an NLRB election, which was held in March 1938. The precarious position of the URW was indicated by the outcome of the election; it won only 3696 votes to 2564 for its newly formed opponent, out of 7534 eligible employees.[36] However, the company renewed its agreement without change, and the Protective Association, after several years of vain effort to obtain a foothold in the plant, disappeared.

In September 1938, the contract with United States Rubber was also renewed. The union achieved minor concessions in the form of time and a half for overtime, union bulletin boards in the plant, and seniority in recalls as well as layoffs. The principal achievement of the agreement, from the union point of view, was maintenance of the prevailing wage level.[37]

Relations with Goodyear

The outcome of negotiations with Goodyear, the giant of the industry, was quite another matter. As the result of an NLRB election on August 31, 1937, Local 2 of the URW won the exclusive right to bargain for Goodyear's Akron employees. The first matter dealt with in collective bargaining was the manner in which layoffs proposed by the company should be arranged. The company refused to commit itself in writing to any solution to this vexing problem, and on November 18, a strike took place. With the help of the regional director of the National Labor Relations Board, an eight-point agreement was worked out on November 21 to provide an orderly layoff procedure, but the company refused to sign the final draft. Instead, in a letter to the NLRB regional director, it referred to the agreement as a memorandum signed by him, and indicated that "in no event could the company predict or discuss the situation beyond the first of the year," which was five weeks away.[38] Such a course of conduct was hardly calculated to create friendly labor-management relationships.

Conferences were held during the following months on specific objections raised by the union to management policy, with the union pressing for a comprehensive agreement on wages and other conditions of labor. The company never refused to meet, and thus fulfilled its legal obligation to bargain, but it took no step in the direction of the union's request. Enraged, finally, at what they regarded as deliberate stalling tactics by the company, the workers, on May 26, formed a picket line around the Goodyear plant, leading to the worst clash in the history of Akron labor relations. These developments were described graphically by the URW newspaper:

The executive board [of Local 2] met with the union committeemen, reported the company had again refused to settle the grievances. As the meeting was in progress a worker ran in, reported the company was moving out more office equipment, ammunition was going in, a fleet of trailers was moving out thousands of tires.

"Shut her down!" someone shouted. "If we're gonna do something, let's do it now before they can whip the pants off us," cried another.

Within ten minutes pickets were patrolling the gates.

At plant 3 a long fleet of loaded trucks drove up to the gate, paused while police commanded the pickets to disperse. . . . The police swung the gates open, the trucks roared out. Pickets flung themselves against the bumpers and fenders, fell back as the trucks gathered speed and rolled down the highway.[39]

All night long, battles between pickets and the Akron police continued. Tear gas was fired into the union headquarters; and the next morning found 50 people in the hospital with club and bullet wounds, while others were treated by private physicians for lesser injuries.[40] Seventy-five AFL and CIO unions in Akron formed a United Labor Defense Council and served an ultimatum that unless picketing was permitted, and efforts made to negotiate a settlement, there would be a general strike. In consequence, the mayor ordered the police withdrawn, picketing was restored, and the company agreed to meet with the union. Some 3600 Ohio National Guard men were alerted to enter Akron in the event of further violence.

An agreement was reached on May 30 in which the company agreed to review all seniority grievances that had arisen since the beginning of the year and to take up wage adjustments with the union before they were put into effect.[41] The union also claimed that the company had agreed to enter into a written agreement with it. However, the company issued a statement to the effect that "any talk in the conference about a signed agreement was limited on our part to a mere expression of willingness to discuss the subject at a future time." [42]

A new series of negotiations began on June 20. They continued for six months, but no final agreement could be reached. Management insisted that the wage clause should be subject to change at short notice and that daily hours be increased from six to eight, which the union rejected because it had attained better clauses in the Firestone and Goodrich contracts.[43] It seems clear in retrospect that the company was bargaining only because the Wagner Act required it to do so, and that it had no real desire to conclude a written agreement.[44] Finally, in December 1938, the union filed charges against Goodyear with the National Labor Relations Board, leading to long, drawn-out board proceedings and court litigation. No conclusive results were reached with Goodyear until 1941.

Effects of the Recession

These events reflected the weakness of the union during the recession years of 1937–1939. Dalrymple told the 1938 Convention that 25,000 members were unemployed.[45] Union membership was down to 59,500.[46] Nor did things improve greatly the following year; union membership in September 1939, had fallen still further to 57,200, and it was revealed that the national union had been operating at a deficit for the preceding ten months.[47] The only favorable developments, from the union point of view, were a new agreement with Goodrich in which wages were maintained; the first contract signed with General Tire and Rubber, providing for sole collective bargaining rights; and a union shop agreement with Seiberling.[48]

During this period the union had to contend with another challenge to the limited foothold it had in the industry: the threat of the major producers to decentralize operations by moving work out of Akron. Actually, this movement had been going on for some time, but between 1936 and 1941, it became intensified. A student of the industry found that:

until very recently the advantages of centralized mass production have been sufficient to restrict effectively decentralizing tendencies in the tire industry. Since about 1939, however, the technological developments in the industry have been to a large extent in the direction of more individualized units of equipment. . . . Technological developments of this nature have thus facilitated the decentralization of the industry by market areas in order to secure transportation and marketing savings. In this respect the tire industry has merely followed the decentralization of the automobile assembly plants.[49]

The controversial aspect of the decentralization movement was whether the union, by its wage and hour policies, had hastened industrial migration out of Akron. Management continually harped on this theme; for example, President Litchfield of Goodyear told a stockholders meeting in 1938 that Goodyear would have to abandon Akron unless it could cut wages.[50] The union, while facing the fact of a shrinking labor market, denied its responsibility, arguing that decentralization would have occurred even in the absence of unionism. Outside observers are in some disagreement on the point. Gaffey found it "exceedingly unlikely that anything like as large or as rapid a decentralizing movement would have developed were it not for the unfavorable position of Akron with regard to labor costs and labor relations. . . . The growth of the union has strengthened the tendency for the industry to decentralize . . . the concentration of union strength in Akron tends to prevent a readjustment which would give Akron a more favorable competitive situation and thus remains a factor favoring further decentralization." [51] Roberts, on the other hand, after a review of the decentralization policies of individual companies during the period, tended to stress other factors, such as cheap plant sites and power, and nearness to the market. However, he does concede that low wage rates and the absence of unions in such places as Clarkesville and Memphis, Tenn., and Wabash, Ind., where major plants were built, also played a role in stimulating movement. He concludes: "Decentralization occurred long before active organization began, but has probably been somewhat accelerated since." [52]

Available statistics indicate a substantial drop in Akron's share of the nation's tire employment. A special study by a federal government economist indicated that between 1935 (average for the year) and February 1938, employment in Ohio tire establishments declined from 68.4 per cent to 58.7 per cent of total U. S. tire employment.[53] Between the 1935 and 1939 censuses of manufactures, the Ohio percentage of employment declined from 68.4 to 56.6.[54] However, the bare data do not lead to any definitive conclusion regarding causality. It would seem reasonable that if for no other reason than management's preoccupation with the issue, the rise of the Rubber Workers' Union was a factor in industrial decentralization. Viewed in perspective, the movement out of Akron during the period 1935–1941 appears to be more properly an episode in a secular geographical move of the industry,[55] ascribable more to the pull of market orientation than to the push of unionization. The expansion of the union outside Akron after the war renders difficult the testing of any hypothesis regarding the autonomous effect of the union, since the period of Akron's isolation as a union city was of so relatively short a duration.

From the point of view of union history, the rubber tire and tube branch of the industry has been the critical center of activity. In 1939 there were 120,740 wage earners employed in the American rubber industry, of whom 14,861 were engaged in the manufacture of rubber boots and shoes, and 51,764 in the manufacture of other rubber products, leaving 54,115 for the tire industry.[56] However, the non-tire plants were much smaller, on the average, than the tire plants, and consequently more troublesome from an organizational and bargaining standpoint. Of 595 establishments manufacturing rubber products in 1939, only 53 were engaged in the production of tubes and tires, and 13 in rubber boots and shoes. Thus, while the URW organized a great many companies outside the tire industry,[57] the focus of its attention has always been tire manufacture in general, and Akron tire manufacture in particular.

Resurgence of the Union

With the improvement of business conditions that occurred in the rubber industry in 1940, the fortunes of the United Rubber Workers took a turn for the better. In February 1940, the national organizing staff was increased from 14 to 22 men, the latter being the largest number ever employed in such capacity by the union. An organizing drive was begun against Goodyear in July 1940, under the leadership of Robert J. Davidson, who was assigned by the CIO for this purpose. The only strike of any consequence during 1940 was one against General Tire and Rubber, lasting for eleven weeks, and resulting in a relatively favorable settlement for the union.[58] On the debit side of the ledger was the loss of the Hood Rubber plant of Goodrich in Watertown, Mass., and the Memphis plant of Firestone to AFL federal locals, both after bitter election campaigns, the latter involving physical violence against URW organizers.[59]

The 1940 Convention was told that although total membership was off by 3000 from the previous year, dues-paying membership had risen by 6000. For the first time in several years, ideological differences cropped up at the convention. A constitutional amendment barring communists and fascists from membership was hotly debated. Dalrymple and L. S. Buckmaster, who became president of the union some years later, spoke strongly in favor of the amendment, which was carried by a rising vote. Endorsement of Roosevelt's third term candidacy was enthusiastically voted, nothwithstanding the current opposition of John L. Lewis.[60]

Immediately after the convention, a staff of eight organizers, four of them on the payroll of the CIO, was assigned to an intensified organizational campaign among the Goodyear plants, in an effort to solve what the union acknowledged was its "No. 1 problem." Slowly but surely the company yielded. Plants at Bowmanville, Ontario, and Los Angeles were brought under signed contract.[61] An agreement limited to wages, providing for an average increase of 7 cents per hour, was secured for the Akron plant in July 1941. This was supplemented by a more comprehensive agreement on October 28, providing for protection of seniority rights, vacation pay, grievance procedure, and a limitation of the famous Goodyear "Flying Squadron," a group of management trainees who were assigned on a rotating basis to various jobs within the plant, to 2 per cent of the total payroll.[62] However, when the URW sent men to organize the Gadsden, Alabama, plant, they were met with violence, as in the past. One of the top union officers, John House, was severely beaten and required 86 stitches to close 15 scalp wounds.[63] Nor did the union succeed in winning bargaining rights at the Jackson, Michigan, plant. Thus, although by 1941, the Rubber Workers had made substantial inroads upon the last major holdout in the industry, there was no dramatic surrender to unionism, as in the case of the Ford Motor Company. It was to take several more years before collective bargaining on a friendly basis was possible between the Goodyear Company and the United Rubber Workers.

During 1941, new contracts were negotiated with all the major producers providing the first general wage increases which the URW had negotiated since its organization, averaging about 7 cents per hour, although it prided itself on having held the line against wage cuts during the 1937–1939 recession. Average hourly earnings for the industry from 1936 to 1941 are shown in Table 5.

Table 5.

Average hourly earnings, rubber industry, 1936–1941 (in cents)

	Tires and tubes	Rubber boots and shoes	Other rubber products
1936	87.3	52.3	53.5
1937	95.0	59.0	59.2
1938	94.8	60.2	59.7
1939	95.7	60.7	60.5
1940	96.7	61.7	62.1
1941	102.8	68.8	68.4

Source: U. S. Department of Labor, *Handbook of Labor Statistics,* 1947 edition, p. 79.

In reporting the conclusion of a new pact with Firestone, the union reported:

Perhaps no other local union suffered more from the layoffs of 1937 and 1938 than did the Firestone local. Nearly 5,000 Akron Firestone employees (approximately one-half the total enrollment) lost their jobs during that period. The fear and despair engendered by this situation, together with the actual loss of membership set this local back on its heels for two or three years. However, with the uptrend in employment and with a rebirth of confidence, Local 7 started a vigorous campaign about a year ago to strengthen its position. . . . More than 3,000 new and rejoining new members have been taken into the fold.[64]

By the end of 1941, membership in the URW had reached 93,000, an increase of 58 per cent for the year.[65] It had under agreement most of the major producers within its jurisdiction, both in tire manufacturing and in other branches of the rubber industry. A few companies were held by AFL federal locals, and several plants of the larger producers were still un-organized, but considering the age of the union, a very substantial degree of unionization had been obtained.

The credit for this must go to the union itself, and to its leadership. Despite the fact that the rubber workers were predominantly unskilled and semiskilled men, they conducted their affairs, after the first hectic sit-down stage, with exemplary responsibility. The turbulence and factionalism that characterized the United Automobile Workers Union during a correspond-ing stage of its existence was almost completely lacking in the URW. The officers of the URW were, on the whole, simple, honest, and sincere men, close to the rank and file because they had themselves just emerged from the shop, democratic in their conduct of union affairs, and ideologically uncommitted, except to the cause of trade unionism. Local unions were accorded considerable leeway in managing their own affairs, despite the geographical proximity of the international offices, and in sharp contrast, for example, to the Steel Workers' Union.

Undoubtedly, the union received important assistance from the govern-ment. From October 1, 1935 to June 30, 1940, the URW participated in 28 NLRB elections, of which it won 20 and lost 8, four of these to AFL unions. It received 70 per cent of all the votes cast in these elections. The URW filed 132 unfair labor practice cases during the same period, of which the majority were adjusted to its satisfaction. However, this assistance merely supplemented its own activities, and was in no sense a substitute. Roberts' characterization of the position of the union at the end of the period with which we are concerned seems a fair appraisal of its achieve-ments:

It has obtained better working conditions, seniority rules, transfer and promo-tion procedures, vacation and grievance machinery. It has developed an intelli-gent leadership which understands the problems of the industry and the needs of the rubber workers. In the brief years since its formation, it has achieved a degree of stability uncommon in so young an organization.[66]

7

The Men's Clothing Industry

The Amalgamated Clothing Workers of America, under the leadership of Sidney Hillman, was one of the founding unions of the CIO, and remained loyal to it until the final merger with the AFL. The break with the AFL was not a difficult one for the Amalgamated to make. It had been established in 1914 as a breakaway group from the United Garment Workers, and remained independent until 1933, when, through the intermediation of John L. Lewis and Daniel Tobin, the Amalgamated affiliated with the AFL. But almost immediately the craft-industrial unionism dispute broke out, with the Amalgamated supporting Lewis strongly on the issue. Suspension from the AFL was accepted with equanimity, and at a CIO board meeting in November 1936, when several CIO members were in favor of renewed peace efforts, Hillman declared:

We made sacrifices to come into the A.F. of L. I appreciate the [negative] feeling of Murray, because during the N.R.A. I saw that failure was due not alone to the Chambers of Commerce but also to the A.F. of L. . . . . Two vice-presidents on the Executive Council openly worked with the Liberty Leaguers, and were not censured. . . . Peace conferences have brought a certain amount of demoralization. If you want a committee, I'd be for it, but I wouldn't be a member.[1]

As one of the principal beneficiaries of the NRA period, together with the United Mine Workers and the ILGWU, the Amalgamated was in a position to render substantial aid to the new industrial unions.

The Amalgamated, the ILGWU, and the United Mine Workers faced one important economic factor in common: a highly competitive price structure, induced by the presence of a great number of small firms. The NRA was effective for a time in restraining product market competition and stabilizing product prices, which made employers much more susceptible to unionization. When the NRA collapsed, the Amalgamated and the ILGWU sought to continue along the price-stabilization line through collective bargaining, while the United Mine Workers, as already noted, relied primarily upon federal legislation. From 1933 to 1935, between

40,000 and 50,000 new members had been added to the union,[2] and the claimed total membership at the beginning of 1936 was 150,000, making the Amalgamated one of the largest unions in the country.[3] The men's clothing industry was 80 per cent organized, and the shirt industry, almost completely nonunion in 1932, was 50 per cent organized.[4] The treasury was replenished by a special assessment of $10 per member levied at the end of 1935; by January 31, 1936, $694,000 had been collected from this source.[5]

Concerned though they were with the affairs of the CIO, and in particular with the organizing drive in the textile industry, Hillman and his fellow officers of the Amalgamated took advantage of the favorable unionization climate to round out organization in the men's clothing industry proper, and to move into a number of allied fields which theretofore had been largely unorganized. During the five years from 1936 to 1941, Amalgamated membership almost doubled, and despite a large investment in the CIO, its resources were greatly augmented. The union also undertook a radical and ambitious revision of the industry's wage and product structure in an attempt to protect its employers in the principal manufacturing centers against competition based upon lower wages, the program being in many ways analogous to that espoused by the United Mine Workers through legislative stabilization measures.

Organizational Activities, 1936–1937

By the end of 1937, the percentage of organization in clothing manufacture had risen to 90, and only half a dozen concerns of any consequence were not unionized. New York City and vicinity, one of the major producing areas, was completely controlled, while the Friedman-Harry Marks Company of Richmond, Virginia, one of the largest nonunion concerns, capitulated soon after the constitutionality of the Wagner Act was upheld.[6] The men's clothing industry was concentrated in nine major centers of which New York was first with about a quarter of all the workers and Philadelphia second with half as many workers. It was characterized, in general, by small producing units, although there were a few large companies manufacturing nationally advertised clothing. "In 1935 the eight largest companies employed only 10 per cent of all workers and turned out only 7 per cent of the total product. . . . Among the thousand or more separate manufacturers producing men's clothing, a concern with a $1 million output is regarded as a good-sized firm. A big majority of all firms are less than half as large. Almost half the workers in the industry are on payrolls which list less than two hundred and fifty employees." [7] There were in 1937 some 158,000 wage earners employed in the industry, of whom slightly more than half were women. In view of the small size of the producing unit and the composition of the labor force, so high a degree of labor organization was a remarkable achievement.

It may be well to mention at this point that the Amalgamated had a competitor in clothing manufacture, the United Garment Workers, AFL, from which it had originally seceded in 1914. This organization, with a membership of around 40,000, was largely confined to the work clothes industry, where the union label was of importance to the manufacturers. Indeed, a perusal of its publications yields the conclusion that its major concern was promotion of the label; very few other unions have had such close and continuing relationships with the AFL union label department. [8] When the Amalgamated affiliated with the AFL in 1933, it was agreed that the Amalgamated should have jurisdiction over suits and overcoats, and the UGW over work clothing. The Amalgamated agreed to use the UGW label on its garments. However, when the Amalgamated was suspended from the AFL in 1936, it decided to reissue its own label, which was promptly boycotted by the AFL. [9] Although the AFL would undoubtedly have liked to harass the Amalgamated by having the UGW expand, the latter organization showed no sign of wanting to venture beyond its traditional stronghold in work clothes manufacture. Thomas A. Rickert, its venerable president, had attained a seat on the AFL Executive Council, and was content to run his organization as an old-line beneficial craft union.

Amalgamated control of clothing manufacture was rounded out by its absorption, in March 1936, of the Journeyman Tailors' Union, an old craft organization, dating from 1860, which catered to highly skilled custom tailors in retail stores. Because of some mobility of labor between clothing shops and retail stores, there had been jurisdictional conflict beween the Amalgamated and the Tailors. The latter organization, with about 5000 members, was accorded the status of a semi-independent department within the Amalgamated. [10] Two years later, the Tailors were reported to have doubled their membership. [11] By affiliating with the Amalgamated, this union forfeited its AFL charter, and its jurisdiction was transferred to the United Garment Workers.

The second largest industry in which the Amalgamated claimed jurisdiction in 1936 was the manufacture of men's shirts and pajamas. In 1937, the census indicated that this industry employed 67,500 wage earners in

529 establishments;[12] while most shops employed less than 100 workers, there were a few very large ones with over 5000 workers each. The cotton garment workers, most of them girls, rushed into the union with the advent of the NRA, and by 1934 25,000 were organized, mainly in New York, New Jersey, and Pennsylvania.[13] The NRA code represented a considerable wage gain for them, but with the Schechter decision, the non-union sector of the industry reverted to the pre-NRA status of a 30-cent per hour minimum and a 40-hour week, in place of the 36-hour week and the higher minima imposed by the code. To put their employers on a competitive basis, the unionized workers agreed to work 40 hours at straight time pay, and to cut in half the wage increases they had received in 1933.[14]

During 1936 and 1937, however, the Amalgamated devoted considerable resources to the organization of the cotton garment industry, a campaign which met formidable obstacles in the form of highly mobile employers, intense competition, and scattered location of enterprise. A number of manufacturers had moved to the South, and the Amalgamated pursued them in cooperation with the Textile Workers' Organizing Committee. Membership of over 40,000 cotton garment workers was claimed in January 1938, including 5000 in work clothing and work shirt factories.[15]

A third major area which the Amalgamated entered was the laundry industry, confining its initial activities mainly to New York City and vicinity. This industry offered even greater structural obstacles to organization than did the cotton garment industry. There were three distinct segments to the industry: (a) the hand laundries, which were small shops using little machinery, and often owned by Chinese; (b) power laundries, the most important sector, which operated on a somewhat larger scale with the assistance of machinery; and (c) the linen supply houses, engaged in renting towels, uniforms, and so on to restaurants and hotels, and not necessarily performing the work of laundering themselves.[16] Most laundry workers were semiskilled or unskilled, and many of them were Negroes, unable to secure work in higher-paying occupations. Wages were very low — $15 a week represented good earnings — and the workers were often obliged to work up to 70 hours a week to achieve even this level.[17] Wage cost approximated 50 per cent of total operating cost, thus placing great pressure upon the wage level. The union summarized its problem as follows:

The favorable aspects of the picture are that, being a service industry, laundries cannot move "out of town" to avoid unionization; further, that cleaning clothes being an all the year round job, the laundry industry has not suffered from seasonal ups and downs to the same extent that other industries have. The unfavorable aspects of the picture that we have briefly described are (1) the ease with which low-skilled workers can be replaced, and (2) the racial and national-istic differences, which has made the development of unity among them difficult.[18]

There were several AFL federal locals in the field, but they were making little headway. The CIO, early in 1937, had chartered a laundry workers' union on the basis of these AFL locals, and this was taken over by the Amalgamated in August 1937, as Local 300. Within a month, after a whirl-wind campaign, 10,000 workers in the linen supply branch were under a closed shop agreement, providing for a weekly minimum wage of $15.75, a rest period of 15 minutes a day, 7 days of sick leave per annum, and arbitra-tion of grievances. By the end of the year, 15,000 workers in the power laundries were under agreement, which gave them a 35-cent minimum hourly wage, a 10 per cent wage increase, and a 44 to 48-hour week.[19] Little progress was made among the small hand laundries. To provide for better administration, Local 300 was split into nine separate locals, but their activ-ities remained coordinated through the Laundry Workers' Joint Board.

It was natural for the Amalgamated to jump from the laundry industry into cleaning and dyeing, which was also conducted, typically, in small establishments engaged in fierce competition. The workers were mainly unskilled, and like the laundry workers, were subjected to long hours at low pay. To make matters worse, there was a considerable amount of racketeering in the industry. The AFL Executive Council was forced to intervene in the affairs of its Cleaning and Dye House International Union at the behest of the Chicago Federation of Labor, which charged that Local 3 of the International was gangster-dominated.[20] The AFL had ordered Federal Local 17742 to enter into the Cleaning and Dye House Workers' Union, and it was this decision which evoked a strong protest by the Chicago Federation of Labor. Local 3 of the Cleaning Union claimed juris-diction, but the workers of the federal local refused to join it. A merger was ordered by the AFL Executive Council nonetheless, and an AFL organizer sent to supervise it. On the night elections were to take place for officers of the combined body, the police arrested the former officers of Local 17742 for assault, on a warrant sworn by officers of Local 3. Although the charges were dismissed, the arrested men could not be nominated for union office because of their absence from the meeting. The Executive Council ordered new elections to be held, and in these, the entire Local 3 slate, which had been accused of gangster-domination, was victorious. The Executive Council took no further action, under the rule of national union autonomy.

During the latter half of 1937, the Amalgamated organized 2000 cleaners and dyers in Boston, 5000 in Detroit and neighboring cities, 4000 in New York, and 1000 additional workers in other cities, giving it a total membership of 12,000, out of an estimated 57,000 workers engaged in the industry throughout the country.[21]

Other industries to which the Amalgamated extended its jurisdiction were men's neckwear, in which there had been an old AFL federal local,[22] and glove manufacture. The latter field had been covered by the International Glove Workers' Union, AFL, which, like the Tailors, came into the Amalgamated as a separate department. The Glove Workers was a small organization, however, and did not swell the membership rolls of the Amalgamated by more than 3000 to 4000 workers.

As the result of expansion into new areas, as well as the filling out of organization in the basic jurisdiction, coats and suits, the Amalgamated claimed a total membership of 225,000 by 1938, an increase of 75,000 over 1936.[23] As in other CIO unions, however, expansion had virtually come to a halt with the onset of the 1937 recession; the big months for organization were April and May 1937. At the end of 1937, the union complained: "Industrial conditions being what they are, most of the factories in our industry are either working on part time basis or have altogether shut down for the present. Under the circumstances, the best that the union can do is to hold its own. But we are doing better than that, in many places. Organizing drives have slackened down to an extent, but have not been given up." [24]

As already noted, the Amalgamated was one of the major contributors to the CIO drive. In the summer of 1936, $100,000 was given in support of the steel organizing campaign. During 1937, $500,000 in cash was donated to the CIO, mostly for textiles, and an additional $500,000 was given in the form of the services of organizers, clerical assistance, and other material help.[25] While this did not match the contribution of the United Mine Workers, it clearly made the Amalgamated the second largest financial angel of the CIO. Despite the magnitude of these expenditures, $786,000 was added to the Amalgamated treasury between 1936 and 1938.

The Stabilization of Wages

The level of wages in the men's clothing industry fell sharply during the Great Depression, from a high of 76 cents per hour in 1924 to 51 cents in 1932. As the result of the NRA, average hourly earnings rose to 66 cents, and by 1938 to 77 cents, largely as a consequence of a general wage increase of 12 per cent negotiated on a national basis in 1937.[26] Hours of labor were reduced from the average of 44 hours per week that had prevailed since 1922 to 36, beginning in 1934, as part of the union's attempt to maintain employment by spreading the available work.[27]

The 1937 agreement, negotiated with a temporary committee of employers representing the major production centers, was the first national wage agreement obtained by the union, and it was hailed as a landmark in the collective bargaining history of the industry. Soon after the effective date of the agreement the industry was hit by a sharp depression, which a union publication ascribed to increased prices in the face of a high degree of price elasticity,[28] and the high hopes of the union were disappointed. In the words of the union's officers, reporting to the 1938 Convention:

Unfortunately, the net results of this wage increase were not as conspicuously beneficial as had been expected. Because of circumstances, over which neither the union nor the employers had control, leading among them the dislocation that began in the woolen market almost on the effective date of the agreement, the clothing industry started its journey downward several months ahead of the general business and industrial recession. With most of the factories closed a great deal of the time, the wage increase didn't show up as it might have, had the industry continued busy.[29]

Nonetheless, the report continued, the agreement was of great importance in paving the way for the long cherished goal of Amalgamated wage policy, national wage stabilization:

of primary importance . . . is the fact that the unionized industry everywhere was placed on a like footing as to the basis of the wage increase. When production is resumed on a normal level we shall have laid the basis for a progressive approximation to a uniform wage policy throughout the industry. . . . The establishment of a national agreement will in time facilitate the working out, in conference, of those details of arrangements which will eventually eliminate competition among manufacturers and markets on the basis of labor's wage. Of course, competition in the industry will not be eliminated, but that isn't our purpose. The union is only concerned about eliminating inequalities in workers' pay as a consideration in competitive calculations.

With the revival of business in 1939, the Amalgamated inaugurated a plan of national wage stabilization which had been some time in preparation. The obstacles to wage uniformity were formidable: garments were produced under a great diversity of manufacturing methods; the final product was subject to almost infinite variation with respect to style, material, and specifications in general; piece work was the well-nigh universal practice in the industry; the actual operation of manufacturing was done in part by manufacturers, and in part by contractors, specializing in coats, vests, or pants of a given quality, and sometimes even more narrowly in such details as buttonholes. Beginning in 1933, the Amalgamated, in concert with manufacturers, undertook to classify all garments into six basic grades, ranging from the cheapest, grade 1, to the most expensive, grade 6, based upon construction features which were correlated with the quality of workmanship. The next step was to determine a standard labor cost for each grade; for example, the labor cost of a grade 1 suit jacket was fixed at $1.70, for a grade 2 jacket, at $2.14. These costs then had to be translated into piece rates, shop by shop, to yield the desired unit cost. Earnings continued to vary with skill, speed, and the nature of the capital equipment at the disposal of the worker, but the cost to the manufacturer remained stable.[30]

Until 1939 the union did not attempt to extend stabilization beyond individual markets, the international generally leaving administration up to the managers of the joint boards.[31] The result has been described vividly as follows:

"I'll go out of business if I have to pay that much for labor costs," a contractor complains. "They don't pay that much in some other place I know. Put the price down a nickel and I'll be able to stay in business." What is the business agent who hears such a statement to do? If he insists on the prices, the contractor may close down and put his people out of work. And perhaps the garment is made for less in some other territory. Those were arguments and considerations that plagued local managers and price makers for years. They wanted to uphold standards, but they didn't want their work going to other markets.[32]

With the market managers given discretion to allow exemption to individual manufacturers, standards quickly collapsed in the intense intermarket "fight for the bundle." To eliminate the competition thus generated, the international union itself assumed control over the stabilization plan. A stabilization department was established under the leadership of a former manufacturing executive, responsible directly to the general president of the union, with authority to establish standards and to ensure their enforcement through periodic investigations. Local organizations were no longer permitted to grant exemptions from established labor costs. As the first step in 1939, the plan was applied only to the cheaper clothing, grades 1 and 2, manufactured chiefly in the East. All manufacturers and contractors producing these grades of clothing were required to register with the union and secure approval of their wage rates before they were permitted to operate.[33] In enforcing the program, the union's stabilization department was given great authority, by agreement with the producers. Investigators were empowered to visit shops unannounced, to interview workers, to inspect work, and, if they deemed it necessary, to examine the books and records of the employer, including his bank account and canceled checks, to make sure that the workers were not undermining standards by kicking back part of their wages.

A year after the centralized scheme had been put into operation, the international union reported:

the union has overcome all of the major problems and . . . national stabilization of grades 1 and 2 has become a successful and permanent achievement. The establishment and rigorous enforcement of minimum national standards for grades 1 and 2 have put an end to the migration of shops or the transfer of work from market to market in search of lower labor costs. No longer is it possible for any market or for any manufacturer to make a bid for business at the expense of the standards of workers. With labor costs equalized on a national basis, intermarket rivalry, jealousy and suspicion have been done away with and our members everywhere are assured of their equitable share of work.[34]

By the end of 1940, the stabilization program embraced 23,000 workers, mainly in the East. It proved necessary to extend control to the medium grades, for some manufacturers of this type of clothing, by paying below-standard rates, were threatening the existence of the producers of the lower grades. During 1941, grades 3 and 4 were brought under the stabilization program, and by the end of 1941, 40,000 workers were covered. According to the union, stabilization did not necessarily redound to the disadvantage of the consumer, since the plan provided accurate quality standards for garments.[35] However, an objective appraisal of the plan during its early stages cast some doubt upon the benefits to the consumer, and also raised the problem of the existence of producer incentives toward greater efficiency in the face of a fixed ratio between the grade of clothing and labor cost.[36] A final judgment upon the wisdom of the stabilization plan, both from the view of the clothing workers themselves and of the consumer, will have to await a more thorough analysis of its operation than has hitherto been available.[37]

One of the initial advantages accruing to the workers from the plan was an increase in wages flowing from the raising of substandard shops up to the standard wage level. The union estimated that the great majority of the workers involved realized wage increases of from 5 to 10 per cent.[38] No further wage increase was requested during 1940 due to poor business conditions, but in 1941, under the impact of rising living costs, wages were increased by 13 per cent for grade 1 garments and by 10 per cent for other grades, the first general wage increase since 1937. The employers also agreed to initiate a study looking toward the establishment of an employer-financed health and welfare scheme, which was finally consummated in 1942.

The wage gains achieved by the Amalgamated were by no means spectacular. The union had to adjust itself to an industrial environment that did not permit it much latitude, and its wage policy was cautious. By 1938, average hourly earnings in men's clothing had just about regained the 1924 level, whereas in manufacturing generally, a substantial increase took place between these two years. Nor did the 1941 general wage increase in clothing match the wage increases that the worker in manufacturing industry as a whole received from 1935 to 1941.[39]

The cotton garment workers received a wage increase of 7½ per cent in March 1937, but the subsequent decline in business made it difficult to enforce. A further increase of 7½ per cent was secured in September 1939, raising average hourly earnings in union shops to a level "somewhat above" the 36-cent minimum of the NRA codes for the industry.[40] The minimum wage rate, established by union contract in 1938, was 30 cents per hour. The union wage scale, constantly threatened by nonunion competition, was bolstered in 1940 by a minimum wage for cotton garments of 32½ cents per hour under the Fair Labor Standards Act, in the enactment of which Sidney Hillman played a major role.[41] It was estimated that the imposition of this wage scale meant increases for 67,000 out of 142,000 employed cotton garment workers, the majority in the South.[42] The legal minimum was raised to 40 cents per hour on September 29, 1941, and a general wage increase of 10 per cent was secured by contract in June 1941.[43] A decade later, however, despite numerous intervening wage changes, the union noted that "wages for shirt and cotton garment workers are still substantially below decent American wage standards. As unionization is extended in this industry, additional economic gains will be secured." [44]

The Amalgamated in Politics

There were few trade unions in the United States which took as active an interest in local and national politics during the New Deal period as the Amalgamated Clothing Workers. Sidney Hillman became labor's principal spokesman in Washington, and no labor leader was closer to President Roosevelt than he. His part in the 1944 presidential camapign was well publicized by the Republican opposition under the slogan "Clear it with Sidney." Even before that, however, he was high in the councils of the

Democratic Party, and his union had made substantial contributions to Democratic victories in all the elections beginning with 1936.

It was natural that the Amalgamated, as one of the principal beneficiaries of the NRA, should rally behind the banner of Roosevelt in 1936. To do this required a considerable break with the past, for part of the tradition of the Amalgamated was a belief in the necessity of an independent labor party. Indeed, there were in the union many supporters of the Socialist Party, though Hillman had never been one of them. When Hillman urged the Amalgamated to support the candidate of the Democratic Party in 1936, he did so in a half-apologetic tone: "I do not take back my faith in a labor party or my readiness to do everything within my power through this organization to bring about a labor realignment in politics. But it is impossible even to think of a labor party with a presidential candidate in this campaign." The only one who arose to oppose Hillman at the 1936 convention was Joseph Schlossberg, the union's secretary-treasurer since its formation, who argued that as a socialist, he had never and would never vote for a nonlabor party. It was rare indeed for a member of the Amalgamated publicly to challenge Hillman, who lost no time in censuring Schlossberg for bringing his views before the convention, and then went on to outline a philosophy of political action which served to bridge the gap between the old "progressivism" and the new pragmatism of the left of center wing of the American labor movement:

It is wrong to draw a line, as was done in this debate, between practical men and idealists. . . . To say that only a man who holds firm to ancient convictions is an idealist is to misrepresent idealism. Convictions! We all have convictions — even political convictions — but we always remember that we are not part of a political party. We are an economic organization, and as an economic organization we must agree, regardless of personal convictions, on that common policy which will best safeguard our interests. . . .

We claim that this is an emergency. We claim that in this emergency the Amalgamated must take a position. Let those who disagree come forward and say whom we shall support. The Communist Party? The Socialist-Labor Party? Any other party? What party? . . .

I believe in independent political action for labor. I have always believed in it. I believe in it more today than ever before. But the building of a labor party must be begun by the labor movement, not by those who have taken the book and read chapter so-and-so. Nor will a labor party be built by resolutions. It will only be built by long, hard effort. . . . Every law for labor has been declared unconstitutional. Labor knows that this is wrong and that the Democratic Party is not an instrumentality that can be depended upon to right the wrong. Labor needs its own party. . . .[45]

Hillman played a leading role in the formation of Labor's Non-Partisan League, the first executive director of which was Eli P. Oliver, a former Amalgamated organizer, whose salary was paid by the Amalgamated. The League raised $1,000,000 for the 1936 campaign, $500,000 of which came from the Mine Workers and $100,000 from the Amalgamated.[46] In addition to the League, which was a national organization, the Amalgamated collaborated with the Ladies' Garment Workers and other New York unions in the formation of the American Labor Party in New York State, with a program basically that of the New Deal.[47] The party mustered 300,000 votes for Roosevelt in the 1936 election, and convinced the garment and clothing workers of the efficacy of independent political action in New York.

In the New York City mayoralty campaign of 1937, the ALP forced the Republican Party to nominate Mayor Fiorello LaGuardia for reelection, and provided him with 482,000 votes on the ALP ticket, LaGuardia's winning plurality margin being 14,000 less than this total.[48] Five members of the American Labor Party were elected to the City Council. The original purpose of the Amalgamated in founding the ALP, which later fell under the control of the communists, was set forth as follows:

We are out to establish a permanent medium of independent and progressive labor action in politics.

The term *independent* we interpret to indicate independence of any group and disassociation from any policy but such as will advance the objectives of the movement as understood by the organized trade unions who joined their forces for this political move. We want to utilize political instrumentalities and our franchise as citizens to accomplish by way of political participation and perhaps thus with greater ease, the aim which we are trying to bring about through organization in trade unions. Consequently, the political party of union labor does not pursue the realization of a philosophic or general social aim which is not implied in the meaning of the word trade union and its stated purposes.[49]

The subsequent history of the American Labor Party is dealt with below. On the national scene, Hillman took an active part in the ill-fated "purge" of 1938, and in the congressional elections of that year. He was among the first of the top labor leaders to come out for a third term for Roosevelt, and in May 1940, the convention of the Amalgamated unanimously adopted a resolution to that effect.[50] During the ensuing campaign, considerable bitterness developed between Lewis and Hillman over the former's espousal of the cause of Wendell Willkie. Potofsky, who had succeeded Schlossberg as secretary-treasurer in 1940, wrote in the journal of the Amalgamated: "As a leading force in the creation of the CIO, we were shocked and indignant when we heard John L. Lewis speak last Friday night. Our General Executive Board, meeting after that speech, voicing the burning conviction of our membership, unanimously repudiated Mr. Lewis' statement, questioned his motives, and rejected his advice. . . . When he marched into the waiting arms of the Girdlers, the Weirs and the Fords, he marched alone." [51] The outcome of the election was a matter of great satisfaction to the Amalgamated, and served further to strengthen the ties of friendship between President Roosevelt and Hillman. The former demonstrated his confidence in Hillman by appointing him first as a member of the National Defence Advisory Commission, then associate director of the Office of Production Management, and finally, head of the labor division of the War Production Board.

The Amalgamated and the CIO

The Amalgamated Clothing Workers Union was one of the founders of the CIO, and next to the United Mine Workers, its principal supporter financially during the first five years of its existence. Yet apart from the organizing drives in textiles and the department stores, which Hillman directed and which were staffed to a considerable extent by Amalgamated organizers, the Amalgamated played a relatively small role in the internal affairs of the CIO. Individuals drawn from the ranks of the Amalgamated, such as Leo Krzycki, Charles W. Ervin, and J. B. S. Hardman, were drawn on occasion into the activities of other CIO unions for special work, and Hillman functioned as mediator in the bitter internal fight that took place in the United Automobile Workers. But until 1940, the direction of the CIO was largely in the hands of one man, John L. Lewis. It was he who planned the strategy, appointed the staff, and participated in the day-to-day administration.

The outbreak of war in Europe and the 1940 election campaign produced the first open rift within the CIO ranks. Lewis, with the support of the communist unions in the CIO, until the invasion of Russia, became an ardent isolationist, while Hillman became closely identified with the nation's defense effort. Nor was Hillman convinced of Lewis' sincerity in conducting negotiations with the AFL looking toward unity of the labor movement. When Lewis recounted to the CIO Executive Board the events of the unsuccessful negotiations of 1939, Hillman declared: "Probably because I am still a novice in these war and peace negotiations and not having been present at the last conference, I am permitting myself to be a bit more optimistic about the possibilities. . . ." [52] Lewis was undoubtedly jealous of Hillman's position in the defense administration, and he complained, "My advice has not been sought, and no conference has been held," and he warned his fellow CIO officials: "I think all organizations should be careful about not making commitments on policies as affecting their own union that can be exploited as tremendous achievements that the administration has accomplished by taking a Northwest Passage around the executive officers of the CIO." [53]

Hillman's public criticism of Lewis' conduct of the AFL-CIO unity talks, delivered to the 1940 Amalgamated convention, and the events of the 1940 presidential campaign, brought the differences between the two men to a head. A week before the 1940 CIO convention, the Amalgamated journal printed an editorial calling for democratization of the CIO: "The six vice-presidents and secretary function in their official capacities as just seven lines of small type on the CIO letterheads. The resolution proposes that the president, the secretary and the vice-presidents of the CIO constitute an administrative committee to exercise CIO leadership throughout the year. . . ." [54] At a CIO Executive Board meeting held on November 15, three days before the convention opened, Potofsky raised the issue of financial reporting by the CIO, leading to a vitriolic interchange between him and Lewis, during the course of which the latter accused the Amalgamated of "sticking the knife into the CIO." [55] At this meeting controversy developed over the New York State CIO Industrial Council, which was in the throes of a fight for control between the Amalgamated and the communist-dominated unions. Gus Strebel, an Amalgamated official who led what was claimed to be the legal faction of the council, declared: "New York State, Brother Lewis, a portion of it, believes rightly or wrongly, that the issue is definitely one of Communism versus our ideas." [56] Lewis ruled, however, that the right-wing forces had attempted to pack the convention of the council, and he appointed Thomas Kennedy as administrator pending a new convention, a ruling which was to the satisfaction of the left-wing group.

The climax came at the 1940 convention. There were rumors that Lewis, who had pledged that he would step down from the presidency of the CIO, was nurturing a "draft Lewis" movement. His appearance on the platform occasioned a tremendous ovation, whipped up by the left-wing unionists, to whom Hillman, now a national defense commissioner, was more than ever anathema. Lewis then proceeded to castigate the needle trades for deserting the CIO:

Yes, five years ago a little group of men representing some eight organizations in the American Federation of Labor in a hotel on the Boardwalk a stone's throw away highly resolved that come high or come low they would go forward with those words — some of them did so and they have kept the faith, while others have fallen by the wayside.

And one of those men was Mr. Dubinsky, representing the Ladies' Garment Workers International Union, who swore by every God that ever sat on high that he, Dubinsky, would never waver in the cause and he signed the scroll and by book, bell and candle vowed to affiliate to this movement. And where is Dubinsky today? Furthermore, where is Rickert? He has crept back into the American Federation of Labor. He abandoned his fellows and he abandoned what he claimed was his principle. And he has gone into that organization on his adversary's terms. He is crying out now and his voice laments like that of Rachel in the wilderness, against the racketeers and the panderers and the crooks in that organization.

And Zaritsky, he was the man representing the Millinery and Cap Workers. And now above all the clamor comes the piercing wail, and the laments of the Amalgamated Clothing Workers. And they say, "Peace, it is wonderful." And there is no peace. . . .

Dubinsky took the easy way. Zaritsky took the easy way. If there is anybody else in the CIO who wants to take the easy way, let them go on.[57]

Hillman was not in attendance on November 19, the day Lewis made this speech, and according to his biographer, was busy with defense matters in Washington and had not intended to be present at the convention at all.[58] However, at the urgent insistence of the Amalgamated delegation, he appeared on November 20 and addressed the convention. Stating that there "has been some wishful thinking outside, and maybe even on the inside of CIO," that the Amalgamated would leave the CIO, he promised that his organization would not desert it. He made no attempt to minimize his differences with Lewis, and delivered a bitter denunciation of the communists in the CIO, whom he termed "a menace to the labor movement." He concluded his speech in the following vein:

I regret that John L. Lewis will not be the leader of this organization. I know there is nothing else that he can do and will do and will agree to do but what he believes to be the best for the organized labor movement. I have greater respect for a man who in every crisis stands by his guns, and I am not making nominating speeches. . . . I hope to be present in your convention at the election of your officers, but I may be called away. . . . I hope you will thresh out your differences and you will elect such officers as will command the confidence of the membership you represent, and it is my considered judgment when John L. Lewis steps down there must be a demand for Phil Murray.

This blunt reminder to Lewis of his pledge to step down was followed immediately by an organized demonstration for Murray, and ended whatever chance Lewis might have thought he had to renege gracefully. It was clear that at least the Amalgamated and the Textile Workers would oppose his reelection. The next day Murray was elected in his place.

The growing animosity between Lewis and Murray during the following year saw the Amalgamated lined up solidly behind the latter. On July 7, at a CIO legislative conference, Lewis delivered a bitter attack upon Hillman, reflecting the intensity of the internal struggle, and elicited this response from the editor of *The Advance*:

Mr. Lewis guessed wrong once — on the presidential election. He guessed wrong once again on the outcome of the election in the CIO convention, in 1940, at Atlantic City. It would seem as if he was now engaged in making another wrong guess, namely about what the nation's organized workers think of the America Firsters' anti-national, anti-defense policies. Of course, he has a personal right to guess wrong as many times as he is trying to guess. But title to leadership wears down with each wrong guess and being, in addition, a bad loser does not help matters at all.[59]

Lewis ascribed all his difficulties with the government during the captive mines dispute of 1941 to Hillman, whom he accused of being actuated by malice against the Mine Workers Union. The withdrawal of the latter organization from the CIO in 1942 resulted in a considerably augmented role for the Amalgamated in the inner councils of the CIO during the following years.

The year 1941 saw the Amalgamated Clothing Workers at the peak of its influence in the American labor movement. Its membership had reached 275,000,[60] making it one of the most powerful unions in the country in terms of numbers. Sidney Hillman, its president, was labor's principal representative in the rapidly growing defense administration, while Potofsky, who was in effect the acting president, was exceedingly influential in the national CIO. The clothing industry was completely organized; 50,000 out of 65,000 dress shirt workers were under Amalgamated contract; the New York Laundry Workers Joint Board claimed 25,000 members.

Although still one of the ten largest unions in the United States, the Amalgamated has since yielded primacy to such giants as the Automobile Workers, the Steel Workers, the Teamsters, and the Carpenters. The simple fact of the matter is that by 1941 the Amalgamated had substantially organized its industry, and while there has been growth since, it has been on the fringes of its jurisdiction. Political action, in which the Amalgamated was a pioneer, has become a matter of routine to the American labor movement.

It would be a mistake, however, to leave the impression that the Amalgamated has merely marked time since 1941. More than 100,000 members were subsequently added to its ranks. Organizing campaigns in the South and Southwest have given the union among the largest bodies of membership of any union in the country in these areas. A comprehensive health and welfare program has been developed, and the union has established a successful insurance company operating on a national basis. The Sidney Hillman Foundation, created after the death of the former president, has carved out new fields of labor activity in the community as a whole.

8

The Women's Clothing Industry

There are many parallels in the history of labor organization in men's and women's garment manufacture during the period with which we are concerned. The International Ladies' Garment Workers' Union, like the Amalgamated Clothing Workers, seized upon the NRA code system, which brought some measure of stability to a chaotic industrial situation, to extend its organization in several swift strokes. Membership rose from 40,000 in 1932 to 200,000 in 1934. The union itself has described this era in the following terms:

The historian of our Union, in viewing its life and progress, will doubtless reach the conclusion that the period of mass-campaigns, of organizing movements which carried in their sweep scores of thousands of workers into our organization, reached its peak in 1933 and 1934, when, under the momentum of the new industrial policies of the first Roosevelt administration, we carried out gigantic drives and established our organization as one of the foremost labor unions in this country. . . . The great crusade of the first NRA year brought into our fold more than 125,000 new members, a new working population, with a psychology, work conditions and industrial surroundings materially different from the older groups in our Union.[1]

During the following years, membership expanded, but the basic organizing job had been done before the inauguration of the great CIO drives in the mass production industries, permitting the ILGWU to play an important role in the CIO. This is not to say that by 1936–1937 the ILGWU had completed its organization; like the Amalgamated, it faced some peculiarly difficult problems in the cotton garment industry, as we shall see. However, it was in a position, together with the Mine Workers and the Amalgamated Clothing Workers, to plow back the financial resources accumulated from 1933 to 1936 into organizational work in other industries.

As in the case of the Amalgamated, the ILGWU devoted a major part of its efforts during the period 1936–1941 to industry stabilization. The women's clothing industry was even more competitive and more speculative, and the average producing unit was on a smaller scale, than men's clothing manufacture. The production of women's clothing was carried on in several partly competitive but nevertheless distinct branches: the traditional cloak, suit, and skirt industry, concentrated in New York City, and employing about 50,000 wage earners in 1939; the silk dress industry, with over 100,000 wage earners in 1932, 82,000 of whom were located in the New York metropolitan area; the cotton dress industry, which had evolved from the production of noncompetitive house dresses into the manufacture of styled garments which threatened the competitive position of silk dresses, with almost 40,000 wage earners scattered throughout the country; and a number of other branches, including the production of undergarments and nightwear (30,000 wage earners); infants' and children's outerwear (24,000 wage earners); corsets and allied garments (17,000 wage earners); blouses (10,000 wage earners); and neckwear, scarves and other accessories.[2] The 1939 Census of Manufactures listed a total of 279,000 wage earners in women's garment manufacture, but this figure excluded the corset, knitted underwear, and knitted outerwear industries with about 80,000 wage earners among them, not all of whom, however, were engaged in the production of women's garments.

The typical producing unit in the industry was small and unstable. In 1940, the average number of workers per shop in the New York silk dress industry was 42, but 80 per cent of all shops employed less than 50 workers each. Only 20 shops employed more than 150 workers, and the largest shop had a total employment of 560.[3] In the cloak and suit industry, the average "inside" shop employed 21 workers, and the "contracting" shop, 25 workers, in 1939. Unit size in the cotton dress industry was somewhat larger; in 1939, average inside shop employment was 57, and average contracting shop employment, 43 workers.[4] In the latter industry, there were some factories employing hundreds of workers each, located mainly outside of New York City.

The typical coat and suit and dress shop required very little capital. It was estimated that the amount of capital investment per worker in the dress industry was $400 in 1939, about one-sixth of the average for all manufacturing. This made for ease of entry, but a high degree of business mortality. A union survey of the New York dress industry revealed that 22 per cent of all producers in business during 1939 went out of business during that year; and that of 984 manufacturers operating during 1939, only 524 had been in business before 1937.[5] The causes of this type of industrial organization have been outlined as follows:

It is the factor of style around which all else in the needle trades revolves. Styles usually originate in the high-priced field, and are soon copied in the lower-priced lines. Style places the industries where they are, and determines whether it is profitable to invent and introduce new machinery. This in turn limits the size of the shop, and lowers the cost of entering business, leading to bitter competition and constant turnover of firms. . . . In men's clothing, although style has assumed more importance with the passing of years, the changes are moderate and subdued, without the same caprice, extravagance, and erratic fits that characterize fashions for women. It is this relative stability in men's fashions that permits a more minute division of labor and the development of moderately large enterprises.

The labor force in the manufacture of women's garments was even more heavily weighted with women than that of the men's garment industry. Apart from the cloak and suit industry, which was predominantly male in the composition of its labor force, women dominated the industry numerically, constituting, in 1939, 77 per cent of all workers in silk dress manufacture, 91 per cent in cotton dresses, 88 per cent in corsets and allied garments, and 90 per cent in children's and infants' outerwear.[6] Despite this fact, the leadership of the union was 95 per cent male, which has been attributed to the low degree of permanent attachment of women to the industry, as well as to the general prejudice against women holding leadership positions in our society.

The ethnic characteristics of the women's garment labor force have had a major impact upon union structure and policies; in fact, their reflection in structure is as explicit as in any American trade union. The New York dress industry was dominated by two large locals, Local 22, 70.5 per cent of its 1937 membership of 29,000 being of Jewish origin, and Local 89, with 33,000 members almost exclusively of Italian origin. The cloak and suit industry was predominantly Jewish, but in other branches of the industry, particularly cotton garments, neither Jews nor Italians figured prominently.[8] For the international union as a whole, it was estimated that 40 per cent of the membership was Italian and 30 per cent Jewish. However, the top leadership of the international was predominantly Jewish, due to what has been aptly termed "the weight of oligarchic continuity,"[9] with the Italian element receiving recognition in the form of the first vice-presidency, a post that was for many years occupied by Luigi Antonini, head of Local 89.

While there were many points of similarity in the development of the ILGWU and the Amalgamated, the parallelism should not be overstated. The market situations faced by the two unions were different in many respects, and their responses varied. Their political ideologies, while in general to the left of the American labor movement as a whole, contained significant elements of dissimilarity. Their views on the AFL-CIO conflict were never identical, and toward the end of the nineteen-thirties became quite different. In fact, after many years of harmonious relationships, the two organizations quarreled bitterly and created an atmosphere of coolness which has persisted, in a diminished degree, until the present time.

The Dress Industry

The manufacture of dresses constituted the largest industrial subdivision within the jurisdiction of the ILGWU. In terms of value of product, it provided about 40 per cent of the industry's total output.[10] Historically, this branch of the industry was divided into two distinct segments: the manufacture of silk dresses, normally sold by the unit in distinct price lines, and the manufacture of cotton house dresses, where the product had so low a unit price that it was normally sold at wholesale by the dozen. However, during the depression years, by improving styling and introducing rayon fabrics, the manufacturers of house dresses reached out for a wider market. "Stress was laid . . . on the evolution of the cotton dress from its lowly position only a few years ago as a house dress or a so-called utility garment to a higher priced rayon product qualifying it for street wear. This general change has made the 'cotton' dress . . . a definite competitor to the silk dress of the lower brackets, a dominant article of production in the New York market and in several other silk dress centers." [11]

The silk dress industry was almost completely organized by a general strike in August 1933. The focus of organization was the New York Dress Joint Board, composed of four locals, with a combined membership of 80,000 in 1936. During the NRA period, the dressmakers had won the closed shop, a 35-hour week, and a guaranteed minimum wage. With the demise of the NRA code for the industry, the union endeavored to substitute its bargaining power for the government compulsion that had been applied to the employers from 1933 to 1935. It made three major demands during the negotiations to renew the collective agreements that were due to expire on January 1, 1936:

Limitation of contractors. Under the system of manufacture prevalent in the industry, garments were produced either by "manufacturers," who engaged in the actual process of manufacturing on their own premises with their own materials, or by "jobbers," who purchased materials, sent them out to "contractors" for manufacture, and then sold the completed garments. In 1939, of 85,000 dressmakers employed in New York and environs,

29,000 worked for manufacturers and jobbers, and 56,000 for contractors, indicating that the jobber-contractor system was the dominant mode of production.

The contractor was the least stable element in the picture. Because of ease of entry, intense competition for the favors of the jobber prevailed among them, and business mortality was high. A union survey undertaken in 1939 revealed that average annual earnings of workers employed by contractors were $935, compared with $1252 for workers employed by manufacturers. The union had long inveighed against the system. "The petty contracting shop, especially in the cheaper lines of dress manufacture, has for years been the bane and curse of the industry. It has been the epitome of insecurity, of haphazard earnings, of industrial waste and inefficiency. In its essence it typifies chaos, confusion, top-heavy overhead costs and bottle-necked production. No one is better familiar with these evils than our workers, no one has paid more for it in fruitless toil, misery and meager returns." [13] From the worker's point of view, the chief evil of the system lay in the fact that the hard-pressed contractor turned to his labor cost as a means of solving his competitive dilemma, thus rendering difficult the enforcement of union wage standards. "Confronted with the problem of how the garments could be produced at the lowest prices and still permit them to operate at a profit, the contractors would attempt to shift the burden to the workers . . . often the prospect of earning a few dollars proved too great a temptation for workers who always lived on the brink of poverty. They accepted work at lower prices without realizing that such acts could only lead to even lower standards for the entire industry." [14] The temptation of the worker to make wage concessions was augmented by the close attachment of the worker to the individual contractor; if the contractor failed to get work, his employees were likely to have low earnings for the season.[15] The union had to contend with the fact that workers, because of the competitive struggle, often felt a greater degree of solidarity with their employer than with workers in other shops.

As a means of curbing unbridled competition among contractors, the union demanded, in 1936, that a limitation be placed on the number of contractors who might work for a jobber. "Under limitation a jobber will be able to work with only the number of contractors he needs for his legitimate production. He will be able to use contractors only to produce dresses. He will be denied the contractors he has used to depress prices. Contractors will work for one particular jobber. We begin to approach the conditions of the inside shop. Since a jobber will be unable to discharge a contractor, he

will be unable to manipulate that the workers of that contractor find themselves discharged without cause. He will be unable to play shop against
shop, setting up vicious competition that places a constant pressure on
prices." [16]

The 1936 agreement, which was signed in February between the Joint
Board and the five associations in which the employers were organized,
went a long way toward meeting the objectives of the union. These organizations were the Affiliated Dress Manufacturers, Inc., which included manufacturers and jobbers producing expensive lines; the National Dress Manufacturers Association, including the producers of medium priced lines; the
Popular Priced Dress Manufacturers Group, including the producers of the
lower priced lines; the United Popular Dress Manufacturers Association,
including the contractors on the cheaper garments; and the United Better
Manufacturers Association, which embraced contractors on the more expensive products.

By the terms of the agreement, contractors working for jobbers as of
January 31, 1936, were designated permanent contractors. A jobber might
manufacture in his own "inside" shop, or he might let the work out to his
designated permanent contractors, but he could not give work to any new
contractor without permission of the Administrative Board, a tripartite
agency created by the agreement, under penalty of fine. Moreover, work
was to be divided evenly among all contracting shops, and no firm was to
open an "inside" shop or enlarge its existing facilities without the consent
of the Administrative Board, nor could contractors enlarge their shops without permission. In the event that increased business rendered the existing
facilities available to a jobber or manufacturer inadequate, he might take
on an additional temporary or permanent contractor, again with the consent
of the board. No contractor could be discharged by his jobber except for
poor workmanship or late deliveries, subject to the decision of the board.[17]

Wage settlement on the premises of the jobber. In a further effort to
remove competitive pressure on wages, the union proposed that the locus of
the settlement of piece rates on garments be moved from the premises of
the contractor, where they had traditionally been fixed, to the premises of
the jobber or to a neutral site. The purpose of this change was to make the
jobber responsible for maintenance of the agreed wages, and to ensure uniformity of rates among shops working for the same jobber. "Here again the
jobber is forced to shoulder the obligations which are rightly his. Under the
new system of price settlement, he is forced to pay uniform prices for labor
regardless of where the garment is manufactured. Prices are settled with the

jobber by a committee representing the workers of all the contracting shops
employed by the jobber." [18] The 1936 agreement embodied this new system
of settlement demanded by the union.

The unit system of wage settlement. Since about 75 per cent of the industry was working under a system of piece rates, it was a matter of vital
importance, if earnings were to be maintained, to prevent *sub rosa* wage
cutting through concessions in the piece rates. The union proposed that
the so-called unit system be adopted, "under which a dress is split up into
its component parts and the time necessary to make each part is carefully
determined. Each item is then listed on a schedule with the number of units
of time, on the basis of 10 to a minute, required to complete it. It is then a
simple matter to determine the units, and from that the number of minutes,
required for each dress. Since the collective agreement fixes the hourly
earnings of the worker, the pay for the dress may be determined quickly." [19]
To what extent this system actually replaced the traditional "grab-bag
method of haggle and bargain" as a result of the 1936 agreement cannot be
determined from the record.

The new contract was hailed by the union as having effected a basic
change in the structure of the industry. "The entire former concept of the
jobber within the structure of the industry had fundamentally been changed
insofar as the Union is concerned. The jobber today has become established
as the employer of the workers in the outside shops that are designated for
his production." A vigorous campaign of enforcement was undertaken, and
underpayment of wages checked. Between November 1935 and December
1936, the number of contractors under the jurisdiction of the Joint Board
declined from 2128 to 1745, compared with virtual stability in the number of
jobbers and manufacturers, indicating that the agreement was having its
effect.[20] A similar index of effectiveness was that whereas in 1935, only 26
per cent of the contractors were working exclusively for one jobber, the
percentage had risen to 67 in 1936.[21] By November 1939, 86 per cent were
in the exclusive employ of a single jobber, and there was a further drop of
26 per cent in the number of dress contractors.[22]

However, if the union had expected that these structural changes would
usher in an economic millennium, it was grievously disappointed. The 1937
recession hit dress manufacturing particularly hard, and the seasons of 1938
and 1939 continued to be poor ones. Between 1937 and 1940, membership of
the locals comprising the Dress Joint Board declined by 12 per cent, in part
because of the general decline in production, and in part due to the increasing inroads of cotton dress shops upon the silk dress industry. Average

hourly earnings, which had risen from 70.5 cents in 1935 to 80.2 cents in 1937, declined to 72.5 cents in 1939. It became evident that the welfare of the workers was basically dependent, as it always had been, upon the economic health of the industry, and that alterations in industrial organization were palliatives at best. The union, therefore, turned its attention to measures which would have the effect of increasing consumer demand for dresses.

The collective agreement was renewed at the beginning of 1939 with little change. To offset the competition of cotton garments, an organizing campaign was undertaken among the workers of this sector of the industry, which had considerably lower wage standards than the silk dress industry. In 1939, for example, average hourly earnings in cotton garments were 38.7 cents per hour compared with 72.5 cents in silk dresses. This drive, inaugurated in November 1939,[23] proved to be unsuccessful. The union later admitted that "since early 1938 no effective organizing activity in this area had been possible. The second industrial slump which occurred three years ago brought about a period of retrenchment, halting all major union campaigns. Scarcity of work, brief seasons, and resulting lower earnings are hardly conducive to trade union progress."

An allied threat to the position of the union was a tendency on the part of some manufacturers and contractors to move out of New York City, where they might escape the union, or even if they operated under union contract, enjoy lower production costs in nonlabor items. The 1936 agreement bound the signatory employers not to move their plants beyond the range of the New York City five-cent fare. Despite this agreement, the "runaway shop" continued to be a vexing problem during this period; fortunately for the union, its magnitude was limited by the many advantages, some of them other than pure cost in character, of a New York City location for manufacturing a highly stylized product.[24]

The most ambitious effort of the union to improve the sales position of the industry was the so-called Hochman Plan, which was presented to the employers in late 1940. Its purposes were two-fold: to reduce costs by increased efficiency, and to increase the general demand for dresses. Hochman, the head of the Dress Joint Board, argued:

Our industry has been built on sand. From the very beginning the employers have not concerned themselves with the production end of the business. They have paid attention to buying and selling, but never to the way the product was manufactured. . . . We also feel that the employers in this industry have failed completely in promoting the product. . . .[25]

On the cost front, he proposed the installation of cost accounting and budgetary control, training of supervisors, and a joint program of industrial engineering to improve methods of manufacture. With respect to promotion, a nationwide advertising campaign to secure recognition for New York City as the style center of the world, to replace Paris, which was then under German occupation, was advocated. Specifically, the union suggested an annual expendiutre of $1,500,000 for this purpose, toward which the ILGWU proposed to contribute $100,000, on condition that its label be affixed to every dress product.

This plan was accepted by the employers, somewhat reluctantly, as part of the revised collective agreement of 1941. The agreement also provided that the employer should operate his shop "at all times in an efficient and well-ordered manner." Specifically, employers committed themselves to the following conditions:

Machinery and equipment shall be maintained in good working condition; the premises shall be kept clean, shall be properly lighted and well ventilated and adequate working room shall be provided for all workers. There shall be provided to the worker in the shop a sufficient amount of supervision and adequate floor service to perform the immediate functions so as to obtain an uninterrupted flow of work, and to enable the workers of each craft to devote their full time exclusively to the work of their craft. . . .[26]

An efficiency engineering department was established in the office of the impartial chairman, the function of which was to advise employers on manufacturing procedures and to investigate union complaints of violation of the efficiency clause. The union created its own management engineering department, which also had as one of its purposes the improvement of production methods. To effectuate the promotional plan, the New York Dress Institute, Inc., was organized, and a combined union and fashion label, the New York Creation Label, was adopted, for which the manufacturers agreed to pay at the rate of one-third of 1 per cent of their monthly sales to finance the program. A leading advertising agency was engaged to launch the promotional campaign, but before it was fairly under way the war intervened and put an end to any real possibilities of large-scale promotion.[27]

These events occurred in a none too favorable economic environment. The year 1940 was the worst year for the dress industry since 1932, from the point of view of production and sales. There was some improvement in the first half of 1941, but the second half of the year witnessed one of the worst production seasons in the history of the industry. Indeed, it was not until 1943 that any substantial improvement took place. Average hourly earnings in dress manufacture were 73 cents in 1939, 72 cents in 1940, and 73 cents in 1941, while employment declined by 8 per cent between 1939 and 1941.[28]

The temporary upswing during the early part of 1941 was utilized by the union for inaugurating an intensive organizing drive in the cotton garment industry outside of New York City. The results of the campaign were described as follows:

This drive, now being terminated after a strenuous run of four months, can be easily set down as one of the most fruitful in the history of the union. Among its direct results are the unionization of a half dozen of very large dress factories which for years had defied the ILGWU and had scorned collective bargaining. Even greater have been its indirect results as scores of non-union dress firms in New York City and vicinity have come to terms with the New York Dress Joint Board without strikes. . . .[29]

In permanent membership terms, however, the gains achieved were not spectacular. For the year 1941, the net membership increase in cotton dress shops was only 3135, and in silk dress shops 1715. It was evident that the problem of the cotton garment industry, which was paying an average hourly wage of only 46 cents in 1941, was far from solved.

The Cloak and Suit Industry

In the branch of the ladies' garment industry devoted to the manufacture of coats, suits, and skirts, the union faced many of the same problems as in dress manufacture: a shrinking market, runaway shops, and the highly competitive jobber-contractor system of manufacture. Its version of the dangerous cotton dress competition was the introduction in out-of-town shops of so-called section work, under which the production of a garment was subdivided into numerous simple operations and allocated among different workers, in distinction to the traditional method employed in the New York shops whereby the same individual fabricated almost the entire garment.

The NRA code for the industry introduced the principle of contractor limitation, jobber responsibility for wages in contractor shops, and the guarantee of equitable division of work among designated contracting shops. When the code system came to an end, it was replaced with a voluntary organization, the National Coat and Suit Industry Recovery Board, with similar functions.[30] Partly as a consequence of the union's policy, there was a considerable shift in employment from the "outside" to the "inside" shop, and a consequent diminution in the number of contractors in the industry. All union employers were obliged to affiliate with the Recovery Board and comply with its standards, the system being policed by the issuance to complying employers of a Consumers' Protection Label. The board has claimed that its membership consistently included over 90 per cent of the firms in the industry, accounting for a somewhat higher percentage of the total output.[31] Among the trade practices which it attempted to regulate was the unlimited return of unsold goods to the manufacturer, subjecting the latter to the costly risks of style changes or a poor season. It also attempted to curb price cutting in the form of preferential discounts.[32]

The labor force in the cloak and suit industry was chiefly male, in contrast to that in dress manufacture, and relatively skilled in its composition. These factors were reflected in the wage level that prevailed in the industry. Following are the average hourly earnings that obtained in coat and suit manufacture from 1935 to 1941:[33]

1935	$1.086
1937	1.139
1938	1.133
1939	1.017
1940	0.92
1941	0.98

While these wages were considerably higher than those paid in dress manufacture, they also displayed a somewhat greater decline from 1937 to 1941 than did dress wages. Some progress seemed to have been achieved with the renewal of the industry's collective agreement in June 1937, when piece wages were raised by 10 per cent and a 32½-hour week was installed in place of the prevailing 35-hour week, effective upon the adoption of a similar reduction in hours by markets outside New York. The union placed great stress on the reduction of the work week, as a device for stretching the working season and for sharing the work among the excessive number of operatives attached to the industry.[34] It proposed that the improvements be paid for by a general price increase:

While opposed to an inflation of retail prices that would badly effect its members as consumers, the Union sees, at times, the necessity of a wholesale price adjustment that would keep the market within a frame of stability. Rather than to see the industry swamped by liquidations and a dangerous turnover of labor with all its attendant evils, the Union is lending a hand to effect a readjustment of wholesale prices that would strengthen the industry all around. By this the Union once again proves that it is one of the basic elements in the industry. . . .[35]

But the recession of 1937 prevented the effectuation of either the wage increase or the reduction in hours, and in 1939 the previous agreement was renewed unchanged.[36] Not until 1942 did coat and suit wages regain the 1937 level, and it required the full impact of wartime inflation to bring about a substantial increase in the money wage level. The lesson of the cloak and suit industry is that in the face of declining product demand, not even the most powerfully organized trade union can arrest a downward movement of labor standards.

The International Union

Membership and finances. Following are the membership statistics of the ILGWU from 1934 to 1942:

1934	198,141	1939	234,825
1935	216,801	1940	239,349
1936	222,369	1941	247,937
1937	242,290	1942	298,756
1938	253,646		

Source: International Ladies' Garment Workers' Union, *Financial and Statistical Report,* May 29, 1944, p. 47.

The upward trend after 1934 was slow, and included a period of retrogression until late 1941, when the membership curve once more began to rise swiftly. Of the period from 1937 to 1940, the union reported:

In contrast to the five years which preceded our [1937] convention, which were marked by rapid accretion of numerical strength, the past inter-convention period has been largely characterized by entrenchment, consolidation and inner growth. . . . You will learn that while this period, since our last convention in 1937, was not identified with great strikes and mass movements, the International Union and its affiliates everywhere were compelled almost daily to battle for the preservation of work standards and for new economic betterment against a rising tide of opposition made sharper by the general industrial recession all over the country.[37]

The membership gain from 1941 to 1942 resulted from the special organizing drives undertaken in 1941, mainly in the cotton garment industry outside New York City.

The ILGWU published, for the years with which we are dealing, the most detailed financial statements of any union in the United States, so that it is possible to trace its financial operations with precision. Following are data on the cash and investments held by the union from 1934 to 1944:[38]

May 1, 1934	$ 528,885
April 1, 1937	2,140,860
April 1, 1940	3,265,957
April 1, 1944	5,228,535

The union's assets were built up through a steady increase in its dues income, beginning with a little over a million dollars in 1934 and rising to almost two million dollars in 1943. Considering the intermittency of employment in the industry, the consistently high ratio of paid to total membership shown by the union's statistics is remarkable, particularly when it is recalled that the check-off was virtually nonexistent in the industry. The absence of any major protracted strike during this period prevented drainage of funds for a purpose which in the past had kept the union's treasury empty.

However, the union spent considerable money for other than pure trade union purposes, reflecting the wide interest in general social and political affairs which has become synonymous with garment unionism. Following is a partial list of major expenditure items during the years 1934 to 1944:

Table 6.

ILGWU expenditures, 1934-1944[a]

	May 1, 1934 to March 31, 1937	April 1, 1937 to March 31, 1940	April 1, 1940 to March 31, 1944
Educational expenses	$176,448	$252,343	$392,123
Steel Workers' Organizing Committee	100,000	. . .	. . .
American Labor Party and Labor's Non-Partisan League	68,500	147,230	168,946
United Textile Workers and TWOC	12,800	112,000	. . .
Aid to Refugees	56,455	247,000	320,000
Charitable contributions	59,912	275,000	335,000

[a] These figures are taken from the various financial and statistical reports submitted to the union conventions. In some cases the data were not presented under precisely the categories shown, and had to be estimated.

Relation with the labor movement. The experience of the ILGWU in relation to the AFL-CIO controversy was unique. One of the original founders of the CIO, the ILGWU soon became disillusioned with that organization, and by 1940 it had once again become affiliated with the AFL.

In this respect, the history of the ILGWU diverges sharply from that of its sister organization, the Amalgamated Clothing Workers.

Part of the explanation, at least, lies in the different pattern of relations with the AFL in the pre-CIO years. Ever since its formation in 1900, the ILGWU had been affiliated with the AFL, whereas the Amalgamated came into the AFL only in 1933, having been regarded until that time as a dual union to the United Garment Workers. Some of the more conservative members of the AFL Executive Council, such as Matthew Woll, who were anathema to Lewis and Hillman, were close personally to Dubinsky and other leaders of the ILGWU, notwithstanding the socialist background of the latter. It was only with considerable disquiet that the ILGWU became a charter member of the CIO, for reasons well expressed in an editorial appearing in its official organ:

Our Union, which was among the first unions to affiliate with the CIO, has gone into this movement without a trace of selfish motives. We are not a mass production industry, and we never had any jurisdictional conflicts with any of the unions affiliated with the AFL during all the 36 years that we belonged to it. For us it was not a matter of gaining new industries or strengthening our position in our own industry. Our Union joined in the CIO movement because of the principle and the idealism involved in it. Long before the CIO was born our membership preached the theory and practice of industrial unionism.

Yet, as earnest and devoted as we are to the principles of CIO and ready to make our contribution and sacrifices in its behalf, just as anxious is the overwhelming majority of our membership for a united labor movement in America. In our case, it must be realized too, it has been a tradition of two generations of working and struggling as a progressive union within the American Federation of Labor. . . .[39]

Of the original CIO leaders, Dubinsky was inclined to be the most cautious in defying the AFL, and the most reluctant to make the final break. He remained on the AFL Executive Council until September 1936, and resigned only after the ILGWU had been suspended from the AFL. In replying to an AFL ultimatum, Dubinsky, on behalf of the General Executive Board of his union, pleaded with the Executive Council to suspend judgment until its 1936 convention assembled, pledging that he would abide by the judgment of that convention on the CIO question. As has already been recounted, the ILGWU officials put considerable pressure on Lewis to meet with AFL peace negotiators in 1936, and favored attendance at the AFL Tampa convention. However, they were outraged by what they regarded as a flagrant breach of the AFL constitution by the Executive Council:

What was most disheartening in this entire tragic procedure is that the leaders of the Executive Council have chosen to motivate their arrogance of power to suspend affiliated unions on the claim of democracy in labor government and on the supposition that a minority of unions had conspired to force their will upon a majority as represented in the opinion of the Executive Council. It is a sad comment upon the logic and sense of fairness of the Executive Council, indeed, that when our Union had proposed to it the only sound and acceptable method of democracy, namely, a decision by convention vote, the upholders of democracy in the Council could think of no other method than of high-handed autocracy, of an order to stand trial without investigation, to submit to a hastily adopted rule of convenience, or to stand suspended.[40]

ILGWU-AFL relations reached their nadir in 1937. Six AFL federal locals in Cleveland, Ohio, under the leadership of a veteran AFL organizer, Coleman Claherty, led a back-to-work movement during an ILGWU strike in the knit goods industry of the city. In a telegram to William Green, Dubinsky discarded the usual tone of friendship with which he had continued to address the AFL leaders, and said:

In view of the fact that these acts of outright scabbery were brought by me to your attention and were condoned by you, I take this opportunity of congratulating you upon the significant success achieved by your agents in their efforts to break our Cleveland strike this morning. The task of escorting and herding scabs used to be the job exclusively of company thugs and strongarm hirelings but it appears to have been now voluntarily assumed for the benefit of anti-union employers by men in the service of the American Federation of Labor. Let me advise you that no orders or efforts on the part of the American Federation of Labor representatives to break our strike nor any amount of slugging and beating up of our pickets by American Federation of Labor representatives or their hirelings will succeed in breaking this strike. . . .[41]

Throughout 1937 the ILGWU continued to support the CIO. Financial assistance of $345,440 was given to various CIO drives,[42] the two principal donations going to the Steel Workers and the Textile Workers. After the breakdown of the 1937 peace negotiations, however, the ILGWU began to manifest some distrust of the CIO leadership. In the issue of January 1, 1938, *Justice*, the periodical of the ILGWU, expressed disappointment over the failure of the AFL–CIO negotiations, and observed that the AFL concession of industrial unionism for the mass production industries seemed to remove all fundamental barriers.[43] On January 11, Dubinsky addressed a meeting of 1500 ILGWU officials and reviewed the position of the organization at some length. He pointed out that there had always been within the ILGWU a strong pro-AFL group which had opposed the original decision to join the CIO, and revealed that the General Executive Board had voted for such affiliation in December 1935, by the close vote of 12 to 10; and that such vote "was due only to my assurance that we would be diligently on the lookout against the development of a dual movement." [44] Dubinsky declared that he was a real representative of the CIO rank and file, because: "We have been paying our share of the taxes, we have made our contribution, we have given of our resources and time to CIO activities; but we have never been consulted as to policy, procedure, issuance of charters and strategy." He reiterated the *Justice* claim that the 1937 negotiations had provided an equitable basis for peace, laid their failure at the door of the CIO, and expressed the hope that the future activities of the CIO would be devoted to organization of the unorganized rather than raiding existing unions.

When informed of this speech, Lewis commented that "Mr. Dubinsky, whom I esteem highly, is apparently giving an imitation of Eliza crossing the ice. Like Lot's wife he is looking backward. He must decide for himself whether he is fish, fowl or good red herring." [45] Whereupon Dubinsky retorted: "Peace and accord in organized labor, in my humble opinion, is looking forward and not backward. Eliza crossing the ice may not have had a very pleasant journey, but as I recall, she had to make that trip getting away from a none too kind overseer and she got to the other side."

After a futile attempt at AFL-CIO mediation through a committee consisting of Antonini, Hochman, and Nagler, all vice-presidents, the ILGWU Executive Board, at a meeting on November 10, 1938, formally broke with the CIO by declining to participate in its constitutional convention. "The formation of a permanent national union to supersede the CIO would, in our judgment, sharpen the conflict in the labor movement and would create greater obstacles for ultimate reconciliation. Traditionally opposed to dualism, we therefore decide not to take part in the move to form a permanent competitive national organization." [46] For the first time in its history, the ILGWU had broken all formal ties with the general labor movement.

Although the ILGWU leaders may have intended to remain neutral, it was not long before they began to move toward the AFL. One of the events which impelled them in this direction was a bitter jurisdictional dispute with the Amalgamated Clothing Workers. Actually, the area of the dispute was on the periphery of each union's jurisdiction, and under ordinary circumstances would have been adjusted amicably. But the coolness engendered by the ILGWU desertion of the CIO, differences between the two unions in the political arena, and assistance rendered by the ILGWU to the Homer Martin faction in the internal dispute that was raging in the Automobile Workers Union, served to raise the jurisdictional dispute to the rank of a major issue. In 1937, when introducing Hillman, Dubinsky told his convention: "I introduce the president of a union that is closer to our Union and closer to our hearts than any other organization within the American labor movement. . . . Our trade unions were always known as the twin unions within the labor movement. . . ."[47] Two years later, the erstwhile twin was being bitterly accused of sanctioning the manufacture of mannish-styled ladies' coats and suits in men's clothing shops, and of undercutting the wage scales of bathrobe workers. Members of the ILGWU picketed the general offices of the Amalgamated, much to the indignation of the latter, with placards stating: "Why has the Amalgamated made a deal with the contractors?", and "Can industrial unionism be decided on the basis of a pocket?" (the latter a reference to the claim of the Amalgamated that the sole distinction between the man's and woman's robe is the location of the pocket).[48] When the Amalgamated offered to send over all women's bath-robes made in the men's shops by parcel post, *Justice* waxed indignant: "We are left wondering. Is this the super-modern trade union 'national policy' of which the 'Advance' article boasts? Is this up-to-date labor statesman-ship? To us in the ILGWU, where old-fashioned union ethics and con-siderations still prevail, this parcel post business, frankly, carries a special and very unsavory odor." But the controversy got beyond the point of logomachy when the ILGWU General Executive Board adopted the fol-lowing resolution, in November 1939:

After examining reports relating to the unjustifiable and deliberate invasion by the Amalgamated of the bathrobe and other industries over which the ILGWU has exercised jurisdiction for a quarter of a century, we are forced to the realiza-tion that the Amalgamated is waging open warfare upon our Union. This inva-sion is a flagrant and bare-faced breach of trade union laws and principles.

We regard it as extremely unfortunate that the Amalgamated has chosen to destroy the traditional friendship which existed for decades between our two organizations by these attempts to capture a few members from our ranks. . . . In view of the recurring acts of hostility on the part of the Amalgamated against the International as evidenced by its repeated invasions of our jurisdiction, the General Executive Board has decided to meet the present challenge and attack of the Amalgamated and to instruct all our local and joint boards to resist, with all means and resources at their disposal, every act of invasion and aggression by Amalgamated officers and organizations to usurp our jurisdictional rights or to lure away employers from signing agreements with our union by offering wage concessions and the abandonment of other work standards.[49]

Fortunately, cooler counsels prevailed, and through the intermediation of Adolph Held, the respected president of the Amalgamated Bank, Dubinsky and Hillman were brought together for a series of conferences, which resulted in a statement deploring the differences that had arisen and pledging that they would personally settle any jurisdictional disputes between the two unions.[50]

Discussions between AFL and ILGWU leaders looking toward reaffiliation of the latter were held early in 1940, and by the time of the ILGWU convention in May, the stage was set. William Green reported to the AFL Executive Council that "President Dubinsky stated he wanted to have a declaration made at the convention and the whole thing acted upon in a dramatic way so that the A.F. of L. as well as his organization could have all the benefit out of it possible, particularly with regard to public opinion." [51] In order to make the affiliation more palatable to his rank and file, Dubinsky set three conditions as the basis for reaffiliation: elimination of the special one cent per capita tax which the AFL had levied to fight the CIO; taking away from the Executive Council the right to suspend affiliates; and AFL action against racketeering in the labor movement. Green gave the necessary commitments on the first two points in a form which was acceptable to the ILGWU, but which later gave rise to controversy when the 1940 AFL convention repudiated them in part.[52]

At the ILGWU convention, the committee on resolutions reported that there had been submitted to it 25 resolutions calling for reaffiliation with the AFL, 16 recommending continuation of neutrality, and one asking affiliation with the CIO. A letter from Green was then read to the delegates, in which the first two of Dubinsky's conditions were met, though no mention was made of the problem of racketeering. The committee then moved that the ILGWU reaffiliate with the AFL, and that its delegates be instructed to seek at the next AFL convention legislation empowering the Executive Council to remove from positions of trust in the labor movement individuals with bad records. With little debate, the convention voted 640 to 12 in favor of the motion, and Dubinsky noted that the twelve dissenters were communists.[53]

The first experiences of the ILGWU within the "house of labor" were not too happy. Dubinsky complained that the Executive Council had refused to honor its pledge with respect to its constitutional authority to suspend affiliates.[54] "Even more disappointing was the action of the New Orleans convention with regard to the antiracketeering resolution introduced by our delegation. The 1940 A.F. of L. convention, leaning heavily upon the autonomous rights of the affiliated international unions, went only as far as proposing to use 'moral suasion' as a preventive measure against malfeasance in office." [55] Dubinsky was physically attacked by Joseph Fay, an official of the Operating Engineers, in the bar of the Roosevelt Hotel in New Orleans, while the convention was in session. "In his cups, Mr. Fay had the courage of his convictions and objected in his favorite manner to Dubinsky's aspersions on racketeering." [56] The ILGWU delegation pointedly refused to vote for the reelection to the Executive Council of George E. Browne, president of the Stage Employees, who was already under charge of malfeasance in office and was subsequently convicted of a criminal offense, together with Bioff, a fellow official. However, the ILGWU was able to integrate itself into the local and regional structure of the AFL without difficulty, and the General Executive Board told the 1944 convention of the ILGWU that "on the whole, our relations with the national office of the Federation have, as in all former years, been of utmost cordiality and cooperativeness." [57]

Political action. During the 1920's, the ILGWU had been a battleground for socialist and communist factions. By 1928, the communists had been defeated, and the socialists were in firm control. The 1936 decision of the General Executive Board, by a vote of 16 to 5, to back Labor's Non-Partisan League thus marked a sharp break with the past. As *Justice* put it: "Until 1936, our Union never directly took a part in politics. From time to time we would support, or express sympathy with, political groups which we felt were close to labor and its objectives; our members would affiliate with such groups or movements, but this all was largely a matter of individual preferment. In July, 1936, however, we chose to cast our strength as citizens and workers with a labor party. . . ." [58] The ILGWU enthusiastically entered the American Labor Party, and Luigi Antonini, its first vice-president, became state chairman of the party.

The record of the ALP in 1936 and 1937 has already been recounted.[59] Because of the concentration of its membership in New York City, the ILGWU became the dominant partner in the party, with the Amalgamated Clothing Workers playing a secondary role. Some coolness developed between the two unions in 1938, when the ILGWU expressed its resentment of a movement that developed within the ALP to run Hillman as a candidate for the U. S. Senate.[60] In that year, the ALP backed Lehman in his bid for reelection as governor of New York State, and endorsed Wagner and Mead for the Senate. Lehman defeated Dewey by a margin of 70,000 votes, having won 350,000 on the American Labor Party line, which gave the latter considerable prominence as holding the balance of power in the state.

But in 1939, an internal dispute arose within the ALP which was eventually to lead to its destruction. The Communist Party ordered its members to register as ALP members, and proceeded to use the primary elections to infiltrate the organization. The fight came out into the open with the signing of the Stalin-Hitler pact in 1939, when the communist faction refused to support a resolution adopted at a state convention condemning the pact and the Soviet invasion of Finland. A group headed by Eugene Connally of the Transport Workers, Sam Watson of the Newspaper Guild, and Joseph Curran of the National Maritime Union, attempted to oust the right-wing state leadership, but was defeated at a state convention held in April 1940.[61] The communists opposed the endorsement of Roosevelt in 1940, but the ILGWU forces were still in control. "Our American Labor Party, naturally and logically, has endorsed President Roosevelt and the New Deal. We have saved the machinery of the Party from the clutches of Communist disrupters who conspired to convert it into a tail to their Party's kite." [62] The ILGWU was jubilant over the 417,000 votes which were cast for Roosevelt under its emblem.

But the rejoicing was premature. The left-wing, under the leadership of Vito Marcantonio, captured the Manhattan ALP organization and began moving out into the other boroughs of New York City. To the ILGWU, "the worst feature of this infiltration, aside from the disintegrating effect of intra-party conflict, was that it imposed on the party the incessant agony of perennial primary contests with their devastating drain of party energy and resources." The 1941 election, in which the party's vote of 435,000 ensured the reelection of Mayor LaGuardia of New York, failed to mitigate the internal strife.

The ILGWU was rather caustic in referring to the role of the Amalgamated in these events: "The Amalgamated's contribution, especially in later years, however, was anything but consistent and its financial assistance was not always dependable, though several of its lesser leaders doubtless had been quite sincere in their allegiance to the party." [63] However, there was no formal break between the two unions until 1942, when the ALP put an independent candidate for the governorship, Dean Alfange, into the field against John J. Bennet, the Democratic Party nominee. Although Hillman backed Bennet, on the urging of Roosevelt, the ILGWU-supported ALP candidate garnered more than 400,000 votes, resulting in the election of Thomas E. Dewey, the Republican candidate. In 1944, in a bitter primary fight, Sidney Hillman, in alliance with the left-wing faction, gained control of the state ALP organization, causing the ILGWU forces to secede and form a new organization, the Liberal Party.[64]

This venture into politics was an expensive one, and the tangible gains were not great. When first formed, the ILGWU leaders looked upon the ALP as the nucleus of an American version of the British Labor Party. However, the ALP never really moved beyond the confines of New York City, and stabilized itself at about 15 per cent of the vote there. Among its handicaps, in addition to the communist attachment, was the suspicion with which it was regarded by the AFL unions, even after the ILGWU had rejoined the AFL. The ILGWU leadership admitted that on many occasions, it had been tempted to withdraw from the party, but the conviction that political action is a necessary supplement to collective bargaining activities not only led the ILGWU to continue its support of the ALP when it was clear that the Communist Party had gained a firm bridgehead in the organization, but to continue on a new and even more costly venture when it was convinced that the ALP experiment had failed.

Internal affairs. The ILGWU had been one of the principal targets of the Communist Party ever since the latter's formation. During the decade from 1920 to 1930 communists attained positions of power in the union, particularly in the large New York dressmakers' Local 22, where a young and able trade unionist, Charles S. Zimmerman, held sway. However, with the change in the Communist Party line in 1928 from "boring from within" to "dual unionism," and the unseating of Jay Lovestone as secretary of the Communist Party, Zimmerman and other left-wing leaders who had been expelled from the ILGWU broke with the communists and returned to the fold. When in 1935, the communists, in another change of line, dissolved the Trade Union Unity League and once more attempted to infiltrate the ILGWU under the cloak of a "Popular Front," they managed only to capture Local 9 of the cloak finishers, an old stronghold, though they were given positions of importance in the cloakmakers Local 117.[65] In Local 22 Zimmerman, who was thoroughly versed in communist tactics, prevented them from gaining control, though in this period he was not averse to collaboration with them. For example, on May 1, 1936, Local 22 participated both in the communist-sponsored May Day parade in lower New York and in a May Day celebration held at the Polo Grounds under the auspices of the International. This action elicited the following comment from Dubinsky:

The Executive Board of Local 22 would have acted more wisely had they adopted no such resolution. The only purpose it can serve is to be broadcast in the Communist press as an example of divided loyalty in our Union. Local 22 may have had technically a right to take part in two May Day celebrations but it is, nevertheless, undeniably true that it was against the spirit governing the life of our organization. . . . Such a course shows that Local 22 is less concerned with a united front with a trade union movement than with a so-called united front with the Communists.[66]

The International itself, though aware of the dangers of communist control, did not favor the expulsion of individual communists. When the United Mine Workers adopted a constitutional provision barring communists from membership, the ILGWU newspaper declared, in an editorial:

We, in the ILGWU, have had more experience with the Communists, a good deal of it sad and tragic, than any other trade union. We, nevertheless, assert that keeping work-people out of jobs and a livelihood because of political affiliation is both unsound and immoral from a labor angle, even though such people are likely to become a nuisance and a danger to the organization. . . .

An intelligent, well-informed membership can be depended upon to keep such an element out of places of responsibility as a matter of self-preservation. . . .[67]

Considering the background of the union, the conventions, beginning with that of 1937, were singularly free of factionalism. True, at the 1937 convention there was some sharp debate over a resolution, backed by the leadership, the purpose of which was to dissolve all so-called clubs and factional political groups within the locals. Zimmerman defended the clubs as essential to the internal life of the larger locals, with 25,000 or 30,000 members each. But Dubinsky argued that they created a privileged caste within the locals which dominated rather than helped, and with the proviso that groupings could be organized three months before local elections, the resolution was adopted.[68] However, this was all. The handful of communist delegates who were elected to this and subsequent conventions were completely unimportant.[69] Zimmerman, once the leader of the left wing, together with Jay Lovestone, who joined Dubinsky's staff, became two of the foremost anticommunist tacticians in the American labor movement.

It would be wrong if the foregoing discussion were to leave the impression that the ILGWU was primarily interested in politics and radical factionalism. In fact, beginning with the New Deal period, the principal energies of the union were devoted to the humdrum business of collective bargaining and the administration of agreements. In this area the union was anything but radical. Thus, when the sit-down strikes were at the height of their prominence, *Justice* wrote that "as far as the garment shops are concerned, the 'walk-outers' have a good bit of an edge on the 'sit-downers.'

The old method having proved quite effective, it would seem quite risky, if not irrational, for us to play with experiments." [70] A jurisdictional dispute between the Dress and Cloak Joint Boards gave rise to far more acrimony than political differences.[71] It would also be remiss to fail to mention the widespread educational and cultural activities carried on by the international and its subsidiary bodies, which included evening classes, choral and instrumental societies, summer recreational facilities, athletic associatons, and dramatic clubs — the latter resulting in the production of *Pins and Needles,* a musical revue with a cast of workers drawn from the shops, which became a Broadway hit, the first trade union dramatic production to attain that distinction.[72]

Wages and employment. There are shown in Table 7 the average hourly

Table 7.

Average hourly earnings in the ladies' garment industry, 1935–1941
(in dollars)

	1935	1937	1938	1939	1940	1941
Coats and suits	$1.09	$1.14	$1.13	$1.02	$0.92	$0.98
Cotton garments	n.a.	0.37	0.39	0.39	0.42	0.46
Dresses (except cotton)	0.71	0.80	0.75	0.73	0.72	0.73
Corsets and allied garments	0.46	0.46	0.46	0.46	0.48	0.51
Knit outerwear[a]	0.46	0.46	0.47	0.46	0.48	0.50
Knit underwear[a]	0.40	0.41	0.42	0.41	0.43	0.46
Other	n.a.	0.45	0.43	0.42	0.45	0.49

Sources: International Ladies' Garment Workers' Union, *Report and Record, Twenty-Fourth Convention* (1940), p. 18; *ibid., Report and Record, Twenty-Fifth Convention* (1944), p. 38.
[a] Includes both men's and women's garments.

earnings for the various industries within the jurisdiction of the ILGWU for the years 1935 to 1941. It is apparent from these data that not only the coat and suit and dress industries, but all other industries under the ILGWU, progressed little in terms of money wages during the period. The imposition of federal minimum wages in 1940, fixed at 35 cents per hour for most branches of the industry, served to raise the lower wage branches somewhat. It should be recalled that except for the coat and suit industry, the labor force in women's garment manufacture was predominantly female in composition. When a comparison is made with the wages of women in other manufacturing industries, the silk dress level of 73 cents per hour is relatively high, in part due to the location of the industry in a high wage area. The cotton dress industry, however, was low by any standard.

The hourly rates tell only part of the story. During the entire period 1935 to 1941, employment was irregular and the season tended to be short. The union was less concerned with raising hourly rates than with providing more employment, and on several occasions locals resorted to the expedient of closing their books to new members for months at a time in order to discourage new entrants. A study of seasonality arrived at the following conclusion:

The generally prevalent custom of dividing the work equally among all workers in the shop during dull seasons, although it mitigates the burden of unemployment suffered by each worker, makes it difficult for the workers to find supplementary employment. Reliance on casual workers or workers from other seasonal industries during periods of peak employment seems not to be common in the dress industry. Consequently the full burden of seasonal fluctuations has to be distributed among the regular workers through sharing the work in dull seasons.[73]

For the entire period 1936 to 1941, in all its branches, the ILGWU was struggling against adverse economic circumstances, which drastically curbed the possibility of improving the labor standards of its members. Concurrently, workers in other manufacturing industries were enjoying substantial wage increases; average hourly earnings in all manufacturing increased by 31 per cent during this period.[74] Despite this fact, the membership not only remained loyal to the ILGWU and to its leadership, but sanctioned the expenditure of large sums of its funds for other than pure trade union purposes. Their acquiescence in this policy may be judged not only from convention actions, but from the success of voluntary drives to raise funds for such diverse causes as the Steel Workers' Organizing Committee, refugees from European fascism, and a general chest for charitable institutions. This is understandable only if it is realized that the ILGWU was a movement rather than a trade union in the narrower sense, and that its members were committed ideologically as well as economically. There were signs, however, that this type of member attachment was giving way to the more traditional attitude by 1941.

Finally, a word is in order about the spread of unionization beyond the confines of New York. Although New York City and the surrounding markets produced a very substantial proportion of ladies' garments, there were important producing areas in other parts of the country. The ILGWU was obliged to invest a disproportionate amount of resources to the organization of these areas, if only to protect its New York employers.

The Philadelphia and Chicago markets were largely organized together with New York. The growing southwestern district, however, demanded close attention. In 1937, this district had 6400 members in 25 locals. By 1940, there were 8000 members in 40 locals. The only city in the area with a substantial production of garments which was largely unorganized by 1940 was Dallas, Texas.[75] The increasingly important Los Angeles area was nonunion in 1940, although four years later it was reported to be largely under union control.[76]

The Southeast represented the greatest stumbling block to the ILGWU, as to most other unions. Located mainly in small towns, employers had little difficulty keeping union organizers away. Some progress in organization was made during the war in the knit underwear industry, but the manufacture of dresses remained solidly nonunion.

9

The Renascence of Textile Unionism

As was the case in the iron and steel industry, textile unionism had a long history behind it when the New Deal appeared on the American scene. Organization began as early as 1850, and continued in various forms without interruption. The American Federation of Labor chartered a national union of textile workers in 1896, and in 1901 this organization was merged with others into the United Textile Workers of America.[1]

The UTW maintained a precarious existence throughout the first decade of the present century, challenged first by the IWW and later by the communist National Textile Workers Union, as well as by numerous craft organizations of nonradical orientation. Its greatest effort came in 1934, when under its auspices, 420,000 textile workers went on strike in protest against the failure of the NRA codes to guarantee them the right to bargain collectively. The strike ended inconclusively, with the United Textile Workers unable to translate this great demonstration of textile labor solidarity into permanent organization. In 1935, the UTW paid per capita tax to the American Federation of Labor on 80,000 members, far less than the 350,000 members claimed on the eve of the general strike of 1934. The union characterized this period as follows:

Many obstacles lay across the path of organization. Community opposition to unions, especially in the South, was even stronger in those days than it is today. The business elements in the mill towns would combine their resources to keep unions out of the community. In those days when there was no Wagner Act to protect the rights of workers, not only was there no legal protection for the right to organize, but the law, in effect, hindered organization. . . . There were also administrative difficulties that hindered the task to be done. Organizational drives cost money and the UTW had none. Trained personnel was also needed but the UTW had only a few organizers on its staff because of its limited financial resources. The UTW had never been a wealthy union. Except for a brief spurt in membership at the time of the 1934 strike, it was one of the smaller unions in the A.F. of L. . . . It was financially weak, not only because of its small membership but also because provincial, craft-conscious elements in the union who insisted on craft autonomy and dues concessions, purposely kept the International Union weak, financially and structurally.[2]

Despite internal problems of craft and industrial federation separatism, the UTW espoused the cause of pure industrial unionism in the craft–industrial union controversy that developed within the American Federation of Labor. Its 1934 convention adopted resolutions in favor of industrial unionism, and Thomas McMahon, its president in 1935, was a charter member of the CIO. The executive council of the UTW came out in support of the CIO in December 1935, and the 1936 convention approved the course of action which led to eventual expulsion from the AFL. Even after its return to the AFL, the UTW justified its 1935 position in the following terms:

The United Textile Workers of America, which had operated on a semi-industrial basis ever since 1901 and now saw an opportunity to secure sufficient funds to organize the 1,000,000 unorganized textile workers, naturally joined in the formation of this Committee. The Executive Council of the A.F. of L., at that time, misunderstood the purposes motivating the UTW in joining the Committee, suspended and finally expelled the UTW and the other nine unions involved.[3]

Formation of the Textile Workers Organizing Committee (TWOC)

At the second meeting of the Committee for Industrial Organization, McMahon told the committee: "We are well fixed in the South — never were in a better position. Our greatest trouble is inability to secure halls. If we could afford organizers, we would build up." [4] This optimism was hardly justified by the facts. There was very little organization among the cotton mill workers of the South and New England, and much of the union's strength lay among hosiery workers and dyers. About one-half of the paid membership of 60,446 during the months of December 1936, and January-February 1937 consisted of workers from these two industries.[5]

The CIO was engrossed with preparations for its steel and auto organizing campaigns during 1936, and little attention was paid to the textile industry. Although John Brophy, CIO director of organization, conferred with the UTW Executive Council,[6] there was no general discussion of the textile situation by the committee as a whole. (This is evident from an examination of the CIO minutes for 1936.) Despite an improvement in business conditions in textiles, little organizational progress was achieved by the UTW operating on its own resources. The force of organizers was cut from 42 in November 1936 to 34 in February 1937, the very time the CIO was achieving its spectacular victories in the automobile industry. The only substantial gains secured were a contract between the rayon workers and the Celanese

Company of America, and unionization of the Reading district of Pennsylvania by the hosiery workers. Apart from contracts in the hosiery and dyeing industries, only nine new contracts were signed between September 1936 and February 1937, for a total of 25. The situation of the UTW at the beginning of 1937 has been well summarized as follows:

The UTWA leaders . . . had gauged the organization's shortcomings and were aware of its needs. They, too, awaited an opportunity to establish a real textile union. . . . Textile workers, they felt, should repeat the record of the rubber, steel and automobile workers. . . .

With immediate aid imperative, the job of organizing textile workers could not be done by a small group. It was a responsibility for the entire labor movement.

The needs of a mass organization were too varied for the group to undertake, no matter how willing and energetic. Of all these needs money loomed as most important. Such qualities as leadership and guidance in addition, formed basic requisites for the permanency and success of a textile workers' organization.[7]

In February 1937, McMahon resigned from the presidency of the UTW to become head of the Rhode Island Department of Labor, and he was succeeded by Francis J. Gorman. The CIO, flushed with victory in steel, autos, and rubber, and looking for new fields to conquer, decided to undertake the organization of the nation's textile workers. The UTW provided an obvious starting point, particularly since it was already a CIO affiliate. After several months of negotiation with Gorman, the following agreement was reached between the UTW and the CIO:

Agreement this ninth day of March, 1937, between the Committee for Industrial Organization and the United Textile Workers of America:

1. A Textile Workers' Organizing Committee shall be appointed by the Chairman of the Committee for Industrial Organization. Such Committee shall consist of a chairman and Secretary-Treasurer, and such additional members as are deemed necessary by the Chairman of the Committee for Industrial Organization, two of whom shall be from the United Textile Workers of America.

2. The Textile Workers Organizing Committee shall have full authority and power:
   (a) To administer outstanding and existing contracts between members of the United Textile Workers of America, or any of its affiliated federations or locals.
   (b) To handle all matters relative to the organizing campaign to be instituted on behalf of all the textile workers of this country.
   (c) To fix the initiation fees and dues for all new members, and to grant dispensation from the payment of initiation fees or dues for present members, and to require, if it so determines, that all initiation fees or dues that may come

into the United Textile Workers of America from any source, shall be turned over to the Textile Workers Organizing Committee for campaign purposes.

(d) To deal with employers of the textile workers and execute agreements on an industry, employer or any other basis in the discretion of the Textile Workers Organizing Committee.

3. The United Textile Workers of America shall turn over its funds to the Textile Workers Organizing Committee to be used in the organizing campaign. The several officers and agents of the United Textile Workers of America shall place themselves under the jurisdiction and orders of the Textile Workers Organizing Committee.

4. The Committee for Industrial Organization shall contribute such sums of money as conditions of the organizing campaign require. The disbursement of the funds shall be made by the Secretary-Treasurer of the Textile Workers Organizing Committee, subject to rules promulgated by such Committee.

5. The Committee for Industrial Organization shall have complete power and authority to determine the details incident to the termination of the organizing campaign, the disbandment of the Textile Workers Organizing Committee, and the re-organization of the United Textile Workers of America for the benefit of its present members and new members who join during the organizing campaign.[8]

This agreement was obviously patterned after the one which had been signed between the Steel Workers' Organizing Committee and the Amalgamated Association of Iron, Steel and Tin Workers. It entailed complete subordination of the UTW and its officers to appointees of John L. Lewis and Sidney Hillman. The Executive Council of the UTW ratified the agreement unanimously, but at least one member, Gorman, did so with some reluctance:

The Executive Board of the UTW received this proposed agreement with the mixed emotions. They fully appreciated the opportunity it provided to organize the unorganized textile workers. They welcomed the offer of financial and other aid, which were so badly needed. But they objected to the inferior position in which the UTW and its officers were placed and to the removal of control of both the UTW and the organizational campaign from the hands of the UTW, a thoroughly undemocratic procedure. They attempted to negotiate better terms but were met by an unyielding "take it or leave it" attitude.[9]

Hillman placed no great confidence in the existing UTW leadership, and he was determined to run things his own way. Cut off from the AFL, Gorman and his associates saw no other way out; refusal to go along with the CIO proposal would have probably resulted in an independent CIO drive. But the demotion rankled, and within a few years led Gorman and others to desert the TWOC.

Problems of Organization and Strategy

Immediately after the agreement was signed, Lewis appointed the following to the TWOC: Sidney Hillman, chairman; Thomas Kennedy, secretary-treasurer; Thomas F. Burns, Charles Zimmerman, and Charles Weinstein. Gorman and Emil Rieve, president of the American Federation of Hosiery Workers, a semi-autonomous industrial federation within the UTW, represented the latter organization on the TWOC.

Hillman was the logical leader of a textile drive. Just as Lewis emphasized the importance of organization in steel to protect an exposed flank of the coal miners, and made this his first order of business, so Hillman felt that a nonunion textile industry constituted a threat to his organization, the Amalgamated Clothing Workers. The official organ of the Amalgamated justified an assessment levied upon the clothing workers to support the TWOC in the following terms:

No group in the American labor movement is more vitally concerned with the success of the textile drive than the wearing apparel unions and foremost among these, the Amalgamated Clothing Workers of America. Divisions of our industry stand elbow to elbow with the textile mills. Cotton garment factories have sprung up under the protecting wing of the powerful open-shopism of the South. A whole area of our country has been turned into a swamp of exploitation by the arbitrary rule of the textile kings. . . . This area has been a threat to the unionized workers of the wearing apparel industries. Organization of the textile workers will clean it out. For our own sakes, as well as for the sake of the laboring people of the country, this textile drive must go over the top.[10]

Considerable care and thought went into the creation of an organizing staff. Eight regional offices were established, four of which were directed by Amalgamated officials. The most critical area, the deep South, was entrusted to A. Steve Nance, a popular southerner who had been president of the Georgia State Federation of Labor. A staff of 650 organizers was assembled, 500 of them directly on the TWOC payroll, 50 furnished by the Hosiery and Dyers federations, 60 by the Amalgamated Clothing Workers, and the remainder by other CIO unions.[11] In the South, an effort was made to recruit idealistic southern intellectuals, ministers and other nonworker elements for the staff, among them Franz Daniel, T. Witherspoon Dodge, and Lucy Randolph Mason, to overcome the allegations that the drive was being led by "communistic Yankees." [12] There was virtually no communist infiltration of the TWOC, despite a long standing communist interest in the low wage textile industry. Hillman and his principal associates were all experienced trade unionists, well acquainted with communist tactics, and had no difficulty in preventing their attaining positions of influence. In this respect, the record of the TWOC paralleled that of the Steel Workers' Organizing Committee, which was run firmly by a group of Mine Workers leaders.

The heterogeneity of the textile industry. In planning its organizational drive, the TWOC faced a number of difficult problems. Textile manufacturing is not a single industry, but rather a group of industries, some of which produce noncompeting products. Table 8 shows employment and earnings in 1937 for the principal subdivisions.[13] The largest of the industry groups was cotton textile manufacturing, a highly competitive industry, and characterized by a high ratio of labor to total cost. As a result, pressure on wages has been traditionally severe: "the individual manufacturer seeks the easiest way out of all of his problems. He thinks immediately of wages. He uses wage cuts to outplay his competitors, and snatch away a part of the market, even though he knows that his competitors will follow suit, depriving him of his temporary advantage and further depressing prices. Sometimes he increases work loads to accomplish the same purpose, and then turns to wage reductions when the savings from the stretchout prove inadequate to meet the even lower prices which might in the meantime have been instituted by other competitors." [14] Average wages of 41.3 cents per hour in 1937 compared with a figure of 64.8 cents average for 105 manufacturing industries compiled by the Bureau of Labor Statistics.[15] The problems resulting from the division of the industry into northern and southern sections will be considered below.

Table 8.

Average annual employment of wage earners and average hourly earnings in textile manufacturing, 1937

Industry	Average annual number of wage earners	Average hourly earnings (cents)
Cotton goods	445,500	41.3
Woolen and worsted	158,841	56.9
Rayon and silk	117,946	45.0
Hosiery	150,460	55.2
Dyeing and finishing	64,781	56.1
Carpets and rugs	44,871	62.2

Sources: Employment—United States *Census of Manufactures* (1939), vol. II, part I.
      Wages—Bureau of Labor Statistics, *Handbook of Labor Statistics,* 1947 edition, p. 70.

The woolen and worsted industry, located mainly in New England and the Middle Atlantic states, while still highly competitive, was characterized by a greater degree of industrial concentration. The American Woolen Company accounted for 20 per cent of domestic wool output in 1937, and ten companies, which employed among them 40 per cent of the industry's labor force, provided some wage leadership.[16] The silk and rayon industry was divided into two principal subdivisions. The section producing natural fibers, heavily concentrated around Paterson, New Jersey, was characterized by chaotic competition among a large number of small producers, and provided low wage standards. The synthetic rayon yarn-producing industry, on the other hand, was "technically the most advanced, industrially the most integrated, financially the most narrowly controlled, and commercially the most monopolistic" [17] of all the textile industries. Out of 57,000 workers in the industry in 1937, the American Viscose Company employed 20,000 and the Celanese Company, 11,000. The industry was in a period of rapid expansion, and paid relatively good wages. The rayon textile industry, as distinct from synthetic yarn production, was neither modern nor particularly concentrated.

Hosiery, dyeing and finishing, and rug and carpet manufacturing had relatively good wage standards. There were in addition a number of minor branches of the industry, including cordage and twine, linen goods and lace goods, all with their unique problems.

The southern cotton textile industry. The decline of cotton manufacturing in New England, and migration of the industry to the South, a traditional stronghold of militant anti-unionism, constituted the TWOC's principal obstacle. New England's share of the nation's spindles in place declined from 68 per cent in 1899 to 24 per cent in 1940, with the South having the balance. Moreover, idle capacity tended to be concentrated in the older New England mills. In 1940 New England had only 19 per cent of the country's spindle-hours, while the South, with 73 per cent of the spindles in place, had 79 per cent of the spindle-hours.[18] The principal southern cotton manufacturing states were North and South Carolina, Georgia, Alabama, and Virginia, while in New England, Massachusetts was the main cotton manufacturing center.

Labor standards in the South were lower than in the North, for a variety of reasons. In 1937, the average hourly wage in southern cotton textiles was only 39.7 cents compared with 50 cents for the North.[19] A study of the migration of cotton textiles from New England to the South yielded the conclusion that the principal cause was the large differential in wage costs between the two areas. The differences in cost were not merely a matter of differences in wage rates. Higher fringe benefits in the North and higher productivity in the South were major contributing factors. The southern advantage was attributed largely to "the large flow of workers from Southern farms (in contrast to the shutting off of immigration, with unfavorable effects on the North); Southern antagonism to trade unionism with favorable results in keeping down wages and fringe benefits and in keeping up work-loads; the concentration of the industry in small and hence low-cost communities; the (related) lower cost of living (a minor factor); the much smaller proportion of industrial workers in the South relative to the population and hence the greater pressure on wage rates in textiles." [20] Failure of New England management to keep up in research, investment, and technology, also contributed to the decline of that area, and other factors were cited as well. But whatever the precise reasons for the shift of industry, it was quite clear that as long as the South remained unorganized, the long run viability of textile unionism remained in question.

Craft and industrial separatism. The textile union had long been plagued with what has well been termed a "balkanization" of the national body. This problem was described in a publication of the United Textile Workers (AFL):

From the very day of its birth in 1901, the UTW had been faced with demands for craft autonomy and the unwillingness of groups to subordinate their special interests to that of the International Union. The UTW had been a weak International in an industry largely unorganized and, therefore, was frequently forced to give way to the demands of those opposed to the development of real authority in the hands of the International. . . . In 1932, these federationist elements . . . succeeded in writing into the UTW constitution provisions recognizing the establishment of autonomous federations within the UTW. These provisions were strengthened in 1934 and 1936.[21]

The TWOC was not prepared to countenance separatism, and all the industry federations with the exception of the Dyers and the Hosiery Workers were simply abolished. The two that were permitted to continue were not only self-supporting, but were able to contribute to the organizing campaign. The men who became the principal executive officers of the Textile Workers of America in 1939, Emil Rieve and George Baldanzi, had been the presidents, respectively, of the American Federation of Hosiery Workers and the Dyers Federation.

To provide coordination among local unions in the various branches of the industry, the TWOC resorted to *ad hoc* industry conferences which however, did not possess any legislative authority. "At these conferences, representatives of local unions within each of the industries gather for a day or two to consider all aspects of their industry's problems, to correlate informa tion from various areas, and to develop uniform policies. . . . These conferences have served to bind the locals together on chords of cooperation and mutual understanding. They have, in addition, dissipated rumors and suspicions. In the last analysis, they pool for the scattered locals all the basic information of the industry." [22]

On the local level, joint boards were created to coordinate activities. By October 1937, there were 16 such boards in which 83 locals were joined. The joint boards maintained central headquarters, thus reducing local expenses. Social, educational, and recreational activities could be planned jointly.[23] Through industry conferences and joint boards, the TWOC hoped to provide the internal coordination that was essential in so diversified an industry as textiles without permitting the rise of permanent functional suborganizations which might eventually challenge the authority of the national union.

Finances. The United Textile Workers had little money when it was taken over by the TWOC. Nor was there any expectation of substantial dues collections from new members. To facilitate organization, the TWOC instituted a policy of postponing dues payments until a contract was negotiated. Workers merely signed pledge cards designating the TWOC as their bargaining agent. A local union was established on a permanent basis only when a collective agreement was finally negotiated, and since there was often a long lapse of time between organization and agreement, particularly in the South, financing was highly uncertain. A regular dues schedule of $1.00 a month was instituted for members covered by agreement, a high rate for textile workers.

A financial statement covering the period March 23, 1937, to March 31, 1939, showed that the principal sources of TWOC financing were as follows:[24]

TWOC locals and joint boards	$442,000
American Federation of Hosiery Workers	183,000
United Textile Workers	126,000
Dyers Federation	60,000
Amalgamated Clothing Workers	523,000
United Mine Workers	198,000
CIO	85,000
International Ladies' Garment Workers	110,000

In addition to these amounts, some $300,000 was spent by various unions, in particular the Amalgamated Clothing Workers, in organizational assistance to the TWOC, bringing total expenditures for the two-year period up to about two million dollars. After steel, this was the best financed of the CIO drives, with the Amalgamated making the major contribution, and the Mine Workers giving a surprisingly large amount in view of its other heavy commitments.

The 1937 Organizing Drive

The drive got under way promptly in April 1937. By May 1, it was reported that agreements had been signed with 127 firms covering 62,000 employees,[25] no mean achievement for so brief a period. The reaction of the industry to the drive was by no means uniformly unfriendly. The editor of *Textile World,* one of the principal trade journals, wrote:

Why then is the industry less agitated than it was a month ago? Primarily, we believe, because the threat of a general textile strike, at least in the near future, has been averted. That threat, in fact, was an imaginary one. It was another one of those nightmares evoked by the Lewis legend. The immediate reaction of every textile manufacturer was to expect an industry-wide strike within the next month or two. They can hardly be blamed for this, in view of their past experience with Francis Gorman. But Hillman plays a different game.

One of his first public statements after assuming the chairmanship of T.W.O.C. was that his aim would be to avoid industrial strife. He was very evidently promising to bury Gorman and all his works when he said that the unionization campaign would be "conducted in an orderly, disciplined and responsible fashion." That, of course, describes exactly the way in which Gorman's [1934] campaign was *not* conducted. In fact, it is apparent that Hillman recognizes as his first job the necessity of taking the "bad taste" out of the industry's mouth, left there since the shameful days of September, 1934. . . .

The textile industry can expect a far more intelligent and effective labor leadership than it has ever had in the past. . . . [Hillman's] plans will not be one of concentration, but rather one of securing separate agreements with individual companies as he progresses with his campaign. . . .

If there is one general impression this reporter has gained from his contacts in the field, it is an agreement that, after all, the textile industry couldn't lose by a change in labor leadership. It just couldn't get a worse deal than it had in the past.[26]

In an attempt to ward off unionization, the industry resorted to several defensive measures. A 10 per cent wage increase, the second such increase within a six-month period, was fairly widespread in April and May. Firms operating on a 50-hour-week basis cut back to 40 hours.

Hillman chose as his first objectives the large manufacturing units in the Middle Atlantic states and New England, rayon and carpet rather than cotton manufacturers. In April, the American Viscose Company, employing 20,000 workers, was brought under contract, and soon afterward, North American Rayon, with 8000 workers. Other important conquests were the Bigelow-Sanford Carpet Company and the J. & P. Coats Company, employing 4000 workers in the manufacture of cotton thread. The first real opposition encountered by the drive, which was proceeding on the momentum of the CIO victories in steel and autos, as well as the Supreme Court decision declaring the Wagner Act constitutional, was in the silk and rayon throwing industry, centered in New York, New Jersey, and Pennsylvania. When a union proposal for an industry-wide agreement elicited little response, a strike was called for August 9, 1937, and 35,000 workers in 60 plants stopped work. By August 20, with the help of the friendly offices of Governor Earle of Pennsylvania, the strike was settled to the satisfaction of the union.[27]

The union's most notable victory was at the Wood and Ayer Mills of the American Woolen Company at Lawrence, Mass., the scene of famous labor struggles. This firm, the leader in the woolen industry, had successfully resisted unionization in the past, despite its location in relatively strong union territory. Great open-air rallies were held in Lawrence; on May 23, 50,000 workers turned out to hear John L. Lewis and Sidney Hillman, and on September 12, a few days before a scheduled NLRB election, Mayor La Guardia of New York was the featured speaker.[28] In sharp contrast to the dramatic events of 1912, the TWOC campaign was peaceful and effective, and in the elections of September 15 and 16 the workers designated TWOC as their collective bargaining agency by a vote of 6814 to 3248.[29] Although a union-shop agreement was negotiated with American Woolen, the union's satisfaction was short-lived, for in October, under the impact of economic recession, the company shut down most of its mills and discharged 75 per cent of its employees.

Some notion of the over-all progress achieved by the TWOC during its initial organizing drive may be gained from the following statistics of workers under TWOC contract (not to be confused with membership):[30]

May 15	81,000
June 30	130,000
September 11	202,000
September 30	215,000

Some of the textile industries were substantially organized; there were estimates of 75 per cent for synthetic yarn, 60 per cent for rug manufacturing, and 75 per cent for silk and rayon, and it was claimed that by July, 30,000 additional hosiery workers had been recruited.[31] But impressive though those achievements were, they could not conceal the fact that progress in southern cotton textile was disturbingly slow. By August 1937, the union had secured signatures on only 16 agreements covering 17,500 workers in southern mills.[32] The TWOC claimed in October that more than 100,000 southern workers had signed pledge cards, but even if this figure had some validity, it was a long step from pledge cards to signed agreements, as subsequent events revealed.

The importance of Federal labor legislation in persuading textile employers to deal with the union cannot be overemphasized. Emil Rieve admitted at the end of 1937: "The story of the organization drive in the textile industry could not be told without reference to the National Labor Relations Board. Obviously, this law did not organize our industry — no law ever did. But it provided a necessary safeguard." [33] Particularly in the South, TWOC strategy was to work slowly to obtain pledge cards, than to seek an NLRB election, and whatever gains it achieved in that part of the country were secured in this manner. By the end of September, the TWOC had won 51 out of 58 NLRB elections in which it participated, a total of 43,000 workers having voted in these elections.[34]

Internally, the TWOC kept a tight rein on its locals. All new locals set up were affiliated directly with the TWOC, rather than with the United Textile Workers, and UTW locals were urged to switch to the TWOC, thus further weakening the position of Gorman and the other officials of the UTW. All agreements were made out directly in the name of the TWOC, rather than the individual local union, and no contract could be signed without the approval of the national organization.[35] The loyalty of the TWOC staff to Hillman and the Amalgamated was assured by the fact that so many of the key TWOC leaders were drawn from Amalgamated ranks.

Economic Recession

The organizing drive was cut short by a severe recession that hit the textile industry late in September 1937. For the next year, the TWOC was engaged largely in a rearguard action to hold the gains it had made. Its immediate goal was to prevent the wave of wage cuts which was the invariable concomitant of a textile slump. For several months, it was successful, and claimed that for the first time, unionism had imparted an element of stability to a notoriously unstable industry.

There is . . . a new note in the industrial picture today, which is becoming increasingly more apparent. In the textile industry, it is the rising importance of the T.W.O.C. . . . Mill owners, in the past, have invariably responded to a business recession with an old, suicidal remedy which was usually labeled — reduction in operating costs. It was accomplished by cutting wages, lengthening hours, adding to the work-load, impoverishing the people who buy, and removing mass purchasing power from the market. The T.W.O.C. is putting a stop to this. Its organizing drive is establishing a firm line of defense against the unscrupulous employers who seek to drive industry to lower levels for its workers. The T.W.O.C. is preventing fierce competition from depressing industry to greater chaos and disorganization. In safeguarding the living standards of the workers and maintaining their purchasing power, the T.W.O.C. serves as the greatest spur to industry.[36]

But these claims were premature. In December 1937, the New Bedford Textile Council, a regional affiliate of the UTW, negotiated a 12½ per cent wage cut with its employers in cotton textiles without the knowledge or approval of the TWOC. The seven local unions constituting the council were suspended, and then expelled from the TWOC, and the workers were urged to reorganize the locals under new leadership and return to the TWOC.[37] The wage cut spread rapidly throughout the industry, and by August 1938, average hourly earnings in cotton were 38.3 cents compared with 42.2 cents the previous year.[38] In woolens, the story was much the same. During January and February 1938, the union called fifteen strikes against firms attempting to institute wage reductions, and for a time checked the movement, but resistance crumbled in April when the large Uxbridge Worsted Company, which was not under contract, announced a reduction in wages. The union noted sadly: "In the woolen industry, the workers have been slow to respond to the call for unionism and the protection of their wage scales. Many remained satisfied with the 10 per cent wage increase in April. Many were blinded to the need of the protection of this wage scale. The industry remained essentially unorganized though workers have for decades learned their helplessness before the concerted conspiracy of employers." [39]

But even strong organization was no proof against the powerful depressive forces that were operating. The Bigelow Sanford Carpet Company, which was under contract with the TWOC, suddenly announced a 10 per cent wage cut on May 4, 1938. Some 70 per cent of the industry was organized, and this was the first company to reduce wages. Six thousand employees of Bigelow Sanford in Amsterdam and Thompsonville, New York, went out on strike in protest. Mass picketing kept the plants closed, and a nationwide boycott against the products of the company was instituted. When the strike was in its third week, the company offered to offset the wage cut by increasing average weekly hours worked from 16 to 19 (the company had been on short time before the strike), but the offer was refused.[40] Finally, after seven weeks of shutdown, it was agreed to submit the wage question to arbitration, and Arthur H. Meyers of the New York State Mediation Board was named as arbitrator. When in October, he reduced the wage cut to 5 per cent, the union hailed his decision as a victory.

However, the depression years 1937–38 were not entirely without gain for the TWOC. The number of workers covered by agreement rose from 173,-000 at the end of 1937 to 190,000 by July 1938, although most of the new agreements were the culmination of long negotiations based upon organizational victories achieved in the summer of 1937. In the South, in the ten months ended July 1938, the TWOC won 43 NLRB elections involving 23,000 workers and lost 19 elections involving 5800 workers. But few of these election victories were translated into agreements, since southern employers were disposed to ignore the mandate of the law with respect to collective bargaining. Perhaps the union's greatest achievement was to weather the recession with few contract losses for the first time in the long history of textile unionism.

July 1938 marked the bottom of the recession in the textile industry. Prices began to turn upward, and with them the confidence of the union. However, recovery proved slower than anticipated, and in April 1939, the union's economist wrote:

The months following August of 1938 have not favored a widespread extension of union organization. With this whole period characterized by slow economic improvement, the near future, furthermore, promises little economic reassurance. Though the wool industry has registered marked gains, the cotton textile and silk and rayon weaving industries revealed but moderate increases, periodically suffering recessions in both business and prospects.[41]

Between July 1938 and April 1939, the TWOC obtained 153 new agreements representing some 37,000 workers, a much lower rate of growth than had characterized the first six months of its existence. The principal gains were in woolen and worsteds, where additional mills of the American Woolen Company, and other sizable producers, were brought under contract. The following organizational percentages were claimed in May 1939:[42]

Carpets and rugs	75 per cent
Woolens and worsteds	27 per cent
Silk and rayon	50 per cent
Velvet	50 per cent
Full fashioned hosiery	90 per cent

In southern cotton, however, the union had but 27 contracts for 27,000 workers, though it had won NLRB elections covering an additional 40,000 workers and claimed that 85,000 workers beyond this had signed pledge cards. The reports of union officials operating in the South at this time were monotonously uniform. The principal obstacle to organization was the fierce resistance of southern employers, taking the form of discriminatory discharge of active trade unionists, coupled with eviction from company houses and the denial of credit at company stores in the smaller textile mill towns; the enlistment of religious revivalists to preach against the CIO; and the use of outright force and violence against TWOC organizers. For example, Witherspoon Dodge, a TWOC organizer, while seated on the porch of the Lee-Grant Hotel in Fitzgerald, Georgia on August 8, 1938, conversing with President Cox of the Fitzgerald Cotton Mills, was seized by a band of men, thrown into a truck, beaten severely, and dumped out of town with the warning not to return.[43] Four mill officials, including Cox, and eleven employees of the mill were indicted by a federal grand jury for this action. However, when special attorneys assigned by the U. S. Department of Justice to prosecute the case arrived in Savannah for the trial, they found that the jury had been selected five weeks prior to the beginning of the trial, as well as other irregularities. The indicted men were acquitted in what the Department of Justice attorneys termed "a complete abortion of justice, extending all the way from the United States District Attorney's office in Savannah through the jury and the presiding judge of the court."

The National Labor Relations Board has documented the anti-union activities of the Alma, Limestone and Hamrick Mills, located at Gaffney, South Carolina.[44] The TWOC, in May 1938, after almost a year of organizational work, petitioned for an NLRB election in the three mills, whereupon anti-union "clubs" were formed under the auspices of the companies to prevent a TWOC victory. When Witherspoon Dodge attempted to hold a public meeting, he was stoned by a mob of 40 men in the presence of local law enforcement officials. "Club" leaders, including foremen, solicited signatures for union resignation cards. Itinerant preachers were encouraged to oppose the CIO, and company trucks were used to transport workers to their meetings. A number of workers were arrested by company policemen on charges of drunkenness, jailed overnight, and discharged from employment the next day. In many cases, such discharge carried with it eviction from company houses without notice. Lucy Randolph Mason, in her autobiography, notes that Gaffney continued to be a rough town even after the NLRB had found the employers guilty of unfair labor practices. In 1939,

Don McKee, a Textile Worker organizer attempting to distribute leaflets, was hit over the head with a brick. When he accompanied a federal wage-hour inspector to Gaffney, a mob gathered around the car in which they were riding and attempted to overturn it. The same thing occurred when he drove to the town with a field examiner for the NLRB. Numerous similar episodes are cited by Miss Mason.[45]

A. Steve Nance, the first southern regional director for the TWOC, was described as "a jolly, modest Southern gentleman in his early forties; for twenty years president of his local of the International Typographers, the American Federation of Labor's oldest union; recently head of the Atlanta, Georgia, central trades body; currently president of the Georgia Federation of Labor."[46] It was his belief when he first went to work for the TWOC that southern employers would be willing to sit down and bargain with him, and he insisted on personally handling all negotiations. In an interview in July 1937, he declared:

> One thing they cannot charge against us — that we are foreigners, Reds, outside agitators or damn Yankees. My great-great-grandfather settled in Georgia. They paid him in land for his services in the Revolutionary War. My grandfather and my father fought in the Confederate Army. I was born and reared in Georgia. . . . Virtually every one of our officers and organizers likewise is of Southern birth and upbringing. This is strictly an American and a Southern movement.[47]

Nance's expectations were doomed to quick disappointment. The negotiations he conducted bogged down, and he became a bottleneck rather than an expeditor. He died several years later a disappointed man, his philosophy of conciliation having proved an utter failure.

Franz Daniel, another TWOC leader in the South, summarized the difficulties he had encountered in an address to the first convention of the Textile Workers Union in 1939:

> In a barrage of propaganda every newspaper in the South, without one single exception, opened up and repeated time after time the same old shopworn slogan that the CIO was Communist, that all of us were Communists, and that we were foreign agitators and we were destroying the peaceful arrangement that the mill owners had made in the South.

> We had to fight the newspapers. We did not think that we would have to fight the church. We no more than stepped into the field when they came like locusts and pitched their tents, revivalists paid by the manufacturers who told the workers that we were the agents of the devil and that the mark of the beast was on our foreheads. Time after time the revivalists were able to destroy our majorities.

We did not think that we would have to fight the Ku Klux Klan. We felt that it was dead and buried, but no sooner had we stepped into the field than they came with the Night Shirts and the fiery crosses.[48]

The TWOC also charged that American Federation of Labor organizers were approaching southern employers who were being organized by the CIO and urging them to enter into AFL contracts as the lesser of two evils.[49]

A realistic management evaluation of the southern position of the TWOC in April 1939, on the eve of its first constitutional convention, concluded that the TWOC could claim about 20 per cent of southern textile workers as card bearing members, namely, somewhere between 50,000 and 65,000 of the South's 350,000 cotton workers; and that no more than 15 per cent of these were paying dues with any degree of regularity. While the TWOC had only a score of signed agreements (the union claimed 27), a somewhat larger number of mills were operating under verbal agreements with the union. It was estimated that only 5 per cent of the total number of spindles in the South had been affected by union agreement, and that one-third of these were no longer in force by April 1939.[50]

From Organizing Committee to National Union

Toward the end of 1938, internal dissention developed within the TWOC. Personal rivalries had existed from the beginning, but the failure of the TWOC to make progress during the recession permitted their translation into organizational fission. Joseph Sylvia, a leader of the old Woolen and Worsted Federation of the UTW, charged the TWOC with unlawful violation of its constitutional rights, and instituted a legal suit in Rhode Island to compel the repayment to local unions of money which had been transferred to the TWOC when the TWOC-UTW contract was entered into. When a lower court ruled in his favor (the decision was later reversed on appeal) Francis Gorman, the president of the UTW, advised all UTW locals that they were no longer under the jurisdiction of the TWOC. "Gorman had been definitely dissatisfied for some time with his position in the T.W.O.C. This has been an open secret. He was demoted from his position as former chief in the textile labor movement to that of a subordinate. Hillman ran the show, very definitely — and other aides than Gorman were his real source of advice." [51] Hillman became seriously ill in November 1937, and was obliged to relinquish the day-to-day operation of TWOC. For the next year, the organization drifted with little leadership from the TWOC. When it became apparent that Hillman had selected Emil Rieve to succeed him as executive head of the union, Gorman decided to make his bid for independence.

Gorman turned to the AFL for assistance. William Green was in a receptive mood; the AFL had organized 80 federal locals of textile workers in various parts of the country, and after conferring with Gorman, Sylvia, and George Googe, the Federation's southern director, it was decided to seek restoration of the old charter of the United Textile Workers.[52] A conference was held on December 28, 1938, attended by twenty-one delegates, which petitioned the Executive Council for a charter, and authorized Gorman to reorganize the UTW.[53] The charter was reinstated in February 1939.

The UTW-AFL began its first convention under the new regime on May 8. In attendance were 131 delegates representing 83 local unions, 32 of which were federal locals and 51 former UTW locals. Most of these must have been paper locals, however, for it was later admitted that the union had but 1500 members at the time. Gorman justified his withdrawal from the TWOC on the ground that the UTW was being systematically destroyed in violation of the TWOC-UTW agreement:

Complaints started coming in during the latter part of April, about organizers insisting that U.T.W.A. charters should be sent to New York to the T.W.O.C. . . . We were told that some of the charters were sent in voluntarily. The facts are that the organizers demanded them, and sometimes took them off the walls. The complaints continued to a point where, in the latter part of the year, we had about 200 charters returned. . . .

In 1938 came more complaints of the practices of the representatives of the T.W.O.C. who had planned to take over the organization entirely, who had subordinated the officers and the organizers of the U.T.W.A. to an inferior position, and assumed complete control with the statement that they were representing Mr. Hillman, and their decisions were final. Any U.T.W.A. organizer who dared to protest was immediately discharged.[54]

The only surprise of the convention came when Gorman declined to run for the presidency. This was not his idea, however. William Green reported to the AFL Executive Council that he had told Gorman that he had not yet lived down his action in taking the UTW out of the AFL, and that therefore it would be unwise for Gorman to become president, and that Gorman had agreed to follow this "advice."[55]

On the other side of the fence, Gorman was denounced as "a pathetic little 'Napoleon' without an army."[56] As soon as his defection became known, he was ousted by the Executive Council of the UTW-TWOC, and replaced in the presidency by George Baldanzi. The remaining UTW officers remained loyal to the TWOC.

Perhaps because of these developments, the TWOC decided that the time was ripe for formalizing its relationship with the UTW. Accordingly, a convention was called for May 15 at Philadelphia to effect a consolidation of the two organizations. When the delegates assembled, they were told that the union represented 424,000 workers, 274,000 of them under union agreement, and 150,000 more without privilege of agreement.[57] Actual per capita membership was not revealed, but in view of the facts (a) that not all workers under union agreement were members, and (b) that TWOC did not require dues payments until members were under agreement, paid membership must have been only a fraction of the figure cited above. The report to the convention stated that the union was still not self-sustaining.

The plan of reorganization consisted simply of the merger of the 302 locals directly affiliated with the TWOC with the 126 locals chartered by the old UTW into a new organization, the Textile Workers' Union of America. Emil Rieve was elected president and George Baldanzi executive vice-president, without opposition. Rieve had made his reputation as president of the American Federation of Hosiery Workers, the most stable and businesslike of the textile unions, and was a pioneer in collective bargaining on a national basis. It was his boast that during his tenure of office, the Hosiery Workers had never violated an agreement. Baldanzi, a younger man, was the organizer and first president of the Federation of Dyers, the other stable subfederation in the UTW. It is an interesting commentary on Hillman's approach to trade union government that he should have selected to lead the new union the two men who were closest to the American ideal of wage-conscious unionism.

Among the achievements upon which the union had cause to congratulate itself were the textile minima that had been set under the recently enacted Fair Labor Standards Act. The Textile Workers' Union, more than almost any other trade union in the United States, was vitally concerned with this legislation as a means of raising the wages of unorganized southern workers to levels more competitive with those paid in the organized mills of the North. In August 1938, cotton textile wages in the North averaged 44.6 cents per hour, compared with 36.6 cents per hour in the South.[58] The industry wage board established under the act set the initial minimum in cotton at 32.5 cents per hour, resulting in an increase for a considerable number of workers, although this rate did not become effective until October 24, 1939. Other minima established were 40 cents for the full-fashioned hosiery industry, the highest figure then possible under the law; and 36 cents for the woolen and worsted industry.

The Stabilization of Textile Unionism

The economic environment in which the Textile Workers' Union found itself during the next few years was less favorable than for American unionism as a whole. The traditional two-year textile cycle reasserted itself with the advent of a new business decline during the first half of 1940, after a considerable degree of recovery had been achieved in 1939. However, growing national defense orders made the 1940 recession a short lived one, and by the summer, business was once more on the upswing. It was reported that the December 1940, consumption of cotton was the greatest in the history of the industry, while wool output was also at a very high level.[59]

During the second half of 1939, the wage cuts of 1938 were largely restored. The 5 per cent reduction decreed by an arbitrator in the carpet and rug industry was revoked in July; a 6 per cent increase spread through the rayon industry after a successful strike against the Celanese Corporation; cotton wages were increased by 7 per cent, which did not match the 12½ per cent reduction of 1938; and wages in the woolen and worsted industry rose by from 7 to 10 per cent in February 1940, after negotiations between the union and the American Woolen Company. A new round of wage increases took place during the second half of 1940 and early in 1941: 2 to 3 per cent in carpets and rugs, 10 per cent in woolens, 10 per cent in northern cotton, and from 5 to 7 per cent in southern cotton.

Slowly, other changes in labor conditions favored by the union found their way into agreements. The 40-hour week was assured by the enactment of the Fair Labor Standards Act. Most of the agreements renewed in 1939 and 1940 provided for vacation pay of one week. Contracts began to provide for joint study of work loads, and for appeal against company established standards to impartial arbitrators. The national union devoted considerable attention to the work load problem, and increasingly provided technical assistance to the locals.

The union relied extensively in its organizational work upon government assistance. Its executive council reported in 1941: "The most important method of securing rights to collective bargaining during the past two years was election victories."[60] In commenting upon organization of the Lane Cotton Mills of New Orleans, long an anti-union firm, a union publication noted: "Our pressure through federal laws was too much for the management. They were beginning to lose government contracts because they were blacklisted and that proved to be the final blow."[61]

Lahne has compiled some election and contract statistics[62] which illustrate succinctly the continuing difficulties of organizing the South, despite governmental help. As of May 31, 1941, the TWUA had won NLRB elections in 46 southern cotton mills employing 32,000 workers, while in the North it won 12 elections in cotton mills employing 14,000 workers. In addition, certification was won at 3 northern mills and 5 southern mills without elections. Of the 15 northern mills, contracts were secured at 13, while negotiations were proceeding at one mill when the tabulation was made. Ten of the 13 northern contracts were still in effect on May 31, 1941, one had expired without renewal, and two were lost to other unions. In the South, by contrast, the union had succeeded in gaining contracts in only 29 of the 51 mills at which it had been certified, and of these 29, only 16 were still in effect on May 31, 1941, 12 having expired without renewal, while one was lost to the AFL.

By way of further contrast, on May 31, 1941, the TWUA had 23 cotton contracts in the South covering 17,000 workers, and 33 in the North covering 26,000 workers. Only 7 of the 23 southern contracts had been secured without NLRB intervention, as compared with 23 of the 33 northern contracts. To quote Lahne:

The North-South contrast indicates that in the Southern section of the industry, which is most important to the success of the T.W.U.A. in its campaign to organize cotton textiles, the anti-union tradition of the employers has scarcely abated. In several cases more than two years of negotiations had failed to result in an agreement, and the NLRB had to order the mills to bargain in good faith instead of systematically rejecting every union proposal without making counterproposals, and to refrain from setting arbitrary and unwarranted limits on the negotiations.

Nevertheless, some progress was made even in the South. The CIO undertook a concerted southern organizing campaign in 1940, with Rieve as chairman of the committee. Among the important producers brought under contract were Marshall Field, Lane Cotton, and the Erwin Mills, the latter having been the first of the "big four" North Carolina cotton mills to be organized.

Even in the North, cotton remained the weakest link in the organizational chain. The New Bedford Textile Council, which had been expelled from the TWOC for agreeing to a wage reduction, remained independent until 1941, when, under the threat of encroachment by the Teamsters, it joined the United Textile Workers, AFL, under similar conditions of loose affiliation as those agreed upon in 1928.[63] The TWUA made no full-scale effort to enter Fall River until 1941, when a drive was initiated to replace the five craft locals affiliated with the independent American Federation of Textile Operatives. On September 19, 1941, the TWUA won a representation election in the Kerr Mills of the American Thread Co., in opposition to the Weavers Protective Association, one of the independent AFTO locals, and thus established a foothold in Fall River. It was not until 1942 and 1943, however, that the TWUA captured a commanding position in these two major northern cotton centers. It was estimated that as of May 31, 1941, the TWUA had enrolled only 55,000 cotton mill workers in the entire country,[64] less than 15 per cent of the cotton textile labor force.

The situation was somewhat better for the union in other industries. It controlled 36,000 workers out of 55,000 in synthetic yarn, or about two-thirds, and the same percentage in the carpet and rug industry. The degree of organization among woolen and worsted workers was much less, about 25 per cent, though the union's influence in the industry was greater than this figure might suggest by virtue of its control of two-thirds of the employees of American Woolen, the wage leader in the industry.[65]

For textile manufacturing as a whole, the TWUA claimed in 1941 to represent 260,000 workers, of whom 230,000 were covered by signed agreement.[66] This may be compared with 160,000 workers under TWUA contract in 1939, indicating that some progress had been made. However, contract coverage should not be confused with actual membership, which was undoubtedly much lower, though no data are available.

Nevertheless, a considerable degree of stability had been achieved during this period. Rieve stated in 1941 that "since our last convention we have received no contribution from any source and we have requested none." The national union collected over one million dollars in dues from June 1939 to February 1941.[67] Even more important than the financial aspect was a new attitude toward trade union function which had spread throughout the textile industry, which is well expressed in the following passage from a TWUA publication:

The failure of textile workers in the past to create lasting unions can be attributed in part to their refusal to accept contractual relations with their employers. Forgetting periodic recessions, they relied almost entirely on their economic strength applied in the form of strikes or threats of strike. Organizations rose and ebbed, and working conditions followed the rise and fall of business. The two-year business cycle in the textile industry restricted favorable economic periods to a maximum of six months every two years. A continuous labor organization, therefore, could be maintained only with great difficulty. Previous unions concerned themselves chiefly with sporadic action against immediate grievances, but built no permanent union and carried on no continuous functions. They grew and waned with the realization of immediate objectives.

TWUA was convinced that responsible unionism was fundamental. The written union contract represents the best method of fixing gains and stabilizing relations, outlining, for a specific period, labor's rights. . . . Under these conditions, employers are more willing to accept collective bargaining as a substitute for industrial conflict. Responsible unionism means that the union is willing to accept its obligations and observe the pledges which it has given. This system of industrial law, developed through collective bargaining, has been one of our major contributions.[68]

Politically, the TWUA hewed to the line marked out by Sidney Hillman and the Amalgamated Clothing Workers. It was one of the first CIO unions to support Roosevelt for reelection in 1940, and never deviated from this stand despite the defection of John L. Lewis. When Lewis came out for Willkie, the TWUA newspaper made what was probably the strongest public attack upon him to appear in any CIO publication.[69] The 1941 convention, with only one speaker in opposition, adopted a resolution barring communists, nazis, and fascists from election or appointment to any office in the national or local unions.

The AFL rival of the TWUA, which had started with only 1,500 members in 1939, claimed to have enrolled 42,000 members by the end of 1941.[70] A good portion of this increase came from the affiliation of the New Bedford cotton locals in March 1941. Some 12,000 dues-paying members were claimed for the woolen and worsted industry, many of whom were employees in the large Arlington Mills of Lawrence, Mass., when the UTW defeated the TWUA in an NLRB election.[71] Another important victory over the TWUA was achieved among the 4500 employees of the American Bemberg Rayon Corporation at Elizabethton, Tenn. However, the UTW was still not self-supporting in 1941, and it was plagued with one of the traditional handicaps of textile unionism — industry separatism. The 1941 convention took some steps to eliminate this condition by depriving the industrial federations within the national union of the power to collect the per capita tax, thus permitting national officers to maintain a greater degree of control by withholding funds from the federations. By constitutional amendment, the federations were made subordinate departments of the national union, with their only function the exchange of knowledge and views on wages and working conditions. This action was resented by some of the federations, and it was some years before a satisfactory solution of this structural problem was achieved.[72] The 1941 convention also saw the restoration of Gorman, who had expiated his sins, to the presidency of the UTW.

The campaign to organize the textile industry must be put down as one of the least successful of the great CIO organizing drives of the nineteen-thirties. The initial momentum generated by the investment of large sums of money and the enthusiasm following CIO victories in steel and automobiles was lost when the recession of 1937 set in, and was never really recovered. A spurt of organization in 1939 was again cut short by adverse business conditions in 1940, and only with the beginning of the defense boom did the curve of unionism once more take an upward turn.

Reasons for the comparative failure of textile unionism during this period are not difficult to find. In steel, automobile, and electrical manufacturing, the CIO faced highly integrated industries, in which organization of a few firms meant that unionism was over the hump. But in textiles there was no United States Steel, General Motors, or General Electric. The nearest equivalent, American Woolen, was in a secondary branch of the industry, and, moreover, did not occupy a position comparable to the industrial giants enumerated above. In textiles, and particularly in cotton textiles, the CIO found numerous middle-sized and small firms, fiercely competitive, and very much alarmed lest their labor costs, which were a substantial part of total cost, be raised to uneconomic levels.

Then there was the South, which proved to be the ultimate stumbling block to American textile unionism. The steel, automobile, and electrical manufacturing industries were located largely in communities in which the unions were able to attain considerable political influence, and thus prevent local pressures from being brought to bear against them. But the textile unions had to contend with a combination of legal and economic force and social mores which were to prove invulnerable to even stronger efforts.

But it is wrong to write the textile drive off as a failure. By 1941, the CIO had established a stable organization of workers in most of the major textile industries other than cotton, and demonstrated its ability to withstand economic adversity, in sharp contrast to the evanescent textile unionism of the past. Upon the foundation built during the years 1937 to 1941, it was able to achieve a substantial growth during the decade following.

10

The Meat Industry

The packing and distribution of meat is one of the major industries of the United States. There were in 1939 about 120,000 wage earners employed in meat packing, but this only begins to define the jurisdictional area of the meat unions. The structure of the old AFL trade union in the field, the Amalgamated Meat Cutters and Butcher Workmen of North America, has been described as follows:

Within it are not only packinghouse workers but retail butchers, sheep shearers, and fish workers; workers in canneries, creameries, butter-and-egg and poultry plants; and workers in sausage factories. In its own economic framework, the Amalgamated is an industrial union which organizes workers in the production of meat products from the stages of slaughtering and processing up to their distribution in retail stores.[1]

The packing end of the industry has long been dominated by the "Big Four" companies: Swift & Company, Armour & Company, Wilson & Company, and the Cudahy Packing Company, the two first named being the giants of the industry. The Big Four companies together controlled over one-half the total output of the industry,[2] the rest being divided up among 600 to 700 smaller concerns, some of which are nevertheless very substantial firms in their own right.[3] On the retail side, there has been a steady trend away from the independent butcher shop toward the retail chain as the principal outlet for meat products. There were in 1935 some 206,740 employees in independent combination grocery and meat stores, and 151,660 in chain stores of the same description. Only a fraction of these employees were butchers, but the ratio gives some notion of the respective importance of the two groups. These figures exclude the shops engaged exclusively in retailing meat and fish, which numbered some 42,000 in 1939. Most of these shops were individual proprietorships with few employees.

The structure of the meat industry posed some special problems for the trade unions associated with it. At the retail end, the problem was obvious.

There are butchers in every city and town in the United States, a few to each shop, even in the large chain outlets. Organizational work involved a tremendous amount of contact with individual workers, though, as we shall see, the Amalgamated Meat Cutters evolved a successful concerted approach to the larger chain stores. With respect to packing, although Chicago has been the historical center of the industry, a trend toward decentralization set in during the 1920's, with the result that there are packinghouses in most of the major urban centers of the country. The Big Four packers together own over a hundred plants,[4] and when the independents, widely scattered geographically, are added in, it is apparent that the unions faced a geographical problem of no mean magnitude. However, it was primarily in the states of the Midwest that the principal early organizational drives were conducted, although even this comprises so large a geographical area as to have posed serious difficulties for labor organizations with very limited resources. The Packinghouse Workers Organizing Committee, for example, felt obliged to appoint twenty regional and subregional directors upon its organization in 1937, although five of these directors were located in the State of Iowa.

The Amalgamated and Industrial Unionism

The Amalgamated Meat Cutters and Butcher Workmen was chartered by the American Federation of Labor in 1897, but despite its long association with the AFL, it was firmly committed to the principle of industrial unionism. The rationale of this commitment was set forth by President Patrick E. Gorman in opening the 1936 convention of his union:

There is no man here who represents a packing plant workers' local union that has not, over a period of years, come in contact with the difficulties that the craft idea in large mass production industries has caused for us. In my own brief connection with the International Union . . . I know that there were times when we seemed to be moving onward to the goal for which we were aspiring, almost to the point where success could be seen, when workers from time to time joined our International Union by the hundreds and by the thousands, only to be discouraged in the end when certain other International Unions who did not contribute a sou to the organization of these people, who did not send a representative to assist in the campaign for organization of the great packing industry, laid claim upon our people and we were forced to turn them over, much to the discouragement of the people of our industry.[5]

Given this predilection, it may well be asked why the Amalgamated remained with the AFL rather than enrolling itself under the banner of John L. Lewis in the crusade for industrial unionism. The history of the relations between the Amalgamated and the CIO, in the first year and a half of the latter's existence, provides an instructive example of the conflicts created by the industrial union controversy within a trade union which was part craft and part industrial in structure; which had behind it forty years of close association with powerful craft organizations strongly opposed to the principle, if not always to the practice, of vertical unionism; but which believed that if the packinghouse workers, predominantly an unskilled group, were ever to be organized, it would have to be on the basis of a single union, without distinction as to craft.

A few months after the formation of the CIO, two independent unions of packinghouse workers, the Independent Union of All Workers of Austin, Minnesota, and the Mid-West Union of All Packinghouse Workers of Cedar Rapids, Iowa, advertised that they were affiliated with the CIO. Dennis Lane, the secretary-treasurer of the Amalgamated, wired Lewis: "You are well enough acquainted with the Butcher Workmen to know that our policy is now and always has been for Industrial Organization. Would you kindly wire me immediately some strong statement that the Committee referred to herein has no connection whatever with your Committee for Industrial Organization and has no authority or sanction from your Committee to use this title." [6] On behalf of Lewis, John Brophy, the CIO director of organization, wired back: "The Amalgamated Meat Cutters and Butcher Workmen of North America is industrial in form and purpose and supported with voice and vote in the AFL Convention at Atlantic City the minority committee report. . . . The independent unions in the packing houses in Austin and Cedar Rapids are not affiliated with the CIO." [7]

In a letter to Brophy written about the same time, Lane described with some bitterness the difficulties the Amalgamated was having with its AFL confrères:

Our Philadelphia strike is not settled as yet. Our President Gorman just returned from the east and he informed me that the teamsters of Philadelphia went into those packers and signed an agreement when they did not have a man connected with these organizations involved in the trouble because every meat driver that was employed by these companies were members of our union and out on strike. . . . That is just another repetition of the same picture we have been confronted with that organization over a period of years, even during the time when we used to organize drivers for them and turn them over to their organization. The only part they played in any of our disputes was to stay on the job and help the packers defeat our organization.

It is such actions as I describe of the I.B. of T. over many years past that has made it difficult for us to organize the packing house workers because they will not join a dozen organizations and be divided against themselves. All organizations within the A.F. of L. that might have any claim of jurisdiction over employees in the meat packing plants would not exceed 10 percent of the total employees, while our organization has always covered 90 percent or more. Yet the 10 percent, or a small number of the 10 percent, are used by the packers as a club to beat our efforts to organize and establish decent conditions for the workers within the industry.[8]

So long as the CIO was absorbed with organizing efforts in automobiles and steel, it was content to leave the meatpacking industry to the sympathetic Butcher Workmen. Thus, in September 1936, Brophy wired the independent union in Austin, Minnesota: "The CIO cannot grant permission to your body to act as CIO groups in organizing packing house workers as this would be contrary to CIO policy. Our advice has been that you affiliate with the AMCBW and work out your problems with them as this organization favors industrial unionism."[9] The Amalgamated was enjoying the best of both worlds. It was basking in the favor of John L. Lewis and at the same time maintaining normal relations within the AFL.

But in the spring of 1937, when, after the victories over U. S. Steel and General Motors, the CIO was seeking new fields to conquer, the skies began to darken. On March 15, 1937, President Gorman of the Amalgamated complained to Lewis that organizers purporting to represent the CIO were appearing on the packinghouse scene and advising against affiliation with the Amalgamated. "We expect soon," he continued, "to have a complete force organized to make a drive in all of the packing centers at the same time and when we are ready we shall certainly appreciate any assistance the CIO can give us." And he added, significantly: "We have not yet been kicked out of the A.F. of L."[10]

This complaint apparently fell upon deaf ears, for a month later Gorman wrote to Brophy that the CIO was active among packinghouse workers in St. Louis, St. Paul, Philadelphia, and Omaha. Gorman asserted that the friendliness shown by his organization toward the CIO was becoming a costly matter, and that the CIO should reciprocate by calling off its organizers:

Several weeks ago we were told by the Federation that we did not have jurisdiction over wholesale and retail fish markets, when as a matter of fact, we have been enrolling this form of membership for years. We are of the opinion that this decision of the Executive Council would not have been made if we had not been so outspoken for the CIO. . . .

In virtually every city where an effort was made by Central Labor Unions to oust the C.I.O. delegates, our local unions have stood with the C.I.O. I don't feel that the activity of the C.I.O. representatives within the field of our International Union is being carried on with the full knowledge of the Washington headquarters of the Committee for Industrial Organization. We can't imagine that you would want to make an already hard road harder for us.[11]

But Lewis was not averse to making the road harder for the Amalgamated. Gorman went to Washington to see whether a personal call upon Lewis might allay the growing pressure of the CIO for a clearcut decision on the part of the Amalgamated. He emphasized the past support the Amalgamated had given to the principle of industrial unionism in general, and to the cause of the CIO in particular, and reported Lewis' response as follows: "When I left him at the first conference he told me if he couldn't help the Butcher Workmen he wouldn't hurt the Butcher Workmen. He suggested that the CIO, with our permission be given the consent to organize the packing house workers for us and then at the opportune time he would turn over this entire membership to the Amalgamated Meat Cutters and Butcher Workmen. Of course I frowned upon that proposition as we want to do our own organizing."[12]

Gorman and Lane paid still another visit to Lewis, in a last attempt to avoid a competitive union struggle in the meatpacking industry:

We even went so far with Lewis as to state that we knew mass production industries should be organized and we felt the CIO was the only safe plan by which it could be done. We said we were willing to do our share, even somewhat in the way of financial help. Lewis replied, "no, you have got to make a decision." He said, "there's one thing you can do. I want you to withdraw from the American Federation of Labor."

Both Secretary Lane and I considered that extremely unfair because he himself did not withdraw from the American Federation of Labor, nor did any of the ten organizations. We thought it was unfair too because of the fact that the Typographical Union is still a part of the Federation and a strong CIO advocate. The same is true of the Brewery Workers International Union.

Lewis said he would withhold charters from the field until he received an answer from us and that if it was not to withdraw from the American Federation of Labor that he was going to issue these charters in the packing centers.

The Executive Board of the Amalgamated, on May 10, 1937, reaffirmed its belief in industrial unionism but declared flatly that there was "no thought in mind of any separation or secession from the American Federation of Labor." Two days later a telegram came from Brophy inquiring what position the Amalgamated was going to adopt, and Gorman replied on the same day: "We have decided to continue our status as is. We are not secessionists for we have always fought secession and are firm believers in settling our disputes within our household." [13] A month later, Gorman wrote Lewis once more, expressing his disappointment over the fact that the CIO was chartering unions in meat packing, and noting that the Amalgamated had refrained voluntarily from sending organizers to Austin, Minnesota, and Cedar Rapids, Iowa, two CIO strongholds, out of a desire to avoid internecine warfare.[14] Lewis replied: 'Of course, the Cincinnati Conference of the American Federation of Labor which declared war on the Committee for Industrial Organization and the later action of the American Federation of Labor in chartering a rival organization to the United Mine Workers of America, have complicated the entire situation. I suggest that it might be well for you to give additional consideration to the subject matter of our conversation when you were in Washington." [15] But the Amalgamated had already chosen sides, and the struggle for control of the meat industry, which was to continue unabated for more than a decade, began in earnest.

Early Amalgamated Organization Policy

The Amalgamated Meat Cutters had received an almost mortal wound in 1921, when a nationwide strike of 105,000 packing plant workers conducted under its auspices was broken after thirteen weeks. Considerable violence characterized the strike, and the hardships experienced by the strikers during bitter winter weather made an indelible impression upon the workers, many of whom laid the blame for defeat at the door of the Amalgamated leadership. Even as late as 1936, the defeat of 1921 was a living memory, and handicapped the Amalgamated considerably in its attempts to organize the packinghouses.

The significance of the 1921 strike was continually emphasized by packinghouse labor officials. For example, one of them wrote:

My feeling is that the 1921 strike was of such major importance that its impact was felt by the Amalgamated and the workers in the industry through the 30's, the 40's, the 50's and even up to now, because the whole character of the Amalgamated bargaining is in relation to this strike experience which they have never forgotten, and the fears that these recollections bring up have inhibited action on many occasions when such action was necessary and desirable.[16]

After the 1921 strike, total membership in the Amalgamated fell to 5000 workers. Although the union managed to survive, membership in 1930 was only 13,000.[17] Six years later, on the eve of the CIO drive in meat packing, it had risen to twice that number,[18] as the result of an organizational drive undertaken during the NRA period. The principal gains occurred among the employees of retail chain stores rather than in the packinghouses. By opposing enactment of federal antichain store legislation, the Amalgamated was able to win the confidence of some of the largest chain operators. This process was described by an Amalgamated vice-president as follows:

International President Gorman went to Washington and appeared before the Congressional Committee dealing with the Patman Bill. He was on the witness stand for three long hours. He held firm to the conviction of the Executive Board that the Patman Bill was a bad Bill. At least four hundred interested parties crowded the meeting places of the Congressional Committee. Among these spectators were Mr. Charles Schwimmatt of the A & P Tea Company, "Navy Bill" Ingram representing the Safeway Stores and many others. They swarmed about President Gorman, congratulating him upon the fine presentation of the Amalgamated's case. The Patman Bill was defeated. . . .

Shortly thereafter a delegation of our International Union was called to New York City. They found themselves in the office of Carl Byor, adviser in A & P operations. We were told that the door was open for A & P organization, not only to the Amalgamated, but also to all other International Unions.

John Hartford, head of the A & P Tea Company, attended the American Federation of Labor Executive Council meeting the following year in Miami, Florida. He sponsored a banquet for the representatives of all labor unions who were present. Within a period of little more than two years after the International Executive Board decided to oppose the Patman Bill, seven divisions of the vast A & P system were almost entirely organized.[19]

Nor was the A & P the only chain which decided that union recognition was a fair price to pay for the support of organized labor in fighting discriminatory legislation. In 1935, Safeway Stores signed a national agreement with the Amalgamated, and the First National chain, the Economy Stores, the American Stores, Food Fair and others were also brought under contract.

The Patman Bill was not without its supporters in the ranks of the Amalgamated. Local unions which had their contracts with small independent retailers tended to take on the economic views of their employers, despite the position of the international union. "Those of our membership who are employed in chain stores too often take the position of their employers and too often the meat cutters employed by the independent merchants consider the chain stores the industry's greatest evil."[20] However, the international union has never regretted its stand on this controversial issue of market structure, and a semi-official chronicler characterized its attitude as "a constructive combination of progressive economic and social policy."[21]

The meat packers, less sensitive to political pressures of this nature, were far less responsive to the conciliatory tactics of the Amalgamated. In 1934, the Amalgamated successfully organized the Sioux Falls, S. D., plant of John Morrell & Company, the largest of the so-called independent packers. Many disputes arose out of the contract, and finally in July 1935, a strike took place over the issue of procedure to be followed in lay-offs. The workers remained in the plant, and left only after the governor of the state had despatched militia to the scene. Negotiations for a settlement broke down over the company's insistence upon the discharge of the men responsible for the sit down.[22]

The Amalgamated then resorted to the product boycott. Morrell products were declared unfair, and butchers throughout the country were urged to refuse to handle them. The union claimed that the boycott was effective. Gorman told the 1936 convention that the company's normal hog kill had been reduced from 700 to 200 an hour, while the Amalgamated Executive Board was informed by one of its organizers that Morrell sales in the Pacific Northwest had declined by 70 per cent, and by 60 per cent in Wyoming, Nevada, and Utah.[23] However, the boycott appears to have been ineffective except in the West, and the strike dragged on until March 1937, when a settlement was finally reached on terms which the union described as fair.[24]

Perhaps as a result of this experience, the Amalgamated displayed caution in subsequent years in the use of what seemed to many locals engaged in desperate struggles with their employers a most attractive weapon. Thus, in 1939, when the Los Angeles locals were embroiled in a dispute with Swift and wanted to declare a boycott, they were informed that "it would have to be handled in a careful manner, that it couldn't be declared a national boycott as the International Union hadn't taken any action on it. . . ." [25] Later the same year, when the dispute had spread to other cities in California, Gorman warned the locals that "a nationwide boycott against the Swift products would be disastrous for our International Union." However, an eleven-month boycott against Swift in Oregon and Washington resulted in the first signed agreement with that company.[26] Thus, under appropriate circumstances, the boycott proved to be an effective weapon, and it may be inferred that in an industry as competitive as meat, no single manufacturer was anxious to run the gauntlet of a boycott, particularly when it could be backed up by an ever growing army of organized butchers at the retail level. The international officers of the Amalgamated were quite shrewd in their handling of a method of economic warfare which was of great potential power, but which might have boomeranged in a very damaging fashion if it had been employed indiscriminately.

Independent Unionism

Alongside the Amalgamated, there grew up during the NRA period and subsequent years a number of independent local unions which eventually became the nucleus for the CIO in the industry. Among the more important groups were those at the Wilson and Company plant in Cedar Rapids, Iowa; at the Hormel plant in Austin, Minnesota; and at a number of packing plants in Chicago.

A considerable number of the employees at Cedar Rapids had at one time been members of the Amalgamated so that a tradition of unionism existed there.[27] In protest against a company-sponsored Employee Joint Representative Committee Plan, many of the employees, in 1933, applied for and received a federal charter from the AFL, but were soon transferred to the Amalgamated, becoming Local 206 of that organization. Although the union claimed the allegiance of an overwhelming majority of the employees, the company refused to deal with it, and finally a strike was called on May 6, 1934. During the subsequent negotiations for a settlement, the company refused to meet with an international representative of the Amalgamated who was directing the strike, insisting that it would treat only with its own employees. The agreement ending the strike provided only for partial recognition, the company refusing to disestablish the Joint Committee Plan.

Early in 1935, the local withdrew from the Amalgamated and established itself as the Mid-West Union of All Packinghouse Workers. Continued efforts to secure a collective agreement under the new auspices were as unsuccessful as under the old. In 1935, according to the union, the company hired one Harold Jacques as an oiler; Jacques immediately indicated an active interest in the union, and urged that a much more militant attitude be adopted in dealing with management. The union's suspicion was aroused by the ease with which it was able to secure a wage increase for him, and an effort was made to learn his background:

it was very difficult as when it came to discussing himself he was very close-lipped, although investigation did prove that he lived at the Y.M.C.A., which had a reputation of harboring scabs and strikebreakers, and that he was in possession of a typewriter. It was disclosed that he was corresponding with people, other than his immediate family. There was an attempt made by trusted members of the union to maneuver him into a position by drinking with him, whereby he would tip his hand. A further attempt was made by one of our respected female members to lure this gentleman into our taverns and pretend to be on friendly relations so that he might disclose some vital information. . . . The last approach met with success for the organization.[28]

The indiscreet Mr. Jacques turned out to have a twin brother employed at Red Wing, Minnesota. A union committee was sent to that city, and posed as fellow employees of Jacques' at the Bell Telephone System, for which it was learned he had worked prior to coming to Cedar Rapids. Jacques' brother revealed that Harold was currently in the employ of an industrial service organization in Chicago. Armed with this information, charges were brought against Jacques at the next union meeting. Jacques tried to escape, but was escorted into another room, where he admitted that he had been sent into the plant for the purpose of fomenting a strike. When he was released, he left town immediately. Company officials denied any complicity in his actions, upon questioning by the union.

As soon as the CIO was formed, the Cedar Rapids union contacted John L. Lewis and asked that it be permitted to affiliate. But the CIO was not yet prepared to move in this field, and was still on good terms with the Amalgamated, so the request was denied. Lewis J. Clark, the head of the Cedar Rapids union, then decided to attempt to organize the entire industry from Cedar Rapids. On May 5, 1937, he wrote as follows to Judge J. Cooney, vice-president of Wilson and Company:

In our conversation in your office on May 1, 1937, concerning the proposed plan of organization for the packing industry, the question was discussed of how such an organization could be brought about and kept free from outside "racketeers" and communistic powers.[29]

Under Clark's plan, Wilson was to grant the Cedar Rapids local a closed shop and the check-off. This "victory" would then be publicized at the Chicago plants of Wilson, the company to do its share by talking with the company union representatives there. "We know that you cannot come out directly and tell them to join our union movement, but you can explain the union at Cedar Rapids, Iowa which is a legitimate labor organization, free from communistic form of operation. You can also make it stronger, for example, explain to them if the union at Cedar Rapids, Iowa, was like some operating organizations, that the Wilson & Company would never consent to a closed shop agreement." Two days prior to a mass meeting to be called by the Cedar Rapids union, Wilson was to announce that its company union plan was being terminated. After several additional meetings, the NLRB would be petitioned for an election. In conclusion, Clark warned:

"I do know that it will have to be handled quickly as other packing centers such as Austin, Minnesota, are worming their way not only into the C.I.O. but have undertaken to organize the Morrell plants. From truthful reports they are making rapid success. Once their caliber gains a foothold in the packing industry, each and every packing house organization will be under communistic control." Wilson apparently refused to go along with the plan, for the Cedar Rapids local shortly thereafter joined the CIO, and Lewis J. Clark, its president, eventually rose to high office in the CIO packinghouse organization, including the presidency for a short period.

Independent unionism at Austin, Minnesota, followed a quite different course from that at Cedar Rapids.[30] In the spring of 1933, under the impact of contemporary events on the national political scene, rumors of unionism spread among the workers in the Hormel plant at Austin. No concrete action emerged until July, when the refusal of two workers to sign for a weekly deduction of $1.20 for a newly instituted old age pension scheme, sparked a revolt. "A large group of protesting, aroused and indignant workers gathered around the supervisor and the killing floor was shut down. They told the supervisor to give the fellow back his card, and let him tear it up and to stop trying to force people to sign the cards, or they would not work. This demonstration was planned in advance, and a large share of these fellows had pledged to stick together even though they didn't have a union." [31] The same evening, a meeting was held, at which 600 workers signed pledge cards.

The leaders of the new organization had far-reaching ambitions for it, as the following extract from its informal history indicates:

The Independent Union of All Workers was organized on an industrial basis following a pattern similar to the I.W.W. (Industrial Workers of the World). This was done because the craft form of organization had shown itself unable to cope with the present day problems and had a tendency to pit one craft against another which made the workers ineffective. . . . The basic unit in the I.U.A.W. was called the Local Unit. The Local Unit was comprised of all workers in one industry or a group of workers closely associated; that is, the garage workers in one city would belong to a local unit, the packinghouse workers in another local unit, etc.[32]

The reference to the IWW was not fortuitous, for the union prided itself on its militancy and its willingness to adopt direct action. The first issue of *The Unionist,* which it published as its official organ, declared that "this paper will be radical and militant, dynamic rather than static, alive rather than asleep. . . . We recognize that we are under a system which perpetuates wage slavery. We will defend the right of free press, free speech and lawful assemblage." [33] Charters were issued to local unions in nearby cities.

On September 23, 1933, after a strike threat, an agreement was reached with Hormel and Company recognizing the union as bargaining agent for its members and providing for seniority in layoffs and rehiring, the principal demand of the union. On November 10, after rejection by the company of a union demand for a wage increase, a strike was called. Picket lines and barricades were set up around the plant, and all officials of the company, including President Jay C. Hormel, were escorted from the plant by the strikers, who placed men from their own ranks in possession. The Austin police were mobilized, and for a time it appeared that a pitched battle was imminent. However, Governor Floyd B. Olson came to Austin,[34] and proposed that the wage demand be submitted to arbitration by the State Industrial Commission, which the parties accepted. The governor then addressed the strikers, and persuaded them to evacuate the plant. In the subsequent arbitration, the workers secured a 10 per cent wage increase, and the union won exclusive bargaining rights.

The prestige of the Independent Union of All Workers was high after its victory in the Hormel strike, which had received national publicity because of the forcible capture of the plant and the refusal of the governor to authorize use of the state militia to eject the strikers. Membership rose to 3700, and included many local workers outside the Hormel plant. However, as was so often the case with the unions formed during the first flush of the New Deal, interest lagged, and this, combined with internal dissention, resulted in a decline of membership and influence. By January 1936, membership was down to 1300 in the entire community.[35] With the formation of the CIO, however, the union's fortunes once more took an upward turn, and after several vain attempts to gain admittance to the CIO, affiliation was finally granted on May 22, 1937, when the independent union became Local Industrial Union No. 183, United Packinghouse Workers. It is interesting to note, however, that there was by no means unanimity on affiliation, the vote at the Hormel plant being 396 for, to 326 against, CIO affiliation.

Chicago, the geographical center of the meatpacking industry, was the scene of sporadic organizational efforts. In March 1933, a group of workers from various Chicago plants formed the Stockyards Labor Council, which had its principal base in the G. H. Hammond plant, a subsidiary of Swift & Company. Disturbed by the events at Austin, Minnesota, Hammond discharged 40 union leaders in January 1934, and although their reinstatement was secured by the NRA Regional Labor Board, the union was seriously weakened, with membership declining precipitously.[36] A conference held in 1934 between the Stockyards Council and the Cedar Rapids and Austin unions failed to produce hoped for unity, partly because of inadequate finances and partly due to rivalry among the leadership of the respective unions.

In addition to the Stockyards Council, the Amalgamated Meat Cutters and the Packinghouse Workers Industrial Union, an affiliate of the Communist Trade Union Unity League, were active among the Chicago packinghouse workers. A unity conference among the three failed, and the Stockyards Council decided to throw in its lot with the Amalgamated in January 1935. However, according to Arthur Kampfert, the president of the Stockyards Council: "The Amalgamated assigned 38 paid organizers, millions of organizational leaflets were distributed, but the packinghouse workers reacted against the Amalgamated. Very few would join the Amalgamated because it had been hated in Chicago since the 1921–22 strike." [36] The Amalgamated was successful in securing agreements with several small packers where labor conditions were substandard, but it was unable to gain a foothold in any of the larger companies.

The CIO Enters Meatpacking

Toward the end of 1936, when the CIO drives in automobiles and steel were in full swing, there was considerable interest among independent local groups of meatpacking unionists to enroll under the CIO banner. Thus, on December 16, 1936, representatives of local unions in Des Moines, Cedar Rapids, Austin, and Mason City, Iowa, entered into an agreement providing for the creation of a federation of meatpacking unions: "The purpose of the proposed organization shall be to seek and obtain affiliation with the Committee for Industrial Organization, and to submit to the properly accredited officers of the aforesaid Committee for Industrial Organization a tentative draft or form of union Organization or Federation of Packing House Workers that will provide for local autonomy for all affiliated groups. . . ." [37] Although there is no record of any further developments along this line, the agreement indicates quite clearly that the CIO did not begin its operations in completely virgin territory, but rather, that it had the advantage of an organizational base among local unions that for one reason or another refused to join or remain within the Amalgamated.

The CIO organization drive appears to have begun in earnest only in the summer of 1937, although there is evidence of earlier activity in a rather haphazard way. For example, Vice-President Jimerson of the Amalgamated reported in May that the CIO was active in the St. Louis area. "The CIO organizers are very friendly toward our organization, and it is doubtful whether or not we can organize the big houses other than CIO, as they all seem to be CIO minded." [38] CIO activity was also reported in Seattle, Los Angeles, Butte, Denver, Fort Worth, and Oklahoma City. The packers were aware that organization was in the air, and attempted to forestall it by raising wages nine cents per hour, which raised the minimum for men to 62½ cents per hour. According to a Chicago newspaper, "The action in the packing industry, taken before John Lewis' Committee of Industrial Organization could rid itself of its steel and motor difficulties and seek to organize packing plant workers, will affect an estimated 82,000 workers throughout the country, about 30,000 here." [39] This increase followed a 7 per cent increase given the previous October.

During the first few months of the CIO drive, the campaign was financed by the national CIO and some of its affiliated unions. Locals were chartered directly by the CIO as local industrial unions, with no uniformity in title.[40] At a conference held in Chicago on October 24, 1937, the Packinghouse Workers Organizing Committee was formally established, under the leadership of Van A. Bittner, a long-time associate of John L. Lewis in the United Mine Workers, and with Don Harris, who had formerly been an organizer for the Hosiery Workers, as Director of Organization. (The other members of the committee were Sam Levin of the Amalgamated Clothing Workers of Chicago; David McDonald; and Walter Smethurst.) For the next four years, Bittner exercised authority over the PWOC in the name of the CIO. Dues of one dollar a month were decided upon (in contrast to $1.50 being charged by the Amalgamated), and regional directors were appointed for twenty areas.

Armour and Company. The strategy of the CIO was to go after the Big Four, rather than the smaller independents, with well publicized campaigns. About 25,000 workers were employed in the Chicago stockyards, the bulk of them by Armour, Swift and Wilson. Armour was chosen as the first target, in part because there had been organizational work among its employees for the previous half year. Swift and Company, the largest and most profitable packer, was paying above-average wages, and provided a more difficult object of attack.[41]

On November 23, a meeting of Armour workers at PWOC headquarters was addressed by Father John Hayes, who told the assemblage: "Every good Christian should join the union, and every Catholic must join, under Catholic doctrine. . . . Thank God the C.I.O. is including all races and all peoples in its ranks. The C.I.O., I am convinced, far from being a racketeering organization, is a strong, militant union working for the good of the working men." This ecclesiastical blessing was extremely important to the new organization, for the Chicago packinghouse workers were predominantly of the Catholic faith. The union appealed to the NLRB to outlaw the Armour company union, which had been reorganized subsequent to the U. S. Supreme Court decision upholding the constitutionality of the Wagner Act, and to conduct a representation election.

The NLRB held extensive hearings on the unfair labor practice charges brought by the union, and on September 15, 1938, ordered the disestablishment of the Armour Employees Mutual Association and the reinstatement of several workers who had been discharged for PWOC activities.[42] An election was held in October, which the PWOC won by the decisive margin of 2840 to 237, and on December 30, 1938, it was certified as exclusive bargaining representative of the workers in the Chicago plant of Armour.[43] However, more than a year was to go by before a collective agreement was finally achieved.

The meatpacking drive was one of the last major organizing campaigns to be undertaken by the CIO during the initial phase of its existence. Initial progress was slow, and although 75 locals were chartered during the first year of its operation, only ten contracts covering 9000 workers were signed.[44] One of the major problems faced by the union, it soon discovered, was the far-flung nature of the packing industry. A drive against the Big Four could not be restricted to Chicago, for the companies followed the policy of refusing national bargaining, and forced the union to fight for each branch plant separately.

Because of its initial foothold in the Chicago plant of Armour and Company, the heart of this great enterprise, the PWOC devoted a considerable proportion of its resources to the 29 meatpacking houses which Armour was operating in 22 states. In Kansas City, the PWOC won a consent election in August 1937, but again had no success in securing a contract. On September 9, 1938, a sit-down strike took place at this plant, arising out of a minor grievance. An estimated $52,000 worth of meat was spoiled before arrangements were made for the strikers to put all meat in process back into refrigerators.[45] The strikers were fed by means of baskets hauled up by rope, and it is an interesting commentary on the temper of the time that the police chief intervened only to the extent of ordering the arrest of anyone found sending beer or liquor to the strikers. Local railroad workers indicated that they would not pull cars with products for Kansas City, and in general, the strikers received considerable support from the local labor movement. After four days, an agreement was reached to submit the original grievance to arbitration, and the plant was evacuated.

At Indianapolis, organizational efforts began at the Armour plant in June 1937, and the familiar pattern repeated itself. The union secured a majority of the workers, but the company refused it a written agreement, confining collective bargaining to the processing of grievances with the union grievance committee. The plant was struck on December 5, 1938, over the administration of overtime, but it was adjusted quickly. The East St. Louis, Illinois, plant was organized in June 1938, and closed down by a strike in December. After an eleven-hour sit-down strike, the company granted the union demand for what amounted to a union shop.[46] This plant was plagued with a series of lightning strikes over grievances in the ensuing years.

An interesting form of direct action was employed at some of the Armour plants where management refused to deal with the union, termed "whistle bargaining" by the union. Every shop steward carried a whistle, and the members were informed that one whistle meant stop, two meant back to work. When a grievance arose, the whistles were blown, and work ceased until it was adjusted.

In September 1938, 51 delegates representing employees at Armour plants throughout the country met in Chicago to fire the opening gun for a national agreement. A policy committee was established, and a conference requested with Robert H. Cabell, president of Armour and Company.[47] Mr. Cabell replied very simply that he was not aware of any issues of importance that required negotiation. At a national PWOC conference held in July 1939, Van Bittner for the first time voiced the threat of a nationwide strike against Armour if the company refused to sign collective agreements. The conference authorized such a strike, and appealed to President Roosevelt to intercede with the company.

At this juncture, the Amalgamated Meat Cutters, fearing the possibility of being frozen completely out of the Armour chain, intervened. In a radio address, President Gorman declared:

this national agreement was to be virtually forced down the throats of this large packing firm and this in opposition to the men and women, who are engaged in the meat packing industry and belong to trade unions affiliated with the American Federation of Labor. . . .

We have studied the situation calmly and carefully and our best analysis is there will be no strike this week nor next against Armour nor any other packer. We feel confident the blustery strike threats are merely a desperate effort on the part of the Congress for Industrial Organization to clutch at a fleeting and lost cause.[48]

Gorman went on to put the blame for the strike threats upon communistic elements within the PWOC, although he absolved Lewis and Bittner of any sympathy toward communism. He warned, finally, that the Amalgamated would not sit idly by while an attempt was being made to take from it what it had been striving for over a long period. When the Chicago City Council called a meeting in an effort to avoid a strike, the Chicago Federation of Labor intervened on behalf of the Amalgamated, claiming that it had acquired a majority at the Chicago Armour plant. Bittner retorted: "Such action on the part of the Chicago Federation of Labor means just two things, insanity or crookedness. I am charitable enough to believe that their action is due to insanity. . . . I am wondering what labor would think of me if I attempted to break a legitimate strike of some A.F. of L. union? I know what I would think of myself. I would think I was a traitor, a coward, and destitute of every element of honor and manhood." [49]

As part of its fight against Armour, the PWOC arranged a mass rally, the largest one in the history of Chicago unionism since the inception of the New Deal. The rally was held on July 16, the featured speakers being John L. Lewis and Bishop Bernard J. Sheil, one of the leading Catholic prelates of Chicago. The appearance of Bishop Sheil on this occasion was a great coup for the PWOC, which was being increasingly harassed on the issue of communism.

By August 1939, the PWOC had been certified for 17 of the 29 Armour packing plants, as well as for a good many smaller branch houses.[50] With pressure mounting, Bittner and a delegation representing all the PWOC plants went to Washington, where they conferred with Secretary of Labor Perkins. She immediately asked Armour representatives to meet with her in Washington, but no progress was made at a meeting held on August 18, 1939.[51] After another meeting with her on September 19, the company agreed to assign responsible officials on a plant-by-plant basis to meet with the PWOC. As part of the settlement, Bittner agreed to withdraw the demand for a national contract. Bittner and his aides justified this action on the ground that the first task was to get a contract, no matter what its form. The left-wing faction in the PWOC was critical of this concession, arguing that unless there was a single contract, one plant could be played off against another.[52] The company, in further negotiations, took the position that the 1938 representation election at its Chicago plant had not been a representative one, since the PWOC received only 2800 votes out of a total employment of 6000 people. PWOC thereupon agreed to a second election, in which the Amalgamated could appear on the ballot.[53]

The election campaign itself provided one of the sharpest rival union clashes that had theretofore taken place in meatpacking. The journal of the PWOC commented:

In several packing centers the Amalgamated Meat Cutters, AFL, have risen from the dead during these past few months. After a deep sleep of 20 years or more while the packinghouse workers went unorganized and were left to be kicked around by two-by-four bosses and sweated to death by stuffed-shirt superintendents, the AFL has turned up to annoy the local unions of the PWOC and to play company union for the bosses. . . . The time has come to drive them out of the packinghouses and back to the butcher shops where they came from.[54]

Shortly before the election, Al Malachi, a former president of the PWOC Armour local, who had been expelled for alleged secret negotiations with the Amalgamated, appeared before a Congressional committee headed by Martin Dies to charge that Henry Johnson, assistant national director of the PWOC, Herb March, the Chicago district director, and Walter Strabawa, financial secretary of the Chicago Packinghouse Workers Council, were members of the Communist Party. In return, the PWOC charged that George Dasho, president of the Amalgamated Armour local, had been convicted, before coming to work at the Armour plant, of grand larceny and illegal narcotics sale.[55] The election, which was held in November 1939, resulted in victory for the PWOC with 4006 votes against 1047 for the Amalgamated, with 1254 workers voting for no union.

The pressure on Armour to enter into an agreement with the PWOC grew. The weight of the United States Government, through Secretary of Labor Perkins, was thrown into the balance. War had begun in Europe, and the increasing demand for American meat rendered the prospect of a work stoppage less palatable than it might have been the previous year. Finally, in February 1940, after almost three years of organizational work, the PWOC secured its first collective agreements with a major packer when Armour and Company signed for its Kansas City and Chicago plants. The minimum male rate of 62½ cents per hour and the scale in general were left untouched. A seniority system was installed, for promotion as well as lay-offs. One of the major union demands was granted: a break of a year, rather than the previous 60 days, was required in order to terminate a worker's seniority, thus affording the worker a considerably greater degree of tenure in employment.[56] Similar agreements were negotiated soon thereafter for the remaining Armour plants controlled by the PWOC.

Armour continued to take the position, however, that it would not bargain on a national basis, leading to a strike threat by the PWOC in July 1941. The case was referred to the National Defense Mediation Board, the union demanding an 82½-cent basic wage (the wage had been raised unilaterally by all the packers from 62½ cents to 67½ cents in April 1941), the closed shop and the checkoff, and formal grievance machinery. Through the good offices of the Mediation Board, an agreement was reached raising the basic wage to 72½ cents (which was matched by the other large packers),[57] granting a grievance setup, and, most important from the union point of view, providing for a single agreement for all plants controlled by the PWOC, covering some 20,000 workers.[58] With this agreement, the PWOC was firmly established in the plants of the nation's second largest packing concern. When the history of unionism in meatpacking, and the intense competition of the Amalgamated Meat Cutters, are taken into account, this was no mean achievement.

Swift and Company. The history of PWOC efforts to organize Swift and Company, the giant of the industry, is quite different from that of Armour. The first battle with Swift came at its Sioux City, Iowa, plant, where the company had recognized the Independent Packing House Workers Union, Local No. 2, a lineal descendant of the Employees Security League of Swift & Co., as bargaining agent for its workers. In April 1938, the PWOC approached the management of this plant with a request for recognition. After several months of fruitless efforts, a stoppage of work occurred on September 29 to enforce the union's demand that the company deal with its grievance committee, the company having taken the position that in any individual grievance case, it would meet only with the aggrieved employee and one representative chosen by him. The employees were immediately notified that unless they returned to work or left the plant within 30 minutes, they would be discharged, and when the deadline had passed, 165 employees were given discharge slips.

At the request of the mayor of Sioux City, the strikers agreed to clean up the killing floor to avoid putrefaction of carcasses that had been left there. However, when they learned that 15 of their number had been removed from the plant and arrested under criminal syndicalism warrants secured by the company, they stopped work once more. Informed that the sheriff was on his way to the plant with warrants for their arrest, the remaining strikers vacated the plant and established picket lines.[59]

Attempts to move strikebreakers and supplies into the plant were met by violent resistance on the part of the strikers. Mass arrests were made, and after union sympathizers had attempted to storm the plant, state troops were sent to the scene to preserve order. The picket line was maintained for several months, but the strike was lost, and with it, any hope of securing an immediate foothold in Swift. The Amalgamated commented on PWOC strategy in the Sioux City strike as follows:

The foolishness of this move can be explained best that the Swift concern operates 46 large packing plants from coast to coast and yet the C.I.O. leadership actually believed some advances could be made by creating stoppage in only one of these 46 plants. This again was asinine.[60]

In retrospect, the Amalgamated had a point in its critique of PWOC strategy. But the strategy was dictated locally, and not by the national office. The packinghouse workers were beginning to flex their muscles, after almost two decades of employer-domination. The importance of grievances was apt to be magnified, and the refusal of the packers to participate in collective bargaining, as they were legally bound to do under the National Labor Relations Act, contributed to the disquiet of the workers. The PWOC attempted to control local exuberance by sending out the following order in January 1939:

First, under no circumstances is there to be a strike or stoppage of work among any of our members of local unions, unless the strike is authorized by the officers of the Packinghouse Workers Organizing Committee; and, Second, under no circumstances will a strike or stoppage be tolerated in plants where we have wage agreements, and all grievances are to be settled in accordance with machinery provided in the contracts for the settlement of grievances.[61]

A local of the PWOC was organized in the large Chicago plant of Swift in 1937. Although it was not sufficiently strong to venture on an NLRB election until 1942, it did engage in day-to-day grievance negotiation, securing, among other things, a seniority system, pay for grievancemen while engaged in handling grievances, and tacit outlawing of discrimination against union members in layoffs and promotion.[62] A national drive on Swift was launched in May 1940,[63] but the close of 1941 came with no concrete record of achievement in the form of a collective agreement with any of the major units of the Swift empire, although a number of Swift plants had been organized and brought successfully through NLRB elections.

Swift & Co. finally signed a master agreement with the PWOC for 15

plants and with the Amalgamated for 8 plants on April 1, 1943, after being
directed to do so by the War Labor Board.

Wilson and Company. The success of CIO unionism in Wilson and
Company, the third largest of the meat packers, was somewhat greater than
at Swift, but not conspicuously so. The first test of strength between the
CIO and Wilson came in New York City, where Wilson maintained eight
branch houses. In November 1938, on the basis of card checks and elections,
the NLRB certified the PWOC as bargaining agent for the employees of
these branches, but contract negotiations broke down over the demand of
the union for a closed shop and an increase in wages. A short strike in
December proved damaging to the union, for 15 of its members who had
been replaced by strikebreakers were refused reemployment. Nothing
daunted, the union continued to press for its original demands, but: "The
union was young and not too strong at Wilson's, management knew it and
was giving the union a time of their life, then too, the workers expected to
gain everything overnight not realizing the financial strength and anti-union
policy of Wilson & Company." [64] Charges of refusal to bargain in good faith
were filed with the NLRB, but they were not sustained. The fact of the
matter was simply that control of a few branch houses did not provide the
union with enough leverage to force concessions from Wilson.

The PWOC was well entrenched at Wilson plants in Faribault and
Albert Lea, Minnesota, and at Cedar Rapids, Iowa. A brief but unsuccessful
sit-down strike occurred at the latter plant in 1938. The union survived,
however, and in 1940, the NLRB ordered Wilson to bargain with it.[65] As
was typical of industry labor conditions at the time, it was a long step
between the legal acquisition of bargaining rights and the achievement of
a signed agreement. After protracted and futile bargaining, a strike was
called on March 24, 1941, affecting 1800 workers. Hanging over the heads
of company officials was an NLRB order finding Wilson in violation of the
Wagner Act, an order that had been sustained by a Circuit Court of Appeals.
The federal government was also exerting great pressure on the company
to settle, but to no avail, the company taking the position that it would
under no circumstances accede to the demand for a union shop. There was
a considerable amount of sympathy with the strikers in the community, and
with the company making no real effort to operate the plant, the strike was
conducted in an orderly fashion. An observer wrote:

The strikers really had a lot of fun around the picket camps and the boys were
housed in as if they expected to be there for a long time. In one camp I saw
practically all the comforts of home, table, magazines, and even pictures on the

walls. All camps had stoves, lanterns or large flash lights. In one camp there sat a picket playing the guitar.

Three strike kitchens were kept busy day and night feeding the strikers. Much credit was given to the girls from the plant and to the Ladies Auxiliary for their efforts in preparing the food. . . . Merchants cooperated to the fullest extent, with donations of rolls, milk, cream, etc.[66]

After 23 days, the company agreed to accord the PWOC sole bargaining rights, and to negotiate a written agreement covering wages and other conditions of labor.[67] This represented the first major contract which the PWOC won from Wilson.

A PWOC local had been chartered in July 1937, at the large Chicago plant of Wilson and Company, and subjected the plant to a number of "quickie" strikes to secure the adjustment of grievances. An organizing drive was conducted in 1938, based upon the success of the CIO in handling grievances, but the economic recession then prevailing made progress difficult. However, the NLRB victory at the Armour Chicago plant spurred the union to new efforts. One of the chief obstacles was the existence of the Wilson Employees' Representation Committee, which commanded a considerable following among the workers. The PWOC felt strong enough to petition for a representation election at the beginning of 1940, and the national organization threw all its resources into the election campaign. When the workers went to the polls on January 26, 1940, the PWOC received only 1545 votes compared to 1890 for the Employees' Representation Committee,[68] a result which was attributed to insufficient organizational work among the many women employees.

The PWOC almost immediately brought charges of company-domination against the Employees' Representation Committee, which it had failed to do before the election because of overconfidence. The charges were sustained, and the end of 1941 found the PWOC preparing once more for an NLRB election in Chicago. Only at Cedar Rapids, however, had Wilson actually entered into a collective agreement with the PWOC.[69]

The Cudahy Packing Company. Cudahy had established a system of company unions in its plants, and soon after the constitutionality of the Wagner Act was upheld, these unions were reorganized in an effort to free them from the taint of company domination. They were quickly accorded collective bargaining rights, and on May 15, 1937, a convention of the independent unions in the Cudahy plants was held in Omaha, Nebraska. At the convention, a blanket agreement covering conditions of employment for all the company's plants was concluded.[70] The company hoped to forestall outside unionism by facing the CIO with a *fait accompli*.

The PWOC nevertheless organized a local at the Sioux City, Iowa, plant of the company in June 1937, and set up in active competition with the independent. Men wearing CIO buttons were kept under surveillance and subjected to discrimination. Beginning with July 1937, a number of active CIO men were discharged, and finally in June 1938, discriminatory discharge complaints were made to the NLRB. In September 1939, the NLRB ordered six of the discharged employees reinstated, and the disestablishment of the company union. However, the president of the PWOC local signed an affidavit stating that he had conspired with the attorney for the NLRB to be discharged for purposes of bringing the action against the company, and the entire proceeding was brought into question. Cudahy not only refused to abide by the NLRB order, but discharged additional active unionists.

After a year and a half had gone by, characterized by guerilla warfare in the plant, a stipulation was entered into providing for the reinstatement of seven discharged workers and the holding of an election to determine bargaining representatives. The independent union was ruled off the ballot as company-dominated, and the PWOC received 671 of the 760 ballots cast,[71] thus becoming the legally designated bargaining agent of the company's employees.

Cudahy's Kansas City plant was won by an overwhelming majority in June 1940.[72] The Los Angeles plant was taken at about the same time from the Amalgamated, which had won representation rights there in 1938. The Denver plant also fell to the PWOC as the result of an NLRB victory, and a victory at Newport, Minnesota, in 1941, reversing a defeat suffered the previous year, rounded out the PWOC sphere of influence. A conference of the Cudahy locals was held at Omaha in January 1941, preparatory to the formulation of uniform demands on a nationwide basis. The goal of a master agreement covering all Cudahy plants controlled by the PWOC was finally achieved in November 1941, the union winning a system of seniority rights, formal grievance machinery, and union security in the form of a maintenance of membership clause.

The Independents. As already noted, the strategy of the PWOC was to drive right for the center of the meatpacking industry, the Big Four packers. "Our policy of concentration on the 'Big Four' packers, who are the heart of the industry, has been successfully carried out," the organ of the

PWOC declared, in 1939, with some exaggeration. A history of meat unionism sympathetic to the Amalgamated Meat Cutters conceded that the PWOC "enrolled a substantial membership in the plants of the Big Four, where it competed for power with the Amalgamated, but it achieved little of importance in the plants of independent packers." [73] This judgment is not entirely correct, for the PWOC did pick up a considerable number of independent packers throughout the country.

To cite a few examples, the PWOC organized the so-called "Little Six" packers in Chicago: the Illinois Meat Company, the Agar Packing and Provision Company, Miller & Hart (after a brief sit-down strike), Robert & Oake, P. Brennan, and the Independent Casing Company. A contract was signed with the Tobin Packing Company of Fort Dodge, Iowa, in October 1939, after two years of intense activity, which included the setback of a lost NLRB election. The Milwaukee plant of Cudahy Brothers Packing Company was captured in 1938 after an NLRB contest with the Amalgamated.[74] At Buffalo, New York, a strike was called in July 1937, against the Jacob Dold Packing Company, the Donahy Packing Company, and the Klinck Packing Company, the last a subsidiary of the Hygrade Food Products Corporation. Although Klinck refused to deal with the union, Dold and Donahy entered into agreements at the conclusion of the strike. However, the victory was short-lived, for in 1939, Dold closed its Buffalo plant, idling 800 workers and leaving the Buffalo local defunct.[75] The Superior Packing Company of St. Paul, Minn., was organized in 1938 after a sit-down strike. Six small packers in Boston were brought under PWOC contract in 1939 following a strike.

Among the large independent packers, the PWOC controlled, by the end of 1941, the Hormel Company; the Ottumwa, Iowa, plant of Morrell, won by an NLRB election in 1937, in which the Amalgamated was defeated; and the Detroit plant of the Hygrade Food Products Corp.

One further organizational event of this period should be mentioned at least briefly: the strike in November 1938, of 685 Chicago stockhandlers employed by the Union Stock Yards and Transit Company. The Amalgamated Meat Cutters had begun organization among this key group of workers in 1933, but it was unable to overcome the opposition of the company. The CIO chartered a local in November 1937, and won an NLRB election a few months later by a slight majority. After futile lengthy negotiations, work ceased in November, paralyzing the stockyards. Faced with pressure from city officials and the packinghouses, Union Stock Yards yielded after two weeks, and entered into a written agreement representing considerable improvement in the wages and working conditions of the stock handlers.

The Response of the Amalgamated Meat Cutters

References in the foregoing pages to Amalgamated intervention in particular disputes has already made it clear that the older organization did not abdicate the meat packing field in favor of its younger rival. Once it had been determined that John L. Lewis would not work on any compromise basis, the Amalgamated set out on a campaign of its own. A nationwide organizing drive was announced on July 1, 1937, in which 22 additional organizers were added to the existing field staff of 31 organizers. The union's journal reported: "The packing plant worker is beginning to realize that there is *magic* in the word *Amalgamated,* the *old, reliable,* and the *one alert, methodical, militant* and *thorough, business-like* organization for the employes in the Butchering trade. The *Amalgamated* is so industrial in its scope, that it covers the entire field from the time the live animal reaches the Stockyards until the finished product is passed from the retail counter to the consumer." [76]

A progress report made to the 1940 Amalgamated convention in June 1940, listed the following achievements:

We have obtained exclusive bargaining rights and are maintaining thriving militant units in fourteen of Armour & Company's main plants.

Our progress has been equally as successful in our efforts to unionize the Cudahy Company employees.

We have accomplished the thorough unionization, under strictly union agreements, of all the main and branch plants operated by Kingan & Company numbering nearly 5,000 workers.

We have negotiated a nationwide understanding with the National Association of Retail Meat Dealers.

We have improved upon our National Agreement with the Safeway Stores.

We have organized, under strictly union conditions, 6,000 of the 93,000 meat cutter employees of the Great Atlantic & Pacific Tea Company.

We have improved our relationship with the Kroger Company, the second largest of the chain systems, so that today nearly 80 percent of all their employees eligible for membership with us are members of our International Union enjoying splendid contracts. [77]

This was by no means the full list of companies under contract with the Amalgamated. A Morrell plant, for example, had been organized earlier,[78] as well as units of Mickleberry's Foods,[79] Oscar Mayer Company, and Hygrade Food Products. Claimed membership in 1940 was 120,000, of which 85,000 were said to be fully paid, compared with only 19,000 in 1936.[80] In October 1941, the Executive Board was informed that dues-paying membership had risen by an additional 12 to 14 thousand,[81] thus putting membership at the end of 1941 within sight of the 100,000 mark. (However, if the lower figure of 73,000 for 1940 is accepted, 1941 membership becomes about 85,000.) The PWOC had won representation rights for 80,000 workers by 1941, but its dues-paying membership was undoubtedly much lower. The increase in Amalgamated membership from 1936 to 1941 probably exceeded the total membership won by the PWOC from its organization in 1937 to 1941, although a substantial proportion of the Amalgamated gain was in the retailing of meat rather than in the packing end.

Internal Problems of the PWOC

Until 1943, the PWOC remained an organizing committee of the CIO. This meant that it was governed by officers who were appointed by the national CIO rather than elected by the membership. In view of the prevalent factionalism, this was in retrospect a fortunate occurrence for the young organization, which might otherwise have been rent by the fratricidal strife which characterized the internal life of other contemporary CIO unions. Even as it was, beneath the CIO directorship there seethed a constant struggle between rival political forces for control of the union.

The Chicago locals, into which had come the remnants of the Communist Packinghouse Workers local, comprised the nucleus of communist power in the PWOC. Although Van Bittner, the first chairman of the PWOC, was a trusted lieutenant of John L. Lewis and thoroughly anti-communist, the first organizational director of the PWOC, Don Harris, was leftist-oriented.[82] Also prominent among the PWOC leaders were Herb March, the director of the Chicago district, who was subsequently a member of the National Committee of the Communist Party,[83] and Henry Johnson, assistant director of the national PWOC and the most important leader of the Negro groups in the organization, who was at least collaborating closely with the communists in the early years of the PWOC.

Stung into action by the repeated charges of communism that were being levied against the PWOC, Bittner removed Harris from the national directorship at the end of 1939, and replaced him with Arthur Kampfert, a veteran unionist who had come up from the ranks of the packinghouse workers.[84] Johnson remained as assistant director, however, and began a campaign for the establishment of a national union to replace the organizing committee, the principal purpose of which was to oust Bittner from the position of top leadership in the union. In February 1940, the organ of the Amalgamated Meat Cutters stated:

Henry Johnson, associate national director, P.W.O.C., is on the "shelf" and also Herb March, district director (Chicago). Incidentally, Henry Johnson and Herb March were hailed before the Dies Committee for their un-American activities in Chicago stock yards. It is also said that Hank Johnson, Herb March and Frank McCarty have staged a "sit down" on Van A. Bittner, the chairman of P.W.O.C. for being "shelved," and they also threaten to start an "Independent Packinghouse Union." [85]

Matters came to a head in November 1940, when the anti-Bittner group, taking advantage of the split in the CIO over the Roosevelt-Willkie election, lined up about 30 of the 85 PWOC locals behind John L. Lewis in his support of the Republican presidential candidate. Bittner, who had thrown his lot in with Philip Murray upon the latter's election as president of the CIO, discharged Johnson and replaced him with Neal Weaver.[86] Johnson refused to leave the scene, however, and intensified his activities among the dissident locals. The so-called "night-rider" group was formed (the name derived from the fact that members of the group would be despatched after working hours to neighboring centers for the purpose of securing support, often involving long automobile rides at night), consisting of Communist Party adherents, pro-Lewis and anti-Bittner elements, united only in their desire to secure Bittner's ouster. Some of the latter group were packinghouse "nationalists" who objected to Bittner's somewhat casual and part-time interest in the PWOC. During the following months, the internal dispute rose in intensity. The opposition locals began to withhold their per capita tax payments from the PWOC. A typical circular put out by this group, signed by 50 PWOC representatives, read as follows:

Bittner is the boss; Bittner is the Financial Secretary; Bittner is the Treasurer. The packing house workers had a Secretary and Treasurer, Mr. Smethurst. To their knowledge, he never handled a dollar. Bittner pushed him aside and took over the job for himself. Bittner hires organizers that will go out and persecute organizers and stewards. To Hell with organizing the unorganized and getting national contracts, so far as Bittner is concerned.[87]

There is some question of the extent to which Johnson could count on the support of the communist bloc in the union. March, the leader of this faction, had been dismissed from his position along with Harris; from there he had been employed temporarily by John L. Lewis in helping organize the Sparrows Point, Md., shipyards, then transferred back to Chicago as an organizer for District 50 of the United Mine Workers. Bittner rehired him in 1941, for the purpose of keeping the Chicago locals, particularly the Armour plant, out of Johnson's control. March appears to have played a somewhat independent role in the events of 1941, swinging his strength against Johnson.[88] At any rate, it seems clear that the Johnson faction had strength beyond the communist-dominated locals of the PWOC. Kansas City and Omaha were strongly in his camp, Sioux City and St. Paul were split; while Austin was firm for Bittner. The Chicago joint council of the PWOC, under the leadership of David MacKenzie, was anti-Bittner, but some of the Chicago locals were on the other side. For example, Swift Local 28 passed the following resolution: "On the grounds that the PWOC Council of Chicago had become the breeding ground for disruption and is controlled in a dictatorial manner by its executive board, Local 28 passed without a dissenting vote a motion to withdraw from the Council." [89]

The dissidents, seeking to take advantage of the Lewis-Murray feud that was then raging within the CIO, sought Lewis' support by proposing that Ray Edmundson, Illinois director of the United Mine Workers, be appointed to replace Bittner. They charged that "every organizer who followed John L. Lewis in the presidential election of November has been fired by Bittner. At that time, Bittner said he would get rid of anyone who supported Willkie and he has done so." [90] Seeking to avert a threatened split in the union, Philip Murray appointed a committee consisting of Allan Haywood, James Carey, and Powers Hapgood to look into the situation. On the recommendation of this committee, Bittner was removed from the chairmanship of the PWOC and replaced by J. C. Lewis, director of the Iowa district of the United Mine Workers as well as of the PWOC, having been given the latter post in the internal shakeup at the end of 1939.[91] Lewis, who had been of great assistance to the Iowa packinghouse workers in their organizing work, was a stalwart backer of John L. Lewis, but he had not been identified with the Johnson faction, so that he was an acceptable compromise in that peculiar period of rapidly shifting alliances in the political life of the CIO. His tenure proved to be a short one, however, for when John L. Lewis quit the CIO in 1942, J. C. Lewis resigned from the PWOC, and was replaced by Sam Sponseller, a CIO staff organizer.

This episode proved to be but a prelude to turbulent factionalism in the

Packinghouse Workers' Union, which received a national charter in 1943. The precise role of various groups in the struggle is more difficult to document than in the case of such organizations as the Woodworkers and the Mine, Mill and Smelter Workers, for the PWOC did not hold conventions, and its newspaper, a special edition of *The CIO News*, was controlled by the Bittner leadership. In its policy, throughout the period 1937-1941, this journal remained apolitical, and provided no clue to the sectarian currents that were agitating the organization. That any progress was made on the collective bargaining front during 1940 and 1941, in the face of PWOC leadership absorption with internal politics, attests to the strength of the desire on the part of the rank-and-file workers to maintain unionism in the industry.

By the end of 1941, trade unionism had attained a firm foothold in meat packing, an industry which had for half a century militantly and successfully resisted the efforts of organized labor to invade it. The Armour and Cudahy concerns, two of the giants of the industry, were fairly well unionized, and had bowed to the inevitable by concluding written collective agreements. A bridgehead had been established in Swift and Wilson, but the former, the largest firm in the industry, had not yet signed an agreement for any of its major plants. The employees of the smaller independent packers were either under union contract, or not far from it.

The meatpacking organizing campaign of 1937 to 1941, starting out inauspiciously at the onset of the 1937 recession, and progressing slowly at first, must nevertheless be accounted as successful from the union point of view. The PWOC was primarily responsible for the inroads made into the Big Four packers, while the Amalgamated concentrated upon the independent packers, and upon its traditional jurisdiction of wholesale and retail meat distribution. In terms of membership, the Amalgamated was larger than the PWOC, although a substantial proportion of its members was in meat distribution rather than in manufacturing.

For the packinghouse worker, trade unionism meant primarily greater job security through formal seniority systems and a mechanism through which grievances could be processed, independent of company control. The Chicago base wage rate rose from 53½ cents per hour at the beginning of 1937 to 72½ cents in 1941, and average hourly earnings from 66.5 cents to 74.1 cents[92] but how much of this increase was due to unionism, or more accurately, in the case of meatpacking, to the desire of employers to avert unionism, cannot be determined. Compared with workers in manufacturing generally, and with those in food processing in particular, the packinghouse worker was well off in 1941. The "Jungle" had given way to a relatively well paid industry, increasingly subject to mechanization, in which the workers, through their own organizations, were vested with the right to a voice in the determination of the conditions under which they were employed.

1 1

The Lumber Industry

In few sectors of American industry has there been as turbulent a labor history as in lumbering. This is hardly fortuitous. A good many of the tasks of the industry are arduous and dangerous, and require men of considerable physical courage and independence of mind. The labor force of the logging camps has traditionally included a large proportion of unmarried, rootless workers, subject to intermittency of employment, to whom the stability of orderly collective bargaining under written collective agreements had little meaning. Living conditions left much to be desired, industrial accidents were frequent and severe. Professor William F. Ogburn of the University of Washington wrote, in 1918, that the chief causes of labor unrest in lumbering were long hours, low wages, unsanitary camps, lack of family life, absence of community life, and unsatisfactory working relationships with foremen; and he indicated that the importance of these factors was inverse to the order in which they are listed.[1] Between 1918 and the inception of the period with which we are dealing, considerable improvement had taken place in labor and living conditions, but some of the basic sociological causes of unrest still remained.

It is important to distinguish between the two major occupational groups in the industry: the loggers and the sawmill workers. "The significant division between sawmill and logging labor is its method of living. Loggers, for the most part, are by necessity forced to live in camps which can be moved about from one center of logging to another. . . . Therefore there are very few permanent living quarters for loggers. This means, of course, that they are, for the most part, unmarried and more or less transient in most of the producing areas. . . . Sawmill workers may be likened, for the most part, to any other factory labor, and in the western areas they are less transient than loggers."[2] It is the lumberjack, rather than the sawmill worker, who is the romantic figure of fiction, and who is largely responsible for the unique flavor of lumber unionism.

Structure of the Industry

Lumber is produced widely throughout the United States. Historically, there have been four major producing regions, the Northeast, the Great Lakes region, the South, and the West. The Northeast and Great Lakes regions have been on the decline since the beginning of the present century, and in 1936, were comparatively small producers. The South, while a significant producer in the nineteen-thirties, was virtually devoid of lumber unionism, and plays no role in our story, which centers in the Pacific Northwest. This area consists of several subregions, the most important of which is the Douglas Fir region, running through Washington and Oregon west of the Cascades. In 1940, the Douglas Fir region alone produced 26 per cent of the lumber, 23 per cent of the wood pulp, and 90 per cent of the shingles produced in the United States.[3] The Western Pine region, which includes the area east of the Cascades, southern Oregon, northern California, Idaho and Montana, and the Redwood region of northern California, constitute important secondary producing areas. Together, the three western regions accounted for almost 40 per cent of the total U. S. timber output in the nineteen-thirties.

The size of the average producing unit in the lumber industry is relatively small. A sawmill with 2000 employees is a giant of the industry, while millwork establishments rarely employ more than 500 men. Logging crews of from two to three hundred men are to be found in some of the larger operations in the West, but the typical crew size is much smaller. Only one lumber company appeared among the 200 largest U. S. nonfinancial corporations in 1935, and this company operated several independent units.[4] Also significant from the point of view of trade unionism is the location of lumber operations. Logging, of course, is scattered widely, depending upon where the timber is to be found. There has been a concentration of sawmills along Puget Sound, in Grays Harbor and Willapa Harbor, and along the Columbia River, particularly in Portland, but smaller mills are spread throughout the entire lumbering area.

There was a chronic tendency toward industrial overcapacity, with intense competition prevailing among the many producing units. During the depression years 1930–1935 inclusive, the industry as a whole sustained net losses; 1936 and 1937 were years of modest net profits, but this upturn was temporarily interrupted by the recession of 1938.[5] Since labor costs constitute a substantial percentage of total costs — the 1939 Census of Manufactures put the ratio of wages to value of products at 31 per cent for sawmills — the wage bill was a crucial factor in the calculations of operators. Thus, from the point of view of ease of unionization, the favorable structural factor of relatively small units of enterprise, making for weakness in the ability of employers to resist, was offset by lack of concentration of workers in large masses, and by the pressure of wages on what were at best thin profit margins.

It is difficult to determine with any degree of precision the "clientele" within the effective jurisdiction of the lumber unions. In 1939, some 360,600 wage earners were employed in U. S. logging camps, sawmills, veneer mills, planing mills, and plywood mills. Many of them were in regions which the unions made little or no attempt to organize, the South in particular. If southern employment in that year is deducted, the remaining pool of eligible employees is reduced to about 190,000 wage earners for the rest of the country. Perhaps 100,000 of these wage earners were located in the Pacific Coast states of Washington, Oregon, and California.[6] In addition to these, allowance should be made for Canadian lumber workers, over whom the American lumber unions exercised jurisdiction, as well as workers in woodworking plants, not included in the above enumeration, to whom the Carpenters' Union in particular laid claim, in computing percentages of trade union organization. In terms of total employment, lumbering was not one of the giants of American industry, but it was extremely important to the economic life of segments of the nation, and to the Pacific Northwest in particular.

One further aspect of lumber employment was of significance to the history of trade unionism in the industry. While there are a great many occupational skills called for, particularly among the loggers, the bulk of the sawmill employees were either unskilled or semiskilled men. A study made in 1933 placed 83 per cent of the total number of sawmill workers in this category.[7] This is a datum to be kept in mind in connection with the craft-industrial union controversy that occurred in lumbering as well as elsewhere.

Early Unions in Lumbering

The American Federation of Labor entered the lumber industry in 1905 when it chartered the International Brotherhood of Woodsmen and Sawmill Workers. In the same year the IWW appeared on the scene, and with its appeal for direct action and the principle of industrial unionism, soon achieved a considerable following among the lumber workers, particularly the loggers. Neither of these unions achieved any great organizational success, but the IWW bequeathed an ideological heritage to the lumber workers which was to play a not inconsequential role. In 1917 an anti-IWW organization, the Loyal Legion of Loggers and Lumbermen (4 L's) was formed under the sponsorship of Colonel Bryce P. Disque, acting on behalf of the United States Army, the government of which was half employer and half employee. The 4 L's survived into the New Deal period, and in 1937, after the constitutionality of the Wagner Act had been upheld, was transformed into the Industrial Employees' Union, Inc. (IEU), with management representation eliminated.

Neither the AFL union nor the IWW survived the twenties. The AFL union surrendered its charter in 1923, while the IWW, after a spurt of activity in 1923, became moribund. The onset of the Great Depression, which hit the lumber industry with particular intensity, found the lumber workers with virtually no organization. Although the NRA code for lumber was drafted without labor participation, the advent of NRA provided a stimulus for organization. A communist organization, the National Lumber Workers' Union, which had been established in 1929, gained some adherents, but the principal beneficiary of the union spirit in the air was the AFL, which chartered 130 federal local unions in the industry. Between 1933 and 1935, thousands of workers joined these locals almost spontaneously, and a new era in the history of lumber unionism began in 1935, when the Executive Council of the AFL decided to transfer the federal locals to the United Brotherhood of Carpenters and Joiners.

In March 1935, a convention of the AFL lumber locals, which had organized themselves loosely into the Northwest Council of Sawmill and Timber Workers Unions, was held at Aberdeen, Washington. A. W. Muir, a member of the Carpenters' executive board, was despatched to assume control. Although he was successful in establishing his leadership at the convention, Muir's position was shaken by the events of a major strike which began in April. His proposals for settling the strike, first accepted by the Longview, Washington, employers, were resisted by a number of local unions, and on June 5, a rump convention of insurgent unions met in order to wrest control of the strike from him. Participating actively in this movement were former members of the communist union, which on April 17 had voted to dissolve and "bore from within" the AFL. However, as Jensen warns us:

The strength of the Communists at this time . . . should not be overemphasized. The key to the truth in the situation at Longview was a genuine dislike for

Muir's leadership, particularly among the rank-and-file loggers who did not relish an outsider directing them.

In an effort to control the situation, Muir revoked the charters of a number of local unions and replaced the insurgents with men loyal to the Carpenters. Slowly the strike declined, and a considerable number of operators entered into agreements with the Muir unions. However, the terms of the settlement were generally unpalatable to the workers, and far from ushering in an era of industrial peace, they were merely a prelude to greater turbulence. The significance of the 1935 strike has been summarized as follows:

The rapid, genuine response to the call to organize and the almost complete support of the strike were surprising. The workers gained unionization, although unity was damaged and they failed to get a standard agreement. For the latter the operators were largely responsible. If the majority of the employers in the industry had had the foresight to go along with the early Longview settlement, standardization might almost have been achieved at a stroke, and the painful weeks of continuation of the strike could have been avoided. By holding out against any settlement with the union the employers opened the way for left-wing elements to enter the industry labor scene. The militant opposition of most employers and the resort to state police and the militia, in some cases, in opening the mills was also shortsighted and contributed greatly to ill will in the industry. The intense dislike of outside leadership among the workers contributed to insurgency, but the problem of leadership could have been solved peaceably in time, once stable relations were established. The course of events, and the bitterness which developed, seriously jeopardized worker unity for many years, and gave an unhappy direction to labor-employer relations in the industry.[8]

Formation of the International Woodworkers of America

In an attempt to consolidate his regime, Muir called a convention of all Sawmill and Timber locals for October 12, 1935. Scheduled initially to meet at Centralia, Washington, the place of the meeting was shifted to Portland in an effort to keep out thirteen insurgent-dominated locals, which had held a preconvention meeting at Olympia. Following the rule of "divide and conquer," the Muir faction decided to abolish the Northwest Council and establish in its stead district councils, modeled on those provided for in the Carpenters' structure. The councils were deliberately kept as small as possible, and there was some gerrymandering in order to split up the opposition.

This tactic was destined to end in failure. On September 18, 1936, without approval of the Carpenters' Union, representatives of all locals in the ten district councils that had been established met in Portland and formed the Federation of Woodworkers. While communists played an important role in the formation of the federation, it was by no means a purely communist endeavor. Groups which remained loyal to the Carpenters, for example, the Puget Sound District Council, were active in the federation prior to the final break with the Carpenters. Harold Pritchett, who was elected president, if not an actual Communist Party member, followed the communist line with the utmost fidelity, but it has been argued that his election was motivated by the desire to encourage the British Columbia unions (he had been president of the British Columbia district council), as well as to prevent friction between the Washington and the Oregon groups.[9]

Despite its illicit existence, the Federation of Woodworkers expressed its fealty to the Carpenters' Union, and urged its constituent locals to send delegates to the Lakeland, Fla., convention of the Carpenters, which opened on December 7. But the lumber workers' delegates were in a rebellious frame of mind; the official organ of the Federation wrote:

There was never a better opportunity to air our grievances than is now presented. The AFL and all affiliated organizations has received a severe and long overdue shock. The Committee for Industrial Organization has challenged rule of the men composing the governing board. This rebellion against undemocratic procedure has widespread ramifications in the Internationals composing the Federation and is finding expression in locals of the Carpenters and Joiners.[10]

This mood was not abated by the action of the Carpenters' Executive Board in denying convention voting rights to the lumber delegates, based upon the fact that the lumber locals had been admitted to the United Brotherhood on a nonbeneficial basis, that is, they were paying only 25 cents a month per capita to the Brotherhood, compared with the 75-cent levy paid by construction locals, a concession that had been necessitated by the lower wage scale of the lumber workers. The latter had renounced any interest in such beneficial features operated by the Brotherhood as a pension plan and a home for retired members, but objected to deprivation of voting rights.

On the second day of the convention, a delegate from the carpenter's local at Kelso-Longview, Washington, moved that the lumber local delegates be seated with a vote on all matters pertaining to their industry. He argued that the Brotherhood constitution made no provision for nonbeneficial membership, and that the lumber workers had been admitted as full-fledged members. He was answered by Frank Duffy, the general secretary of the Brotherhood, who reviewed the history of organization among the lumber workers, emphasizing the malignant effects of industrial union sentiment, and closed in the following vein:

Now, what do you want? Do you want to stay with the United Brotherhood or do you not? We have done more for you that you have done for us. . . . Let me tell you this — and this is no threat. Go on out of the Brotherhood, and we will give you the sweetest fight you ever had in your lives. First of all, we will notify all local unions not to take any notice of you, not to give you any support, moral, financial, or otherwise. The next step will be that we will notify all the big firms with which we have contracts covering hours, wages and working conditions for the timber workers that if they want to continue employing you outside of the Brotherhood we will put them on the unfair list and your manufactured stuff won't be handled elsewhere.[11]

The lumber delegates were seated as fraternal delegates, without the right to vote. A subcommittee of the general executive board was appointed to confer with them, and recommended to the convention that a thorough investigation of the lumber industry be conducted prior to any "hasty decisions"; that a union label be designed for lumber; that certain firms be placed on the "unfair" list of the Carpenters; that an organizing campaign be conducted, using lumber workers as organizers; and that the lumber delegates be requested to address the convention to present a picture of their situation.[12] This did not satisfy the lumber delegates, and when the convention had ended they journeyed to Washington, where they conferred with John L. Lewis and John Brophy. However, the CIO at the time had its hands full with the steel and auto campaigns, and the lumber workers apparently received little encouragement.[13]

The Woodworkers' Federation called a second convention to consider the report of the delegates. It assembled at Longview, Washington, on February 20, 1937. The delegation told the convention that "the results gained at the Lakeland Convention should be accepted as a distinct advantage towards an effective organization program." Pointing to the union label and the cooperation of the Carpenters in boycotting recalcitrant firms, it urged that the federation remain a part of the Carpenters' Union, but at the same time "maintaining our unity at all costs and not [permitting] the disruption and disintegraion of our organization by craft union raids on our membership." [14] This recommendation was adopted by the convention, and Pritchett was at pains to assert that the federation was acting wholly in conformance with the constitution of the United Brotherhood.

But this uneasy truce did not last. The spectacular victories of the CIO in the spring of 1937, and the transformation of that organization into a full-fledged rival to the AFL, resulted in mounting sentiment among the lumber workers for CIO affiliation. Lewis was now more receptive; flushed with victory over some of the great corporations of the country, he may have welcomed the opportunity of carrying the fight into the territory of his arch-enemy, William Hutcheson, president of the Carpenters' Union. A conference of district officials was called for June 7 to consider a resolution passed by the Grays-Willapa Harbor District favoring a transfer of allegiance to the CIO.[15]

The conference invited William Hutcheson and John Brophy, both of whom were in the Northwest at the time, to address it. Brophy accepted the invitation, and seconded by Harry Bridges, promised the lumber workers a national CIO charter, as well as financial assistance to the tune of $50,000. Hutcheson refused to appear before the conference on the ground that it was not a part of the Brotherhood, but sent Muir in his stead. The latter received a very cool reception.

A resolution was introduced calling for a referendum among the members of the Federation of Woodworkers on affiliation with the CIO. Some of the delegates were opposed to a referendum on the ground that the conference had not been empowered to adopt any such action. When the resolution was adopted by a majority vote, and a referendum scheduled, members of five district councils left the conference, among them Al Hartung and Don Helmick of the Columbia River District Council, one of the largest in terms of membership.[16] Most of these dissenters were suspicious of the intentions of Pritchett and the activist group within the federation, but on the other hand they were bitterly opposed to the craft policy of the Brotherhood. As Duffy stated a few months later, "President Hutcheson told them they would have to respect the jurisdiction claim of the Boilermakers, the Blacksmiths, the Machinists, and any other trade that might be within the confines of where they worked. They didn't like that." [17]

The CIO, in a further effort to win the lumber workers, sent a check for $5000 to the federation as a first instalment on its promise of financial aid. Pritchett and O. M. Orton called upon John L. Lewis in Washington to learn what the CIO would do for the federation if the referendum turned in that direction. While the referendum was in progress, the executive officers of the federation issued a pro-CIO statement, which said, in part:

Hutcheson and his agent Muir have used every possible means of selling us out by boss collaboration. In the case of the Longview workers during the '35 strike who were courageously fighting the largest lumber concern in the world, Muir was meeting in hotel rooms with the company stooges and formulating the infamous McCormick agreement and when the workers refused to accept this agreement in all of its silliness, Muir yanked their charter and destroyed their unity.[18]

The federation convened in Tacoma on July 15 to consider the outcome of the referendum, in which the workers had voted 16,754 to 5306 in favor of joining the CIO. There was considerable opposition both to the CIO and to the leadership of the Pritchett group, but after five days of argument, a majority of the delegates favored application for a CIO charter. Those who opposed the CIO thereupon left the convention. On July 20, the new union convened as the International Woodworkers of America (IWA), and proceeded to elect Pritchett and his supporters as the principal executives. The Columbia River District Council, which was the nucleus of the opposition to the Pritchett regime in the ensuing years, objected to the way things were railroaded through the convention, but their dislike of the Carpenters prevented their splitting off from the IWA.

The Carpenters' Union retained real strength mainly in the Puget Sound region, the IWA dominating the remainder of the Northwest, and commanding the allegiance of a decided majority of the lumber workers.[19] But Hutcheson set out to show that this affront to the most powerful international union in the AFL, the leadership of which had spearheaded the fight against the industrial union movement, would not be received passively. Under date of August 11, 1937, a circular letter was sent out to all Carpenter locals, which said, *inter alia:*

The committee [of the General Executive Board] found that there were Communists and adverse influences boring from within for the purpose of trying to destroy the activities of the United Brotherhood . . . to combat this dual movement it becomes necessary to notify all our Local Unions, District, State and Provincial Councils of the Brotherhood that our members must not handle any lumber or mill work manufactured by any operator who employs C.I.O. or those who hold membership in an organization dual to our Brotherhood. . . . Let your watchword be "No C.I.O. lumber or mill work in your district," and let them know you mean it.[20]

Thus was ushered in one of the most bitter rival union conflicts in the history of American labor. The Carpenters soon made it clear that they were not going to stop at logomachies. A list of mills organized by the Woodworkers was circulated to retail lumber dealers, many of whom were quick to take the hint and cancel orders. On August 21, the Carpenters convened a meeting of its remaining adherents at Longview and organized the Oregon-Washington Council of Lumber and Sawmill Workers. Legal action was resorted to in an attempt to retain control over the assets of the seceding IWA locals.

The first major pitched battle between the two organizations took place at Portland, Oregon, where six large sawmills were involved — the Jones

Lumber Company, the West Oregon Lumber Company, the B. F. Johnson Company, the Portland Lumber Mills, the Inman-Poulsen Lumber Company, and the Eastern and Western Lumber Company. The employees of these mills were organized in a single local, which had changed its affiliation from AFL to CIO. On August 16, AFL pickets appeared before the mills, and they were closed down in what the IWA claimed was a lockout by the employers. A week later, the IWA notified the employers that it represented a majority of the employees involved, and filed unfair labor practice charges with the NLRB. On August 27, after mediation by the regional director of the NLRB, the employers agreed to reopen the mills under the conditions prevailing on July 1, pending a representation election. The IWA agreed, but the Carpenters did not, and when the mills opened on August 30, they bent every effort toward shutting them down again. Members of the Teamsters' Union entered the fray on the side of the Carpenters; they refused to deliver lumber and fuel, and overturned trucks driven by IWA men. Workers' homes were stoned, and individuals on both sides beaten. The Carpenters placed the mills on their unfair list. The AFL picketed the rivers with small boats, and logs could not be brought in because AFL sailors refused to go through the picket lines. As a result, the mills began to close down once again.[21]

On October 21, the NLRB certified the IWA as exclusive bargaining agent for the employees of the six mills involved, on the basis of a check of membership cards. The AFL replied by denouncing the board as an ally of the CIO, and tightened its boycott. In retaliation, CIO longshoremen instituted a boycott of AFL produced lumber at the Portland docks. Far from settling anything, the NLRB certification merely served to exacerbate the controversy.

Jensen found it surprising that the operators made no effort to open the mills in view of the undoubted CIO strength. He concluded: "The probability that the operators were delaying in favor of the A.F. of L. is borne out by the fact that other mills in the area were running without difficulty, and the boycott never seemed effective. On the other hand, the operators could not afford to start up unless they were reasonably sure of continuous operation, and the Carpenters had not officially applied the boycott everywhere." [22] It might also be added that recession had struck the lumber industry in September 1937, and the employers were therefore able to remain closed without much financial sacrifice.[23]

In December, Governor Martin of Oregon entered the dispute by announcing that he was going to conduct an independent representation election at the Inman-Poulsen mill. Several years later, he clarified his motives in ordering this election in the face of the NLRB certification:

I was told by the employers in the Poulsen mill, which is the biggest mill and which has a great export business. I was told by Van Duzer and his partners that a decided majority of that mill was A.F. of L. . . . I said, "I am not going to call an election here unless I know that you have a majority, because I want this election to be a cinch. I don't want to get licked. I want this thing to go A.F. of L." . . . I made those fellows — I had to wait two weeks to bring me the cards that the A.F. of L. would carry that election, and at last they produced them. . . . Well, of course, we had to go C.I.O. with that mill, and that spoiled the whole business, and then, of course, immediately your boycott was slapped on.[24]

Martin was referring to the fact that the IWA carried the election by a vote of 376 to 183, after which he was obliged to condemn any further obstructive tactics by the AFL. During January 1938 the mills began to reopen, but without entering into agreements with the IWA. The Carpenters intensified their activities within some of the plants, chartering new locals in some cases, but they removed their boycott. The struggle continued during 1938 and 1939, with claims and counterclaims, charges and countercharges being presented to the NLRB. It was not finally resolved until 1939, when as the result of NLRB elections, the Carpenters were certified for B. F. Johnson, Portland Lumber and Jones Lumber, whereas the IWA eventually won West Oregon Lumber and Eastern and Western Lumber and Inman-Poulsen.[25] After February 1938, however, the controversy proceeded along peaceful lines, and the employers were not subjected to the harassment of rival union claims expressed on the picket line, together with the attendant financial loss. The president of the Jones Lumber Co. estimated that between September 1, 1937 and April 1, 1938, the mills in Portland suffered an average loss of three months of operation.[26] However, these were all months of low business activity, so that they cannot be taken as net losses. It is quite probable that there would have been some shutdowns even in the absence of strikes.

The IWA Convention of 1937

The first regular convention of the IWA, which opened in Portland on December 3, 1937 presaged the stormy internal life for the new CIO union that did in fact materialize. Although the IWA claimed membership of 100,000, it was admitted that current per capita paying membership was only 45,000.[27] Pritchett conceded that the Carpenters had considerable strength in the Puget Sound area, Longview, and Coos Bay, and claimed the Columbia River and the Grays-Willapa Harbor districts, as well as British Columbia, as the major centers of IWA power. Some 155 locals had been chartered, but 40 of them had never made financial reports to the International.

The principal issue in debate was that of communism. The issue first arose when a delegate argued that in excluding the press from certain sessions of the convention, an exception should be made for the *Daily Worker*, the official Communist Party newspaper, on the ground that it was the only paper which championed the CIO cause. Don Helmick, a leader of the Columbia River District, charged that ". . . there are certain things within the International Woodworkers that reveal the presence of a Communistically controlled machine. . . ." The communist press representative was permitted to remain by a vote of 136 to 106. Another delegate from the Columbia River area alleged that O. M. Orton, the IWA vice-president, had introduced him to a Communist Party organizer, who had attempted to enroll him in the party.[28] However, the communist-oriented faction was clearly in control of the convention, and beat off all attacks, although Pritchett, as presiding officer, was conciliatory rather than dictatorial in his handling of the opposition.

One of the interesting incidents of the factional fight revolved around the events of a strike that had occurred in November 1937. In support of a strike against the Carnation Lumber Co. at Forest Grove, Oregon, an IWA picket line had been established at the Portland docks to prevent the handling of lumber produced by this mill. The local longshoremen, who were in the left-wing International Longshoremen's and Warehousemen's Union, honored the picket line. The Portland Waterfront Employers Association threatened to close the entire port unless the lumber was loaded, and Harry Bridges, who feared a coastwide lockout, prevailed upon Pritchett and Orton to go to Portland and remove the picket line, the effect of which was to smash the Forest Grove strike. When they were denounced for this action on the floor of the convention, the executive officers argued that the strike had been ineffective from its inception, and the Longshoremen could not be expected to carry the burden of IWA strikes. Harry Bridges himself argued the same point frankly before the IWA convention in 1939, two years later:

We did say, and we still say, we'll support the IWA and any other union with every means within our power, and up to that point where support does any good, but we're not going to make every fight a finish fight without considering the consequences to our organization, to your organization, and to the CIO. . . .

We made this proposition to your men — after the longshoremen are locked out, what's the next step? Tell us what it is, and we'll go. They had no answer. We were just told that they don't think the employers would lock us out. We're not gambling any part of our organization on what somebody thinks or doesn't think, and that may as well be understood now. . . . We're not worried about the coastwise strike of the longshoremen or the rest of our affiliated unions under our International. We get into enough of them. We gamble our entire organization sometimes for the protection of one or two men. When we know we've got a chance to win, but we're not dumbbell enough to gamble it when there's a good chance of losing. And we don't throw good money after bad, and that Carnation mill was operating and it looked very much to us like we were going to go out on a limb if we were going to do what these fellows said we were going to do, and we'd all sink or swim together, with the emphasis on the sink. . . .

I was told by your officials your membership doesn't believe in agreements. Well, maybe you fellows don't believe in agreements, but we do, and we're not going to risk them for a bunch of people that don't believe in agreements. . . . And those people that talk about not believing in agreements, they believe in direct action all the time. It was only plain to me they were carrying out the plan they believed in direct action and economic strength, but it was our economic strength, not their own. . . .[29]

The closing section of Bridges' remarks was a slap at the alleged IWW tendencies of some opposition leaders. While it is true that there were still some remnants of the IWW philosophy of emphasis upon direct strike action and opposition to written agreements among the lumber workers,[30] and that some of the leaders, administration as well as opposition, had an IWW background — for example, Worth Lowery, who became the first anticommunist president of the IWA, had once been an IWW member — there is no evidence that by the time of the IWA period, there was any real rejection of orthodox collective bargaining based upon syndicalist principles.

A final major topic discussed at the 1937 IWA convention was that of relations with the Carpenters. The Washington-Oregon Council of Lumber & Sawmill Workers, the organization which had been established in opposition to the IWA, submitted a proposal for unity under the banner of the Carpenters' Union, based upon a guarantee of autonomy for the lumber workers, the right to use the Carpenters' label, the commitment that all organizers would be men from the lumber industry, and a reasonable return of per capita tax paid to the Carpenters to the Northwest.[31] A year earlier, these concessions might have been sufficient to prevent a split in the ranks of the lumber workers, but coming with an independent IWA already in existence as a CIO union, it was clearly little more than a public relations tactic. The proposal was rejected summarily as one that could not "be accepted or even considered as good will proposal by the delegates in Convention. The return to the Brotherhood does not mean peace to the workers in the industry. . . . It is our opinion that in order to establish and share the greatest gain it is not a question of the I.W.A. moving backwards to join the Oregon-Washington Council to the United Brotherhood but precisely the opposite." [32]

Under the IWA constitution, officers were nominated by the convention and elected by a referendum of the membership for two-year terms. In the voting that followed the convention, Pritchett and Orton were reelected over the candidates of the opposition, Hartung and Woodruff. As a matter of policy, the precise outcome of the balloting was not announced, so that it is difficult to judge the strength of the opposition among the rank and file at this juncture.

The Depression of 1937–1939

As already noted, the depression that began in the summer of 1937 affected the lumber industry, which was heavily dependent upon the volume of building construction, with particular severity. Thus, no sooner had the IWA achieved independent status as a CIO affiliate, than the possibilities for organization were drastically curtailed. Employment conditions continued poor until July 1938, when a slight upturn occurred. However, it was not until October 1939, with the stimulus afforded by the European war, that lumber employment began to climb to 1936–1937 levels.

Average hourly earnings in the Douglas Fir region rose from 58.3 cents in 1934 to 74.6 cents in 1937, largely as a consequence of two waves of increases, the first in the middle of 1935, the second in March and April of 1937.[33] In 1938, however, the problem was to maintain existing wage rates, rather than to seek any further increases. Both unions set themselves firmly against wage cuts, and on the whole were successful in this policy; average hourly earnings remained virtually unchanged during 1938.

One attempted wage cut produced particularly serious consequences. At the beginning of July 1938, the Red River Lumber Company, which was the chief enterprise in the town of Westwood, Cailfornia, announced a wage cut of 17½ cents per hour. In March 1938 the NLRB, after an election, had certified the IEU, the successor of the 4 L's, as bargaining agent for the plant. A majority of the IEU members voted against acceptance of the reduction, whereupon the national office revoked the local charter. At this point the IWA assumed leadership of the workers, and a meeting called under its auspices for July 12 was attended by 1400 of the 2000 company employees.[34] The next day, a reign of terror began at Westwood. An IWA picket line which had been established at the plant was broken by an armed mob. Bands of men armed with guns and clubs roamed the town, rounded up known CIO men, took them to the center of town, and gave them a "trial." They were then ordered to leave the town; between 500 and 600 persons, including wives and children of the workers, were thus deported. They returned to their homes some days later with an escort of state highway police.

The plant was reopened, but the IWA men who appeared for work were told to leave the plant. A few days later, the AFL established a local at Westwood, and enrolled 1300 employees, mostly former IEU men. The director of the California Department of Industrial Relations testified that the leaders of the new local were the same as those of the IEU, and concluded: "The facts permit of only one conclusion: The so-called A.F.L. union at Westwood is nothing but a company union." This was denounced indignantly by a representative of the California Federation of Labor, who denied that the AFL had any connection with the "purge" of CIO members.[35]

The Westwood situation continued for some years to constitute an irritant to IWA-Carpenter relationships, if any was needed. Because of pending unfair labor practice charges, the NLRB refused to call an election, and in February 1940, the AFL union called a strike, which was accompanied by so much violence that Governor Olsen threatened to send troops to protect IWA men. An election was finally held in May 1941, which was won by the AFL, 1059 to 432 votes. "The A.F. of L. local was certified and the I.W.A. men began to pack up their belongings so that they might seek jobs elsewhere." [36]

Another scene of acute AFL-CIO rivalry was Bellingham, Washington. A majority of the Carpenters' local there had gone over to the IWA, but the former retained minority support. During 1938, the IWA local leadership was split on the advisability of accepting a wage cut to reduce unemployment. The group favoring the reduction seceded, formed an independent union, and in December, was granted exclusive bargaining rights by the Bloedel-Donovan Lumber Company, the principal employer. The IWA called a strike, whereupon the Carpenters granted a new charter to the independent group, quite separate from the existing AFL charter in Bellingham. In an NLRB election held in March, the new Carpenters' local received 538 votes to 447 for the CIO, whereupon it was immediately granted a union shop, which had the effect of eliminating all IWA influence.

The Seattle convention of the IWA, held against the background of depression conditions, saw a resumption of the intense factional strife that had characterized the previous convention. Although the IWA still claimed 100,000 members, per capita payments to the International had fallen to about 20,000.[37] Early in the convention, a resolution to add to the IWA constitution a clause to the effect that nothing in it conflicted in any way with the Constitution of the United States was defeated after an acrimonious debate in which the sponsors of the resolution were accused of red-baiting. Another resolution which would have barred from union office members of "antidemocratic" parties was defeated without debate.[38] A resolution introduced by the Columbia River group censuring Vice-President Orton for his role in the Carnation Mills strike[39] was also defeated, but only after a long debate in which Al Hartung warned the administration forces:

Certainly, we have had a lot of dissention in the two different Conventions that we've had. We came this time to try and build a program that was constructive to the movement of the I.W. of A. . . . Every proposal that the Columbia River District delegates have been opposed to has been crammed down our throat. No consideration has been given to any of the problems that confront our District. Now, possibly the International does not want the membership from the Columbia River area.[40]

Despite this truculence, there was no immediate move toward secession, although factionalism continued unabated. In April, *The Timberworker*, in an editorial titled "The Disruptionists — An Enemy Within the Walls," said:

. . . in our very IWA there is a "fifth column" at work. . . . Every diversion from the main issues of trade unionism should be sharply questioned. Recognizing such diversion as the work of the "fifth column," workers should lose no time in taking action against those who conduct such sabotage. The enemy within the walls is far more dangerous than the one outside.[41]

In reply, H. I. Tucker, president of the Aberdeen local and a leader of the opposition group, urged that *The Timberworker* devote less space to attacks upon nazism, fascism, and red-baiting; and agreed that there was a fifth column at work: "They have been at work for a long time. We differ only in opinion as to who are the members of this 'fifth column.' "[42] Two weeks later, the paper printed a letter from Ernest Kozlowski, defending the Communist Party, and concluding: "As a Communist I feel that Communists need no defense, but that our unions and our democratic organizations do need defense. In trade unions, especially, I have noted that it is not the Communists who raise the issue of Communism, but those who seek to destroy the trade union movement itself." The climax came on June 3, when under a banner headline, "Expose IWA Wreckers," the executive officers of the international union, Pritchett, Orton, and McCarty, accused the leadership of the Aberdeen local of conspiracy with employers to destroy the IWA. The specific charges, which were later dropped as based upon insufficient evidence, need not concern us. What is of interest is that the editorial, couched in violent terms and full of epithets characteristic of the communist press — traitors, wreckers, agents of Wall Street — seemed to presage an all-out war against the opposition. However, Pritchett chose instead to adopt a policy of conciliation, perhaps for fear of isolating the left-wing bloc.

The 1939 convention was devoted almost entirely to the issue of communism, which had become more acute with the outbreak of the war in Europe, referred to by Pritchett, in his opening address, as "this imperialistic world war." [43] The administration had little to show for the previous year; paid membership was still around 20,000, and wages had remained almost stationary. Pritchett, who was a Canadian citizen, had secured a visa to enter the United States for the purpose of attending the convention only with great difficulty, and a number of prominent citizens had formed a committee for the purpose of helping him secure a permanent entry permit.

On the second day of the convention, Bob Williams, an administration supporter, began the long debate by accusing the opposition of having caucused the previous evening for the purpose of capturing the convention. The temper of the convention may be judged by the following excerpt from the transcript:

Brother Williams. . . . Every delegate has instructions from Don Helmick to watch these men and vote the way he votes, and if he doesn't vote the way he votes Don Helmick says he'll get them. They also have a watching committee to watch them. (Much booing)

Some Delegate. You're a God damned liar, he never said that.

Williams also reported Helmick, a leader of the opposition, as charging that the IWA program had come directly from Moscow; that the IWA leaders were liars in claiming 100,000 members; that the communists were maintaining control by financing a number of paper locals; and that the previous referendum had been dishonestly counted. Helmick, a logger, arose to make charges against the IWA administration that went as far as any that had been made by the Carpenters:

Yes, I am opposed to the Communist Party, and I'll tell you why, because I as a logger believe that I have the free right to oppose the Communist Party or any other political group, and that when Harold J. Pritchett says that I'll either get in the Party or they will run me out of the industry, then I say they have asked for a fight. . . . Somebody says this is red-baiting, we hear this cry. Every time that the question of whether Communists are actually and bonafidely controlling or attempting to control a given organization, if anyone mentions red — ah, ah, communism, they are red-baiting. Almost to the extent that if you accuse somebody who might be a comrade of stealing sheep and you caught him with the sheep, they would still cry that you were red-baiting . . . when people tell me either to join the Communist party or they will run me out of the industry . . . I will fight back and when people like Jim Murphy, the Director of the Communist Party in Portland, who as far as I know wouldn't know a chocker from a frying pan is going to participate in laying down policy for unions then I object, and if Rapport, one of the leading officers of the Communist party of Seattle is going to meet with woodworkers in regard to political affiliation of their persons O K let them meet. More power to them. But if they are going to meet and lay down policy for the IWA there are many of us that object.

In an impassioned defense, Pritchett accused Helmick, at the very outset of the IWA, of having said to him: "I'll dump you out of the Federation of Woodworkers or my guts will hang on the road." He admitted having introduced Murphy, "an old logger with much more experience than Brother Helmick ever had in the industry," to Helmick in a casual fashion, but he denied having ever invited Helmick to join the Communist Party, as well as his own membership. Claude Hale, a delegate from the large Portland local, accused the administration of following "a policy of dirty rotten slimy under-handed tactics, of discrediting and discriminating against any member who won't go down the line with them on a Communistic program." Ed Benedict, who was to become secretary-treasurer of the IWA a few years later, was even more specific in his charges:

. . . as we know very well International officers, members of the office staff, former district officers have over a long period of time been under the influences some of whom are actually members of the communist party (*sic*). . . . That they consult from time to time with Morris Rapport, Section Organizer of the Communist Party, with headquarters in the Smith Tower Building in Seattle. We know they consult with Lou Sass, Organizational Secretary of the Northwest District, that's his official title.

The issue was disposed of, for the time being, by referring the whole controversy to a committee consisting of the International executive board, the officers of the Columbia River District, and the CIO directors for California, Oregon, and Washington, Harry Bridges, William Dalrymple, and

Richard Francis respectively. The opposition voted against this move, but was defeated in a roll call, 123 to 107. A meeting was held in an attempt to bring about a reconciliation, but the opposition delegates walked out when Pritchett, after several hours of wrangling, informed them they had no right to vote.[44] On the recommendation of administration supporters, the three CIO state directors worked out a unity proposal with the following principal points:

1. The official journal of the union should be devoted to the problems of the industry, and never to the persecution of individual members.

2. Procedures should be adopted to ensure fair counting of referenda.

3. Complaints against national officers should be diverted to CIO regional directors, and not to national CIO officers.

4. It was recommended that the IWA declare itself in agreement with CIO policy, namely, "The CIO is an industrial union organization and an American institution, with its national policies and decisions arrived at by Conventions, and by Executive Board meetings and Executive Officers between such meetings, and through no other medium."[45]

This program was adopted, but immediately afterward an altercation ensued on a proposed amendment to the IWA constitution barring communists from membership. Harry Bridges was given the floor to speak against the amendment, and in the course of a long speech he made the following remarks:

when [witnesses] were asked to give one single example of how the Communist Party was wrecking the Labor Movement, there wasn't one of those experts on Communism could give one single example and that's a matter of official government record. . . . I'd say you ought to cut out the funny business and do some constructive work. And you've got a job to do, and the better you do that job, the better it is for the CIO and the better it is for my own Organization. There's Communists in that Organization and they're staying there. And its a pretty good Organization, a darn good Organization. But God help the person that starts kicking out Communists, or anybody else. Because the Organization will take care of him.

A motion not to concur in the amendment was carried, and the convention adjourned soon thereafter. However, this was not the end of the match, but simply another round.

Recovery and Union Growth

The Carpenters, too, were not without their internal problems, which prevented them from capitalizing to a greater extent than they did on the

IWA schism. Early in 1940, the Carpenters levied a special assessment to fight the antitrust prosecution which had been brought against the organization. The assessment was levied on the individual lumber locals without going through the Oregon-Washington Council. When the Grays Harbor District Council refused to accept the tax, a subcommittee of the Carpenters' executive board came out to the Northwest and told the Council that it would have to pay or local charters would be revoked. After this, there was little enthusiasm for the AFL in the Grays Harbor area.[46]

The Timberworker, the IWA organ, while for a time modifying the tone of its attacks on the opposition, continued to follow the twists in the Communist Party line assiduously. As early as June 1939, the Executive Board of the IWA had endorsed Roosevelt for a third term, and during the following months, article after article appeared in pursuit of this theme.[47] Suddenly, with the signing of the Hitler-Stalin pact, the paper became conspicuously silent on this issue, only to resume early in 1940 on the other side of the fence. An editorial of February 17, 1940, stated:

The road the Roosevelt administration travels today, and has travelled since renouncing the New Deal, can take this nation to but one destination — war.[48]

The attack grew in intensity. A few months later, *The Timberworker* editorialized on its first page:

The imperialist profiteers in the United States have launched their "total war" against the struggle of the American people to keep this country out of war. The "big push" of the war-mongers to take this nation into the bloody conflict between German and Anglo-French imperialism gains momentum with every day.

This, of course, was sheer piracy from the *Daily Worker,* the official U. S. Communist Party newspaper, and illustrates the degree of control exercised by the communists over the IWA. The IWA sent delegates to the 1940 Chicago convention of the Committee to Defend America by Keeping Out of War, a communist enterprise. The slogan, "The Yanks are not coming," was stressed time and again. Just prior to the 1940 presidential elections, *The Timberworker* printed in full John L. Lewis' radio address endorsing Willkie, and concluded: "We have viewed Roosevelt's foreign and domestic policies with the suspicion and misgiving that they have but one destination — war. Our organization has pledged full support to the CIO program of peace and security for the American people. In our opinion the address of John L. Lewis, though he spoke unofficially, furthered that program." [49]

Such blatant examples of communist control aroused the opposition to even more intensive activities.

The referendum following the 1939 convention returned Pritchett, Orton and McCarty to office, though Worth Lowery, an opposition leader, was elected to the newly created post of second vice-president. However, the Columbia River Council protested the election, and recommended to its affiliated locals that they withhold their per capita tax payments to the IWA. Lowery refused to take office. At this juncture, when a formal split in the union seemed inevitable, the national CIO office intervened. Michael Widman, then CIO director of organization, was sent to the Northwest to mediate. The opposition group proposed that the CIO launch an organizing drive under the direct supervision of Widman, but the majority insisted that the IWA officers must retain control over all activities of the international union. After some negotiations, the IWA was obliged to sign an agreement with the CIO providing for a campaign under the direction of a man designated by the CIO, the CIO director to have complete charge over organizing personnel, including the right to hire and fire. Adolph Germer, a veteran CIO organizer, who had figured prominently in many CIO drives, was named director by Lewis. Lowery was induced to assume the office of vice-president.

When Germer arrived on the Coast, he reported that he was asked time and again, "Who is going to hire the organizers and who is going to handle the money," whenever he appeared before local unions to urge an affirmative vote in a referendum on a special assessment to finance the organizing drive.[50] Germer set to work in typical CIO style; he concentrated the first attack upon the Everett mills of the Weyerhaeuser Timber Co., the largest single operation in the lumber industry. Although the AFL had some strength in other Everett mills, the IWA managed to organize the Weyerhaeuser mills, and on October 31, 1940, signed its first agreement with the company, gaining exclusive bargaining rights, and putting it far ahead of the AFL in this important lumber center.[51] Another focus of the campaign was Longview, where there were sizable units of the Long-Bell and Weyerhaeuser companies. Despite a bitter internal fight in the local there, during the course of which the opposition group, acting in alliance with Germer, secured a legal injunction against the administration-supported faction, the IWA won a decisive NLRB election victory in both mills in March 1941, giving it control over 5000 men.[52]

Apart from the CIO drive, wages began to move up during 1940 on the heels of a heightened demand for lumber products. The IWA promoted the idea of an area-wide agreement for the Douglas Fir competitive region, and established an International Policy Committee, composed of representatives of each of the districts involved, to enter into negotiations with an employer group, the Lumbermen's Industrial Relations Committee, which claimed to represent the employers of 40,000 men. After several months of negotiation, the committee revealed that it had no authority to sign agreements for its members, and this first attempt at industry bargaining collapsed.[53] Collective bargaining continued on a district-wide basis, and agreements were concluded late in 1940 providing for wage increases of 4 to 5 per cent.[54] The Carpenters, not to be outdone by the IWA, made demands on behalf of their members in the Douglas Fir area exceeding the IWA settlement. When the employers refused, a strike of all AFL operations in the area was called, during the course of which the Carpenters entered into collaboration with the anti-administration forces in the IWA, which were reluctant to accept the IWA-negotiated settlements. The strike was eventually settled on about the same terms as the IWA had secured.

While these events were taking place on the collective bargaining front, factionalism within the IWA continued unabated, despite CIO intervention. Not only Germer, but Francis and Dalrymple, the Oregon and Washington CIO directors, joined forces with the opposition group. In August 1940, Dalrymple sent a letter to the IWA denouncing a Communist Party circular that had been sent to lumber workers and stating that "the Industrial Branch of the Multnomah County Communist Party is not speaking for the CIO and its affiliates in the State of Oregon and we are here and now telling them to keep their hands off the affairs of our organization." [55]

The 1940 IWA convention was again devoted largely to the issue of communism. It was presided over by Orton, Pritchett having been denied admission to the United States by the immigration authorities. An increase of 6000 per capita dues-paying members over the previous convention was claimed, and total membership was later revealed to have been 33,700.[56] Hardly had the convention begun when a resolution was introduced demanding that the Communist Party cease interfering in the internal affairs of the IWA. During the debate on the resolution, a delegate from Portland accused Orton of having attempted to induce him to join the Communist Party in 1937, "with a threat if I ever expected to go any place in the labor movement, it would be necessary for me to sign a card. He assured me that I would never advance in the I.W. of A. . . . A special trip was made from

Seattle to Portland to force me into the Communist Party. A trap was set for me, and I was just recently elected President of my Local Union." James Fadling, who later rose to the presidency of the IWA, said: "If smoking the reds out, and if talking about Communism where it truly exists is red-baiting, then I am a pioneer at red-baiting, because I helped smoke a lot of them out in my time." A delegate from the Raymond, Washington, local, which went into the IWA in 1937 with 1500 members, admitted that he had been a member of the communist unit within the local, and had watched it dwindle to 200 members under communist domination.[57] Many examples were cited of diversion of local union funds for Communist Party purposes, and constant solicitation of funds for communist-sponsored organizations. After several days of debate, a compromise resolution was adopted.

The next day, however, the issue was reopened by the proposal of a constitutional amendment excluding communists from membership. After another long debate, in which the same arguments were repeated, the communist faction succeeded in beating the proposed amendment by the close vote of 134 to 124. The opposition was now stronger than at any time in the past, but the communist machine, based largely upon the control of numerous small locals away from the major lumber producing areas, was still in the majority.[58]

During the last hour of the convention, a resolution was brought in which in effect abrogated the organizational agreement between the CIO and the IWA. Orton cut the debate short, called for a vote, declared it adopted amid protests from the floor, and declared the convention adjourned *sine die*.[59] This was followed a few days later by a decision of the IWA Executive Committee ordering the immediate removal of Germer as director of the organizing drive, and instructing Orton, who had been elevated to the presidency immediately after the convention (Pritchett having delayed his resignation until then to avoid new elections), to confer with John L. Lewis "with the view of obtaining a man who will refrain from interfering in the administrative and internal affairs and policies of the International union as well as one more capable of directing the organizing work of the IWA." [60]

In throwing down the gauntlet to the right wing, the communists may have hoped to receive support from John L. Lewis, whose political line they had followed in the 1940 national election campaign. But if this was their purpose, they miscalculated, for with the ascendancy of Philip Murray to the CIO presidency in November, the weight of CIO influence was thrown to the opposition group in the CIO, and was a deciding factor in the ultimate triumph of the latter.

On December 5, 1940, the IWA executive board addressed a letter to Germer, informing him that he no longer had any authority or connection with the IWA. Not only Germer, but the CIO regional officials, came in for bitter criticism:

The duty and responsibility [to build the CIO] has been forgotten or ignored by two regional directors on the West Coast, Richard Francis of Washington and William Dalrymple of Oregon, who, in collaboration with Adolph Germer, have pursued the policy of injecting themselves into the internal affairs of not only the IWA, but of the Int'l. Longshoremen & Warehousemen's Union and other unions. . . .

From almost the beginning of the organizing drive . . . it became apparent that Adolph Germer had interests which he placed far above that of organizing.

In selecting men as organizers, those who were supposedly aligned with certain individuals within the IWA were given preference. Upon hearsay, rumors and whispered slander, men who have contributed much to the IWA were ruled out as organizers by Germer. . . . The counsel and advice of elected officers of the IWA went unsolicited by Germer. The motive of Germer was obvious. It was to make more secure, at the expense of the IWA membership and its elected officers, his own precarious place in the labor movement and, in cooperation with Dalrymple and Francis, to further personal ends.[61]

The answer of the opposition to this personal attack upon the ace organizer of the CIO was to secure a court injunction tying up the funds that had been raised by special assessment, on the ground that the assessment was predicated upon CIO control of the organizing drive. Philip Murray then appointed a committee of three, consisting of Reid Robinson, Sherman Dalrymple, and J. C. Lewis, all prominent CIO officials, to look into the situation. This did little to allay the controversy. In February 1941, the IWA formally terminated its organizing agreement with the CIO. The opposition responded by creating the CIO Woodworkers Organizing Committee, which began to publish its own newspaper, *The Woodworker*, and financed its activities by a 50-cent assessment on the locals, primarily in the Columbia River Districts, which aligned themselves with it. When these funds were exhausted, the national CIO office contributed funds to keep organizational work going.[62] Thus, during the first half of 1941, the IWA was in fact split into two virtually independent parts, one controlled by the Communist Party, and the other, strongly anticommunist, supported by the CIO.

The Triumph of the Right Wing in the IWA

Contract negotiations in all sectors of the industry were initiated in February 1941; those involving the so-called "Twin Districts" of Northern Washington and Grays-Willapa Harbors were destined to achieve national notoriety. Union demands included a 7½-cent per hour wage increase, the elimination of piecework, a union shop, and vacation with pay. These negotiations were being conducted under the auspices of the communist-controlled group in the IWA. Parallel discussions were taking place under the aegis of the Columbia River Council and the Carpenters' locals, complicating the collective bargaining pattern.[63] The AFL, through the good offices of the National Defense Mediation Board, settled for a 7½-cent per hour wage increase, and a maintenance of membership clause. A similar agreement was reached with the Portland mills. However, in the Twin District negotiations, the employers flatly refused to grant the nonwage demands of the union, and limited their wage offer to 5 cents per hour, which would have put the IWA workers on a parity with the AFL locals, based upon September 1940. This offer was immediately rejected by the union, and a strike began on May 9, involving an estimated 22,000 workers.[64]

The manner in which this strike was handled did much to undermine the left-wing leadership of the IWA. It will be recalled that at this time, the Communist Party line favored resistance to defense preparations, and in a number of industries, communist-controlled unions were taking a "tough" line in collective bargaining. An editorial appearing in *The Timberworker* in February 1941, justified at considerable length the Vultee aircraft strike and urged militant action in support of labor demands. A headline in an April issue shouted forth: "Defend the Right to Strike." The events of the Twin District strike can be understood much more readily against this background.

The dispute was certified to the National Defense Mediation Board, which appointed a panel to formulate recommendations for a settlement. The panel proposed a wage increase of 7½ cents per hour for workers in the minimum brackets, with lesser increases for those in the higher paid brackets, a maintenance of membership clause, a modified vacation allowance, and the appointment of a commission to study other aspects of labor conditions in the industry. The employers' negotiating committee accepted this proposal, but it was rejected by the union representatives. The NDMB requested the union to reconsider its decision in the light of national defense exigencies, and Orton was recalled to Washington for further discussions, at the request of Chairman Dykstra and Philip Murray, a board member. Orton refused to budge from his position, and publicly referred to the board as "an all-out labor-busting and strike-breaking device." *The Timber-worker* supported him in the following vein:

Is it patriotic for American workers to submit meekly to coolie terms of labor in order that a handful of profiteers can enrich their already vast personal fortunes? It is a sad commentary on the Roosevelt administration that the newly created National Defense Mediation Board should boldly throw its weight on the side of these greedy profiteers. And it is a national scandal that American troops should be ordered into Inglewood plant to force coolie standards upon American workers.[66]

Philip Murray then stated publicly that despite his personal recommendation, the IWA leaders had refused to accept the board's terms. He accused them of having engaged "in a campaign of misrepresentation, slander, and abuse," and characterized Orton's denunciation of the board as "a most reprehensible, lying defamation." [67] When Orton laid plans to resist, despite the opprobrium which had been heaped upon him by Murray, the pro-communist group within the CIO, apparently alarmed by the rapidly deteriorating situation in the IWA, arranged another conference in Washington between Orton and Murray, which was also attended by Joe Curran and John Brophy, among others. As a result of this meeting and further board negotiations, the strike was called off and bargaining with the employers was resumed. Though no agreement was actually reached until the middle of August, following the appointment of a commission to make recommendations, the invasion of Russia at the end of June produced an immediate about face on the part of the IWA leadership. No longer was there any question of "coolie laborers" being exploited by "warmongering profiteers." Instead,

it becomes increasingly important for the speedy completion of negotiations. The spread of fascism continues to be a threat to trade unions of every land and to the freedom of the common people in all nations. . . . The Office of Production Management calls for increased production in the lumber industry to speed the defense program. Rapid settlement of the Twin District negotiations is a vital step in order that our membership may effectively meet the demands of the national emergency.[68]

The final settlement was not far in its terms from that originally recommended by the NDMB.

Taking advantage of the newly cooperative spirit of the communists, Allan Haywood, CIO director of organization, called a conference of the leaders of the opposing IWA factions to see whether unity could be achieved. A committee of four was established, consisting of Orton and McCarty on one side and Hartung and McSorley on the other. Under the guidance of the CIO, the committee agreed upon a joint proposal for the conduct of the forthcoming convention. The principal recommendation governed the method of convention voting; in place of the old system, each local was to have as many votes as it had members, thus permitting the larger locals to exercise the full power of their membership. It was also agreed that a constitutional amendment would be submitted to the convention providing for a similar method of voting on the executive council, and for an increase in the per capita tax to the international union. Further, it was recommended that money collected by the CIO Woodworkers' Organizing Committee and expended for legitimate union purposes be credited to the locals thus contributing in lieu of their per capita debt.[69]

By these far-reaching concessions, the communist faction virtually renounced control of the IWA. The new method of voting meant that they could no longer control the convention. We can only guess at the motives behind their surrender; they may have felt that the tide was running against them, and simply bowed to the inevitable. The Communist Party, in its new "unity" phase, may have cold-bloodedly sacrificed the IWA in its general retreat on the trade union front. Certainly the strong pressure of the national CIO contributed toward the new attitude of sweetness and light that prevailed at IWA headquarters. No longer was *The Timberworker* truculent in dealing with the conduct of American foreign relations. Instead, "The IWA is confident that President Orton expressed the united sentiments of woodworkers when he wired congratulations following President Roosevelt's Labor Day address. 'Your expression of the necessity for the crushing defeat of Hitler fascism has our wholehearted approval,' the telegram said." [70] And the Neutrality Act, once a bulwark in the struggle to prevent American involvement in the "imperialist war," now became a "direct blow at the seamen who are manning the ships carrying supplies to nations fighting Hitler."

At the 1941 convention, with IWA membership having reached the 51,000 mark,[71] it soon became clear that the opposition had gained the upper hand. An appeal from a ruling by Orton, who was chairman, carried by a vote of 19,983 to 13,385, and from that point on, there was no doubt that a change was imminent. A resolution to submit to a referendum of the membership a constitutional amendment barring communists, nazis, and fascists from IWA membership was divided into three separate resolutions at the suggestion of Michael Widman, who was at the convention with what was obviously a considerable degree of authority from the CIO to settle all disputes. Despite Orton's plea that this proposal was undemocratic, it was adopted on a voice vote, and for the first time the membership of the IWA was given an opportunity to express itself on the issue of communism.

A plan for conducting a new organizing drive under the auspices of the CIO was presented and adopted. The CIO was again to appoint a director, vested with sole authority over organizing personnel. It was provided that the agreement could not be altered or suspended except by consent of the CIO president, in order to prevent a repetition of the Germer incident.[72]

Two slates were nominated for the executive positions, with Orton running for vice-president rather than president. Prior to the referendum, the left-wing group attempted to promote a "unity" slate, in which the right wing would have the presidency and one vice-presidency, while the communist group would retain the other vice-presidency (Orton) and the post of secretary-treasurer. This maneuver was rejected by the right wing, which succeeded in electing all its candidates by majorities of approximately 3 to 2, although the race for the secretary-treasurer was extremely close.[73] Worth Lowery, a well-respected logger, became the new president,[74] and for the first time the IWA was under a nonpolitical leadership. The anticommunist constitutional amendment was adopted by a vote of 2 to 1, thus providing a clear indication of how the rank and file of the union viewed this question.[75] The new administration immediately signed an agreement with the CIO, setting an organizing drive in motion, with Adolph Germer as director, and the circle came to a full close at the end of 1941.

The precise strength of the IWA and the Carpenters in the lumber industry at the end of the period with which we are dealing is difficult to estimate. As we have seen, the IWA claimed about 50,000 members at the time of its 1941 convention. At the end of 1940, the Carpenters claimed that they had 35,000 members in lumber locals working under closed shop agreements, and "several thousand" additional members not working under contract.[76] A study conducted by the Bureau of Labor Statistics in 1944 yielded the conclusion that of the 130,000 workers currently employed in the basic lumber industry of the Far West, four-fifths were working in unionized operations, slightly more than half under IWA contract and the remainder under Carpenter contract. The IWA had the preponderance of the workers in the Douglas Fir region, while the AFL controlled almost all the California pine and redwood regions.[77] These figures lend credence to the rival claims for 1940 and 1941, in view of continued organizing efforts during the war. Unionism remained largely confined to the West, with the important Southern pine area largely untouched by organization.

The Carpenter-IWA struggle, which was waged so violently from 1937 to 1941, quieted down considerably thereafter, and was replaced by a "fairly well-defined system of collective bargaining . . . which encompasses the two competing unions. A more 'mature' form of rivalry has developed in which representational questions are settled through National Labor Relations Board machinery and legal channels rather than on the picket line." It has been claimed by a student of the industry that the "mature" rivalry led to a greater degree of organization and higher wages than would have prevailed in the absence of rival unionism.[78] Whatever the validity of this argument, there can be little doubt that the type of interunion controversy which prevailed up to 1941 was beneficial neither to the public, the unions, nor the industry, but rather marked one of the more destructive periods of industrial relations in the annals of American labor.

Two things stand out in the history of lumber unionism from 1936 to 1941. One was the ability of the Carpenters' Union, after a severe initial defeat, and in face of the strongly flowing CIO tide, to fight its way back into the industry. There are at least three factors behind the ability of the Carpenters to remain in the race. The first, and probably the most important, was the intense distrust with which many lumber workers regarded the blatantly procommunist policies of the IWA. As between craft unionism and communism, the former easily represented the lesser evil, particularly when the Brotherhood softened the blow by installing a modified form of industrial union structure through the regional council device. A second factor was the boycott. "The Brotherhood boycott and the support which the Carpenters received from other AFL unions during the jurisdictional fracas were probably the most effective tactics used in recouping the losses suffered by the Carpenters in the initial switch." [79] A final factor was the generally pro-AFL attitude of the average employer when confronted with the choice between AFL and CIO.

The second notable event of this period was the political situation within the IWA. In almost all the CIO unions in which communists attained dominant positions, it proved impossible to eliminate them except through desertion by the top leadership or by the drastic method of expulsion. In the IWA, however, there was a persistent rank-and-file anticommunist faction which the communists were unable to suppress, despite intense efforts to do so, and which eventually bested them. The IWW tradition among the lumber workers, particularly the loggers, may have had something to do with this; if nothing else, it rendered them less willing to accept the slavish and often ridiculous adherence of the IWA leaders to the twists in the Communist Party line. The lumber workers had been exposed to one brand of radicalism which immunized them, to a certain extent, from another with a widely varying philosophy.

It would be incorrect, however, to lay too great a stress upon this factor. Certainly, without the help of the national CIO, the anticommunists might not have succeeded in capturing the union in 1941. They were also fortunate in having a centralized base in the Columbia River District, which was impregnable to outside attack, and which was one of the most solidly organized areas within the jurisdiction of the IWA.

1 2

The Petroleum Industry

One of the least successful of the major CIO organizing campaigns was that conducted in the petroleum industry. On several occasions between 1936 and 1941, considerable publicity was given to attempts to unionize the oil workers. Each time these efforts came largely to nothing; they petered out against the resistance put up by the industry. By the end of 1941, the major producers were still operating on a nonunion basis, and the union had little more than a foothold among the million or so workers employed in the production, transportation, refining, and marketing of oil.

The union involved in these abortive campaigns was the International Association of Oil Field, Gas Well and Refinery Workers' Union, a name later simplified to the Oil Workers' International Union. This organization had been chartered by the American Federation of Labor in 1918, and in 1921 attained a membership of almost 25,000, mainly in California. Refusal of the oil companies to continue bargaining led to a progressive decline in strength, until a low of 400 members was reached in 1932, in the depths of the depression.[1]

In the oil industry, as in many others, the National Industrial Recovery Act provided an impetus to organization. The Petroleum Labor Policy Board, established under the Petroleum Code, investigated numerous complaints of discrimination against union men and certified the union as collective bargaining representative after elections or payroll checks. "Courageously [it] outlawed many a company union and upheld the right of workers to join the union. Many OWIU locals gained representation through elections held by this board in 1934-35." [2] With the help of this board, and through energetic organizing efforts, the Oil Workers' Union made rapid headway. The 1934 convention, the first since 1926, was attended by 152 delegates from 32 locals. It came on the heels of the most successful coup the union had achieved in all the years of its existence: the negotiation of a national agreement with the Sinclair-Consolidated Oil Corporation, covering about 10,000 men, and providing for the check-off of union dues, vacations with pay, time and one half for overtime, and substantial wage increases.[3] Sinclair was the first of the major integrated producers to recognize the Oil Workers' Union, an action that has been attributed to the favorable attitude of Harry F. Sinclair toward the New Deal.[4]

During the following year, however, the tide of adversity once more set in. Although centers of unionism had been established at Hammond, Indiana, where refineries of Cities Service, Shell Petroleum, Sinclair, and Socony Mobil were unionized; at Houston, Texas; at Long Beach, California, and at several other refining centers, "these were but storm-wracked islands of unionism in a sea of open-shop oil."[5] At the end of 1935, the union's newspaper was suspended for lack of funds, and officers were obliged to work without pay. While the union claimed to represent 42,800 workers, largely in refining and pipe-line operation, actual dues-paying membership had fallen to 16,000.[6] It was at this low ebb of its fortune, virtually bankrupt, and increasingly threatened by the AFL Metal Trades, which were demanding that the Oil Workers' Union turn over the skilled craftsmen among its members to the craft unions with appropriate jurisdiction, that the OWIU cast its lot with the newly formed CIO.

The Industrial Background

The key to failure of the oil organizing campaign lay in the structure of the oil industry. For the year 1939, which may be accepted as roughly representative for the period with which we are concerned, the following estimates of wage-earner employment were made by the American Petroleum Institute:[7]

Drilling and production	155,000
Pipe-line transportation	23,100
Refining	85,840
Wholesale marketing	106,875
Retail marketing	385,500
Total	756,315

While these figures are very rough, they are sufficient for our purposes, to indicate the potentialities of the area over which the Oil Workers' Union claimed jurisdiction. However, these various branches of the industry were by no means equally promising from the standpoint of union organization. The employees engaged in marketing oil products were scattered throughout the country in units of typically small size, and for this as well as other reasons have not proved susceptible to unionization. Indeed, the Oil Workers' Union has never made any serious attempt to invade this segment of the industry; only the Teamsters' Union has made sporadic and largely unsuccessful forays. Pipe-line employment was also distributed widely geographically, and again without any large concentrations of manpower. Production operations were concentrated in oil fields in some 13 states, but here other obstacles appeared. The labor force is divided rather sharply between skilled well drillers and rig builders and unskilled helpers. Many of these men are mobile, moving among fields as drilling operations expand and contract. Moreover, some of them are in the direct employ of specialized drilling contractors rather than the oil companies; it was estimated that from 30,000 to 35,000 of the 155,000 wage earners in drilling and production in 1939 were doing such contract work. The problems involved in organizing the oil field workers were well brought out by a delegate to the 1939 Oil Workers' convention:

We are scattered in a large area. If you don't know what large areas are come down to Texas. In the lower section of that country it is largely populated with mainly foreign labor. It has a very low wage rate. There are field workers all over the area and I might say their base pay is more or less based on the opposition that is offered. I might say that the rig builders have been struggling in that particular area to organize. . . . It is almost impossible to get organization until some organization has taken place in the field workers. The rig builders are getting $1.75 per hour and they are told "Look what we are paying these other men out here." We feel that it is necessary that the conditions which exist among the field workers should be thoroughly studied and some action taken on it.[8]

The branch of the industry which most closely approximated the condition of stable manufacturing employment was refining, and it was in the refining end that the union was most successful. Even here, however, industrial structure was not propitious for organization. As of January 1, 1939, there were some 435 refineries in operation throughout the United States, scattered among 30 odd states, but with some concentration in California, Illinois, Indiana, Kentucky, New Jersey, Ohio, Oklahoma, Pennsylvania, and Texas, particularly in the last named.[9] Some of the larger refineries, such as the Baytown (Texas) plant of the Humble Oil and Refining Co., with 3500 employees, or the Houston (Texas) plant of Shell Oil, with 1200 men, afforded the union a large group of prospective members in a single location, but most of the refineries were smaller and employed only a few hundred men each. The situation faced by the union, for the entire industry, was well summarized by a trade journal:

So far in its drive for mass organization of industrial workers, C.I.O.'s efforts have been directed to the thickly populated centers in which workers live. Only a minor percentage of the industry's employes live under conditions most adaptable to C.I.O.'s organization methods and this alone is relied upon heavily by oil executives to maintain a majority of employe bargaining on a strictly inter-industry [sic] basis.[10]

Location was by no means the only economic factor militating against unionism in the oil industry. Perhaps of equal importance was the combination of a high profit structure in production and refining and relatively low labor costs, enabling the industry to pursue a policy of paternalism aimed directly at thwarting outside unionism. As early as 1918, Standard Oil of New Jersey, the giant of the industry, introduced a company union in its New Jersey refineries, and during the ensuing years, the practice spread. By 1933, in addition to Standard of New Jersey, company union plans had been adopted by Standard of Indiana, the Texas Company, Shell Oil, Standard of California, Phillips Petroleum, Sun Oil, Atlantic Refining, Tidewater Associated, Standard of Ohio, Pure Oil, Sun Oil, and Standard of Ohio, among the major companies.[11] Standard Oil of New Jersey set the pace for the industry in establishing welfare plans for its employees. By 1935, they enjoyed sick benefits, old age annuities, death benefits, a stock subscription plan to which the company contributed, vacations with pay, and termination allowances. Such practices were by no means confined to Standard Oil of New Jersey, but were followed by many other companies as well.

The wage level was also a factor in inhibiting unionism, as the Oil Workers' Union itself pointed out on numerous occasions. In 1940, for example, President Coulter told his associates:

We must take into consideration the fact that the workers of the oil industry are ahead of many other industrial workers as to wages, working conditions and especially hours. . . . Consideration must be given to the state of apathy prevailing among the workers of the oil industry; the facts must be faced that the average oil worker compares his conditions, his wages, his hours with those of workers in other adjacent industries; he reads or hears about workers being out of work or working for much less than what he is receiving; he at once realizes that other groups are fighting for and striking for conditions, wages and hours below what he already is enjoying and he does not, because of this fact, join the Union upon his own initiative. . . .[12]

Average hourly earnings of petroleum refinery workers in 1936 were 82.7 cents, and of workers in crude oil production, 76.8 cents, compared with an average of 55.6 cents for all manufacturing.[13] Seasonal fluctuations were small, making for high annual earnings; thus, in 1935, annual earnings in petroleum refining were estimated at $1416, compared with $1061 for all manufacturing, and $1401 for automobiles, the next highest industry.[14] However, the petroleum workers enjoyed a 36-hour week, which had been established under the NRA code and continued even after the expiration of the code, compared with 40 hours for most other manufacturing industries. Commissioner of Labor Statistics Lubin, after hearing the industry testimony on wages before the TNEC, commented: "I think the conclusion is self evident, that the labor conditions in the industry are very, very good." [15]

One of the consequences of the favorable conditions of labor, both wage and nonwage, was a very stable labor force, particularly in the refining end. For the six-year period 1932 to 1937 inclusive, the average annual quit rate in oil refining was 5.67 per cent of total employees, compared with 10.78 per cent for all manufacturing and 14.40 per cent for automobiles.[16] The larger integrated companies tended to follow seniority in layoff and rehiring, so that long-service employees were virtually guaranteed life time jobs, at a time when unemployment was the chief concern of the American worker.

The labor standards enjoyed by petroleum workers were facilitated economically by a combination of two factors: a low ratio of labor cost to total cost, and rapid increases in labor productivity. A rough estimate put the ratio of wages to the retail price of gasoline at about $2\frac{1}{2}$ per cent.[17] As far as productivity is concerned, it was estimated that between 1929 and 1937, output per manhour increased $26\frac{1}{2}$ per cent in production, 11 per cent in pipe line transportation, and 63 per cent in refineries.[18] An upward bias was imparted to the wage structure of the industry by the increasing skill component, accompanying mechanization of operations. One large company estimated that in its refineries, between 1929 and 1938, the number of skilled workers rose from 27 to 52 per cent of the labor force; semiskilled worker employment decreased from 48 to 36 per cent; and unskilled worker employment decreased from 25 to 12 per cent.

Although there are a great many petroleum companies, a considerable degree of concentration exists, so that the union was facing some very powerful employers. In 1940, for example, the 21 major integrated companies held 75.8 per cent of the crude oil refining capacity of the industry, while the six largest owned 45 per cent of the capacity. In production (1939) the 21 majors were responsible for 52.2 per cent of total crude oil output.[19]

The First CIO Drive

In August 1936, prior to the inception of the first organizing drive under CIO auspices, the Oil Workers' Union had 64 collective agreements, most of them with small independent companies.[20] Among the important agreements were the national contract with Sinclair and those covering eight refineries of Cities Service, five of Shell Oil, six Texas Company plants, and two subsidiaries of Socony Vacuum Oil.[21] The union had not succeeded in establishing bargaining relationships with Standard Oil of New Jersey for any of its operations. Of the 21 largest integrated oil companies, contracts had been secured with only four, and except for Sinclair, in no case did the contracts cover all the refineries of these companies. Production operations were hardly organized at all.

The 1936 convention of the union was a much less enthusiastic and hopeful affair than had been the previous convention in 1934. Dues-paying membership was down to 14,000.[22] There was considerable criticism of the national administration for the decline in union fortunes. The union constitution was revised in the direction of greater "rank-and-file" control: the international executive council was to be composed of seven members, each representing a geographical district, who were barred from accepting a paid position in the International Union. Their function was to check the activities of the International officers, and to report back to newly created district councils. To keep the organization solvent, a constitutional provision was adopted limiting expenditures in any month to 80 per cent of the income in the preceding month. However, Harvey Fremming was reelected to the presidency, while John L. Coulter became vice-president and Emmet C. Conarty secretary-treasurer. There developed at this convention a split between the conservative unionists, including Fremming and the Coulter brothers from California, who had kept the union alive during the lean years of the twenties, and a more radical group, including Conarty and O. A. Knight, who came into the union during the hectic days of the early New Deal. The top leadership of the latter group was not committed to any left-wing political party, though the communist element within the union, which was never in a commanding position, favored it over the right wing.[23] Differences between the two wings of the union centered about trade union rather than political matters. The Hammond local, the largest in the union until 1938, from which Conarty and Knight came, was critical of the high union overhead, the lack of planning, and the absence of any unit at the International Union level with authority to review the actions of the officers, and it was able to win a majority of the convention delegates to its point of view largely because of the failure of the union to make any progress between 1934 and 1936.

Fremming, in his capacity as president of the Oil Workers' Union, was one of the charter members of the Committee for Industrial Organization, and his union suffered the same fate as the other organizations which defied the AFL Executive Council in refusing to desist from alleged "dual" activities. At the beginning of 1937, when the CIO campaign in automobiles and steel was going into high gear, plans were laid for a drive in oil. In January 1937, Fremming addressed a letter to the various associations of oil operators asking universal establishment of the 36-hour week and a $5 per day minimum wage, but elicited no direct response.[24] An indirect reply to the anticipated CIO drive came, however, in the form of a general wage increase of about 6 per cent instituted by the major companies. This wage policy was not new, and was used with good effect upon numerous subsequent occasions. The Oil Workers' newspaper later carried a cartoon in which it epitomized this problem; it showed a Standard Oil personnel manager saying to a company unionist: "Now we want you to go and find out when the Oil Workers' Union is going to propose an increase in wages and we will raise our men before they do." [25]

A formal CIO drive was launched on April 5, under the auspices of a Petroleum Workers' Organizing Committee, consisting of Fremming, Philip Murray, and Charles Howard. The CIO contributed a number of organizers, including Adolph Germer, who later played so important a role in the lumber industry. The focus of the attack was the great refinery of the Humble Oil Co. at Baytown, Texas, a subsidiary of Standard of New Jersey. Just prior to the holding of a mass meeting at nearby Houston, Humble Oil unilaterally announced a wage increase totaling almost $1.5 million annually.[26] The plant management granted Fremming an interview, after which it issued a public statement to the effect that "the company's policy of long standing with respect to collective bargaining is unchanged and that no change is now contemplated."

Shortly after the National Labor Relations Act had been upheld by the U. S. Supreme Court, Humble Oil announced the discontinuance of the company union at the Baytown refinery. Ten days later, however, a new organization, the Employees' Federation of the Humble Oil and Refining Company, was formed. In its newspaper, which began to appear soon afterwards, the rationale of the independent federation was set forth in the following terms:

True, the Humble companies are making money, thank God for that. If they were not we wouldn't receive more pay than the employees of other oil companies operating in this area, we couldn't possibly receive, in addition, 10.7 per cent of our wages in the form of annuities, stock, sickness benefits, vacations, full pay for jury duty, etc. Regardless of fancy words or threats, and promises of a pot of gold, we Humble employees have sense enough to know that the people who furnish the money to start, and still furnish the money to run, the Humble companies have the right to a fair return on their investment. . . . Striking and forcing men to join any organization is un-American and unpatriotic, it smacks loudly of communsm, and we want none of it.[27]

It was reported that 58 per cent of the employees at Baytown had joined the new plan. A private ballot was taken among the employees, in which 2516 were reported as favoring the federation, with only 79 opposed.[28] The movement spread to other Standard companies, with the same pattern of reorganized company unions appearing. The Sohio Council, the company union of Standard Oil of Ohio, adopted dues of 50 cents per month and cut itself loose from dependence upon the company.[29] Although some of these plans were later declared to be company-dominated by the National Labor Relations Board, the board was overruled by the federal courts and the validity of the plans generally sustained. This was true both at Baytown and at the Beaumont, Texas, refinery of Magnolia Petroleum, a subsidiary of Socony Vacuum. The Oil Workers' Union, unable to win sufficient worker support either to call strikes or to utilize the election machinery of the NLRB, was effectively stopped by this transformation of the company unions into independent employee federations.

Why the company unions in the Standard Oil companies were so much more successful in transforming themselves into genuine independent unions than was true of most of the rest of the oil industry, or of industry generally, has never been explored adequately. Certainly, the willingness of Standard management to keep hands off the new independents, plus their wage and personnel policies, which convinced many of their employees that it would be more advantageous to continue on an independent basis, were important factors.

In other areas, particularly where local support could be secured from CIO unions, greater success was attained. An agreement was reached with a Gulf refinery at Toledo, Ohio. The Richfield Oil Corp. agreed to recognize the union as bargaining agent for its members, the first major operating company apart from Sinclair to grant a company wide agreement. Other refineries brought under contract were those of the Skelly Company at El Dorado, Kansas; the Cities Service refinery at Linden, N. J.; the Texas

Company refinery at Lockport, Illinois; and plants of Shell, Associated, Texas Company, Union, and Wilshire at Long Beach, California. This is by no means the entire list, but one thing is notable about it: the absence of refineries of any of the Standard companies among those organized.[30]

While the CIO drive was underway, the American Federation of Labor attempted a counterattack. John Frey, president of the Metal Trades Department, announced that the AFL would enter into one contract with each oil company covering all workers. Each craft union involved was to retain immediate jurisdiction over its members, but over-all administration of the contract would rest with the Metal Trades Department.[31] While there is nothing to indicate that Frey's proposed substitute for industrial unionism proved effective, some of the AFL crafts, notably the Boilermakers and the Operating Engineers, did augment their membership among oil workers.

The 1937 convention of the Oil Workers' Union was held while the organizing drive was still in full swing. Membership had risen to 27,000, double the number at the previous convention, and the union's debt had been cut from $31,000 to $11,000.[32] To answer AFL charges that the Oil Workers' Union was communist-dominated, a constitutional amendment barring communists and fascists from membership was adopted with virtually no discussion.[33] Under pressure of the "rank-and-file" group that had dominated the 1936 convention, the constitution was further amended to require ratification of contracts by the membership before they could be signed by officers, despite the objections of President Fremming that this would handicap the union in collective bargaining.[34] The Hammond group also elected one of its members, Ben Schafer, a vice-president, along with John L. Coulter, indicating its further progress toward control of the union.

Depression and Retrenchment

With the economic recession that began in the last half of 1937, the oil organizing drive came to an abrupt close. The upward trend in union membership leveled off almost immediately after the June 1937 convention, and beginning with December, started to decline.[35] Some 21 organizers who had been contributed by the CIO in connection with the drive were laid off at the end of the year.[36] Companies with which collective bargaining relationships had been established became more difficult. After ten months of fruitless collective bargaining with the Shell Oil Co. for its Houston refinery, a strike was called on November 19, and lasted until December 23, when the company recognized the union as sole bargaining agent and set up seniority and arbitration procedures.[37] On May 13, 1938, a strike was called against the Pure Oil refinery in Toledo; it was the most bitter strike that had been fought in the North up to that time, lasting four months and costing the international union $20,000. At its conclusion, the OWIU won a written agreement.[38] The executive council of the OWIU advised all its locals to renew agreements without change, "due to the unstable economic conditions and the tendencies of industry to reduce wages wherever possible."

Even where agreements had been reached, however, collective bargaining responsibilities were often acknowledged more in the breach than in the observance. At the Houston Shell refinery, for example, 78 discharge complaint cases were filed with the NLRB against the company from 1938 to 1941, a majority of which were won by the union, with the company also required on one occasion to post notices that it would cease discriminating against union men.[39] At Gulf Oil, in Toledo, the union had won a posted set of working rules in lieu of a contract in May 1937. In 1939, the company refused to renew even this limited agreement, and a strike ensued, complicated by AFL intervention. After five months out, Gulf signed its first written agreement with the union. The only bright spot among the larger companies was Sinclair; the large local at Sinclair, Wyoming, for example, has enjoyed friendly relations with the company from 1937 to the present time, and helped make the town a model among oil refining centers.

The 1938 OWIU convention saw a continuation of the internal squabbling that had characterized its predecessors. Fremming was taken sharply to task for having intervened in negotiations for a new Sinclair contract; he had urged the locals not to reopen the existing contract in the light of poor business conditions. Nevertheless, he was reelected, as were the remaining officers.

But the worst was yet to come. On December 22, 1938, a strike was called against the refinery of the Mid-Continent Petroleum Corporation at Tulsa, Oklahoma. Mid-Continent, one of the smaller integrated companies, had signed an agreement with the OWIU in March 1937. However, grievances piled up which the union was not able to get adjusted. The president of Mid-Continent refused to meet with Fremming and other officers of the union, despite intervention of the U. S. Conciliation Service. Finally, when a strike began on the night of December 22, about 150 union men took possession of the turbo-electric plant, and remained in for six hours, when they were finally persuaded to leave. For two days the plant entrance was blockaded, during which time airplanes were used to fly in food and supplies to nonstrikers who had remained in the plant. The National Guard was sent in to maintain order, and the plant resumed full operations.

The company accused the union of planning a sit-down strike and of sabotage, and declared that none of the men who had participated in the seizure of the turbine plant or was guilty of violence would be rehired.[40] The union protested these charges as false:

We shut the property down in a proper manner. We protected it against sabotage. We met at designated places and marched out in a group. . . . There was no intention of a sit-down and if there had been, had we wanted to sit-down there was not anything to have kept us from it because those four or five hundred armed guards and those they wish to call "loyal employees" did not have the guts to come to the turbine plant and come in and take us. . . .

At the refinery gates were hundreds of people, men, women, and children, not members of our organization, certainly some of them were members but the great majority were just common curiosity seekers. The police department of the city of Tulsa . . . had thrown tear gas into that crowd. A number of people were injured. We treated forty-eight in our Union Hall.[41]

Subsequent events served only to embitter relations still further. Several of the company's pipe lines were dynamited, the company accused the union of complicity, and the latter alleged that those episodes were actually attempts to frame the union.[42] One hundred and six strikers were indicted for unlawful assembly. Governor Phillips of Oklahoma told a press conference that "in his opinion, the oil workers' strike is an activity of a minority of the employees, and that he is convinced that the committee that has been acting for the employees is without authority since . . . there had never been an election at the Mid-Continent plant on the question of representation." [43] Both the Tulsa newspapers were hostile to the union, and community opinion was against it as well. "Judges before whom strikers have been brought for attacks on non-strikers have been anything but easy in the matter of bonds." The union offered to submit the entire dispute to arbitration, but the company refused to consider any action that might result in the reinstatement of the employees it held guilty of sabotage.

The CIO resorted to the only weapon that seemed likely to be effective, a boycott of Mid-Continent's products. Thousands of letters were sent out to both CIO and AFL unions, urging them not to purchase D-X gasoline and 760 motor oil, the trade names under which the company marketed its products. The indicted strikers were acquitted in May 1939, but 17 of the leaders were indicted for inciting to riot, a more serious charge on which a jury eventually disagreed. The Tulsa Central Trades and Labor Council, AFL, refused to cooperate with the strikers, which made their position more difficult. To support the strikers, the international union exhausted its entire defense fund; through August 1938 it expended $84,000 for this purpose.[44] Many of the locals contributed directly, and money was also received from other CIO unions. One writer puts the total union expenditure for the Mid-Continent strike at $500,000,[45] but this is probably an exaggeration. Nevertheless, considering the size of the OWIU, the strike was a financial drain that all but threw it into bankruptcy.

The 1939 convention of the Oil Workers was devoted largely to a discussion of the events of the Mid-Continent strike, which by then had lasted more than eight months, and to the formulation of plans for its prosecution. So desperate was the situation of the union, the executive officers revealed, that on August 4, 1939, they had met with John L. Lewis and made two proposals to him: (a) that the CIO take over and direct an organizing campaign; (b) and that the OWIU become a district of the United Mine Workers. Lewis told them that the CIO, currently engaged in a packinghouse campaign, was unable to go into the oil industry, but indicated that he might have some interest in the latter proposition if it were approved by the convention. However, the delegates were not interested in going into the United Mine Workers, and instead authorized the officers to seek a loan from the CIO.[46] Membership as of June 30, 1939, stood at 28,000.[47]

The report of the Executive Council to the convention, even aside from the Mid-Continent strike, was a report of failure. An organizing campaign in the fall of 1938 in the Sabine district of Texas came to a standstill when an election at the Port Arthur plant of the Gulf Refining Company was lost by a narrow margin. Assignment of extra men to the East Texas oil fields failed to yield any results. "In some areas where we have a few Local Unions that are strongly entrenched, we find the anti-union opposition such that company unions are actually trying to invade our well-organized plants for the purpose of destroying our footholds. This is particularly true in the Gulf Coast country." [48] With respect to over-all membership, it was admitted: "In viewing the membership for the past fourteen months' period, we find a slight and almost constant decline. There has [sic] been several spontaneous organizational successes, but these membership increases have not been able to offset the membership that has dropped from the union."

John L. Coulter, one of the veterans of the Oil Workers' Union, was elected president in place of Harvey Fremming, who had been absent on sick leave since the preceding summer. Another union pioneer, R. H. Stickel, became vice-president, together with Harry Staton. The situation of the union during the following year has been described vividly in the following terms:

In the dark and bitter winter of 1939–40, the Mid-Continent strikers held on heroically. Whatever money the International could scrape together was sent in to keep the picket kitchens going. But slowly the life blood of the union was being drained away. There was nothing left for organizing. The locals began to ignore the repeated assessments. . . . Small locals began disintegrating; larger ones showed a steady decline. Not since the 1920's had OWIU faced such a crisis, one in which for the first time some despaired.[49]

The degree of organization achieved by the CIO and the AFL in 1939 was indicated in a special survey of 14 major companies, operating 128 refineries, undertaken at the behest of the Temporary National Economic Committee. This survey revealed that of 66,657 employees in these refineries, some 80 per cent of national refinery employment of wage earners, 9054 in 20 refineries were covered by CIO agreements and 4116 in 7 refineries by AFL agreements, 13.6 per cent and 6.1 per cent, respectively, of the total employment. Since June 1935, the two organizations had secured agreements in only six refineries of the larger companies, representing less than 3000 workers. In addition, the CIO or AFL was recognized as collective bargaining agency, but without contracts, in 10 refineries employing 4023 employees. On the other hand, independent unions represented 34,100 employees in 53 refineries under formal agreement. It was also brought out that from 1936 to 1939 the CIO had raised its percentage of representation in refineries from about 10 per cent to the current 13.6 per cent; that of the AFL had increased by a few percentage points; while the share of independent unions had risen from 20 per cent to 47.8 per cent.[50] Thus, on the basis of this very substantial sample, three years of organizing efforts on the part of the CIO and AFL, in the midst of a general upsurge of union membership throughout the country, had succeeded only in raising the percentage of organization among oil refinery workers from about 15 to 20 per cent. About 80 per cent of the refinery workers, representing the most highly concentrated segment of the petroleum industry, still remained outside the orbit of the two major labor movements.

The only bright spot in the picture, from the viewpoint of the union, was the termination of the Mid-Continent strike in March 1940, after fifteen months. Under the terms of the agreement, the company agreed to reemploy all strikers with seniority rights except for the 247 men who had been discharged for alleged sabotage, if and when jobs became available. The discharged individuals were to have their cases reviewed by management within 60 days, during which time hearings on NLRB charges of unfair labor practices were to be suspended.[51] Since the union had been holding out for reinstatement of all the strikers, the settlement represented, in the words of a union officer, "ignominious defeat." In fact, the union had been offered virtually the same terms a year earlier, and refused them.

The aftermath was as unfortunate as had been the strike itself. Only about 40 of the strikers were reemployed immediately; a year later the number had risen to 200, leaving about 600 men still out of work. At its convention in September, the union resolved to place the company products on the unfair list, and levied a new monthly assessment to support the former strikers who had not secured other employment.[52] The company had signed an agreement with the AFL for its maintenance work, thus further limiting the number of jobs available for CIO members. A member of the executive council told the OWIU in September 1940: "During the past year, we have been engaged in a strike that has drained our financial resources and consumed the energies of most of our organizing staff. Our lesson is not yet learned, nor is it over; yet it has cost us up to the present, $160,000 in round figures and much human suffering and hardships. We hope that our membership will now better understand the importance of more careful planning. . . ."[53]

During the following year, the international union disbursed an additional $44,000 for the relief of the former Mid-Continent strikers, representing almost 25 per cent of its total income.[54] It was not until 1942 that most of the men were able to secure other employment. But even as late as 1950, it was reported that payments were still being made to disabled men and to widows and children of the strikers.[55]

It was not surprising, under the circumstances, that the smoldering dissention within the OWIU should burst into flame. At the 1940 convention, Secretary-Treasurer E. C. Conarty told the delegates: "It is very true that John Coulter [president of the OWIU] and I have not gotten along all year. Not only this year but preceding years and I don't suppose as long as John Coulter and I are in the Oil Workers' International Union, and we continue to think the way we think that we are going to get along. . . ." Coulter replied bitterly that "early in this year, in February, to my great surprise, I found that the Secretary-Treasurer had sent out communications . . . stating that a number of members of this organization had decided that a program must be worked out by which our organization could go forward and possibly we would have to clean the slate of officers, making a statement that a meeting was to be held at a certain place and that this matter was secretive."[56]

The program of the insurgent group was essentially an extension of the notion of "workers' control" which had dominated the 1936 convention.

There was a strong feeling that if only the leadership had been more responsive to the rank and file, if only there had been a greater opportunity for the voice of the individual member to be heard, failure would have been turned into success. In actual fact, it was most unlikely that any leadership, or any complex of constitutional provisions, could have achieved better results, given the economic circumstances of the industry from 1936 to 1940. Fremming, Coulter, and Stickel were experienced unionists, veterans of the era when trade unions were a marginal group on the American industrial scene. They were much like the redoubtable group of men whom Lewis and Hillman sent out of the Mine Workers' Union and the Amalgamated Clothing Workers to organize the basic industries of the country.

It was soon apparent that the insurgents controlled the 1940 convention by a margin of about two to one. Their program was carried into effect; it included election of officers and executive council members by referendum rather than by convention; exclusion of officers from membership on the executive council; shift of the power to remove other officers and fill vacancies from the president to the Executive Council; and appointment of international representatives by the two vice-presidents rather than by the president. Coulter, seeing the handwriting on the wall, declined to run for reelection, and he was replaced in the presidency by O. A. Knight, who had come originally from the Hammond local, and served since 1936 as an international representative. Sam Beers and A. R. Kinstley were elected vice-presidents, giving the union a new set of officers, except for the secretary-treasurer. Coulter was voted a pension by the convention in recognition of his services. However, he joined forces with the Operating Engineers' Union against the OWIU in an election contest at the Port Arthur Refinery of the Texas Company early in 1942, apparently embittered by his ouster.

The Organizing Drive of 1941

Membership in the Oil Workers' Union in March 1940 had fallen to 19,873.[57] The secretary-treasurer remarked when he was presenting his report: "I am just as ashamed of the figures in that report as you are. After twenty-two years of organization work we have to print in the officers' report that we have some twenty thousand members." [58] The first task of the new leadership was to rouse the union from the lethargy into which it had fallen.

Fortunately, the economic climate was propitious for a new organizing endeavor. The demand for petroleum was rising, though embargoes on shipments to some foreign countries tempered the improvement in domestic business. The first important break came in February 1941, when the Shell

Oil Co., under threat of a strike, granted a 5-cent wage increase to the employees of its Pasadena, Texas refinery.[59] This wage pattern spread throughout the industry; it was the first general upward adjustment since early in 1937. In September, after a 60-hour strike, the East Chicago refinery of Cities Service granted a wage increase of 10 cents per hour, followed shortly by the Socony-Vacuum and Sinclair plants in the area. The union pointed out somewhat proudly: "This is the first time that wage rates in the organized refineries has exceeded the Standard Oil Company rates." For the first time in several years, the membership trend turned up. Between September 1949 and June 1941, the union claimed a membership increase of 6520, certainly not spectacular, but in the right direction. Between the 1940 and 1941 conventions, 20 new local unions were chartered.

The September 1941 convention was the occasion for launching a more concentrated organizing drive on the pattern of the old CIO campaigns, which it was hoped would finally overcome the still unsurmounted barrier of employer opposition. The problem, and the plans, were well summarized by President Knight in his report to the convention:

It is increasingly evident that our union cannot attain a proper degree of effectiveness in the oil industry until the employees of the Standard Companies have been organized. We are, therefore, attempting to work out with the National Office of the C.I.O. a program whereby the C.I.O. will assume the task of Standard organization. We have made a survey of Standard properties and of the organizational possibilities. We have made definite recommendations as to the number of men needed and the places for concentration. We have suggested to the C.I.O. that it would be wise to start organization of Standard properties in refineries first, picking five concentrated areas, including the New Jersey area of Bayway and Bayonne; Whiting, Indiana; San Francisco or Richmond, California; El Segundo, California; and the Texas Gulf Coast. We have pointed out to the National Office of the C.I.O. that the Standard Companies constitute the one great 'open-shopper' still operating without proper labor relationship and without proper contracts.

The convention voted to levy an assessment of 50 cents a month per member to help finance the drive. To clear the decks, the Mid-Continent strike was declared officially terminated, although, as noted above, relief payments continued for some years thereafter.

The issue of communism came in for discussion at the 1941 convention. Shortly after the 1940 convention, the *Chester Wright Washington Newsletter,* which was devoted largely to labor news, stated that the outcome of that convention meant that the Communist Party had gained control of the Oil Workers' Union. Knight charged that the letter had been prompted by someone close to the union, who had been present at the convention.[60] He stated to the convention:

I feel certain that every delegate and every member of this organization is determined that people who are in the organization and delegates to this convention shall be the type of people who are acting to foster this union, and the delegates who come from any outside group, whether it be Fascist, Communist, Nazi, or whatever they might call them, they are not welcome and I personally deny any allegation that any member of this Union is working on behalf of subversive influences.[61]

The union decided not to sue for libel on advice of counsel that the resultant publicity might be unfavorable. It may be noted in passing that between 1936 and 1941, there is no evidence in the union newspaper, the resolutions adopted at conventions, or elsewhere, of any communist influence in the Oil Workers' Union. This does not mean, of course, that, despite the constitutional provision barring communists, there were no communists in the organization. But when the record of the Oil Workers is compared with that of some of the communist-dominated unions, such as the United Electrical Workers' Union or the National Maritime Union, it is quite clear that no parallel existed.

In November, with considerable fanfare, an organizing drive was announced. Appointed to lead it was Edwin S. Smith, a former member of the National Labor Relations Board. The CIO contributed the services of Smith and four organizers, while the OWIU put in an estimated $10,000 a month.[62] The AFL Operating Engineers counterattacked by enlisting within its rank former President Coulter; a former vice-president, Robert L. Bruce; Ralph Farmer, secretary of District Council 3; and several other Texas officials of the OWIU.[63] However, the Engineers were badly defeated at an NLRB election at the Port Arthur, Texas, refinery of the Texas Company; the OWIU received 1351 votes, the AFL union, 67; and neither union, 781.[64] This was the most important refinery victory the OWIU had won up to that time. Other elections were won at the Southport and Pan-American refineries at Texas City, the latter a subsidiary of Standard Oil of Indiana. Continental Oil signed a statewide agreement for California. During the war, membership continued to grow, and by 1944 the union claimed 50,000 members. It was not until after the war, however, that the OWIU was able to offer a successful challenge to some of the Standard companies.

From 1936 to 1941, wages in the petroleum industry rose somewhat more slowly than in industry generally. In refining, average hourly earnings increased from 82.7 cents per hour in 1936 to $1.034, 25 per cent; in crude oil production, from 76.8 cents to 93.4 cents, 22 per cent. By way of contrast, wages in all manufacturing increased by 31 per cent during the same period from 55.6 cents to 72.9 cents; in durable goods manufacturing, by 38 per cent, from 58.6 cents to 80.8 cents.[65] Some would read into the relative lag of petroleum wages the absence of a vigorous independent trade union operating in the industry; others would point to the high level of petroleum wages already prevailing at the beginning of the period, or to the failure of the petroleum industry to share equally with other manufacturing, and particularly durable goods manufacturing, in the boom occasioned by the initial stages of the United States defense program. The Oil Workers' Union would argue that while it did not achieve any substantial results through collective bargaining until 1941, its very existence, by posing the threat of unionization, forced the major oil companies to maintain wage levels higher than those which would have prevailed had the organization been disbanded. While these are controversial matters for which no easy answer is forthcoming, there can be no dispute over the statement that from 1936 to 1941 the oil industry employers successfully stopped the CIO from making any significant inroads into their domain, one of the few major industries in the country to achieve this feat.

13

The Maritime Industry[1]

The American maritime industry, which is taken to include all activities directly connected with shipping, does not bulk large as a contributor either to employment or to national income. Gross receipts from shipping constitute less than one-half of 1 per cent of national income.[2] In 1938, the number of workers engaged as seamen, deepsea fishermen, and longshoremen was estimated roughly at 300,000. Of these, 140,000 were unlicensed seamen, with most of the remainder engaged in stevedoring work.[3]

Maritime workers are sharply divided into two groups, those who work aboard ship (offshore personnel), and those who work on shore. The shipboard workers fall into two main groups, licensed and unlicensed personnel. Among the former are officers, engineers, and others who possess special skill and training. Both the seamen and the longshoremen are also classified, on the basis of their home port or place of work, into workers on inland waterways, the Atlantic Coast, the Pacific Coast, the Gulf Coast, and the Great Lakes. All these subdivisions are of great significance for trade union structure.

If industrial size were the sole selection criterion, it might not be necessary to include the maritime industry in a general labor history. But as every student of the labor movement knows, some of the most notable events in the history of American trade unionism centered about the efforts of seamen and longshoremen to organize. The seamen and longshoremen have occupied a special niche in the labor movement of every country. Both have been problem groups, generally radical in their political orientation, prone to take direct action rather than to engage in collective bargaining. Each of the groups is able, by withholding its labor, to inflict considerable damage upon the economy, so that maritime labor disputes have attracted considerable public attention.

The history of maritime unionism naturally divides itself into four distinct parts: East and West Coast longshore work, and East and West Coast offshore work. Within each, the offshore sector in particular, there are further subdivisions based upon craft, but the four divisions enumerated constitute the main stream of the story. However, it is impossible to discuss each of these separately. On the Pacific Coast, seafaring and longshore unionism were intimately related for a time, while the rivalry between the East and West Coast seamen's unions is one of the focal points of their history. Only the East Coast longshoremen, controlled by a corrupt union, remained isolated from the events that accompanied the rise of maritime unionism commencing in 1933.

The Revival of Maritime Unionism

Throughout the nineteen-twenties, organization among maritime workers was at a low ebb. Membership in the AFL International Seamen's Union fell from 115,000 at the height of the post-World War I boom to 15,000 by 1926, and dipped even further to 5000 as a result of the Great Depression.[4] The longshoremen were no better off. On the Pacific Coast, independent unionism ceased to exist after 1921, and management possessed sole discretionary power to fix all conditions of labor.[5] In the East, the International Longshoremen's Association (ILA) managed to maintain some semblance of organization, but only at the expense of virtually abdicating the collective bargaining function, and concentrating instead on providing lucrative jobs for a few union officials.[6]

The enactment of Section 7a of the National Industrial Recovery Act revived maritime union activity. Although no NRA code was ever adopted for the shipping industry, the union fever that was in the air stimulated the West Coast longshoremen to repudiate employer-dominated unions and organize under the banner of the ILA. Latent grievances now became explicit: the speed-up, heavy loads, frequent accidents, split shifts without standby pay, excessive working hours, the casual nature of employment. Harry Bridges described these conditions in the following terms:

Men have dropped dead from exhaustion. Stevedores are paid by the hour. Every minute is checked on him. Every minute counts. From the time you go to work in the morning until evening you are driven like a slave. If you try to get yourself insured every company will refuse you. Physical strain is too much. Life is too uncertain. You have no chance of living as long as people of other walks of life. Speed-up production — the loads that we have to sling out of the ships make it too dangerous. And all these evils center around one thing — fear of losing your job.[7]

The union's principal demand was for control of the hiring hall, which it was felt would be the first step toward elimination of employer pressures and domination. To quote Bridges once more:

We have been hired off the streets like a bunch of sheep standing there from six o'clock in the morning, in all kinds of weather; at the moment of eight o'clock, herded along the street by the police to allow the commuters to go across the street from the Ferry Building, more or less like a slave market in some of the Old World countries of Europe.[8]

When the employers refused the union demands, a strike was called for March 23, 1934. It was delayed at the request of President Roosevelt, but when a mediation board appointed by him failed to work out a settlement, the strike commenced. Within a few days, 12,000 longshoremen all along the West Coast had left their jobs. The seamen began to quit their jobs in sympathy, and forced the International Seamen's Union, in turn, to declare a strike. Violence occurred in both Los Angeles and San Francisco when the employers attempted to use strikebreakers.

Joseph P. Ryan, president of the ILA, came to San Francisco and worked out a compromise agreement, but the rank and file rejected it, and the leadership of the strike passed entirely into the hands of the executive board of the San Francisco ILA local, which refused to countenance anything less than a union-controlled hiring hall. It was during this strike that Harry R. Bridges, a member of the local strike committee, came to the fore as the undisputed leader of the longshoremen.

After negotiations had completely broken down, President Roosevelt, on June 26, appointed a National Longshoremen's Board to mediate once more. The employers, however, remained adamant in their opposition to the union hiring hall, and on July 3 began a new attempt to break the strike. Violence once more flared up, and two longshoremen were killed in clashes with the police. The Battle of Rincon Hill, as this fracas was termed by the longshoremen, was followed by a funeral parade through the streets of San Francisco, which raised labor sentiment to a fever pitch. Even the conservative San Francisco Labor Council could not resist the emotional appeal of these events, and on July 16, a general strike of all union labor in the San Francisco Bay area began, probably the most extensive strike in American history.[9]

The general strike lasted for three days, and persuaded the employers of the futility of following the tactic of violent resistance. They agreed to arbitrate all issues in dispute, including the union hiring hall, and the strike ended on July 31. The National Longshoremen's Board was designated as the arbitration agency, and on October 12, 1934, it handed down a decision which represented a substantial victory for the union. In particular, a jointly operated employer-union hiring hall was to be established in each port, but the dispatcher was to be selected by the union, which in effect gave it control of job assignment. With the acceptance of this decision by the employers, the union was firmly and permanently established.

As part of the strike settlement, it was agreed that the demands of the seamen for union recognition and other conditions also be submitted to arbitration. Although the National Longshoremen's Board conducted a representation ballot among the seamen, the shipowners agreed in December 1936, to recognize the ISU without awaiting the results. After negotiation and further arbitration, the shipowner-controlled hiring hall was abolished, and employers were given a choice between hiring through a union hall or directly from the dock. The latter alternative was soon nullified by "job actions," or wildcat strikes, against shipowners who refused to hire through the union hall. As in the case of the longshoremen, unionism came into being swiftly and successfully among the Pacific Coast seamen.[10] For the next several years, job actions became the accepted method of doing business in offshore labor relations. Between 1934 and 1936 there were some 470 incidents of this character, arising out of differences in interpreting the 1934 award, or out of union attempts to improve on the award.[11]

The success of the joint seamen-longshoremen action in 1934 led the two groups, in 1935, to form the Maritime Federation of the Pacific. In addition to the ILA and the Sailors' Union of the Pacific (SUP), which was the West Coast affiliate of the ISU, the Federation included the Marine Cooks and Stewards and the Marine Firemen, Oilers, Watertenders and Wipers, also affiliated with the ISU; the Marine Engineers' Beneficial Association; the Masters, Mates and Pilots; and the American Radio Telegraphists' Association. All the original member organizations were affiliated with the AFL. While the constituent unions retained their autonomy, the constitution of the Maritime Federation called for joint action in collective bargaining and strikes.[12]

The first president of the Maritime Federation of the Pacific was Harry Lundeberg, who was destined to play a major role in maritime unionism. Lundeberg had sailed out of Seattle for 12 years prior to the 1934 strike, and he was strongly influenced by the remnants of the IWW philosophy that persisted in the Pacific Northwest. This meant that he favored industrial unionism and direct strike action, and was generally opposed to political activity. In 1934 he emerged as the rank-and-file leader of the seamen, which

soon brought him into conflict with the officers of the ISU. Paul Scharren-
berg, the long time lieutenant of Andrew Furuseth, the famous leader of
the ISU, had been entrusted with control over the SUP, but he was no
match for Lundeberg, and was expelled from the SUP in 1935. In retaliation,
the ISU revoked the charter of the SUP in January 1936, putting the latter
out of the AFL. Furuseth, from his death bed, wrote a pathetic letter to the
1936 ISU convention, its final one, in which he said in part:

It is with deep sorrow but under absolute conviction of necessity that I urge you
all to vote unanimously for the expulsion, and that I urge upon all the loyal
members with whom I have lived and toiled for some fifty years for the improvement of the seamen's conditions on shore, on the ships, and in legal status under
the law, to immediately affiliate with the union to be chartered.[13]

The other strong personality in the Maritime Federation was the Aus-
tralian-born Harry Bridges, who was strongly influenced by the philosophy
of the Communist Party and was to follow the communist line undeviat-
ingly for a quarter of a century. It was not long before trouble began to
brew within the Federation. Bridges favored centralization of authority in
the Federation, which he hoped to control, and elimination of the job action
as a tactic, while Lundeberg was strong for individual union autonomy.[14]
Bridges urged the SUP to remain within the ISU in 1936, which would
have meant submitting to ISU control, unpalatable to Lundeberg. Nor
would Bridges support Lundeberg's desire to merge the organizations of
marine cooks and marine firemen with his own, for fear of further an-
tagonizing the ISU and the AFL.[15]

Temporary harmony was reestablished in 1936, under renewed pressure
from the employers. The 1934-1935 awards for both seamen and longshoremen were due to expire in the fall of 1936, and it was widely reported that
the shipping companies were preparing for a showdown in order to secure
the ouster of Bridges and Lundeberg. The principal issue, again, was the
control of hiring. The employers demanded neutral administration of hiring
halls, and an increase in the number of registered men, to eliminate the
overtime payment that had become common on the docks with the introduction of a six-hour straight time day in 1934. The seagoing crafts, for
their part, sought outright union hiring halls to replace the formally biparti-
san administration provided by the 1934-1935 agreements.[16]

The United States Maritime Commission intervened in the dispute, and
sought to delay the calling of a strike. A division between Lundeberg and
Bridges on the proper tactical response to the request of the Maritime Commission was resolved by a referendum among the workers, which resulted

in overwhelming approval of a strike. Faced with this result, the waterfront employers conceded virtually all the demands of the longshoremen, but refused to grant a union hiring hall to the seamen. Efforts to split the two groups were in vain, however, and on October 30, 1936, a complete maritime stoppage began on the Pacific Coast.[17]

The tactics of the employers this time were to attempt to starve the unions out rather than to operate the docks and ships with strike-breakers. They also sought to weaken the already wavering unity of the two major groups involved. They entered into separate negotiations with Lundeberg, and on December 18 a tentative agreement was reached meeting all of the seamen's demands. Bridges accused the SUP of sabotaging the strike, by negotiating separately, but Lundeberg promised that the seamen would not return to work until the other maritime crafts had won their demands. The strike dragged on for 97 days; not only were 40,000 maritime workers idle, but many logging operations and sawmills were shut down, and the entire economy of the West Coast was slowly being strangled.

Agreement with the longshoremen was finally reached on February 4, 1937, and the strike ended. Sailors, cooks, and firemen won a union-controlled hiring hall, from which employers were to secure all men. The mates, engineers, and radio operators had to settle for mere union recognition. The longshoremen retained all their 1934-won hiring control, and in addition, made progress toward coastwise uniformity in working conditions when the employers agreed to a joint commission to establish maximum sling loads and uniform penalty rates.[18]

The practices of the union hiring hall, the source of so much controversy, have been well described as follows:

The fundamental policy is equal treatment of all union members with equal qualifications with strict adherence to the principle of "first come, first job." Members are prohibited from hiring through channels other than the union, and are dispatched to jobs for which they are qualified (the general rule is that a man must not sail below his rate) in the sequence in which they registered their availability. With the exception of rush orders for replacements, a member may retain his rank on the shipping list by appearing at the hall only at certain hours during the day when jobs are "called." A member may retain his position on the shipping list while working at certain stand-by shore jobs and some relief or short voyages.[19]

The importance of the hiring hall to the union was that it provided a form of union security almost the equivalent of a closed shop. With the signature of the 1937 agreement, and the full acceptance by employers of collective bargaining, a new era in Pacific Coast labor relations began, not peaceful and untroubled, but one in which mutuality of authority finally replaced the *ancien régime,* based as it had been upon employer authoritarianism.

Formation of the National Maritime Union

Throughout these years of turbulence on the West Coast, things had not been standing still in the East. In 1930, the Communist Party had organized the Marine Workers' Industrial Union as part of an ambitious attempt to set up a full-fledged federation paralleling the AFL. The moribund status of the ISU, and the deterioration of wage standards during the depression, provided the MWIU with an opportunity to extend its influence somewhat. By 1934, it claimed a membership of 12,000, but it was unable to capitalize on the NRA enthusiasm to become a true mass organization.[20]

The ISU approached shipping employers in 1934 with the warning that rejection of its overtures might lead to stronger demands by more radical organizations. Under pressure from the MWIU, the ISU called a strike on the Atlantic and Gulf coasts for October 8, 1934, but the strike was called off when 28 companies operating 450 ships agreed to recognize the ISU. The MWIU protested this recognition, and called a strike of its own on October 8, but it proved to be a failure, and was soon called off. Collective bargaining between the ISU and the shipowners resulted in agreement with 41 companies on December 21, 1934, with 20 additional companies signing up in the following months.[21]

At about this time, the international communist line changed from "dual unionism" to "boring from within," and the MWIU offered to merge with the ISU on the condition that all its members would be accepted into the new organization with full rights. The ISU, of course, rejected this offer, and the MWIU "decided to dissolve and carry through the merger from below in spite of the ISU officialdom." [22] By these tactics, the communists were able to place within the ISU a nucleus of skilled organizers who came to exercise a dominant influence upon the East Coast seamen.

The 1934 agreement negotiated by the ISU was less favorable in many respects than the terms secured by the West Coast seamen in April 1935. The base rate of $57.50 a month for able seamen and firemen was $5 less than the West Coast rate; there was no provision for overtime pay; and while ISU members received preference in hiring, men could still be secured through company employment offices and the much disliked shipping masters (crimps), who had long been the bane of the seaman's existence.

The entrance of the MWIU cohorts into the ISU led to the almost immediate establishment of an "ISU Rank and File Committee," with its own publication and program. The ISU leaders attempted to suppress this challenge to its authority by resorting to packed election meetings and expulsion of dissidents. The opposition group, capitalizing upon the dissatisfaction of the East Coast seamen with terms of employment less favorable than those prevailing on the West Coast, raised the banner of revolt in 1936 when the ISU officials indicated their willingness to accept a renewal of the 1934 agreement without change. Port meetings all along the coast forced submission of the issue of contract renewal to a referendum, the result of which showed opposition to this step by a three to one margin. The ISU then asked the employers for a $5 increase in the interest of industrial stability.[23]

At this juncture, an incident occurred which was to have profound repercussions on the history of East Coast unionism. On March 2, 1936, while the intercoastal liner *California* was tied up in the West Coast harbor of San Pedro, a group of sailors under the leadership of Joseph Curran, a member of the crew, refused to sail unless they were guaranteed the West Coast rates. The tieup was ended by the personal intervention of Secretary of Labor Perkins, who assured the strike committee by telephone that she would see to it that their point of view was placed before the ISU negotiating committee, and that she would use her best offices to ensure that there would be no discrimination against the strikers. While the *California* was on its return journey, the ISU signed an agreement with fourteen companies, providing for a $5 per month increase, but without a union hiring hall or any provision for overtime. To make matters worse, Secretary of Commerce Roper requested the Justice Department to take action against the *California* strikers for mutiny, and the ISU leaders denounced the strike as a violation of contract. When the ship arrived in New York, twenty-five members of the crew were logged six days' pay apiece, discharged, and given unfavorable character ratings, which meant blacklisting from future employment. However, the charges of mutiny were never formally raised.

A rank-and-file strike committee, under Curran's leadership, prevented the *California* from sailing on its next scheduled voyage, and moved to extend the strike to other ships. The strike was denounced by the ISU leaders, who expelled Curran and eighteen others on the grounds of communist influence. It was called off after nine weeks, when the ISU agreed to help prevent discrimination in employment against the strikers, to implement the grievance procedure provided by contract, and to intercede with district unions for the restoration to membership of expelled strikers. The opposition then resorted to legal action against the ISU leaders. David Grange, president of the Cooks and Stewards affiliate of the ISU, who had amended his union's constitution to give him completely dictatorial powers, was brought into court and asked to account for $144,000 in union funds that had disappeared between January 1, 1935 and June 1, 1936. An election dispute within the Marine Firemen enabled a rank-and-file slate to oust the incumbent secretary, Oscar Carlson, with the help of the courts.[24]

A Seamen's Defense Committee, under the chairmanship of Joseph Curran, continued to represent the opposition among the major group, the seamen. After visiting the West Coast in October 1936, where preparations for a strike were going on, Curran called a rump meeting in New York which empowered the Defense Committee to call a strike in sympathy with the West Coast. The ISU attempted to restrict the strike, but the initiative passed from its hands, and a strike was declared effective November 6, with the seamen encouraged to sit down to prevent the use of strikebreakers. The Defense Committee was supported by the Masters, Mates and Pilots, the Marine Engineers, and the Radio Telegraphists, all of whom voted to go out in support of their West Coast locals.

The shipowners, with the active support of the ISU, tried to break the strike. Joseph P. Ryan, president of the East Coast longshoremen's union (ILA), announced that he would not furnish labor to any company which dealt with the insurgents. In retaliation, a coastwise meeting arranged by the Defense Committee in December voted to expel the ISU leaders, and elected trustees to administer the affairs of the union until elections could be held. But the Defense Committee was forced to call the strike off on January 24, 1937; it later reported that "out of 30,000 members that registered in the beginning of the strike, we wound up on January 24th with less than 3,000 men left up and down the entire Coast. Presumably, the rest of the guys finked out." [25]

The shipowners attempted to consolidate their victory by bolstering up the ISU leadership through wage and overtime concessions, and by blacklisting strike activists, with the cooperation of the ISU. However, the rank-and-file committee still had considerable support among the seamen, and the existence of a *de facto* dual center boded ill for the stability of the old union. The Executive Council of the AFL, alarmed by the possibility of CIO intervention, received a delegation representing the insurgents at its February 1937, meeting, and endeavored to bring the two factions together, but to no avail. The Council ordered President William Green to supervise an election for officers in the sailors' union, thus recognizing the charges of undemocratic practices levied by the rank and file.[26]

But events were moving too swiftly for the slow internal processes of the AFL. The rank-and-file group turned to the National Labor Relations Board, and charged that the shipping employers, by dealing with the ISU, were depriving the workers of their freedom to bargain collectively. A sitdown strike was called on the *President Roosevelt* in April 1937 to protest the refusal by the International Mercantile Marine Company, one of the leading shipping companies, to recognize the rank-and-file leadership. Similar job actions enabled the insurgents to gain limited recognition from a number of companies. The die was cast on May 5, 1937, when the rebels announced the formation of a new union, the National Maritime Union.

The ISU, faced with a growing tendency on the part of ship owners to accord recognition to the NMU, petitioned the NLRB for representation elections, an act born of desperation which turned out to be its final tactical blunder. After some months of balloting, the NMU had carried 52 shipping lines with 18,947 votes, compared with six lines and 3015 votes for the ISU.[27] In August 1937, Joseph P. Ryan appeared before the AFL Executive Council; though on the extreme right wing of the labor movement, he argued that the leadership of the ISU was bankrupt, and would have to be replaced if the AFL were to remain a factor in East Coast shipping. The Executive Council issued a statement announcing the resignation of all ISU officials, and designated a new executive committee consisting of Ryan, William Green, and an AFL representative to be named by Green, to undertake an organizing campaign.[28]

The demise of the ISU marked one of the few instances in recent history in which an established AFL union was driven out of business by a rebellious group. With the death of Andrew Furuseth, the ISU had lost all capacity for leadership. Run as a sinecure for incompetent and corrupt officials, it proved no match for the energetic and enthusiastic young rank and filers, backed by experienced communist functionaries. The seamen flocked into the NMU, which by the time of its constitutional convention in July 1937, claimed 35,000 members.[29]

The NMU, at its inception, was divided into divisions representing the deck, engine, and stewards' departments, and into three autonomous districts — the Atlantic, Gulf, and Great Lakes. The National Council, consisting of the national officers and the district officers, was authorized to act only on matters of national import. The constitutional convention voted to recommend acceptance of a CIO charter, giving the union jurisdiction over all seagoing personnel except licensed officers and radio operators, a recommendation which was confirmed overwhelmingly by a referendum vote.

Even as early as the constitutional convention, an issue was raised which was to plague the NMU for the next decade, that of communist domination. A delegate arose to complain: "I just came in this morning, and as I look around here, I see quite a few of the Party men seated here — quite a bloc of them here this morning. . . . Boys, let's get new blood and throw out these men of the Party." [30] But he had little support, and the convention went on record in condemnation of his remarks.

The Breakup of the Maritime Federation of the Pacific

The strike of 1936–1937 was the last unified action of the West Coast maritime unions. Discord soon developed between the longshoremen and the seamen, and centered initially in a dispute over the editorial policies of the *Voice of the Federation,* the official organ of the Maritime Federation. Harry Bridges accused Barney Mayes, who had come to the editorship after having run the *Northwest Organizer* for the Dunne brothers in Minneapolis,[31] of attempting to destroy the unity of the federation. Mayes retorted that the attacks on him were made in retaliation for his resistance to Communist Party efforts to control the *Voice,* but he was removed. He was succeeded for a brief period by Jim O'Neill, who in turn yielded to Ralph Chaplin, whose apprenticeship had been served in the IWW.[32] Chaplin lasted exactly two months, and in his final issue, took this parting shot at the Bridges group:

The blow has fallen at last. Following a process of slow and deliberate strangulation, the stooges of the Communist Party have the *Voice* right where they want it — on the rocks. . . . With this issue of the *Voice,* the present editor steps out. He refuses to serve as scapegoat for the cunning plot hatched by the local Moscow wrecking crew.[33]

Thereafter, the *Voice* was controlled by Bridges. But while this was symptomatic of the growing fissure within the federation, it was by no means the cause. The rise of the National Maritime Union, and the political affinity between Curran, head of the NMU, and Bridges, posed a threat to the SUP, which was considerably smaller than its East Coast counterpart. The SUP, moreover, was without any federation affiliation after its expulsion from the AFL in 1936, whereas the NMU was backed by the militant CIO.

Early in 1937, Lundeberg had discussed with John L. Lewis the possibility of getting a CIO charter for the SUP. A referendum among SUP members on the question of affiliation with the CIO was undertaken in June 1937, but the ballots were never counted. Instead, the SUP manifested increasing hostility to the prospect of alliance with the CIO.[34]

The 1937 convention of the Maritime Federation of the Pacific, a marathon affair which lasted five weeks, was marked by continuous bickering between the forces of the SUP and the supporters of the Longshoremen. The principal issue about which debate centered was affiliation with the CIO. John Brophy was present as CIO representative, and was subjected to a barrage of unfriendly questions from the Sailors. The convention then went on record "as recommending that each organization affiliated with the Maritime Federation take a referendum ballot of their membership on the matter of affiliating with the C.I.O. as soon as possible according to the rules of each organization. . . ."[35]

But on the specific issue of the form of affiliation, wide differences of opinion were manifested. The Longshoremen advocated an immediate unity conference of all maritime crafts, including the East Coast seamen, under the auspices of the CIO, but the SUP insisted that such a step should await a referendum among the East Coast seamen on the selection of a union to represent them. It was evident that Lundeberg had a profound antipathy to Curran and the newly formed NMU. When the charge was made by Bridges that the SUP was infringing upon the jurisdiction of the NMU, he said: ". . . we would like to know what the I.L.A. has got to say about whose jurisdiction the ships should come under. They would get along a lot better on this Coast if they would mind their own business and not start jurisdictional squabbles." To another charge, he replied: "As for the Sailors Union Pacific [sic] maintaining a hiring hall in New York that is our business. We will open up a hiring hall in Hell if we want to and nobody is going to tell us what we can and can't do in that respect."

While the convention was still in session, the CIO called a meeting of the maritime unions in Washington, which was attended, among others, by Bridges and Curran. A five-point program was adopted, calling for the following action:

1. The ILA to become a national union affiliated with the CIO.
2. A conference of all unlicensed seafaring unions to be held for the purpose of forming a CIO national industrial maritime union.
3. All licensed crafts to join the CIO or units.
4. Fishermen to receive a national CIO charter.
5. Upon appropriate action by all unions, a CIO maritime federation to be formed.

The SUP observer at the meeting wired Lundeberg: "I got blasted for stating SUP position which they branded as stalling tactics which might be expected from us. Bridges accepted the program without qualifications as did Curran for NMU. . . . My personal reaction is that our jurisdictional problems are still an important issue which they have to consider. . . ." The SUP lost no time in attacking the program, and succeeded in having a motion adopted to the effect that since the affiliates of the Maritime Federation were autonomous bodies which had not yet polled their membership on the CIO, the Federation could not endorse the program. On this inconclusive note the convention ended, the last one to be truly representative of the West Coast maritime industry.

So far as Bridges was concerned, the die was cast. On August 11, 1937, his ILA district became the International Longshoremen's and Warehousemen's Union (ILWU), affiliated with the CIO. He had some initial difficulty in securing bargaining recognition from employers, and was obliged to resort to the NLRB to substantiate his claim of membership majorities. A year later, in June 1938, the NLRB ruled that the entire Pacific Coast, with the exception of three small Puget Sound ports which the ILA managed to have excepted, constituted a single unit appropriate for collective bargaining, and certified the ILWU as the bargaining agent.[36]

The CIO plan for holding a national conference of the unlicensed seamen in order to bring the SUP and NMU together never materialized. Lundeberg did not relish the prospect of joining forces with a numerically larger organization to form a new union in which he was sure to be outvoted. Moreover, several incidents occurred which brought him into direct conflict with Bridges, who had been named West Coast director for the CIO.[37] One of these involved the Shepard Line, an intercoastal steamship company, which had been organized by the SUP in 1935, but switched to East Coast crews during the 1936–1937 maritime strike. Although the SUP signed a closed shop contract with Shepard in 1937, the NMU won certification on the line through an NLRB election, and provided men for Shepard ships. When the Sea Thrush, a Shepard ship, anchored at Portland in April 1938, the SUP began to picket it. When the ship moved on to San Francisco, it was picketed once more, but this time CIO longshoremen went through the sailors' lines.[38] The SUP charged that Bridges was using the Maritime Federation to force the SUP into the CIO.

Another source of controversy was jurisdictional disputes directly between the SUP and the ILWU. These involved loading and unloading of coastwise steam schooners and ship-scaling work. The longshoremen claimed that the sailors were doing both of these types of work below the longshore wage scale, and had even crashed picket lines to enforce their right to the work.[39] These disputes persisted for a number of years; in 1940, Lundeberg suffered a fractured jaw leading his men through a picket line of ILWU ship scalers.[40]

The dispute came to a head at the June 1938 convention of the Maritime Federation of the Pacific, when the SUP issued an ultimatum that it would withdraw unless the Tacoma longshoremen, who had remained loyal to the old ILA, were admitted to the convention. The ILWU was adamant in refusing to cooperate in any way with the ILA. Bridges delivered a free-swinging attack on that organization, saying, *inter alia:*

If any of the guys here went back there and seen the conditions, and the way they sweat and graft on the East Coast longshoremen, the poor devils, the various nationalities that can hardly speak English, and make four or five bucks a week and thirty or forty cents grafted off of them to pay people like this here. You see men working there ten times worse than we ever worked here, and five per cent of their pay paid to racketeers alone. They all take out their cuts, the gangster takes his, the saloon keeper and the clothing store and the red light birds and everything, they all take it off the poor guys. These people [from Tacoma] get their cut and they are here today on that money. . . . They hold a meeting of 19 men out of a local of two thousand and vote sixteen thousand bucks to you people to carry on your activity. . . .[41]

The SUP delegates thereupon withdrew, taking with them some delegates from the Firemen, the Masters, Mates and Pilots, and the Marine Engineers, and the Maritime Federation became an undisputed province of Harry Bridges. Shortly thereafter, the SUP formally withdrew from the Federation, and voted to affiliate with the AFL.

The AFL, after the demise of the ISU, had put its small remaining membership among the East and Gulf port seamen under the jurisdiction of a federal local. This local held ten contracts under NLRB certification, inferior in terms to those on the Pacific Coast. Under an agreement worked out between William Green and Lundeberg, the old ISU charter was to be revoked and a new one issued to the SUP. The SUP, in turn, was to issue a district charter to the Atlantic and Gulf Coast groups. After an initial organization period, the Atlantic and Gulf Coast district, and a Great Lakes district to be established, were to be accorded local autonomy in the direction of their affairs. The agreement was effectuated when the 1938 convention of the AFL formally revoked the charter of the ISU and issued a new one in the name of the Seafarers' International Union.[42]

That there was a very poor base from which to build an East Coast AFL seamen's union is evident from a letter written by Lundeberg to the AFL Executive Council early in 1939, in which he stated that the former federal local officials had greatly exaggerated their strength. "Shipowners have also taken a hostile attitude towards the new International, almost from the start they have bucked us and still are. . . . No doubt they must have had a 'comfortable agreement' with former ISU and AFL-SU officials, because they never raised such objections in the past when dealing with these organizations." [43]

The beginning of 1939 found the major maritime unions set in a more or less permanent mold, after five hectic years. The East Coast seamen and West Coast longshoremen, under Curran and Bridges, respectively, were firmly in the CIO camp. The West Coast seamen and the East Coast longshoremen, under Lundeberg and Ryan, were affiliated with the AFL. This cross-pattern of organization was hardly conducive to industrial peace and orderly collective bargaining, as the events of subsequent years were amply to demonstrate.

The smaller maritime unions, caught in the crossfire, went various ways. The Marine Cooks and Stewards, once a department of the ISU, became a satellite of the Bridges group, and received a CIO charter in 1938. The Pacific Marine Firemen preferred to remain independent. Bridges tried to get both these groups to affiliate with the NMU. He warned them:

If the Firemen, the Cooks and others, cannot see their way clear and cannot see the advantage or the immediate necessity of getting lined up on a national basis with the N.M.U., it is just going to be too bad as far as I can see, and as far as the I.L.W.U. is concerned. If they want to be sentimental and maintain their small organizations, they are going to pay for it the hard way in the long run. . . . As far as the I.L.W.U. is concerned, we are going to look ahead and protect ourselves in every way possible because it is necessary. . . .[44]

But his efforts were to no avail. Both unions persisted in their desire to maintain separate organizations. The radio operators formed the American Communications Association in 1937, and followed Bridges into the CIO. Of the licensed crafts, the Masters, Mates and Pilots, which had been in the AFL for many years, retained their affiliation, while the Marine Engineers' Beneficial Association, after a long period of independence, joined the CIO in 1937.[45]

The NMU and East Coast Collective Bargaining

The formation of the NMU coincided with the end of the temporary economic boom of 1936–1937, and for the next few years the young union was on the defensive. Fortunately, the AFL was completely demoralized in the East, and the shipowners had little alternative but to deal with the NMU. They reorganized their existing loose association, the American Steamship Owners' Association, into the American Merchant Marine Institute, and after almost a year of negotiation, reached an agreement with the NMU covering East Coast dry cargo vessels, on October 31, 1938. The union secured the equivalent of a union hall, and wage and hour provisions comparable to those prevailing on the West Coast.[46]

It was less successful in negotiating with tanker operators, the other large factor in the merchant fleet. In January 1938, an agreement had been negotiated with this group, covering 17,000 men employed on 300 ships. It did not contain provision for a union hiring hall, and when the agreement expired in 1939, the rank-and-file bargaining committee decided to push for the hiring hall, despite warnings from Curran that this demand was premature. The union was forced into a strike, which it lost when the companies were able to man the ships, and it had to call the strike off without securing an agreement.[47]

Weakened externally, the NMU faced another challenge from within. An opposition group, organized into the informal Mariners' Club, and with its own newspaper, charged the union with being communist-dominated. In the 1938 referendum for officers, the opposition won a majority of the national offices, but failed to capitalize on this advantage because of inexperience. Jerome King, who had won the post of national secretary, "was suspicious and uncommunicative. Moreover, he was either unable or unwilling to get assistance from those acquainted with Communist tactics." The King forces charged that Ferdinand C. Smith, a national vice-president and one of the leaders of the communist group, had remained at work during a strike in 1934, but the charges were dismissed. The Curran forces then took the offensive, and in May 1939, preferred charges of disruption, seeking to put the union in the AFL, and collaboration with shipowners, against King and several of his followers. The King group was expelled despite protestations that their only offense had been opposition to communist control of the NMU.[48]

This took place shortly before the 1939 convention of the union, at which the only challenge to administration control came from a group of Gulf district delegates. A pro-administration slate from the Gulf was seated at the convention, and the Gulf opposition was eliminated by the expulsion of its leaders.

There can be no doubt that at this point, the Communist Party achieved full domination over the NMU. Joe Curran, the president of the union, followed the party line assiduously, though he has denied ever being an actual member.[49] Among the other national officers were Hedley Stone, Frederick (Blackie) Myers, who was termed by William Z. Foster "one of the finest elements of our party," and Ferdinand Smith, all of them members of the Communist Party.[50] Other leaders, such as Howard McKenzie, were close to the party if not actually members. Communist control continued until 1946, when Curran broke with the party and in a bitter fight that lasted for two years, managed to rid the NMU of all communist officials. After the events of 1946–1948, Curran became one of the top leaders of the CIO, and was seriously considered for the CIO presidency after the death of Philip Murray.

The 1939 convention undertook a drastic reorganization of the NMU structure in the interests of centralization of authority. The geographical and craft divisions, a heritage from the ISU, were abolished. The organization was to consist only of branches, or locals, at major ports; the National Council, composed of national officers and the port agents; and the national office. The National Council was given broad authority in collective bargaining involving more than one ship or more than one branch, which meant authority over all significant wage movements.[51] Thus streamlined, the NMU turned to the task of reestablishing itself, faced now with opposition from an AFL union revitalized by a transfusion of SUP blood from the West Coast.

The dry cargo operators, mindful of the success of the tanker operators in forestalling the union hiring hall, demanded that they be permitted to hire nonunion men who would then be required to join the union. Negotiations continued from September 30, 1939 to January 1940, when a two-year agreement was reached, essentially renewing the previous agreement. The union regarded this as a victory, with some justification in view of its current fortunes.[52]

Reestablishment of control over the tanker fleet was a more difficult matter. Three of the larger operators, Standard Oil of New Jersey, Socony Vacuum, and Tidewater had established independent unions to replace the NMU. The latter filed charges of company domination with the NLRB, but the independent unions were held to be genuinely free of employer control. The NMU then concentrated on securing the reemployment of ex-strikers, in preparation for NLRB representation elections, which were held on May 6, 1940. The NMU was decisively defeated on the Tidewater lines, but the results were inconclusive on Standard Oil and Socony Vacuum. Run-off elections resulted in victories for the independent unions on these lines as well. However, the NMU succeeded in gaining representation rights for the maritime employees of Continental Oil, Texas Oil, and Pure Oil, in April 1941.[53]

The Atlantic and Gulf District of the SIU held its first organizational meeting in August 1939, and launched a membership campaign shortly thereafter. By the end of 1940, membership of 6000 was claimed for this district.[54] However, the SIU remained largely a West Coast union, though its presence on the East Coast posed a constant threat to the NMU and forced the latter into somewhat more aggressive action than it might otherwise have taken.

West Coast Developments

After the coastwide strike of 1936–1937, the longshoremen on the Pacific Coast were not involved in a major strike until 1946. In 1938, for the first time, an agreement was negotiated without a prior work stoppage, continuing the previous agreement unchanged except for the creation of impartial arbitration machinery. The following year, the union demanded higher wages, but the employers refused to make any concessions unless the ILWU would agree to take effective measures against the frequent job actions which characterized this period.[55] Negotiations lasted for fifteen months, and were finally consummated in November 1940, with the intermediation of the Maritime Labor Board. The new agreement committed the union to stop job actions, and conditioned wage increases upon increased productivity. In February 1941, an efficiency wage increase was granted, but in August 1941, the employers refused any increase on the ground that there had been no demonstration of increased efficiency. The case was taken to the impartial umpire, Wayne L. Morse, who awarded an increase on the ground that a productivity study made by the employers was deficient in some respects.[56]

In Pacific offshore employment, too, labor relations were much more peaceful after the 1936–1937 strike. There again, sporadic job actions continued to be the major source of friction; there were 144 between February 1937 and June 1939, arising out of grievances.[57] All agreements were renewed between 1937 and 1939 without change, since the unions were not prepared to act aggressively because of the poor economic conditions that prevailed. The contracts were extended indefinitely in 1939, but with a sixty-day reopening clause, in order that modifications could be made in the light of developments occasioned by the European war.

Relations between the seamen and the longshoremen continued to deteriorate. Lundeberg, who came to power with a syndicalist ideology, abandoned this philosophy for a tough-minded business unionism once his organization had obtained job security. But he reserved a special measure of dislike for his old collaborator, Bridges, and in 1941 testified at the latter's deportation hearing that he knew Bridges to be a Communist Party member. The trial examiner relied heavily on Lundeberg's testimony in finding Bridges subject to deportation, but the Supreme Court eventually overruled the decision.[58]

Whatever the truth was with respect to the Communist Party status of Bridges, there is no doubt whatsoever that the ILWU was under the complete domination of this organization. Prior to 1939, the union stood for collective security against nazism, an embargo on shipments for Japan, and the shipment of arms to Europe. With the signing of the Russo-German pact of 1939, isolationism became the order of the day. For example, in 1940 the Maritime Federation of the Pacific, which was by this time an instrument of ILWU policy, adopted a resolution on neutrality which read in part:

Whereas: It becomes increasingly clear that the war in Europe is not a war for the advancement of democracy in any part of the world, but a war whose sole purpose is the further enrichment of the few who would gain new and profitable economic positions from such a war. . . .

Resolved: That this 6th Annual Convention of the Maritime Federation of the Pacific calls upon the American people to fight each and every action, large and small, subtle and significant, which ignores our stated policy of absolute neutrality in the present conflict, whether by selling munitions to one side or the other, or attempting to drum up public sympathy for either side; and that the organizations represented at this conference continue to cooperate on issues of common interests tending to spread the message to all the world that *The Yanks Are Not Coming*.[59]

Immediately after the German attack upon the Soviet Union, the ILWU became militantly prowar, and even urged a declaration of war against Germany prior to Pearl Harbor.[60] Nor was this the only evidence of communist domination. A CIO committee which investigated the ILWU in 1949 reported that "the policies of the International Longshoremen's and Warehousemen's Union are consistently directed toward the achievement of the program and the purposes of the Communist Party rather than the objectives and policies set forth in the CIO Constitution." [61] The ILWU was among the unions expelled from the CIO on the issue of communist domination.

After the withdrawal of the SUP, the Maritime Federation of the Pacific maintained only a nominal existence, with no real function. In 1941, the ILWU proposed that it be abolished. Harry Bridges stated frankly:

The Maritime Federation as such, up to some time ago, was an organization that fitted the occasion and was something of great value to us. The value of that organization has gone; we have only the name and the structure left now.

The federation ceased to exist in 1941, and whatever coordinating functions it performed were taken over by the CIO Maritime Committee. This body, established in 1938, had failed of its purpose in creating nationwide industrial unions of maritime workers, and confined its efforts largely to furthering legislation of interest to the maritime unions.[62]

The Impact of War

The outbreak of war in Europe affected the American maritime industry more drastically than almost any other industry in the country. American ships, although forbidden by the Neutrality Act of 1939 from entering combat zones, were able to take over trade routes vacated by the belligerent nations. Many American ships were transferred to foreign flags at very profitable rates. Under these circumstances, the attitude of shipowners toward their employees underwent a marked change.

To the seamen, this situation carried mixed blessings. Job opportunities for seamen fell, though the burden of the impact fell on the East Coast rather than the Pacific.[63] Efforts to induce the government to prevent the transfer of ships to foreign registry failed. It was not until the United States entered the war that job opportunities increased.

In May 1940, the SUP secured a war emergency increase of $7.50 a month for deepwater runs and $10 for intercoastal runs, raising the basic monthly wage of the ablebodied seamen to $82.50.[64] The NMU immediately demanded, and won, similar increases, although it was operating under a contract which still had several months to run. The increasing severity of interunion rivalry made it dangerous for either union to lag behind, and with the deepening of the war emergency, and the diminishing resistance of the now affluent shipowners, the race sharpened.

In January 1941, the NMU took the initiative and secured a further increase of $7.50 a month. According to the union: "This marked the first time the NMU had assumed indisputable leadership in securing higher wages on both coasts."[65] This was matched almost immediately by the Pacific coast operators. In November, an additional $10 a month was added simultaneously on both coasts, raising the basic rate to $100 a month, a figure which remained unchanged for the duration of the war.

These changes in the basic rate were overshadowed by the introduction of a war risk bonus. Immediately upon the outbreak of war in Europe, the

NMU demanded a war risk bonus for ships entering combat zones. After a few sit-down strikes, the U. S. Maritime Commission granted a 25 per cent bonus for its own ships, but the union was soon able to secure more favorable terms from private operators, including insurance against death and injury. The war risk bonus was extended to the Pacific Coast in 1940, with the spread of hostilities.[66]

Pressure for an increased bonus mounted during 1941, with the heightened war risk. Each union sought to outdo the other, and demands were frequently backed by work stoppages. In August 1941, the Maritime Commission sought to tie war risk bonuses to the cost of ship insurance, and thus bring about national stability, but it was unable to secure agreement except for licensed personnel. On September 13, 1941, the East Coast SIU, anxious to make a showing of militancy, struck twenty-five ships scheduled to leave for war zones, at a time when strikes were virtually proscribed. The Maritime Commission threatened to seize the struck ships, but was defied by the SIU president:

As the first week of the strike ended and we were bombarded with threatening telegrams from Admiral Land of the Commission, I wired him our ultimatum. I told him that the Commission had forfeited all respect of maritime labor and that henceforth the Atlantic and Gulf District of the SIU would sit at no conference table with the shipowners when the Commission was represented.[67]

The National Defense Mediation Board intervened, and after twelve days, the strike was called off. The board settled the dispute on the basis of an increase in the bonus from $60 to $80 for African and Far Eastern runs, and a bonus of $100 for the port of Suez, a particularly hazardous run.[68] The SIU noted with satisfaction that although it had not won all its demands, "[no] one can deny us the honor of a militant and solid strike action, of permanently shelving the Maritime Commission, and of obtaining again direct negotiations with the shipowners. . . . It was, by every standard, an honorable and successful strike and it gave us pride and assurance in our strength." [69] The SIU, clearly, was doing its best to live down the reputation of its ancestry.

The National Maritime Union, when it assembled in convention in July 1941, also had reason for satisfaction. In 1939, the union had been obliged to borrow $25,000 in order to hold a convention; now, it had a cash balance of $35,000. President Curran reported that ablebodied seamen were currently earning 60 per cent more than in 1935, plus overtime pay, which had not been paid in 1935, and exclusive of war risk bonuses. There were still a few militant anticommunists within the ranks,[70] but they had no influence, and the threat of a split which had hung over the 1939 convention was completely dissipated. The convention went a step further in the direction of centralizing authority by empowering the National Council to transfer local officers from one port to another, without consulting the local port membership concerned. In effect, all local officials were henceforth to be agents of the national, rather than the local union.[71]

A word is in order about the East Coast longshoremen, of whom very little has been said in foregoing pages. The fact of the matter is that in the midst of all the tumult and the shouting on both coasts, the formation and reformation of unions, they remained incredibly quiescent within the old ILA, an organization which was eventually to be expelled from the AFL because of corrupt influence. It was revealed later that Joseph P. Ryan, the ILA president, began collecting secret contributions from longshore employers in 1935 "for a confidential fund to be used to fight Communism on the waterfront," all the proceeds of which went into Ryan's personal bank account.

The period of the mid-1930's was the one in which underworld elements, unemployed by the repeal of the Prohibition amendment, invaded the waterfront. By a process of action and interaction, a substantial number of ex-convicts secured jobs on the docks, and these men, often grateful for an opportunity to hold jobs, however intermittent and ill paid, remained loyal to their gang bosses, many of whom in turn had criminal records. The following incident, too, may help explain why the ILA hold was unbroken:

In 1937, six Brooklyn locals controlled by Albert Anastasia were amalgamated without an election. Pete Panto, a young longshoreman, led the opposition to Anastasia's seizure and by 1939 had rallied more than a thousand supporters of his demands for regular meetings and elections when he suddenly disappeared from the waterfront. A year later, his body was found in a lime pit. District Attorney William O'Dwyer, in the course of the murder investigation, arrested several ILA officials and interrogated hundreds of longshoremen. He reported that gunmen had taken over the six locals, looted their treasuries of hundreds of thousands of dollars, and destroyed the books. Panto's murder was never solved, nor were convictions obtained for other crimes described by O'Dwyer.[72]

It was not until after the war that increasing restiveness among the rank-and-file longshoremen, in part a rebellion against the "shapeup," a method of hiring which gave rise to the worst forms of favoritism and exploitation of workers, focused attention upon the waterfront, and led to remedial government action. The contrast between East and West, between racketeer control and communist control of the longshore industry, has often been commented upon, but there is still no fully adequate explanation, economic, sociological, or other, of why longshore unionism should tend toward polar extremes.

Government Regulation of Maritime Labor

There is no American industry in which government has played a more important role, both in a regulatory and an entrepreneurial capacity, than in shipping. The relation of the industry to national defense, coupled with the inability of American shipowners to compete on a purely commercial basis with the other major maritime nations, dictated a policy of government assistance, first through a mail subsidy, then through construction aid and operating subsidies on essential routes. Government operation of the merchant marine during World War I, through the United States Shipping Board, introduced detailed federal intervention into every aspect of the industry's operation, including labor relations, which was never wholly relinquished. When the Shipping Board was replaced by the United States Maritime Commission by the Merchant Marine Act of 1936, the authority of the federal government in maritime labor relations was, if anything, heightened. The maritime unions were forced, in consequence, to devote a considerable part of their energies to legislative matters. Indeed, the major contribution of the ISU, under the leadership of Andrew Furuseth, was in the legislative area.

One of the principal legislative issues during the period under consideration was that of the government discharge book. The unions had succeeded in eliminating employer-issued continuous discharge books, in which the entry of character ratings at the conclusion of a voyage provided each subsequent employer with a seaman's complete employment record, and permitted victimization of militant individuals. These were replaced by individual discharge certificates issued at the conclusion of each voyage.

The Seamen's Act of 1936 provided for the issuance of government continuous discharge books. "The book was to include such personal information as the seaman's description, photograph, age, address, nationality, and signature. Upon a seaman's discharge, the shipping commissioners were to enter in his book such notation as the name and type of vessel he had just sailed on, the nature and length of voyage, and the kind of job he had filled." [73] There was no place for any reference to the seaman's ability or character.

The new leadership of the maritime unions seized upon the issue of the "Copeland fink books," as the government discharge books were called, after the author of the Maritime Act, as a means of demonstrating their militancy. Harry Lundeberg in particular denounced the government books as merely a veiled reinstitution of the hated employer-issued books, that would enable shipowners once more to blacklist active union men by revealing breaks in service during maritime strikes. Lundeberg advocated outright refusal to accept the government books in violation of law, but the issue was laid to rest in March 1937, when Congress amended the law to give seamen the option of individual discharge certificates in place of the continuous discharge book.

The controversy soon gave way to another in the realm of hiring practices. In 1938, when Admiral Emory S. Land became chairman of the Maritime Commission, the commission directed that crews for forty government owned, privately-operated ships be secured exclusively through government hiring halls, to the exclusion of the union hall. The theory on which the commission made this rule was that the seamen thus employed were government employees, and not entitled to collective bargaining rights, in the face of a contrary ruling by the National Labor Relations Board.[74] The government "fink hall" immediately replaced the "Copeland fink book" as an object of union attack. The National Maritime Union first directed its members to boycott the government hiring bureaus, but then relented for fear that AFL and nonunion workers would monopolize the jobs concerned.[75] The SUP first became involved in 1939, when the Pacific Northwest Oriental Line, with which it held a contract, was designated by the Maritime Commission as a government contractor to operate its ships. After futile efforts to negotiate a settlement, four ships were tied up by picketing, leading the commission to cancel its contract with the Oriental Line. The SUP remained defiant, even in the face of this action. Its newspaper declared:

All right. The Sailors' Union of the Pacific will take the blame. Six thousand members . . . say we are right. Five Maritime Commissioners say we are wrong — and are attempting to inflict on 6,000 American seamen their idea of what they think is right. Who in hell do they think they are to attempt to put chains around us again . . . we do not believe the American taxpayers want to see the American seamen forced to register at crimp joints and go back to the old system of sea slavery just in order to get a job . . . we sail the ships — and we, and nobody else, will tell us how and where we will sell our labor.[76]

Under pressure from Seattle business interests, the Maritime Commission renewed the contract and reached an agreement wherby its contractors could hire through the union halls, a significant victory for the unions, and particularly the SUP.

The turbulence of maritime labor relations in 1936 and 1937 led to congressional demand for federal regulation, and in 1937, bills were introduced into both the Senate and the House for the purpose of extending railway industrial disputes legislation to shipping. Charges of communist infiltration into the merchant marine, coupled with a well-publicized refusal of seamen to refuse to handle cargo on a government-owned ship unloading at Montevideo, Uruguay, in sympathy with striking longshoremen, provided support for the proponents of legislation. The unions vigorously opposed the legislation, and were supported by Secretary of Labor Perkins, who urged that legislation be deferred until the maritime unions had a chance to settle down.[77]

A law enacted on June 23, 1938, created a Maritime Labor Board, with authority limited to mediation of labor disputes. The board began to function in September 1938. Between that date and June 30, 1941, it was involved as mediator in 118 disputes, as adviser in 40, and as observer in 37.[78] The Sailors' Union of the Pacific refused to deal with the board at all, relying instead on the U. S. Conciliation Service. The NMU was more friendly, and in particular, praised a report issued by the board in 1940 which reviewed existing legislation and made recommendations for changes. Curran declared: "It [the report] proved to have been long needed. Its recommendations were, generally speaking, progressive. With one exception, its main proposals included things for which the NMU had been fighting ever since it was organized." [79] Limited to three years by the initial legislation, the board's life was extended for a year in 1941, but the following year it was allowed to expire, "unsung and unwept." [80] It has been remarked that "the vast majority of American seamen were unaffected by the existence of the Maritime Labor Board, primarily because of the increasingly stable labor relations which characterized the period of the board's existence." [81] Its major contribution was the 1940 report, a lengthy historical study of maritime labor relations.[82]

Attempts to extend unemployment compensation and workmen's compensation to seamen failed of enactment because of the failure of unions and employers to agree upon specific measures. With respect to the latter, the seamen already enjoyed favorable opportunities for bringing tort actions in the federal courts under the Jones Act of 1920, and were reluctant to trade this type of benefit for the far less generous pattern of workmen's compensation. The seamen were accorded old age benefits under the Social Security Act in 1939.

Relations between the unions and the U. S. Maritime Commission were strained in yet another area: the training of seamen. In 1938, the commission established the United States Maritime Service to train personnel in government schools. The unions regarded this program as superfluous at a time when considerable unemployment prevailed among seamen, despite the fact that in the initial stages of the program, the Service restricted enrollment to experienced men. The SUP, true to form, refused to cooperate in any fashion, a policy it was to continue even during the war, when it established its own training school.[83] The NMU first endorsed the program, then rejected it when it was given no voice in the selection of personnel and the determination of curriculum.[84] However, the NMU cooperated with the government in training seamen during the war.

What emerges from this brief review of federal legislation and legislative efforts is, on the one hand, the numerous ways in which federal activities affected maritime labor, and on the other, the failure of the federal government to establish any successful particularistic system of maritime labor relations to govern the industry. Failure stemmed partly from the fact, as Goldberg has pointed out, that while the general labor agencies of the government, the Department of Labor and the National Labor Relations Board, were seeking to stabilize industrial relations through the furtherance of collective bargaining, "the agencies primarily concerned with the technical aspects of shipping operations, such as the Maritime Commission and the Department of Commerce, frequently showed impatience at the pangs attending the birth of collective bargaining . . . although the activities of the maritime agencies were generally restricted to the periphery of maritime labor relations, they frequently stimulated serious reactions on the part of the unions." [85]

The unions were by no means powerless in the legislative arena. They staved off restrictive legislation in 1937 and 1938, despite public clamor against alleged lack of discipline on American ships, and maintained in Washington an effective lobby with respect to the numerous bills affecting shipping which were considered by the Congress.[86] This effectiveness stemmed in large measure from a sense of guilt which the American people felt toward the men who manned the nation's merchant ships, a guilt induced by the miserable conditions of labor, the poor wages, and the unstable employment which had long characterized the maritime trades. When the seamen, and the longshoremen as well, were finally able to channel their resentment in a purposive fashion, the vigor of this expression was accepted as a natural reaction of men engaged in rough and hazardous work.

Membership, Employment, and Wages

In 1936, membership in the West Coast maritime unions, based upon per capita tax payments to the Maritime Federation of the Pacific, was as follows:[87]

International Longshoremen's Association (later the ILWU)	12,999
Sailors' Union of the Pacific	6,800
Masters, Mates and Pilots	1,217
Marine Firemen	5,000
Marine Cooks and Stewards	4,000
Marine Engineers' Beneficial Association	2,161

At the end of 1941, the SUP reported 5496 members in good standing.[88] Whether this represented an actual decline from 1936 is difficult to determine in the absence of more information about the validity of the 1936 per capita report. It is likely, rather, that 1941 SUP membership was higher than that of 1936, if anything, in view of the facts: (a) that the West Coast seamen were almost completely organized in 1936, and (b) that total offshore employment increased somewhat between 1936 and 1941.[89] The same generalization probably holds true for the remaining seagoing crafts.

The ILWU claimed a dues-paying membership of 11,192 in September 1937, shortly after its transformation from a district of the ILA into an independent CIO union.[90] By 1939 the membership total had risen to 21,000, the ranks having been swollen by the acquisition of warehousemen in the famous "march inland." [91] No figure was released in 1941, but since, on the one hand, the number of registered longshoremen declined slightly between 1939 and 1941,[92] and on the other, the "march inland" was halted by the Teamsters, it is unlikely that 1941 membership exceeded the 1939 level. A thousand or so members should be added to these totals for Hawaii, although serious organizational efforts were not made in Hawaii by the ILWU until 1944.[93]

The National Maritime Union claimed 35,000 members at its 1937 convention, and 51,300 in December 1938, of whom 12,800 were unemployed or not working for some other reason, leaving 38,500 working members.[94] No membership data were reported to the 1941 convention, though in 1943 it was stated that "our records show that at the [1941] convention the financial report proved that for the fifteen months prior to the convention only 1500 new members joined the union." [95] Whether this represented gross or net accretion was not made clear; if the former, 1941 membership would undoubtedly have been below that for 1939, in view of membership turnover. To the NMU data should be added 12,000 Atlantic and Gulf Coast members of the SIU, claimed for 1941.[96]

The International Longshoremen's Association increased its AFL per capita tax based from 40,000 members in 1936 to 66,300 in 1939, and then suffered a reduction to 61,500 in 1941 as a result in the decline of overseas shipping.

According to the 1940 Census of Population, there were 73,612 longshoremen and 45,017 sailors either employed or seeking work in the United States.[97] These figures may be compared with membership claims of roughly 87,000 by the two longshore unions and 57,000 by the two seafaring unions *circa* 1940. Even allowing for the fact that the ILWU had enrolled several thousand warehousemen, and that included in the NMU membership figure were stewards and enginemen, in addition to seamen, the union claims were impossibly high compared with the census data. On the other hand, a 1938 estimate of maritime employment had yielded a figure of 300,000 (including fishermen),[98] and it may be that the Population Census concept was unduly restrictive. One thing may be said with certainty, however: between 1934 and 1941, the maritime workers organized themselves for the first time into powerful trade unions, and were able to corner the labor market through the device of the union hiring hall. By 1941, there was scarcely an unorganized man working at sea or on the docks. This transformation of status within a brief span of years, after decades of vain and often violent effort, was little short of revolutionary. In few other American industries was the transition so abrupt and so thoroughgoing.

Wages. It appears from Table 9 that in terms of percentage wage increases, the seamen did relatively well during the period 1935 to 1941. The longshoremen, on the other hand, lagged behind workers generally.

These data are subject to numerous qualifications, however. In the first place, the seamen started from a very low base. The monthly base rate of an ablebodied seaman on the East Coast was $55 in 1935,[99] whereas a railroad worker, on the basis of average hourly earnings of $0.643, would have earned over $100 a month. The seamen also experienced less employment stability than the railroad worker, or than the manufacturing employee. Thus, the rapid increase in the index of seamen's wages from 1935 to 1941 marked a catching up process on the part of a traditionally low paid group of workers, and not a spurt ahead in any absolute sense.

Table 9.

Indices of wage rates of maritime workers, 1935 to 1941, compared with straight-time hourly earnings of railroad workers and average hourly earnings of manufacturing employees
(1935 = 100)

Year	Pacific Coast seamen	Atlantic Coast seamen	Pacific Coast longshoremen	Atlantic Coast longshoremen	Class I Railroad employees	Manufacturing employees
1935	100.0	100.0	100.0	100.0	100.0	100.0
1936	100.0	109.0	100.0	105.3	100.8	101.1
1937	116.0	116.4	100.0	110.5	103.6	113.5
1938	116.0	134.5	100.0	110.5	109.3	114.0
1939	116.0	136.4	100.0	110.5	109.5	115.1
1940	132.0	152.7	100.0	115.8	109.8	120.0
1941	160.0	166.4	105.3	126.3	114.5	132.5

Sources: Pacific Coast seamen: Gorter and Hildebrand, *The Pacific Coast,* p. 350.
Atlantic Coast seamen: National Maritime Union, *Proceedings of the Third National Convention* (Cleveland, July 7–14, 1941), p. 124.
Pacific Coast longshoremen: Gorter and Hildebrand, *The Pacific Coast,* p. 350.
Atlantic Coast longshoremen: Bureau of Labor Statistics, Wage Chronology Series, series 4, no. 17 (1953), p. 2.
Railroad employees: Bureau of Labor Statistics, *Handbook of Labor Statistics,* 1950 edition, p. 83.
Manufacturing employees: Bureau of Labor Statistics, *Handbook of Labor Statistics,* 1947 edition, p. 54.

Second, it is important to note that the maritime data are in terms of base rates, the others, in terms of average hourly earnings. Between 1939 and 1941, seamen received additional pay equal to about 8 per cent of their base rates for overtime penalty work.[100] Moreover, the war risk bonus added greatly to their earnings beginning in 1940. Thus, if the seamen's wage index had been calculated in terms of average hourly earnings, their terminal position would be more favorable than is indicated in Table 9.

The longshoremen, on the other hand, appear to have fared relatively poorly. But several modifying factors must be taken into account. The West Coast longshoremen obtained a basic six-hour day in 1934, which meant a much greater opportunity for overtime than was available to workers generally. Secondly, in 1937 penalty rates were added to the basic rates for working certain kinds of cargo. Finally, maximum sling-loads were introduced in 1938, reducing the labor input per man-hour worked. "Although the longshoremen clearly fell behind the six offshore groups so far as basic wage rates were concerned, their true position was thus somewhat better than their wage rates indicate. At the same time, however, the lag was large." [101]

Among the explanations that have been advanced for the longshore lag are the greater demand elasticity for the services of longshoremen, due to the relatively high component of total costs attributable to wages; the government policy of subsidizing foreign trade shipping; and what may have been a deliberate policy on the part of employers to favor Lundeberg over Bridges on political grounds.[102] However, an even more important factor was probably the same force of equalization that brought seamen nearer manufacturing and railroad workers. The basic hourly rate of both East and West Coast longshoremen in 1935 was $0.95, and although they worked fairly intermittently, their economic status was superior to that of the seamen.

An interesting fact that emerges from Table 9 is that the racket-ridden ILA was able to raise the basic wage of East Coast longshoremen more than the communist-dominated ILWU on the West Coast, both starting from a rate of $0.95 an hour in 1935. One may speculate on the reasons for this disparity, but no firm conclusion seems possible without a detailed comparison of conditions on the two coasts. For one thing, Atlantic shipping was an advancing, and Pacific shipping a declining industry. Thus, total tonnage imported and exported on the Atlantic Coast rose from 32.3 million in 1935 to 47.4 million in 1940, while Pacific tonnage fell from 12.4 million to 11.9 million.[103] Secondly, and of critical importance, base rates, again, cannot be taken as an adequate expression of total earnings. The West Coast longshoremen were working a shorter regular-time day than the East Coast longshoremen, and therefore had greater opportunities for overtime pay. The Western hiring hall versus the Eastern "shape up," with the consequent implications of decasualization versus a highly casual labor market, meant quite different things to the individual worker. Study of a later period (1949–1951) revealed that the high New York hourly rate meant very low annual earnings for the average longshoreman, whereas a lower hourly rate was translated into much higher annual earnings for Seattle longshoremen.[104] The West Coast union policy of decasualizing the industry conferred greater economic benefits upon the individual than the East Coast policy of relying primarily upon higher basic rates.[105]

This brief review of the economic experience of maritime workers from 1935 to 1941 can be summarized as follows: the seamen, organized for the first time in powerful, aggressive unions, made great strides in raising their conditions of labor from what was a substandard level, by any criterion, to a standard more in consonance with that generally prevailing in shoreside employment. This was accomplished through both an increase in basic wages and an improvement in fringe benefits and in physical conditions of labor. The longshoremen on the West Coast used their newly won bargaining power to decasualize employment, thus promoting employment stability and increasing annual earnings for the remaining workers.

Professor John T. Dunlop has catalogued the major motifs running through the history of maritime unionism as follows:

1. The continuing struggle against diversity, toward unity in organization and collective bargaining.
2. The important role played by the federal government in the industry's economy in general and industrial relations in particular.
3. The long-term improvement in wages and other conditions of labor.
4. The distinctive character of the maritime collective bargaining system.[106]

No historical period begins with a *tabula rasa;* the events of earlier years inevitably play an important determining role in the unfolding of subsequent events. But the period 1934 to 1941, in the opinion of the present writer, was the most fateful era in the history of maritime labor, creating a pattern that has persisted for almost a quarter of a century and that bids fair to continue into the indefinite future.

The early years of the CIO seemed propitious for the realization of the old ideal of national unity among seamen and longshoremen. Inherited organizational barriers were burst asunder, the whole industrial union philosophy of the CIO favored unitary organization. But the actual effect of CIO entrance into the maritime industry was precisely the opposite. The unity of the old ISU, however tenuous, was replaced by open and bitter warfare between the forces of Joe Curran and Harry Lundeberg. Similarly, the monopoly of the quiescent ILA was shattered by the rise of Harry Bridges. Natural jurisdictional rivalries were exacerbated by the three cornered ideological conflict among communism, anarcho-syndicalism, and corrupt business unionism. Although the cast of characters has changed — Harry Lundeberg and Joe Ryan are gone from the scene, allegiances have shifted, and Joe Curran rid his organization of communists — organizational division and conflict of ideology are still characteristic of the maritime union movement.

The appropriate role for the federal government to play in maritime affairs was a subject for some experimentation during the latter half of the nineteen-thirties. The unsuccessful career of the Maritime Labor Board put an end to the possibility that maritime labor relations would be regulated by a special system of rules similar to those provided in railroad labor legislation. The limits of governmental intervention acceptable to employers and unions were worked out by a sometimes painful process of trial and error, and they have remained pretty well unchanged.

The significance of the years 1934 to 1941 in the secular advance of the maritime worker toward economic equality with his shoreside confrere has already been commented upon. While the trend was to continue unabated in later years, the first major steps toward equality belong to this period.

Finally, the present system of collective bargaining in the maritime industry was largely determined by the labor market institutions established after 1934. This period marked the beginning of the acceptance of true collective bargaining by maritime employers, after many years of dealing with weak organizations or, more often, with the individual worker. The union hiring hall, which survived the seemingly incompatible Taft-Hartley Act, provided the basic framework against which bargaining took place. The present complex of union and employer bargaining techniques, while they have undergone modification over time, can be traced back to the tempestuous days in which maritime unionism first emerged as an effective force in the American economy.

14

The Teamsters

The International Brotherhood of Teamsters has become the colossus of the labor world. With its jurisdiction extending into almost every industry in the country, and controlling the most vital of economic links — motor transport — its coercive power has become almost legendary. American trade unionism has watched the growth of this organization with some trepidation. A number of unions "voluntarily" ceded portions of their membership to the Teamsters, a very rare event in the annals of the American labor movement. The fate of the Brewery Workers' Union, which refused to accede to the jurisdictional demands of the Teamsters, provided an object lesson which other unions have taken to heart.

The power of the Teamsters is taken so much for granted that it is easy to forget its relatively recent origin. In 1932, total membership was only 82,000.[1] After an organizational drive undertaken during the NRA period, membership rose to 135,000 in 1935. The 1935 convention was told: "we stand today in this Convention having the highest membership over a period of one year that we ever enjoyed in the history of the International Union." [2] Yet at the time it was estimated that intercity trucking alone provided employment for about one million people,[3] and while employment data are not available for intracity trucking, there must have been at least that number again engaged in such employment. It was only in the years after 1935 that the Teamsters' Union began to realize its organizing potential. By 1941, it had attained a dues-paying membership of 530,000, having achieved a rate of growth more rapid than that of any other major union in the country. Thus, the period of the nineteen-thirties was characterized fully as much by the rise of the Teamsters as it was by the establishment of the CIO.

Trade Union and Industrial Structure

The Teamsters' Union is a multi-industrial organization. Within cities, it asserts jurisdiction over drivers in general local trucking, as well as over men engaged in driving furniture vans, building construction trucks, coal trucks, hearses, retail delivery trucks, Railway Express trucks, milk wagons, bakery wagons, beer and other beverage trucks, and laundry trucks, among others. Between cities, there is the important over-the-road trucking industry and log hauling. But jurisdiction is by no means confined to truck drivers. For various reasons, the Teamsters have asserted jurisdiction over warehousemen, service station and other automotive employees, brewery and beverage workers, cannery workers, dairy workers, department store employees, vending machine repairmen, as well as many other groups. It should be pointed out here that some of these jurisdictional claims are contested by other unions. (Several such cases are developed below.) Yet the Teamsters have always asserted that they are basically a craft group. Daniel J. Tobin, who presided over the union's fortunes during the years of its most rapid growth, said in this connection:

As far as industrial or craft unionism is concerned there is no argument at all for us on this question, because our organization is a craft union. Driving a truck is today a craft necessitating skill, training and intelligence second to none in any trade. . . . In addition to this we are a part of every other craft because we touch every business, hauling raw materials into manufacturing plants and hauling materials out after the products are finished.[4]

In 1936, the strength of the Teamsters' Union was concentrated among local drivers in the larger cities. The men engaged in driving milk, bakery, laundry, and general cargo trucks were traditionally organized into separate locals for the major trades where the number of members warranted a multi-local structure; otherwise, and particularly in the smaller cities, single locals embraced drivers in a multitude of trades. There was no uniform rule governing local structure; new locals were chartered as the need for them arose.

To coordinate the activities of local unions within an area, where more than one local existed, a second echelon of organization termed the "joint council" exists. Membership in the joint council is compulsory for all locals within its jurisdiction. Again, the precise geographical limits of the area covered by the joint council vary with the circumstances. For example, the Pacific Coast is divided among five joint councils, one covering Washington, one Oregon, with three in California. Nor has there been any uniformity of function, the precise role of the joint council depending largely on the local leadership. The Pacific Coast joint councils developed into powerful administrative units under the tutelage of Dave Beck:

Centralized research and legal services were established; frequent, regular meetings of the secretaries and business agents provided useful communication channels; better coordination of collective bargaining strategy and tactics was achieved; the experience and advice of the seasoned leaders was made available to the newer and less experienced.[5]

In some areas, joint councils have taken over the collective bargaining function from the locals, and entered into master agreements containing identical provisions for all industries except for wages, which are then negotiated separately by industry.[6] The joint council has also been an important political unit, a stepping stone by which ambitious local leaders have been able to move into a wider arena.

Of relatively recent origin are the regional conferences, embracing numerous joint councils and independent locals within broad geographical areas of the country. The rise of the conference form of organization after 1936 is the most important structural development within the Teamsters' Union in recent times, and will be dealt with in some detail below.

The International Brotherhood of Teamsters itself was formed by a merger of two earlier organizations in 1903, and has ever since been one of the pillars of the American Federation of Labor. Catering to an industry which until recent years was oriented largely toward the local market, it never became a highly centralized organization, such as the steel or automobile workers' unions. Locals enjoyed a good deal of autonomy, and the national union on occasion had to tolerate local leadership whose ideals and practices were obnoxious to it. The Minneapolis locals, which will be considered later, provide a good case in point, though many others might be cited.

In 1937, the minimum dues scale chargeable by local unions was $2 a month. The International Union received 30 cents of this, of which half went to a strike fund, three cents to the AFL and its departments, leaving only 12 cents to the International for its general purposes.[7] President Tobin once complained of this distribution of funds: "Our local unions have the largest degree of autonomous rights of any local unions in the American Federation of Labor. We permit you, under our present laws, to hold in your local treasuries at least 90 percent of the money you collect from the membership. Many organizations of labor take at least 50 or 60 percent of the total collection from the membership into the International treasury." Notwithstanding this pattern of allocation, the International increased its net assets from $2.2 million to $6 million between 1935 and 1940.

It would be wrong to leave the impression that the International was an impotent body. There was always the possibility of suspending or revoking local charters as a means of discipline, though whether this weapon was effective depended in part upon local union politics. Dave Beck, in particular, used charter revocation quite freely; it was reported that at one period 39 out of 43 Teamster locals in Los Angeles were in receivership, with the concurrence of the International union.[8] The power of the International organizer, a key official of the union, was defined as follows:

The Constitution is very strict on the recognition of International organizers and representatives and on the right of the representatives of the International Union to enquire into the affairs of any local in the district; and while the International representative does not have the power to discipline, he has the power to recommend and is compelled to report any wrongs within any local union within its jurisdiction, to the International Executive officers. . . .

The organizer has the right to walk into any union at any time and whenever he deems it necessary and inquire of the officers of the union regarding any matter or subject. He has the right, if he so desires, to attend meetings of local unions or Joint Councils and must be given the floor whenever he believes it necessary to make a statement in the interest of the union, or to set forth an order of the International Union. The organizer in the district has the right to sit in on all wage scale discussions with employers. . . .[9]

At the 1940 convention, Tobin had a constitutional amendment introduced which would have given the president of the International the right to revoke a local charter if he suggested that a labor dispute be settled by arbitration and the local refused. Had it been adopted, this amendment could have made the International the arbiter of all local wage scales. When Dave Beck, then a vice-president of the International, rose to defend the proposal, time was called on him by a delegate, an unprecedented occurrence. Tobin attempted to permit Beck to continue, but there were continued interruptions from the floor, whereupon Tobin chided the delegates: "Now, Brothers, don't act like a lot of children. Listen to the proceedings and the regular order of business." [10] A delegate retorted: "There are 1800 members in this convention, and it appears to the 1800 or a good majority of the 1800 that the Chair and the committee on the platform are acting a whole lot more childish than the delegates to the convention." Beck was unable to continue speaking, and the amendment was referred back to committee.[11] Another proposed amendment giving the president power to approve or disapprove all local wage scales met a similar fate.[12] The International thus failed to secure this ultimate central power over its locals, though the conferences were later able to exercise *de facto* authority to this effect.

The history of the Teamsters cannot fully be understood without some knowledge of the structure of the trucking industry. First and most important is the fact that in both major divisions of the industry, local and over-the-road trucking, the average unit of enterprise has been small. It was estimated in 1939 that 80 per cent of all enterprises engaged in long-distance hauling owned one truck, and that the number of trucks per operator was only 1.8.[13] Comparable figures are not available for local trucking, and though there are segments of this industry which are carried on by large fleet operators, for example, milk delivery, the small owner-operator is an important factor.

Capital requirements for entry into the industry have been small, which has contributed to intense competition and a high business mortality. As one observer noted:

The small owner-operator or "gypsy" needs only enough capital to make a down payment on a truck and is free to offer his services at whatever rates he may be willing to accept. In order to protect his equity in his truck he tends, under competitive pressures, to progressively lower his rates until he is taking a bare subsistence for his own wages and is providing inadequate reserves for repairs, maintenance, or replacement. He works long hours, attempts to do his own repair work, often disregards health and safety requirements and load restrictions. . . . He often loses his truck through inability to maintain payments; or when it wears out he has no funds accumulated for another.[14]

A common characteristic of the entire industry is the high incidence of labor costs. These represent about 35 per cent of the total cost of operating a trucking firm, on the average.[15] The wage policy of the Teamsters' Union is therefore a critical item in the calculations of the trucking employer.

Both within local and long distance trucking there are noncompetitive groups, paying widely varying wages for comparable work. Drivers of newspaper delivery trucks, building material trucks, bakery wagons, soft drink trucks, and beer trucks have tended to enjoy higher wages than drivers of coal trucks, ice trucks, and department and retail store delivery trucks. In long-distance hauling, common carriers pay lower wages than private carriers, by virtue of the fact that the rates of the former are regulated by the Interstate Commerce Commission; that they are more directly in competition with the railroads than are the private carriers; that private firms typically add to their transportation revenues through merchandising and manufacturing; and that common carriers are not able to schedule customers or cargoes as accurately as private carriers.[16] It has been pointed out that these wage differences are by no means transitory, but reflect the basic nature of the product market.[17] Ability of the industry to pay, based upon the nature of the demand for its products, is a major consideration in determining the appropriate wage level, though there are many instances of wage differentials which are seemingly irrational, if this factor is viewed as a sole determinant.[18] The problem is further complicated by the existence of quite different methods of wage payment within the industry: day rates, trip rates for over-the-road tracking, and commission payments where selling is important, as in milk and bakery delivery.

The average trucker is concerned more with the relation of his wages and other costs to the levels prevailing in his immediate competitive group than to the general industry level. Union wage policy has been increasingly directed toward the equalization of costs within competitive segments of the industry through a combination of government action and collective bargaining. There is little individual bargaining, since employers handle their labor contracts through a ubiquitous network of employer associations, organized on the basis of mutual competition. The Teamsters' Union has been a major influence in furthering employer association, in order to simplify the problem of controlling the numerous small employers.

Major Union Policies

The Teamsters' Union of the 1930's was in transition from old to new style American unionism. Dan Tobin, its president, had assumed office when the union was a small, struggling organization of underpaid workers, near the bottom in the industrial scale, dependent upon the assistance that could be rendered by the American Federation of Labor. He was an important member of the AFL Executive Council, if not of its inner circle. Dave Beck, harbinger of the new era, was still a local chieftain, building up an independent power base on the West Coast. Tobin was clearly unhappy about the new developments, but was powerless to stop them.

The role of Tobin in the AFL-CIO controversy has already been recounted. Although he supported the expulsion of the CIO unions, he was by no means a die-hard opponent of industrial unionism, and he became somewhat critical of his fellow AFL leaders for some of their policies toward the CIO. For example, when during the 1937 General Motors strike, AFL leaders attempted to impede a settlement with the CIO, Tobin wrote:

No labor man should, because of his disagreement personally with someone representing the C.I.O., do otherwise than pray and hope that the union will be successful, because if you let that personal feeling enter you, you are not honest with the rank and file whom you represent. Whether you like them or not, those men now leading this fight against this monstrous corporation which has made hundreds of millions in profits after covering up everything they could — this group of labor men are the only ones that ever gave this national corporation a battle for the right to organize.[19]

As time went on, he became a proponent of labor unity. In 1940, he wrote: "Neither side has to sacrifice very much in order to bring about a settlement. Less than one dozen men on both sides are responsible for the division of eight million workers." The peculiar interest of the Teamsters in bringing about a cessation of hostilities was specified as follows:

We are caught between two fires, between the two contending parties, the A.F. of L. and the C.I.O. We haul in and out of every plant and every corporation. We must preserve and protect and carry out our contracts. Many organizations on both sides are continually requesting us to lend them help here and there. . . . We find it very embarrassing to have to refuse, but the very life of our organization in some instances is in danger.[20]

Politically, there was no labor organization more committed to the New Deal than the Teamsters' Union. In 1936, Tobin was appointed chairman of the Labor Division of the National Democratic Committee, and was not backward in urging members of the union to vote for Roosevelt. In the summer of 1940, he took leave from the union to accept an appointment as administrative assistant to the president, a position he soon resigned to become once more the Democratic Party labor chairman. Upon assuming the latter position, he received the following letter from President Roosevelt:

Dear Dan:

I have your letter of August twenty-third in which you advise me that Ed Flynn has asked you to again assume the position of labor's representative in the headquarters of the Democratic National Committee for the duration of the campaign. I have no alternative and therefore I reluctantly accept your resignation as Administrative Assistant to the President, effective September 9, 1940.

Ed's gain is my loss! . . .

I will continue to count on your advice on all matters affecting labor and government, with particular relationship to national defense.

The famous "Fala" speech of Roosevelt, which was his opening gun of the 1940 election campaign, was delivered at the Teamsters' convention, which was then in session. Tobin was widely regarded as an advocate of the Democratic administration, and he often took positions at variance with those held by the AFL in this cause; an example was his support of the National Labor Relations Board at a time it was under AFL attack for alleged CIO partisanship.

On the economic side, the International Union was constantly urging restraint and responsibility upon its locals, many of which were newly organized, and inclined in their inexperience to rely too heavily upon their strike effectiveness. As the power of the organization grew, it was Tobin's constant fear that the power to tie up transportation was inherently so great that unless the union acted with caution, government would step in with restrictive regulation. It was this that led to the attempt to impose arbitration upon the local unions at the 1940 convention.

The Teamsters' leaders were also conscious of the restraints imposed upon wage increases by the economic position of the product market. During the 1938 recession, Tobin wrote:

We are going to try and maintain our present wage scales wherever we can, and where those wage scales are below the average scale for the same kind of work in the same kind of city or district we are going to endeavor to balance the wage scales and put truck owners on an equal competitive basis. In the meantime we are going to be exceptionally careful and slow in endorsing a strike for any local union while this serious unemployment condition prevails.

And even when the defense boom had removed the threat of unemployment, the local unions were cautioned:

Our organizations have it in their blood that every time a wage contract expires there must be an increase in wages in the new contract. I now state to you that there is a point of saturation for wages and hours, and that if you go beyond that point, or even if you reach that point in some instances, you can rest assured if you go any further you will destroy the employment and thereby destroy yourselves. . . . We have had more than one experience where railroads have marked down the hauling of freight in order to recapture the work our truck drivers were doing.

These warnings were necessitated by the fact that most local business agents were not particularly aware of any relationship between wages and employment, and were inclined toward the opportunistic policy of charging what the traffic would bear in each locality at a particular time.[21] Frequently, the result was violation of the contract wage scale. One of the methods of ensuring competitive uniformity and preventing undercutting of prices and wages was union stimulus to employer association, a policy that has already been mentioned. Gillingham has indicated the following advantages to the Teamsters' Union arising out of this policy:[22]

1. The administrative and procedural difficulties of collective bargaining were reduced by bargaining with an association rather than many small employers. Individual bargaining would have entailed great burdens upon the union's staff.

2. Enforcement of the agreement and grievance settlement were simplified by association bargaining. Rebellious employers could be brought into line by the association.

3. The union's position in relation to independent operators not belonging to the association was strengthened, in that insistence upon their acceptance of the association contract seemed a reasonable union demand.

4. ". . . the Union recognizes that in such an industrial structure, a strong, inclusive employer or trade association is a necessary precondition for any effective self-regulation or general policy for the promotion or protection of the industry as a whole. . . . Unregulated entry and cutthroat price competition in industries such as laundry and dry cleaning, trucking, or automotive service, means a threat to employment conditions; likewise, there are external competitive threats, for example, the railroads. . . . The employer association becomes a prime instrument from the Union's point of view to combat the pervasive threat of excessive competition internally and of competitive menaces of various sorts externally."

A cardinal principle of Teamster bargaining policy was sanctity of the collective agreement. Because of the character of their work, the Teamsters are involved potentially in labor disputes conducted by other unions, and indeed, Teamster cooperation is often a critical factor in determining the outcome of such disputes. Some organizations, for example, the Retail Clerks, have been able to organize largely on the basis of Teamster support. The Teamsters had to balance the gain to fellow trade unionists flowing from their refusal to cross picket lines against their own wage losses and the resentment of their employers. Increasingly, the tendency was to give more weight to the latter considerations, a policy strongly espoused by the International. In 1938, Tobin urged his local leaders:

I am giving this warning to our people everywhere. Mind your own business and don't jump in breaking agreements or tying up firms in behalf of some other union. . . . Also in reference to picket lines. Whenever you have an agreement with your employer you remain at work regardless of picket lines of any other union, unless you receive the sanction of the International Union to stop hauling or delivery to that plant that is picketed . . . tell your members what to do, and if they are afraid to go through the lines, get them some assistance, and if they are still weak towards preserving their employment and their signed contracts, find other men for their jobs. The whole sum and substance of the story is that the Teamsters' Union has been injuring its own organization by taking up everybody's fight, and it must stop from now on.[23]

However, the Teamsters' Union was not reluctant to use the strike weapon for its own purposes. Particularly during the period 1933–1940, short strikes over minor grievances were quite common, and locals had to be warned constantly not to overreach themselves.[24] A particularly effective device was the discriminating strike, in which the union permitted some companies to operate while closing down others, thus placing great economic pressure on the recalcitrants.[25] Even before the advent of the regional conference, locals often aided one another by refusing to work with non-union trucks from other cities. Once collective bargaining relationships were established, strikes became rare, and were discouraged by the International Union with every means at its disposal.[26]

Throughout the 1930's, the International Union aggressively pursued expansion of the Teamsters' jurisdiction, although often the quest for broader jurisdiction was a defensive reaction against the expansion of other labor organizations. The jurisdictional dispute with the Brewery Workers' Union, one of the classic internal disputes of American labor, will be dealt with below in some detail. In 1938, the Teamsters received jurisdiction over gas station employees over the opposition of the Gasoline Station Operators' National Council, a group of AFL federal locals with about 5000 members.[27] Jurisdiction was secured over warehousemen as a countermove to the march inland by the West Coast longshoremen.[28] The Retail Clerks were frequently the target of Teamster encroachment. In 1939, for example, they complained to the AFL that the Teamsters had been organizing automobile salesmen in Seattle and San Francisco. "Representative [Dave] Beck contended that it was necessary for the Teamsters to take in these workers because the Retail Clerks organization was not the kind of organization that could take part in the fight they have been up against on the Pacific Coast and make any progress. . . . He stated that unless he did something the CIO would go in so a charter was granted to these automobile salesmen from the Teamsters." [29] In this case, the Teamsters agreed to turn the salesmen over to the Retail Clerks, but on later occasions they were not as accommodating. The Teamsters were also involved in a bitter dispute with the Railway Clerks over control of American Railway Express drivers. In 1941, refusal of the Teamsters to accede to a National Mediation Board certification of the Railway Clerks as bargaining agent for the Detroit Railway Express drivers led to considerable violence, which was ended only after President Roosevelt twice demanded that the Teamster stoppage be terminated.[30]

Consistent with the demand that all men who drove trucks, whatever the industry to which they were attached, belonged to the Teamsters, the International was insistent that local unions admit all drivers. In 1940, the General Executive Board issued the following pronouncement on transfer cards, an important issue because of the high job mobility prevailing among teamsters:

That insofar as it is humanly possible the transfer card be recognized by all local unions . . . that under no circumstances should any applicant for entrance into another union be charged extra fees or initiation in order to have his transfer card accepted; that the foundation of the International Union was based upon the acceptance of transfer cards, and if today any local union may hesitate about accepting a transfer card because of the unemployment among their members, that some local union may be refused recognition by another local union in the very near future. . . . We find that the local union membership in many instances is narrow and selfish. The great principle upon which the International Union is founded, involving the recognition of transfer cards, must always prevail over and above any local prejudices and desires.

The International Union opposed high initiation fees for new members as a policy which endangered the stability of the organization. Tobin warned: "When a working man is charged an enormous amount of money to join a union simply because the fellows who are inside do not want anyone else in, or because the management of the union believes this is an easy way to make the fellow who wants to come in, pay the price, then it is in most instances not only bad business judgment but it eventually brings those responsible into disrepute or trouble." He urged that in cases of severe local unemployment it was better frankly to close the union to new entrants than to impose high initiation fees which might continue even after employment conditions had improved.

The Teamsters' Union, during the period with which we are dealing, was already concerned with the problem of internal corruption which in later years was to produce a crisis in the American labor movement. Because of the small size of the business enterprises with which the Teamsters deal, the extreme inconvenience of even a temporary interruption in deliveries, and the marginal, if not illegal, character of some businesses in which the Teamsters became involved (for example, pinball machines and juke boxes), opportunities for graft exist which are not ordinarily present in manufacturing industry. "It is easier for a loader in a brewery, in collusion with a driver, to throw a few extra cases of beer on a truck and then split the proceeds than it is for an assembly-line worker in an auto plant to walk out the gate with a new bumper for his car. In the same way it is likelier that a trucking-industry employer will offer a bribe to a Teamster business agent, with whom he deals alone, than that the president of an oil company will attempt to bribe a representative of the oil workers union, who does his negotiating flanked by a committee of refinery employees." [31]

The small trucker certainly has less power of resistance to dishonest union officials than his counterpart in large industrial enterprises. Operating in a highly competitive industry, often on a marginal basis, he can ill afford even a temporary stoppage of work, particularly when he is singled out from competitors and subjected to special pressure. The existence of a relatively casual labor force also contributes to the possibility of corruption, for it is easier to victimize workers who move from one job to another, and are thus dependent upon the goodwill of union officials, than steady workers, who can look to their employers for some degree of protection.

As early as 1941, *Fortune Magazine* wrote that "More than most American unions, the Teamsters' has been accused of crimes and offenses against the public welfare, to say nothing of crimes and offenses against its own members." [32] Tobin defended the Teamsters vigorously against these charges, and in particular, spoke up in behalf of Dave Beck, who was already coming into the national spotlight as a result of his West Coast operations:

During the course of the article you speak of Dave Beck, a General Organizer for the International Union in the western district, and you endeavor to insinuate that he is such a boss, a dictator, that you throw out the impression that he is anything but an honest, decent, God-fearing representative of labor. Dave Beck has worked under my direction and supervision. I appointed him as a General Organizer. He can be discharged at a moment's notice. I prevailed upon him to go to work for the International Union when the employers at that time offered him twice the salary that we were able to pay him. [33]

At the same time, Tobin was aware that the charges of corruption levied against the Teamsters had a substantial basis in fact. For example, officials of New York Locals 202 and 138 were currently being prosecuted for criminal acts. In a number of editorials in the Teamsters' official journal, Tobin warned against the admission to membership in the union of men who had been convicted of crimes or were known to be associated with racketeers. Thus, he wrote in the following vein:

The Labor Movement was created and founded for the purpose of helping the workers of our country. It cannot and must not be made a place for racketeers and degenerates who do not want to work, who do not belong as associates in the membership of the Labor Movement in company with honest, clean-living men. Get rid of any such individual as I have attempted to describe herein. If you do not, we will get rid of your charter. [34]

He urged that not only convicted criminals, but men indicted for criminal acts, be expelled from membership, and suggested that the International constitution be amended to make expulsion mandatory. The 1940 convention followed this recommendation to the extent that actual conviction for criminal offenses was made the basis for expulsion.[35]

While Tobin's personal honesty was never challenged, he opened the door to practices which were later to flower into the Teamster brand of "business" unionism. For example, the 1940 convention adopted a constitutional amendment according the International president full discretion in the manner of performing his duties and providing "fully and liberally" for all expenses incurred by him, including vacations and travel in the United States and abroad, and for the expenses of his wife as well. Such an act contributed to blurring the line between the personal funds of union officials and the treasury of the organization.

The Rise of the Conference

The outstanding development in the Teamster history of the nineteen-thirties was the development of a new structural unit, the regional conference. So long as trucking was largely a local industry, there was little need for intercity cooperation beyond that which could be secured by occasional informal contact. But with the growth of over-the-road trucking, occasioned by improvement in vehicles and roads, the industry's center of gravity began to move away from the local market, and some new mechanism was needed to coordinate the activities of far-flung local units.

A trucking company can just as well run from a terminal in city A to city B and back to A, as the reverse. If the wage rates are different in A and B, men driving the same routes will be paid different wages, depending upon the accident of initial location. The tendency would be for all trucking companies to locate their terminals in the lower wage city, thus endangering the higher union rate in the other. This was one of the factors that impelled the development of new collective bargaining forms to secure the equalization of wage rates within competitive geographical areas.

The origin of intercity trucking was to be found "in the gradual extension of the field of operation of trucks engaged in local drayage. As highways were constructed and the carrying capacity of trucks increased, the prospect of eliminating loading and unloading operations in the transfer of freight between truck and railroad car led naturally to the creation and expansion of intercity truck haulage." [36] Table 10 shows how rapidly intercity trucking expanded in the years 1935 to 1941. By 1940, intercity truck traffic provided employment for somewhere between one million and 1.5 million men.

Table 10.

Index of freight traffic, for-hire intercity trucking (ton miles)
(1939 = 100)

Year	Index	Year	Index
1935	45	1939	100
1936	54	1940	122
1937	69	1941	128
1938	80		

Source: Harold Barger, *The Transportation Industries* (New York, 1951), p. 40.

The regional conference, contrary to popular conception, was not the invention of any one individual or group. It arose simultaneously in various parts of the country in response to roughly similar economic conditions. Essentially, the conference owed its origin to the need for a new unit of collective bargaining. As often in the past, trade union structure proved quite responsive to the requirements of collective bargaining. The precise structural form which developed varied from one area to another on the basis of particular sectional circumstances, the abilities and aspirations of the regional leadership, and the history and age of different local unions. The three major groupings which will be treated here are those which developed on the Pacific Coast, in the Midwest, and New England.

The Western Conference. There was a rapid growth of intercity trucking in the Pacific Coast area from 1929 to 1935. Competition among the truck operators, many of whom were owner–drivers, was intense, and this, combined with ease of entry, led to poor conditions of labor. The enactment of the Motor Carrier Act of 1935 mitigated some of the worst evils, such as unbroken driving shifts of 18 to 20 hours, but wages remained low. In February 1935, representatives of 76 Teamster locals met at Portland, Oregon, to plan a highway driver organizing campaign. Dave Beck, who was head of the Seattle Joint Council, was the guiding genius of the new organization from the start, a position which was confirmed in 1937 when he succeeded Michael Casey as West Coast organizer for the International Union.

It is difficult to determine why the leadership for West Coast organization came from Seattle rather than San Francisco, the traditional Pacific stronghold of organized labor. Part of the explanation may lie in the fact that the 15,000 Teamsters in the Bay Area's 33 locals, secure in their agreements and led by conservative unionists, were satisfied with their situation and not particularly threatened by the lower wage intercity trucking industry. Whatever the reasons, the San Francisco Teamsters remained aloof from the Western Conference, and did not participate fully until membership in the conference became compulsory by action of the 1947 IBT convention.[37] This was the only enclave in eleven Western states to evade Beck's control.

At first the International Union viewed with suspicion the growth of a potential competitor from within its own ranks. In March 1937, Tobin wrote:

The International Union can only sanction or charter the establishment of local unions and joint councils. There are no other bodies or organizations chartered by the International Union. We have no objection to conferences being held in any district by the officers of unions for the purpose of devising ways and means of helping out in a certain situation or meeting a certain organizing condition, but these conferences should observe and keep within the laws of the International Union and should not become either a clique or an inside ring for local political purposes.[38]

Beck was able to persuade Tobin that the Western Conference scheme offered no threat to the authority of the International, for the first formal conference session was held in Seattle in June 1937, with the latter's blessing. Tobin visited the West Coast in 1938 to look into the matter further, and gave the conference a clean bill of health from the standpoint of the International constitution.

The original purpose of the conference, and its relationship to the parent organization, was described as follows:

It came into being because of organizational needs of these Local Unions in the West. Long distances between cities and the growing chain operations in the West coupled with the comparatively sparsely settled nature of the Western country necessitates close cooperation among Local Unions in the West for the purpose of meeting conditions which, before the organization of the Western Conference of Teamsters had made organization very difficult. . . . The Western Conference of Teamsters does not infringe upon the autonomous rights of Local Unions, nor of Joint Councils and in no way does it supersede the International Union. The Western Conference meetings are not conventions. They are business meetings of the representatives employed by the Local Unions.[39]

The Western Conference was soon differentiated into functional subdivisions, termed trade divisions. By 1941, twelve such divisions had been created,[40] reflecting the major industries in which the Teamsters operated. The divisions, in turn, created trade councils, for the purpose of coordinating organizing activity within the jurisdictions of the trade divisions, establishing central offices, and employing organizers directly. The Western Conference Policy Committee, composed of twenty-five representatives of trade divisions and geographical areas, provided the formal governmental mechanism of the conference between the annual meetings of the conference itself, though all major decisions were made by Beck and Frank Brewster, the secretary-treasurer of the conference.

The conference proved to be a very effective organizing device. By 1942, almost 150,000 men belonged to locals affiliated with it, a 50 per cent increase over the membership at the beginning of 1940.[41] One of its major achievements was the organization of Los Angeles, traditionally an open-shop city. Beck explained how this was done in urging that the conference technique be applied to the Midwest and East as a means of organizing the Southeast:

We would then be in a position to shut off the South completely from boat, rail and truck merchandising with the rest of the country. We could tie up the flow of freight by rail and boat, merely by refusing to transport goods to the docks or railroad stations destined for shipment to the South. And we could refuse to move shipments from the South after they arrived at Northern or Western rail or water terminals . . . the same system was used in organizing Southern California. This was accomplished by labor pressure in the strongly organized cities of the North and East where the Southern California companies did business.[42]

Once highway employers learned that trouble with their local Teamsters would subject trucks to boycott and other action at the points of destination, they proved more amenable to organization. The conference, in turn, prided itself upon its realism and businesslike attitude in collective bargaining. Beck asserted proudly in June 1942, that the conference had not had a strike in the previous twenty months, and ascribed it to the care with which the Teamsters studied their industry and appreciated its problems. "We are practical people. We take our livelihood out of those industries and we want them to be prosperous. . . ."[43] Indeed, there was a growing tendency for the line between union and employer to blur. When the Teamsters organized groups of employers, they proceeded to keep "independents" from competing on a price basis. The Seattle laundries, for example, were obliged to join the Associated Laundries of Seattle, which audited their books and made certain that they were not undercutting the standard prices. William H. Short, one of Beck's lieutenants, was put in charge of the association.[44] This device bore many resemblances to those adopted by the garment unions to solve a similar problem:[45] the limitation of competition in an industry with small units of enterprise, easy entry, and easy departure via bankruptcy, placing great pressure upon the union wage scale.

It should be emphasized that the conference as such did not engage in collective bargaining. Contracts continued to be negotiated on the local level, though the Highway Drivers' Council did endeavor to secure uniformity of highway rates.[46] At the end of 1941, however, a considerable diversity of wage rates continued to exist even in this branch of trucking, as well as within local, noncompetitive product markets.

One of the major preoccupations of the Western Conference of Teamsters during its formative years was a vendetta with the longshoremen's organization headed by Harry Bridges. In the San Francisco general strike of 1934, and again in the coastwide maritime strike of 1936, the Teamsters supported the longshoremen, who were then affiliated with the AFL International Longshoremen's Association.[47] The support was rendered largely because of rank-and-file pressure, against the wishes of the Teamster officials. The natural antipathy between the left-wing longshore leaders and the conservative Teamster leaders was finally focused into active rivalry in the fall of 1936, when the longshoremen began to organize warehouses in a variety of industries away from the waterfront, the famous "march inland." By the end of 1936, about 3000 inland warehousemen in San Francisco and Oakland were in the longshoremen's union, this having been accomplished without any Teamster opposition. Belatedly, the San Francisco Teamsters realized that this strategic maneuver had placed a potential enemy at both ends of many of their truck routes, and they began countermoves. Tobin, on their behalf, asked the AFL Executive Council to extend the jurisdiction of the Teamsters to warehousemen, arguing:

the Longshoremen have gone away from the wharfs into the center of the city, have organized warehouses without any right to do so under their charter and in many places on the Western Coast have tied up our trucking concerns . . . we are caught in a trap in the loading and delivery of merchandise between the Longshoremen on the wharf — in many instances controlled by radicals — and warehousemen at the other end.[48]

With the longshoremen moving toward the CIO, the AFL granted the jurisdictional extension, but it was too late to stop the longshoremen in the San Francisco Bay area, for they were solidly entrenched. In April 1937, the longshoremen called a strike at a number of canneries in the East Bay, and Teamster Local 70, in Oakland, refused to go through their picket lines. The local charter was revoked by Dave Beck, who had been empowered to act for the International Union, and a receiver installed. The suspended Teamsters received the support of the local labor movement, the Alameda County Central Labor Council refusing to seat the newly appointed delegates from Local 70, whereupon the council in turn was reorganized by the AFL, and all elements sympathetic to the CIO excluded.

Despite legal action taken by the deposed officers of Local 70, and the loyalty to them evinced by a substantial segment of the rank and file, Beck was able to gain control of the local, and on June 7, he directed an attempt to break through the longshoremen's picket line at the California Packing Company in Oakland. The drivers were stoned, and sporadic violence ensued for several days, not only at Calpac, but at other plants as well.

Events on the national scene were moving to exacerbate local relations. The Pacific Coast longshoremen received a charter from the CIO as a national union, and Harry Bridges became the West Coast director for the CIO. What had before been a jurisdictional dispute was now transformed into a holy war. Beck told the first meeting of the Western Conference of Teamsters: "We can clean up communism in any kind of a fight, under the rules that the communists like to use. If we have to go out in the arena and use physical force, aided by the American Legion and the Elks, we can." [49] Tobin similarly stressed the high ideological justification for the Teamsters' actions:

Unless the Teamsters took action now the entire Labor Movement on the Pacific Coast will be controlled by this dangerous, un-American, radical, Communistic group headed by Bridges. The Teamsters are the keynote to the saving of the workers and their organizations from these foreign influences. . . . And if Bridges' doctrine, backed by the C.I.O. and by foreign influences, spread to the Atlantic ports our government will be seriously inconvenienced, and it may result in revolution, necessitating our government being forced to shoot down innocent men and women in order that the flag of our country might still float in freedom throughout the land.[50]

After finding their access to the California Packing Company plants blocked by the pickets of the new International Longshoremen's and Warehousemen's Union, the San Francisco Teamsters decided on a counteroffensive in September 1937. John McLaughlin, head of the San Francisco drivers' local, announced: "They've been looking for a fight. Now they have it and it's going to be a fight to the finish. The waterfront group have been attempting to dictate to the teamsters for four years. . . . They deny us the right to do the work that is rightfully ours and we are not going to put up with it." The Teamsters' weapon was to refuse to haul cargo from the docks in San Francisco. Although they put picket lines across the water-front, the longshoremen and other maritime workers reported for work as usual. Arrayed in military formation, 2000 longshoremen marched along the waterfront, with the individual gangs moving through the Teamster picket lines in flying wedges. Miraculously, no violence occurred, in view of the fact that at one time the Teamsters' pickets totaled 4000 men.

The waterfront employers, who were cooperating with the ILWU, had railroad cars brought up to the docks in greater than usual volume, affording the longshoremen increasing employment and reducing the impact of the Teamster blockade. Local business was much harder hit than long-distance transport, but even here the severity of the strike was mitigated by the exemption of perishables from the embargo. Feelings in the local labor movement ran very high; for example, John Shelley, an official of the Bakery Wagon Drivers Local 484 (Mr. Shelley later was elected to the United States Congress) was assaulted and beaten at the convention of the State Federation of Labor for his advocacy of AFL-CIO unity.[51]

On September 29, 1937, the Teamsters announced that they were terminating the blockade at the request of the Associated Farmers of California, in order to save the crops. In fact, their assault on the longshoremen had failed; the latter remained firmly in control of the inland warehousemen whom they had organized. An uneasy truce set in, and the Teamsters established warehouse locals which gained a foothold in the area. The San Francisco locals managed to prevent Beck from engaging in open warfare with the ILWU in their jurisdiction.

Elsewhere along the Coast, the Teamsters were more successful in combating the longshoremen's march inland. In August 1936, the Seattle and Portland Teamsters began aggressive organizing drives among warehousemen, and refused to haul for firms that had recognized the longshoremen. Though the ILWU managed to retain a few small employers, through NLRB victories, the Teamsters' tactics proved much more effective than they had in San Francisco.[52]

By 1939, the Teamsters had 68 warehouse locals in the eleven Western states, and a warehouse trade division was established as part of the Western Conference. Only in San Francisco did the ILWU continue to be the dominant organization in the warehouse field. In 1940, the Teamsters joined the Retail Clerks Union in a drive on the Montgomery Ward Company, and after a strike of more than half a year, succeeded in gaining recognition.[53] Hostilities between the Teamsters and the ILWU abated during the war, only to flare up once more in 1947.[54]

The Western Conference of Teamsters was in many ways a pioneering institution, and it may fairly be said to have been largely the work of one man, Dave Beck. It was Beck who first clearly formulated the principle of organizing by the long-distance boycott, and who had the ruthlessness and energy to weld the disparate elements that constituted the Western teamsters into a centralized, hard-hitting organization. Beck's trade-union philosophy, which characterized the Western Conference from its very inception, was brought out clearly in the following abstract from a speech to the conference in 1942:

There is only one thing in the world that you men, and the people you represent, own, and that is labor. You haven't anything else to sell but labor. We are trying to formulate a policy of operating a business organization to sell that labor. . . .

I have a world of admiration for the Standard Oil Company because it is efficient. . . . I think we ought to run ours along the same business lines.[55]

That Beck's conception of unionism proved effective cannot be gainsaid; by the time of the outbreak of the war in 1941, the Western Conference, after four years of operation, was a going concern, and Beck had become one of the most powerful trade union leaders in the United States. But as subsequent events were to demonstrate, a union conceived of as a business organization selling labor was not without its grave dangers, not only to the workers concerned, but to the community at large.

The Minneapolis Teamsters and the Central Conference

The Central Conference of Teamsters had its origin at the opposite end of the political spectrum. The story begins in the spring of 1934, when the seemingly moribund Local 574 of the Teamsters Union conducted a successful strike among the coal drivers of Minneapolis. Bill Brown, international organizer and head of the Minneapolis Teamsters Joint Council, entrusted the leadership of the strike to a group of dissident communists, adherents of the Trotskyist Communist League of America. This remarkable group of men, Karl Skoglund, Farrell Dobbs, and the Dunne Brothers — Vincent, Miles and Grant[56] — quickly seized upon this initial victory to lay plans for further organization work among the drivers. With unionism in the air, the local signed up 3000 truck drivers within a few months, and in May 1934, it called a strike which paralyzed the economic life of Minneapolis.[57] Pitched battles ensued between police and hastily sworn-in deputies, on the one hand, and mobs of strikers and sympathizers on the other. Floyd B. Olson, the Farmer-Labor governor of Minnesota, was unwilling to use force against the strikers, and the employers were obliged to capitulate. The union won recognition, a minimum wage, seniority, and arbitration for future wage changes.

But peace proved to be short-lived. The Citizens' Alliance of Minneapolis, a militantly antilabor organization of employers, organized a counteroffensive against unionism, with Local 574 and its radical leadership the focus of the attack. Local 574, in turn, accused the employers of failing to live up to the agreement, and demanded an additional wage increase of 2½ cents an hour. On July 16, 1934, a second general strike of drivers began, this one lasting five weeks. Again, there was considerable violence, and several men were killed. When the employers refused to accept a proposal worked out by Federal conciliator, Governor Olson, terming the Citizens' Alliance a "sinister group [which] repeatedly prevented a settlement of this and the former strike," [58] proclaimed martial law. After first stopping the trucks from running, he authorized the militia to permit them to operate once more under a permit system. When the union defied the militia and attempted to halt all truck operations, the leaders of the strike, including James P. Cannon and Max Schachtman, national leaders of the Trotskyist Party, were arrested. At the same time, the governor issued an ultimatum to the Citizens' Alliance to the effect that he would revoke all permits for truck operation unless an agreement was reached within a specified period. The strike ended on August 21 with a substantial victory for the union.

Once the dust had settled on these events, the International Teamsters' Union, alarmed at the character of the leadership of the Minneapolis local, revoked the charter of Local 574, and set up a new Local 500 in an attempt to keep the membership intact. A committee representing eleven local unions which belonged to the Minneapolis Central Labor Union called upon President Dan Tobin to urge him to reinstate Local 574, but was informed that expulsion of the radical leadership was an absolute condition for reinstatement. "At this stage an agreement was reached between the Executive Board of the Central Labor Union and Local 574 so that there would be no friction regarding membership jurisdiction. Local 574 asked only that it be accorded the same jurisdictional rights it held before the charter revocation. The Central Labor Union approved this as a reasonable request." [59] With the support of the local labor movement, the leadership of Local 574 was able not only to hold its membership, but to push out into new fields. Several years before the Teamsters' Union had received jurisdiction over warehousemen, Local 574 was busy organizing, in addition to drivers of all

character, "those workers in the large warehouses, stores, and small manufacturing and distributing establishments who rightfully belong with the
truck drivers because of the close relationship of their jobs to the transportation of goods on the streets and highways."

Alarmed at the success of the independent local, the AFL Executive
Council instituted an inquiry into the situation. Secretary Lawson of the
Minnesota Federation of Labor informed the council in October 1935:

The menace of this situation has continued to grow and has now reached the
stage, in our opinion, that requires drastic action upon the part of the American
Federation of Labor unless the city Central Labor Union of Minneapolis is to
be known as being controlled by dual organizations and Communists. While not
accredited delegates to the Central Labor Union, these people are permitted to
attend the meetings and are instrumental thereby in creating disturbances that
are destroying the effectiveness and work of the Central Labor Union.[60]

Meyer Lewis, one of the top organizers for the AFL, reported to the
Council after an on-the-spot inquiry:

The entire labor situation in and around the Twin Cities is very critical and
serious, due to the efforts being made by the suspended organization of the
Teamsters and Chauffeurs to create in and around these parts a single labor
organization, that will take in everyone and anyone, regardless of any jurisdictional bounds. This organization has made a great deal of progress, due to its
ability to appeal to unfortunate individuals who are victims of the economic
conditions of the present day.

Meyer Lewis was despatched to Minneapolis with the task of breaking
up Local 574. There were mutual accusations of beatings and gangsterism.
Among others, Vincent Dunne and George Frosig, a vice-president of Local
574, were severely beaten with blackjacks in May 1936, at the height of the
controversy. Alarmed by the possibility that the newly formed CIO might
become interested in the Minneapolis Teamsters as a nucleus for industrial
organization in the Midwest, the AFL decided to compromise. Vincent
Dunne was invited by Meyer Lewis to talk matters over, and after three
weeks of discussion, Locals 574 and 500 were merged into a newly constituted Local 544, to be governed initially by an executive board consisting
of three officials from Local 574, three from Local 500, with the secretary
of the Teamsters' Joint Council as neutral chairman.[61] This arrangement
was actually a face-saving device for the AFL, for it was soon evident that
the Trotskyist leaders of the old Local 574 were firmly in control of the
new organization. Moreover, it was consummated in the face of a 1935
Teamsters' International convention resolution denying membership to

communists, and although the Minneapolis Teamster leaders were dissident rather than orthodox communists, Tobin had not theretofore made any such fine distinctions.

Even before their return to the Teamsters' fold, the group in control of the Minneapolis Teamsters exhibited a keen appreciation of potentialities for organization among the highway drivers. The official newspaper of Local 574 carried a long article on February 19, 1936, which outlined the obstacles to organization among this group of workers:

In the first place, they do not work in a group where they have an opportunity to discuss their problems with each other. Second, the present rates of pay and the hours of work vary so greatly that it is almost impossible to get two of these drivers to agree on what constitutes fair wages and decent working conditions for the line drivers. Minneapolis is one of the greatest truck terminals in the Northwest. It is estimated that no fewer than 2,000 overland truck drivers make Minneapolis their headquarters.[62]

As soon as the internal conflict had been patched up, the newly constituted Local 544 began to agitate for an organizational drive among the highway truckers, arguing that Minnesota constituted an ideal proving ground for such an experiment. The plans bore fruit in January 1937, when the North Central District Drivers Council was established with Farrell Dobbs of Local 544 as secretary-treasurer and general sparkplug. The council initially consisted of representatives from 13 locals in North and South Dakota, Iowa, Minnesota, Wisconsin, and Michigan and had as its formal purpose "to promote the organization of workers engaged in truck transportation throughout the entire district and to establish uniform wages, hours and working conditions." *The Northwest Organizer*, the well-edited publication of Local 544, was adopted as the official organ of the Council.

The progress of the North Central Council was slowed initially by the economic recession of 1937. However, in the spring of 1938, with a membership that had expanded to 46 locals from eleven states (in addition to those listed above, Ohio, Indiana, Illinois, Missouri, and Nebraska), a committee was established consisting of one representative from each state, charged with the task of laying the ground for a uniform over-the-road wage contract.[63] A proposed agreement was presented on March 5, 1938, to the American Trucking Associations, Inc., which promptly responded by dissolving its Labor Relations Committee and refusing to hold joint meetings.

Some of the allegedly unfair wage practices which the union sought to alleviate in the standard agreement were described as follows:

the employer may allow a flat payment of a certain sum for a designated run and this is what the driver receives, irregardless [sic] of the amount of actual time worked. He may lose time because of a breakdown, or he may be forced to lay over, or he may be tied up waiting for freight. . . . An even more vicious method of exploitation is employed by forcing the driver to work on a tonnage basis . . . the driver is subjected to every form of swindling in computing operation cost and, in the best event, is directly dependent on the ability or inability of the employer to efficiently manage the operation.

Several employer groups within the American Trucking Associations, Inc., a federation of state employer associations, proved to be more amenable to persuasion than the parent federation, with the result that an eleven-state agreement covering 250,000 men and 2000 operators was signed in August 1938. The agreement had been preceded by a series of key strikes in strategic centers, demonstrating clearly the striking power of the union. Under the terms of the agreement, drivers on through runs were to receive 2¾ cents per mile, plus 75 cents per hour for time lost in pickup and delivery, and special compensation for breakdowns, deadheading, layovers, and impassable highway conditions. A permanent committee was set up by the union to enforce the contract, with Farrell Dobbs as secretary.[64]

The area pact was renewed in 1939, with the mileage rates raised to 3 cents, and hourly allowances to 80 cents. In 1941, the regional organization was renamed the Mid West Central Highway Drivers Council and made into a permanent organization. Its wage movement of that year could not be settled between the parties, and landed eventually in the lap of the War Labor Board.[65]

The Dunne Brothers and Farrell Dobbs, who were instrumental in forging what was to become the most powerful organizational unit within the International Brotherhood of Teamsters, were equally successful in building a stronghold in Minneapolis. They made no effort to conceal their political views; Vincent Dunne, for example, visited Leon Trotsky in 1938,[66] and spoke at many open meetings of the Socialist Workers Party. Local 544 was engaged in a constant feud with the Communist Party. It supported the Machinists' Union when the communist-dominated United Electrical Workers was attempting to take away Machinists' locals at Minneapolis Honeywell Company and other local plants, arguing:

The Minneapolis crisis is not a CIO question, not an industrial union question. This is the question: Is the Minneapolis labor movement to be split up and clubbed into the dirt, all for the purpose of feeding the appetites of the self-seeking Stalinist clique that, having failed to rule the Minneapolis labor movement through fair and honest competition for leadership, is now seeking a violent rupture and open warfare to gain its ends? [67]

In December 1937, Patrick Corcoran, head of the Minneapolis Teamsters' Joint Council and the original neutral chairman of the reorganized Local 544, was murdered, a crime which was never solved. The communists charged that the leaders of Local 544 were responsible for the crime, a charge which John Dewey, the noted educator, termed an example of the Moscow frameup technique. A year later, Bill Brown, the president of Local 544, was shot and killed by a mentally deranged organizer for the union. In 1941, Grant Dunne, under Federal indictment, committed suicide. Thus, three of the top leaders of Local 544 came to violent ends within the space of four years.

Tobin had never forgiven the Dunnes for the defeat which they had administered to him in 1936, and he bided his time until he could move against them. In 1938, a group within Local 544 brought suit to oust the leadership on the basis of the anticommunist clause in the International constitution, but the suit was dismissed on the ground that the followers of Trotsky were hostile to the Communist Party. But in May 1941, without warning, an editorial appeared in the Teamsters' journal to the effect that membership in the Socialist Workers' Party might lead to expulsion from the Teamsters.[68] The executive board of Local 544 replied that the Teamsters' constitution applied specifically to the Communist Party and to no other organization, and concluded: "The names, the record, the ideas and the general attitude of the leading staff of Local 544, collectively and individually, are and have been no secret to anybody, including President Tobin." [69] The officers of Local 544 were given a hearing before the International Executive Board, after which Tobin demanded that the local be placed under receivership pending reorganization under different leadership.[70] When the local refused to act, Tobin revoked the charter and reconstituted it under new officers.

The Dunnes, who had been so hostile to the CIO a few years earlier, accepted a charter from the United Construction Workers Organizing Committee, headed by Denny Lewis, who apparently believed that the Minneapolis group might be used as a nucleus for drawing away other teamster locals. John L. Lewis wired Local 544: "Please convey to mass meeting of truck drivers in Minneapolis area . . . my compliments and my congratulations upon their forward step in joining the Congress of Industrial Organizations. It is my hope that their action in joining the CIO is a forerunner of an intensive drive to bring all truck drivers in the United States into a free and democratic organization." [71] Headquarters for an organizing drive were established in Minneapolis, and the Teamsters' locals in Austin, Minnesota, and Ottumwa, Iowa, switched allegiance to the CWOC. Despite claims of progress among truck drivers in centers dominated by the Automobile Workers' Union, the rival trucking union failed to make any real progress against the Teamsters.

The Teamsters' Union did not take the CIO attack lying down. The following quotation from a Minneapolis newspaper exemplifies the manner in which their counteroffensive was carried out:

Scores of cars, carrying an estimated 200 AFL men cruised the warehouse district and the larger plants, putting the pressure on, where necessary, to sign up drivers and helpers. There were a few fist fights. . . . But on the whole, leaders of the AFL organizers said they experienced little difficulty in ascertaining that the men pledge allegiance to the AFL and the International Brotherhood of Teamsters. One big caravan in the mop-up consisted of several cars with Michigan license plates. . . . The Michigan cars bore nearly a score of labor huskies who were very determined and very tough. . . . In each instance these huskies simply accosted 544 men, persuaded them to accept the new AFL-544 buttons, and sign up with the new AFL set-up. [72]

The IBT imposed a national boycott on trucks driven by CIO men, and persuaded employers to sign contracts with the reorganized local. The National Labor Relations Board refused to intervene at the request of the CIO, but a Minneapolis state conciliator, under prompting from Governor Harold Stassen, who was cooperating with Tobin, certified the AFL group as the bargaining agent for the Minneapolis teamsters. [73]

Even more telling assistance was given to Tobin by the federal government, in what seemed to some contemporary observers a reward for his services to the Democratic Party in the 1940 election campaign. On June 13, Tobin sent the following telegram to President Roosevelt:

The withdrawal from the International Union by the truck drivers union Local 544 and the other small union in Minneapolis, and their affiliation with the CIO is indeed a regrettable and dangerous condition. The officers of this local union . . . were requested to disassociate themselves from the radical Trotsky organization . . . we feel that while our country is in a dangerous position, those disturbers who believe in the policies of foreign, radical governments, must be in some way prevented from pursuing this dangerous course. [74]

In reply, Stephen Early, on behalf of the president, stated that the latter condemned jurisdictional raids. Following swiftly upon the heels of this rebuke, the Department of Justice secured an indictment against 29 current and former leaders of the Socialist Workers' Party, including the Dunne

Brothers, Farrell Dobbs, George Frosig, Kelly Postal, Ray Rainbolt, Carl Skoglund, and Nick Wagner, all officers of CIO Local 544, charging a conspiracy (1) to overthrow the United States Government by force and violence; (2) to spread disaffection among the armed forces; (3) to engage in private military training with arms for the purpose of overthrowing the government. The indictment was based partly upon a Civil War sedition statute and partly upon the newly enacted Smith Act. In a letter to Attorney General Francis Biddle the American Civil Liberties Union, over the signatures of John Haynes Holmes, Roger Baldwin, and Arthur Garfield Hayes, made the following charges:

It is reasonable to conclude that the action . . . taken by the government arose from the President's reaction to Mr. Tobin's request. . . . It may be argued that Mr. Tobin merely called the government's attention to a situation which in itself warranted federal action. But it seems more reasonable to conclude that the government injected itself into an inter-union controversy in order to promote the interests of the one side which supported the administration's foreign and domestic policies. In our judgment, this is a highly improper use of the criminal law. Our conclusion is reinforced by the fact that it has been a matter of common knowledge for some years that the Socialist Workers Party, an insignificant little group of extremists, has been strongly represented in the Minneapolis labor movement — alone of any city in the country. Nothing charged in the indictment is of recent origin. The situation in Minneapolis is no different now from that obtaining over the past five or ten years.

The Department of Justice denied that there was any trade union background to the affair, terming the timing of the indictment purely fortuitous. The trial was held in the fall of 1941, attracting national attention. One of the accused, Albert Goldman, a veteran of the 1934 Minneapolis strike and the principal intellectual light of the Socialist Workers Party, acted as attorney for his codefendants.[75] The jury, after deliberating for 56 hours, found 18 of the defendants guilty of advocating armed revolution, as defined in the Smith Act, but found for the defendants on the other counts, including that of forming a workers' militia.[76] Among those acquitted were Miles Dunne and Kelly Postal, while charges against Frosig and Wagner had been dismissed during the trial for lack of evidence. Twelve of the convicted men were sentenced to 18 months' imprisonment, and six to 12 months' imprisonment, sentences which were upheld on appeal.[77]

The indictment and trial, following upon a campaign into which the International Brotherhood of Teamsters threw all its resources, proved too much for the Trotskyist group, despite the fact that most of the officers of Local 544 were actually acquitted. At the end of 1941, the *Northwest Or-*

ganizer (which had been renamed the *Industrial Organizer* a few months earlier) ceased publication for lack of funds after almost six years without missing an issue. The first — and only — experiment in American Trotskyist trade unionism had come to an end, leaving behind as a monument the Central Conference of Teamsters.

The New England Teamsters.[78] The coordination of Teamster activities in New England took a somewhat different form than in the West and the Central States. In 1933, the only locals still alive in New England were Local 25 in Boston and a small local in Lynn, Mass. Elsewhere, unionism among the truck drivers had been completely eliminated by the depression. Even Local 25, with only 16 contracts, was moribund.[79]

A spurt of organization occurred in 1933. Because of the small geographical area of New England and the contiguity of its cities, the Boston Teamsters recognized from the start that to raise Boston wages, they would have to raise wages in the rest of the region. Employers were able to shift to low wage terminals with greater ease than in the western part of the country. Within a few years, locals had been established in 17 New England cities, and by 1941 there was scarcely an unorganized truck driver, local or over the road, in the entire area. The New England locals were also successful in organizing warehousemen, reacting swiftly to a CIO drive among these workers. The process of organization has been described as follows:

The unionization of most of the men in the transportation part of the trucking industry seems to have been accomplished with relative ease. In a short period of three or four years at least 90 per cent of all eligible employees were organized. This was brought about by several factors. The first and most important were the long hours and low wages universal in the industry prior to the advent of the union. The hours were probably of more importance than the wages. Prior to organization, it was not unusual to hear of truck drivers falling asleep at the wheel because of long hours of labor. Many of them literally made their trucks their homes, except for very brief intervals. . . . With the advent of the N.R.A. and Section 7a, many of the fears of employer discrimination because of union membership were removed and it became possible to organize a union in the industry. The men flocked into the locals rapidly.[80]

It should not be inferred that labor relations in New England trucking were uniformly peaceful. Early in 1939, there was a general trucking strike in Boston, tying up the entire city. Not a truck entered or left Boston during the week the strike lasted. A few months later, nine locals in southern Massachusetts, Rhode Island, and Connecticut engaged in a three-week strike to force the adoption of a uniform agreement for the area, in order to eliminate jurisdictional controversies among the locals. Although the

economic gains achieved through this strike were meager, a uniform contract was adopted, including the establishment of a tri-state Fair Practice
Board to enforce and interpret the agreement.[81]

The principal wage policy problem faced by the New England unions
prior to the war arose out of intercity wage differentials. The relatively high
wage Boston local, for example, lost 500 jobs to surrounding areas between
1935 and 1939 as a result of operators shifting their bases of operations. The
obvious answer was regional uniformity of wage rates, particularly for
over-the-road truckers. The problem was complicated by the fact that because of the closeness of urban centers, there was often no clear line between
local and highway trucking, as there was in the West. There, uniform
highway rates could be established without too much regard for differentials
in local rates. But in New England,

the presence in the group of a large number of local men, who in reality are road
drivers and do a great amount of intercity hauling, renders the adjustment
[equalization] of rates for local drivers more imperative . . . than it would be
if the term local driver were applied only to persons doing strictly local work
and never moving outside of a small radius. It would not matter greatly if
persons doing work in metropolitan Boston received wages higher than those
doing work within the confines of the city of Worcester, except insofar as road
drivers from Worcester could be substituted for local Boston drivers on local
work at lower rates of pay. If this could be done, however, jobs would tend to
move from Boston to Worcester even on local work.[82]

The need of the New England Teamsters' locals for coordination of
collective bargaining policy was as great, if not greater, than that which
gave the initial impetus to the Western and Central conferences. But New
England lagged behind in the regionalization of authority, and one of the
important reasons appears to have been the necessity of first eliminating
gross differences in local wage scales as a condition precedent to uniformity
in highway hauling wages. In 1938, Boston earnings for a 60-hour week
were $44.68, compared with levels ranging from $33.85 to $40.85 for southern
New England and $30 for New Hampshire and Vermont. An obvious first
step was the unification of southern New England rates, which came about
with the tristate agreement of 1939. Certainly the Fair Trade Practices
Board established under this agreement represented as formal and effective
a mechanism for ensuring wage equality as either of the conferences which
were organized at about the same time. As Hill observes:

The regional contract was designed to eliminate wage differentials between
locals, and has succeeded in large measure. As we have seen, the Board has

enforced the wage scale. Thus locals have been freed from the many controversies which arose prior to the uniform contract, as a result of employers turning
runs around to take advantage of favorable wage rates of the low wage locals.

Among other reasons for the failure of New England to develop a full-
fledged conference may have been the ease with which organization was
achieved. Both in the West and the Midwest, the conference developed
initially as an organizing device, and only later took on collective bargaining
as its primary function. Growth of the area of standard bargains in New
England had to wait upon further leveling of local wage scales.

The principal reason for the failure of the East to develop a conference
paralleling those in the West and Midwest was probably the fact that its
over-the-road trucking was neither so large, relatively, nor so strategic as
in the two latter areas. The logical center for an eastern conference was New
York City, but the locals there were content to operate in that great enclave,
largely unaffected by the conditions prevailing in over-the-road trucking
entering New York. In many ways there is a parallel between New York
and San Francisco; the latter, it will be recalled, stayed outside the Western
Conference of Teamsters for many years, though as the most highly organized West Coast center, it would have seemed an obvious focal point for
regional organization. And it will also be recalled that it was Minneapolis,
not Chicago, which took the lead in midwestern regional organization.
Chicago, like New York, was so big a trucking market that the local unions
had neither the desire nor the need to look outside. The same may be said
of Philadelphia, which might have provided eastern leadership.

The Teamsters and the Brewery Workers

A history of the Teamsters' Union would not be complete without at
least a brief account of the fierce jurisdictional fight which it waged against
the Brewery Workers' Union. The latter organization, which was formed
in 1886, early adopted an industrial form of structure, which brought it in
conflict with a number of craft unions. In 1907 its charter was revoked after
it had refused to surrender to the appropriate craft unions the firemen,
engineers, coopers, and teamsters employed in breweries, but the reaction
within the AFL was so strong that the Executive Council was forced to
reinstate it the following year.[83] In 1913, the Executive Council assigned
beer drivers to the Brewery Workers and whiskey and water drivers to
the Teamsters, a solution which led to an uneasy truce until 1918, when the
issue became academic because of the adoption of the prohibition amendment.

When the brewing industry revived in 1933, the AFL, at the demand of the Teamsters, awarded jurisdiction over the beer truck drivers to the Teamsters' Union. The Brewery Workers refused to accept the decision, and trouble began immediately, particularly in the Pacific Northwest. The Teamsters, under the leadership of Dave Beck, negotiated an agreement with 27 brewing and distributing companies in the area, and in retaliation the Brewers, in October 1933, called a strike against the Hemrick Brewing Company of Seattle to force recision of the *de facto* grant of jurisdiction to the Teamsters. The latter union, in turn, supplied inside men to replace the strikers and keep the plant running. Similar action took place in Portland and Salem, Oregon, and in Vancouver and Spokane, Washington. The Brewery Workers also resorted to court injunctions, and a number of Teamsters were jailed for violation of the injunctions, adding fuel to the fire.[84]

The locus of the fight in the Pacific Northwest came to be centered upon the Northwest Brewing Company, operated by one Peter Marinoff. Marinoff had signed with the Teamsters in 1933, but in 1934, after failing to reach a new agreement with the Teamsters, switched his allegiance to the Brewery Workers. A number of brewers were beaten while driving trucks, and damage was inflicted upon establishments using Marinoff beer. When the Northwest Brewing Company was placed on the unfair list by the Washington State Federation of Labor and the Seattle Central Labor Council, Marinoff capitulated and signed with the Teamsters.

Trouble broke out again in 1935, however, when the Teamsters accused Marinoff of contract violations, including the use of Brewer drivers to make deliveries through Teamster picket lines. A strike was called, and Marinoff attempted once more to operate with Brewery Worker drivers. On May 24, 1935, a Teamster picket was fatally wounded by an armed guard conveying a Marinoff truck in Seattle, leading to a hardening of labor opinion against the Brewery Workers, who were revealed to have lent Marinoff $150,000 to help keep him in business. The Seattle Central Trades Council expelled the Brewery Workers local from membership, an action which was first reversed by the AFL Executive Council, and then upheld under pressure from Beck.[85] The Brewery Workers protested to the Executive Council against their exclusion, alleging that, among other things, the Teamsters had supplied false union labels to employers against whom the Brewery Workers had struck. An old-time Brewer told the Council:

The members of the Brewery Workers feel they had this jurisdiction and they still hold that the conventions have no right to take over beer drivers. That is the sentiment of the rank and file and you cannot change that any more than we can. I have known them for 46 years. The brewery worker feels he is entitled to work in every department making beer. How can he then believe he can scab on anybody else? You can talk from now to doomsday, you cannot tell brewery workers they scab in a brewery.

The council affirmed its earlier decision, nonetheless. The Northwest Brewing Company was forced out of business, and was taken over and operated by the Brewery Workers' Union as the United Union Brewing Company. By 1936 the Teamsters had gained control of the brewing industry in Washington and Oregon, including inside workers as well as drivers. The Brewery Workers then attempted to label Teamster-produced beer unfair, and to promote the importation of beer from California and the Midwest, whereupon the Teamsters imposed an embargo on all beer coming into the region, which was later modified to admit beer bearing the Teamster label. The Brewery Workers protested to the AFL that the Teamsters were not in manufacturing and therefore not entitled to the use of a label; and that the Teamster label was an almost indistinguishable copy of its own.[86] But the Executive Council upheld the Teamster label, and the embargo, as modified, continued in effect. It was some time before outside beer began to come in to Oregon and Washington, forced mainly by injunctions secured by the Brewery Workers and employers.[87]

Although the Teamsters in the Pacific Northwest carried on the most aggressive and successful warfare against the Brewery Workers, trouble was by no means confined to this area. In the Midwest, the Brewery Workers were supported by a number of central labor councils. The AFL Executive Council, on a motion by Tobin, with Lewis and Coefield opposed, directed the local councils to cease such action under penalty of having their charters suspended.[88] As between the powerful Teamsters' Union and the newly-reorganized Brewery Workers, there was no question where the choice of the Executive Council would lie. After 1933, the AFL consistently backed the Teamsters at every juncture.

Tobin did not hesitate to use any weapon against the Brewery Workers, including the entirely unmerited charge of communism. Thus, he wrote in 1936:

All Communists with any influence are favoring the Brewery Workers and are opposed to our International Union and consequently are opposed to the decisions of the American Federation of Labor. We wonder why. Certainly it is because the Brewery Workers must be closely allied or in sympathy with the Communist leaders who hate and despise the American Federation of Labor and its policies. . . . All the Communists and radicals and all the other men who hate the United States and its government, but who will not leave here, are opposed to the Teamsters and in favor of the Brewery Workers and the industrial form of unionism.[89]

In 1938, open hostilities broke out once more, this time in Detroit. After the Teamsters had chartered a local of brewery drivers there, the Brewery Workers secured an injunction ordering employers to live up to their contracts with the latter union. The Teamsters called a strike, effectively tying up the breweries of the city, but were persuaded to submit the dispute to Frank Martel, president of the Detroit Federation of Labor, for arbitration. Much to the surprise of all concerned, Martel ruled in favor of the Brewery Workers. Tobin waxed indignant at this unexpected turn of events:

No one has a right to arbitrate decisions made on our jurisdiction by the American Federation of Labor, but we have endeavored to give you the reasons above why the Teamsters agreed to such procedure, which again we repeat, was because, as they state themselves, that they were given to understand, either directly or indirectly, that if they did agree the decision would be in their favor, and that by such a decision it was giving the courts and the brewery owners and others a chance to find a way out.

The AFL Executive Council informed Martel that his decision was contrary to AFL laws, and directed the Detroit Council to support the Teamsters. Martel replied that his decision was made in a personal and not an official capacity, and that it was taken because "the trucks of the breweries having attempted to go on the street have been destroyed, many men have been beaten up, and many have been arrested on both sides. . . . The nature of the controversy was one that was bringing extreme discredit upon the labor movement as represented by the American Federation of Labor unions in this city." [90] Martel was nevertheless directed to reverse his decision.

In October 1938, Tobin informed the AFL Executive Council that unless all Brewery Worker locals had been suspended from city councils and state federations by December 1 of that year, his organization would withdraw from all such bodies. At the urging of William Green, he agreed to withhold action until the constitutionality of the matter had been investigated. When the general counsel of the AFL reported that suspension of the Brewery Workers' locals from local AFL bodies would have to be preceded by suspension of the international union from the AFL itself, the Executive Council voted to recommend such action to the 1939 convention. The Brewery Workers would probably have been suspended in 1939 had they not managed to secure a federal court injunction restraining the AFL from interfering with their jurisdiction on the ground that such action violated a contract right conferred upon them by their AFL charter of affiliation.[91] The AFL convention voted to appoint a conciliation committee which was to report to the Executive Council in 30 days, and empowered the council to take whatever action it deemed necessary if no agreement could be reached.[92] A vice-president of the Teamsters explained frankly the adamancy of his organization in the following terms:

Well, some people may say, why should the Teamsters bother with a handful of men in the Brewery Workers' organization? They have a big organization of over 400,000 members. It is true we have, and we expect to have a million workers some day. We expect to have any man who drives a vehicle in this country. . . . If we were to relinquish this jurisdiction, if we were to let the brewery workers go their way with this matter, what will every other organization do, what will every other organization think? Are they any better than the bakery workers who gladly — not gladly but willingly, when the Council decided so — relinquished their jurisdiction over the men driving bakery wagons?

The conciliation committee reported back to the council that both organizations had refused to make any concessions, leading the Executive Council to adopt a statement in condemnation of the Brewery Workers, and indicating that the organization would be expelled from the AFL as soon as the Federal injunction had been lifted.[93] In 1941, the injunction was set aside by the U. S. Circuit Court of Appeals, this decision being sustained by the U. S. Supreme Court. The 1941 AFL convention, by an overwhelming majority, voted to suspend the Brewery Workers, although a substantial number of delegates, including those representing the Bakery Workers, the Iron Workers, the Railway Clerks, the Electrical Workers, and the Butcher Workmen, were recorded as not voting.[94] Many of these organizations had themselves been involved in jurisdictional disputes with the Teamsters, and had been forced to cede jurisdiction to avoid the fate of the Brewery Workers.

This was by no means the end of the matter. During the war there was a temporary truce, but in 1946 the Brewery Workers affiliated with the CIO and the controversy was transformed from a jurisdictional into a rival union dispute. The Teamsters pressed the advantage which their greater resources afforded them and, by the time of the AFL-CIO merger, had succeeded in winning most of the beer drivers and a large proportion of the inside workers as well. The outcome of this dispute provided an object lesson for other unions with jurisdictions impinging upon the sphere of organization claimed by the Teamsters. In this case, as well as all others, "the Teamsters protected their claims by whatever means were feasible or necessary. They disregarded picket lines, conducted organizing campaigns behind picket lines, collaborated with employers against the rival union, recruited personnel to replace strikers, and applied damaging secondary boycotts against rival unions and employers dealing with such unions." [95]

The membership claimed by the Teamsters at various times during the period 1936 to 1941 was as follows:

January 1936	150,000[96]
December 1936	180,000
June 1937	250,000
January 1938	300,000
October 1939	450,000
June 1940	500,000
January 1941	500,000
August 1941	530,000

However, these figures included all members carried on the books, and they must be revised downward to allow for dues delinquencies and normal turnover. Thus, average annual dues paying membership for the year 1939 was estimated at about 350,000, and at about 450,000 for the first six months of 1940. By any measure, the Teamsters' Union tripled its membership from 1936 to 1941, and emerged as the largest national union in the American Federation of Labor, if not in the entire American labor movement. It had asserted jurisdiction successfully over truck drivers in every industry, and over many other categories of workers as well. Whereas at the beginning of the preceding decade, Teamster locals had been confined to a few of the major cities of the country, by 1941 there was scarcely a town of any size into which the Teamsters did not reach. In addition to the national journal, ten local Teamster newspapers were being published in various parts of the country.[97] Even this impressive record of growth was to be dwarfed, however, by the tremendous surge in membership and power that took place in the decade of the nineteen-forties.

Although there were signs of a radically new brand of labor philosophy within it, particularly in the Western Conference, where Dave Beck held sway, the prewar Teamsters' Union, for all its aggressiveness and militancy, remained traditionally AFL in outlook and in its ethical preconceptions. While there were bad local situations, the national leadership, at least, continued to practice the mixture of business unionism and idealism that had characterized the approach of Samuel Gompers, of whom Daniel Tobin always spoke with warm respect. But Tobin was fully aware of the dangers, as well as the advantages, which such tremendous power as the Teamsters were able to mobilize carried with it, and he was constantly urging caution, responsibility, and honesty upon his membership. With the ascendancy of Dave Beck, James R. Hoffa, and Frank Brewster within the national organization, the restraining ties with the past were broken, and a type of pure business unionism, unadulterated by any shred of even the Tobin brand of idealism, emerged. The consequences of trade unionism *sans doctrines* for the American labor movement have become all too evident.

15

The Machinists

The International Association of Machinists was an organization which, up to the mid-nineteen-thirties, was having trouble making up its mind on structure and jurisdiction. It was torn between a loyalty to craft unionism, on the one hand, and the desire to organize manufacturing establishments on an industrial basis on the other hand. Apart from William Hutcheson, no member of the AFL Executive Council was more bitterly opposed to industrial unionism in 1935 than A. O. Wharton, the Machinists' president; nor was any member inclined to be less compromising in his attitude toward the CIO. In arguing for the expulsion of the CIO unions in 1936, Wharton said: "I do not know of any International that would tolerate a condition within its own ranks that the American Federation of Labor is now confronted with. . . . There is no institution in the country that has not the right through its duly constituted authority to protect itself against insurrection within its ranks." [1] The *Machinists' Monthly Journal* commented editorially on the CIO soon after its formation as follows: "The I.A. of M., through its responsible officers, cannot . . . do other than resist with all the power at its command, any attempt on the part of the so-called C.I.O. to organize in Industrial Unions, or any other unions than the I.A. of M., those employed on work over which it claims jurisdiction. If machinists, or those eligible to the I.A. of M. are to be parceled around among several unions, industrial or otherwise, it means the beginning of the end for the I.A. of M., whose members now find employment in every industry no matter what its character may be." [2]

Yet when faced with the alternative of permitting organization by rival unions, the Machinists' Union unhesitatingly admitted to membership workers whose classification as machinists was feasible only by a construction of that term which would have delighted the heart of the most rabid industrial unionist. While the most obvious example of this policy was the organization of the aircraft industry, the union had in effect been moving in this direction for many years. Initially it was an organization of highly skilled craftsmen engaged in the construction, repair, and maintenance of locomotives, marine and stationary engines. A period of apprenticeship was required for entrance to the trade, and apprentices were admitted to membership only during their last six months in such status. In 1904, however, the bars were let down with the absorption of the Allied Metal Mechanics, a group of specialist rather than general machinists, and the process of broadening jurisdiction continued with the admission of semiskilled automobile and aircraft workers under the impact of technological changes which were destroying old skills. Thus, by 1936, the Machinists' Union had established a dual craft–industrial structure, which is well reflected in the following pronouncement by its president:

Speaking of our own organization, I have frequently said it is more of an industrial organization than many which claim to be industrial organizations. . . . Our organization is industrial; at least semi-industrial. . . . The aircraft industry has just come under the jurisdiction of the International Association of Machinists by the decision of the American Federation of Labor. . . . We have various other branches of the trade, such as tool makers and die sinkers, that are highly specialized. We are going into the production field and doing some splendid work in those plants where we have been successful.[3]

The stake of the IAM in craft unionism was clear. It had members who were engaged in the railroad industry, historically the most important branch of its jurisdiction; in shipyards and government navy yards; in the construction of newspaper printing presses and office equipment; and in many other metal fabricating plants. But its approach to the automobile and aircraft industries was more that of a vertical organization. The IAM claimed jurisdiction over automobile repair shops as a whole; over shops producing automobile parts (on the theory that such shops were engaged in the fabrication of parts for other industries as well); and over virtually all workers in aircraft plants. In large measure, the story of the IAM from 1936 to 1941 is concerned with the relative strengthening of its proclivities toward industrial unionism, of its conversion from a predominantly craft-oriented organization into one of the great mass production trade unions of the country, in the face of strong internal pressures to preserve the traditional multicraft form.

The rapid growth of the CIO in the first years of its existence was paralleled by the expansion of many AFL unions; the history of Teamster growth has already been recounted. The International Association of Machinists was another of the old-line unions which availed itself of the opportunities presented by the combination of the economic upswing and a favorable climate of public opinion, reflected in a federal government administration friendly to the aspirations of organized labor. In 1935, average dues-paying membership was 88,887. There was an increase to 105,063 in 1936, and to 152,022 in 1937.[4] In commenting upon the record of the year 1937, which, it will be recalled, was the period of the first CIO drives, IAM Vice-President C. F. Grow said: "it is a great satisfaction and pleasure to note that the I.A. of M. has made more gains in all fields of activity than in any previous single year; 1937 was truly a banner year."[5]

In the first instances, expansion came about by the dubious expedient of absorbing small unions which were under the domination of the Communist Party through affiliation with the Trade Union Unity League. These were the Federation of Metal and Allied Unions, led by James Matles, and the Transport Workers' Union of New York City, of which Michael Quill was president. In explaining the admission of production workers and New York subway guards to the IAM, Wharton noted that "the doors of the I.A. of M. are, and have been for many years, open to all persons — male and female — who are actively engaged in or *connected* with the Machinists' trade." It is interesting to find Wharton, one of the strongest apostles of conservative AFL craft unionism, speaking in the following vein of Matles, Quill, Santo, and others who were closely identified with the Communist Party:

We cannot pass this opportunity to pay tribute to the representatives of the Federation of Metal and Allied Unions; the Machine Tool and Foundry Workers' Union, and to those of the Transport Workers' Union. We found them live, intelligent, energetic young men, whose conduct during the negotiations leading up to the agreement, was at all times dignified and gentlemanly; they proved themselves well qualified to carry on the negotiations for those they had the honor to represent.

The agreements with these organizations,[6] dated February 18, 1936, brought into the IAM about 10,000 members. However, the new recruits came in as a bloc, retaining intact the majority of their locals and officers, and were never integrated into the IAM. By May 1937, the "live, intelligent, energetic young men" had led the Transport Workers and the former Metal and Allied Union into the CIO, in response to a change in the line of the Communist Party from "boring from within" the AFL to affiliation with the CIO. The Machinists must have been aware of the political background of the newly acquired unions, for they subsequently showed considerable sophistication in dealing with communist infiltration of their local lodges. Indeed, Matles, as a local IAM leader, had earlier taken several locals out of the organization into the Communist Trade Union Unity League, while Santo had edited the Hungarian language newspaper of the Communist Party.[7] The Machinists' leaders may have planned to eliminate these left-wing leaders after weaning their followers away, but the rise of the CIO deprived them of the opportunity to carry out such an operation.

The Remington Rand Strike

Early in the period with which we are dealing, the IAM became embroiled in what was to become one of the notorious strikes of the era, directed against the Remington Rand Company. Organization work among the employees of this corporation was undertaken in 1933,[8] and after a brief strike in 1934, Remington Rand signed collective agreements with local unions which were either affiliated with AFL international unions or were directly affiliated with the AFL. The Machinists' Union, which held contracts for the plants at Middletown, Connecticut; Ilion, Tonawanda and Syracuse, New York; Norwood, Ohio; and Cambridge, Massachusetts, had the lion's share of the employees. In the fall of 1935 the various unions involved formed the Remington Rand Joint Protective Board of the District Council of Office Equipment Workers, under the auspices of the AFL Metal Trades Department, in order to present a united front to the company.[9]

In November 1935, the IAM learned that plans were afoot to concentrate the company's operations in a new plant at Elmira, New York. It was also rumored that the new plant would be operated on a nonunion basis. President Rand refused to meet with union representatives, but a company representative did meet with the unions on April 24, 1936 in a noncommittal interview, at which a union request for increased wages was discussed inconclusively.

The unions conducted a strike vote among their members, at which over 75 per cent of the organized employees voted in favor of a stoppage of work. The company replied by conducting its own strike ballot, which was boycotted by the unions, and announced that the overwhelming majority of the employees desired to remain at work. After a brief sit-down strike at the Syracuse, New York, plant, the company discharged sixteen union leaders and shut its plant down. The Joint Council in turn called a strike at all the plants for May 26, 1936.

Remington Rand then initiated a campaign designed to rid itself of unionization which the corporation itself proudly advertised as the "Mohawk Valley Formula." The events at Ilion, New York, a town of 10,000 people largely dependent upon Remington Rand for employment opportunities, can be taken as a typical application of the "Formula." Shortly before the strike was called, a group of Ilion business men met with James H. Rand, Jr., the president of the corporation, in New York City, and were told that Ilion had been a good place to operate until the union came into the picture. While the discussion was under way a group of Rand employees from Ilion was ushered into the room, and assured Rand that the Ilion workers were opposed to the American Federation of Labor. Rand informed both groups that he would not again personally meet with AFL representatives.

On May 26, all the employees, about 1800 in number, went on strike. Although there was no disorder, 100 guards supplied by the Foster Industrial and Detective Bureau and the Burns Detective Agency appeared at the plant, armed with clubs. Immediately the situation became tense, but the mayor refused to deputize the plant guards as law enforcement officers. To put pressure on the local authorities, the company announced that it was selling the plant, and began to move machinery out as evidence of its intention. Barney Allen, the leader of the business group that had conferred with Rand, visited Rand again and was told that the plant would be reopened if a majority of the employees returned to work under adequate police protection. The mayor of Ilion and officials of nearby communities were brought together with Rand, and were given the same assurance.

The entire police force of Ilion numbered only six, falling far short of Rand's requirements. Governor Lehman of New York State refused to supply state police. The business group then approached the local sheriff, and arranged to have 300 men sworn in as special deputies.

On June 8, the businessmen's group and a newly formed Ilion Typewriter Employees' Association held a joint meeting and called upon the mayor and the police chief to clear the streets and drive union organizers out of town. After first refusing, the mayor, under further pressure, agreed to cooperate.

The evening of that same day Mayor Whitney met with two of the leaders of the Ilion unions. He explained to them, tearfully, "that he was being compelled to do things that he didn't want to do, because these particular interests had and could wield an influence which would ruin him." The Mayor was one of the largest property owners in Ilion "and was afraid of this committee, members of which included bankers, . . . he could easily be a ruined man and have nothing left but his hat, coat and pants if these people were to clamp down on him as they were able to do and in a manner which he felt fearful they would do."

An advertisement appeared in the local newspaper, inserted by the Employees' Protective Association, stating that when enough applications to return to work had been secured, the association would petition Rand to reopen the plant. On June 10, arrangements were made for a meeting to be held at the plant of employees desirous of returning to work. All the streets surrounding the plant were roped off, deputies and police were present in force. Disturbances "were treated with a severity completely beyond necessity, thereby heightening the intimidation worked by the display of force." Tear gas was used in dispersing the crowd. About 500 employees entered the plant, and Rand personally appeared to congratulate them upon their decision.

Preparations were made to open the plant in earnest the next day. The mayor declared that a state of emergency existed, additional deputies were sworn in, all roads leading into the town were blockaded, and only persons with passes issued by the association were permitted to enter the town. The headquarters of the Ilion unions were padlocked. Foremen visited the homes of employees, promising them $5 in cash and $10 later for merely entering the plant. The result was foregone; on June 12, about 1200 employees entered the plant, and the strike was effectively broken. A celebration was held there the next day, at which businessmen and town officials made jubilant speeches. Rand congratulated the town for its action. "Two million business men have been looking for a formula like this and business has hoped for, dreamed of and prayed for such an example as you have set," an example that "would go down into history as the Mohawk Valley Formula." The National Association of Manufacturers picked up this phrase, and gave it nationwide publicity. Subsequent investigation revealed that the back-to-work movement had been fostered by "missionaries" in the employ of Pearl Bergoff, a notorious strikebreaker.[10]

Events at other plants of Remington Rand followed much the same course, with President Rand supervising the company's campaign in each city involved. In Middletown, Connecticut, he enlivened things by personally riding along the picket line with a motion picture camera and photographing the pickets. Labor spies were used in large numbers, and picket line disturbances were deliberately fomented. By the end of 1936, Remington Rand was operating with a full complement of men at all its plants, without a union contract.

Up to the beginning of September 1936, the Machinists' Union had contributed $123,600 toward financing this strike.[11] It continued to support the strike until March 1937, when an agreement was reached with the company providing that strikers were to be reemployed if jobs were available for them, while all those not replaced were to be paid $10 a week each for a maximum of six weeks.[12] The corporation refused to enter into a collective agreement with the union, and many active union men were denied reemployment. The IAM continued to maintain some organization at Remington Rand plants, while the National Labor Relations Board pursued the company through the courts in an endeavor to force disestablishment of company unions and abstention from interference with the employees in the exercise of their bargaining rights. In 1940, a boycott was instituted against Remington Rand products,[13] but the outbreak of war in 1941 found the IAM still outside the company's plants.

The Grand Lodge and the Locals

The history of the International Association of Machinists was made to a great extent by the local lodges rather than by the Grand Lodge, as the international union is termed. Unlike the new CIO unions, which at least in the early stages of their development, were built and controlled from the top, the Machinists' organization developed first on a local basis. There is in this organization, as in many other old AFL unions, a strong tradition of local autonomy, which has on occasion led to conflict when locals were following policies deemed inimical to the welfare of the national union by the Grand Lodge. Several of these conflicts were important enough not only to leave an imprint upon the internal political life of the union, but to have a significant effect upon collective bargaining relationships as well.

The Grand Lodge, by virtue of its control of the union's strike funds, exercises a considerable degree of authority over collective bargaining. The IAM constitution provides that before a strike can be called, three-fourths of the workers who will be involved in the strike must give their approval by secret ballot. Then, "the recording secretary of the local lodge shall prepare a full statement and history of the matters in controversy and forward the same to the International President, who shall thereupon in person or by deputy visit the local lodge where the controversy exists, and, with a member of the local lodge whose members are involved, investigate the controversy and if possible effect a settlement." [14] The dispute must then be submitted to the Executive Council of the Grand Lodge for strike sanction; declaration of a strike without permission of the Executive Council means not only deprivation of strike benefits, but is cause for suspension of the local lodge charter. A major function of the IAM Executive Council is thus the review of wage and hour grievances from local lodges and the determination of whether they are serious enough to warrant strike action.

Beginning in 1936, relations between the Grand Lodge and its locals in the San Francisco area became strained. Lodge 68 in San Francisco and 284 in Oakland had called strikes without complying with the strike vote procedure in the union constitution,[15] after President Wharton of the International had been unable to reach agreement with the employers. The Executive Council had proposed that the dispute be submitted to arbitration, but the local leadership rejected this advice. Nothwithstanding the unconstitutional action of the locals, the Grand Lodge ultimately sanctioned the strike, the outcome of which was a victory for the unions. Local Lodge 68 actually had a long history of disobeying the constitution and the Grand Lodge with respect to the calling of strikes. It had taken the bit in its teeth in 1919, and again in 1931. One reason for this was the fact that Lodge 68 had not been organized by the IAM, but affiliated with the latter when already organized. It considered itself older than the IAM and exempt from the rules that were binding on ordinary lodges.

During the summer of 1936, Oakland Lodge 284 became involved in a dispute with 37 employers. A strike vote was conducted in an illegal manner, according to the Grand Lodge. Although an International representative was on the scene and conferring with employers, the strike of 1800 men became effective on July 20. In consequence, the IAM Executive Council revoked the local charter and suspended its officers from membership. In partial justification for this action, it was alleged that the local business agent had employed Communist Party leaders to work out of his office, and that they had been fomenting trouble in the area.[16]

E. F. Dillon, the business agent of San Francisco Lodge 68, appeared before the Executive Council to protest the manner in which his close ally had been handled. He argued that the Oakland local was striking to secure the conditions prevailing in San Francisco, and that the action of the International was proving detrimental to the conduct of the strike. The following colloquy took place at the meeting of the Executive Council:

Wharton: There is a general attitude of disrespect for the Grand Lodge. That goes for you and the members of 284 who seem to think the Grand Lodge is an alien group and does not have the interest of the organization at heart. . . .

Dillon: After all is said and done, who do you think is in the best position to best judge a local situation of this kind?

Wharton: That all depends upon the circumstances. The difference between you and the Grand Lodge would be this — that you assume that the Grand Lodge does not know anything about the situation in San Francisco and apparently you assume that the attitude of the Grand Lodge is not sympathetic toward the membership. You are wrong again.[17]

The issue was debated for a day and a half at the 1936 convention of the IAM. Dillon and other West Coast delegates asserted that the International representatives who had been assigned to the situation did not have the confidence of the workers; that the allegations of communism were vague and unsubstantiated; and that the International had overstepped the bounds of propriety in conducting secret negotiations with employers.[18] The International officers contended that the local had acted in an insubordinate and unconstitutional manner, and that the revocation of its charter was fully merited. The convention sustained the action of the Executive Council.

However, this proved to be merely the beginning rather than the end of the controversy. The expelled Local 284 became the East Bay Machinists' Union, and received a charter from the CIO Steel Workers' Organizing Committee. Despite the efforts of the Grand Lodge to take over its membership, the old local retained the allegiance of the machinists within its jurisdiction. It was aided by the refusal of San Francisco Lodge 68 to break off relations; not only did Lodge 68 continue to recognize the working cards of the East Bay Machinists' Union, but it even provided financial assistance on occasion. Nor was it only the San Francisco group which persisted in this attitude. In 1938, in a letter to Wharton, the California State Conference of Machinists urged that Lodge 284 receive its charter back, and continued:

in going over this situation, we want to inform you, in no uncertain terms, that we find that while the boys in old 284 made mistakes, they are not alone in this. We find that the Representatives handling this situation also made some very costly mistakes, and had this matter been handled by one with a bit of diplomacy, this situation would never have occurred.[19]

Negotiations for the reaffiliation of Lodge 248 foundered on the refusal of the Grand Lodge to agree to reinstate all members of the expelled local with full rights dating from the time of expulsion, and to permit all officers to continue to hold positions of leadership. The issue was debated again at considerable length at the 1940 Convention of the IAM. Dillon once more took up the cudgels for Lodge 248, and explained the reluctance of the California Machinists to break with this local:

let me advise you, whether you know it or not, that the San Francisco Bay Area, all the sea-going trades with the exception of the sailors, are C.I.O. organizations.

The warehouse men have a local of some 8,000 members in the City of San Francisco. We have any number of our men in the maintenance shops who work with these C.I.O. warehouses. We have 100 or 150 men that go to Alaska every year in the Alaska salmon-canning season. They ship up there with a solid contingent of C.I.O. cannery workers, fishermen, and other workers — some of the highest paying jobs that our members have.

Now, do you think for one minute that it doesn't constitute a very serious proposition when you begin to talk about opening up a feud with all of those solidly organized groups? Nobody else in San Francisco is doing it. Even the teamsters' union group works with the C.I.O., not because of desire, but because of necessity.[20]

The East Bay Machinists' Union remained outside the IAM, but relations between the parent organization and its San Francisco local improved somewhat as a consequence of the events of a national defense strike in which the local became embroiled in the spring of 1941. On April 23, 1941, the Metal Trades Department, with which the IAM was affiliated, had entered into a master agreement covering all shipbuilding workers on the West Coast. The Bethlehem Shipbuilding Corporation refused to accept several provisions of the agreement, in particular a clause providing for double pay for overtime work and a union shop provision, whereupon Lodge 68 of the IAM declared a strike against it.[21] The remaining metal trades locals in the area honored the IAM picket lines at first, but then returned to work at the direction of their respective international unions.[22] The Grand Lodge of the IAM gave reluctant approval to the strike, which involved one of the major shipyards of the country, engaged at the time entirely in national defense work. On June 9, Harvey Brown, who had succeeded Wharton as president of the IAM, was called to the White House by President Roosevelt and asked to call the strike off in the national interest. In deference to this request, the Grand Lodge, on June 12, ordered the termination of the work stoppage, but this order was rejected by the strikers by a vote of 385 to 370, whereupon the Grand Lodge discontinued financial assistance to the local. The IAM was under intense pressure from the American Federation of Labor to take this action; the AFL Executive Council had adopted a resolution insisting that the strike be terminated, and the IAM International representative on the Pacific Coast wrote as follows of AFL policy in this situation:

The Bethlehem Company had refused to be a party to the master agreement but insisted on their right to accept such parts of the agreement as they chose to apply. . . . This, our machinists refused to do. Now the rest is history, during which we witnessed one of the most unprecedented spectacles where John P.

Frey, President of the Metal Trades Department of the A.F. of L., advertised himself as a new Moses, leading strikebreakers through the picket lines.[23]

Allegations of communism and radicalism against the strikers by the press did little to put them in a conciliatory frame of mind. However, when E. C. Davison, the IAM secretary-treasurer, arrived on the Pacific Coast armed with a promise from Sidney Hillman, in his capacity as associate director of the Office of the Production Management, that Bethlehem would be obliged to meet all the terms of the Shipbuilding Master Agreement, the strikers voted to return to work. Davison stated that he "failed to find the slightest evidence of any connections between our local leadership and subversive or Communist groups. It was apparent that there were a great many radical individuals engaged in this strike, but their radicalism was directed toward the preservation of the American standards of living. . . ."[24] The tactful manner in which the international union handled this strike, in sharp contrast to the heavy-handed diplomacy of Wharton in the earlier Oakland situation, did much to allay hostilities within the organization.

Several other incidents involving friction between the international union and local unions arose out of communist infiltration into local situations. In 1934, the Minneapolis locals of the IAM fell under the domination of active communists, led by Harry Mayville and William Mauseth. Although suspended from membership in 1936, they continued to play an active role in the affairs of the locals. In the fall of 1937, they succeeded in taking substantial portions of the local membership into the United Electrical Workers' Union, CIO, for which Mauseth became an organizer. One of the arguments used with great effect by the communist group was that the local Machinist groups, which had organized the Minneapolis-Moline and other machinery manufacturing plants on an industrial basis, were going to be parceled out among the AFL craft unions, an eventuality which was strongly opposed by the workers. Vincent R. Dunne, the Trotskyist leader of the Minneapolis Teamsters, appeared before a Machinists' investigating committee and offered the cooperation of the Teamsters in cleaning out the communists. "Brother Dunne suggested that a public declaration should be made by the Executive Council that the policy of the International Association of Machinists is — that the organization will continue its present policy of taking into membership all of those engaged in, or connected directly or indirectly with the Machinery Industry, as had been done in the past."[25] Thus, the Machinists' Union was involved, although somewhat tangentially, in the bitter political sectarian strife that rent the Minneapolis labor movement for almost a decade.[26]

The issue of communism arose again in connection with Seattle Lodge 751, which represented the employees of the Boeing Aircraft plant in that city. Charges of communism had been levied against several active members of this strategically placed union late in 1940, and local trial committees were appointed to hear the charges, but the proceedings were so dilatory as to suggest deliberate obstruction by the local officials. The international union decided to step into the picture, and President Harvey Brown was despatched to Seattle in April 1941. In an open letter to the members of Local 751, written soon after his arrival on the scene, Brown wrote:

Subversive forces are deceptively working to obstruct the National Defense Program. Recently, there was plotted a program to cause a stoppage of work, to bring idleness to all employees of the Boeing Aircraft Company. The time has come for you to call a halt. Developments demand that every loyal member, worthy of our American institutions, cooperate to the utmost in cleansing Lodge No. 751 of the Communist element now gnawing at its vitals.[27]

A few days later, he wrote in the same vein that "Aeronautical Mechanics Lodge 751 has been a long suffering victim of Communist strategy, character assassins, deliberate lying; in fact, perjury to create confusion, prejudice, hate, bitter feeling among members." The matter was handled by revoking the charter of the local, expelling the communist activists, and splitting the local into six separate lodges in order to prevent reassertion of communist control.[28] This was a delicate operation, since the Machinists were locked in a bitter struggle with the United Automobile Workers for hegemony over the aircraft industry, but it was carried out successfully.[29]

These were some of the highlights in the internal life of the Machinists' Union between 1936 and 1941. Of the relatively uneventful, day-to-day relationships among the hundreds of locals and the Grand Lodge there is little that the general historian can say, although they were of the essence of the Machinists' development. It must be left to the historian of the IAM to record the less spectacular but more fruitful details of local organizing and collective bargaining, aided by a large staff of Grand Lodge representatives,[30] which transformed the IAM into one of the giants of American trade unionism.

The Aircraft Industry

The International Association of Machinists first received jurisdiction over mechanics in the aircraft industry in October 1934, by a decision of the AFL Executive Council. There was little organization in what was then a small industry; there were only a few AFL federal locals, which were transferred to the IAM. The potentialities of the situation were not entirely lost on other AFL craft unions, however. In 1936, the Sheet Metal Workers protested to the Executive Council that the term "aircraft mechanics," as interpreted by the Machinists, included men who were engaged in the fabrication of sheet metal.[31] Wharton, at the time one of the leaders in the fight against the CIO unions, promised that the Machinists were "willing to work with any organization and would not hold tight to this action of the Council," whereupon the Executive Council adopted the following resolution:

Having been informed by the representative of the Machinists' Union that in the enforcement of jurisdiction granted to it over aircraft mechanics the Machinists' Union did not intend to do violence to the legitimate and practical claims of any organization affiliated to the American Federation of Labor, and was prepared to take up any possible grievances, it is moved the Sheet Metal Workers be so advised.

Two years later, however, the Machinists were in a much less conciliatory frame of mind, faced with the realities of organizing the industry. In a reply to further protest by the Sheet Metal Workers, they declared:

The Sheet Metal Workers have done nothing in organizing the air craft mechanics in the commercial aviation field, while the Machinists have gone out to organize against the CIO on the only basis that could be successful and that is, taking in all mechanics. President Wharton further states that if this method of organization is interfered with, the Machinists could not continue to organize in this industry.

After this, there was no further talk of the "legitimate and practical claims" of craft unions in the aircraft industry. The Machinists operated there on as fully an industrial union basis as its principal competitor, the United Automobile Workers, uninhibited by the paper jurisdictional claims of fellow AFL unions, and with little protest by the latter until after the war.

When the IAM and the United Automobile Workers began organizing campaigns in the aircraft industry early in 1937, the industry employed only about 30,000 men, of whom about 12,000 were in Southern California, which was to become the major center of airframe construction. By the beginning of 1941, total employment had risen to more than 200,000, and during 1941, employment rose rapidly under the pressing demands of defense and war production.[32]

The Machinists had early organized the Boeing Aircraft Company plant in Seattle, and consolidated its status there by securing a closed shop contract, which placed it in an impregnable position. With 8000 members, the Seattle lodge remained the largest single aircraft unit of the IAM until the outbreak of the war.[33] Having thus established itself on the Pacific Coast, the burgeoning Southern California area was a natural next step for the Machinists. But here they came into conflict with the young and ambitious United Automobile Workers' Union, flushed with victory over the giants of the automobile industry.

In February 1937, an independent union, the Western Mechanics' Industrial Union, organized a few hundred employees at the Douglas Aircraft plant in Santa Monica and asked the company for a collective agreement. Douglas replied by discharging several union leaders, whereupon the UAW stepped in, assumed control of the independent union, and engaged in a sit-down strike. The sit-downers threatened to set fire to the plant if any attempt were made to evict them, but eventually withdrew when 345 men were indicted for forcible entry and occupancy, without having achieved their objective of a collective agreement.

The CIO turned its attention next to the Lockheed Aircraft Corporation in Los Angeles. This company, alarmed by the events at Douglas, decided that if there had to be a union, the IAM was preferable to the UAW. ". . . the C.I.O. men were arrested by the local police, while the Machinists' representatives, called in by some Lockheed workers, managed to sign up 800 or 900 of the then 1,000 employees and to negotiate a contract with a cordially acquiescent management, all within the space of three weeks." The contract was a very liberal one for the time, providing the highest wage rate in the industry: a 48-cents an hour hiring rate, compared with 40 cents being paid by Douglas. The union received a voluntary checkoff, but the company balked at granting a union shop. The Lockheed lodge of the IAM became its second largest aircraft local in the prewar period. The Machinists also managed to gain bargaining rights for the employees of Consolidated Aircraft at San Diego,[34] as well as at such aircraft motor concerns as Curtiss-Wright and Canadian Car and Foundry. In April 1940 they claimed 19,741 members in 17 aircraft lodges, the majority of them at Boeing and Lockheed.[35]

The UAW, after its initial defeats at Douglas and Lockheed, was confined at first to some of the smaller concerns in the industry: Bell, Lycoming, Brewster, and the engine plant of the Packard Motor Company.[36] In 1940, however, it inaugurated a concerted organizing drive under the leadership of Wyndham Mortimer, who was succeeded the following year by Richard Frankensteen. The UAW secured collective agreements with the Vultee Aircraft Company, after a strike; with the Ryan Aeronautical Company; and with North American Aviation, the scene in 1941 of a notorious communist-inspired antidefense strike;[37] and in other parts of the country, with Bell Aircraft in Buffalo, Vought-Sikorsky in Stratford, Connecticut, and the Goodyear aviation plant in Akron.[38] But attempts to organize the main Douglas Aircraft plant in Los Angeles, dubbed "the Ford of the aviation industry," proved unavailing at this time.

The outbreak of the war found the IAM and the UAW about equal in strength in the aircraft manufacturing industry. Both organizations profited from the great expansion in aircraft production during the war, and have continued to divide the industry along much the same pattern as that which was established during the period of intense interunion warfare between 1937 and 1941. In 1950, the IAM and the UAW entered into a no-raiding agreement, in which each organization pledged itself to refrain from attempting to organize plants represented by the other. However, intense competition continued at the many new plants that were being established, and to prevent harmful interunion rivalry, a new mutual assistance pact was signed in 1953. Pursuant to its terms, the unions agreed to conduct joint organizing campaigns, to coordinate their collective bargaining demands, and to exchange information regularly. This pact has done much to curb rivalry between the two unions.[39]

The Machinists also entered the air transport industry, but encountered difficulty in attracting the mechanics employed in the repair and maintenance of commercial aircraft. By 1940, it had contracts only with Eastern Air Lines and Pan American World Airways, covering 201 men.[40] A projected merger in 1940 with the independent Air Line Mechanics' Association, an organization of 1250 men with eight major airline contracts, failed to materialize.[41] Five years later, although claiming 2500 members in this industry, the IAM acknowledged: "Company dominated unions and misguided employees in so-called independent unions have retarded the system-wide organization of the airlines."[42]

Jurisdictional Difficulties

The International Association of Machinists, because of the multiplicity of industries in which its members are employed, and also because of the elastic concept of the term "machinist" — an essential elasticity because of the rapidity of technological change in this trade — has been involved in numerous jurisdictional disputes with fellow members of the American Federation of Labor. During the period with which we are concerned, for example, the Blacksmiths complained, unavailingly, that the Machinists were asserting jurisdiction over their work in automobile repair shops.[43]

The Machinists, in turn, complained that the Street Car Workers were asserting jurisdiction over bus mechanics who belonged in the IAM.

But there were few jurisdictional disputes in the history of the American Federation of Labor which aroused more animosity, and were the subject of more protracted negotiation, than that between the Machinists and the Carpenters' Union over the work of installing machinery. The 1914 convention of the American Federation of Labor had adopted a resolution which read, in part:

Whereas the International Association of Machinists has jurisdiction over the building, assembling, erecting, dismantling and repairing of machinery in machine shops, or elsewhere, where machinery may be used; and

Whereas the United Brotherhood of Carpenters and Joiners is attempting to do this work and taking advantage of every opportunity to place the members of the United Brotherhood of Carpenters and Joiners on same. . . .

Resolved, that the United Brotherhood of Carpenters and Joiners be and is hereby instructed to discontinue the infringement complained of; and be it further

Resolved, that the President and Executive Council of the American Federation of Labor stand instructed to render every possible assistance in enforcing the intent of this resolution.

The Carpenters refused to accept this edict, and year after year the issue was brought to the floor of the AFL convention without producing anything more than the pious recommendation that the two organizations should meet and adjust their differences. A joint committee was established in 1931, and although it could not find a solution, it agreed that there was no line of demarcation between the work of millwrights belonging to the Carpenters' Union and Machinists, that it was impractical to do the work of installing machinery with mixed crews, and that all the work should be given to one of the competing organizations.[44] Despite this recommendation, presidents Wharton and Hutcheson arrived at a tentative agreement on October 15, 1931, for dividing the work, and it appeared as though the long-standing controversy was finally at an end. On April 14, 1933, however, Hutcheson wrote to William Green that because of objections raised to the agreement by some building trades unions, the Carpenters were cancelling it.[45] Wharton later claimed that the alleged objections were only a pretext, and that the circumstances which had in fact caused the cancellation were threats by local unions of the Carpenters to force the calling of a special convention over the issue, at a time when unemployment was very severe among the Carpenters and Hutcheson feared that he might not have been invulnerable from attack.[46] Be that as it may, the effect of the Carpenters' action was to restore the situation to the *status quo ante*.

During the next few years, disputes over the installation of machinery arose all over the country, and became a major problem for the AFL. At a meeting of the Executive Council in February 1938, the jurisdiction of the Machinists as set forth in the 1914 resolution was in effect affirmed, and William Green, upon request, sent telegrams to employers caught between the two organizations setting forth the nature of that resolution.[47] Hutcheson thereupon told Green that the Carpenters had never recognized the 1914 decision, and would withhold further *per capita* dues payments to the AFL until Green ceased sending out such telegrams. Since the Carpenters were then paying $72,000 a year to the AFL, the telegrams stopped. Repeated attempts by the Machinists to force the AFL Executive Council to act were unsuccessful. In 1940, when the Carpenters were under indictment for violation of the antitrust laws, an indictment that grew out of a dispute between the Carpenters and the Machinists over the erection and dismantling of machinery at the Anheuser-Busch Brewery in St. Louis, in which the Carpenters had instigated a boycott against the products of the brewery after the work had been awarded to the Machinists, the Executive Council deferred action until the results of the indictment were clarified.[48] The increasing irritation of the Machinists is evident from the following public statement by a Machinist vice-president, Eric Petersen:

Some of the worst offenders have outdone the C.I.O. in forcing on our members compulsory membership in plant unions, organized in many instances from the top down, and completely under the domination of the employers. . . . The right of the I.A. of M. to represent machinists and machine shop workers as the collective bargaining agency in many plants — a right guaranteed by the NLRA — has been completely nullified by the high-handed piracy of these self-constituted purveyors of benevolent labor despotism, and in this nefarious activity they have been aided and abetted indirectly by the between-convention policy makers of the A.F. of L. . . .

Unless organizations committed to a policy of "might makes right" are willing to play the game fair or agree to cooperate in the establishment of a jurisdictional tribunal and abide by its decisions, our membership probably will be called on before the end of the year to decide the course the I.A. of M. shall pursue.[49]

The dispute was once more treated to a full-dress debate at the 1941 AFL convention. Despite the threat of the Machinists to withdraw from the AFL unless the 1914 decision was reaffirmed, the entire subject matter was referred back to the Executive Council with instructions to arrange

further negotiation between the two unions.[50] The matter was further complicated by the action of the AFL Building Trades Department in sending
letters to employers with the advice that only its members (the Machinists
were not affiliated) had jurisdiction over construction projects, thus barring
the Machinists from the installation of machinery on new construction.[51]

This dispute was conducted with unabated vigor on both sides for almost fifteen more years, during the course of which work on many important construction projects was held up by the inability of the two organizations to adjust their differences. The Machinists several times stopped paying
dues to the AFL in protest, and it was only after the federal government
began to intervene in the disputes pursuant to the Taft-Hartley Act, plus
the factor of new leadership in each of the unions, that the two organizations
finally sat down and negotiated an agreement over the work in controversy.[52]

Growth of the Machinists until the War

The 1937–1938 depression called a temporary halt to the growth in membership which had characterized the two preceding years. Membership
declined somewhat in the early part of 1938, but then began to rise once
more. Average actual dues-paying membership for the years 1938 to 1942
was as follows:[53]

1938	155,267
1939	161,828
1940	187,738
1941	284,514
1942	444,892

The Machinists utilized the services of the National Labor Relations
Board in its organizing activities to an unusually high degree. From October
1, 1935 to June 30, 1940, the IAM was the initiator of 976 NLRB cases, 669
involving unfair labor practices and 307, questions of representation, involving 125,544 workers in all. The IAM won 81 and lost 59 of the elections in
which it participated, 26 of the 59 losses having been to CIO unions, and 18
of the victories having been at the expense of CIO unions. It gained 113
contracts as a direct result of NLRB proceedings.[54]

On the eve of the war, the Machinists' Union was the third largest union
in the American Federation of Labor, coming after the Teamsters and the
Carpenters. Its growth during the period 1936 to 1941 compared favorably
with that of most CIO unions. Commanding perhaps the largest staff of

international organizers of any AFL union, the IAM capitalized upon the favorable political and economic climate not only to strengthen its hold on the industries which had traditionally been within its jurisdiction, metal fabricating plants, machine tool plants, and maintenance departments of industrial establishments, but to enter such new and growing industries as aircraft manufacture. Its important role in the railroad industry will be dealt with below. Only in automobile manufacture, in which the IAM displayed an early interest, did this hard-hitting organization fail to make any impression, faced as it was with the spectacular victories of the United Automobile Workers in the early part of 1937, and the consolidation of those victories in the form of contracts with General Motors and Chrysler.

The Machinists' Union operated with little fanfare, but, capitalizing upon experience in organizational work and an intensely loyal membership, it became in the course of five years one of the giants of American trade unionism, against opposition not only from competitors in the CIO, but also from erstwhile allies within the AFL. This achievement demonstrated beyond question that the Gompers brand of unionism was still alive and vigorous.

16

The Building Trades

The building trades constituted the hard core of the American Federation of Labor prior to the expansion of AFL membership in the years following 1933.[1] Among the first to organize in the nineteenth century, the workers engaged in building construction displayed a consistent though by no means complete adherence to the principle of trade unionism thereafter. The power of building unionism rose sharply during the first World War, but it was affected adversely by the decline in building activity during the depression. Membership in building unions fell from 800,000 in 1928 to 500,000 in 1933.[2] By 1936, membership had once more risen. Unions affiliated with the Building Trades Department of the AFL reported an average of 650,000 members in good standing during that year.[3] During 1936, contract construction offered employment to about 1.1 million workers.[4]

The term "building trades" is a convenient label for a heterogeneous group of national unions, varying in structure from craft to semi-industrial, in size from tiny to giant, and in jurisdiction from narrow building construction to multi-industry. Between 1936 and 1941 there were nineteen separate unions affiliated with the Building Trades Department, ranging from the Marble Polishers, the Asbestos Workers, the Stone Cutters, the Roofers, and the Granite Cutters, with between 4000 and 5000 members each, and confined entirely to the construction industry, to the Carpenters' Union, which straddled the construction, lumber, and furniture industries. The larger and more powerful unions were, in addition to the Carpenters, the Electrical Workers, the Laborers, the Painters, the Plumbers, and the Bricklayers. The Teamsters' Union was affiliated for that portion of its membership which was engaged in building construction. In addition to the national unions, there were affiliated to the Building Trades Department about 500 local and a dozen state building and construction trades councils.

It would be manifestly impossible, within the confines of a general history, to trace through in any detail the experiences of all the building trades unions. All that will be attempted, therefore, is a summary of some of the problems faced by the building trades in common, with a few more specific comments on the larger organizations.

The Building and Construction Trades Department

Just before the period with which we are concerned, a serious split occurred within the building trades. On one side stood the Carpenters, the Bricklayers, and the Electrical Workers, and on the other the remainder of the building unions. The issue was one of personalities and factions plus the perennial question of jurisdiction; all three of these unions had left the Building Trades Department in protest against department jurisdictional rulings. Since they were at the time the three largest building unions, their departure seriously impaired the functioning of the department. In 1934, the smaller organizations refused to admit the "triple alliance" to membership, lest they be swamped, whereupon the AFL chartered a second building trades department, which managed to secure the allegiance, in addition, of the Operating Engineers, the Laborers, and the Teamsters. Fearful of the impending warfare that might ensue, and faced by the threat of the CIO, the AFL forced the two groups to merge. A series of conferences under the chairmanship of George Harrison resulted in agreement on details, including an equal division of officers between the two factions.[5]

This uneasy balance did not last long. "As a result of a series of hotel-room caucuses Hutcheson [president of the Carpenters' Union] kicked the 1936 settlement to shambles. In a move that 'verged on the insulting' to the smaller craft unions, he made one of his allies president and another secretary-treasurer. He then lifted for his side five of the eight vice-presidencies, modestly reserving the eighth for himself. Never again, during the period covered by this study [to 1941], did he lose control of the Department."[6] Hutcheson, incidentally, killed two birds with one stone when he secured the election of J. W. Williams, a member of his union, as president of the Building Trades Department in 1936. Williams later expressed the conviction that "Brother Hutcheson put him in that job to side-track him" from any presidential possibilities within the Carpenters' Union.[7]

One of the principal reasons for the willingness of the Carpenters and their allies to patch up their quarrel with the smaller organizations was the knowledge that the federal government was determined that the perennial jurisdictional squabbling should not hinder its efforts to lift the building industry out of its doldrums. The unity plan of 1936, which reestablished a single Building Trades Department, provided for a referee with authority to make awards.[8] But the habits of a lifetime could not be changed so easily; the president of the Building Trades reported to the 1937 convention:

During the early part of this year jurisdictional disputes were so prevalent that they were a real menace to the building and construction industry. A dispute would appear at the least provocation and the Department was besieged with complaints from all parts of the Country requesting settlement of the same.

The referee under the plan, John A. Lapp, reported that there were many violations of the jurisdictional award agreement.[9] After almost two years of operation, he had decided only ten cases, with many still smoldering and occasionally bursting out into active controversy.[10] Lapp resigned as referee when the Operating Engineers refused to abide by the plan after having lost two decisions, and was succeeded by William Carroll of the Cleveland Building Trades Employers' Association.[11] The 1939 convention of the Building Trades attempted to bolster up the effectiveness of the plan by providing for initial mediation by the local building trades council, and a year later it was reported that a reduction in jurisdictional strife had taken place.[12]

Coincidentally, in late 1939 and early 1940, the Anti-Trust Division of the United States Department of Justice launched a major offensive against the building trades for the purpose of encouraging competition by the elimination of jurisdictional strikes, feather bedding, extortion, union refusal to work on new materials, and collusive price fixing.[13] Twelve indictments involving some 35 AFL unions were secured.[14] The Carpenters were indicted seven times, among other things for attempting to prevent the use of lumber produced by the rival Woodworkers' Union, for refusing to work on sash, frames, and doors that did not bear their label, and for interfering with the operations of the Anheuser-Busch Co., a brewer, because the latter employed members of the Machinists' Union on work claimed by the Carpenters.[15] In the Anheuser-Busch indictment, which became the key case in the government's campaign, the grand jury charged:

Beginning so many years ago that the Grand Jurors are unable to fix the date, United Brotherhood of Carpenters and Joiners of America has been engaged, and it is still engaged, in a so-called jurisdictional dispute with International Association of Machinists . . . the said combination and conspiracy was formed . . . not to obtain higher wages, shorter hours of labor, or any other legitimate objective of a labor union, but only with the unlawful and wrongful object and purpose of inducing and coercing an employer to violate a contract with one group of employees and to replace them with another group. . . .[16]

The AFL responded with great indignation against this challenge to the practices which were so fundamental to the successful organization of its principal affiliates. The Executive Council declared: "It is . . . noteworthy that the first batch of anti-trust indictments against building trades unions of the American Federation of Labor was strangely timed to coincide with the inauguration of a C.I.O. drive to raid A.F. of L. membership in the building trades." [17] Joseph Padway, general counsel of the AFL, charged that the indictments were "the most reactionary, vicious, outrageous attempt in the last dozen years on the part of any department of the Government to bring labor unions under the provision of the Anti-trust laws. Labor stands aghast and horrified at this bold attempt." [18]

The motivation behind this government attack upon the building trades is not altogether clear. The investigations conducted by the Temporary National Economic Committee had highlighted some unsavory practices in the construction industry, and Thurman Arnold, who headed the Anti-Trust Division of the Justice Department, had become convinced, and may have convinced President Roosevelt, that the only way to restore competition and stimulate activity in building construction was by a wholesale campaign against the unions. But the practices had long prevailed, and the indictments might have been expected to result in violent AFL reaction against the administration on the eve of a national election campaign.

The entire labor movement was not equally horrified by the indictments. The CIO, which was endeavoring to gain a foothold in the construction industry, greeted it with undisguised satisfaction. Many small AFL unions, harassed by the imperialistic tendencies of larger organizations, must have welcomed it as well, although they could not openly say so. For the administration, the antitrust campaign constituted an excellent answer to the charge that it was prolabor. It could appear before the country as a champion of free enterprise and an opponent of monopoly, whether the latter was attempted by big business or big labor. A critic of the Carpenters' Union has suggested still another motive: the furtherance of internal democracy within trade unions. He quotes Thurman Arnold as saying:

The right of collective bargaining is being enforced in favor of labor organizations which are using the right for illegitimate purposes, against the interests of consumers, against the interests of efficiency, and against the interest of labor itself. Industrialists found themselves forced to deal with unions many of which are nothing more than corrupt political machines that use the right of collective bargaining against the interests of the rank and file of laborers. Many unions are interested in restricting output, in building trade barriers between states, and even in discriminating against working men themselves for the advantage of a few. Many of these unions are undemocratic in organization and their leaders maintain themselves in power by coercion. Such types of organizations inevitably lead to corruption on a large scale.[19]

Whichever, if any, of these motives was predominant, Hutcheson chose to regard the entire affair as a political attack upon the AFL in general and upon the Carpenters' Union in particular. In an open letter to his membership, written September 24, 1940, he accused the administration of "persecuting, not prosecuting" members of the union, and continued:

> It seems strange indeed that although the law referred to [the Sherman Act] has been on the Statute Books for fifty years no administration prior to the New Deal administration has ever attempted to say, or even inferred that men exercising their rights as Trade Unionists and as free Americans would be violating the provisions of said law. The acts of representatives of the New Deal administration clearly show that they are not friends of our Brotherhood. Therefore the members of our organization should remember and follow the long practice and custom of the American Federation of Labor: namely, "Assist your friends and defeat your enemies." [20]

A number of the indicted unions pleaded *nolo contendere* to the charges and paid relatively small fines. The Carpenters were determined to resist, however. A special assessment of fifty cents a month was levied on each member for six months, and a prominent member of the New York Bar, Charles H. Tuttle, was retained as chief defense counsel. The government decided that the Anheuser-Busch case was its strongest one, and when the indictment was dismissed by a lower court, took direct appeal to the United States Supreme Court. That tribunal, in February 1941, held that neither the Sherman Act nor the Clayton Act prohibited the conduct complained of, the jurisdictional dispute in particular.[21]

This decision resulted in a collapse of the government antitrust campaign against the unions. A few days after its promulgation, President Roosevelt suggested to William Green that the AFL general counsel meet with Attorney General Jackson to agree upon a plan to bring about the termination of the proceedings.[22] The estrangement between the Roosevelt Administration and the AFL proved to be temporary, and soon gave way before the urgent necessity for cooperation occasioned by the mounting defense crisis.

The Organization of Construction Workers

One of the principal concerns of the Building Trades Department and its affiliated organizations was to spread unionism among a greater proportion of building and construction workers. On June 30, 1936, the Carpenters'

Union reported that out of a total membership of 301,800, only some 160,700 were "beneficial" members, i.e., employed in building and fully entitled to all the fraternal benefits provided by the union, while the rest were "non-beneficial" members, employed mainly in lumbering.[23] Membership in the Bricklayers' Union fell from 110,000 in 1928 to 53,000 in 1936; moreover, the latter total included 20,000 members not currently paying dues.[24]

The degree of unionization varied considerably among the major sectors of the construction industry. Some organization existed in government-financed, industrial, and commercial building, but residential construction was largely being done on a nonunion basis. In smaller communities, it was not unusual for all work to be nonunion.[25]

One obvious method of increasing union membership was to increase employment on public construction. The value of federally-financed construction increased from $1.478 billion in 1935 to $2.316 billion in 1940, then soared to $5.931 billion the following year. In 1940, more than half of the labor required for on-site construction was being absorbed by public construction work.[26]

The building unions were in the forefront of the drive to raise the quantity of public construction.[27] At the same time, they were very careful to protect union standards, and thus their status, on such work. The Bacon-Davis Act, as amended in 1935, provided for the payment of the prevailing rates of wages on all federal contracts in excess of $2000 involving the construction of public works. The determination of prevailing wages was a function of the Department of Labor, and the building trades always maintained close liaison with the unit within the department responsible for making determinations, to the end that union contract rates should be chosen as representative. Both the Public Works Administration and the Works Progress Administration were committed to the payment of prevailing wages, although the unions constantly complained that local administrators often selected rates considerably below the union contract level. In the case of the former, regional labor advisers were appointed in 1938 to assist in local determinations, with the result that the level of PWA wages took a sharp upward turn.[28]

Relations with WPA were less satisfactory, from the union standpoint. After repeated protests by the Building Trades Department that unskilled workers were doing the work of skilled mechanics, and that prevailing rates were not being maintained, Harry Hopkins, the WPA administrator, issued instructions in 1938 that such practices were to be terminated.[29] The following year, however, Congress, in the face of strong labor opposition, abolished the prevailing wage requirement for WPA work, and authorized the Works Progress Commissioner to fix wages in such a way that the monthly earnings schedule would not substantially affect the national average labor cost per person on the WPA. The purpose was to provide as much employment as possible with the funds available, but the Building Trades complained bitterly:

In its general effect, W.P.A. continued to give relief employment to relief workers in the building and construction field under substandard labor provisions. With the continued growth of such activity in the construction field, these W.P.A. projects were in effect taking away potential employment opportunities at union standards from our membership and diminishing the scope of private construction activity for the membership of our trades in the future. By training handymen and laborers to perform skilled operations on W.P.A. projects, it became the accepted policy of the program to undermine the skill qualifications and the standards of the trades built up in the industry over a period of years and accepted on private construction.[30]

Organizational efforts were hampered by the considerable amount of unemployment that prevailed among building workers until the defense boom of 1941. The short recovery of 1936–1937 provided no substantial measure of relief. It was reported near the close of 1937: "More men are employed today on building and construction work than were employed a year ago, yet there is no shortage of mechanics or laborers. To the contrary, we find there are still a great number of idle mechanics and laborers who have formerly been employed in the Building and Construction industry."[31] The depression of 1937–1938 reduced employment quite sharply, and not until the latter part of 1940 was there any marked improvement.[32]

Membership in the Building Trades Department, as reported by affiliated unions, was as follows, for the years 1936 to 1941:[33]

1935–1936	650,566
1936–1937	686,985
1937–1938	789,852
1938–1939	822,593
1939–1940	844,016
1940–1941	893,173

Reference has already been made to the inadequacy of these data. Imperfect though they are, however, the figures indicate that the periods of major expansion were during 1937 and, to a lesser extent, in 1940. The great CIO push of 1937 was accompanied by a rise of building trades membership as well, though monthly figures would undoubtedly have recorded a drop during 1938. The Carpenters' Union reported a total membership of 309,500 on June 30, 1937,[34] a slight increase over the total for the previous year despite the defection of the woodworkers of the Pacific Northwest in the meantime, and implying, if accurate, a substantial increase in construction membership. The Bricklayers, on the other hand, reported a slight decline in membership between 1936 and 1938, from 53,280 to 52,749.[35] Their policy during this period was described frankly in the following terms:

No organizing campaign was put into effect by our International office to recruit membership in wholesale lots, such as was being practiced by other organizations who, for publicity purposes, herded recruits into unions in droves upon payment of initiation fees as low as one dollar and, in many instances, no fee at all. This mushroom growth, just for numerical strength, had no appeal for your officers. We insisted that our unions function for the benefit of those who had remained loyal to the organization through times of stress and that they be the first to enjoy the fruits of loyalty by being employed on the small amount of work under construction.[36]

This attitude toward organization was not confined to the Bricklayers. The secretary of the International Brotherhood of Electrical Workers reported to his members, on June 30, 1941:

[Membership] has been on the increase during the last two years. However, we have not made the increases in membership that other labor organizations seem to be making, for the reason that in many localities our locals do not seem to want to increase their membership for one reason or another. Two reasons seem to be dominant: one, new members might change the political complexion of the local; second, when business gets normal, there would be more members for fewer jobs.[37]

On the basis of per capita tax payments to the AFL, membership of the Electrical Workers rose only from 170,000 in 1936 to 201,000 in 1941. Despite the active expansion of its jurisdiction into electrical manufacturing, utilities, and radio broadcasting, the IBEW thus remained fairly static from 1936 to 1941. The Building Laborers, on the other hand, representing unskilled labor and having no fears about the effects of admitting new members into the privileged islands of employment which the skilled unions regarded as their exclusive preserves, pursued a much more active policy. Their membership rose from a low of 26,500 in 1933 to 281,300 in 1941, a rate of growth equaled by few American unions.[38]

On July 31, 1939, there occurred an event which resulted in a considerably different attitude toward organization of new members by the skilled trades: the CIO announced the formation of a Construction Workers' Organizing Committee. A. D. Lewis, a brother of John L. Lewis, was put at the head of the committee, the other members of which were Philip Murray, James Carey, R. J. Thomas, and Sherman Dalrymple. Dues were set at $1.50 a month, much lower than the average being charged by the AFL building unions, and initiation fees were dispensed with altogether.[39]

Behind this move on the part of John L. Lewis was undoubtedly the intent to hit back at the AFL for its attempted harassment of the United Mine Workers through chartering of the Progressive Miners; invasion of the heart of the CIO was to be met by a thrust at the holy of holies in the American Federation of Labor. While there were some grave doubts within the CIO of the wisdom of entering an area in which the AFL was so firmly entrenched,[40] the left wing was delighted with the opportunity to attack the most "reactionary" element in the labor movement. Harry Bridges, head of the West Coast longshoremen, told the CIO Executive Board:

I think if we look at it from a practical point of view, as far as the PWA is concerned all over the nation, we would be better off if they were non-union than to follow the principle that any union is better than none. We are looking at it from that realistic attitude in certain locations, and if we can make them non-union, so that we can move in and take over, that is what we intend to do. We are following the basic, fundamental principles of unionism when we take that attitude, because the objectives we are trying to reach are somewhat in the future, and the only thing on which we differ is the technique or the method we use.[41]

Saying that the support of the building trades was needed for the municipal elections in San Francisco, Bridges added: "Up to next November naturally we will make no great attack on the building trades in San Francisco, but afterwards it is another story."

The essential strategy of the CIO was embodied in the following offer to employers of building labor:

The contractor using CIO labor does not worry about having to bargain with 20 separate craft unions. One single union speaks for every worker on the job. Since there are no jurisdictions he does not have to worry about jurisdictional strikes. There are no regulations against the use of new materials. Hourly rates are calculated on a reasonable basis.[42]

A uniform daily scale of $9 for skilled workers, $6 for helpers, and $5 for laborers was established, in contrast with the complicated schedules prevailing in the building trades. Employers were promised that there would be no interference with new methods of production, including prefabrication, and in fact, the Construction Workers' Committee cooperated in the construction of some prefabricated housing projects.[43] Charges of corruption and racketeering against the AFL unions were made repeatedly, and there were numerous allegations of violence being used against CIO men.

At the end of a year of operation, the CWOC claimed 150 local unions in 30 states, though no membership data were revealed. Whatever strength the CWOC had appeared to be concentrated in maintenance and repair work in CIO-controlled factories, in residential building located in areas where the CIO was strong, and on some road construction work where the bulk of the labor was unskilled. Efforts were made to enlist building teamsters, in order to prevent the tieup of deliveries to CIO jobs, and eventually the CWOC acquired the expelled Minneapolis Teamsters' local run by the Dunne brothers.[44]

The AFL was clearly concerned with the CIO drive in construction, although, as we shall see, it did not materialize into a real threat. But there was no way of telling that at the time. There were hundreds of thousands of unorganized construction workers, many of them in the low-paid, unskilled bracket, of a type with whom the CIO had had considerable success in other industries. The situation was particularly bad in residential housing, which was beginning to pick up after a decade of inactivity.

One of the obstacles to organization was the wage differential between union and nonunion work, which was most marked in small residential construction. A survey conducted in 1936, for example, showed that for bricklayers, the average union rate was 39 per cent in excess of the nonunion rate; for electricians, 58 per cent; for plumbers, 34 per cent. Even in the case of common laborers, there was a differential of 50 per cent.[45] It was manifestly impossible to bring nonunion rates up to the union level at once without seriously affecting the volume of construction; yet union members were understandably reluctant to compromise the levels which they had maintained through the depression years.

In a number of areas, a solution was sought through the recognition of a so-called "secondary" rate. In Philadelphia, Washington, St. Louis, Detroit, Boston, Cincinnati, and Columbus a number of the building unions set a lower scale for real estate developments of one or two family houses. This differential was to be temporary, to be eliminated when a sufficient degree of organization was achieved.[46] Not all the unions went along with the scheme, however, and considerable resistance was manifested within some of the unions that did. For example, in the Philadelphia area, the local bricklayers' union refused to cooperate with the other trades in the campaign, resulting in the employment of nonunion bricklayers on otherwise union jobs. Many of these men were former members of the Bricklayers' Union, and to fore-stall their organization by the CIO, the international union chartered a new local in the area to cater to them.[47] This action was severely criticized at the 1940 convention of the union, and in particular, by the New York local, which had voted eight to one against the establishment of a secondary rate. As one of the New York delegates put it:

How can we accept this secondary rate of wages? It is impossible, Mr. Chairman. I went to a lot of these fellows working on these scab jobs, rat jobs, or whatever you want to call them. I put the question to them. As far as joining the organiza-tion again, it is impossible. They are satisfied the way they stand today.[48]

President Bates, after pointing out that in city after city, a very substan-tial portion of all bricklaying was being done on a nonunion basis, warned:

Unless we can clean up the lot situation and raise the wages of these men on the lots, we will not be able to establish our union wage scale as the prevailing wage for the purpose of the Bacon-Davis Law or the Walsh-Healy Act. Unless we control this class of work sooner or later the number of men employed on the type of work will exceed the number of members in our organization.

The convention sustained the action of the international union, and President Bates later reported that the program bid fair to organize the resi-dential field until the outbreak of war terminated residential construction. After the war, the position of the building unions was much stronger, and the state of the labor market greatly altered, making a dual rate unnecessary.

The Defense Construction Program

The inception of the defense program marked a new phase in the history of building unionism. Federally-financed construction jumped from $1.5 bil-lion in 1939 to $5.9 billion in 1941; the annual average of construction employment rose from 1,150,000 to 1,790,000 between these two years.[49] Even more important from the point of view of the unions, the expansion in employment occurred primarily in just that sector of the industry in which the unions were most strongly entrenched, public construction.

The AFL unions moved swiftly and surely to consolidate their positions in the defense program. Despite their dislike of Sidney Hillman, who was the labor member of the National Defense Advisory Commission, represen-tatives of the building unions agreed to serve on his Labor Policy Advisory Committee. The AFL was not informed in advance of Hillman's appoint-ment as labor's chief representative on the Commission, and its initial reac-tion was negative when asked to designate a representative to cooperate with

Hillman. President Roosevelt then phoned William Green and informed him that an AFL man would be appointed as assistant to Hillman, but the AFL remained skeptical. However, the pressure was increased when Daniel Tobin was made Administrative Assistant to the President, and Joseph Keenan, a building trades man from the Chicago Federation of Labor, became Hillman's assistant. Dan Tracy, head of the Electrical Workers, and Harry Bates, of the Bricklayers, informed the AFL Executive Council that they felt it their duty, in the interest of their organizations, to cooperate with Hillman.[50] Though the AFL refused officially to sanction the Hillman appointment, it ceased opposition.[51] A labor policy to govern defense work, including a 4-hour week and full compliance with the provisions of the Bacon-Davis and Walsh-Healy Acts, was soon agreed upon.[52] Repeated claims were made that the Defense Commission had recognized the Building and Construction Trades Department as having exclusive jurisdiction in the industry. This was hotly denied at first by Sidney Hillman in the following statement:

The statement that the AFL has been given control of defense building is just silly. I have never at any time said or written anything upon which such an assumption could be based. Nor could an AFL official worthy of his office have come to such a conclusion from any remark of mine.[53]

Nonetheless, the government turned increasingly to the AFL in dealing with construction problems. On July 22, 1941, an agreement was reached between interested government agencies and the Building and Construction Trades Department providing for uniform overtime rates and uniform shift pay on all national defense projects. The unions gave up more advantageous overtime rates, and agreed that there would be no work stoppages because of jurisdictional disputes, or for any other reason. In return, the government agreed that general contractors would be required to use specialty contractors in accordance with customary practice, and promised to use more realistic area rates in predetermining wages under the Davis-Bacon Act. "Perhaps greatest significance should be attached to the fact that the unions secured unprecedented recognition from the Federal Government that they represented the workers of the construction industry." [54]

The CIO was highly indignant at what it regarded as an unfriendly act by Sidney Hillman, who negotiated the agreement. The Construction Workers' Organizing Committee complained that the agreement demonstrated "an utterly unfair attitude on the part of Hillman toward the UCWOC since this union was not advised that such an agreement was planned." [55] The AFL trades, on the other hand, were jubilant. In introducing Hillman to the 1941 convention of the Building Trades Department, President Coyne declared:

he openly stated to his Advisory Committee that there was no question about the permanency of the established groups that were predominant in building and construction work, that so far as he was concerned, while he was acting in the capacity, he would recognize only the Building and Construction Trades Department of the American Federation of Labor.[56]

The indignation of the CIO's construction union changed to anguish in the late fall of 1941 when one of its major employers, the P. J. Currier Lumber Company of Detroit, was denied a contract for defense housing despite the fact that its bid was very substantially below that of the next lowest bidder. Hillman was accused of being a labor czar, of consistent discrimination against the CIO, of acting as a recruiting agent for the AFL. Senator Harry Truman, after hearings had been held before his investigating committee, denounced Hillman's action as one that was in violation of long-established government policy:

I cannot condemn Mr. Hillman's position too strongly. The United States does not fear trouble from any source; and, if trouble is threatened, the United States is able to protect itself. If Mr. Hillman cannot or will not protect the interests of the United States, I am in favor of replacing him with someone who can and will.[57]

The position of the AFL was that the award of the job to Currier would result in widespread industrial warfare in Detroit, and might endanger the entire construction stabilization agreement.[58] Despite considerable Congressional pressure, the administration remained firm, and when the United States entered the war, the AFL enjoyed, and continued to enjoy, a central position in federal construction, with the CIO relegated to unimportant fringe jobs. In June 1942, the Construction Workers lost its identity and became part of District 50 of the United Mine Workers,[59] a clear acknowledgement by John L. Lewis that his foray into the construction industry had failed.

Average hourly earnings of construction workers are compared with those for manufacturing workers in Table 11. Percentagewise, manufacturing workers gained somewhat more between 1936 and 1941 than did construction workers. In comparing the two groups, however, the differences in absolute wage levels and the continued slump in building activity, right up to the defense boom, must be taken into consideration.

By the outbreak of the war, the AFL building trades had more or less

Table 11.

Average hourly earnings in manufacturing and construction, 1936 to 1941
(in cents)

Year	Manufacturing	Construction
1936	55.6	82.4
1937	62.4	90.3
1938	62.7	90.8
1939	63.3	93.2
1940	66.1	95.8
1941	72.9	101.0

Sources: Bureau of Labor Statistics, *Handbook of Labor Statistics,* 1947 ed., p. 54; Bureau of Labor Statistics, *Construction During Five Decades,* Bulletin 1146 (1954), p. 56.

recovered their predepression membership strength. The Carpenters were somewhat above their 1929 level;[60] the Bricklayers were still far below their predepression peak.[61] Only the Laborers, among the larger unions (apart from the Carpenters), experienced a marked growth, from a predepression peak of 117,000 to 281,000 in 1941.[62] However, it would not be correct to conclude that the years between 1936 and 1941 constituted a period of stagnation for the building trades. They were, it will be recalled, among the most powerful of the trade unions in the nineteen-twenties, and suffered greatly during the depression years. Until 1941, total construction employment was considerably behind the 1921–1929 average, so that the construction unions were catering to a smaller potential clientele. It may be said that the task of the building trades in the nineteen-thirties was reorganization rather than, as in the case of most manufacturing unions, organization.

By 1941, the reorganization process had been completed. Even more important, the AFL building trades had maneuvered themselves into a strategic position from which they could capitalize upon the rising demand for construction. Thus, by 1950 they had about two million members, more than double the 1940–1941 average, and more than keeping pace with the increase in employment, although a considerable sector, perhaps one-third, of all residential construction was still nonunion.[63]

The building trades were notably aggressive in their collective bargaining policy; for this they have always been known. But it is not generally realized to what extent they have been active politically. During the New Deal period, when the federal government first became a major consumer of construction, the building trades were careful to maintain close contact with the Roosevelt Administration. The antitrust suits of 1940 marked only a temporary breach in the cordiality of the relationship. Such men as Dan

Tobin of the Teamsters, a union which was deeply involved in construction, and Harry Bates of the Bricklayers, were high in the counsels of the Democratic Party. Daniel Tracy, president of the Electrical Workers' Union, became assistant secretary of labor in 1940, a strategic position in view of the fact that the Department of Labor determined prevailing wage rates on government construction under the Bacon-Davis Act. Joseph D. Keenan, also from the Electrical Workers, became one of the key men in the defense production administration.

The major holdout was William L. Hutcheson of the Carpenters' Union. He supported Landon for the presidency in 1936, almost alone among labor leaders to do so, and Willkie in 1940, although in the latter year he was joined by his erstwhile foe, John L. Lewis. When he was attacked for his political stand by a delegate to the 1940 convention of the Carpenters' Union, Hutcheson replied:

Just a moment. If the delegate who has just spoken cares to renounce his rights of citizenship merely because he was elected business agent of a local of the Brotherhood, I don't, that does not apply to the General President. . . . I will not renounce my Americanism, because in all the 38 years I have been a member of the Brotherhood I have been a union man unreproached — get that! [64]

At the 1936 convention of the union, J. W. Williams, at the time president of the Building Trades Department, was nominated in opposition to Hutcheson, but he withdrew for reasons not made public.[65] The same thing happened in 1940, this time the opposition nominee being H. Schwarzer.[66] In the meantime, Hutcheson had elevated his son, Maurice A. Hutcheson, to the post of first vice-president, and the latter succeeded his father to the presidency in 1951.

Under the impact of the CIO drive, some of the building unions dropped their policy of craft exclusion and broadened their jurisdictions to cover semiskilled workers, mainly in manufacturing. The construction locals, however, continued to exclude semiskilled men in general. The Carpenters, in addition to claiming lumber workers, also established a furniture worker department. The Electrical Workers went after workers in electrical manufacturing and public utilities. But not all the building trades were equally enthusiastic about this policy of expansion. The president of the Bricklayers' Union told his membership that "the future strength of this International Union and its growing effectiveness depend upon confining our membership to the skilled and qualified mechanics represented by the different branches of our trade." [67] Neither the expansion of the CIO nor the "Roosevelt revolution" could budge such unions from their policies of exclusiveness, based upon a fierce pride in craftsmanship, and handed down over a century of organization.

The real significance of the period 1935–1941 for the building trades was the spread of unionism to new fields. The unions grew outward from the big metropolitan centers to smaller cities. They expanded their scope from commercial work to smaller operations. They began to capture industrial building, and, most important of all, they made a real dent in heavy and highway construction, which more and more took on the dimension of a large-scale industry. A landmark in highway construction labor relations was the conclusion of an agreement in 1939 between the Construction Association of Western Pennsylvania and the Heavy Engineering, Railroad Contracting and Highway Construction Council of the AFL (the latter comprised as its members the Carpenters, Operating Engineers, Laborers, and Teamsters), marking the first major inroad of unionism into what had been a traditionally open shop industry. Most of the workers involved were unskilled and semiskilled men, and it may have been the threat of the CIO which induced the building unions to stake their claims in heavy and highway construction work.

1 7

Printing and Publishing

The Typographical Union

Trade unionism in the printing and publishing industry had already achieved a considerable degree of success and stability by 1936. With collective bargaining long accepted by a very substantial proportion of newspaper publishers and a somewhat smaller percentage of book and job printers, the impact of the NRA and the Wagner Act upon employment relationships and union development in the industry was less severe than in manufacturing generally. The period 1936 to 1941 represents merely one episode, albeit an important one, in the long evolution of printing unionism, rather than the revolution that characterized events in such industries as steel and automobiles.

The mechanical, as distinguished from the editorial workers in printing, are organized into six unions: the International Typographical Union, the International Printing Pressmen and Assistants' Union, the International Brotherhood of Bookbinders, the International Stereotypers' and Electrotypers' Union, the Amalgamated Lithographers' Union, and the International Photoengravers' Union.[1] Editorial workers are organized in the American Newspaper Guild. Of these organizations, the Typographical Union is the oldest, largest and most stable; indeed, the others were originally offshoots of it.[2] Because of the difficulty of dealing with a complexity of small unions, this chapter will be concerned primarily with the International Typographical Union (ITU) as the most representative organization of the mechanical trades, and with the American Newspaper Guild, a new departure in white collar unionism originating in the nineteen-thirties.

The ITU, while a relatively small trade union, is one of the most celebrated in the American labor movement. Formed in 1852, it was the first international union to be established in the United States on a stable basis. It is known for the vigor with which it enforces its working rules, and even more, for the almost continuous existence within its structure of a two-party political system. The latter institution is a unique one in the American labor movement, and has been the subject of extensive comment.[3]

The industry within which the ITU operates is in fact a bifurcated one, with sharply differing economies. Daily newspaper printing, one of the two main branches, is characterized by relatively large production units enjoying a considerable degree of local monopoly. The fact that unit costs diminish sharply with increasing volume has contributed to the gradual stifling of competition and a reduction in the number of newspapers published. Since newspapers produce for a local market, and must ordinarily be printed close to the market, the existence of lower wage rates and nonunion shops in other markets does not constitute a serious competitive problem for the publisher or the union. Mechanical labor costs ranged from 10 to 20 per cent of the total cost of production in the nineteen-thirties,[4] a relatively low figure, serving further to mitigate the economic effects of union wage pressures. Moreover, "the mass of newspaper revenue throughout the 1899–1939 period was derived from advertising linage. Resistance to a wage demand which plunged mechanical departments into a strike could easily prove disastrous to circulation, upon which advertising rates depended. . . . In newspaper printing . . . the gross income from sale of the printed product, the actual newspaper, was not expected to cover production costs and greater importance was placed upon advertising receipts for net returns." Newspaper publishing has been a relatively prosperous industry, and even during the depression years, newspaper income held up quite well.[5]

Book and job printing, by contrast, was a less stable and profitable, and a more competitive industry. It is composed of a large number of producing units, the great majority of them small. However, the larger units, which produce mail-order catalogues, telephone directories, and periodicals and books, were engaged in national rather than local competition, so that geographical wage differentials were often of crucial significance. The fact that mechanical wages were running over 32 per cent of total costs of production served as a further bar to union wage demands. "The connection between labor costs and total or net income was thus more important for book and job proprietors than for newspaper publishers. Not only was the employing printer in the commercial field more sensitive financially to demands for wage increases, but he could more easily pull up stakes and flee the union's jurisdiction."

It is not surprising, in view of these facts, that the organizational status of the ITU in 1936 was entirely different in the two main branches of its jurisdiction. In 1935, some 372 out of 435 newspaper establishments which belonged to the American Newspaper Publishers' Association operated their composing rooms under union conditions. These establishments published 455 daily and 192 Sunday newspapers, as against 71 daily and 19 Sunday papers published by the nonunion shops, which were generally smaller newspapers, with an average circulation of 7000.[6] Comparable details are not available for book and job printing, but for mechanical workers as a whole, the percentage of organization was only about 40 per cent in 1935.[7] Some of the largest commercial printers, such as R. R. Donnelley and Sons, which printed catalogues for Montgomery Ward and Sears Roebuck, as well as telephone books for many affiliates of the Bell System, were operating militant open shops.

The interesting fact about the Typographical Union in the period 1935 to 1941 was the relatively slow tempo of its progress, both organizationally and economically. The relevant membership figures are shown in Table 12. It

Table 12.

Membership in the International Typographical Union,
1935 to 1941

Year	Average per capita paying membership	Total membership
1935	73,586	74,276
1936	73,375	74,311
1937	74,781	78,489
1938	78,886	80,919
1939	79,362	79,970
1940	79,347	80,681
1941	79,308	81,069

Source: *The Typographical Journal* (July 1941), Supplement, p. 134.

appears from these that ITU membership increased either 8 per cent or 9 per cent between 1935 and 1941, depending upon the measurement used. This was far less than the comparable growth of the American labor movement in general, and of old and well established AFL craft unions in particular. For example, the Bookbinders reported a membership increase of 90 per cent for the same period; the Printing Pressmen, of 43 per cent; and the Photoengravers, of 20 per cent.[8] Of the printing trades, only the Stereotypers failed to grow more rapidly than the Printers. Almost every building trades union showed greater progress. To cite a few examples: membership in the Iron Workers tripled, that of the Electrical Workers almost doubled, and the Carpenters experienced a 50 per cent increase. In railway transportation, hardly a rapidly expanding or poorly organized industry, the Brotherhood of Railway Clerks registered a membership increase of more than 50 per cent, and the Railroad Trainmen, of 37 per cent. Much the same picture emerges on the wage side, as will be seen below.

What are the reasons for this apparent failure of the ITU to participate in the great upswing in organization of the late nineteen-thirties? An inquiry into the causes can scarcely yield precise results, for the skein of events is too tangled. Nevertheless, the problem is worth examining for the light it may throw upon some aspects of union development and structure.

It might be argued that the ITU, as the oldest national union in the United States, operating in an equally old industry, had attained so stable and commanding a position by the inception of the New Deal as to render further expansion unlikely and unnecessary for the welfare of its membership. While the nineteen-thirties appear to mark the coming to maturity of a large segment of American unionism, should not a comparable episode in the life-cycle of the ITU be dated three decades earlier?

Percentages of organization, to which some reference has already been made, help us in approaching this question, but only in part. The estimated number of compositors and machine operators enrolled in the ITU rose from 23 per cent in 1900 to almost 40 per cent in 1930. But the global figures conceal a wide discrepancy in the degree of organization prevailing in the two principal branches of the industry: newspaper printing was firmly organized, whereas book and job printing had a major nonunion sector. In fact, after the union had lost a strike for the 44-hour week in 1921, the open-shop sector of the industry expanded; one estimate put it in 1931 at double the 1919 level.[9] Even in newspaper publishing, the American Newspaper Publishers Association maintained an open-shop department, established in 1922, the chief function of which was to furnish strikebreakers.[10]

Trade union maturity may be defined as the attainment by a union of sufficient control of the labor supply within the product market in which it operates so that competition from nonunion producing units does not constitute a significant factor in influencing collective bargaining decisions. Obviously, a union need not have organized to the very limit of its jurisdiction to have achieved maturity, in this sense. Even in the most strongly organized of industries there will usually exist a nonunion fringe which it does not pay to attack. Precisely when a union "matures" cannot be determined with any degree of precision, but it is not difficult to discern from trade union periodicals when nonunion competition ceases to be an important economic issue.

Measured by this touchstone, it is possible to say that by 1936 the ITU had reached maturity in newspaper publishing, but fell decisively below it in book and job printing. President Howard, in his annual report to the membership of the ITU, stated:

During the period of unemployment there has been a growing opposition on the part of union members to admitting into membership those who make application. The attitude is injurious to union success. With an inexhaustible reservoir of nonunion printers available, it is more difficult to negotiate acceptable wage scales.[11]

In the newspaper industry, the strength of the union position was augmented by the characteristically local nature of the product market. Militantly nonunion local centers such as New Orleans and Los Angeles, as well as unorganized shops in small towns, did not provide harassment for such union strongholds as New York and Chicago. But in commercial printing, the situation was far different. President Howard may be quoted once again, this time from his 1938 report:

Decentralization of the printing industry has been a development which has increased the difficulties of applying an effective solution [for unemployment]. Concerns producing publications with a large national circulation have found it necessary to remove from the congested areas that previously had been large printing centers. The new locations generally have been in unorganized territory or jurisdictions where lower wage rates prevailed. One of the difficult problems with which the union has been confronted was to maintain union contracts with these concerns and secure acceptable wage rates and conditions.[12]

Attempts at organization during the depression were largely ineffective. Opposition candidates in the 1936 union elections charged that all the 31 strikes undertaken by the ITU from 1929 to 1936 had been lost. Union membership between these two years declined from almost 77,000 to 74,300. Certainly in 1936 there was within the ranks of the ITU a clear recognition of the urgent need for greater organizing efforts. "To maintain effective control of the supply of competent labor," stated President Howard, "we must return to the condition where every member will recognize that he and she is a volunteer organizer." The hypothesis that the status of the ITU in 1936 was so commanding as to lead to complacency is clearly not tenable. There were large numbers of nonunion printers whose enrollment was essential to the economic welfare of the union members.

In fact, a considerable amount of organizing work was undertaken with the support of the international union, and as the membership data indicate, there was some success. But even within the ITU, there was a strong feeling of inadequacy. Vice-President Baker wrote in the following vein in January 1937:

the record of the last full fiscal year of our organization is not one of growth. Despite the psychology of organization which seems to be everywhere evident, the International Union actually lost membership insofar as journeymen printers are concerned. . . . Valuable and dear to us who have been members for years as the pension and mortuary may be, it is still difficult to "sell" a shroud or a funeral to prospective members still in their twenties. And it is just as difficult to make him anticipate economic needs forty years in the future. . . . Greater stress should be placed upon the economic value of the organization.[13]

A drive was undertaken at the beginning of 1937 to add 10,000 members by the end of the year. Howard claimed that during the years 1936 and 1937, some 600 printing shops had been organized, bringing 12,000 new members into the union.[14] However, reference to Table 12 makes it clear that the claim must have been gross rather than net accretion. The 1937–1939 recession temporarily reversed the upward trend in membership, but a very moderate rise commenced once more in 1940, continuing until 1943, when the membership curve once more took a downward turn.

Several major campaigns, directed at specific targets, were undertaken during this period. One of them involved R. R. Donnelley and Sons, the nation's largest commercial publisher, which was operating on a nonunion basis. A joint printing organizing committee was established in Chicago, to which the ITU contributed funds and organizers, but to no avail.[15] An attempt to secure a national boycott of magazines printed by Donnelley was successful to the extent of removing two national sports magazines and the New York telephone book from Donnelley to union concerns, but the economic impact was not sufficient to change the company's attitude toward unionism.

Another bad situation, from the union point of view, prevailed in New Orleans, where the local newspapers operated on a nonunion basis. President Baker described the significance of the New Orleans campaign as follows:

If you could unionize the papers, and if you can today, it is worth $100,000 to us, because there never was a major strike in the last twenty-five years that special cars of strikebreakers did not leave New Orleans. They went into Albany, Hackensack, Patterson, Minneapolis. I saw them there in the hotel lobby being paid off by H. W. Flagg. That was where they kept them ready for what they termed "gold rushes."[16]

In 1941, the ITU won an NLRB election among the employees of the New Orleans *Item,* but the remainder of the industry continued on a nonunion status.

To summarize: the ITU, in 1936, was still in a phase of its development in which organizational work was essential to the economic welfare of the union. There was clear and abundant recognition of the need to organize among both the leadership and the membership.[17] That there were serious obstacles to organization cannot be denied. President Baker pointed out that "printing and publishing is a 'sheltered' industry, made up of a multitude of units. In those respects it differs from the so-called mass production industries. Consequently, organizational achievements are not spectacular since relatively small numbers of craftsmen are engaged in plants which are brought under union jurisdiction. It must also be borne in mind that with each union chartered or plant unionized, the field of growth is decreased."[18] But these same considerations applied in other industries as well, and against the background of American labor developments from 1936 to 1941, the organizational performance of the ITU must be regarded as a relatively poor one.

The wage performance is much more difficult to assess. Although newspaper publishing was only moderately affected by the depression, book and job printing was quite adversely affected, although not as much as the generality of manufacturing industry. Not only did advertising volume fall off directly, but cheaper substitutes for letterpress printing reduced employment opportunities for printers. While a few of the larger firms operated profitably, most of the smaller firms functioned within an intensely competitive environment, close to the margin of financial solvency.[19] By 1937, although employment of wage earners on newspapers and periodicals was 4.2 per cent above the 1929 level, employment in book and job shops was still 6.7 per cent below 1929.[20] However, the secular trend of employment in the industry had been upward, despite sharply rising productivity occasioned by technological change, reflecting the increased demand for printing products.

Before considering the course of printing wage rates from 1936 to 1941, it is well to examine their history during the depression. Table 13 compares hourly wage rate indexes in printing with those in manufacturing as a whole from 1929 to 1936. It appears from this table that union printing wage rates fell much less during the depression than manufacturing wages generally, but that the rapid rebound of manufacturing rates brought them almost up to the printing level, relatively, by 1936. Within the printing

Table 13.

Indices of hourly wage rates in manufacturing and union hourly
wage rates in printing, 1929 to 1936
(1929 = 100)

Year	All manufacturing	All printing	Book and job	Newspaper
1929	100.0	100.0	100.0	100.0
1930	97.5	101.5	101.8	101.0
1931	91.3	102.1	102.5	101.3
1932	78.8	101.3	101.4	101.1
1933	78.1	95.3	95.8	94.5
1934	94.0	97.3	98.4	95.8
1935	97.2	101.0	100.6	101.6
1936	98.2	103.3	103.5	103.1

Sources: Bureau of Labor Statistics, *Handbook of Labor Statistics,* 1941 and 1947 editions;
Bureau of Labor Statistics, Bulletin No. 675 (1940), p. 5.

industry, the wage experience of commercial and newspaper printing did
not differ greatly in regard to average hourly earnings. With respect to the
welfare of the printing workers, it was the conclusion of a careful observer
that "the maintenance of depression hourly earnings in newspaper and
periodical plants nearer to the 1929 level than was true of manufacturing
industries as a whole did not plunge production and man-hours worked
to the depths plumbed by the generality of manufacturing industries." [21]

ITU statistics indicate that for its members, wage rates in 1936 were
90.7 per cent of the 1929 level, while actual weekly earnings were 79.2 per
cent of 1929.[22] However, these figures were calculated in a manner different
from those cited above, and are not comparable with them.

The conclusion appears to be, on the basis of the data in Table 13, that
printing workers were only slightly better off in 1936, compared with 1929,
than manufacturing workers generally, so that a substantial corrective
adjustment of wage rates in favor of the latter would not necessarily have
been anticipated.

Turning to the period with which we are more directly concerned, Table
14 indicates that printing trades wage rates lagged rather far behind manufacturing and building trades wages, but that their correspondence with the
rise in wages paid to railroad workers was fairly close. This may be part
of the general narrowing of differentials that has occurred in the United
States, for printing was traditionally a trade with a high absolute wage
level. There is evidence, however, that this was more than a mere narrowing
of differentials, for printing dropped from first to tenth place, in terms of

Table 14.

Indices of hourly wage rates in selected industries, 1936 to 1941
(1936 = 100)

Year	Manufacturing	Newspapers and periodicals	Book and job printing	Building construction	Steam railroads
1936	100.0	100.0	100.0	100.0	100.0
1937	112.2	104.3	104.2	106.9	102.6
1938	112.7	107.1	107.5	116.5	108.0
1939	113.8	108.9	108.4	117.3	108.4
1940	118.9	112.0	109.3	119.2	108.8
1941	131.1	116.0	110.9	123.5	113.9

Sources: *Manufacturing and Printing:* Bureau of Labor Statistics, *Handbook of Labor Statistics,*
  1947 edition, pp. 54ff.
  Building Construction: W. S. Woytinsky, *Employment and Wages in the United States*
  (New York, 1953), p. 584.
  Railroads: Jacob J. Kaufman, *Collective Bargaining in the Railroad Industry* (New
  York, 1954), p. 91.

the height of wages paid, among manufacturing industries, between 1923
and 1939.[23] Whatever the cause the fact is undeniable that workers in the
printing trades fared relatively poorly in the years following the depression.

Some notion of the comparative situation among the various crafts within
printing can be garnered from Tables 15 and 16. In conjunction with these

Table 15.

Indices of union hourly wage rates, selected printing trades, book and job printing, 1929–1939
(1929 = 100)

Year	Machine compositors	Cylinder pressmen	Bookbinders	Photoengravers
1929	100.0	100.0	100.0	100.0
1930	102.7	101.8	101.2	100.2
1931	103.2	102.5	101.6	100.5
1932	103.3	99.8	97.9	103.5
1933	96.9	93.6	94.4	101.5
1934	97.0	96.3	97.9	103.1
1935	98.6	97.5	99.3	109.6
1936	102.0	101.5	100.6	112.3
1937	104.8	105.1	103.4	113.7
1938	107.7	108.2	107.2	116.6
1939	108.0	109.0	109.3	117.5
1940	108.8	109.7	109.9	118.4
1941	109.7	110.5	111.5	118.9

Source: *Monthly Labor Review* (December 1941), p. 1538.

Table 16.

Indices of union hourly wage rates, selected printing trades, newspapers, 1929–1939
(1929 = 100)

Year	Machine compositors	Web pressmen	Photoengravers	Stereotypers
1929	100.0	100.0	100.0	100.0
1930	100.8	101.7	101.6	100.8
1931	100.9	102.3	102.6	101.2
1932	100.2	103.6	103.8	100.2
1933	93.7	97.0	96.0	94.6
1934	94.9	97.2	100.5	96.0
1935	101.2	102.5	105.3	100.5
1936	103.9	103.1	107.9	102.0
1937	107.3	106.5	109.9	105.2
1938	109.7	109.3	115.5	108.8
1939	110.5	111.7	117.8	109.9
1940	112.6	114.4	119.1	113.0
1941	113.7	116.0	119.6	114.8

Source: *Monthly Labor Review* (December 1941), p. 1538.

tables, it is well to point out that in book and job printing, the ranking of the crafts in terms of the absolute level of wages (July 1, 1939) was: photo-engravers ($1.564); compositors ($1.276); pressmen ($1.246); and book-binders ($1.032). Among the newspaper crafts, the rankings were: photo-engravers ($1.703); compositors ($1.356); stereotypers ($1.241); and pressmen ($1.239). In book printing, the compositors fared somewhat better than the pressmen during the depression years, but the latter came back more strongly after 1936, though this may have been a function of their slightly lower position on the wage scale. In newspaper printing, the press-men did consistently better than the typographers, except for the years 1937 and 1938. The highly paid photoengravers in both branches of the industry made a considerably better showing than the compositors.

The results which emerge from these data are not conclusive. As already stated, printing wage earners as a group did not do particularly well eco-nomically during the years 1936 to 1941. ITU members, in particular, fared slightly less well than the pressmen in terms of the rise in their average hourly earnings. This does not suggest the presence of an aggressive, dy-namic, organization of printers, alert to the opportunities afforded by the favorable conjuncture of government encouragement to collective bargain-ing and the possession of a $657,000 defense fund [24] available for organiza-tional purposes. It tends to reinforce, rather, the impression created by the membership data cited earlier.

Union democracy. A recent study of the International Typographical Union concluded on the following note:

To the sympathetic student of the labor movement, the ITU stands as a model of the trade union in a democratic society. In the ITU he sees the image of the democratic processes he prizes in the national body politic, in the organization through which printers exercise some control over the conditions of their livelihood. . . . The ITU and its democratic political system *is:* to know what makes and has made it what it is may help make possible the development of organizational democracy elsewhere.[25]

An earlier study of the ITU reached much the same conclusion:

The compositors' union is known for the battles which have raged between rival political factions for the control of its international administration during the twentieth century. The high degree in which political arguments of all shades find free and unhindered expression in the campaigns for I.T.U. offices constitutes a bright page in the history of union democracy.[26]

The ITU was not unique in having internal factionalism, as the foregoing chapters have amply demonstrated. It was unique, however, in that factionalism crystallized into well defined political parties which have persisted throughout most of its history. It has often been argued by some students of the labor movement, as well as by most practitioners of trade unionism, that factional strife is not necessarily correlated with union efficiency in attaining the ends for which its members joined. Indeed, the usual assumption has been that the degree of internal factionalism was apt to be inversely correlated with success in collective bargaining.

If it could be shown that the economic cost to ITU members of internal political strife was negligible, or actually yielded increased dividends, the argument for institutionalizing political factions within the labor movement would be unanswerable. If, on the other hand, this type of union government was revealed to have its costs, the argument would become a much more complicated one. From a theoretical welfare point of view, union members would have to make the choice between more democracy and less wages or more wages and less democracy. Unfortunately, despite all the attention that has been devoted to the ITU in recent years, this crucial question has not been considered. It is simply taken as axiomatic that the ITU is doing a first-rate collective bargaining job.[27]

A general history is no place to consider this question in any depth; that must wait upon a full-scale monographic account of the fascinating organization which the Printers have built. But even a brief discussion of the political situation inside the ITU from 1936 to 1941 may suggest that party politics in trade unionism can be a costly affair.

The 1936 elections were won by the Progressive Party, which had been in firm control of the organization since 1928. Charles Howard, the president of the Progressives, carried a full slate into office with him, including Claude M. Baker as first vice-president and Woodruff Randolph as secretary-treasurer. From 1930 on, Howard had been under fire within his own party, the Progressives, for being too conservative. This stemmed in part from his opposition to sharing the available work with unemployed members. The New York and San Francisco Progressive Clubs actually campaigned to deny him renomination, and he generally ran behind the ticket, particularly in New York, where the powerful communist-dominated Amalgamation Party disliked him. Claude Baker was the candidate of the left-wing Progressives, while Woodruff Randolph was considered a militant trade union officer by the same group. The opposition Independent Party had accused the Howard administration of failing to make organizational progress, of laxity in enforcing the 5-day week, and of giving insufficient assistance to striking locals.[28]

The internal situation was complicated by the fact that Howard became secretary of the CIO in a personal capacity. His party, the Progressives, was friendly to the CIO, but feared to take the issue to the membership. Among other things, cooperation with the other printing crafts, particularly as it affected use of the union label, might have been endangered by an abrupt break with the AFL. The ITU leadership opposed suspension of the CIO unions, arguing that the AFL lacked any authority to determine jurisdictional questions in the first place.[29] When Howard was attacked by the Independents for devoting time to CIO affairs, he replied:

I have devoted no time away from my duties as President of the International Typographical Union and I receive no compensation whatever from the C.I.O. My influence is being used to assist in unionizing unorganized workers without neglecting my many duties as President of the International Typographical Union.[30]

That Howard would have liked to take the ITU into the CIO is clear from a letter published after his death by political opponents.[31] Randolph, too, was quoted as writing to Lewis and Hillman in March 1937, advising them as to the proper course to be taken in the Stalinist-Trotskyist controversy then raging in Minneapolis.[32] However, although the 1936 ITU convention endorsed the organizational efforts of the CIO among industrial workers, and criticized the AFL executive council for suspending the CIO unions, it took no action toward affiliation with the CIO.[33]

Woodruff Randolph, who increasingly became the chief spokesman for the Progressives, advanced an argument at the 1936 convention which he was to repeat many times in the future: that the ITU, as one of the founders of the AFL, had never been chartered by the parent organization and could therefore not have its charter withdrawn. He maintained that the ITU had received merely a certificate of affiliation from the AFL. While this argument was excessively legalistic, it apparently appealed to the printers, who were proud of the record of their organization as a pioneer of the labor movement.

As the AFL-CIO fight increased in bitterness, the position of Howard became increasingly untenable. William Green appeared at the 1937 ITU convention and challenged its officers to submit the question of its affiliation to a referendum vote. He declared:

it seems to me most contradictory and inconsistent for a great organization such as yours to be loyal and devoted to the American Federation of Labor, functioning as a part of it, helping to shape its policies and formulate its organization work and at the same time the President of your organization serving as an officer of the Committee for Industrial Organization.

The convention merely adopted a resolution calling upon the AFL to respect the rights of the autonomous unions comprising it.[34] However, as the 1938 election campaign approached, the Independent Party centered its fire upon Howard's role as a CIO official. In an attempt to dispose of the issue before the election, the ITU executive board asked the membership to vote on the questions of whether the ITU should pay the special assessment that the 1937 AFL convention had levied to fight the CIO, and whether the ITU should continue to assert its "historic" independence from AFL control. Claude Baker, the ITU first vice-president, who had become increasingly estranged from Howard after his election in 1936 on the Progressive ticket, attacked the referendum as unnecessary and ill-advised, and introduced for the sole purpose of influencing the outcome of the election.[35] But the fact that payment of the assessment might have meant higher dues, linked with the popular issue of autonomy, made the outcome certain: the members voted overwhelmingly against payment of the assessment and in favor of the traditional autonomy of the ITU.

Baker, who became the standard-bearer of the Independent Party, nevertheless continued to attack Howard for "misuse of the prestige attaching to the office of president of our great union in fomenting discord in the labor

movement and with allied crafts." Quite surprisingly, in view of the outcome
of the referendum, Baker defeated Howard in the 1938 election by a decisive majority (Howard died of a heart attack shortly after the election).
However, he was able to carry in with him only the second vice-president,
the Progressives winning the first vice-presidency and the secretary-treasurership. Baker, who implied that he favored a policy of further distribution
of work to the unemployed members, undoubtedly gained a great many
Progressive votes because of this stand. Secretary-Treasurer Randolph, who
was regarded as a more militant Progressive than Howard, was reelected
handily, and later rewarded his left-wing supporters by giving an international vice-presidency to Elmer Brown, who had been the leader of the
Amalgamation Party in New York City. These four officials, together with
a vice-president representing the Mailers, a small group of semiskilled
workers over whom the ITU exercised jurisdiction, comprised the ITU
executive board. This meant that for the next two years, the principal executive body of the union was to be split equally between the two parties, with
the deciding vote residing potentially in the hands of a man representing a
group which customarily did not interfere in the affairs of the craft-conscious printers. The result was almost inevitable: internal guerilla warfare
from almost the first day following the announcement of the election results.

Under the arrangement then in effect, the secretary-treasurer acted as
editor of the union's official organ, *The Typographical Journal*, which was
sent to every member. However, each officer was permitted to furnish a
column free from censorship by the editor. The *Journal* increasingly became
a battleground, with the officers attacking one another on every conceivable
issue, some of them of an exceedingly petty nature.[36] This may have come
under the head of healthy debate, but it must nevertheless have been discouraging to organizers in the field and to local unions facing hostile employers.

The question of affiliation with the AFL continued to occupy the center
of interest. The Baker administration introduced a resolution at the 1938
ITU convention calling for another referendum on payment of the AFL
assessment. Baker argued: "I think we have too long been the victims of a
high-powered propaganda campaign. Now, it is a moral question. What do
you think of a man that deliberately permits himself to continue delinquent
and be kicked out?"[37] The resolution was defeated by a close margin, leaving the ITU in a peculiar status.

Prior to the 1938 AFL convention, the Teamsters strongly protested to
the AFL Executive Council against seating the ITU at the convention.

William Green conferred with Baker, and suggested that the ITU delegates refrain from submitting their credentials in the interest of convention harmony. Baker replied that he intended to arrange another referendum as soon as possible, a step which could be done on the initiative of a certain proportion of local unions, and urged that the delegation be seated lest the opposition be furnished with more ammunition. Green told the AFL Executive Council:

Under the circumstances it seems to me it is an extraordinary situation. I do not suppose we ever had a case like this. It is not like a union positively refusing to pay, it is a situation where a new president is coming into a new position on the eve of a convention, and is confronted with an impossible situation. He is willing to pay and wants to pay and he is going to make a determined effort to pay.[38]

In the light of this plea, the ITU was seated at the convention. But Baker was unable to secure a referendum on the issue, which was debated fully once again at the 1939 convention of the ITU. Baker accused his predecessor in office of misleading the membership, of withholding the truth from them, with the purpose of exacerbating relations with the AFL.[39] A resolution was finally adopted advising the AFL that continued affiliation could not be dependent upon the ITU paying the special assessment, and warning that if the AFL refused to seat ITU delegates at its next convention, no further per capita tax would be paid. This resolution was a substantial victory for the Progressives, who favored a complete breach of relations with the AFL, but did not consider it politic to come out openly with this view.

As a consequence, the ITU delegates were refused admittance to the 1939 AFL convention. Following the convention, Green notified all AFL central bodies that the ITU was no longer in affiliation with the AFL, but he did not order that ITU locals be disassociated from such bodies, urging that the pro-AFL forces in the ITU be given another chance to work for regularization of the ITU status. The AFL Executive Council, however, insisted that all ITU locals be suspended from AFL central trade councils and state federations of labor.[40]

This was by no means the only issue which created friction within the ITU. Vice-President Barrett, a Progressive, told the membership in his 1939 report that he was deprived of a secretary to open his mail while he was away, with the result that important correspondence had been delayed. He accused Baker of having engaged in wholesale dismissals of ITU office employees on assuming office, and concluded:

Where we have a secretary appointed by the President, in a position where he can nullify any order of a vice-president, who is elected by the membership, then I say you are placing those officers where they may not be able to carry out the will of the membership. *Particularly is this so where you have two political parties in office.* [Italics mine]

Secretary-Treasurer Randolph also accused President Baker of interfering with the proper performance of his duties, and asked that the next convention take measures to rectify the situation.[41]

As the 1940 ITU elections approached, mutual recrimination reached a new height. Vice-President Conley accused Randolph of having "conspired to destroy the relationship of the I.T.U. and the A.F. of L. and that he actually participated in the scheme to destroy an old established A.F. of L. labor council and supplant it with a C.I.O. unit, even though Mr. Randolph knew and disclosed that the C.I.O. movement was saturated with Communism from top to bottom." [42] Some damaging correspondence which the Baker administration had found in the files on assuming office was printed, although it was revealed that Howard adherents had taken some care to remove from the files material which might prove embarrassing to them. The issue of subversion was dragged into the election campaign. President Baker wrote, for example:

The International Union can not be destroyed even by officers heavily obligated to almost every subversive group in the country. . . .

Whenever [Vice-President] Barrett called a strike it was lost and usually the union virtually destroyed. . . .

Insist that the opposition disavow the support of the same Communists and fellow travelers whom a few years ago the Progressive leaders so vigorously denounced.

Vice-President Conley, who was running against Randolph for the secretary-treasurership, produced a memorandum from the War Department showing that in 1917 Randolph had claimed exemption from the draft as a conscientious objector because of membership in the Socialist Party. He reproduced a letter from Norman Thomas, the head of the Socialist Party, to Charles Howard, dated October 19, 1937, in which Howard's aid was solicited in securing employment for Liston Oak, an ex-Communist, from which Conley drew the following moral: "Now there might be some difference between Socialism and Communism, but it is difficult to determine where one ends and the other begins. After all, Russia is a Socialist Republic." The administration also published a letter from an international representative to Vice-President Barrett, who was running against Baker for the presidency, complaining that a recently organized local had turned against the Progressive Party. Barrett replied:

I can't understand what could have happened at Greensburg, Pa., and it seems to me since you were responsible for the organization of this union, you should develop some reason to visit the jurisdiction and find out why they have taken this attitude toward the administration who organized them and improved their working conditions. Contacts could be established in those places that voted adversely against us and an effort made to bolster up our position in those localities.

A majority of the printers voted for Barrett, who was defeated by the margin of the Mailer votes, which went heavily for Baker. The election was a repetition of the previous one. By very slender margins in all cases, the Independents captured the presidency and the second vice-presidency, while the Progressives elected the first vice-president and the secretary-treasurer, thus continuing the deadlock on the executive board. A few months after the election, President Baker published the following commentary on the result:

Since Mr. Randolph chose to analyze the vote of members of the International Union and whine because there were those who consistently have opposed him, it is well that members know that Mr. Randolph owes his re-election in 1940 solely to the bloc vote of German and other hyphenated unions. Analysis of the vote in May will show that Randolph's opponent received a clear majority of the votes of the members of other unions. The "bloc" vote of the hyphenated, foreign language unions re-elected Mr. Randolph. Thus his election by such unions is clearly established. Mr. Conley made no appeal for Nazi or Communist support.[43]

Matthew Woll appeared before the 1940 ITU convention and disclosed that the AFL was prepared to make some concessions in the direction of curbing the authority of its Executive Council to suspend affiliated unions. The convention empowered the international officers to meet with the AFL for further discussions of the feasibility of ITU reaffiliation. In these discussions, the ITU representatives demanded that the AFL adopt a clear requirement of a two-thirds vote of the convention for suspension of an affiliate; a restatement, by constitutional amendment, of lack of AFL power to determine jurisdiction; and elimination of the right to levy assessments.[44] The AFL, in return, presented a memorandum acknowledging the autonomy of affiliated unions, and making certain other concessions to the ITU position. This statement was submitted to the ITU membership through a referendum, with the Independents strongly advocating that it be approved as the basis for ITU reaffiliation with the AFL. However, the Progressives urged that the ITU remain outside the AFL until the latter's constitution was redrafted to specify clearly that affiliated unions were not subordinate to the parent federation. The proposal was defeated by a sizeable margin, and another effort to bring the ITU back into the AFL collapsed. It was clear from the debate on the issue that there were no longer any real principles at stake, the main purpose of the antagonists being to squeeze some party advantage out of the matter.

The foregoing account records but a few of the highlights of the internecine party warfare that was waged continuously in the ITU during the years 1936 to 1941. Enough has been quoted, however, to demonstrate the degree of personal animosity that prevailed among men who were closely associated with one another in what was presumably a common endeavor. It must be remembered that the ITU executive board was not a legislative body, but an executive and administrative agency, engaged in making immediate decisions of importance to the union. Only a detailed examination of the events occurring at the local level during this period can establish whether or not party strife proved costly to the membership. But there is at least a *prima facie* case that it did not add to the effectiveness of the union as a collective bargaining agency.[45]

To conclude this brief account of ITU history on a negative note would be to create an erroneous and unwarranted impression in the mind of a reader. Measured by any absolute scale, the ITU had achieved a remarkable degree of control over working conditions in the substantial segment of the industry which was organized. The wage rates specified in its agreements were among the highest in American industry. The issue is not whether the ITU was a powerful and stable union, but whether its efficiency was adversely affected by the persistence of internal politics.

A considerable amount of attention has been devoted to the system of collective bargaining that has developed in the printing trades over the course of a century,[46] and little can be done in a general history other than to note that the system continued to operate with little change. A few economic problems became particularly acute, among them the trend toward decentralization of production in book and job printing, with New York in particular feeling the impact of the movement.[47] The New York local organized a regional scale conference in 1937, which urged that typographical wage differentials be limited to a maximum of 10 per cent in all cities within 100 miles of New York, and that all employers moving their shops be compelled to pay the wage scale prevailing in the jurisdiction which they had left, but the problems raised by these efforts were so formidable that no action was taken by the international union.[48] A later attempt by New York to secure boycotts against employers moving from a jurisdiction in order to secure a lower wage scale met with a similar fate.[49] The demise of the Open Shop Division of the American Newspaper Publishers Association, as a result of the Wagner Act and the Byrnes anti-strikebreaking law, should also be noted.

The American Newspaper Guild

Although not a large organization, the American Newspaper Guild merits a distinct place in a general history of unionism because of its success in organizing a group of workers who would have seemed to be very poor union material from an objective viewpoint. The Guild is not the only union of professionals; organization exists among teachers, actors, musicians, architects, and engineers. But the Guild faced certain obstacles in addition to the reluctance of professionals to associate with manual workers, and the usual resistance of employers. Newspaper men are among the most sophisticated trade groups in the country, and might have been expected to view with suspicion, if not cynicism, the discipline imposed by unionism. Moreover, newspaper publishers felt strongly that organization of the men and women who write the news would inevitably endanger freedom of the press. The board of directors of the American Newspaper Publishers Association warned its members, in 1936:

While it is impossible for the Government to destroy or even restrict the freedom of the press, it is not impossible for an individual publisher by agreement to do so insofar as his own newspaper is concerned by a course of conduct or by contractual arrangement.

The chief function of the press being the gathering and dissemination of information, it is imperative that publishers should take every proper step to make certain that their news and editorial departments are manned by efficient personnel, working under conditions mutually satisfactory to employes and employer alike.

Any agreement restricting the publisher's control of his editorial and news departments necessarily restricts him in the performance of this function and his obligation to the public, and it is the board's opinion that no such agreement should be entered into.[50]

On the credit side of the Guild ledger was the fact that the mechanical employees of newspapers were strongly organized, and publishers had long engaged in collective bargaining with them. The collective agreement was not a new and frightening concept to the newspaper owner, as it was to most manufacturing employers. Nevertheless, the success of the Guild, despite all the obstacles in its path, not the least of which was virulent political factionalism, constitutes a considerable achievement.

The origins of the Guild. Significant among the factors which were responsible for breaking down resistance to unionism among newspaper men was their relatively poor economic status before and during the depression. Prior to 1930, the wages of editorial employees failed to rise as rapidly as those of mechanical employees. Between 1930 and 1934, their earnings had declined by about 12 per cent,[51] considerably more than among the mechanical employees. Moreover, a great deal of employment retrenchment in editorial departments had occurred, and the employees enjoyed little job security. The Guild was one of the pioneers among labor organizations in securing dismissal pay for its members.

Prior to 1933, there had been some attempts to organize newswriters by the American Federation of Labor. In 1923, after vain efforts at organization, the International Typographical Union formally relinquished jurisdiction over this category of newspaper employees, and the AFL remained in the field through the medium of federal locals.[52] Several of these locals eventually became affiliated with the Guild.

The Guild owed its inception to the wave of union sentiment that accompanied enactment of the National Industrial Recovery Act. Within a few months, local newswriters unions had sprung up throughout the country, and on December 15, 1933, representatives of 21 local bodies met in Washington to form the American Newspaper Guild. The guiding spirit of the organization, which was initially independent of the American Federation of Labor, was Heywood Broun, one of the most widely read newspaper columnists of the time, ably assisted by Jonathan Eddy, the full-time executive secretary.[53] The original conception of the organization was that of a loose association of local bodies. All local bargaining was reserved to the local guilds, with the national Guild restricted to bargaining with press associations and national syndicates. The membership was generally opposed to a centralized organization with full-time officers and a national treasury.[54]

At first, the Guild concentrated upon use of the NRA code machinery to improve wages and other conditions of labor. It was not long before disillusionment with what the federal government was prepared to do set in, however, and early in 1935, when President Roosevelt issued an order forbidding appeal from the Newspaper Industrial Board, which the Guild claimed was publisher-dominated, to the National Labor Relations Board, Guild disenchantment became complete. Heywood Broun wrote:

We feel that it is impossible to dodge the fact that the newspaper publishers have cracked down on the President of the United States, and that Franklin D. Roosevelt has cracked up. . . . The President made no attempt to learn from the Guild its bill of complaints against the stupidities and the iniquities of the Newspaper Industrial Board.[55]

Initially, publishers did not react in an overtly unfriendly manner to the new organization, although there was no rush to sign agreements with it. The first contract was with the *Philadelphia Record* whose publisher, J. David Stern, had demonstrated consistent support of the guild idea. But when the Guild, during the course of 1934, began to act more like a trade union and less like a professional association, a marked change of attitude began to occur. A successful boycott against the *Long Island Daily Press* to secure the reinstatement of discharged employees, followed by an 18-week strike against the *Newark Ledger*, during the course of which the Guild employed mass picketing and the secondary boycott of advertisers, hardened the attitude of the publishers.[56] *Editor and Publisher*, the trade journal of the industry, wrote:

Editors and publishers need no longer regard the American Newspaper Guild as an independent body of responsible professional newswriters and editors, a "guild" with an economic program. It is a radical trades-union, at least insofar as its national officers are concerned. They bring discredit to many local Guilds that deserve recognition.[57]

Difficulties began to crop up throughout the country. Several Guild members were discharged by the *Oakland Tribune* (California), and despite strong support from the local labor movement, the Guild was unable to secure their reinstatement.[58] Differences developed with the management of the *Cleveland News*, which had entered into an agreement with the Guild after nine months of negotiation. A strike was called against the *Lorain Journal and Times Herald* (Ohio) over an alleged lockout of seven Guild members. The question of affiliation with organized labor became more prominent in Guild circles, with Jonathan Eddy, the executive secretary, pushing strongly for this move.[59]

The second annual convention of the Guild, held in Cleveland in June 1935, moved a considerable distance in the direction of transforming the organization into a traditional trade union body. The convention empowered the national executive board to draft a model contract for the guidance of local guilds, and gave it authority to disapprove any collective agreement which the board held to be in violation of the constitution and the collective bargaining principles adopted by the convention. The bargaining program included the forty-hour week, a minimum wage, the preferential Guild shop, time and one half for overtime, and dismissal compensation. However, local guilds were warned against accepting wage arbitration, widely practiced by the mechanical trades, "for the history of arbitration is a history of losses for labor."

The major issue at the convention was affiliation with the American Federation of Labor. The proponents of affiliation argued that the Guild was a labor organization and belonged in the organized labor movement. They pointed to the importance of the support that might be secured from other unions, particularly the printing crafts, during Guild strikes. The opponents attacked the AFL as a weak and nonrepresentative body, and maintained that affiliation would be of little benefit and much potential harm by alienating publishers and prospective members who feared that such ties might endanger the traditional political neutrality of newspaper men. It was eventually agreed that the question should be submitted to a national referendum, with a two-thirds majority required for affiliation. The referendum gave 1 per cent less than the required majority, and the Guild remained independent for the time being.

Because of a low dues structure, the national organization was experiencing constant financial difficulties, and in September 1935, all organizational activities were suspended and a special assessment levied. This precipitated an internal fight, with the opponents of centralization opposing attempts to increase the amount of funds at the disposal of the national body. The administration had its way, and a defense fund was started in preparation for an intensive organizing drive.

From a bargaining point of view, 1935 was not a good year. Three strikes were called against small papers, two of which resulted in agreement, while one was lost. The *Newark Ledger* strike, which cost the Guild $25,000 in support, was lost when the local unit abandoned the Guild.

The year 1936 saw a stepup in Guild activities. Early in the year, the Guild became involved in a strike against the *Wisconsin News* (Milwaukee), the first of a long series of disputes with the Hearst chain. William Green promised the strikers AFL support, and urged the Milwaukee Federated Trades Council to render what assistance it could. Mass picketing was employed, but the refusal of the mechanical crafts to leave their jobs enabled the paper to continue in operation, and the strike dragged on until

September, when the strikers were reinstated without having gained recognition for the Guild. The Guild was quite critical of the printing trades for their role in this and other strikes, accusing them not only of failing to cooperate directly, but of even attempting to prevent other unions from lending support to the Guild.

Affiliation with the American Federation of Labor. The support proffered by the AFL in the Milwaukee strike, and the failure of the Guild to make any real progress on the collective bargaining front, led to increasing sentiment for AFL affiliation. This step was finally taken by a vote of 83 to 5 at the June 1936 convention of the Guild, authorizing the executive board to seek a charter. The Guild became affiliated with the AFL on July 22, after entering into a series of jurisdictional agreements with the other printing crafts. The Federation immediately lent the Guild $2000, and put a Guild organizer on the AFL payroll. John L. Lewis, not to be outdone, extended the Guild a loan of $4000 as evidence of CIO interest in the young organization of newsmen.

Affiliation with organized labor was greeted with a blast of disapproval by publishers. The trade journal of the industry wrote:

Editor & Publisher continues in the belief that affiliation with organized labor is a mistaken and futile move for organized editorial employes. It violates a tradition still held dear by many editorial men and women that their pursuit is not a trade, but a blend of the arts and professional skill. . . . It [the Guild] still represents a minority of journalistic thought that has small chance of becoming a majority. It represents a philosophy we cannot accept, and which we believe will be rejected by most of our colleagues in daily journalism.[60]

The 1936 convention took a further step in the direction of centralization by authorizing the creation of nine councils to coordinate collective bargaining activities with the major newspaper chains.[61] The councils were not specifically authorized to negotiate on a chain-wide basis, but it was the obvious expectation that they would eventually evolve into bargaining units. This form of organization developed very slowly, however, with the Scripps-Howard chain council leading the way. Organization of the national wire services was made the responsibility of the national executive board, in view of the fact that many employees of the services worked in areas where local guild units did not exist.

Shortly after affiliation with the AFL had been consummated, the Guild became involved in one of the major labor disputes of its entire history. Thirty-six members declared a strike against the Seattle *Post-Intelligencer,* a Hearst paper, to protest the discharge of two employees, allegedly for union activity. The paper was forced to suspend when the Guild picket line was reinforced by teamsters, longshoremen, and woodworkers, under the leadership of Dave Beck, at that time the head of the Seattle teamster organization. After several months of vain negotiations, the Executive Council of the AFL intervened, and on the basis of a report made by John P. Frey, proposed that the strike be terminated and all issues referred to a committee consisting of William Green and a representative of the Hearst management, except that the fate of the two men whose discharge had brought about the strike be left to the NLRB. The council proposal was brought about largely because of pressure brought to bear by Charles P. Howard, president of the Typographical Union, who wanted an end to the strike in the interests of his members. The Guild insisted that it would not accept the proposal unless the two discharged men were first reinstated, and a Guild representative were included on any arbitration committee. It protested vigorously against the invasion of its autonomy by the Executive Council, and received strong support for its stand from the Seattle Labor Council.[62]

The strike was finally settled on November 25, 1936. The Guild was recognized as representative of its members in a management statement of policy — not a collective agreement — and concessions were made in wage scales and vacations. However, the men whose discharge constituted the *casus belli* were not reinstated.[63] While this was far from an unqualified victory for the Guild, it represented a considerable gain in view of the previous adamancy of the Hearst chain against collective bargaining.

This period marked the first real breakthrough achieved by the Guild on the bargaining front. The Scripps-Howard San Francisco *News*, after bargaining with the Guild, made concessions in the form of a bulletin board statement, followed shortly by the San Francisco *Chronicle* and the San Francisco *Examiner*, the latter a Hearst paper. A formal agreement was signed with the New York *Daily News,* a newspaper with the largest circulation in the United States, including, *inter alia,* provision for a Guild preferential shop, while more limited agreements were signed with the Peoria (Ill.) *Journal-Transcript*, and the Boston *Herald* and *Traveler.* The Guild's prestige received a further boost in January 1937, when Mrs. Eleanor Roosevelt, the wife of the President, became a member, being eligible by virtue of her daily syndicated column. When asked about her action, she declared:

I have always believed in the Guild, and I don't suppose I ever would go on strike, but because I couldn't do any picketing, in the immediate future at least, or other things sometimes required of members that I couldn't, under present circumstances, do, I had to make that clear before joining. But I do believe in the things the Guild is trying to do and I was told that I could join on that basis and did so as a member-at-large of the New York Guild.

A major victory was won in April 1937, when six Scripps-Howard papers entered into agreements with the Guild. This action followed on the heels of the decision in the Associated Press case, in which the U. S. Supreme Court rejected the contention of the publishers that the National Labor Relations Act menaced freedom of the press.[64] The great CIO organizing drive which took place early in 1937 also helped create an atmosphere favorable to the aspirations of the Guild.

External progress occurred in the face of increasing dissention within the Guild. Hardly had the Guild received its AFL charter when Heywood Broun, the Guild president, conferred secretly with John L. Lewis about the possibility of affiliating with the CIO. On August 10, the CIO passed a resolution "that Mr. Broun be admitted to membership on the C.I.O. and that this action be kept confidential until released by Mr. Broun." [65] Broun announced that he intended to resign from the Guild presidency and stand for reelection on the issue of affiliating the Guild to the CIO. He was prevailed upon to withdraw his resignation, but insisted on retaining individual membership in the CIO, pointing out that Charles Howard occupied a similar position.[66]

The issue was hotly debated within the Guild until the June 1937 convention. The convention, by a vote of almost two to one, voted to switch affiliation to the CIO immediately, without reference to a membership referendum. This convention marked the clear ascendancy to power within the Guild of a radical, procommunist machine, based primarily upon the large New York local guild. In joining the CIO, the Guild extended its organization to commercial employees of newspapers, a step that was bitterly opposed by some of the more skill-minded members. The Guild was also committed to independent political action through a "farmer-labor" party, the current line of the Communist Party, and to support of the Spanish Loyalists, in each case over the objection of a vociferous minority.

The convention adopted new bargaining rules requiring submission of proposed contract changes to the international executive board in advance of presentation to the employer, and provided for suspension of any local which accepted contract terms less favorable than the minimum program of the Guild (including the Guild shop and the five-day forty-hour week) without the board's permission. To strengthen the hand of negotiators, it was provided that in local bargaining, the entire local, rather than the particular newspaper concerned, should represent the Guild, with the smaller unit entitled only to observers on the negotiating committee. With these actions, the Guild put aside the last vestiges of the professional association concept and became a full-fledged trade union.

An immediate response to the new bargaining program came in the form of an emergency meeting in Chicago, attended by 565 publishers and editors. The meeting was unanimous in opposing the Guild shop as a threat to freedom of the press, and the publishers in attendance agreed to fight it on that basis.[67]

The reply of the AFL, too, was not slow in coming. Dave Beck, who had been the mainstay of the Guild in the *Post-Intelligencer* strike, warned the Guild to stay away from circulation employees, and to emphasize the point, made the first move of a counterattack by demanding that 20 circulation managers of the Seattle *Star* join the Teamsters' Union despite their unanimous vote to remain in the Guild. When the men in question were discharged, the Guild declared a strike. This time the Seattle Central Labor Council denounced the strike as illegal, and Mayor Dore limited the Guild to two pickets when Guild picketers, reinforced by CIO longshoremen and lumber workers, clashed with Teamsters who were going through the picket line.[68] The strike continued for seven months until February 1938, when an agreement was reached assigning the 20 discharged men to other jobs until the NLRB ruled upon their status. The contract with the newspaper was a favorable one from the Guild standpoint, and although Beck achieved his immediate objective, the outcome was by no means a defeat for the Guild.

On another front, the AFL undertook the formation of a rival newswriters' union. In a statement issued on September 12, 1937, William Green invited all news and editorial employees to join AFL federal locals, promising the full support of the mechanical trades. State and central bodies of the AFL were instructed to expel local Guild chapters from membership and to refuse to give them any cooperation.[69] An immediate organizing drive was undertaken, and all AFL organizers were directed to concentrate on this campaign. The first unit to organize was in Los Angeles, where the AFL claimed between 150 and 200 members, including 130 employees on the staff of the Hearst *Examiner*. In November 1937, the *Examiner* entered into an agreement with the AFL group, the first contract gained by the AFL.[70]

The decisions of the 1937 Guild convention were also challenged by the minority within the union itself. Availing itself of a constitutional provision on referenda, this group forced submission to the membership of ten major questions, including affiliation with the CIO, support of Loyalist Spain, independent political action, the controversial Roosevelt plan for enlarging the U. S. Supreme Court, and expansion of jurisdiction to include commercial employees. In the vote, CIO affiliation was carried by a two to one majority, but independent political action, expansion of jurisdiction, and the court reform plan won only by narrow margins. The members voted against the pro-Spanish Loyalist resolution, however, thus reversing the action of the convention. Several questions having to do with the centralization of collective bargaining were approved by large majorities, indicating clearly how the members stood on this score.[71]

This experience indicated forcefully the value of the policy referendum in checking a national administration which was politically out of step with the sentiment of most members. At conventions, the procommunist group came in with a solid bloc of New York votes, and thus controlled almost one-third of the convention. But in the referendum, the large minority bloc in the New York guild was able to make its voice felt; on the Spanish question, for example, there were 574 votes against the convention resolution to 787 votes for it. However, the qualification must be added that the electorate involved was a highly literate and politically interested one, deeply concerned with issues going beyond narrow union interests. There is no evidence that the referendum by initiative has operated as a potent curb on leadership where this condition did not hold.

Collective bargaining, 1938–1941. The recession of 1937–1939 slowed the organizational progress of the Guild. As part of the CIO affiliation arrangement, the CIO had agreed to furnish the Guild with ten organizers. At the end of 1937, this assistance was discontinued for reasons of economy. The efforts of the Guild went primarily to the maintenance of its existing territory, rather than to the exploitation of any new area. In a few relatively unimportant actions, the CIO was able to assist it. In Wilkes-Barre, Pa., for example, the center of a coal mining area, the Mine Workers' Union forced suspension of a newspaper engaged in a labor dispute with the Guild, and helped the Guild secure a closed shop on all the city's newspapers. A similar result obtained in Superior, Wisconsin. A strike at the Duluth, Minnesota, *Herald and News Tribune,* which resulted in considerable picket line violence, was won when Governor Benson of Minnesota, a farmer-laborite, sent state troops in to protect the picket lines, which had previously been broken by local police. In May 1938, Guild Vice-President Eddy acknowledged that "the Guild has faced financial difficulties during the recent period. Although we have made steady progress despite them, these difficulties have embarrassed the work of the union and affected its ability to protect the gains of the membership and to win new ones."

The Guild attempted, wherever possible, to enlarge the bargaining unit, in order to secure wage uniformity among newspapers and to centralize bargaining control in the higher echelons of the organization. The two principal units were the local labor market and the newspaper chain. Thus, a uniform contract was negotiated with five papers in San Francisco and Oakland, including three papers belonging to the Hearst chain. No agreements were obtained with chains *per se;* with these, the Guild's strategy was to apply pressure nationally in an effort to force settlement in particular local markets. This policy was most successful in the case of the Scripps-Howard chain, which by the end of 1938 had become reconciled to bargaining with the Guild, but the Hearst newspapers continued to resist the Guild, abetted in some cities by AFL federal locals.

The National Labor Relations Board was of great assistance to the Guild during this critical period of its existence. In some of the larger newspapers, such as the New York *Daily News* and *Daily Mirror,* NLRB certifications were the medium by which the Guild achieved the enlargement of its jurisdiction to commercial employees. The secretary-treasurer, in his report to the 1938 convention, stated:

Just as there can be no doubt that the real or imagined protection of the NRA gave impetus to Guild organization at its very beginning, the protective machinery of the NLRB acted in many instances as a brake to anti-Guild dismissals and company union moves. Where a Labor Board action used to be a rarity, it became during the past year a commonplace necessity. Well over a third of our locals have had to prosecute Labor Board action of one kind or another.

The Guild shop provision, which was part of the minimum bargaining program adopted by the 1937 convention, fell by the wayside. It was acknowledged that in most contract renewals, the international executive board was obliged to waive this requirement at the behest of locals. "In most guild negotiations, it has been a bargaining point to be defended lightly and abandoned for other considerations if the publisher's stand against it was evidently firm." [72]

The AFL counteroffensive began to show some results in 1938. In Boston, the *American* and *Daily Record* units of the Guild voted to secede and accept an AFL charter (both were Hearst papers). In an NLRB election, the new AFL local defeated the Guild by the resounding margin of 103 to

28. An AFL charter was issued to a group of employees of the Chicago *Herald* and *Examiner,* also Hearst papers. The Guild struck the two papers in December 1938, in an effort to gain recognition, and was met by the full force of the Chicago AFL. The Teamsters repeatedly broke the Guild picket lines, clearing the way for AFL newswriters and mechanical employees. John A. Fitzpatrick and Joseph D. Keenan, officials of the Chicago Federation of Labor, termed the strike "basically a fight of the CIO guild against the regular trade unions and in defiance of the NLRB." The strike became a Guild *cause célèbre,* costing the national union $125,000, leading to repeated violence, and lasting for 17 months. As part of the settlement, 115 strikers were reinstated while 52 were discharged with severance pay. The Guild was recognized for its members only, pending an NLRB election. The election, held in September 1940, resulted in an overwhelming defeat for the Guild, and the certification of AFL locals to represent both the editorial and commercial employees.

As an aftermath of this victory, the AFL created the American Editorial Association, a national council of 15 federal locals. Frank Fenton, one of the Federation's crack organizers, was made president. The association was limited to editorial employees, and made much of the Guild's alleged pro-communism. However, it was never successful in gaining the status of an autonomous union, or in becoming a major threat to the Guild.

With the improvement of economic conditions in 1939, the Guild once more began to show some progress. Gain came mainly from solidifying the cities already partly organized, rather than from the conquest of new areas.[73] Faced with innumerable small shops in every city and town in the country, a constituency quite different from that of almost any other CIO union, the Guild concentrated upon a few areas:

It certainly seems an unhealthy thing to continue indefinitely without commercial organization on a paper where we have an established editorial group, or to allow indefinitely one paper to remain unorganized in a town where the other one or two papers are organized and under Guild contract. Every completely organized town becomes a virtually unchallengeable base from which we can proceed to spread out.

In July 1940, the Hearst chain entered into a contract with the Guild covering 14 newspapers, including among its terms a modified Guild shop. In return, the Guild agreed to arbitration of all contract disputes, a two-year term, and contract recognition of the management prerogative to make dismissals for reasons of economy. This settlement with the largest of the newspaper chains, and the one which had been most virulently anti-Guild, marked the beginning of a new phase of Guild history.

About the same time, the Guild negotiated its first contracts with the Associated Press, the largest of the wire services. The United Press had entered into an agreement with the Guild in 1938, after 14 months of negotiation,[74] but AP proved to be a more difficult nut to crack. Success was achieved only after strike threats in San Francisco and New York, backed by the powerful locals in those cities.[75] With these contracts, the Guild had finally received some degree of recognition from every major employing unit in the newspaper industry. By June 1, 1941, the Guild had 100 contracts covering 127 daily and Sunday newspapers. Almost half of these included a union or closed shop provision. There were, in addition, 10 contracts with wire services.[76]

Guild membership on the books at the time of each annual convention from 1935 to 1941 was as follows:[77]

1935	5,250
1936	5,830
1937	11,112
1938	16,797
1939	18,755
1940	17,210
1941	17,286

Included in these totals were the following number of commercial, as distinct from editorial employees:

1938	3,292
1939	5,028
1940	5,694
1941	6,477

The membership decline from 1939 to 1940 resulted from a concerted campaign to clear inactive members from the books; during this period, 3200 inactive members were removed from local rolls.[78] Nevertheless, the figures do indicate a relative stagnation in Guild membership after the organizing push of 1936–1937. More than half of the membership increase from 1937 to 1938 was due to the broadening of jurisdiction to commercial employees. The data for subsequent years to 1941 indicate a decline, if anything, in Guild influence among editorial employees, a state of affairs with which internal factionalism, shortly to be considered, had much to do.

The extent of Guild collective bargaining power, and the general pattern of its organization, were shown in a survey made by the American Newspaper Publishers' Association at the close of 1939. Of 266 cities with Association papers, the Guild was established in only 79. There were Guild locals in 88 per cent of cities with populations in excess of 200,000, in 39 per cent of cities whose populations were between 100,000 and 200,000, and in only 10 per cent of the smaller cities.[79] The Guild was essentially a big city organization, based upon several strong points, and extending into smaller communities mainly where these were already strong union territory.

The growth of factional strife. The internal political warfare that absorbed much of the energies of the Guild officialdom from 1937 to 1941 was undoubtedly a major factor in inhibiting the organization's growth. As already noted, the New York Guild was the power base of the procommunist machine that gained control of the national organization. Coming into conventions with a solid bloc of New York votes, the administration needed only a few other cities to wield a working majority.

Unlike most other communist-dominated unions, in which adverse political comment was generally suppressed, the *Guild Reporter*, the official organ of the Guild, printed some letters critical of the administration. For example, Reuben Maury, the chief editorial writer of the New York *Daily News*, wrote:

Only the Guild rank and file, by concerted action at an opportune time, can toss out the Red and Pink politicians, Lewisolators, neurotics, professional smearers, born soreheads and plain damned fools among our national leaders, and replace them with men and women chiefly interested in newspaper workers' problems and the general welfare of our general meal ticket, the newspaper business.[80]

Heywood Broun, while president of the organization, did much to allay criticism of the leadership. He was not himself a communist, though he generally followed a left-wing line. However, he was one of the outstanding personalities in the world of journalism, and wielded a powerful pen, of which the following reply to a vitriolic attack by Westbrook Pegler is an example:

I was one of the founders of the American Newspaper Guild and it is the only important work I ever did in my life. I am proud of the fact that I have been five times unanimously elected as president. That doesn't mean that I have made great sacrifices for the Guild. I haven't. In the last couple of years I have loafed shamefully. But once upon a time I worked hard on Guild business. Self-interest actuated me. The Guild has given me more than I could ever give the Guild. When the Guild came along I was just a fat slob. Now I'm not all slob.

In 1939, the left-wing forces gained a considerable victory when Milton Kaufman, who had been executive secretary of the New York guild, defeated Jonathan Eddy, one of the Guild founders, for executive vice-president. Since the presidency was not a paid job, the executive vice-presidency was the key administrative position in the union, and the Kaufman regime marked the high water of communist influence. There was a noticeable falling off of critical correspondence in the *Guild Reporter*.

With the death of Heywood Broun in December 1940, the political pot began to bubble anew. Kenneth Crawford, an officer of the strongly anti-communist Washington, D. C. local, was selected by the executive board to fill out the remainder of Broun's term. Shortly before the 1940 convention, six international vice-presidents and a number of additional local leaders made public a long indictment of the Kaufman leadership, which was accused of failure to make organizational progress, acquiescence in substandard agreements, and administrative ineffectiveness in general. "The *Guild Reporter*, the newspaper man's newspaper, is characterless, humorless, ineffective. It falls far below the level of many union publications. It does not command the respect of members; it does not encourage frank discussion of Guild questions; it does not handle Guild news with fairness and impartiality." [81]

One of the major battles at the 1940 convention involved an attempt by the anti-administration forces to enact a resolution condemning communism and fascism as equally inimical to the purposes of the Guild. Their argument was that this step was essential to the health of the Guild; "Here is our chance to tell the country and to tell the employers that we are not a Red organization and refuse to be branded with such a label." [82] The resolution was defeated when the Philadelphia local, second only to New York in voting strength and theretofore considered in the anti-administration camp, came out in opposition to it.[83] The St. Louis local, which had also been counted on the right wing side, took a similar stand. With the opposition thus split, the administration made a clean sweep of the elections to office. Donald Sullivan, up to that time almost unknown outside the Boston local, was elected to the presidency over Crawford as a front for the left-wing group. Kaufman was reelected executive vice-president, and the administration won every position but one on the executive board.[84]

But the growing discrepancy between the Communist Party line on war and defense and the beliefs of the average newspaper man did not permit the administration to enjoy the fruits of its victory in peace. The New York guild became a battleground of the opposing forces, with the anti-administration group receiving the open support of Mrs. Eleanor Roosevelt for its platform, which included the following plank:

We oppose the present leadership of the New York Guild on the ground that — regardless of whether the individuals concerned are enrolled members of the Communist Party or not — their actions over a period of years have paralleled the Communist Party line.[85]

The administration slate was victorious in New York by the narrow margin of 1062 to 898, the closest race in the history of that key local. An anticommunist slate was elected in Los Angeles, which had also been a communist stronghold. Making use of the referendum device once more, the anti-administration faction forced submission to the membership of a resolution condemnatory of communism which had been rejected by the 1940 convention. As a counterfire, the international executive board placed on the ballot a resolution affirming the Guild's "traditional independence of control by any political party or group whether Communist, Socialist, Democrat, Republican, Nazi or Fascist."[86] The anticommunist resolution carried by a vote of 3655 to 1284, the anti-all party resolution by the smaller margin of 2611 to 2085, marking a severe defeat for the administration. The New York guild voted 986 to 481 for the anticommunist resolution, a striking reversal of the stand taken by its delegates to the 1940 convention.

The opposition groups, which had splintered so badly in 1940, formed a solid coalition at the 1941 convention. They were helped by the fact that two days before the opening of the convention, Russia was drawn into the war by the German attack, resulting in confusion and disorientation in the communist camp. At the 1940 convention, most of the personal accusations and counteraccusations had been aired at an executive session, but the 1941 convention consisted of a series of explosions on the issue of communist domination which were made a matter of public record.

Vice-President Kaufman was the principal target of the attack. He was condemned for his public support of the North American Aviation strike, a communist-inspired affair which had been denounced by the CIO leadership.[87] An affidavit signed by Ferdinand Lundberg, a free-lance writer, was read to the convention, in which it was alleged that Kaufman had been a member of the Communist Party and had written for the *Daily Worker* under a different name. Kaufman denied the allegations categorically, though defending his position in the North American strike. An attempt to censure him by passing a resolution instructing Guild officers "not to interfere in the affairs of other friendly CIO unions, and specifically not to promote, endorse or encourage strikes officially condemned by the CIO and CIO duly-elected officership as outlaw or wildcat or due to the operation of Communist Party leadership" failed by the narrow margin of 85 to 79 votes.[88]

The chief subject of debate, however, was a minority committee report critical of the *Guild Reporter*. Among other things, the report stated:

The committee minority has come regretfully to the conclusion that *The Guild Reporter* no longer represents truthfully the American Newspaper Guild, but is concerned definitely with the promulgation of the Communist Party line. The committee minority finds it most strange and significant that those locals which are most viciously and consistently smeared are those which are most aggressively and consistently anti-administration and anti-communist.

Dillard Stokes, a well-known Washington correspondent, charged the leadership with driving away a third of the membership within the two previous years by its political line, citing events concerning the Washington guild to prove his point. The anticommunist president of the Los Angeles guild asserted that "it has been the policy of the *Guild Reporter* even to refuse to print the official actions of various locals with whom the administration was on antagonistic terms." The minority report was defeated 80 to 91, but again, New York provided 34 of the majority votes. Almost every other major Guild stronghold — Philadelphia, San Francisco, Washington, Seattle, Los Angeles, Minneapolis — voted solidly with the minority, with Chicago alone supporting the majority.

Another hotly debated issue was a Guild strike currently being waged against the New York *Jewish Day*. David Dubinsky, in a telegram to the convention, denounced the strike as "a Communist-inspired dual-unionistic venture and not as a struggle for the betterment of the workers." Frank Rosenbloom and Jacob Potofsky, of the Amalgamated Clothing Workers, sent a telegram in similar vein, recalling the past assistance which the Amalgamated had rendered the Guild, and concluding: "The CIO was founded to organize the unorganized, not to split other bona fide unions. That is what the New York Guild, in a moment of folly and as a result of factional advice, sought to do in the *Jewish Day* situation." Notwithstanding these protestations, the convention voted approval of the strike.

Apparently fearing the temper of the convention, the administration, in a major strategic error, agreed to a constitutional amendment providing for election of officers by referendum rather than by convention. However, it was successful in securing the continuance in office of the existing leadership until the referendum could be held.[89] Rival slates of candidates were nominated, with Milton Murray of Detroit and Sam Eubanks of San Francisco chosen by the opposition to contest the presidency and the vice-presidency.

Midway during the election campaign, the procommunist group proposed a "unity" plan in which its candidates for secretary-treasurer and four vice-presidencies would be withdrawn, to permit the opposition appropriate representation. The anti-administration forces refused to agree to this plan, particularly since neither Sullivan nor Kaufman, running for the two top positions, were withdrawing; despite the fact that the administration withdrew the five candidates unilaterally, a full opposition slate was maintained.[90] The election, held in October, resulted in a smashing victory for the opposition. Its entire slate was elected by a margin of about five to three. The New York guild, which because of communist machine control had been without minority representation at the convention, gave Murray 1055 votes against 1213 for Sullivan. It was the large New York minority, finally making itself felt through the medium of direct elections, which was largely responsible for unseating the administration.

As soon as the new executive board met, it instituted a housecleaning at Guild headquarters. The editor of the *Guild Reporter,* the research director, and the director of organization were discharged and replaced by anticommunists. The Guild thus successfully rid itself of its national left-wing leadership, and unencumbered by a political philosophy repugnant to the great majority of newspaper men, paved the way for a rapid membership increase at the conclusion of the war.

It would not be correct to infer from the foregoing account that the Guild, during the first eight years of its existence, failed to make any progress in collective bargaining; the point is rather that internal political factionalism reduced its influence and effectiveness. On the positive side, the Guild gained some contractual recognition from all major employers of newswriters. Virtually all agreements contained some provision for dismissal pay, usually one week's pay for each 30 weeks, 8 months, or one year of service. Grievance machinery was established, and employees were protected against arbitrary or unfair discharge. A study of contract minima indicated that "the Guild appears to have secured higher wages in the lower paid classifications and on starting jobs, and to a lesser degree for those workers with long years of experience who are in the upper wage brackets." [91]

Perhaps even more important than these specific gains was the firm establishment of the principles that members of the "fourth estate" could affiliate with organized labor without loss of dignity, and that unionization of newsmen for collective bargaining purposes did not impair freedom of the press. The Guild conception of the proper form of journalistic organization, much of the credit for which must go to Heywood Broun, the founder of the Guild, was, and continues to be, an important precedent in white collar unionism.

1 8

Railroad Unionism

The railway unions were already well established at the inception of the New Deal. Once one of the nation's most turbulent labor relations arenas, the scene of numerous strikes and sharp repression against workers who attempted to organize, the rail carriers, or at least a great majority of them, had become reconciled to collective bargaining. Government operation during World War I, and the twin threats of bankruptcy and nationalization, had served to tame railroad management to an extent unknown in manufacturing.

However, the situation should not be idealized. Although company unionism had been dealt a severe blow by the Supreme Court's interpretation of the Railway Act of 1926,[1] many so-called "system" unions continued in existence. It required the 1934 amendments to the Railway Labor Act, a little Wagner Act for the railroads, to break their hold. Between 1933 and 1935, national unions replaced 550 company unions on 77 Class I roads. By 1941, the company unions had all but disappeared.[2]

The standard trade unions were in far from an enviable position in 1933. For most of them, membership had declined rather than risen during the 1920's, and dropped precipitously during the depression. To take the Brotherhood of Railway Clerks, the largest of the railroad unions, as an example, membership declined from 170,000 in 1921 to 60,000 in 1933. In the latter year, there were about 207,000 employees over whom this union claimed jurisdiction. The Brotherhood held contracts with only 73 out of 149 Class I roads, and even for the roads under contract, coverage was spotty.[3]

The activities of the railroad unions were sharply circumscribed by the poor economic position of the industry. The index of freight ton-mile carried fell from 100 in 1929 to 52.3 in 1932, and by 1936 had risen only to 75.8. The recession of 1937–1938 resulted in a further decline to 64.8 in 1938, and while there was a marked improvement in the following years, operations remained below the predepression level until the advent of United

States participation in war.[4] The decline in activity was only partly cyclical in character. A number of secular factors were combining to produce a long-run reduction in the demand for railroad services, among them the development of hydro-electric power, the increasing replacement of coal by natural gas, the more efficient use of coal, and the growing competition offered by pipe lines and trucking.[5]

Employment was affected to an even greater degree than output, due to rising productivity. The index of total employment fell from 123 in 1920 (1929 = 100) to 57.5 in 1938, and rose only very slightly in the next three years.[6] This meant a loss of about one million jobs from 1920 to the mid-thirties, a halving of the labor force. In addition, there were severe seasonal fluctuations in employment, adding to the insecurity of the workers, particularly the younger ones, for an almost universal system of seniority had been established.

The Growth of Unionism

Against this unpromising background, the railroad unions launched organizing campaigns and benefited from the benevolent atmosphere created by the NIRA and the Wagner Act, although they themselves were not directly covered by either of these pieces of legislation. It should first be explained that although there are some 50 labor organizations which have collective bargaining agreements with American railroads, many represent only small groups of workers. The 21 organizations which represent the great majority of the workers are commonly referred to as the standard railroad labor organizations. They are listed, together with estimated membership on the railroads (in 1939) in Table 17. Their affiliations in 1939 are also shown; with one exception, the operating crafts (that is, the men who operate trains) were independent, whereas most of the nonoperating unions were affiliated with the AFL.

Membership data are not available for all these unions. Even those which were affiliated with the AFL tended to understate their membership in *per capita* reports to the Federation, often showing a virtually unchanged level of membership (for example, see the reports of the Railway Carmen and Railroad Telegraphers). However, the growth of the Brotherhood of Railway Clerks may be traced through the period in which we are interested with some degree of accuracy. While this union was more aggressive and successful than most of its associates, its history does exemplify the response of railroad unionism to new opportunities.

In 1933, as already pointed out, membership in this once large organiza-

Table 17.

Railroad unions and railroad membership in 1939

	Estimated membership
Operating unions	
Brotherhood of Railway Trainmen (Ind.)	140,000
Brotherhood of Locomotive Firemen and Enginemen (Ind.)	80,000
Brotherhood of Locomotive Engineers (Ind.)	60,000
Order of Railway Conductors (Ind.)	35,000
Switchmen's Union (AFL)	8,000
Non-operating unions	
Brotherhood of Railway and Steamship Clerks (AFL)	185,000
Brotherhood of Maintenance of Way Employees (AFL)	65,000
International Association of Machinists (AFL)	n.a.
International Brotherhood of Boilermakers and Blacksmiths (AFL)	n.a.
Sheet Metal Workers' International Association (AFL)	n.a.
International Brotherhood of Electrical Workers (AFL)	10,000
Brotherhood of Railway Carmen (AFL)	65,000
International Brotherhood of Firemen and Oilers (AFL)	27,000
Brotherhood of Railroad Signalmen (Ind.)	9,000
Order of Railroad Telegraphers (AFL)	35,000
National Organization of Masters, Mates and Pilots (AFL)	n.a.
National Marine Engineers' Beneficial Association (CIO)	n.a.
International Longshoremen's Association (AFL)	n.a.
Hotel and Restaurant Employees' International Alliance (AFL)	n.a.
American Train Dispatchers' Association (Ind.)	2,500
Railroad Yardmasters of America (Ind.)	n.a.

Source: Harry D. Wolf, "Railroads," in Twentieth Century Fund, *How Collective Bargaining Works* (New York, 1942), p. 332.

tion had fallen to 60,000. As a result of an organizing campaign undertaken after the enactment of the 1934 amendments to the Railway Labor Act, membership rose to 72,500 in 1935.[7] That the Brotherhood participated in the great organizing campaign of 1936–1937 is indicated by the fact that its net membership increased by 20,000 from April 1936 to April 1937. The Brotherhood's journal made the following comment about this period:

We pinch ourselves occasionally to make sure we're not dreaming as the reports of new members come across our desk. For more than a year the stream of applications has been unbroken and each passing month shows a big net increase in our membership.[8]

During the two years between September 1935 and September 1937, net membership rose by 35,800. President George M. Harrison, in accounting for this increase, acknowledged:

we benefited from the wave of organization sentiment throughout the country which resulted from the influence of a pro-labor President. His conception that the organization of workers is a stabilizing factor in our economic system and a great aid in bringing about a more equitable distribution of the nation's wealth, is the most progressive and constructive stand taken by a President in our history.

The 1938 recession, which was accompanied by large reductions in force on the railroads, slowed membership growth, but did not stop it entirely. President Harrison reported to the May 1939 convention of his organization that during the preceding four years, there had been a membership growth of 53,800 to a total of over 140,000.[9] At that time, the Brotherhood held contracts covering 95 per cent of the total employment under its jurisdiction; only about 8000 workers were outside its contracts. However, many of the workers covered by Brotherhood agreements were not members of the organization, and the winning of this large pool of prospective enrollees was the next task. Parenthetically, it may be noted that the national union spent $380,000 for organizing expenses during 1935–1939, while local lodges spent additional substantial sums.[10]

A substantial group of workers was barred from Brotherhood membership by reason of color, for the constitution of the union restricted membership to white workers. About 100 locals of colored railway clerks had been chartered directly by the AFL, but this could obviously not be a permanent solution. The 1939 convention authorized the Grand Executive Council to set up machinery to permit the absorption of the 6000 workers involved into the Brotherhood. This was accomplished by the creation of a new auxiliary, separate from the main structure of the Brotherhood, to which the AFL transferred its federal locals. By 1943, there were 12,000 Negro members in 246 auxiliary locals.[11] The barring of Negroes from membership was common among the railroad unions at the time, reflecting the southern origin and strength of many of the organizations.

With the quickening of economic activity attendant upon the outbreak of war in Europe, the membership curve of the Brotherhood of Railway Clerks once more took an upward turn. By 1943, at the time of its next convention, total membership was over 200,000, the net gain in the four-year period 1939–1943 exceeding that for 1935–1939 by 8000 members. Thus the Brotherhood, in the course of a decade, more than tripled its membership, reaching a higher level than it had ever before enjoyed despite a drastic reduction in railroad employment. By 1941, it represented the employees on 98 per cent of total railroad mileage, virtually complete coverage.[12]

The Brotherhood of Railway Clerks was by no means alone among the railroad labor organizations to experience rapid expansion at this time. The Brotherhood of Maintenance of Way Employees, second among the non-operating unions in size, doubled its membership from 1933 to 1939.[13] The growth of the operating brotherhoods, already comparatively well organized in 1936, was more modest. The largest of the operating crafts, the Brotherhood of Railroad Trainmen, increased its membership from 123,000 in 1935 to 169,000 in 1941, while the Locomotive Firemen and Enginemen grew from 66,000 to 99,000 in the same period. However, the Conductors and the Locomotive Engineers failed to record any appreciable expansion during these years.[14]

Organization for Collective Bargaining

Historically, collective bargaining on the railroads was carried on mainly in an atomistic fashion, each of the crafts dealing separately for itself. As far back as 1910, however, the various operating crafts started cooperating with each other in wage movements. While these arrangements were informal and *ad hoc,* they were often very effective.

Two major cooperative organizations had been established, the Railway Employees' Department of the AFL, and the Railway Labor Executives' Association, but neither was primarily a bargaining agency. The department, first chartered in 1909, consisted by 1938 of only the shop craft unions, all of the other organizations having either resigned or failed to join. Its purposes had been primarily to further legislation and to bring about uniformity in working rules. Only after the amendment of the Railway Labor Act in 1934 did the department emerge as a major bargaining group, though on the system rather than the national level.[15] Nationally, the constituent unions worked alone or with other railroad organizations in the larger wage movements.

The Railway Labor Executives' Association was founded in 1926 by the standard railway labor organizations, coincident with the enactment of the Railway Labor Act, and in large measure for the purpose of watching over the administration of that legislation. It consists of the chief executive of each of the member organizations, with each member entitled to one vote, regardless of size. No member is bound by any action of the association inconsistent with the laws and policies of the organization he represents, but every organization is obligated to submit to the association in advance any proposal affecting railway legislation which may vitally affect the interests of other unions. In general, the association has not engaged in collective bargaining, but certainly its monthly meetings provided the leaders of railway labor with a convenient opportunity for informal discussion of mutual problems.

However, the association did become involved directly in the first instance of nationwide collective bargaining on the railroads, in 1932. A committee representing the major carriers proposed to it that as a means of preserving employment opportunities, wages be reduced. The outcome was an agreement, effective February 1, 1932, for a period of one year, reducing the pay of all railroad employees by 10 per cent. This pact was later extended until February 1934, when it was agreed that one-fourth of the deduction was to be restored on July 1, 1934; another fourth on January 1, 1935; and the balance on April 1, 1935.[16] This was the full extent of the wage concessions made by the railroad unions during the depression.

Although the Railway Labor Executives' Association as an organization remained aloof from subsequent wage movements, it continued actively to participate in legislative lobbying, and was also involved in the negotiation of a remarkable compact, the Washington Job Protection Agreement of 1936. Concerned with the loss of employment occasioned by railroad consolidations which were being encouraged by the government as a matter of economy, the unions secured in 1933 an amendment to the Emergency Railroad Transportation Act limiting the number of employees who might be discharged as a result of consolidating lines. This legislation was terminated in June 1936, whereupon the Association proposed to the Association of American Railroads that its labor provisions be extended by agreement. Failing to make any progress, legislation was introduced into Congress at the behest of the unions, and fearful that its passage was certain, the employers preferred to negotiate an agreement. According to its terms, employees, retained after a consolidation, were assured, for a five-year period, of not being transferred to a less favorable job. Transferred employees were to be reimbursed for all moving costs. Those employees who were discharged as a result of consolidations received either monthly or lump sum dismissal pay, the amount depending upon previous length of service.[17] Many of the provisions of the Washington Agreement were incorporated into the Transportation Act of 1940. Considering the time when this Agreement was negotiated, the degree of job security gained by railroad workers justifies the claim, made at the time by George M. Harrison, Chairman of the Association, that "we have found the best possible solution for this most difficult problem through the Agreement instead of by legislation."

On the employer side, no single formal organization designed to represent the carriers in collective bargaining arose to parallel the Railway Labor Executives' Association. Basically, the bulk of bargaining is done on the individual railroad. Collective agreements in the industry have no terminal dates and may be opened for renegotiation at any time. Since a large proportion of railroad agreements relates to local rules and conditions, there is a great deal of negotiation at local levels.

However, there has been an increasing tendency to broaden the unit of bargaining on basic rates and working rules, and three regional multi-employer conferences emerged to handle this function. The conference bargaining committees — eastern, southeastern, and western — are *ad hoc* in character, and represent only those roads which give them a power of attorney. In addition, each of the conferences established permanent regional organizations, which service their member roads on all matters relating to labor matters, but do not participate in the negotiation of new agreements.

On a national basis, there is the Association of American Railroads, which dates in its present form from 1934, created by the merger of several preexisting organizations. While the interests of this organization are broad, the area of labor relations is generally beyond its scope.[18] However, many of its officials participate in the activities of the regional labor relations organizations, and some of them are normally members of the *ad hoc* conference committees.

National Collective Bargaining, 1936–1941

The restoration of the last instalment of the 1932 wage cut in April 1935 left railroad workers at their predepression money wage levels. In this respect they were about on a par with manufacturing wage earners. In absolute terms, however, they were more fortunately situated; average hourly earnings of railroad wage earners in 1936 were 69.8 cents, compared with 55.6 cents for manufacturing wage earners. Within the railroad group, of course, there were wide differences. Operating employees averaged $1.021 per hour, compared with 58.3 cents per hour for the nonoperating group.[19]

Pressure for an increase in wages began to develop during 1936. On the initiative of George M. Harrison, the Railway Labor Executives' Association discussed the question at a meeting in December 1936. "At this meeting it developed that arrangements could not be made for a general national wage increase movement as the Five Transportation Brotherhoods felt the interest of their membership required a separate movement by that group."[20] The operating brotherhoods presented a demand for a 20 per cent increase to the individual roads, which met with considerable resistance. The unions then asked the Association of American Railroads to designate a national bargaining committee, along the lines of the pattern established in 1932, and this was done under the threat of a strike. After months of negotiation, a settlement was reached in October 1937, providing for an increase of 44 cents a day in basic rates.[21]

The nonoperating crafts, in the meantime, had formulated a joint program calling for a wage increase of 20 cents an hour. The dispute was settled on August 5, 1937, by an increase of five cents an hour. This meant a slight relative improvement for the operating crafts vis-à-vis the nonoperating unions, but scarcely enough to justify the belief of the former that their economic power could be brought to bear more strongly in separate bargaining.

Hardly had these settlements been reached when the railroads began to experience a severe decline in revenue as a result of the economic depression. To offset the loss, they applied to the Interstate Commerce Commission for a 15 per cent rate increase. In this petition they were strongly supported by the railroad unions.[22] The ICC denied the general increase, but allowed upward adjustments on specific commodities which yielded an average increase of 5.3 per cent.[23]

The carriers then turned to the unions and suggested a 15 per cent wage cut. The unions were adamant in their refusal even to consider this possibility. Efforts to secure financial assistance from the federal government failed, and the carriers filed formal notice of a 15 per cent reduction effective July 1, 1938. However, the effective date was postponed pending further negotiation. The carriers suggested arbitration, the unions refused. A national strike was called for October 1, 1938, the newly set date for the effectuation of the wage cut.

To avert the strike, President Roosevelt appointed an emergency board pursuant to the provisions of the Railway Labor Act. The board, after holding hearings, issued a report on October 29, 1938. It concluded that wages in the railroad industry were not high relative to wages in other industries;[24] that a wage reduction would run counter to the trend of wage rates in industry generally; that a horizontal reduction of wages on a national scale would not meet the financial emergency of the industry; and that the recession showed signs of lifting. The carriers bowed to this report, and withdrew their proposed wage reduction, no doubt influenced by increasing signs of an economic revival.[25]

In the upswing of 1939-1941, railway wages failed to keep pace with those in manufacturing. Average hourly earnings of wage earners in manufacturing rose by 16.3 per cent from 1938 to 1941, compared with 4.7 per cent for railroad workers.[26] In May 1940, nonoperating unions served notice of a demand for two weeks' vacation with pay. Conferences continued for the rest of the year, without result. The National Mediation Board intervened in March 1941, and was unable to bring about an agreement, but both parties announced their willingness to submit the dispute to arbitration.

However, at about the same time, the operating unions, acting independently of the nonoperating crafts, voted to demand a 30 per cent increase in all basic daily rates, and the nonoperating group immediately followed suit with a demand for a 30 cent increase in hourly rates and a minimum hourly wage of 70 cents. At the time, the minimum established under the Fair Labor Standards Act for railroads was 36 cents an hour. The western and southern carrier conferences countered these demands by requesting changes in the working rules, which were little short of sacred to the workers; what they wanted was greater flexibility in assignments, in starting shifts at irregular hours, and other changes which the unions characterized as an attempt "to virtually wreck existing working conditions agreements."[27] The unions, in turn, withdrew their agreement to arbitrate the vacation dispute.

A strike vote was conducted among both operating and nonoperating workers, resulting in an overwhelming majority in favor of such action in the event that an adjustment could not be secured. On September 10, 1941, President Roosevelt appointed an emergency board under the chairmanship of Wayne Morse, then Dean of the University of Oregon Law School, to hear both disputes. Public hearings began on September 16, and continued until October 22, the most extensive hearings in any railway labor dispute to that time. The union based its arguments on the lag of railroad wages behind those in manufacturing, the increased cost of living, the increases that had taken place in productivity, the spread of paid vacations in other industries, and the favorable financial situation of the railroads. The carriers relied heavily upon the inflationary repercussions that would be created by an increase in wages, and argued that the defense boom might result in only a temporary improvement in their ability to pay higher wages.

The emergency board acknowledged that the wages of railroad workers were lagging, but was strongly influenced by the inflation argument:

it is not fair or reasonable to expect or insist that the labor of one industry should have imposed upon it a sacrifice in the form of low wages before there has been shown a firm determination to formulate and execute measures involving equal sacrifices on the part of all groups. There is no justification for asking railway labor to become martyrs. On the other hand, to adopt the reverse policy and measure the adequacy of railroad wages by the highest discovered wage rate would serve but to accelerate the spiral of wages, costs and prices. A temporary expedient seems therefore to be the only possible course, pending the evolution of defense policies to the point where the threat of inflation may be moderated and a policy of equality of sacrifice among those able to share in that sacrifice is devised.[28]

Consequently, the board recommended temporary pay increases, extending through 1942, of 7½ per cent for the operating employees and 9 cents per hour for the nonoperating employees. A new minimum wage for Class I roads of 45 cents per hour was suggested, as well as a 6-day annual vacation with pay. It recommended, further, that the carriers' request for amendment of the working rules be resubmitted for further negotiation.

The carriers accepted the recommendations, but the unions rejected them indignantly. In a joint statement, the nonoperating crafts termed the wage award "astounding" and "disappointing." The temporary bonus notion "is no answer to this question, nor can it be tolerated by railroad labor." The 6-day vacation was termed "a disgrace to an industry that gains a large share of its business from vacation activities of the people." [29] With the procedures for governmental intervention provided by the Railway Labor Act exhausted, the unions declared a nation-wide strike, to be effective December 7, 1941 (the day on which the Japanese attacked Pearl Harbor).

This gave rise to an unprecedented situation. Up to that time, all recommendations of emergency boards appointed pursuant to the Railway Labor Act, while they did not carry any compulsive effect, had been accepted by both parties. The cornerstone of the law was the theory that neither party could afford to flaunt the force of public opinion created by an impartial investigatory body appointed by the president of the United States. Yet the railroad unions were doing just that, and threatening to tie up the entire transportation system of the country at a time when foreign relations were becoming ever more critical. Obviously, the government could not step aside and permit the issue to be decided by economic force.

Two weeks after the issuance of the emergency board report, President Roosevelt invited the top leaders of railway labor and management to meet with him. Four conferences were held, in addition to meetings directly between the parties, but no agreement could be reached, despite the prestige of the mediator. The carriers stood on the emergency board report, the unions insisted that it was unacceptable. Finally, the president took the unprecedented step of reconvening the emergency board to hear the parties once more, and to render a supplemental report. On the second day of the rehearing, the board offered its services as mediator, and after an uninterrupted mediation session of two days, worked out an agreement acceptable to both parties. The originally recommended increases were to be given retroactively from September to December 1941. Effective December 1, 1941, however, wages for operating employees were to be increased by 9½ cents per hour rather than the 7½ per cent in the original award, while the nonoperating employees were to receive an increase of 10 cents an hour, rather than the original 9 cents. The increases were to be permanent rather than temporary. Clerks and telegraphers were granted more liberal vacations, and the minimum was raised to 46 cents per hour.

The changes were estimated to involve the carriers in a wage cost increase of 14 per cent, compared with 12 per cent in the original award.[30] However, the principle established was an important one. Although the emergency board was careful to define its second recommendation as a mediation agreement, the unions, by threatening to strike, had successfully defied the "public opinion" supposedly created by the original report, and at a time when strikes were deemed subversive of the national interest. To quote a student of the industry:

It has become obvious that the very existence of the emergency boards has completely broken down collective bargaining between the two parties. On the one hand, the railroad unions have, at times, entered the negotiations with the attitude that they can depend on their political power to obtain more than that offered by an emergency board or even by negotiations. Thus, the emergency board's recommendations have become a springboard from which they could obtain further concessions.

It may be that the original conception of the emergency board as a quasi-judicial body, performing a function somewhere between voluntary and compulsory arbitration, but nearer the latter, was incompatible with American collective bargaining institutions, and would have eventually broken down in any event. However, the emergency board of 1941 certainly hastened the demise of this concept by promulgating an award which was clearly unacceptable to one of the parties. In considering itself, rather rigidly, as a quasi-judicial agency, and attempting to mete out social justice on the basis of vague and arbitrary standards, rather than merely seeking to solve a serious labor dispute at a critical juncture in American history, the board made a major contribution to what has been described as the virtual collapse of collective bargaining in the railroad industry.[31]

Other Union Achievements

The railroad unions had long been accustomed to use legislation, both federal and state, as a means of advancing their immediate economic interests. A major example of this method of operation during the nineteen-thirties was in the field of social security. During the depression, a campaign was undertaken to protect railroad workers from the vicissitudes of unemployment and an impecunious old age. The Washington Job Protection Agreement, already referred to above, was one outcome of this campaign. On another front, the unions secured the enactment by Congress, in 1934, of the Railroad Retirement Act, which provided annuities to employees who were 65 years of age or had served for thirty years. However, in May 1935, the U. S. Supreme Court declared the Act unconstitutional on the ground that it appropriated future earnings of the railroads for past services already compensated.

The unions immediately set about revising the legislation to meet the Court's objections. A few months later, the Railroad Retirement Act of 1935 was enacted, this time restricted to persons who were employees after the date of enactment. The carriers refused to concede its constitutionality, however, and court contests were immediately undertaken. A lower court granted an injunction against collection of the tax which had been levied to support the system, once more throwing the entire scheme in doubt. As a way out of the dilemma, President Roosevelt urged that railroad labor and management confer for the purpose of working out a pension agreement. A series of meetings yielded an agreement which was embodied in the Railroad Retirement Act of 1937. The new law, which is still in force, with some amendments, was never challenged in the courts, although the Supreme Court majority of 1937 would undoubtedly have upheld its validity. The benefit structure was more generous than that provided by the original Social Security Act, its contemporary.[32] George M. Harrison, who led the union forces in the fight for its promulgation, said of it at the time:

One of the most generous pension plans to be found anywhere in the world, its beneficial effects are just now beginning to be felt. Faithful employes are guaranteed old age security far more generous than under the Social Security Act. . . . In the first place, the pensions are higher because union wage scales are higher than for industry in general. Second, under the working of seniority rules the employe at retirement age is generally drawing his highest wage, instead of his lowest as is frequently the case where the rules of seniority do not apply.[33]

The railroad unions then turned to unemployment insurance, attempting to apply the same technique of legislation by agreement that had proven successful in old age pensions. A series of conferences was held with a committee designated by the Association of American Railroads, but agreement proved impossible. The Railway Labor Executives' Association thereupon had legislation introduced in Congress, which was enacted into law over the opposition of the carriers.[34] At the time of its enactment, the benefit structure was more generous than those of most state unemployment compensation systems.[35] The Act was liberalized substantially in 1940 in line with what was happening in the country generally.

The legislative successes of railroad labor during this period [36] suggest that the unions were active politically, and were able to build a strong lobby. Actually, until 1947, when Railway Labor's Political League was formed, there was no formal mechanism dedicated to political activity. However, the railroad unions were continually active in both state and national politics; their philosophy was well summed up in the following statement, made in 1938:

Because of the impact of state and federal regulation of railway transportation, upon their wages and working conditions, railway workers long ago learned the importance of political action and through the years have developed a degree of political solidarity, unique in the American Labor movement. By the intelligent use of their political power in support of candidates without regard to party affiliations but pledged to the public welfare; and by their support of constructive social legislation for the benefit of wage earners and farmers, the railway labor organizations have won the respect and friendship of large and influential blocs in State Legislatures and the Federal Congress. Proof of the efficacy of our plan of political action can be found in the record of legislative accomplishments, particularly during the recent past.[37]

The railroad unions were jealous of their political power, and strongly objected to attempts by such organizations as Labor's Non-Partisan League, which was controlled by the CIO, to appropriate it for purposes unrelated to the immediate welfare of railroad workers.[38] On the other hand, there was no hesitation in plunging into partisan political activities in furtherance of these interests. There were few unions more dedicated to the reelection of Franklin D. Roosevelt, in his several campaigns, than the majority of the railroad brotherhoods. They made powerful friends in Congress who served them well; for example, in introducing the then Senator Harry S. Truman to the 1943 convention of the Brotherhood of Railway Clerks, President Harrison termed him "a particular friend of railroad workers, one who has never failed the railroad employees when they sought his sympathetic consideration and assistance on problems in the public interest." [39]

The economic gains of the railroad workers during the nineteen-thirties were achieved with a minimum of industrial strife. Contemporary observers heralded the railroad situation as the harbinger of a new era in American industrial relations. To quote one of the best informed:

This record of almost complete freedom from strife for nearly a score of years is all the more remarkable, in view of the number of employers and employees in the industry, the trying circumstances under which they have operated, and the experience of other industries during the same period.[40]

Subsequent events made it clear, however, that the millennium had not yet arrived for railroad labor relations. Despite the intense pressures generated against interruptions to railroad service, the industry has had its share of strikes, to say nothing of strike threats. Maturity in trade union organization and collective bargaining relationships constitute no certain guarantee of industrial peace.

The record of the 1930's[41] appears to have been due to the conjunction of several favorable circumstances. The industry was spared the chaos that accompanied manufacturing labor's efforts to establish the right of collective bargaining, beginning in 1933. Organizational strikes were almost unknown on the railroads. The company union gave way before the orderly election procedure provided for by the 1934 amendments to the Railway Labor Act. Secondly, railroad workers were relatively well situated economically until the defense period, when they began to get restive. Railroad wages were stable during the depression, with the exception of the wage cut in 1932, which was restored by 1935. While there was considerable unemployment among railroad workers, the strict system of seniority concentrated the unemployment on the younger workers. The older men, who remained at work and controlled the labor organizations, enjoyed a degree of job security prevailing in few other industries. Finally, railroad labor had come to regard political and legislative action as an alternative to direct economic action, and were much more successful in this strategy than almost any other labor group. The separate social security system established for the railroads during this period was more liberal than that for industry generally, and what was of perhaps even greater importance, the railroad unions could demonstrate to their members that such legislation was an immediate result of their activities.

This period marked the rise of the nonoperating unions to a position of parity with, if not superiority to, the operating unions in the politics of railroad unionism. Traditionally, the operating brotherhoods had looked down upon their lower-paid brethren. The engineer, the conductor, even the fireman, were the aristocrats of the railroad world. This was expressed somewhat resentfully by the official journal of the Clerks:

Although cooperation in matters affecting the common interests of railway workers has for years been one of the distinguishing characteristics of the railway unions, there was nevertheless much room for improvement in their working relations. For a long time their joint activities were controlled largely by the train service organizations, and the rest of the unions sort of tagged along when they were invited to do so.

The rapid growth of the two large nonoperating unions, the Clerks and the Maintenance of Way Employees, redressed the balance of power in their favor. George M. Harrison, president of the Clerks, chairman of the Railway Labor Executives' Association from 1928 until 1940, and one of the most influential members of the AFL Executive Council, became the recognized spokesman for American railroad labor. To quote *The Railway Clerk* once again: "An obscure and impotent member of the family of railway labor organizations for many years, the rise of the Brotherhood of Railway Clerks to its present influential position in the labor world has been greatly accelerated by the effectiveness of Brother Harrison's leadership in the councils of the Railway Labor Executives' Association." [42]

The spectacular rise of the industrial unions from 1936 on tends to obscure the significant advances made by some of the older organizations outside manufacturing. Data already presented show that railroad unions participated in the growth of the American labor movement under the New Deal. While complete organization had by no means been achieved by 1941, the brotherhoods represented almost all railroad employees for purposes of collective bargaining. Only in the case of some of the shop crafts were there employers who were still not covered by union contract.[43] All this had been achieved, moreover, without union security provisions in agreements, prohibited by railway labor legislation until 1951. The long fight for recognition had been won almost completely, and the unions were left with the task of persuading nonmembers whom they represented of the desirability of joining and paying dues.

Close attention to the economics of the industry was forced upon railroad unionism at an early date, and this continued unabated. The secular decline in employment that began after World War I exercised a depressive effect upon trade union ambitions. The wage cut of 1932 was accepted for the explicit purpose of augmenting employment, and when it failed to have that effect, the unions lost any lingering belief in the efficacy of a low-wage solution. They turned instead, in part, to the government, joining with management in seeking rate increases, regulation of competing carriers in the interest of the railways, and loans and subsidy.[44] The philosophy behind these efforts is well expressed in the following passage:

the railway labor organizations in these circumstances have in recent years turned more and more to a consideration of these changes taking place in the industry. While they were primarily management problems, they nevertheless affected labor very directly. Not forgetting that their job is first and foremost to represent the employes, union leaders have had the good sense and foresight to realize that the unions would operate under a severe handicap as long as these problems of the industry remained unsolved.

Recognizing the mutuality of interests between labor on the one hand, and management and owners on the other, in the preservation and prosperity of the industry, cooperation between the interested parties has developed to the point where the President of the United States entrusted to a committee composed of railway managers and union leaders the responsibility of advising him and the Congress what needed to be done by government to aid the railroads in their difficulties.[45]

The foregoing passage, it should be recalled, was written at a time when unionism embraced only a minority of American industrial workers.

The railroad unions also sought a way out of the employment dilemma by attempting to protect jobs through their economic power. The Washington Job Protection Agreement was one example of this method. Consolidations and mergers were consistently opposed, and in some cases prevented, even despite the protection afforded by this agreement. Rigid insistence upon a complicated network of working rules, some of them obsolete and undoubtedly of a make-work character,[46] is another facet of the same policy. The Diesel-manning problem, which became a famous case in the history of labor and technology, first arose in 1934 and continued with increasing virulence as Diesels replaced steam locomotives.[47] What effect these rules have actually had upon railroad costs and employment can only be surmised; the fact of the matter is that in 1956, railroad employment stood at 1,043,000, compared with somewhat less than one million at the depth of the depression.

A word is in order about some of the peculiar problems involved in organizing railway workers. Unlike most industrial workers, they are scattered throughout the length and breadth of the country in small groups, making it expensive to contact and service them. The operating crafts established an organizing tradition before the turn of the century — indeed, trainmen the world over have been pioneers in trade unionism — but the union idea was not widespread among the nonoperating employees until the New Deal.

The Railway Clerks had special difficulties all their own: ". . . easy entrance to their trades, the absence of apprenticeship rules, a pronounced lack of trade consciousness among the workers, the white-collar philosophy of clerks, and the employment of women." [48] It overcame these by the concentration of its membership drives. The entire force of national organizers, usually around fifteen, would be sent to a single area, and then moved on when the practicable limits of organization had been reached. Annual recruiting contests were held, with awards for the local lodges and members bringing in the most new members. Success of organization despite factors ordinarily regarded as adverse has been a source of great pride to the Brotherhood. To quote President Harrison:

It hasn't been so long ago when many people thought and many people said, "Well, those white collar fellows — they generally have a wishbone instead of a backbone. You'll never make trade unionists out of them." But we have emerged from that period of growing, expanding, developing, until we now claim that we are the largest organized group of railroad and express workers on the North American continent. Yes, my good delegates, officers, and friends, you have here now the congress of the largest group of white collar workers any place in the world.[49]

19

Some General Aspects of the Labor Movement

Membership

The measurement of trade union membership is beset with many pitfalls. There are not only mechanical problems involved in securing and processing data, but very thorny conceptual difficulties as well. The first problem need not concern us, but some attention must be devoted to the second in order that the figures which are presented below may be evaluated properly.[1]

Unions regard as members, basically, those persons who maintain themselves in good standing by paying their dues regularly. But workers who are unemployed, underemployed, sick, on strike, on military leave, retired, or temporarily working as employers, may be exonerated from the payment of dues for specified periods without losing their good standing status. During an economic downswing, therefore, membership is apt to be overstated. Seasonal fluctuations in employment will also affect the membership data; two unions of equal size may report identical membership totals and yet receive varying amounts of dues, because of differences in the stability of employment.

There are situations in which unions are interested in exaggerating claimed membership. This is apt to be most true during their formative years, when they are seeking status, and during organizing campaigns, when they want to impress recalcitrant employers. Both these conditions prevailed in the case of most CIO unions during the nineteen-thirties, and therefore the public CIO membership statements must be regarded with great caution. Some of the newer CIO unions claimed as members workers for whom they bargained, without regard to actual membership, and it may be suspected that on occasion, they simply inflated membership claims without regard to underlying fact at all. On the other hand, it would be a mistake to define the true influence of the mass production unions as being coterminous with fully paid membership. The Steel Workers' Union, for example, dispensed with initiation fees during its early organizing years, and was not overly assiduous in pressing lower paid workers for dues. Yet many nondues-paying workers were undoubtedly good union members in the sense that they were loyal to the organization. There are varying degrees of attachment to a union, from regular dues-paying membership ranging down to willing-ness to support the union during a strike and mere passive acceptance of the union as legally designated collective bargaining agent. Ordinarily, unions distinguish between regular members and those nonmembers within a bar-gaining unit who are represented for collective bargaining purposes, but in the past, this distinction has not always been made by unions desirous of inflating their publicly claimed membership.

A few examples may serve to indicate the nature of the magnitudes involved. The Steel Workers' Organizing Committee voted on the basis of 535,000 members at the 1940 CIO convention.[2] But Philip Murray, shortly after the conclusion of the convention, informed the CIO Executive Board that the SWOC had 350,000 members in good standing and a steady dues-paying membership of nearly 250,000.[3] The Automobile Workers voted on 412,000 members at the 1940 CIO Convention, although only a few months earlier the membership had been informed that there were only 294,000 dues-paying members.[4] The Textile Workers' Union voted on 314,000 mem-bers in 1940. However, the TWUA did not require members to pay dues until they were covered by union agreement, and not long before the union had claimed that there were only 160,000 textile workers under union agree-ment, not all of whom were union members. Following are some additional comparisons between 1940 convention voting strength and per capita claims for the same year derived from other sources:[5]

	1940 Convention strength	Membership claims, 1940
United Electrical Workers	207,000	92,000
United Rubber Workers	55,406	54,200
Oil Workers' Union	40,647	19,873
Mine, Mill and Smelter Workers	70,000	34,000
Longshoremen's Union	35,000	21,000 (1939)

Since all the CIO unions were not studied in detail, it is impossible to build up a total CIO membership figure from individual union data. How-ever, there is some information available which enables us to arrive at a more realistic membership total than that which was presented by the organization publicly. Table 18 compares Bureau of Labor Statistics data on CIO membership, which were based upon CIO claims, with confidential statements made by Philip Murray to the CIO Executive Board, covering per capita tax payments to the CIO. Comparing 1936 and 1940, Murray said: "So, with all our wind and with all our puffing and blowing we had increased our dues-paying membership by about 500,000 in five years, or perhaps 600,000 members." [6] However, in giving the figure of 1,700,000 for 1939, he indicated that many affiliates were not paying their per capita fees to the CIO, and that actual membership might be as high as 3,000,000.[7]

Table 18.

Alternative estimates of CIO membership, 1936 to 1941

Year	(1) Bureau of Labor Statistics	(2) Philip Murray
1936	—	800,000
1937	3,718,000	n.a.
1938	4,038,000	n.a.
1939	4,000,000	1,700,000[a]
1940	3,625,000	1,350,000[b]
1941	5,000,000	2,850,000[c]

Sources: Bureau of Labor Stastics: *Brief History of the Labor Movement* (October 1947), pp. 17–19.

Philip Murray: Congress of Industrial Organizations, *Minutes of the Executive Board* (November 18, 1938), p. 26; (June 3–5, 1942), p. 532.

[a] Average for the period November 1938 to May 1939. A figure of 1,796,900 for 1939 is given in Leo Troy, *Distribution of Union Membership Among the States, 1939 and 1953*, National Bureau of Economic Research (1957), p. 5.
[b] For month of November.
[c] For month of February 1942.

The deflated data seem more credible than the convention voting strength. The 1936 figure represents roughly the combined membership of the Mine Workers, the Amalgamated Clothing Workers, and the ILGWU, the principal founders of the CIO. The terminal figure of 2,850,000 for February 1942, included 537,000 members of the United Automobile Workers, "under" 500,000 Steel Workers, almost 300,000 members of the Amalgamated Clothing Workers, about 180,000 Electrical Workers, and about 100,000 Rubber Workers. It also included 550,000 members of the United Mine Workers, which did not formally withdraw from the CIO until later in the year. The remaining membership of 700,000 was scattered among the thirty-odd other unions affiliated with the CIO.

AFL membership data for the period are firmer than those of the CIO, but are not without some ambiguities of their own. The standard source is per capita tax payments which affiliated unions are required to pay to the federation. However, some national unions understated, and others overstated their true dues-paying membership for this purpose. To cite a few examples: the Carpenters' Union paid per capita tax to the AFL on exactly 300,000 members for every year between 1936 and 1941, understating their membership for most of the period. The Teamsters paid on 393,700 in 1940 and 408,300 in 1941, although claiming 450,000 dues-paying members during the first six months of 1940.[8]

But there is little doubt that the AFL data were much more reliable than the CIO data for this period. The AFL unions had less need, and less opportunity, to issue extravagant membership claims. The AFL, unlike the CIO, was not living on the largesse of a few large organizations, and every affiliate was required and was able to pay its way, with few exceptions. Pressure was brought to bear against unions which systematically paid less than their proportionate share of per capita tax, while on the other hand overstatement of membership entailed a financial burden which few unions were willing to undertake.

Membership statistics for independent unions entail problems of a different order. Some independent unions were national in scope and functioned in precisely the same way as AFL or CIO unions; the railway brotherhoods were good examples. But most of the independents were small organizations, local in scope, often teetering on the brink of employer domination. They owed their existence to a variety of factors, among them secession movements from standard labor unions because of ideology, corruption, or other issues; resentment of outside interference in local affairs; fear of strikes by workers; employer persuasion or influence. Characteristically, local independents followed a mild collective bargaining policy, rarely engaged in strikes, and concentrated upon the processing of individual grievances. Few had full-time officers or substantial funds.[9]

The available data on independent union membership, together with those for the AFL and the CIO, are shown in Table 19. The four railway operating brotherhoods accounted for about 40 per cent of the 1941 independent total, postal workers and other federal employee unions for about 20 per cent, telephone unions for about 13 per cent, with the balance scattered among numerous small organizations.

For reasons already indicated, the figures in Table 19 should not be endowed with attributes of precision which they do not possess. Particularly

Table 19.

Estimated membership in AFL, CIO and independent unions, 1936 to 1941
(in thousands)

Year	(1) AFL	(2) CIO	(3) Independent	(4) Total	(5) Total (Leo Wolman)
1936	3,422[a]	800[a]	742	4,164	4,075
1937	2,861	1,580[b]	639	5,080	6,334
1938	3,623	1,717[b]	604	5,944	7,342
1939	4,006	1,700	974	6,680	7,735
1940	4,247	1,350	1,072	6,669	8,101
1941	4,569	2,850	920	8,339	8,614

Sources: AFL: American Federation of Labor, *Report of the Proceedings of the Sixty-First Annual Convention* (Seattle, 1941), p. 44.

CIO: Table 18.

Independent: Bureau of Labor Statistics, *Brief History of the American Labor Movement* (October 1947), pp. 17–19.

Leo Wolman: Irving Bernstein, "The Growth of American Unions," *American Economic Review* (June 1954), p. 303.

[a] CIO membership included in the AFL total for this year.
[b] Estimated by applying the ratios of the data in Table 18, column 1, to the absolute figures in Table 18, column 2.

questionable are the CIO figures for 1937 and 1938, which are merely rough interpolations. There is little doubt that many more than a million and a half workers were affiliated with the CIO in some way in 1937. In all probability, CIO membership fell, rather than rose, from 1937 to 1938. Similarly, the decline shown from 1939 to 1940 is of doubtful validity.

Looking at the total membership data in column (4), one would be inclined to raise the 1937 membership figure, so that 1938 showed a decline rather than an advance, and either to reduce the 1939 total or increase the 1940 total in order to show a steady upward trend from 1938 on. The series in column (5), the details of which were not given in the source, present what is probably a more realistic picture of the trend for the years 1938 to 1941, though the absolute magnitudes appear somewhat high.

The relative positions of AFL and CIO are consistent with the non-quantitative evidence adduced in the preceding pages. The CIO leaped forward in 1936 with the AFL in a state of stunned inactivity. But the AFL, concentrated in industries of less cyclical instability than the CIO, was less affected by the 1937–1938 recession, and spurred by the threat of the rival federation, it began to gain in relative strength. After 1937, there was never any doubt as to which federation was numerically dominant, though at the time it was widely believed that the CIO was the larger and more powerful of the two organizations, due in part to superior CIO publicity. During the latter half of 1936 and the first half of 1937, the AFL faced the most serious threat to its hegemony since its encounter with the Knights of Labor. Had it not been for the 1937 recession, the outcome of the 1937 Little Steel strikes, and the exhaustion of CIO financial resources — all interrelated — the outcome of the struggle might have been different. But as it was, the AFL was able to draw upon its superior resources and greater experience to outdistance its rival and attain by the close of the decade a commanding lead which continued to widen until the 1955 merger. A careful analyst of the period wrote of AFL progress as follows:

Only a relatively few AFL unions, in fact, were so adversely affected by the Great Depression that they failed to be stimulated by the pro-union New Deal atmosphere . . . A . . . union to achieve a phenomenal growth in the 1930's was the Hotel and Restaurant Workers Union which moved from a membership of only 38,000 in 1929 to 185,000 in 1939. A semi-industrial union covering all except the mechanized trades in the field, it took advantage of the repeal of the Eighteenth Amendment to regain an extensive membership among bartenders and waiters, which it once held, and to expand into the hotels and restaurants of the larger cities. On a smaller absolute scale but often attaining even greater percentage increase in membership were such diverse unions as the Retail Clerks, the Meat Cutters and Butcher Workmen, the Building Service Employees, the Bakers and Confectionery Workers, the two Pulp and Paper Mill Unions, and the Pottery Workers.[10]

According to Table 19, American trade union membership just about doubled between 1936 and 1941. But this is an inadequate index of the increased strength of organized labor. In terms of the increment in political influence and economic power, a much greater factor would be appropriate. A consideration of some of the structural aspects of union membership may help explain this discrepancy.

Table 20 contains estimates of trade union collective bargaining strength, by industry, as of April 30, 1935. This is not the same thing as membership, for many nonmembers were covered by union agreements. The data point to the absence of unionism in heavy industry; iron and steel and transportation equipment are scarcely unionized. The foci of unionism were the needle trades, coal mining, printing, and public utilities (excluding communications). Two additional union strongholds were the railroads, with 71 per cent of the workers under union agreement in April 1935, and building construction.[11]

The situation prevailing in 1941 is shown in Table 21. While exact per-

Table 20.

Estimated percentage of workers covered by trade unions in establishments dealing with
some or all workers through trade unions, by industry, April 1935

	Per cent
All industries covered	26.1
All manufacturing industries	19.5
Durable goods	12.2
Iron and steel	10.6
Machinery	7.0
Transportation equipment	16.9
Nonferrous metals	11.8
Lumber and allied products	8.8
Stone, clay and glass products	42.4
Nondurable goods	26.1
Textiles	28.1
Fabrics (except hats)	19.6
Wearing apparel	54.6
Leather	35.8
Food	28.6
Cigars	25.0
Paper and printing	33.4
Chemicals	13.0
Rubber products	7.2
Miscellaneous nondurable goods	71.3
Miscellaneous manufactures	7.7
Service	6.4
Public utilities	47.7
Mining	86.6
Retail trade	0.9
Wholesale trade	3.5

Source: Leo Wolman, *Ebb and Flow in Trade Unionism* (New York, 1936), p. 128, based on
a survey by the Bureau of Labor Statistics.

centages of coverage are not available for that year, the conclusions to be
drawn are clear enough. Durable goods manufacturing moved from low to
high on the organizational scale, with less, though significant, progress in
the nondurable sector. In nonmanufacturing, there was one important addition to the well organized trades, the maritime industry. The service trades
still remained largely nonunion.

The expansion of trade unionism from 1936 to 1941 had one overriding
characteristic: it extended the power of labor into new, and strategic sectors
of the economy. Wolman had noted at the commencement of the period:
"It is probably one of the most significant facts concerning union membership in the United States that unions in manufacturing industries should

Table 21.

Proportion of wage earners under written union agreements in 1941

(1) Almost entirely	(2) Large proportion	(3) About half	(4) Moderate proportion	(5) Almost entirely without
		Manufacturing Industries		
Automobiles	Aircraft	Agricultural implements	Canning and processing	
Breweries	Aluminum	Baking	Chemicals	
Clothing — men's	Clothing — women's	Book and job printing	Cigars	
Fur	Electrical machinery	Cement	Clay products	
Glass — flat	Glass containers	Cigarettes	Clocks and watches	
	Iron and steel, basic	Furniture	Concrete, gypsum and plaster	
	Machinery, excl. agricultural and electrical	Glassware	Confectionery products	
	Millinery and hats	Hosiery	Cotton textiles	
	Newspaper printing and publishing	Iron and steel products	Flour and grain products	
	Nonferrous metals — smelting and refining	Leather products, excl. shoes	Gloves	
	Rayon yarn	Meat packing	Jewelry and silverware	
	Rubber products	Nonferrous metals — rolling and drawing	Lumber	
	Shipbuilding	Pottery	Machine tools	
	Sugar refining — cane	Railroad equipment	Petroleum and coal products	
		Shoes	Pulp and paper products	
		Sugar — beet	Silk and rayons	
		Woolens and worsteds	Toys	

Nonmanufacturing Industries

(1)	(2)	(3)	(4)	(5)
Actors and musicians	Bus and streetcar, local	Bus lines, intercity	Barber shops	Agriculture
Airline pilots and mechanics	Longshoring	Construction	Building service and maintenance	Air transport, excl. pilots and mechanics
Maritime — licensed and un-licensed	Radio technicians	Telephone	Cleaning and dyeing	Beauty shops
Mining — coal			Crude oil and natural gas	Domestic service
Motion picture production			Dairy products	Iron mining
Railroads			Fishing	Laundries
			Hotels and restaurants	Office, technical, professional employees
			Light and power	Retail trade, excl. food
			Motion picture theatres	Wholesale trade
			Newspaper offices	
			Nonferrous metals mining	
			Nonmetallic mining	
			Retail trade — food	
			Taxicabs	
			Trucking	

Source: Florence Peterson, "Extent of Collective Bargaining at Beginning of 1942," _Monthly Labor Review_ (May 1942), p. 1066.

[591]

represent so slight a fraction of total membership." Five years later, the centers of heavy industry had been invaded successfully, and either completely or partially conquered. Cities such as Pittsburgh, Detroit, and Akron, which had been strongly anti-union, were transformed into strongholds from which unionism could spread. The growth of organization in the traditional AFL trades, more imposing numerically, was less significant from a strategic point of view than the CIO concentration in vital centers of American industrial might.

Tables 22 and 23 serve to emphasize the magnitude of the CIO achievement. It was manufacturing, quite clearly, in which union member-

Table 22.

Percentage of nonagricultural wage and salaried employees organized, selected years

	1930	1935	1940
All nonagricultural industries	10.9	13.1	24.5
Manufactures	8.8	13.3	34.1
Transportation, communication and public utilities	23.4	26.4	48.2
Building	54.3	56.5	65.3
Mining, quarrying, oil	21.3	54.4	72.3
Services	2.7	3.1	6.7
Public service	8.3	8.5	10.2

Source: Leo Wolman, "Concentration of Union Membership," *Proceedings of Fifth Annual Meeting of the Industrial Relations Research Association* (1952), p. 216.

Table 23.

Percentage of production workers organized in manufacturing industry, selected years

	1935	1937	1939	1941
All manufactures	16.3	33.1	43.0	36.6
Metals	10.2	40.9	51.0	43.3
Clothing	47.6	60.9	67.9	64.4
Food, liquor, tobacco	11.3	13.1	31.1	32.5
Paper, printing, publishing	30.3	29.0	38.0	41.0
Leather and leather products	12.4	31.0	34.1	34.0
Chemicals, rubber, clay, glass, stone	4.7	9.4	15.4	15.4
Textiles	7.5	10.2	25.0	14.3
Lumber and woodworking	6.5	19.7	26.3	11.8

Source: Leo Wolman, "Concentration of Union Membership," *Proceedings of the Fifth Annual Meeting of the Industrial Relations Research Association* (1952), p. 216.

ship increased the most, and within manufacturing, in the metals group. Light industry lagged behind in terms of growth rates, either because of a previously high degree of organization (clothing, printing), or because of obstacles to organization (textiles).

It would be exceedingly interesting to trace the changes in the geographical distribution of trade union membership from 1936 to 1941, but the necessary data are unfortunately unavailable. However, a recently completed study shows the geographical situation in 1939, subsequent to the great organizing drives of 1936–1937.[12] The data relevant for our purposes are shown in Table 24. In 1939, almost half the total U. S. union membership

Table 24.

Trade union membership and extent of organization, by region, 1939

	Membership		
	(1) Number (thousands)	(2) Per cent of total	(3) Per cent organized
New England	331.1	5.1	12.8
Middle Atlantic	1,899.0	29.1	23.5
East North Central	1,659.7	25.4	24.2
West North Central	467.8	7.2	19.1
South Atlantic	474.5	7.3	13.2
East South Central	232.6	3.6	16.2
West South Central	207.0	3.2	10.4
Mountain	157.9	2.4	19.9
Pacific	676.7	10.4	27.1
Not distributed	411.4	6.3	—
United States	6,517.7	100.0	21.5

Source: Leo Troy, *Distribution of Union Membership Among the States, 1939 and 1953,* National Bureau of Economic Research, 1957, pp. 8, 22.

was to be found in the Middle Atlantic and East North Central states, a concentration out of proportion to their share of the industrial labor force, as can be seen from the percentages of organization in Table 24, column (3). The somewhat lower degree of organization shown for New England may be attributed to concentration in that area of textiles, leather products, and light manufacturing, which were everywhere less well organized than heavy manufacturing.

The degree of organization was least in the South, which should come as no surprise to readers of the foregoing pages. Some southern states had extremely low percentages of organization: North Carolina, 4.2 per cent; South Carolina, 4.0 per cent; Mississippi, 6.5 per cent; Georgia, 7.0 per cent. Had it not been for border states such as Alabama (16.1 per cent), Kentucky (22.5 per cent), and Tennessee (15.3 per cent), the regional average would have been much lower.

An analysis of southern trade union membership in October 1938 indicated how little impact the initial CIO organizing drive had upon this part of the country. The Textile Workers' Organizing Committee claimed 100,000 members, but it held only 25 written agreements, and its claim was grossly inflated. The United Mine Workers, with 82,000 southern members, was the region's largest labor organization, followed by the Carpenters with 20,000 and the Railway Trainmen, the Railway Clerks, and the Machinists with about 16,000 members each. Apart from these, there were only small numbers of organized workers.[13]

The reasons for the absence of unionism in the South were detailed in earlier chapters, particularly that dealing with the textile industry. Among the impediments to the advance of unionism were the relatively rural character of the South; the prevalence of small manufacturing establishments, except in textiles; the company-dominated mill town; the racial issue; regional hostility to northern-controlled unions; the highly competitive nature of the principal southern industries; and probably the most important cause, the surplus labor force in agriculture which, combined with a very wide income differential between industry and agriculture, provided a large and willing pool of potential strikebreakers.[14]

Labor was painfully aware of the special character of the southern problem, and devoted particular attention to it. The constitutional convention of the CIO, in 1938, discussed the southern situation at some length, and resolved that a coordinated southern organizing drive should be initiated.[15] A conference held in Washington in December 1939 created a coordinating committee, but an appeal to affiliated unions to assign special organizers to the drive proved disappointing. A regional CIO office was established in Atlanta, Georgia, the following year,[16] but a report to the 1941 convention indicated that progress had been slight.[17] Engrossed with other problems, the CIO was not willing to devote any considerable amount of resources to organizing the South, where the achievement was likely to be small.

The formation of the CIO made the AFL seem more attractive to some southern employers than it had been before. In March 1940, the AFL held a Southern Labor Conference at Atlanta, at which William Green made the principal address. Green was greeted on his arrival by the governor of

Georgia and the mayor of Atlanta, a wholly unprecedented event. Preston S. Arkwright, president of the Georgia Power Company and one of the most influential industrialists in the South, also spoke to the conference.[18] Notwithstanding these demonstrations of friendship, the AFL made no remarkable strides.

But to conclude that there was no southern organization at all would be erroneous. The following summary aptly describes the status of trade unionism in the South before, during, and after the New Deal years:

The writer, while doing the field work for a study on southern labor published in 1930, found in 1928 not a trace in four of the South's major industries, viz., furniture, cotton textiles, lumber and logging, and steel. Ten years later in 1938 unions had begun to make headway in this area. Twenty years later, in 1948, Southern labor is beginning to catch up with labor organization in the rest of the country.[19]

Union Finances

The financial resources of the American labor movement are largely concentrated in the national unions. Wherever individual union data were available, these were set forth in the foregoing chapters. The purpose of the present brief section is to summarize the available information on the financing of the federations.

The American Federation of Labor has published relatively complete financial statistics for many years. The main categories of assets, income, and expenses are summarized in Table 25, for the years 1935 to 1941. Considering income first, the principal single source was the per capita tax paid to the federation by national unions. Column (3) indicates that per capita receipts fell somewhat with the expulsion of the CIO unions in 1936, though the decline was by a lesser amount than the reported decline in membership, for reasons which are not apparent from the data. Total income, after a decline from 1935 to 1936, rose during the two following years. The major categories of income, in addition to the per capita tax, were subscriptions to the *American Federationist,* per capita tax and initiation fees from federal locals, and special assessments, which were particularly important as a source of revenue between 1937 and 1941.

For all years between 1938 and 1941, organizing expenses constituted more than half of total AFL expenditures. The very sharp jump in the absolute amount spent for organizing in 1937–1938 is particularly noticeable. It was this fiscal year (September 1 to August 31) in which the AFL began its counteroffensive against the CIO, and the figures reflect the renewed vigor

Table 25.

Financial data for the American Federation of Labor, 1935 to 1941

(1) Year	(2) Total cash balance on hand [a]	(3) Total receipts	(4) Receipts from per capita tax	(5) Total expenses	(6) Organizing expenses	(7) Balance in Defense Fund
1935	$ 622,954.53	$1,032,475.31	$ 454,839.05	$ 975,227.14	$ 338,576.42	$587,578.43
1936	569,405.99	924,390.38	453,817.37	977,938.92	293,692.88	510,623.86
1937	586,567.41	1,184,478.99	440,139.91	1,167,317.57	457,787.92	533,138.72
1938	443,631.19	1,844,203.37	580,813.45	1,987,139.59	1,174,014.58	436,774.96
1939	546,504.36	1,800,249.70	583,972.13	1,697,376.53	889,549.66	501,963.54
1940	716,151.82	1,938,483.85	629,499.11	1,768,836.39	953,481.38	627,488.86
1941	1,007,149.96	2,126,971.57	1,075,309.33	1,810,973.43	1,039,758.98	800,054.15

Source: Annual reports of the secretary-treasurer, American Federation of Labor.
[a] As of August 31.

of the AFL. The latter part of 1937, in particular, must have involved very heavy organizing expenses, for William Green reported to the Executive Council in February 1938, that he had laid off 70 organizers and was cutting expenses to the bone.[20] Three months later he reported the discharge of an additional 21 organizers.

The sharp increase in per capita tax receipts from 1940 to 1941 was the result of the temporary conversion of a special assessment into a per capita tax. Just prior to the 1940 convention, George Meany, the new secretary-treasurer of the AFL, recommended that the per capita tax be increased from one cent to two cents per month. The Teamsters and the Carpenters, the two largest unions, wanted the increase limited to $1\frac{1}{2}$ cents per month, but the majority of the council voted for the two-cent level.[21] Under pressure from the larger unions, the 1940 AFL Convention voted to set up a fact-finding committee to study the matter anew. In the meantime, the per capita tax was increased to two cents, but a special one-cent assessment was discontinued. The committee recommended a tax of $1\frac{1}{2}$ cents to the Executive Council, but on a motion by William Hutcheson, the council adopted a resolution recommending a tax of $1\frac{1}{2}$ cents per member for membership up to 300,000, and one cent per member in excess of 300,000.

The convention debated the council's recommendation at some length. A representative of a small union complained of the dispensation which the new proposal gave to the larger unions. Daniel Tobin of the Teamsters answered him by citing the great financial burden which the larger unions were carrying, arguing, *inter alia:*

the Federation is not a financial institution; it never was intended to have large amounts of moneys in its treasury, and the founders of the Federation so agreed. It was merely to take from the general membership each year enough to run the Federation for the coming year. . . .[22]

Needless to say, the views of the larger organizations prevailed, and the per capita tax was raised permanently to $1\frac{1}{2}$ cents up to 30,000 members, and retained at one cent beyond that figure.

The Defense Fund, which constituted from 80 to almost 100 per cent of AFL liquid assets during the years 1936 to 1941, was built up from per capita taxes paid by federal locals to the AFL. With respect to the servicing of these locals, the AFL occupied the position of a national union, and the Defense Fund was in a real sense the treasury of the 1,500 odd local unions directly affiliated to the AFL at the time. From 1936 to 1941, $625,000 of Defense Fund money was used for general operating purposes or for special organizational work.[23]

One of the complaints of the increasing number of federal locals organized after 1933 was that they were paying for more than their share of AFL expenses, even allowing for the fact that the AFL, as a federation, stood *in loco parentis* to them. For example, from 1938 to 1940, AFL receipts from federal locals constituted about 30 per cent of the combined receipts from federal locals and per capita dues from affiliated national unions, whereas the membership of the federation locals was only about 4 per cent of total AFL membership. The CIO, in attacking AFL policies, made much of the alleged use of federal local funds to pay the ordinary operating expenses of the AFL, thus sparing the national unions the necessity of raising their per capita contributions. The AFL retorted that expenditures from its Defense Fund were used in large part to service the federal locals, though it was conceded that some of this money went into special organizing drives.

Despite a doubling of its budget from 1936 to 1941, the total assets of the AFL rose by 60 per cent between these two years. Total expenses over the entire period were $10.4 million; total organizing expenses, $5.1 million. These magnitudes are better appreciated against the perspective of CIO financial expenditures.

The CIO published no financial statements in its early years. Moreover, when John L. Lewis was chairman, all the finances were handled by his brother-in-law, who was responsible only to him, and maintained what was apparently a complicated set of books. There are no precise data similar to those available for the AFL.

Before the CIO was formally established as a rival federation to the AFL, its revenues were derived from voluntary contributions by affiliated unions, without regard to any criterion other than ability and willingness to pay. From November 9, 1935, to November 1, 1936, the CIO received $50,000 and spent $41,000, exclusive of funds appropriated to the steel organizing drive.[24] The committee was just getting under way at the time, and operated on a small budget. Thus, in April 1936, John Brophy, the CIO director of organization, told Hillman that the CIO could operate on a monthly budget of $2,600 and maintain its activities.[25]

When the CIO expanded its activities early in 1937, it augmented its staff and its expenses. Organizing expenses were borne, in part, by affiliated unions, which assigned organizers to work under central CIO direction. A headquarters' staff of 50 people was soon built up, and, effective June 1, 1937, a per capita tax of five cents per member was installed, which may be compared with the two cents (one cent per capita plus one cent special assessment) then being charged by the AFL.[26] This tax was written into the constitution of the new Congress of Industrial Organizations in 1938.

From November 1935 to February 1938, various affiliates advanced a total of $1,883,354 to the CIO. Of this sum, the United Mine Workers contributed $1,665,000; the ILGWU, $102,000; and the Amalgamated Clothing Workers, $90,000, with other affiliates making mere token payments.[27] The Mine Workers Union later claimed that its contribution was a loan, not a gift, and demanded repayment, but the CIO refused to acknowledge the indebtedness.

There is some conflicting testimony on the state of CIO finances after 1938. John L. Lewis told the CIO Executive Board in June 1940 that since February 1938 the CIO had balanced its budget and paid its own way.[28] On the other hand, Murray later told the same board that when he assumed office as CIO president in November 1940, there was no money in the treasury, and that it had been necessary to borrow $30,000 from the United Mine Workers and $20,000 from the Steel Workers to finance the 1940 convention. However, between that time and March 1942, the CIO had not only been able to repay its debts, but had accumulated a treasury of $322,000.

Table 26 contains what purports to be a complete catalogue of assistance rendered by the CIO to its affiliates from the date of its formation to September 30, 1941. The total does not include some contributions made directly by one CIO affiliate to another, without the intermediation of the CIO. For example, the Amalgamated Clothing Workers reported giving over $500,000 to the Textile Workers' Organizing Committee.

Nor do the data in Table 26 portray total CIO expenditures adequately, since they do not include the cost of running the CIO itself. A rough estimate of total expenditures may be secured from the following data, which show total contributions made to the CIO up to the end of 1941 by the major affiliates:

United Mine Workers[29]

Monthly per capita at $30,000 per month	$1,680,000	
Services to CIO paid for by UMW	3,904,304	
Loans to CIO	1,665,000	7,249,304
Amalgamated Clothing Workers[30]		2,500,000
ILGWU [31]		345,000
Total		10,094,304

Table 26.

Assistance given by the CIO to national affiliates, including services of CIO organizers,
November 1935 to September 30, 1941

Aluminum	$ 29,585	Newspaper Guild	$ 40,836
Architects	44,322	Office and Professional	
Automobile	7,018	Workers	65,674
Auto (aircraft)	40,990	Oil Workers	116,922
Auto (Ford)	13,741	Packinghouse	92,615
Barbers	2,662	Stone and Allied	1,328
Cannery	88,416	Radio and Telegraphists	33,430
Communications	68,109	Retail and Department	120,616
Construction	313,254	Rubber	23,235
Die Casters	12,816	Shoe	81,657
Distillers	29,513	State, County and Municipal	134,459
Farm Equipment	71,857	Steel	1,018,613
Federal Workers	107,707	Textile	132,845
Flat Glass	13,822	Toy and Novelty	53,255
Furniture	54,139	Utility	75,841
District 50	110,007	Woodworkers — Midwest	155
Inland Boatmen	9,192	Woodworkers — Miscellaneous	85,164
Iron, Steel and Tin	19,670	Cafeteria	500
Longshoremen (California)	28,656	Studio Technicians	4,000
Marine Engineers	1,191	Optical	3,524
Marine Shipbuilders	52,392	Electrical and Radio	52,403
Maritime Committee	49,364	Cannery (Hefferly)	12,168
Maritime Union	71,733		
Mine, Mill and Smelter	62,154	Total	$3,451,551

Source: Congress of Industrial Organizations, *Executive Board Minutes* (June 3–5, 1942), p. 519; United Mine Workers of America, *Proceedings of the Thirty-Seventh Constitutional Convention* (Cincinnati, October 6–14, 1942), pp. 152–53.

While other CIO unions paid per capita after June 1938, it is doubtful whether their total contribution was very great. Most of them were not self-sustaining until after 1941, and the CIO had to help them either through remission of their per capita obligations, or through gifts and loans.

It would thus appear that the CIO spent in the vicinity of $10 million from 1936 to 1941, compared with $10.4 million of AFL expenditures. If from the AFL total, expenditures for 1935 and 1936 are deducted, in order to abstract from the years in which the CIO was operating as a small propaganda committee rather than a rival federation, the relevant sum for the AFL becomes $8.5 million.

The conclusion is that upon a much smaller dues-paying membership base, the CIO raised and spent more money than the AFL, an older organization with a well-established bureaucracy and consequently high fixed operating costs. This does not mean, however, that the same ratio of expenditures would necessarily prevail if the total funds spent by the AFL, national unions and federation, were matched with the comparable CIO figure. The CIO was the creature primarily of two men, Lewis and Hillman, and they ran it as a centralized organizing body, appropriating to it such funds as were necessary to achieve their goals. The AFL, on the other hand, was conceived of as a loose federation with limited functions, new organization being one of the less important of them. Most of the funds for organizing in the AFL were spent directly by the national unions themselves, though on one unusual occasion, in 1938, the Carpenters' Union received credit on a special assessment due the AFL because of extraordinarily large expenditures being made to fight the CIO in the Pacific Northwest.[32]

Of course, it would not be correct to conclude that none of the new CIO unions financed its own activities. Table 26 shows that a number of large unions — Auto, Glass, Longshore, Rubber, Electrical and Radio — received relatively little assistance from the CIO.[33] But it was probably true that per capita, expenditures by AFL national unions exceeded the CIO level. It would be interesting to compare the cost of organizing a worker for the AFL and the CIO, but unfortunately, the necessary data are not available. In their absence, we can only conclude that there was no royal road to expansion. Cash was an essential ingredient, and if to John L. Lewis goes the credit for the first million-dollar organizing drive (steel), it must be said that the AFL leaders responded by loosening their normally tight purse strings when faced with the challenge of the CIO.

Work Stoppages

The trend of work stoppages in the United States is shown in Table 27. The series begins in 1929 in order to provide a contrast for the period 1936 to 1941, in which we are primarily interested. The most notable aspect of the series is the peak for the year 1937, reflecting the great CIO drive in the spring of that year. A second peak, not quite as high as the first, was reached in 1941, accompanying the national defense program. The large number of workers involved in strikes in 1941 is attributable to the nationwide coal strike called by the United Mine Workers.

The average duration of strikes tended to be inverse to their number. Thus, in 1938, when the strike wave abated considerably as a result of the economic recession, the average duration rose to 23.6 days, compared with 20.3 days the previous year. In 1941, average duration fell with an increase in volume. The explanation is probably that unions are more prone to call

Table 27.

Work stoppages in the United States, 1929 to 1942

	Work stoppages		Workers involved		Man-days idle		
Year	Number	Average duration (calendar days)	Number, in thousands	Percentage of total employed	Number, in thousands	Per cent of estimated working time	Per worker involved
1929	921	22.6	289	1.2	5,350	0.07	18.5
1930	637	22.3	183	0.8	3,320	0.05	18.1
1931	810	18.8	342	1.6	6,890	0.11	20.2
1932	841	19.6	324	1.8	10,500	0.23	32.4
1933	1,695	16.9	1,170	6.3	16,900	0.36	14.4
1934	1,856	19.5	1,470	7.2	19,600	0.38	13.4
1935	2,014	23.8	1,120	5.2	15,500	0.29	13.8
1936	2,172	23.3	789	3.1	13,900	0.21	17.6
1937	4,740	20.3	1,860	7.2	28,400	0.43	15.3
1938	2,772	23.6	688	2.8	9,150	0.15	13.3
1939	2,613	23.4	1,170	4.7	17,800	0.28	15.2
1940	2,508	20.9	577	2.3	6,700	0.10	11.6
1941	4,288	18.3	2,360	8.4	23,000	0.32	9.8
1942	2,968	11.7	840	2.8	4,180	0.05	5.0

Source: W. S. Woytinsky and Associates, *Employment and Wages in the United States* (New York, 1953), p. 655.

strikes on the upswing of the cycle, at a time when employers are most willing to settle in order to avoid an interruption to their business.

Historically, 1937 was one of the greatest strike years ever experienced by the United States. There were more strikes in several postwar years, 1944, 1945, 1946, and 1950, but never more in comparison with the number of organized workers, with the possible exception of 1917. The unrest unleashed by the Great Depression, after a preliminary outburst during the NRA years, finally culminated in the 1937 strike wave. Unlike previous waves, this one left a permanent residue of organization when it withdrew.

Table 28 contains a breakdown of the strike record by affiliation of the participating labor organization. In every year, the AFL conducted more strikes than the CIO, but typically, the CIO strikes involved a greater number of workers, on the average. The CIO man-days lost figures for 1937, 1939, and 1941, which are extreme, reflect, for the first year, the steel and automobile strikes, and for the two latter years, the coal strikes, which were to continue on a biennial basis for a decade. Independent union strikes, while they reached respectable totals in several of the years, did not involve many workers and were of relatively short duration, facts which are revealed graphically by the statistics for the year 1939.

There was a marked contrast in the character of labor disputes between the period 1936 to 1941 and the postwar years. This is brought out by the data in Table 29. Although the basis of the classification was a rough and ready one, and the categories were not always mutually exclusive, it is evident that prior to the war, union organization was the major issue in work stoppages, whereas after the war, the economic strike supplanted the organizational strike as the principal cause of industrial strife. The contrast is particularly marked when one compares the years 1936 and 1937, when 60.2 per cent and 76.4 per cent, respectively, of the man-days of strike idleness were due to organizational strikes, with 1949 and 1950, when the comparable data are 3.5 per cent and 6.0 per cent, respectively.

Unions in National Politics

The traditional policy of the AFL in political affairs was one of nonpartisanship. This did not imply, as is often mistakenly assumed, a lack of interest in politics by the American worker. On the contrary, organized labor continually evinced keen interest in both national and local affairs. But it did mean the rejection of independent political action on the European model. The American Federation of Labor was convinced from its inception that American conditions were not suitable for the growth of a labor

Table 28.

Labor organizations involved in strikes, 1936 to 1941

Number of strikes

Year	AFL	%	CIO	%	Other	%
1936	1,780	82.5	—	—	376	7.5
1937	2,301	48.7	1,825	38.7	594	2.6
1938	1,385	50.1	1,121	40.4	266	3.1
1939	1,312	49.7	764	29.0	563	16.4
1940	1,541	61.9	689	27.6	263	5.6
1941	2,343	54.3	1,581	36.1	390	1.7

Number of workers involved

Year	AFL	%	CIO	%	Other	%
1936	590,419	83.1	—	—	119,329	7.9
1937	583,063	30.0	1,163,515	59.8	199,167	11.2
1938	242,975	35.3	376,770	54.9	67,884	4.6
1939	371,822	31.6	704,031	59.7	102,030	3.9
1940	306,541	53.5	222,858	38.9	43,965	5.1
1941	584,442	29.7	1,641,044	69.5	38,811	3.9

Number of man-days idle (thousands)

Year	AFL	%	CIO	%	Other	%
1936	10,059	88.0	—	—	1,373	9.7
1937	10,868	35.2	18,440	59.8	1,540	2.2
1938	3,210	36.0	4,638	52.0	1,078	2.7
1939	4,057	21.9	13,265	71.7	1,199	3.3
1940	3,632	54.5	2,668	39.9	380	3.2
1941	6,970	30.3	14,904	64.8	1,135	1.1

Source: Bureau of Labor Statistics, *Handbook of Labor Statistics*, 1950 ed., p. 155.

Table 29.

Causes of work stoppages, prewar and postwar
(per cent of total)[a]

	Number of strikes			Workers involved			Man-days idle		
	Wages and hours	Organization	Other	Wages and hours	Organization	Other	Wages and hours	Organization	Other
1936	35.1	50.2	14.7	35.3	51.4	13.3	32.2	60.2	7.6
1937	29.9	57.8	12.3	22.4	59.8	17.8	15.7	76.4	7.9
1938	28.0	50.0	22.0	36.7	32.6	30.7	34.8	44.4	20.8
1939	26.5	53.5	20.0	29.9	54.4	15.7	17.9	74.7	7.4
1940	30.2	49.9	19.9	41.0	33.1	25.9	46.3	40.8	12.9
1941	35.6	49.5	14.9	46.9	31.5	21.6	45.4	43.8	10.8
1945	42.4	20.5	36.9	43.7	21.8	34.5	44.4	29.4	26.2
1946	44.9	32.4	22.5	75.1	11.5	13.4	81.9	15.2	2.9
1947	46.3	29.8	23.1	37.2	43.0	19.3	43.9	49.0	7.0
1948	50.8	22.8	25.3	61.9	11.6	26.2	73.9	17.6	8.3
1949	46.6	21.7	30.8	51.0	2.7	46.0	78.7	3.5	17.8
1950	52.8	19.0	27.3	60.7	5.4	33.6	83.8	6.0	10.0

Source: W. S. Woytinsky and Associates, *Employment and Wages in the United States* (New York, 1953), p. 654.

[a] For some years, the figures do not total 100 per cent in the source.

party,[34] and devoted itself instead to the support of those major party candidates who promised to help further its legislative objectives.

The election of Franklin D. Roosevelt to the presidency in 1932 served to heighten labor's interest in political action, if only because the acquisition of power seemed so much more possible than ever before. It was heady wine for labor leaders, long accustomed to a relatively low social status, to have ready access to the president of the United States. In industrial states and municipalities, trade unionists won public office with increasing frequency, and occasionally this played an important role in organizational campaigns. A good example is provided by the election of Thomas Kennedy, the secretary-treasurer of the United Mine Workers, to the lieutenant governorship of Pennsylvania, and the assistance he was able to give in the steel organizing drive.[35]

The ILGWU introduced a resolution at the 1935 AFL convention calling upon the Executive Council to "study the subject of independent labor political action, with the view of taking the initiative in the formation of such a labor party." [36] In reporting its nonconcurrence with the resolution, the Committtee on Resolutions referred to the pending report of the Executive Council which reiterated the AFL political slogan: "The American labor movement is not partisan to a political party; it is partisan to a principle, the principle of equal rights and freedom." The resolution was defeated, with Kennedy of the United Mine Workers arguing strongly against it on the ground that nothing should impair the unity of labor in support of the Roosevelt candidacy during the 1936 election campaign.

The formation of the CIO permitted those who advocated a more active political line greater freedom to act than had been possible within the AFL. On April 2, 1936, the formation of Labor's Non-Partisan League was announced, pledged initially to the reelection of Roosevelt. Although George L. Berry, president of the AFL Printing Pressmen's Union, was made president of the organization, John L. Lewis and Sidney Hillman were actually in control. Eli P. Oliver, a former organizer for the Amalgamated Clothing Workers, became executive vice-president.[37]

The League, with the cooperation of 59 international unions, AFL as well as CIO, spent over a million dollars in the 1936 campaign, half of which was contributed by the United Mine Workers. In general, it eschewed independent political action, except in New York, where it launched the American Labor Party.[38] It soon became clear that the League was CIO-dominated, and with the resignation of Berry as chairman in 1937, it became formally the political arm of the CIO. In September 1937, William Green informed all AFL local bodies that the AFL considered the League as a CIO political machine, to which no cooperation was to be accorded.[39] Nevertheless, some AFL unions continued to give the League their support, and at the 1938 AFL convention, the Hotel and Restaurant Workers' Union introduced a resolution condemning the Executive Council's action in withdrawing AFL assistance. George Meany, then a delegate from the New York State Federation of Labor, spoke strongly against the resolution. He said, among other things:

I want to say now that the American Federation of Labor in that state [New York] today is non-partisan and is going to stay non-partisan. . . . A labor party such as we see it in New York State is a class party, and there is no place in America for a party founded on class or caste lines . . . we are going to carry out the policies of Gompers and not bow to any political boss, no matter what party label he may bear, even if it bears the honored and sacred name of labor.[40]

A few delegates rose to the defense of the League, but the resolution was defeated overwhelmingly. Charges of communist infiltration into the League were made by Meany and others, charges which were to be repeated with increasing vehemence in later years.

The CIO, on the other hand, affirmed its loyalty to the League,[41] which was active in local elections in 1938, particularly in New York State, where the American Labor Party provided Herbert H. Lehman the margin of victory over Thomas E. Dewey in the gubernatorial election. At the 1939 CIO convention, John L. Lewis boasted:

Let no public representative or citizens underestimate the tremendous power and influence now being exercised by labor in the political realm of the nation, and let no politician assume that he can ignore Labor's Non-Partisan League, nor ignore the mandates and the ideals and the objectives of organized labor, without being held to strict accountability in that inevitable day when elections come again.[42]

But the split within the CIO during the 1940 election campaign rendered Labor's Non-Partisan League ineffective. Although most CIO leaders were pro-Roosevelt, Lewis controlled the League, and with the aid of the Communist Party, then in its "neutralist" phase, he carried on a campaign which had as its purpose the defeat of Roosevelt. The aftermath of the election was a bitter one. At a meeting of the CIO Executive Board, Potofsky of the Amalgamated Clothing Workers accused the Lewis forces of spending CIO money for Willkie. Allan S. Haywood, head of the New York State Industrial Council and a Lewis supporter, countered: "Some of your representatives, Brother Potofsky, have stated the [per capita tax] was held back for political reasons. No CIO money was spent for Willkie, not a dime." Potofsky retorted: "You work for the CIO, and you supported Willkie." [43] The American Labor Party in New York was increasingly split over the communist issue.[44]

Lewis would probably have liked to commit the CIO to a third party venture after 1940. The CIO convention of that year, held shortly after the elections, adopted a resolution authorizing the Executive Board to "give serious consideration to this problem looking toward the formulation of a program which would guarantee and assure an independent political role for organized labor." [45] But the growing estrangement of Lewis from the CIO militated against the commitment of the CIO to any such goal. The CIO leadership, headed by Murray and Hillman, who had given Roosevelt their unqualified support in 1940, continued to follow the pro-Democratic Party policy initiated in 1936. When Lewis withdrew from the CIO, he took Labor's Non-Partisan League with him, leaving a vacuum in the CIO which was not filled until the formation of the Political Action Committee in 1943.

Confirmed in its traditional nonpartisanship by the activities of Labor's Non-Partisan League and the American Labor Party, the AFL adopted a statement in January 1940, which termed acceptance of CIO endorsement by any candidate the "kiss of death," and warned: ". . . we caution the members of the American Federation of Labor not to be misled by the endorsements or blacklists of the so-called Labor's Non-Partisan League. This league is a sham. It is merely a paper organization, a puppet of the CIO. It has been entirely discredited and its political power is nil. . . ." Committees were appointed to attend both Democratic and Republican conventions in order to present the views of the AFL on appropriate plat- form planks. Although the AFL as such maintained its traditional neutral- ity, there was a sharp division of opinion among its leaders. Thus, Daniel Tobin, who served as head of the Labor Committee of the Democratic Party, called the attention of the Executive Council to a public attack upon the New Deal issued by ten AFL officials, and complained that this had given rise to the impression that the AFL was opposed to Roosevelt. Upon a motion by George Meany, it was declared that the statement did not emanate from the Executive Council.[46] On the other hand, William Hutche- son, like John L. Lewis, warmly supported the Willkie candidacy, and it is a commentary upon the nature of American politics that the two great antagonists of 1935, whose angry clash on the floor of the AFL convention had signalized the formation of the CIO, were once again united in opposition to the man for whom a substantial majority of American workers consistently voted.

The great Roosevelt victories of 1932, 1936, and 1940 effectively dampened the third-party sentiment that prevailed in some labor quarters, particularly among the unions with a socialist background. The garment unions, not to be denied, had their fling in the form of the American Labor Party locally while supporting the Democratic Party nationally. Against the third-party proponents, the Roosevelt supporters could argue that the Roosevelt Administration had brought to the American worker social benefits and protection of trade union rights that would have seemed utopian to the most ardent socialist at the depths of the depression.

It cannot be said that there was ever any chance for a third party during the nineteen-thirties. For one thing, the AFL was firmly and consistently opposed to any deviation from its traditional nonpartisanship. For another, John L. Lewis, the only labor leader with enough prestige to lead the newly organized industrial workers into untried political paths, was fundamentally a conservative, who strayed into the Roosevelt fold in 1936 to his subsequent regret. The Socialist Party was, by 1932, a mere shadow of its former self, while the communists, veering between "United Front" and independent political action, were too far removed from American realities to have any lasting influence, and killed whatever organizations they touched.

But to conclude that the New Deal marked no change in the political attitudes of organized labor is to misread history. For the first time, American trade unions began to work systematically at the precinct level within the framework of the established political parties. For the first time, they tasted the fruits of electoral victories for which they could fairly claim credit, and these fruits, in the form of greatly enhanced legislative influence, were sweet indeed. The AFL of Samuel Gompers was a humble supplicant before the Congress of the United States on a very limited range of matters.[47] The AFL of William Green, and the CIO of John L. Lewis and Philip Murray, were constant visitors in the halls of Congress, and it required the shock of the Taft-Hartley Act in 1947 to bring them to the realization that labor's political milennium had not yet arrived. Nonpartisanship in 1932 meant that the labor movement was at liberty to present its views to the national conventions of the Democratic and Republican parties, and to have these views generally disregarded. Nonpartisanship in 1940 meant a voice in the selection of many state and local candidates, invitations to meet publicly with the president of the United States and his Republican challenger, nationwide radio broadcasts by labor leaders, and attendance at trade union conventions by the highest officials of the nation, including the president himself.

In part, of course, the increased political influence of organized labor was a function of its numerical growth and its greater financial resources. But beyond this, there had come about an awareness by even the most old-fashioned of the AFL leaders of the augmented role of the federal government in the labor market, and the consequent acceptance of the need for institutionalizing the means of influencing government decisions. Political action had become a necessity, and in the light of what the two parties stood for, this implied pro-Democratic partisanship. A few staunch Republicans in the top leadership of the AFL managed for a time to ensure the preservation of the old Gompers slogans as official AFL policy, but in reality, the AFL, together with the rest of the labor movement, ceased to be neutral after 1936. The New Deal has effectively, and seemingly permanently, destroyed the possibility of an American labor party constructed on the British model, but only at the expense of bringing about a basic alteration in the nature of the Democratic Party. An acute observer of the American political scene has summed up the reciprocal impact of labor politics and Democratic politics in the following words:

The ever developing close relationship between the labor movement and the Democratic Party has had its effect on both groups. It has served to temper and provide a realism to the political philosophy and objectives of the trade unions. It has also served to mobilize, democratize, and humanize the Democratic Party in those northern midwestern states where the labor movement has been influential. The objective of this relationship, however, has not been the transformation of the Democratic Party into a labor party. The development of trade union political consciousness . . . has left the concept of a labor party behind and, furthermore, the Democratic Party itself is much too large and heterogeneous a body to allow itself to be so parochialized or fractionated. Both understand that a labor party would be doomed to the status of a minority party in the American political scene. The relationship, therefore, is based on a marriage of convenience and compatability of ideas.[48]

American Labor and Legislation

The mainstream of the American labor movement, committed always to the American system of political democracy, manifested from its very beginning a keen interest in the laws enacted by the Congress and by the state legislatures. The subject of trade union legislative activity during the New Deal period, when for the first time the unions became a potent political force, is a vast one requiring separate monographic treatment. All that will be attempted here is a brief sketch of union action regarding several pieces of federal legislation which were of key interest to the labor movement, and toward which the AFL and the CIO manifested radically different attitudes.

In terms of importance to the labor movement, star billing must be given to the National Labor Relations Act, which was enacted in 1935 after the futile NRA attempt to safeguard the right of collective bargaining through voluntary agreement among employers. The declaration by the U. S. Supreme Court in April 1937, that the NLRA was constitutional was a major factor in making that year one of the most memorable in the annals of American labor. There is grave doubt that without the NLRA, the new industrial unions could have survived the economic recession of 1937–1939.

During the years 1936 to 1941, almost 24,000 unfair labor practice charges were made against employers, and almost 14,000 representation petitions were filed (see Table 30). Some 6000 elections were held, in which

Table 30.

National Labor Relations Board activities, 1936–1941

Fiscal year ended June 30	Cases filed		Elections and cross checks held	
	Unfair labor practice cases	Representation cases	Number	Votes cast
1936	865	203	31	7,572
1937	2,895	1,173	265	164,135
1938	6,807	3,623	1,152	343,587
1939	4,618	2,286	746	177,215
1940	3,934	2,243	1,192	532,355
1941	4,817	4,334	2,568	729,933
Total	23,936	13,862	5,954	1,954,797

Source: Harry A. Millis and Emily Clark Brown, *From the Wagner Act to Taft-Hartley* (Chicago, 1950), p. 77.

nearly two million votes were cast. The flood of cases during the fiscal year 1937–1938 reflected the 1937 Supreme Court decision, as well as an ebb in direct economic action by labor unions. A majority of the unfair labor practice charges involved alleged discrimination for union activities, with refusal to bargain the second major category. During the early years, the CIO made greater use of the facilities of the act than did the AFL, but as the latter organization increased its organizing activities, its recourse to the National Labor Relations Board became more frequent.

The NLRA was of major assistance to the labor movement in helping secure the elimination of the company-dominated unions that had been established in great number during NRA days. Thousands of workers were reinstated to their jobs with back pay after having being discharged for joining unions. In 1937, unions won 94 per cent of all elections conducted by the NLRB, securing 87 per cent of the votes, and for the entire life of the National Labor Relations Act, up to 1947, won more than 80 per cent of all elections.[49] These figures do not tell the whole story, however. For every worker who was reinstated, many more were not discharged in the first place; for every election held, employers in other cases were willing to recognize unions without the formality of an election. As with any law, the statistics of enforcement are only an imperfect index of effectiveness.

Prior to the split in the labor movement, the AFL strongly supported the National Labor Relations Board.[50] But with the formation of the CIO, the AFL came to the belated recognition of the fact that the traditional method of assigning jurisdiction through the internal processes of the labor movement had been replaced by decision through government-conducted election. Through its determination of the unit appropriate for collective bargaining, the NLRB was often in a position to decide whether a particular group of workers was to be reserved for AFL craft unions or merged with a CIO industrial union. As early as 1937, the AFL sought to secure an amendment to the NLRA which would have made it mandatory upon the board to separate crafts out where a majority of the craftsmen desired separate representation.[51]

Any residue of friendliness to the NLRB evaporated under the impact of frequent board unit determinations which established industrial units in the face of AFL jurisdictional claims. The AFL charged that two of the three members of the board, Edwin S. Smith and Donald W. Smith, were biased in favor of the CIO, and not only on the matter of unit determination. In August 1938, the following was reported to the AFL Executive Council:

President Green stated he spent an hour with President Roosevelt and went over the entire situation and expressed our opposition to the policy of the Board. President Green stated he advised President Roosevelt we were not demanding repeal of the law because we feel that the law is all right if it were properly administered. . . . President Green stated he advised President Roosevelt that Donald Wakefield Smith is not judicially minded and there ought to be some man on the Board who is judicially minded.[52]

The Executive Council then went on record against the pending reappointment of D. W. Smith to the board. President Roosevelt replied rather curtly as follows:

I am sorry that the Executive Council of the American Federation of Labor voted formally to oppose the reappointment of Mr. Donald Wakefield Smith as a member of the National Labor Relations Board.

The telegram expressing the opinion of the Executive Council in referring to his record states that he has shown a bias. That, of course, standing by itself, means nothing, and as a mere expression of opinion does not accord with the opinion of thousands of people who know Mr. Smith and have appeared before him in connection with his official duties.

It is an interesting fact that complaints relating to decisions of the National Labor Relations Board have come from employers and employees representing almost every organization of capital and labor which happens to have lost their case before the Board. There are just as many complaints from labor organizations not affiliated with the American Federation of Labor as from organizations affiliated. I suppose that is a very human and natural attitude to take.[53]

Green expressed the view that this letter was "uncalled for," and the council replied with a long bill of particulars, spelling out its grievances in detail.[54] Although President Roosevelt indicated his intention of reappointing D. W. Smith, the AFL lobbied so effectively against him that his name was never submitted to the Senate. Instead, President Roosevelt nominated William L. Leiserson, at the time chairman of the National Mediation Board. The CIO, which had supported Smith, was very suspicious of the new member. Philip Murray told the CIO convention in 1939 that "the recent appointee, some individual named Leiserson . . . to give credence to the report which is nationwide now, was going to do a job on the CIO when he got on the Board. . . ."[55]

The AFL offensive continued unabated, despite its success in preventing Smith's reappointment. It sponsored a series of amendments to the NLRA which would have made a craft unit rule mandatory upon the board, prevented the board from invalidating agreements with AFL unions notwithstanding a finding that they were collusive, and replaced the existing board by a new five-man board with a mandate to overhaul the staff.[56] The amendments were opposed vigorously by the CIO, and although they were adopted by the House of Representatives, the Senate failed to take action upon them.

While the AFL continued to advocate amendments to the NLRA, its objections were largely satisfied by changes in personnel and administration.

It successfully opposed the reappointment of Chairman J. Warren Madden in 1940 and greeted with satisfaction his replacement by Professor Harry A. Millis. In 1941, it attacked board member Edwin S. Smith as "openly hostile to the interests of the Federation from the very beginning of the formation of the dual labor movement. No private individual has done as much as this public official to encourage opposition to the American Federation of Labor and to enhance and strengthen the development of a dual and rival organization." [57] The CIO, on the other hand, strongly urged Mr. Smith's reappointment. In a letter to President Roosevelt, Philip Murray declared:

The provisions of the Labor Act can be rendered meaningless through a weak administration. It is therefore essential that the type of administration represented by Mr. Smith be continued. A failure to reappoint Mr. Smith would disastrously discourage public officials who are selected to administer labor legislation in a manner consistent with its basic policies.[58]

For a third time, the AFL was successful in opposing an NLRB appointment, thus making a clean sweep of the original board personnel. It was doubly convinced that its objections in the case of E. S. Smith had some merit when Mr. Smith became a CIO organizer directly after leaving the board.

Under Millis and Leiserson, the NLRB underwent drastic changes in administration and policy. In particular, craft groups were given greater opportunity to establish separate bargaining rights, and AFL contracts were accorded a greater measure of protection against CIO charges of collusion.[59] The extent to which the policy shift went is indicated by AFL characterization of the administration of the act, in 1941, as "fair and impartial" and "a vast improvement over the previous administration," [60] as well as by CIO condemnation of the Millis-Leiserson majority.[61]

Although they were sharply divided over administration of the representation provisions of the NLRA, both wings of the labor movement were firmly united in support of the unfair labor practice provisions, behind the protection of which organizational activities could be conducted without fear of employer reprisal against militant trade unionists. The act undoubtedly had profound effects upon American industrial relations, helping to bring about a change of employer policy from anti-unionism to the acceptance of collective bargaining.[62] Its effects upon the unions themselves, though less obvious, were no less important. Government-sponsored elections replaced organizing strife in many instances, giving rise to an entirely

new technique of bringing workers into unions, which was used with particular effect by the newer CIO unions. The necessity of defending policies
before the challenge of rival unions, manifested by the filing of election petitions, forced many unions into more vigorous collective bargaining policies,
and helped eliminate corrupt and undemocratic organizations. Union structure was influenced by the unit policy of the NLRB in numerous ways, still
not fully explored.[63] Whether the American labor movement could have
attained the size and stability it had in 1941 without such federal government assistance as was furnished by the National Labor Relations Board is
a question that has often been raised but never answered. A review of bargaining history during the years 1936–1941 makes it clear that a negative
position, that is, the thesis that the NLRB was a *sine qua non* for the degree
of organizational success attained, is at the very least an arguable one.[64]

Another major piece of legislation on which there was considerable controversy within the labor movement was the Fair Labor Standards Act of
1938. A powerful group within the AFL was opposed to any federal legislation on wages, among them Hutcheson, Coefield, and Wharton.[65] John
Frey, president of the AFL Metal Trades Department, said that his members
"were disturbed with the fear that the enactment of such legislation would
very materially interfere with the free functioning of the trade union movement." They "were opposed to any additional legislation at this time which
would give any powers to any commission or board which would enable
them to in any way fix minimum wage rates and determine those for individual employers." Williams, president of the Building Trades, expressed
himself as being in full agreement with Frey, but Tracy, president of the
Electrical Workers' Union, while opposing wage boards, said: ". . . there
are many underpaid workers in this country today who probably could be
taken care of by such a law but those industries would have to be carefully defined. . . ."

Against this traditional mistrust of government wage determination by
the craft unions the CIO interposed an urgent plea for regulation on behalf
of the workers it represented, particularly in such industries as textile and
garment production. This placed the AFL in a dilemma, for to heed the
advice of the craft unionists would have placed it in a difficult position vis-
à-vis the mass production workers. Some AFL people, like George Harrison
and William Green himself, were reluctant to commit the AFL negatively
on a piece of legislation which had such immediate and widespread appeal
among prospective constituents.

The compromise line chosen was to oppose the original Black bill which was enacted by the U. S. Senate, on the ground that instead of a simple statement of minimum wages and maximum hours, it contained obnoxious administrative features in its grant of discretionary wage-fixing power to a government board. When the House Labor Committee reported the bill out in December 1937, with the support of the CIO, the AFL wired every member of the House, urging its recommittal, and succeeded in having this done by the narrow margin of 216 to 198 votes. The AFL then submitted its own bill to the House Labor Committee, calling simply for a uniform minimum wage of 40 cents an hour and a maximum 40 hour week. President Green told the committee:

Its provisions are clear cut. There is no possibility of escaping or twisting out of them by any manner of interpretation. The law stands on its own feet. It is uniform throughout the Nation. It requires no administrative board or machinery to make it effective. It provides for quick punishment of any violation.

We are unalterably opposed to a complex system of Federal wage and hour regulations and their administration by a new Federal board, as contemplated by the Black-Connery Bill. Labor, industry and the public are fed up with Federal boards. We have had extremely disappointing and disillusioning experiences with the National Labor Relations Board.[66]

A bill along the lines urged by the AFL was enacted by the House, but the Senate forced return to a 25 to 40 cent minimum range, industry boards, and a federal administrator, all features which the AFL considered obnoxious. The CIO was very critical of AFL "sabotage" of the law, arguing that it was the best that could be secured at the time.[67] The AFL quickly became reconciled to the Fair Labor Standards Act, and soon joined the CIO to defend it against attempts at emasculation.[68]

The basic conservatism of the AFL in its approach to government can also be seen in its attitude toward the United States Supreme Court. The action of the court in declaring unconstitutional several pieces of New Deal legislation gave rise to a demand within the labor movement that its powers be curbed. Although several AFL conventions went on record to this effect, the Executive Council, in 1936, expressed considerable concern lest in curbing the Supreme Court, the Congress might acquire absolute authority to fix wages and hours: "The question is whether we want a centralized form of Government and control rather than state organization. Experience of the past is that form of society is extremely dangerous to the masses. . . . If we give one Congress the authority to enact legislation favorable to labor, we cannot prevent another Congress passing legislation unfavorable to labor." [69] After a good deal of discussion, the following resolution was adopted by the Council:

The American Federation of Labor non-partisan political committee be directed to include in its demands to be presented to both political conventions the request or the statement that we favor a constitutional amendment that no law may be declared unconstitutional by the U. S. Supreme Court except by at least a two-thirds vote.[70]

When President Roosevelt advanced his proposal that the Supreme Court be enlarged as a means of guaranteeing a New Deal majority, the AFL Executive Council was split, notwithstanding the imminence of court decisions involving the National Labor Relations Act, in which most lawyers, under the stimulus of propaganda issued by the Liberty League, an employer-financed organization, expected a declaration of unconstitutionality. Rickert of the United Garment Workers, Duffy of the Carpenters, and Coefield of the Plumbers opposed the "Court packing plan"; Bates of the Bricklayers thought that while the president should not have asked for such power, the AFL would have to support him. On a motion to approve the plan, there were nine votes in favor and three against, with two abstentions.[71] That there should have been a majority in favor of the plan is not surprising; what is remarkable is that after decades of trade union animosity toward the Supreme Court for its decisions in labor injunction and antitrust cases, among other things, there were still labor leaders who opposed efforts to limit its powers.

An interesting sidelight on the AFL attitude toward government wage regulation is provided by the following incident. In February 1941, Assistant Secretary of Labor Dan Tracy appeared before the Executive Council and informed it that President Roosevelt had been sold on the practicability of a minimum annual wage of $1500 for building workers. Tracy advised the council that "it might be well to explore the matter with the President and try to get the idea out of his mind." William Green met with Roosevelt, who said that

we ought to begin to consider a plan of calling upon industry and industrial management to guarantee forty-eight weeks work per year and then the balance to be paid as vacation with pay which would be from two to four weeks per year. President Green stated he told the President that it is a splendid idea but that he was not sure we would work that out . . . in his opinion it might be considered a bit revolutionary to talk about it at this time, but the President replied that he thought the time has come when perhaps this could be made a part of our administrative program.

The foregoing were by no means the only examples of labor concern with the details of legislative policy and administration. On every issue which impinged upon the interests of workers, the labor movement expressed itself in no uncertain terms, even though this might entail sharp conflict with New Deal policy.[72] But all these activities paled into insignificance beside the degree of government involvement in labor affairs attendant upon the defense program, and then the war.

The AFL, despite the coolness of its relations with the federal administration, engendered by its opposition to the National Labor Relations Board and to the original Fair Labor Standards Act, as well as by Thurman Arnold's efforts to apply the Sherman Anti-Trust Act to its activities, was more alert than the CIO to the necessity of maintaining close governmental relationships. This was due in no small measure to the ascendancy within its ranks of George Harrison of the Railway Clerks and Dan Tobin of the Teamsters, each of whom now headed a large, powerful organization, which had grown greatly in the five years preceding the defense emergency. Moreover, the building trades, which might have been expected to maintain a policy of aloofness, were more affected than any other labor group by the defense program. The CIO, on the other hand, was hopelessly split into isolationist and interventionist wings, which served to reduce its influence.

Early in 1940, the AFL Executive Council adopted a confidential resolution urging that any government agency established to deal with the emergency be truly representative of labor, management, and the public; setting up a committee to consult with the Assistant Secretary of War on defense planning; and stating:

should a crisis arise which requires national planning because of a national emergency, that the American Federation of Labor should place itself in a position before such a crisis develops, as will assure its recognition and its participation in all governmental planning agencies having to do with civilian activities.[73]

A few months later, the council recalled the readiness of the American Federation of Labor, in 1917, to assist in the prosecution of war, and once more pledged its "active and cooperative support with industry and with every appropriate governmental agency having to do with the production and the construction of material for national defense." There was a feeling of outrage, therefore, when President Roosevelt appointed Sidney Hillman as the sole labor member of the seven-man National Defense Advisory Commission. The AFL dismay was matched by that of John L. Lewis, who apparently had not been informed in advance of the Hillman appointment, and who undoubtedly felt that he, if anyone, should have had the post.[74] Hillman was the *bête noire* of the communist-dominated unions in the CIO, so that all in all, this choice did not seem to augur well for union-government relationships in the defense crisis.

Yet things went surprsingly well, due in no small measure to Hillman's skillful administration, and to his conviction that all partisan considerations would have to give way to the necessities of defense production. An AFL-CIO labor policy advisory committee functioned amicably as an advisory body to Hillman.[75] AFL resentment of Hillman's further elevation to the post of associate director-general of the Office of Production Management in December 1940, putting him second in command to William S. Knudsen as administrator of the entire defense production program, was mollified by Hillman's agreement with the AFL Building Trades relative to defense construction.[76]

The CIO appeared less satisfied with the defense setup than the AFL. In 1940 it asserted that the "deplorable absence of any effective CIO representation in the national defense program must be ended," [77] a demand that was reiterated in November 1941.[78] The CIO advocated the institution of the so-called Murray Plan, under which an industry council, composed equally of labor and management representatives with a government-designated chairman, would be established for every basic industry. The council was to be endowed with very broad powers, including the coordination of production facilities, the allocation of materials, and price fixing. Needless to say, this scheme, which was formally proposed to President Roosevelt in December 1940, was not well received by either management or the AFL.[79]

There were many specific matters relating to defense production in which labor was influential during 1940 and 1941, among them programs of industrial training, and policy with respect to award of government contracts to firms which were in violation of national labor policy. But the following summary of its status is well justified:

As the months wore on, it became increasingly evident that, despite Hillman's position in the formal organization of OPM, in practice labor's influence was vastly inferior to that of management spokesmen; and as OPM passed into history and as defense and then war agencies multiplied, labor's share in the formulation and administration of government defense policy further diminished. Occasional labor vice-chairmen and more frequently labor advisory committees gave labor but limited influence over governmental policy.[80]

On the narrower questions of labor relations, the trade unions were of course in the center of the picture. Strikes in defense industries during 1940, some of them politically motivated, produced a Congressional demand for antistrike legislation. Alarmed at the prospects of drastic legislation, the AFL Executive Council at its meeting in February 1941, came out strongly against compulsory arbitration of labor disputes, and made the following positive suggestions:

Organized labor has indicated its willingness to conciliate, mediate and voluntarily arbitrate its labor differences. In the last war, a Board with equal representation on the part of labor and industry was created by Presidential proclamation and not through Congressional enactment. That Board and its procedures were devised to protect the rights of free enterprise and of free labor. It brought about conferences on the part of the employers and workers and their representatives. Through procedure, the basis of which was wholly voluntary, the parties met and adjusted their differences. The history of the last war proves the effectiveness of this method. . . . In such a program, the Government will have the wholehearted support of the American Federation of Labor and its affiliated organizations.[81]

The CIO vigorously defended the right to strike, arguing that its abolition would cause more labor trouble than its maintenance.[82] In response to Congressional pressures, President Roosevelt, by executive order, created the National Defense Mediation Board on March 19, 1941. The board was tripartite in structure, and operated in most cases through mediation rather than arbitration.

The AFL was fairly well satisfied with the board and its procedure. In May 1941, it called upon all affiliates to "refrain for any reason whatsoever from calling a strike interfering with national defense production until full opportunity has first been given to the Conciliation Service of the Department of Labor and to the National Defense Mediation Board to bring about a peaceful settlement of the dispute." [83] Later in the year it renewed its approval of the board, promising to give "hearty support to the Board in its work to promote our national welfare, and it will zealously safeguard as a function of that board its work of promoting voluntary arbitration, and inferentially of opposing mandatory arbitration." [84]

The experience of the CIO with the NDMB was less happy. During the first months, several of its left wing unions wrangled with the board over national defense strikes. When the communist line changed abruptly in June 1941, John L. Lewis took up the cudgels by calling out his membership in the captive mines during the fall of 1941.[85] And when a majority of the board, including the two AFL representatives, voted against the union shop clause demanded by the miners, the two CIO representatives, Philip Murray and Thomas Kennedy, resigned, so that the board's effectiveness was

Sitdown strikers in the Flint General Motors plant, 1936.

The riot at the Chicago Republic Steel Company plant, 1937.

Reuther and Frankensteen after the battle of the Ford overpass, 1937.

Lewis and Murray during the Little Steel strike, 1937.

The leaders of the Steel Workers' Organizing Committee, 1937. Seated: Murray, McDonald. Standing: Mitch, Golden, Bittner, Pressman.

Photographs from Wide World Photos

The leadership of the CIO in 1937: Brophy, Howard, Lewis, Hillman.

Members of the Executive Council of the AFL, 1941. Seated: Meany, Green, Hutcheson. Standing: Flore, Bates.

Tobin and Green study the expulsion of the CIO unions, 1937.

Roosevelt and Lewis during the 1936 Presidential campaign.

Roosevelt and Green on Roosevelt's birthday, 1941.

The AFL-CIO Unity Negotiating Committee, 1937.

AFL and CIO leaders with Secretary of Labor Perkins, 1941.

Lewis and Taylor concluding the captive mine strike, 1941.

AFL Executive Council members at the White House, 1939: Lynch, Bugniazet, Green, Ornburn, Bates, Frey.

destroyed. The result was renewed activity in Congress on the part of those who were hostile to the labor movement. On December 3, 1941, the House of Representatives, by a vote of 252–136, enacted a fairly extreme antistrike bill.[86] Only the attack on Pearl Harbor four days later prevented similar action by the Senate. On January 12, 1942, President Roosevelt created the National War Labor Board by Executive order, and labor's no-strike pledge helped to forestall the proponents of restrictive legislation.

Corruption in the Labor Movement

The much publicized exposés of the McClellan Committee have given rise to the notion that labor corruption is a new phenomenon. This is not the case; from the days of P. J. McGuire,[87] the trade unions have been wrestling with the problem, and it will probably be with them as long as men are frail enough to yield to temptation, and as long as the institutional conditions which permit racketeering to flourish — namely, small unit size of enterprise, intense competition, a high degree of labor mobility, and an ethic among both employers and workers which regards this type of conduct as a normal way of doing business — continue to exist. Not only was the period of the nineteen-thirties no exception to the rule, but it was one in which the misdeeds of dishonest labor leaders received a great deal of publicity in the press, thanks to the indiscriminate attacks of Westbrook Pegler, a well-known newspaper columnist.

During the nineteen-thirties, the problem was made more serious by unemployment among gangsters occasioned by the repeal of the Prohibition Amendment. Labor unionism seemed to be a lucrative and relatively safe field of operation. Most of the infiltration by racketeers occurred in the service trades of a few large cities, but they did succeed in gaining control of two international unions affiliated with the AFL — the Building Service Employees' International Union and the International Association of Theatrical and Stage Employees. In 1934, with the help of the Capone gang in Chicago, George Scalise, an ex-convict, was made vice-president of the Building Service Union, and succeeded to the presidency in 1937 upon the death of the incumbent. He was not elected on either occasion, having been elevated by action of the executive board of the union. As a result of unremitting attacks on Scalise by Westbrook Pegler, the former appeared before the AFL Executive Council in 1940 to defend his record. Scalise admitted to having been in prison between the ages of 17 and 21 years, but attributed this to youthful mistakes. He vehemently denied ever having had any dealings with organized crime.[88] Although no action was taken by the council, Scalise was convicted soon thereafter of stealing $60,000 of union funds.[89]

The Capone gang was also instrumental in arranging for the election of George E. Browne to the presidency of the International Alliance of Theatrical Stage Employees in 1934. Browne, with the active assistance of William Bioff, a convicted panderer, proceeded to extort money from the large movie chains by threatening to harass them with strikes and such other unpleasantries as the throwing of stench bombs. Bioff received $50,000 a year from the larger movie companies and $25,000 a year from the smaller ones until he and Browne were indicted for extortion in 1941. It was revealed at the trial that Browne and Bioff had collected over one million dollars from the industry. Both men were convicted, Bioff receiving a ten-year term, and Browne, eight years.[90]

Browne had been a member of the Executive Council of the AFL, and after his indictment, the following cryptic note appeared in the minutes of the council:

The Council discussed the indictment of Vice-President George Browne on charges of extortion and possible reaction due to his position on the Council. Vice-President Hutcheson offered a motion that the matter be left in the hands of the President to the end that he work it out to the best interests of the labor movement. Carried.[91]

The 1941 AFL convention ran concurrently with the opening of Browne's trial. Browne was nevertheless nominated for another term as an AFL vice-president. However, at this point, an extremely unusual event occurred: another candidate, Edward Flore, was nominated to run against him. Without any discussion, Flore was elected by a vote of 37,950 to 421, with 3455 abstentions.[92] Thus, Browne ceased to be an AFL vice-president prior to his conviction, though the margin of time was not great.

These events, and many others on the local level, put increased pressure upon the AFL to undertake a housecleaning in its ranks. But the reply, as always in the past, was that the federation lacked jurisdiction over the internal affairs of its affiliates, that the federation's sole weapon was expulsion, too draconian a measure to be used against local malefactors. In its report to the 1940 convention, the AFL Executive Council, after denouncing racketeering and gangsterism, stated:

In dealing with this question, however, it must be pointed out that national and international unions chartered by the American Federation of Labor are autonomous organizations, exercising full and complete authority over their own administrative policies. . . . The American Federation of Labor could not confer upon these organizations full and complete power to administer their own affairs and at the same time reserve to itself the right to exercise dictatorial control. Such attitude would be contradictory. However, the Executive Council urges that the membership of national and international unions select and elect men of character, of known honesty and integrity to official positions, and prevent those with criminal records from either holding official positions or from representing them in any capacity whatsoever.

Nevertheless, the International Ladies' Garment Workers' Union, which had just reaffiliated with the AFL after breaking away from the CIO, introduced a resolution which would have given the AFL summary power to remove corrupt officials of affiliated organizations.[93] For his temerity in pushing this resolution, David Dubinsky, the ILGWU president, was rewarded by a punch delivered in a hotel lobby by Joseph G. Fay, a vice-president of the International Union of Operating Engineers, who spent a long term in the New York State penitentiary some years later.[94] The resolutions committee reported a much weakened version of the ILGWU proposal, merely recommending that all affiliates adopt appropriate provisions for dealing with corruption, and empowering the Executive Council, whenever it "has valid reason to believe that a trade union official is guilty of any such offense, and the National or International Union in question seemingly evades its responsibility, the Executive Council shall be authorized to apply all of its influence to secure such action as will correct the situation." [95]

This resolution, adopted by the convention, was soon put to the test in a case involving a colorful character, Jacob ("Jake the Bum") Wellner. Wellner, a close associate of notorious gangsters, had become business agent of Local 102 of the International Brotherhood of Painters in 1924, and proceeded to engage in wholesale extortion from employers. Efforts to induce the international union to remove him proved unavailing. Finally, in 1935, Wellner and three fellow officers were convicted of extortion and sentenced to indeterminate penitentiary terms.[96]

But this did not end Wellner's labor career. Upon his release from prison, after serving fifteen months, he was reinstated as head of the local union. Painters' District Council 18 of New York refused to recognize this action, but was threatened with charter revocation by the Executive Board of the Painters' Union unless it agreed to acknowledge Wellner's official position. The District Council appealed to the AFL Executive Council for protection against its own international union. Lawrence E. Lindelof, president of the Painters' Union, appeared before the Executive Council and argued that the only issue at stake was an internal fight over dues between Wellner and Sam Freeman, secretary-treasurer of the District Council; that Wellner, who was now completely rehabilitated, was merely acting to protect the interests of his membership. The Executive Council delegated Matthew Woll, one of its members, to determine whether the Painters' Union was living up to its responsibilities under the 1940 racketeering resolution.[97]

The Woll report, delivered several months later, made it clear that the 1940 resolution had not altered in any way the AFL policy of noninterference in the affairs of its affiliates. Woll pointed out that the 1940 convention had rejected the ILGWU resolution, and that no disciplinary power had been vested in the Executive Council. He urged Painters' District Council 18 to exhaust the constitutional processes of its organization by appealing to the convention from the ruling of the Painters' Executive Board, but he concluded that, if the appeal were rejected: "Even then it is not clear how the Federation can do other than use its good influence should it find 'an evasion of responsibility on the part of the General Executive Board' of the Brotherhood. . . . The Federation has no compulsory or disciplinary power. The power delegated to it is that of the use of its influence." The Executive Council approved the report and referred the entire matter to William Green, who was to use his "good influence" with Lindelof.

The AFL acted somewhat more vigorously against corrupt officials of federal locals directly under its control. For example, officers of a Scrap Iron local in Chicago and a Fish and Sea Food Workers' union in New York (in the latter case, a notorious gentleman named Joseph "Socks" Lanza) were removed. But the 1941 convention reasserted with emphasis the traditional barrier of autonomy between the AFL and corruption, and decried the "columnists and labor-hating newspaper publishers" who demanded that "the officers of the American Federation of Labor be dictators, punish men, regardless of law and lawful procedure, who they believe are guilty of the commission of crimes. They demand that the officers of the American Federation of Labor be dictators when they feel said officers should be dictators, but denounce them if they assume dictatorial power." However, all AFL central bodies were directed to refuse to seat any delegate who had been convicted of a serious wrong doing, as evidence of continued AFL concern.[98]

The problem of labor corruption remained an unsolved one at the time of United States entry into war in 1941. Another decade of exposure and constant attack from outside was to ensue before the shibboleth of autonomy began to crumble in the face of so obvious an evil.[99] And it was not until there occurred a drastic shift in internal power, occasioned by the merger between the AFL and the CIO, that the American labor movement fully assumed its responsibility for eradicating the stain of corruption that had so long afflicted it.

Trade Unionism and the Negro[100]

There was considerable diversity of policy among American trade unions with respect to their treatment of Negroes, before the inception of the New Deal. A number of important unions, including the International Association of Machinists and the operating brotherhoods on the railroads, excluded Negroes from membership by constitutional provision. Others kept them out unofficially; to this group belonged the Electrical Workers and the Plumbers. Still others established auxiliary "Jim Crow" locals in which Negroes were segregated and permitted to pay dues, but often denied proportional representation, or any representation, in union affairs. The Railway Clerks, the Boilermakers, and the Sheet Metal Workers fell into the latter category.[101] On the other hand, some trade unions operating in industries which employed a considerable amount of Negro labor maintained an open-door policy toward the Negro and accorded him full membership status. The industrial unions generally belonged to this group — the United Mine Workers, the men's and women's clothing workers — but also such craft unions as the Bricklayers and Laborers in the building trades.

The reasons for these variations in the treatment of a minority group are as diverse as the reasons for the discrimination against Negroes in society generally. The nature and geography of employment, the social philosophy of union leadership, the structure of the union, the fund of employment opportunities, are some of the relevant factors specific to the labor movement. We cannot concern ourselves here with the general problem, which has been the subject of a number of monographs.[102] Rather, we shall concentrate on the racial attitudes of the top echelons of the labor movement, and indicate briefly the modifications both in attitude and policy which accompanied the rapid expansion of organization during the nineteen thirties.

It may be well at the outset to point out that the problem involved almost exclusively the American Federation of Labor and the independent railway brotherhoods. Northrup found that "no national CIO union excludes Negro workers from membership nor segregates its colored members into Jim Crow local unions. Moreover, the national officers of the CIO unions have, by and large, a consistent record of practicing what they preach in regard to the treatment of Negroes." [103] Successful industrial organization in industries employing sizable numbers of Negroes was premised upon equality of treatment. But this is far from the whole story; the leading members of the original CIO, the miners and the garment workers, were consistent exponents of racial equality, and they carried with them into the new organization a strong ethical belief in nondiscrimination which was imparted to the newer unions.

The evolution of AFL racial policies during the nineteen-thirties was profoundly influenced by a remarkable individual, the outstanding Negro trade unionist in American labor history, A. Philip Randolph. Randolph, a socialist intellectual, became interested in the plight of the Negro railroad worker, and in 1925, aided in the formation of the Brotherhood of Sleeping Car Porters, an all-Negro organization which he has headed from the date of its organization to the present writing. William Green became interested in the Brotherhood, and sought to bring it into the AFL. [104] The Brotherhood applied for an international charter in 1928, but the application was blocked by the Hotel and Restaurant Employees' Union, which claimed jurisdiction over Pullman porters. As a compromise, the Brotherhood locals received federal charters from the AFL. Randolph was strongly criticized within Negro circles for accepting this status, but he felt that the long-run interests of the porters could better be advanced from within the AFL.

From 1928 to 1933, the Brotherhood declined in strength, but beginning in 1933, it made a comeback, and in June 1935, won exclusive bargaining rights for Pullman porters in a National Mediation Board election. In 1934, the Brotherhood once more sought an international charter, only to have the AFL Executive Council grant jurisdiction over Pullman porters to the Order of Sleeping Car Conductors, a small union which restricted membership to whites. This union catered to combined conductor-porters who were gradually being eliminated from service. In attempting to protect the jobs of its members it had, among other things, appealed to southern race prejudice by intimating that women and children were not safe in sleeping cars manned only by Negro porters. Partly as a result of this propaganda, a number of southern states decreed that white Pullman conductors would have to be in charge of cars operated within their jurisdictions.

The Sleeping Car Porters refused to accept this jurisdictional award, and informed the AFL that it would withdraw unless granted a charter. The Executive Council bowed to this demand in August 1935, though the charter was not finally presented until almost a year later because of the necessity of compromising several conflicting jurisdictional claims. On June 7, 1938, the Brotherhood became the first Negro international union ever to receive a charter from the main body of organized labor in the United States.

Even before this event, which was hastened by the growing challenge of the CIO, Randolph had emerged as the principal spokesman for Negro labor within the councils of the AFL. The 1934 AFL convention, largely as a result of his prodding, directed the Executive Council to appoint a committee "to investigate the conditions of the colored workers of this country and report to the next convention." [105] The committee held hearings in Washington, D. C., and made a three-point recommendation: (1) all international unions practicing discrimination in any way should take up the Negro question at their next convention and bring their constitutions, rules, and practices in harmony with the official AFL position on racial equality; (2) all charters issued by the AFL should be in conformity with this position; (3) all AFL officers and publications should carry on an educational campaign in order to "get the white worker to see more completely the weakness of division and the necessity of greater trade union unity between white and black workers to the end that all workers may be organized."

The Executive Council referred this report to George H. Harrison, president of the Railway Clerks, a union which excluded Negroes from membership. Harrison's report was not submitted to the convention until its last day, and probably would not have come up at all had not Randolph raised the issue sharply on the floor of the convention. The recommendation made by Harrison and backed by the Executive Council was merely that in view of the autonomous status of AFL affiliates, action should be confined to an educational campaign. Randolph argued for the original committee recommendation, but his voice, and that of his colleague, Milton P. Webster, were the only ones raised in its defense. William Green embroidered upon the autonomy theme, while George M. Harrison admitted that the exclusionist policy of his union, the Railway Clerks, was a wrong one, but stated that it had not yet been possible to convince his membership to change it.[106] Needless to say, the recommendation of the Executive Council was adopted.

Randolph continued his campaign at the annual conventions of the AFL. In 1936, he charged that nothing at all had been done to implement the educational campaign resolution adopted in 1935.[107] Two years later he was successful in getting the convention to concur in the intent of a resolution calling upon all AFL affiliates to end discriminatory practices.[108] But the resolutions were not backed by deeds, and there is no evidence to indicate that the Executive Council gave the question any serious consideration throughout this period.

In 1940, amidst a growing demand for governmental action to protect the rights of Negro workers, Randolph tried a new approach. He proposed that the AFL create an interracial committee to investigate charges of trade union discrimination against Negroes, and recommend appropriate action to the Executive Council. Similar committees were to be appointed by city central bodies. To the argument that the international union leadership could not control its southern membership on the racial issue, Randolph retorted:

Well, we are down here in the South in New Orleans, and I think we had just as well start here on a program of educating the Southern white workers, because the Southern white workers are in the midst of a fight themselves. Thousands and millions of them are in poverty and ignorance and superstition. The only difference between a black worker and a white worker in the South is the color of the skin. Southern white workers are victims of exploitation, just like the black workers of the South, and they have not yet realized that unity in the labor movement between the black and the white workers is the only remedy for this exploitation.

This plea, like the earlier ones, fell on deaf ears. Negro feelings were further exacerbated by a protest by federal unions of Negro freight handlers against transfer to the Brotherhood of Railway Clerks on an auxiliary basis, without the right to handle their own grievances or send delegates to national conventions.[109] William Green promised Randolph, on the floor of the convention, that there would be a letter from George Harrison, president of the Railway Clerks, guaranteeing the Negro workers full membership rights, but he was unable to explain how this letter could be sent out in contravention of specific Brotherhood constitutional provisions. When, a few months later, several federal locals refused to surrender their charters, the charters were revoked. Some of the Negro freight handlers declined to go into the Railway Clerks and set up an independent organization, the National Council of Freight Handlers, Express and Station Employees, but it was unable to win any bargaining rights under National Mediation Board rules, and gradually declined, eventually affiliating with the CIO Utility Workers' Organizing Committee.[110] The locals which agreed to join the Railway Clerks received auxiliary status.

Another group of workers, the red caps, was more successful in breaking away from the jurisdictional dominance of white AFL unions. In 1936, the

Chicago red caps secured a federal local charter from the AFL, and the following year, took the initiative in calling a conference of red-cap locals that had sprung up in a number of cities. Out of this conference emerged the International Brotherhood of Red Caps, an independent union. For the next few years, the Brotherhood concentrated on winning regular employee status for its members, and on substituting a basic wage for the tipping system then in effect. The first goal was achieved on September 29, 1938, when the Interstate Commerce Commission held that red caps were employees under the Railway Labor Act. By the end of 1941, the Brotherhood, which had changed its name to the United Transport Service Employees of America in 1940, held 33 collective agreements, most of them providing for a regular basic wage.[111]

The Brotherhood of Railway Clerks, which claimed jurisdiction over red caps, tried to block the spread of the new organization. The result was that in 1942, the Transport Employees Union secured a CIO charter, one of the few footholds the CIO was able to gain among the nation's railroad workers.

Leaders of the Negro community decided that internal appeal to the labor movement was not likely to be effective. In the spring of 1941, a representative group, under the leadership of A. Philip Randolph, resolved to call upon 50,000 Negroes to march on Washington in protest against their exclusion from defense industry. President Roosevelt, in order to head the march off, issued Executive Order 8802 on June 25, 1941, which stipulated that all defense contracts contain nondiscrimination clauses, and set up a Committee on Fair Employment Practices to police the requirement. The committee, which had no enforcement authority and a very small budget, proved ineffective, but in 1943 it was reconstituted and given broader authority.[112]

Armed with a governmental declaration against discrimination in defense production, Randolph returned to the attack at the 1941 AFL convention, and precipitated the most bitter debate on the racial issue that had theretofore taken place in the labor movement. This time Randolph cited specific instances of the exclusion of Negroes from defense work: among the unions he named as barring Negroes locally were the Painters, the Plasterers and Cement Finishers, the AFL metal trades exercising jurisdiction over shipyards, the Machinists, the Boilermakers, and the Carpenters. He issued personal challenges to some of the top AFL leaders. Of John Frey, the head of the Metal Trades, he declared: "Now, no doubt we all know that Mr. Frey has a fine spirit and believes in sound trade union

principles, but when it comes to the application of these principles with relation to the Negro they do not always seem to hold up." Referring to exclusion of Negroes from the Boeing aircraft plant, he said to Harvey Brown,
president of the Machinists' Union: "Brother Brown has an obligation to
make a statement to America on this matter," and then continued: "if the
Machinists Union is going to persistently defy the President's executive order, then the American Federation of Labor ought to put the Machinists
Union out. We ought to have some way of washing the hands of the American Federation of Labor of the stigma of discrimination."

Some of the leaders of the accused unions took the floor of the convention in self-defense. John Frey delivered a vitriolic *ad hominem* attack on
Randolph:

The delegate [Randolph] . . . has an advantage over every other delegate who
is present. He is the only one who has had the full advantages of an education
in Harvard University. He studied logic, he studied philosophy, he studied ethics,
he studied the humanities and human nature as well, and I again express regret
that a trade union delegate should rise and present the type of indictment which
this highly cultured individual presented this morning.[113]

Frey, and other speakers on the same issue, advanced well-worn arguments: that the AFL did not create racial prejudice, but rather had helped
mitigate it; that raising the matter to public prominence would tend to
inflame anti-Negro opinion; that an AFL committee would be powerless
in the face of the constitutional autonomy of AFL affiliates. President
Hutcheson of the Carpenters' Union summed up the objections to the
Randolph resolution neatly:

If the situation were reversed and a resolution was introduced to this convention
to try to direct the internationals as to what their membership could consist of,
what does he or any other delegate think the internationals would say to this
convention? As far as our organization is concerned, we would tell you to go
plumb to and stay there, if you chose.

Despite the continued refusal of the AFL to meet the racial issue
squarely, it would be wrong to conclude that the Negro worker had not
benefited from the upsurge of unionism that preceded American entrance
into the war. Negroes were accorded full membership rights and privileges
in the industrial unions in the automobile, steel, meat packing, coal mining,
and longshore industries, where they constituted a substantial proportion of
the labor force. Outside the South, the position of the Negro building crafts-
man improved vis-à-vis organized labor.[114] Only on the railroads, where the
situation was complicated by a drastic decline in total employment, was there

retrogression rather than progress toward racial equality. Northrup, after a careful study, delivered the following verdict on railroad unionism:

The Negro railroad worker suffers from serious discrimination by employers and unions — discrimination that is assisted by the policies of government agencies. . . . In no other industry has collective bargaining had such disastrous results for Negroes. . . .

No labor law can provide "a model labor policy, based on equal rights and equitable relations," if it is used as a means of economically disenfranchising a minority race. Yet the Amended Railway Labor Act has served such a purpose. Under it, the National Mediation Board often designates as exclusive bargaining agent for Negroes a union which excludes Negroes, or affords them only inferior status. . . . The record of the National Railroad Adustment Board is even more open to criticism.[115]

The record of the AFL on the Negro question during the nineteen-thirties was not one of which the organization could be proud. Yet there were hopeful signs of change. At the beginning of the decade, the AFL top leadership treated the issue quite cavalierly. As A. Philip Randolph continued to prod the conscience of the labor movement on its dealings with the black worker, the AFL became more and more defensive on the issue, and was forced to give it serious consideration. By the technique of threatening to name offending unions on the floor of the convention, Randolph was able to secure a considerable improvement in the practices of many "autonomous" internationals. This unremitting moral pressure is a factor not to be underestimated in assessing the reasons for change. Many an international officer, personally in favor of extending equality of membership rights to Negroes, was induced by the fear of public exposure to go before his executive board and an often recalcitrant membership to argue a position on which he might have preferred to remain silent for internal political reasons.

Agricultural Unionism[116]

During the early nineteen-thirties, the Communist Party, through its Trade Union Unity League affiliate, the Cannery and Agricultural Workers Industrial Union, dominated the field of trade unionism in agriculture. With the change of the communist trade union line 1935, this organization was abandoned, and a National Committee for Unity of Agriculture and Rural Workers was substituted to work for affiliation of local farm unions to the AFL. By the summer of 1935, some 23 federal labor unions had been chartered by the AFL.

The 1935 AFL convention resolved that the Executive Council should

plan a national organizing campaign in agriculture.[117] But the main drive
for organization came from left-wing organizers operating under the banner
of the AFL. This group pressed aggressively for a national charter at the
1936 AFL convention, claiming that there were 62 agricultural locals in
existence, more than sufficient to warrant autonomy.[118] The convention
refused to grant the charter, referring the matter instead to the Executive
Council. When the matter finally came up before the Council, William
Green told it:

I think all of us having had experience in matters of this kind and realizing
fully the complications that are ever-present in the establishment of a local union
of Agricultural and Cannery Workers agree that the establishment of an international union would be premature. They apparently are not ready for that.
They cannot pay much dues. They are a temperamental and diversified group
and might possibly break up. You might leave the matter in my hands again of
assembling a conference of Agricultural and Cannery Workers for the purpose
of establishing a national council as a preliminary step to the formation of an
international union at a later date.[119]

In California, where a considerable number of cannery workers had been
organized, a tug of war developed between the proponents of industrial
unionism, backed by Harry Bridges' longshoremen, and those who favored
separate organization of the more stable cannery workers, who were supported by the California State Federation of Labor and the Teamsters'
Union. A pro-CIO California Federation of Agriculture and Cannery
Unions, formed in 1937, took the initiative in calling a national convention
in Denver during July 1937. There, a new organization, the United Cannery, Agricultural, Packing and Allied Workers of America, received a national charter from the CIO. "It included such diverse occupational and
sectional groups as cannery workers from Maryland, landscape and cannery workers from the Middle West, mushroom workers from New York,
sharecroppers and cottonfield laborers from Arkansas and Alabama, beet
workers from the Rocky Mountain States, citrus workers from Florida, and
fruit, vegetable and fish cannery workers from the North Atlantic and
Pacific Coasts." [120]

Aided by the CIO finances,[121] the United Cannery Workers made rapid
progress. A membership claim of 125,000 was made at the time of the 1938
CIO convention, but this figure was doubtless exaggerated. Its principal
strength was in commodity processing rather than in primary agriculture.
Attempts to organize field workers were costly and not successful. Not only

was there vigorous opposition from associations of farmers, but strife with the AFL constituted a serious obstacle in many parts of the country.

AFL activities in agriculture were concentrated in California, where a National Council of Agricultural and Cannery Workers, dominated by the Teamsters, was set up in 1937. Aided by the economic power of the Teamsters, some 20,000 agricultural workers were organized in 64 federal locals by the latter part of 1938. But adverse economic conditions slowed organization by both CIO and AFL. The CIO Cannery Workers Union was obliged to reduce its organizing staff because of a lack of funds, and began to decline in strength. Efforts to reach field workers were abandoned, and the meager resources available were concentrated on holding processing centers near urban communities. The cause of the CIO agricultural workers was not strengthened by the fact that the union was from its inception under the domination of the Communist Party; its president, Donald Henderson, later admitted to Communist Party membership.[122] This ideological commitment was used effectively by anti-union employers and by rival organizations.

The AFL continued to be active in the agricultural field, though without conspicuous success. The Executive Council reported to the 1940 convention only that progress was being made;[123] no reference at all was made to the agricultural labor situation the following year. An organizing drive was carried on in California in 1940 and 1941, culminating in a citrus-fruit strike that ended in defeat for the union after five months, despite boycott assistance from the Teamsters.[124]

An interesting organization which developed along different lines was the Southern Tenant Farmers' Union, organized in 1934 under Socialist Party influence among the tenant farmers of western Arkansas and eastern Oklahoma. Despite strong opposition from farm owners and the complications caused by the mixed laborer-tenant composition of its membership, the union made considerable progress during its early years. On January 1, 1937, it claimed 30,827 members in 328 locals. It affiliated with the United Cannery Workers in 1937 on the promise that its autonomy would be respected, and during subsequent years functioned more as a pressure group and legislative agent for its members than as a trade union. In 1939, the Cannery Workers' Union attempted to exercise a greater degree of control over its affiliate, with the result that a majority of the Tenant Farmer locals seceded. Those that remained in the Cannery Workers were integrated into the structure of the union, and were abandoned within a few years.[125]

The seceding locals sought to join the AFL. Their representatives told the AFL Executive Council in 1940 that there were 72 functioning locals with almost 3000 paid members, two-thirds of them working on cotton plantations and the rest tenant farmers. David Dubinsky, whose organization was then active in the South, urged that the Southern Tenant Farmers be chartered by the AFL, but the Executive Council refused to accede.[126] In 1941, the union's executive secretary, H. L. Mitchell, recommended that the organization concentrate entirely on political activity in the interests of the small farmer, and abandon all attempts to operate as a trade union. He stated:

There is no basis for trade-unionism in southern agriculture with conditions such as prevail. No method can be devised whereby an organization of economically insecure people such as tenant farmers, sharecroppers, and farm laborers on southern plantations can bargain with an industry that is disorganized, pauperized, and kept alive only by Government subsidy as is cotton and tobacco production today.[127]

The organizing drives of 1937–1941 left little permanent impression upon agriculture proper. In 1944, the Cannery Workers' Union changed its name to the Food, Tobacco and Allied Workers of America, emphasizing its complete withdrawal from farming. It was subsequently expelled from the CIO because of communist domination. The various AFL agricultural locals that survived the war, when there was little union activity, were chartered as the National Farm Labor Union, and under the guidance of H. L. Mitchell, who had once headed the Southern Tenant Farmers' Union, devoted itself primarily to educational and legislative work, after an unsuccessful major effort to organize the giant Di Giorgio ranch in California.[128]

The American labor movement was thus unable to duplicate in agriculture what it had achieved in industry. Neither communist, socialist, nor pure business unionism succeeded in solving the problem of creating a viable organization that could hold the allegiance of the rural worker. There are many hurdles in the way of agricultural unionism, among them the lack of skill among farm workers, making for ease of substitution; the small unit size of the average agricultural operation; the great heterogeneity of the farm labor group; the instability of farm employment; the sharply downward secular trend in the demand for farm labor; the temporary nature of much farm employment; the strongly anti-union attitude of most farm employers; and the difficulty of charging sufficiently high dues to support effective organization.[129] Not even the great burst of energy released by the New Deal could overcome these obstacles. The great decade of trade union organization left behind it virtually no result in field work. Only in the manufacturing operations allied with agriculture, the processing plants and canneries, was there any residue of the most ambitious attempt in American history to bring unionism to the farm.

Foreign Affairs

During World War I, the American Federation of Labor, like the rest of the country, was drawn into the vortex of international affairs. Samuel Gompers played an important role in the reestablishment of the International Federation of Trade Unions, but he and other AFL leaders quickly became alienated by what they regarded as the excessive radicalism of the organization, and by its tendency to regard affiliates as subordinate bodies rather than completely autonomous units. After some initial hesitation, the AFL refused to affiliate with the IFTU, and slipped back into the isolationism characteristic of the time. Absorbed with domestic problems — the employer offensive of the nineteen-twenties and the consequent serious decline in organizational strength — the American labor movement maintained for a decade and a half only a mild and occasional interest in what was taking place abroad.[130]

The advent of Hitler to power in 1933, and the smashing of the powerful German trade unions, gave rise to apprehension within the AFL, and created a new interest in European affairs. In 1934, the United States government joined the International Labor Organization, and the AFL was designated as the agency to select labor representatives to the annual conferences. The following year, the convention of the AFL adopted a resolution empowering the Executive Council to enter into negotiations with the IFTU looking toward eventual AFL affiliation.[131]

Negotiations lagged, for there were many members of the Executive Council who distrusted the European socialist trade unionists and wanted nothing to do with them. Thus, in May 1936, the council decided "that we do not deem it an appropriate time to affiliate with the International Federation of Trade Unions." [132] The IFTU, however, weakened by the loss of its German affiliate and increasingly pressed by the international communist movement, was exceedingly anxious for American participation in its councils, and sent Walter Citrine and Walter Schevenels to argue the matter with the Executive Council. These two representatives of international trade unionism, armed with plenary power, promised the AFL that it would not have to pay the high dues to which it had long objected, and guaranteed full autonomy in every respect. As a result, the AFL Council despatched Matthew Woll, its most internationally-minded member, to a meeting of the IFTU at Warsaw in July 1937, with instructions to apply for admission.

This about-face was not caused by any sudden change of heart on international relations, but was rather the result of the CIO threat on the domestic front. When Woll arrived in Warsaw, he found that Leon Jouhaux of France and Corneille Mertens of Belgium were working for CIO affiliation, which would have given the new rival to the AFL considerable prestige. However, the British threatened to withdraw from the IFTU unless the AFL was admitted, and this decided the issue. The AFL became the sole United States affiliate of the IFTU, and agreed to pay half the standard per capita tax. This action was affirmed by the 1937 AFL convention.[133]

Thwarted at Warsaw, the CIO attempted to gain a foothold at the ILO in Geneva. Robert Watt, a Massachusetts AFL official who was regarded as not unfriendly to the CIO, was pushed by the latter as a compromise candidate for the ILO governing board. The Executive Council of the AFL was not particularly happy over Watt's election to the post, but was obliged to approve him lest the CIO, which at the time had closer relationships with the Roosevelt administration, secure the right to represent American labor in Geneva.[134]

Despite affiliation with the IFTU, the AFL continued to view involvement in international affairs with its traditional mistrust. In 1938, Citrine asked the AFL to join with European unions in an embargo on the shipment of arms to Japan and a boycott of Japanese goods, in retaliation for the Japanese foray into China. William Green told the Executive Council:

It appears to me we could advise them that while we are sympathetic toward any plan that has for its purpose the promotion of world peace and against war including the aggression of Japan in China that we are reluctant to take any action that might involve our own nation in war and that we propose to carry on the boycott ordered by our convention as aggressively as possible and go just as far as we can in the application of that boycott.

The council informed Citrine that while it favored the boycott, it could neither participate in an international boycott and embargo conference, nor make formal representations to the United States government.

The AFL was very much disturbed by negotiations in 1937 and 1938 looking toward the admission of the Russian trade unions into the IFTU. When an IFTU committee which included Jouhaux and Schevenels negotiated a conditional agreement with the Russians, the AFL Executive Council adopted a strong resolution in opposition to admission of the Russians under any conditions. Citrine, the head of the British trade union movement, sent personal reassurances to the AFL:

You can judge my amazement when I read in the newspapers that an agreement for a United Front had been come to. . . . I regret to say that it seems to me that the delegation went much further than they were entitled to do, and that their attitude has seriously compromised the I.F.T.U. Executive . . . there is not the remotest chance that the I.F.T.U. Executive will accept their proposals even if this necessitates our publicly repudiating the delegation.

In May 1938, by a vote of 16 to 4, the IFTU executive rejected Soviet affiliation, and on a motion by Woll, agreed that no further negotiations should be undertaken with the Russians.[135] At a meeting of the Congress of the IFTU in July 1939, the British, in view of the changed situation and the imminence of war, reversed their stand and urged that the Russian trade unions be invited to join, but this resolution was narrowly defeated by a vote of 46 to 37.[136]

On the issue of the Spanish civil war, which became a major campaign in the communist-controlled CIO unions, the AFL remained neutral. When Matthew Woll, on his way to an IFTU meeting in Europe in 1938, asked for instructions, it was reported that William Green was under tremendous pressure to commit the AFL to the cause of the Loyalist government, but had refrained from taking any position. Green told the AFL Executive Council:

If there are no objections, Brother Woll will follow that course, maintaining a neutral attitude towards the civil war in Spain and maintaining the traditional policy of the American Federation of Labor.[137]

The reaction of American labor to the outbreak of war in Europe did not differ in any significant respect from the reaction of the American people generally. The AFL, in 1939, expressed itself as "unalterably opposed to our own nation becoming involved in European conflicts." [138] The CIO resolved "that organized labor is emphatically opposed to any involvement of the United States in the European war." [139] When the Low Countries were invaded, in 1940, the AFL Executive Council adopted the following statement:

The Executive Council of the American Federation of Labor does not see how the entry of the United States into the European war would serve the cause of peace. On the contrary, we feel that if we steadfastly maintain our neutrality we will be in a better position to aid in the reconstruction of Europe when the war is over. On behalf of the workers of this country, we make the flat declaration that the United States should remain out of the war.[140]

Within the ranks of the CIO, there was a greater polarity of viewpoints on the European war. At a meeting of the Executive Board in 1940, when a resolution for presentation to the next convention was being discussed, Thomas Burns of the Rubber Workers wanted the CIO to condemn aggression, arguing: "I don't think we can remain neutral completely today. There comes a time when there is a decision that must be made on the question of right or wrong." But John L. Lewis quickly quelled an incipient revolt against his uncompromising neutralism, saying: "The committee felt slightly incapable of passing judgment on all the quarrels of Europe. I know I do. . . . I doubt that the committee in a very brief document expressing the matter of policy could undertake to pass on all the events that have transpired in Europe or may transpire in Asia." [141] He was backed by Philip Murray, who emphasized the neutrality policy of the CIO, and by Michael Quill, who followed the communist line in describing the war as a profiteering, imperialist war.

When the resolution was presented to the 1940 convention, several delegates were somewhat critical of its basic philosophy, although they did not openly oppose it. Walter Reuther, for example, stated:

We are involved in a situation in the world today where everything we are fighting for is affected, and we talk about Indians and buffaloes, but it does not change the fact that just this week the war mongers of Europe, Hitler, Stalin and Mussolini, are planning how they are going to carve up the rest of the world that still remains.[142]

Buckmaster of the Rubber Workers echoed these sentiments: ". . . let's be honest, let's not kid ourselves, let's not get the idea in our heads that we have a choice between war and peace." However, the convention, under the domination of John L. Lewis, merely resolved against any entanglements which might involve the nation in war.

With the deepening of the European crisis, the American labor movement began to lose its confidence in the validity of neutralism. The 1940 AFL convention came out in favor of all possible assistance to Britain short of war.[143] After the German invasion of Russia, the AFL advocated assistance to the latter "for practical reasons alone, and without the slightest pretense that the United States and Soviet Russia are friends or can be friends." [144]

The German attack solved an incipient crisis over foreign policy within the CIO. Prior to June 1941, the communist wing, allied with supporters of John L. Lewis, were militant advocates of isolation in foreign affairs, and opposed even economic aid to Britain. Another wing, led by Sidney Hillman and including Walter Reuther, favored all-out aid to the embattled democracies, although not going so far as to advocate the entrance of the United States into the war. Philip Murray, although his sympathies were with the Hillman wing, remained quiet in deference to his old chief. However, when the communists switched over to an extreme interventionist policy, Lewis remained alone; even Murray became antagonized by his attempted machinations within the CIO. Consequently, delegates to the 1941 CIO convention vied with one another in support of a resolution offering complete support to the Roosevelt policy of furnishing aid to Great Britain, the Soviet Union, and China, "which are the nations now carrying on the struggle to rid the world of Nazism, the enemy of mankind." [145]

It may fairly be said of the American labor movement during the five years prior to American entry into the war that apart from the ideologically motivated elements, it was neither more nor less interested in foreign affairs than the American public. There was little awareness of the significance of contemporary events in Europe and Asia for the future of the American worker. Despite a sense of uneasiness generated by the crushing of European trade unionism, and despite the renewed association of the AFL with the international labor movement, organized labor in the United States made no effort to lead the country into a more active antitotalitarian position. Gestures of sympathy were forthcoming, and even resolutions in favor of economic boycotts — resolutions which fitted in well, in any event, with the immediate economic interests of the American worker — but the foreign policy of the United States was determined with neither the help nor the hindrance of the labor movement. Generally speaking, foreign affairs were of interest primarily in their impact upon domestic politics. Thus, the AFL, in rejoining the IFTU, and the CIO, in seeking to establish foreign contacts, were engaged in a struggle for a measure of prestige that might influence the outcome of their internecine struggle. Of concern for foreign policy *qua* foreign policy there is no evidence in the record. It required four years of active participation in war and the emergence of the United States as the dominant world power to awaken the American labor movement to its responsibilities not only in international labor affairs, but even more generally, in the formulation of American foreign policy.

In historical writing, there is always the danger of losing one's way in a maze of facts, and of failing to make out the broad design of events. Wherever possible, we have endeavored, in treating individual trade unions and industries, to present sufficient background material to obviate this danger.

The final chapter considered some aspects of a more general nature. It now remains only to delineate the main trends and to make a few observations that may serve to render the detail more meaningful.

It would be gratifying to be able to fit the events that have been described into a neat theoretical pattern. A simple general theory is always more satisfying than a series of variables which do not behave properly when confronted with empirical data. Professor Selig Perlman, whose name is linked with a well known theory of American labor, professes to see in the events of the New Deal period a confirmation of his theoretical structure. He sums the period up in the following terms:

The American labor program, indicative of its basic philosophy, has shown remarkable steadfastness through times of rapid external change. The objective . . . is unaltered from Gompers' day — the methods, even outside the immediate vicinity of the job, showing no more change than could be accounted for by the changing environment.[146]

The matter would seem much more complicated; there is no clear image of a straight-line trend of trade union development running through the cataclysmic events of the nineteen-thirties. It is difficult to see in the labor movement that emerged from the New Deal a recrudescent Gompersism, and difficult to accept the notion that job control and exclusive jurisdiction occupied the same central role that they once undoubtedly did in labor thinking. On the contrary, the watchword of the period was change, induced partly by growth and partly by radical alteration in the political and economic environment. Nor is it easy to perceive any simple, unifying principle that provides a key to the tangled skein of facts. A number of currents run through the total picture, but no one of them can be regarded as the ultimate determinant.

On the important issue of exclusive jurisdiction and the AFL, Professor Dunlop has said, with justification:

The will to make final decisions, the machinery to enforce decisions, and the consequences of non-agreement or expulsion all led to a gradual abandonment of decision making and to a greater resort to pressure for agreement, postponement and ad hoc solutions to particular situations. Internally, the system of exclusive jurisdiction had seriously declined in its vitality before it was challenged from outside.[147]

The traditional concept of jurisdiction was rendered obsolete by the rise of the CIO and the assumption by the federal government of the function of determining the unit of collective bargaining, which had earlier been the exclusive prerogative of the labor movement itself. The obsession with carving out and holding fiercely to a job territory, which had been characteristic of such dominant AFL figures as William L. Hutcheson, Arthur Wharton, and John Frey, gave way to a concept which permitted conflicting union claims to jurisdiction legitimately to exist.

Structurally, as well, the labor movement underwent great changes under the New Deal. The issue of craft versus industrial unionism, hotly debated within the labor movement for decades as a theoretical issue, was quickly settled in practice when the CIO overran the mass production industries. Unions which were in the forefront of the ideological struggle against the industrial form of organization, the Carpenters, the Teamsters, and the Machinists, found themselves transformed into multi-industrial giants by the pressure of circumstances. The principal cause of the CIO split, the unwillingness of the craft unions to relinquish jurisdiction in large industrial establishments, faded into obscurity as the AFL unions, one by one, eagerly welcomed the semiskilled factory workers as members, and faced new problems of internal government and structure.

How much of the change can be ascribed to economic factors, how much to politics, and how much to such fortuitous circumstances as personal ambitions, quality of leadership, and the concatenation of other events that went to make up a particular situation, cannot be determined easily. It would be foolish to deny the relevance of underlying economic forces. Indeed, if there is one lesson to be drawn from the foregoing pages, it is the powerful influence exerted by economic developments. At every turn, ambitions were furthered or thwarted, political disputes resolved, institutions altered by business fluctuations. Such factors as size and location of enterprise, the nature of product competition, and the elasticity of product demand were seen to be crucial determinants of organizational success. Unions in the grip of alien political philosophies sometimes succeeded where traditional democratic leadership failed, depending upon the economics of the particular situation encountered.

But to look upon trade unions as being in the grip of immutable, impersonal economic forces, unable to effect any basic alteration in underlying market relationships, is grossly to misread the lessons of history. Certainly, neither wage nor other union policy can be formulated successfully without regard to current business conditions. It is abundantly clear from the record that trade union officials are careful students of the labor and product markets in which they operate. But this is far from being the entire story. The introduction of trade unionism has had profound effects upon the entire social life of the factory, upon management practices and prerogatives, upon every term and condition of employment. Some of the things that led men to organize have been well described by Walter Reuther:

As the curtain rose on CIO, injustice was as commonplace as streetcars. When men walked into their jobs, they left their dignity, their citizenship and their humanity outside. They were required to report for duty whether there was work or not. While they waited on the convenience of supervisors and foremen they were unpaid. They could be fired without the necessity for a pretext. They were subjected to arbitrary, senseless rules — no smoking, no eating, no resting. Men were tortured by regulations that made difficult even going to the toilet. Favoritism was endemic to the factory. Men were fired to make way for supervisors' nephews, foremen's brothers-in-law, college chums. Long years of employment entitled workers to nothing. When men slowed down at forty or forty-five they were laid off without hope of recall. After layoffs there was never any assurance that a man would get his job back if work started up again, or if he did get his job that he would return to work at his old pay.[148]

Such type of grievance was fully as "economic" as anything related to wages. But even beyond this, trade unions have often been able to modify the institutions of the product market as well as the labor market, and thus to alter their economic capabilities. To make statistical correlations of union strength and wage trends, and to conclude therefrom that basically, union influence has not been great, is to accept a static model of labor organization. Looking backward, there can be very little doubt that trade unionism has had profound effects on the performance of the American economy.

The rate of growth of unionism during the New Deal period was not constant. It came rather in the form of several short, explosive bursts, and each time a decline to the previous level was prevented by a ratchet-like effect. The first advance came in 1933 as a consequence of the enactment of the National Industrial Recovery Act. This episode paved the way for later progress by creating stable organization among the coal miners and garment workers. A second wave, the most important of all, came early in 1937, when the CIO successfully invaded heavy industry. The recession of this tide left intact nuclei of organization in steel, autos, electrical manufacturing, rubber, and the maritime trades, which were enlarged as soon as the defense boom offered a suitable opportunity.

The successive waves of organization resulted from a conjuncture of favorable circumstances. In 1933, the political repercussions of the Democratic electoral victory played a leading role. Workers were told that President Roosevelt, widely regarded as the savior of the nation from utter economic collapse, wanted them to join unions. But many of the hopes of this period were dashed against the persistence of widespread unemployment and business stagnation, and trade unionism failed to spread far beyond its traditional bounds.

A necessary, though not a sufficient condition for the organizing drive of the breakthrough year, 1937, was provided by improving economic conditions. What was needed above all was dynamic leadership, willing to run great risks in the assault upon the citadels of the open shop. The AFL bureaucracy did not see the opportunity, and it remained for John L. Lewis, perhaps the greatest entrepreneur of American labor organization, to step into the breach. Lewis had on his side a highly favorable climate of public opinion and a benevolent federal government, armed with the powers of the Wagner Act. The drive was carefully planned and well financed. All the elements seemed to add up to so great an advantage for labor that the United States Steel Corporation surrendered without a struggle. One after another, the giants of American industry — General Motors, Chrysler, General Electric — fell into the CIO fold. But the seemingly invincible CIO was stopped short by the violent resistance of Little Steel, motivated by an almost pathological hatred of unionism and fortified by a downturn in the demand for steel.

There was a pause of several years, during which many employers continued to oppose the introduction of unionism into their plants, though with somewhat different methods than had been possible before the days of the National Labor Relations Board and the La Follette investigating committee. When national defense activities made it possible for labor, the AFL as well as the CIO, to take the offensive once more, new tactics were used. To supplement the direct assault technique which was the hallmark of John L. Lewis, federal government pressure was applied against employers eager for defense contracts, with Sidney Hillman placed in a strategic position to direct the pressure. One after another, the bitter end holdouts, Ford, Republic Steel, Bethlehem Steel, Westinghouse, were unionized, and a new era dawned for American industrial relations. Only the South remained as a symbol of the *ancien régime*.

That this could have been achieved without a radical change in labor's attitude toward national politics is very doubtful. The CIO threw itself wholeheartedly on the side of the Democratic Party. The AFL, more reserved, tried to hew to the Gompers line of nonpartisanship, but this became increasingly difficult as the New Deal delivered direct benefits to its members in the form of social legislation. Some of the leading statesmen of the AFL were high in New Deal counsels, and the few Republicans who remained were gradually shorn of influence. The fact that a dozen American trade unionists had ready access to the president of the United States, that they could call upon him for assistance in an emergency, was a critical element in organizing success.

Those who believed that the AFL had signed its death warrant in expelling the CIO unions must have been surprised at its vigorous renascence. Competition for workers may be as beneficent for society as competition for customers. It would be justifiable to assert that the shock of the CIO was necessary to the rejuvenation of the AFL, and that if it had not been for the intense struggle between the two organizations, the United States might have entered the war with its labor force largely unorganized. The CIO demonstrated convincingly that no employer was powerful enough to resist organization, if sufficient resources were thrown into the struggle. The AFL absorbed this lesson quickly, and used its greater experience to maintain its dominant position. New CIO unions were no match for well-established AFL competitors. The manner in which the AFL building trades disposed of an ambitious attempt by John L. Lewis to invade their field provides a classic example of AFL flexibility and fighting ability.

Almost a quarter of a century has gone by since the beginning of the great labor drama at the AFL convention in Atlantic City. Most of the *dramatis personae* are gone from the scene, and the original issues are dead and buried. But the repercussions still persist, and their final effect is not yet evident. The CIO is no more, but the AFL-CIO of George Meany bears little resemblance to the AFL of Gompers and Green. In absorbing its rival, the AFL also took over features that would have been anathema to the members of the Executive Council who sat in judgment on the CIO rebels in 1936. The principle of national union sovereignty has been diluted, if not destroyed, by the codes of ethical practice adopted by the AFL-CIO in 1956 and 1957. Dual jurisdictions have been legitimized by constitutional provision. The Federation staff has achieved a size and authority much more reminiscent of the CIO than the AFL. A permanent political adjunct has been created, and its partisanship is scarcely concealed.

Whether the new order can surmount the centrifugal tendencies always so strong in the American labor movement remains to be seen. That the leaders of American labor are certain it can is clear from the fact that the overriding consideration of the past, the prevention of dualism, of splintering, has yielded its paramountcy to other objectives in which broader social interests are reflected.

Notes

Notes

Chapter 1   Background of the Struggle

1. International Ladies' Garment Workers' Union, *The Position of the International Ladies' Garment Workers' Union in Relation to CIO and AFL, 1934–1938* (December 1938), p. 13.

2. For example, Bryn Roberts, *The American Labour Split and Allied Unity* (London, 1943), p. 44, says: "At this informal conference no definite conclusions were reached."

3. Committee for Industrial Organization, *Minutes* (November 9, 1935), typewritten.

4. Harvey C. Fremming, president of the Oil Workers International Union, later asserted that "the Committee for Industrial Organization was born over a steak at Harvey's Restaurant in Washington. The principals present were Phil Murray, John Lewis and myself." Oil Workers International Union, *Poceedings of the Eighth Convention* (June 7–12, 1937), p. 7. Fremming placed the date of this meeting after the Atlantic City convention, however, and the probable purpose of the meeting was to secure his attendance at the November organizational meeting.

5. At the time Zaritsky was head of the Cap and Millinery Department of the Hatters' Union. The status of his union in relation to the CIO remained a matter of doubt for several years.

6. When McMahon was later asked by the AFL to disaffiliate from the CIO, he stated that his executive board had instructed him to associate with it. American Federation of Labor, *Minutes of the Meeting of the Executive Council* (May 5–20, 1936), p. 237. These minutes are referred to hereafter as AFL Executive Council Minutes.

7. The Typographers never affiliated with the CIO, nor did the Hatters as an international union.

8. AFL Executive Council Minutes (January 15–29, 1936), pp. 207–214.

9. Committee for Industrial Organization, *Minutes* (February 21, 1936), typewritten.

10. Letter from A. A. Myrup to Charles Howard, March 13, 1936 (CIO files).

11. Bryn Roberts, *American Labour Split*, p. 46.

12. Brookwood Labor College was established in 1921 by intellectuals and trade unionists critical of the policies of the AFL leadership. The orientation was socialist, though there was no formal affiliation with the Socialist Party. Thirteen national AFL unions supported the college at one time or another, and many of its graduates subsequently became prominent union leaders. For a history of the college, see James O. Morris, *The Origins of the CIO*, Ph.D. Thesis (University of Michigan, 1954), Ch. IV.

13. *The Position of the International Ladies' Garment Workers' Union*, p. 13.

14. Committee for Industrial Organization, *Minutes*, December 9, 1935 (typewritten).

15. AFL Executive Council Minutes (April 30–May 7, 1935), p. 115. At the time of the CIO formation, the AFL Executive Council consisted of the following: William Green, president; Frank Morrison, secretary-treasurer; Frank Duffy, Carpen-

ters' Union; T. A. Rickert, United Garment Workers; Matthew Woll, Engravers' Union; John Coefield, Plumbers; Arthur O. Wharton, Machinists; Joseph N. Weber, Musicians; G. M. Bugniazet, Electrical Workers; George M. Harrison, Railway Clerks; Daniel J. Tobin, Teamsters; William L. Hutcheson, Carpenters; John L. Lewis, Mine Workers; David Dubinsky, Ladies' Garment Workers; Harry C. Bates, Bricklayers; Edward J. Gainor, Letter Carriers; William D. Mahon, Street Railway Workers.

16. For the text of this letter, see American Federation of Labor, *Report of the Proceedings of the Fifty-Sixth Annual Convention* (1936), p. 70.

17. For the full text of this letter, see *ibid.*, pp. 71–73.

18. United Mine Workers of America, *Proceedings of the Thirty-Fourth Constitutional Convention* (1936), p. 63.

19. AFL Executive Council Minutes (January 15–29, 1936), p. 51.

20. United Mine Workers of America, *Proceedings of the Thirty-Fourth Constitutional Convention* (1936), p. 64.

21. Committee for Industrial Organization, *Minutes* (December 9, 1935), typewritten.

22. American Federation of Labor, *Report of the Proceedings of the Fifty-Sixth Annual Convention* (1936), p. 74.

23. *Union News Service,* January 20, 1936. This one-page clipsheet was the only official publication of the CIO until the first issue of the *CIO News* appeared on December 7, 1937. After that, the *Union News Service* contained material taken from the *CIO News.*

24. AFL Executive Council Minutes (January 15–29, 1936), p. 56.

25. Green urged the Council: "Some may say we have not hit back hard enough. It is not the time to hit back. We have kept our heads and I believe we will be given credit for keeping our heads. There may come a time when it will be necessary to hit back but this is not the time. We are trying to conciliate and placate. I hope that we ourselves will encourage others and inspire others to observe the laws of the American Federation of Labor by obeying the laws ourselves." AFL Executive Council Minutes (January 15–29, 1936), p. 56.

26. American Federation of Labor, *Report of Proceedings of the Fifty-Sixth Annual Convention* (1936), p. 75.

27. AFL Executive Council Minutes (January 15–29, 1936), p. 91.

28. United Mine Workers of America, *Proceedings of the Thirty-Fourth Constitutional Convention* (1936), pp. 164, 172.

29. *Ibid.,* p. 309.

30. Letter from Howard to Hillman, February 3, 1956 (files of Amalgamated Clothing Workers of America).

31. Letter from Hillman to Howard, February 7, 1936 (files of Amalgamated Clothing Workers of America).

32. *Union News Service,* February 24, 1936.

33. *Union News Service,* March 9, 1936.

34. *Ibid.,* May 18, 1936.

35. The letter was dated May 20, 1936. For the full text, see *The Position of the International Ladies' Garment Workers' Union,* p. 17.

36. AFL Executive Council Minutes (May 5–20, 1936), pp. 241, 245.

37. Amalgamated Clothing Workers of America, *Proceedings Eleventh Biennial Convention* (1936), p. 367.

38. *Union News Service,* June 1, 1936.

39. *The Position of the International Ladies' Garment Workers' Union,* p. 20.

40. *Union News Service,* June 29, 1936.

41. AFL Executive Council Minutes (July 8–15, 1936), pp. 17–18.

42. AFL Executive Council Minutes (July 8–15, 1936), pp. 125–127; see also pp. 129, 131.

43. *Ibid.*, p. 190.

44. For the text of the formal charge, see American Federation of Labor, *Proceedings of the Executive Council in the Matter of Charges Filed by the Metal Trades Department* (1936), p. 3.

45. *Ibid.*, pp. 11–13.

46. This is based upon the voting strength of unions shown in American Federation of Labor, *Report of Proceedings of the Fifty-Sixth Annual Convention* (1936), pp. 44–45.

47. The evidence is set forth in American Federation of Labor, *Proceedings of the Executive Council in the Matter of Charges Filed by the Metal Trades Department* (1936). In the course of his testimony, Frey referred to an interview of John L. Lewis by Louis Stark which appeared in the *New York Times* on July 28, 1935, in which Stark obliquely quoted Lewis as saying: "Where the struggle between the industrial and the craft unions will lead is unpredictable. If it eventually leads Mr. Lewis and his union out of the American Federation of Labor by voluntary choice, or through defeat at some Federation Convention, the Miners will be prepared for that step, even if it means the setting up of another and rival labor federation comprising the industrial unions" Frey stated that Stark was prepared to testify that the interview was passed upon by Lewis before its publication. *Ibid.*, p. 61.

48. AFL Executive Council Minutes (August 3–5, 1936), p. 2.

49. *Ibid.*, pp. 57, 60.

50. For the text of this resolution, see American Federation of Labor, *Proceedings of the Executive Council of the American Federation of Labor in the Matter of Charges Filed by the Metal Trades Department* (1936), pp. 134–136. The following ten unions were affected: United Mine Workers; Amalgamated Clothing Workers; Oil Field, Gas Well and Refinery Workers; Mine, Mill and Smelter Workers; International Ladies' Garment Workers; United Textile Workers; Flat Glass Workers; Iron, Steel and Tin Workers; United Automobile Workers; United Rubber Workers.

51. *Union News Service,* August 10, 1936.

52. Committee for Industrial Organization, *Minutes of the Meeting of August 10, 1936* (typewritten).

53. *Union News Service,* August 17, 1936.

54. *Union News Service,* September 7, 1936.

55. *Ibid.,* August 31, 1936.

56. *Proceedings of the Eightieth Session of the International Typographical Union* (September 12–19, 1936), pp. 84, 99.

57. *Ibid.,* p. 102. The ITU has remained faithful to its position on autonomy. For example, its representatives, led by Woodruff Randolph, voted against the expulsion of the Teamsters' Union at the 1957 AFL-CIO convention, and served the following notice on the convention, "The International Typographical Union will be guided only by its own Book of Laws and will flatly reject any resolution, law, rule, regulation, mandate or directive of the AFL-CIO which is contrary thereto. The International Typographical Union will exercise full and complete autonomy in all phases of its relationship to the AFL-CIO or any other labor organization. This is a restatement of the historical position of the International Typographical Union first stated to the AFL in 1886." *Proceedings of the Second Constitutional Convention of the AFL-CIO* (1957), p. 473.

58. AFL Executive Council Minutes (October 8–21, 1936), pp. 151–159.

59. *Proceedings of the Eighty-Third Session of the International Typographical Union* (August 19–26, 1939), p. 78.

60. *Proceedings of the Second Convention of the United Hatters, Cap and Millinery Workers International Union* (October 7–11, 1936), pp. 88, 103.

61. AFL Executive Council Minutes (October 8–21, 1936), pp. 52, 127.

62. *The Position of the International Ladies' Garment Workers' Union*, pp. 29, 30.

63. *Proceedings of the Third Convention of the United Hatters, Cap and Millinery Workers International Union* (1939), p. 203.

64. Committee for Industrial Organization, *Minutes* (November 7–8, 1936).

65. The text of these telegrams is contained in American Federation of Labor, *A.F. of L. vs. C.I.O., The Record* (Washington, 1939), pp. 40–41.

66. Committee for Industrial Organization, *Minutes* (November 7–8, 1936).

67. In the case of the Steel Workers' Organizing Committee, the appearance of regularity had been preserved by working through the AF of L chartered Amalgamated Association of Iron, Steel and Tin Workers.

68. Committee for Industrial Organization, *Minutes* (November 7–8, 1936).

69. *Report of Proceedings of the Fifty-Sixth Annual Convention of the American Federation of Labor* (1936), p. 121.

70. *Ibid.*, pp. 502–503, 538.

71. *Union News Service*, March 15, 1937.

72. AFL Executive Council Minutes (April 19–22, 1937), p. 14.

73. *Proceedings of the Thirty-Seventh Constitutional Convention of the United Mine Workers of America* (1942), Vol. I, p. 154.

74. For the text of the call, see *Report of Proceedings of the Fifty-Seventh Annual Convention of the American Federation of Labor* (1937), pp. 101–106.

75. AFL Executive Council Minutes (May 23–30, 1937), p. 118.

76. *Ibid.* (January 24–February 8, 1938), p. 238.

77. AFL Executive Council Minutes (April 19–22, 1937), p. 16.

78. In a speech on the preceding Labor Day, Lewis had put CIO membership at 3,718,000.

79. See Kenneth D. Roose, *The Economics of Recession and Revival* (New Haven, 1954), Ch. 3.

80. Report of John Brophy to the National Conference of the CIO (October 11, 1937), mimeographed; *Proceedings of the Thirty-Seventh Constitutional Convention of the United Mine Workers of America* (1942), pp. 149–150.

81. Committee for Industrial Organization, *The Program of the C.I.O.* Washington (1937), p. 21.

82. AFL Executive Council Minutes (May 23–30, 1937), p. 5.

83. *Report of Proceedings, Twenty-Third Convention of the International Ladies' Garment Workers' Union* (1937), pp. 154–155; p. 300.

84. *The Program of the C.I.O.*, p. 26.

85. *Ibid.*, p. 16.

86. *Ibid.*, p. 29.

87. AFL Executive Council Minutes (October 3–16, 1937), p. 39.

88. *The Position of the International Ladies' Garment Workers' Union*, pp. 40–42. The CIO proposal was dated October 12, the AFL reply, October 14, 1937.

89. AFL Executive Council Minutes (October 3–16, 1937), p. 78.

90. *Proceedings of the First Constitutional Convention of the Congress of Industrial Organizations* (1938), pp. 92–93.

91. *A.F. of L. vs. C.I.O.*, p. 55.

92. *The Position of the International Ladies' Garment Workers' Union*, pp. 43–44.
93. *A.F. of L. vs. C.I.O.*, pp. 55–56.
94. *Proceedings of the Third Convention of the United Hatters, Cap and Millinery Workers International Union* (1939), p. 374.
95. In the CIO memorandum referred to below, this read "Fur Workers."
96. *The Position of the International Ladies' Garment Workers' Union*, pp. 49–63.
97. *Proceedings of the Third Convention of the United Hatters, Cap and Millinery Workers International Union* (1939), p. 374. Howard vehemently denied the validity of Woll's statement. He stated: "It is utterly untrue that the committee representing the C.I.O. at any time accepted the proposal of the A.F. of L. or that there was agreement that the suspended international unions would reaffiliate with the A.F. of L., and subcommittees be named to agree upon conditions under which the 20 other international unions composing the C.I.O. would secure affiliation. The statement that this agreement was reached at a meeting when Chairman Murray was absent is unqualifiedly false." *Union News Service*, February 11, 1938.
98. *Proceedings of the First Constitutional Convention of the Congress of Industrial Organizations* (1938), pp. 93–95.
99. *The Position of the International Ladies' Garment Workers' Union*, pp. 58, 59.
100. *Proceedings of the Twelfth Biennial Convention of the Amalgamated Clothing Workers of America* (1938), p. 347.
101. *Proceedings of the Thirty-Fifth Constitutional Convention of the United Mine Workers of America* (1938), p. 98.
102. *Ibid.*, p. 125.
103. *Proceedings of the Twenty-Third General Convention of the United Brotherhood of Carpenters and Joiners of America* (1936), p. 57.
104. *Report of Proceedings of the Fifty-Seventh Annual Convention of the American Federation of Labor* (1937), p. 383.
105. *Ibid.*, p. 473.
106. *Proceedings of the Twelfth Biennial Convention of the Amalgamated Clothing Workers of America* (1938), p. 293.
107. *The Position of the International Ladies' Garment Workers' Union*, p. 54.
108. Max D. Danish, *The World of David Dubinsky* (Cleveland, 1957), p. 113.
109. *Ibid.*, p. 65.
110. AFL Executive Council Minutes (August 22–September 2, 1938), p. 13.
111. *Report and Record, Twenty-Fourth Convention, International Ladies' Garment Workers' Union* (1940), pp. 38, 39.
112. AFL Executive Council Minutes (October 2–14, 1938), p. 34.
113. *Report of Proceedings of the Fifty-Eighth Annual Convention of the American Federation of Labor* (1938), p. 385; p. 380.
114. AFL Executive Council Minutes (October 2–14, 1938), p. 34.
115. *Proceedings of the First Constitutional Convention of the Congress of Industrial Organizations* (1938), p. 96.
116. AFL Executive Council Minutes (January 30–February 14, 1939), p. 119.
117. Frances Perkins, *The Roosevelt I Knew* (New York, 1946), pp. 308–312.
118. AFL Executive Council Minutes (January 30–February 14, 1939), p. 122.
119. *Ibid.*, p. 293.
120. *A.F. of L. vs. C.I.O.*, pp. 63–64.
121. Tobin withdrew temporarily, and Rickert was named to replace him. Tobin returned to the committee after the first meeting, at the insistence of the White House.
122. *The CIO News*, March 13, 1939, p. 3.
123. For the text of the AFL reply, see *A.F. of L. vs C.I.O.*, pp. 67–69.

124. AFL Executive Council Minutes (May 10–19, 1939), p. 27.

125. Congress of Industrial Organizations, *Minutes of Meeting of the Executive Board* (June 13–15, 1939), p. 110. This source is cited hereafter as CIO Executive Board Minutes.

126. *A.F. of L. vs. C.I.O.*, pp. 69–71.

127. CIO Executive Board Minutes (June 13–15, 1939), p. 118.

128. *A.F. of L. vs. C.I.O.*, pp. 71–72. See also the statement of Matthew Woll in International Ladies' Garment Workers' Union, *Report of Proceedings,* Twenty-Fourth Convention (1940), p. 250.

129. *The CIO News,* March 27, 1939.

130. CIO Executive Board Minutes (June 13–15, 1939), p. 118.

131. Congress of Industrial Organizations, *Minutes of the Meeting of the Executive Board,* June 3–5, 1940, p. 260. It may be noted parenthetically that advertising in the *American Federationist,* the official AFL journal to which Murray referred, was discontinued in June 1940, in view of "misunderstanding on the part of business corporations as to the propriety of advertising in labor publications and many other evils in connection with this activity which have, in the past, caused labor to be criticized." AFL Executive Council Minutes (May 13–21, 1940), p. 46.

132. CIO Executive Board Minutes (June 13–15, 1939), p. 136.

133. See Congress of Industrial Organizations, *Conspiracy Against Labor,* Publication No. 41 (March, 1940). The AFL indignantly denied the accusation of liaison with the NAM, and said that Padway had merely conferred with a personal friend who happened to have employers among his clients.

134. CIO Executive Board Minutes (June 13–15, 1939), pp. 110, 118.

135. *Ibid.,* p. 136.

136. *Ibid.,* p. 26. See *infra,* p. 583, for a consideration of CIO membership data.

137. AFL Executive Council Minutes (May 10–19, 1939), p. 176.

138. *A.F. of L. vs. C.I.O.*, p. 75.

139. *Report of the Proceedings of the Fifty-Ninth Annual Convention of the American Federation of Labor* (1939), p. 402.

140. *Daily Proceedings of the Second Constitutional Convention of the Congress of Industrial Organizations* (1939), p. 171.

141. CIO Executive Board Minutes (June 3–5, 1940), p. 238.

142. AFL Executive Council Minutes (January 27–February 9, 1940), p. 145.

143. On February 18, 1940, the White House press bureau indicated that Lewis had never replied to the letter addressed to the CIO convention. This assertion seems to have been erroneous, since Lewis had replied under date of October 15, 1939. See *CIO News,* February 19, 1940, p. 6.

144. Frances Perkins, *Roosevelt,* pp. 126–127, 312.

145. *Proceedings of the Thirty-Sixth Constitutional Convention of the United Mine Workers of America* (1940), p. 104.

146. *Proceedings of the Thirteenth Biennial Convention of the Amalgamated Clothing Workers of America* (1940), p. 554. The *CIO News,* May 27, 1940, p. 5, in reporting Hillman's speech, gave the impression that Hillman saw eye to eye with Lewis on the unity talks.

147. CIO Executive Board Minutes (June 3–5, 1940), p. 238.

148. Thomas later asserted that he had been offered the Secretaryship of Labor if he would support Willkie. CIO Executive Board Minutes (June 3–5, 1942), p. 129.

149. *CIO News,* November 4, 1940.

150. CIO Executive Board Minutes (November 15–23, 1940), p. 7.

151. *Ibid.,* p. 14.

152. *Ibid.,* p. 49.

153. CIO Executive Board Minutes (January 24, 1942), p. 94.

154. For the role played by Hillman in preventing a "draft" of Lewis for the CIO presidency, see *infra,* p. 297.

155. Congress of Industrial Organizations, *Daily Proceedings of the Third Constitutional Convention* (November 18–22, 1940), p. 136.

156. CIO, *Third Constitutional Convention,* pp. 159, 160.

157. International Ladies' Garment Workers' Union, *Report of Proceedings, Twenty-Fourth Convention* (1940), p. 449.

158. American Federation of Labor, *Report of Proceedings of the Sixtieth Annual Convention* (1940), p. 446.

159. *Ibid.,* p. 447. Dubinsky quoted a letter from William Green, dated May 30, 1940, which said in part: "The Executive Council decided . . . to recommend to the Sixtieth Annual Convention of the American Federation of Labor that all suspensions of international unions in the event such action seems absolutely necessary, be ordered by a majority vote of the delegates in attendance at an annual convention of the American Federation of Labor. This would mean, if the recommendation of the Council is followed, that the power and authority to suspend national and international unions would be vested exclusively in conventions of the American Federation of Labor." *Ibid.,* pp. 449–450. At the immediate preconvention meeting of the Executive Council, however, Hutcheson had suggested that this commitment be qualified in the manner in which the recommendation was finally submitted to the convention. AFL Executive Council Minutes (September 30–October 10, 1940), p. 10.

160. William Green attempted to reconcile his earlier letter with the Executive Council recommendation (see AFL *Proceedings,* p. 457), but a fair reading of the relevant documents and argumentation leads one to the conclusion that the two are contradictory.

161. American Federation of Labor, *Report of the Proceedings of the Sixty-First Annual Convention* (1941), p. 68.

162. AFL Executive Council Minutes (October 5–17), 1941, p. 2.

163. American Federation of Labor, *Report of the Proceedings of the Sixty-First Annual Convention* (1941), pp. 394, 505.

164. *Ibid.,* p. 62.

165. AFL Executive Council Minutes (September 30–October 10, 1940), p. 48.

166. American Federation of Labor, *Report of Proceedings of the Sixtieth Annual Convention* (1940), p. 209.

167. AFL Executive Council Minutes (September 30–October 10, 1940), p. 49.

168. See CIO Executive Board Minutes (June 3–5, 1940), p. 211; *Daily Proceedings of the Third Constitutional Convention* (1940), pp. 46 ff.

169. Joel Seidman, *American Labor from Defense to Reconversion,* Chicago (1953), p. 29.

170. *American Federation of Labor Weekly News Service.* October 28, 1941.

171. *The CIO News,* November 3, 1941, p. 3.

172. *The CIO News,* November 17, 1941.

173. American Federation of Labor, *Report of the Proceedings of the Sixty-First Annual Convention* (1941), p. 312.

174. For the full text of the agreement, see *ibid.,* pp. 56–57. This document constitutes a good restatement of the position of the AFL *vis-à-vis* its affiliates.

175. AFL, *Sixty-first Annual Convention,* p. 58.

176. These facts were given to the author by a participant in the convention.

177. CIO Executive Board Minutes (June 3–5, 1942), pp. 72, 101.

178. CIO Executive Board Minutes (January 24, 1942), p. 67.

179. United Mine Workers of America, *Proceedings of the Thirty-Seventh Constitutional Convention* (1942), p. 188. Lewis was undoubtedly correct in his assertion that he could have continued as CIO president. In all probability, only the Amalgamated Clothing Workers and the Textile Workers would have opposed him.

180. For the text of this letter, see American Federation of Labor, *Report of Proceedings of the Sixty-Second Annual Convention* (1942), p. 52.

181. Congress of Industrial Organizations, *The CIO and Labor Unity,* Publication No. 62, p. 14.

182. CIO Executive Board Minutes (January 24, 1942), pp. 8, 94.

183. *Ibid.,* pp. 84, 147.

184. *The CIO and Labor Unity,* p. 19.

185. United Mine Workers of America, *Proceedings of the Thirty-Seventh Constitutional Convention* (1942), p. 188.

186. American Federation of Labor, *Report of the Proceedings of the Sixty-Second Annual Convention* (1942), p. 54.

187. CIO Executive Board Minutes (June 3–5, 1942), p. 458.

188. American Federation of Labor, *Report of the Proceedings of the Sixty-Second Annual Convention of the American Federation of Labor* (1942), pp. 56, 57. The AFL reply was dated June 23, 1942.

189. AFL Executive Council Minutes (August 4–13, 1942), p. 9.

190. American Federation of Labor, *Report of the Proceedings of the Sixty-Second Annual Convention* (1942), pp. 59, 61.

191. CIO Executive Board Minutes (March 24, 1942), p. 268.

192. CIO Executive Board Minutes (June 3–5, 1942), p. 72.

193. United Mine Workers of America, *Proceedings of the Thirty-Seventh Constitutional Convention* (1942), p. 419.

Chapter 2   The Organization of Steel

1. Amalgamated Association of Iron, Steel and Tin Workers, *Annual Reports of International Officers to the 61st Annual Convention* (1936), pp. 22, 113.

2. American Federation of Labor, *Report of Proceedings of the Fifty-Fourth Annual Convention* (1934), p. 587.

3. Amalgamated Association of Iron, Steel, and Tin Workers, *Annual Reports of International Officers to the 61st Annual Convention* (1936), p. 23.

4. AFL Executive Council Minutes (January 29–February 14, 1935), pp. 189, 190–191.

5. *Ibid.,* pp. 245, 247.

6. American Federation of Labor, *Report of the Proceedings of the Fifty-Fifth Annual Convention* (1935), p. 97.

7. Interview with John Brophy, March 19, 1955. Those present at this meeting, in addition to Brophy, were Kathryn Lewis, Philip Murray, and Ora Gasaway.

8. American Federation of Labor, *Report of Proceedings of the Fifty-Fifth Annual Convention* (1935), p. 539.

9. For the text of the proposal, see Amalgamated Association of Iron, Steel and Tin Workers, *Annual Reports of International Officers to the 61st Annual Convention* (1936), p. 132.

10. American Federation of Labor, *Report of the Proceedings of the Fifty-Sixth Annual Convention* (1936), p. 86.

11. *Union News Service,* January 20, 1936.

12. For the full text of this letter, see *Proceedings of the Executive Council of the American Federation of Labor in the Matter of Charges Filed by the Metal Trades Department* (August 3, 1936), pp. 37–41.

13. *Union News Service,* April 13, 1936.

14. AFL Executive Council Minutes (May 5–20, 1936), pp. 36, 50.

15. *Union News Service,* April 20, 1936.

16. American Federation of Labor, *Report of the Proceedings of the Fifty-Sixth Annual Convention* (1936), p. 88.

17. *Ibid.,* pp. 89–91.

18. Amalgamated Association of Iron, Steel, and Tin Workers, *Journal of Proceedings of the International Lodge* (1936), p. 2779.

19. Amalgamated Association of Iron, Steel, and Tin Workers, *Annual Report of International Officers to 62nd Annual Convention* (1937), p. 123.

20. Robert R. R. Brooks, *As Steel Goes* (New Haven, 1940), p. 73.

21. Amalgamated Association of Iron, Steel and Tin Workers, *Annual Report,* 1937, pp. 125, 126.

22. *A.F. of L. vs. C.I.O., The Record* (1939), p. 31.

23. For the text of the agreement, see *ibid.,* p. 31.

24. *Union News Service,* June 15, 1936.

25. Interview with John Brophy, March 19, 1955.

26. Minutes of the Organizational Meeting of the Steel Workers' Organizing Committee, Pittsburgh, June 17, 1936.

27. Reproduced in Vincent D. Sweeney, *The United Steelworkers of America* (1956), p. 16.

28. Minutes of a Meeting of the Steel Workers' Organizing Committee, September 29, 1936.

29. Amalgamated Association of Iron, Steel, and Tin Workers, *Annual Report of International Officers to 62nd Annual Convention* (April, 1937), pp. 139, 160, 339.

30. *Ibid.,* p. 3.

31. U. S. Senate, 77th Congress, 1st Session, Committee on Education and Labor, Report No. 151, 1941, p. 10.

32. In 1929, the five largest firms controlled 68.2 per cent of the steel ingot capacity of the industry, a pattern of concentration which remained approximately unchanged in 1936. *Ibid.,* p. 10.

33. The employment data, which include white collar employees as well as wage earners, are from Gertrude G. Schroeder, *The Growth of Major Steel Companies, 1900–1950* (Johns Hopkins University, 1952), pp. 216–222.

34. For an account of the establishment and operation of company unions in steel, see Carroll R. Dougherty, Melvin G. de Chazeau and Samuel S. Stratton, *The Economics of the Iron and Steel Industry,* Vol. II (New York, 1937), Ch. XX.

35. Edward Levinson, *Labor on the March* (New York, 1938), p. 192.

36. Robert R. R. Brooks, *As Steel Goes,* Chap. 1.

37. John A. Fitch, "A Man Can Talk in Homestead," *Survey Graphic* (February, 1936), p. 71.

38. Steel Workers' Organizing Committee, *Proceedings of the First Wage and Policy Convention* (1937), p. 31.

39. On August 22, 1936, Clinton Golden, director of the Northeastern region, asked all his field workers to forward to him the following information:

"1. The name and address of every company union or employee representative in the mills in the territory in which you are working.

"2. Indicate by the use of the letters O.K. placed opposite the name of each employee those with whom you have had personal contact and who you feel are entirely sympathetic with the purposes of our present organizing drive."

United States Senate, 74th–76th Congress, Committee on Education and Labor, Hearings Before a Subcommittee on Violations of Free Speech and Rights of Labor, p. 10610. These hearings are hereinafter referred to as *La Follette Committee Hearings*.

40. Robert R. R. Brooks, *As Steel Goes*, pp. 92–94.

41. A participant in the SWOC drive recently indicated his doubts as to the importance of the infiltration of company unions: "Those company unions represented no one and there was scarcely a person in the organization who believed they did. Our maneuverings with the ERP's were more feint than anything else. Once in a while ERP men would come over to us, but they didn't necessarily bring any membership with them. . . . We got the top men of the Jones and Laughlin Aliquippa employee representation plan to come over to the union. That was all very well, but we still had to organize the employees one by one." Letter from Meyer Bernstein to the author, February 10, 1958.

42. *Steel Labor* (September 25, 1936), p. 1.

43. Fairless pointed out that a 10 per cent wage increase would absorb almost all the profits of Carnegie-Illinois for the first half of 1936, and wrote at length of his responsibility to the stockholders, which was a tactical blunder in the face of the current economic status of the workers, many of them on part time. *The Iron Age*, September 17, 1936, p. 82.

44. *Ibid.*, p. 2.

45. Brooks, *As Steel Goes*, p. 99.

46. Myron C. Taylor, *Ten Years of Steel*, p. 39.

47. The precise amounts of the increase varied from job to job. The percentage increase was to total slightly less than 10 per cent, with individual adjustments to eliminate wage inequities. The sliding scale arrangement tied wages to the B.L.S. cost-of-living index on a quarterly basis.

All the other leading steel companies made similar adjustments at the same time, though without the sliding scale feature. See *Iron Age*, November 12, 1936, p. 72.

48. *Steel Labor*, December 5, 1936, p. 1.

49. See Myron C. Taylor, *Ten Years of Steel*, p. 40.

50. *Steel Labor*, November 20, 1936, p. 1.

51. *The Iron Age*, January 14, 1937, p. 68.

52. *Steel Labor*, January 9, 1937, p. 3.

53. *The Iron Age*, January 7, 1937, p. 192.

54. This committee was to have "full powers of investigation and will be in a position to 'crack down' on any supervisor or superintendants who refuse to cooperate in collective bargaining as set forth in the plan of employee representation." *The Iron Age*, January 14, 1937, p. 68.

55. *The Iron Age*, February 18, 1937, p. 74. It is intimated in the source that Carnegie-Illinois was prepared to make a wage adjustment along these lines.

56. Letter from Meyer Bernstein to the author, February 10, 1958.

57. Myron C. Taylor, pp. 40–42.

58. For a background reconstruction of the conversations, see *Fortune* (May, 1937), p. 91. According to Lewis, his first contact with Taylor was at the Mayflower Hotel in Washington, D. C., in October 1936. Lewis and Senator Guffey were having breakfast, and Taylor, who was sitting with his wife at a nearby table, invited Lewis over. Mrs. Taylor asked, "When is the trouble going to stop?" "When your husband sits down

and writes an agreement," replied Lewis. Taylor said, "What are you doing tomorrow?" and this led to a luncheon meeting the next day. This was the first of a series of meetings, which broke down several times, but were kept going through the intercession of Tom Moses of the Frick Coal Company. Interview with John L. Lewis, November 12, 1954.

59. *Steel Labor*, March 6, 1937, p. 1.
60. *Steel Labor*, March 20, 1937, p. 2.
61. Gertrude G. Schroeder, *The Growth of Major Steel Companies*, p. 216.
62. Myron C. Taylor, *Ten Years of Steel*, p. 43.
63. *Fortune* (May 1937), p. 92.
64. See Edward Levinson, *Labor on the March*, p. 199.
65. Saul Alinsky, *John L. Lewis* (New York, 1949), p. 149.
66. *The Iron Age*, March 11, 1937, p. 107; March 18, 1937; April 1, 1937.
67. *Fortune* (May, 1937), p. 179.
68. *Steel Labor*, March 6, 1937, p. 4.
69. *Steel Labor*, March 6, 1937, p. 3.
70. Tom M. Girdler, *Boot Straps* (New York, 1943), p. 226.
71. U. S. Senate, 77th Congress, 1st Session, *Violations of Free Speech and Rights of Labor*, Report No. 151 (1941), p. 117.
72. This section is based in part upon the hearings and reports of a subcommittee of the Committee on Education and Labor of the United States Senate, under the chairmanship of Senator Robert M. La Follette, Jr. These hearings, held over a period of several years, constitute an extraordinary episode in the annals of labor history. Although at times quite partisan in its efforts to ferret out evidence of wrongful labor practices on the part of the steel companies, the subcommittee accumulated thousands of pages of information and testimony on industrial relations in the steel industry during the years 1935 to 1939.
73. *Steel Labor*, April 10, 1937; May 1, 1937.
74. The SWOC claimed two out of three members of a Special Grievance Committee of the Bethlehem plan, and by April, 1937, 150 out of 250 plan representatives. *Steel Labor*, January 23, 1937; April 10, 1937.
75. *Steel Labor*, January 9, 1937.
76. Robert R. Brooks, *As Steel Goes*, p. 135.
77. *La Follette Committee Hearings*, pp. 10425–10426, 13792.
78. In the Matter of Jones & Laughlin Steel Corporation, 1 NLRB 503 (1936), p. 503.
79. *The Iron Age*, May 13, 1937, p. 103.
80. Robert R. Brooks, *As Steel Goes*, p. 123.
81. *The Iron Age*, May 27, 1937, p. 92.
82. *Steel Labor*, June 5, 1937, p. 1.
83. Robert R. Brooks, *As Steel Goes*, p. 134.
84. La Follette Committee Report No. 151, p. 117.
85. For the text of this statement, see *La Follette Committee Hearings*, p. 13908.
86. La Follette Committee Report No. 151, p. 124. There was some evidence that the calling of this strike was premature, and that the SWOC would have preferred not to have become embroiled with the second largest producer in the industry until it had finished with Republic and Youngstown. The local union called the strike in sympathy with the local employees of a captive railroad controlled by Bethlehem Steel, who had gone on strike the previous day in protest against refusal of the company to bargain.
87. *The Iron Age*, June 3, 1937, p. 86A.

88. *The Iron Age,* May 13, 1937, p. 117.

89. It is difficult to trace precisely the curve of economic activity for the industry during the period of the strike because of the influence of the strike itself. The evaluation in the text is based upon discussion of the business outlook that appeared in *The Iron Age,* the weekly trade publication of the industry.

90. On May 27, 1937, the day after the outbreak of the strike, Girdler was elected president of the American Iron and Steel Institute. Eugene Grace, the outgoing president, remarked cryptically that "there was a real contest in this election and you will appreciate the choice of the directors," and "it was left to his listeners to assume that present labor policies in the industry had an influence in the election of new officers." *The Iron Age,* June 3, 1937, p. 32.

91. Tom M. Girdler, *Boot Straps,* pp. 317, 358–359, 449–450.

92. Pierce Williams, "Essence of the Steel Strikes," *Survey Graphic* (October, 1937), p. 516. Meyer Bernstein, a participant in the Ohio drive, doubts that the Ohio State Federation was powerful enough to have made any difference in the final outcome.

93. The facts concerning this incident are taken primarily from United States Senate, 77th Congress, 1st Session, Committee on Education and Labor, Report No. 46, Part 2, 1937, pp. 14, 21, 31–34.

94. *The Iron Age,* June 17, 1937, p. 94.

95. United States Senate, 77th Congress, 1st Session, Committee on Education and Labor, Report No. 151, 1941, pp. 229–252.

96. *Ibid.,* p. 252; pp. 164–199, 324.

97. *The Iron Age,* July 1, 1937, p. 66C.

98. *The Iron Age,* June 17, 1937, p. 90B.

99. *The Iron Age,* June 24, 1937, p. 91A.

100. *Proceedings of the First Wage and Policy Convention of the Steel Workers' Organizing Committee* (December 1937), p. 34.

101. This was the figure given in the La Follette Committee Hearings, Report No. 151, p. 260. *The Iron Age* put the figure at 3,000, and indicated that while the mill was not operating at capacity, all departments were working. *The Iron Age,* June 17, 1937, p. 91.

102. "The mayor had absolutely no records of any funds received by him or of any expenditures made therefrom during the strike. . . . No honest and conscientious public official would have received the sum of over $31,000 from private sources during a strike without having kept the most careful record in order to prove, beyond a doubt, that the funds had been devoted to legitimate public purposes. . . . There is a strong probability that had he kept vouchers and receipts for his expenditures they would not have accounted for the use of these funds in full." La Follette Committee Report No. 151, pp. 271–272.

103. *The Iron Age,* July 8, 1937, p. 101.

104. *Steel Labor,* July 7, 1937, p. 1.

105. La Follette Committee Report No. 151, p. 323.

106. *The Iron Age,* July 8, 1937, p. 1.

107. Pierce Williams, "Steel Strikes," *Survey Graphic.*

108. *Steel Labor,* March 18, 1938.

109. *La Follette Committee Hearings,* pp. 13938, 13941.

110. The reply of Republic Steel said, in part: "Republic cannot, and will not enter into a contract, oral or written, with an irresponsible party, and the C.I.O. as presently constituted, is utterly irresponsible. Therefore any discussion of this subject is futile. . . . The suggestion has been made by Secretary of Labor Perkins that operations be

kept at 'status quo.' This would mean that thousands of employees who want to return to their jobs would not be permitted to do so. This company cannot, and will not, be a party to any such arrangement." *La Follette Committee Hearings,* p. 13936.

111. *The Iron Age,* June 24, 1937, p. 91B.
112. Tom M. Girdler, *Boot Straps,* pp. 357–358.
113. Vincent D. Sweeny, *United Steelworkers,* p. 32.
114. La Follette Committee Report No. 151, pp. 330–331.
115. United Mine Workers of America, *Proceedings of the Thirty-Seventh Constitutional Convention* (1942), pp. 150–155. The loan and $960,000 of the advances were received by the SWOC during 1936 and 1937. The loan of $601,000 was repaid by 1941. United Steel Workers, *Proceedings of the First Constitutional Convention* (1942), p. 35.
116. United Mine Workers, *ibid.,* p. 188. This figure was quoted by Lewis after his break with Philip Murray, and was undoubtedly exaggerated.
117. Robert R. R. Brooks, *As Steel Goes,* p. 160.
118. *Steel Labor,* December 31, 1937, p. 6.
119. *The Iron Age,* January 27, 1937, p. 72.
120. *Steel Labor,* September 25, 1941, p. 6.
121. Steel Workers' Organizing Committee, *First Wage and Policy Convention* (1937), p. 49.
122. Robert R. R. Brooks, *As Steel Goes,* p. 160.
123. Philip Taft, *The Structure and Government of Labor Unions* (Cambridge, 1954), p. 222.
124. Steel Workers' Organizing Committee, *Proceedings of the First Wage and Policy Convention* (1937), p. 10.
125. *Ibid.,* p. 144.
126. Several years later, the proportion of dues retained by the national union was reduced to 50 per cent.
127. *Ibid.,* p. 104.
128. *Steel Labor,* July 28, 1939.
129. Steel Workers' Organizing Committee, *Proceedings of the First Wage and Policy Convention* (1937), p. 132.
130. See the statement by John L. Lewis in *Steel Labor,* February 18, 1938, p. 2.
131. Republic Steel Corp., 9 NLRB 219 (1938); 9 NLRB 783 (1938).
132. 14 NLRB 539 (1939); 27 NLRB 441 (1940); 32 NLRB 1145 (1941).
133. *Steel Labor,* May 13, 1938, p. 2.
134. Mimeographed report from Ralph Hetzel to Philip Murray, November 13, 1937.
135. Steel Workers' Organizing Committee, *Proceedings of the Second Wage and Policy Convention* (1940), p. 6.
136. Congress of Industrial Organizations, *Minutes of the Executive Board* (November 23, 1940), p. 207.
137. Steel Workers' Organizing Committee, *Proceedings of the Second International Wage and Policy Convention* (1940), p. 132.
138. Amalgamated Association of Iron, Steel, and Tin Workers, *Annual Reports of International Officers to 64th Annual Convention* (1939), p. 218.
139. Amalgamated Association of Iron, Steel, and Tin Workers, *Minutes of the First Policy Board Meeting* (October 29–30, 1938), p. 13; *ibid., Minutes of the Second Policy Board Meeting* (February 11, 1939), p. 22; *ibid., Minutes of the Fourth Policy Board Meeting* (August 19, 1939), p. 4.
140. *Ibid., Minutes of the Sixth Policy Board Meeting* (March 2–3, 1940), p. 8.

141. Steel Workers' Organizing Committee, *Proceedings of the Second International Wage and Policy Convention* (1940), p. 137.

142. *Ibid.*, p. 63.

143. *Steel Labor*, February 23, 1940. As early as 1938 and 1939, other companies, including the Little Steel group, had begun to deal with local SWOC lodges in the handling of grievances, even though refusing to enter into signed agreements.

144. Robert R. R. Brooks, *As Steel Goes*, p. 147.

145. Vincent Sweeney, *United Steelworkers*, p. 50.

146. *Steel Labor*, August 29, 1941, p. 1.

147. *Steel Labor*, March 20, 1941, p. 1.

148. For the complete text of the agreement, see *Steel Labor*, April 18, 1941, p. 3.

149. *Steel Labor*, September 24, 1941, p. 1.

150. *Steel Labor*, June 30, 1942, p. 8.

151. *Steel Labor*, July 31, 1942, p. 6.

152. *The Iron Age*, May 14, 1942, p. 87. The company had at first refused to obey the order of the NDMB, and its Kearny, N. J., plant was seized by the federal government and operated from August 25, 1941 to January 7, 1942, when the company bowed to the inevitable and regained control of its facilities.

153. *The Iron Age*, July 30, 1942, p. 93.

154. Tom M. Girdler, *Boot Straps*, pp. 374–375.

155. *Steel Labor*, June 30, 1942, p. 2.

156. Congress of Industrial Organizations, *Minutes of the Executive Board* (June 3–5, 1942), p. 532.

157. United Steelworkers of America, *Proceedings of the First Constitutional Convention* (1942), pp. 36, 41.

158. *Steel Labor*, August 30, 1940, p. 1.

159. Amalgamated Association of Iron, Steel, and Tin Workers, *Annual Reports of International Officers to 65th Annual Convention* (1940), p. 146.

160. Amalgamated Association of Iron, Steel, and Tin Workers, *Minutes of the Fifteenth Executive Policy Board Meeting* (April 3, 1942), pp. 2, 6.

161. United Steelworkers of America, *Proceedings of the First Constitutional Convention*, 1942, pp. 206–208, 221, 223–226, 267, 291–302.

Chapter 3   The Automobile Industry

1. Selig Perlman and Philip Taft, *History of Labor in the United States, 1896–1932* (New York, 1935), p. 587.

2. Philip Taft, *The Structure and Government of Labor Unions*, Cambridge (1954), chap. VI.

3. See Edward Levinson, *Labor on the March* (New York, 1938), pp. 82–88.

4. AFL Executive Council Minutes (January 29 to February 14, 1935), p. 56.

5. *Ibid.*, pp. 67, 205, 212, 213, 215, 221.

6. Francis J. Dillon, one of the top organizers on the AFL staff, had been assigned by Green in 1934 to supervise the activities of the federal locals chartered by the AFL in the automobile industry.

7. United Automobile Workers of America, *Proceedings of the First Constitutional Convention* (Detroit, August 26–31), 1935, pp. 38, 66.

8. See Edward Levinson, *Labor on the March*, p. 92.

9. *Proceedings of the First Constitutional Convention*, pp. 71, 116.

10. *Automotive News* (*1948 Almanac Issue*), June 7, 1948, p. 74. This figure represents average employment of workers in automobile, body, and parts plants, and was estimated by applying the Bureau of Labor Statistics employment indices to the 1933 Census of Manufactures.

11. U. S. National Recovery Administration, *Preliminary Report on Study of Regularization of Employment and Improvement of Labor Conditions in the Automobile Industry* (January 23, 1935), p. 51.

12. Clayton W. Fountain, *Union Guy* (New York, 1949), p. 41.

13. The higher figure is from *Automotive News* (*1948 Almanac Issue*), p. 74, the lower from *The United Automobile Worker* (August 21, 1937), p. 19.

14. National Recovery Administration, *Preliminary Report*, pp. 9, 66.

15. William Heston McPherson, *Labor Relations in the Automobile Industry* (Washington, 1940), p. 102.

16. Harry Bennett, *We Never Called Him Henry* (New York, 1951), p. 108.

17. Keith Sward, *The Legend of Henry Ford* (New York, 1948), p. 353.

18. National Recovery Administration, *Preliminary Report*, p. 52.

19. McPherson, *Labor Relations*, p. 8.

20. National Recovery Administration, *Preliminary Report*, p. 49.

21. U. S. Senate, Committee on Education and Labor, 75th Congress, 2d Session, Report No. 46, Part 3, pp. 14, 23, 52, 66, 70.

22. AFL Executive Council Minutes (October 5–21, 1935), p. 109.

23. The account of this convention is based in part upon an unsigned memorandum in the files of the Industrial Relations Library of Harvard University, containing a competent and accurate analysis of the events that occurred.

24. AFL Executive Council Minutes (May 5–20, 1936), p. 192.

25. Quoted in Irving Howe and B. J. Widick, *The UAW and Walter Reuther* (New York, 1949), p. 53.

26. Howe and Widick, *The UAW*, p. 52.

27. These biographies appeared in *The United Automobile Worker*, May 1936.

28. *Ibid.*, July 7, 1936.

29. *United Automobile Worker*, August 1936, p. 1.

30. *Ibid.*, November 1936, p. 4.

31. Louis Adamic, "Sitdown," *The Nation* (December 12, 1936), p. 702.

32. *Monthly Labor Review*, May 1937, p. 1235.

33. *United Automobile Worker*, December 10, 1936, p. 1.

34. *The New York Times*, December 2, 1936.

35. *United Automobile Worker*, December 10, 1936, p. 1.

36. *The New York Times*, December 23, 1936, p. 12.

37. Henry Kraus, *The Many and the Few* (Los Angeles, 1947), pp. 78–79.

38. Joel Seidman, *Sit-Down* (New York, 1937), p. 21.

39. *The New York Times*, January 1, 1937, p. 10.

40. *The New York Times*, January 3, 1937, p. 2.

41. *The New York Times*, January 5, 1937, p. 14; January 10, 1937, p. 34.

42. See Edward Levinson, *Labor on the March*, p. 155; and *Automotive Industries* (January 16, 1937), p. 73.

43. Fisher Body No. 2 was a Chevrolet assembly plant without the key significance of Fisher Body No. 1. However, the union was less well established there, and the company apparently felt that its recapture would constitute a damaging blow to union morale.

44. Levinson, *Labor on the March*, p. 157.

45. *The New York Times,* January 18, 1937, p. 2.

46. Quoted in Howe and Widick, *The UAW,* p. 58.

47. *The New York Times,* January 26, 1937, p. 1.

48. *The New York Times,* January 27, 1937, p. 1.

49. For an account of this episode by Robert Travis, in charge of organization at Flint, see *The United Automobile Worker,* February 25, 1937, p. 4. See also Henry Kraus, *The Many,* Chapters 10, 11.

50. *Automotive Industries,* February 6, 1937, p. 171.

51. United Automobile Workers, *Proceedings of the Fifth Annual Convention* (July 24–August 6, 1940), p. 104.

52. Henry Kraus, *The Many,* p. 267.

53. *The New York Times,* February 12, 1937, p. 19; *Automotive Industries,* February 13, 1937, p. 209.

54. *The New York Times,* February 12, 1937, p. 19.

55. Edward Levinson, *Rise of the Auto Workers,* United Automobile Workers of America, p. 10.

56. Russel B. Porter in *The New York Times,* April 4, 1937, IV, p. 10.

57. AFL Executive Council Minutes (February 8–19, 1937), p. 43.

58. *The New York Times,* January 8, 1937, p. 2.

59. AFL Executive Council Minutes (February 8–19, 1937), p. 52.

60. *Ibid.,* p. 43.

61. *The New York Times,* February 12, 1937, p. 19.

62. See *Monthly Labor Review,* May 1939, p. 1130, for a tabulation of sit-down strikes for the years 1936 to 1938. In 1938 there were 52 sit-down strikes involving 28,700 workers, compared with 477 strikes and 398,000 workers in 1937.

63. William Weinstone, *The Great Sit-Down Strike* (New York, 1937), pp. 29–32. Weinstone was at the time secretary of the Michigan district of the Communist Party.

64. *The United Automobile Worker,* January 22, 1937, p. 3.

65. National Association of Manufacturers, *Labor Relations Bulletin,* No. 18, March 21, 1937, p. 7.

66. Louis Adamic, "Sit-Down," *The Nation,* p. 704.

67. Quoted in Levinson, *Auto Worker,* p. 182.

68. *Monthly Labor Review,* August 1938, p. 362. The CIO was involved in 293 of such strikes.

69. *The New York Times,* March 29, 1937; April 3, 1937.

70. Quoted in National Association of Manufacturers, p. 7.

71. *The New York Times,* March 27, 1937; April 8, 1937.

72. N.L.R.B. v. Fansteel Metallurgical Corporation, 306 U. S. 240 (1939).

73. *The New York Times,* April 1, 1937.

74. *Automotive Industries,* July 3, 1937, p. 4.

75. Interview with John Brophy, March 19, 1955.

76. United Automobile Workers of America, *Proceedings of the Second Annual Convention* (1937), p. 66. This was the claimed paid membership for June 1937.

77. For details of the contract negotiations, see *Automotive Industries,* February 20, 1937, p. 246; February 27, 1937, p. 350; March 6, 1937, p. 386; March 20, 1937, p. 445.

78. The percentage of passenger cars produced by each of the major producers in 1936 was as follows: General Motors, 42.0 per cent; Chrysler, 25.0 per cent; Ford, 22.8 per cent; other, 10.2 per cent. *Automotive Industries,* February 27, 1937, p. 276.

79. *The New York Times,* March 9, 1937, p. 1.

80. *Automotive Industries,* April 3, 1937, p. 511.

81. *The New York Times,* April 7, 1937, p. 4.

82. Levinson, *Rise of the Auto Worker*, p. 268.
83. *The New York Times*, April 7, 1937, p. 4.
84. See *infra*, p. 178.
85. Memorandum by Frank Winn, March 28, 1958.
86. *The New York Times*, October 19, 1938, p. 3.
87. Benjamin Stolberg, *The Story of the CIO* (New York, 1938), p. 161.
88. Memorandum of March 28, 1958.
89. *The New York Times*, April 7, 1937, p. 4; Levinson, *Auto Worker*, p. 269.
90. *United Automobile Worker*, June 26, 1937, p. 4.
91. *The New York Times*, April 3, 1937, p. 2.
92. *The New York Times*, June 18, 1937.
93. Howe and Widick, *The UAW*, p. 68.
94. *United Automobile Worker*, May 22, 1937, p. 4; June 19, 1937, p. 1; July 17, 1937, p. 3.
95. United Automobile Workers of America, *Proceedings of the Second Annual Convention* (1937), p. 284.
96. The proposal was to give each local one convention vote for 200 members or less, one additional vote for the next 300 members, and one additional vote for each additional 500 members, with a maximum of five votes per local. The convention instead voted simply to give each local delegation one vote per 100 members.
97. *The New York Times*, August 31, 1937, p. 10; *West Side Conveyer*, August 31, 1937.
98. *United Automobile Worker*, August 14, 1937.
99. United Automobile Workers of America, *Proceedings of the Second Annual Convention* (1937), p. 131.
100. *Automotive Industries*, December 4, 1937, p. 791; January 1, 1938, p. 2; January 15, 1938, p. 64.
101. *Automotive News* (1948 Almanac Edition), p. 74.
102. *United Automobile Worker*, September 18, 1937, p. 1.
103. Memorandum from Frank Winn, March 28, 1958.
104. *Automotive Industries*, November 27, 1937, p. 766.
105. *United Automobile Worker*, November 27, 1937, p. 6; December 18, 1937, p. 5; March 12, 1938, p. 6.
106. *West Side Conveyer*, March 15, 1938.
107. *United Automobile Worker*, April 2, 1938, p. 1; March 5, 1938, p. 1.
108. *West Side Conveyer*, March 15, 1938.
109. *The New York Times*, February 4, 1938, p. 1.
110. Howe and Widick, *The UAW*, p. 75; Stolberg, *The CIO*, p. 179.
111. *Automotive Industries*, May 14, 1938, p. 652; May 28, 1938, p. 709.
112. Howe and Widick, *The UAW*, pp. 74–75; Stolberg, *The CIO*, p. 180. In April 1938, the communists, after first agreeing to support Victor Reuther for secretary-treasurer of the Michigan CIO Council, deserted him in favor of the Progressive candidate, Richard T. Leonard. See Clayton W. Fountain, *Union Guy*, pp. 83–85, for an account of this episode.
113. *The New York Times*, June 14, 1938, p. 1.
114. *United Automobile Worker*, July 9, 1938, p. 1.
115. *Automotive Industries*, July 2, 1938, p. 1.
116. *United Automobile Worker*, July 9, 1938, p. 6.
117. *Ibid.*, July 30, 1938, p. 1.
118. Howe and Widick, *The UAW*, p. 75.
119. *United Automobile Worker*, February 11, 1939, p. 5; February 18, 1939, p. 3.

120. *The New York Times,* August 7, 1938, p. 1.

121. Fountain, *Union Guy,* p. 97, said of these letters: "For a time the use of these letters was a great joke in the inner circles of the union. It was no secret that the Stalinists had obtained the letters by the simple device of sending their agents to break into the living quarters of Lovestone. A small thing like a burglary and the invasion of the privacy of a man's home were all in the day's work for the Stalinist agents."

122. *The New York Times,* August 7, 1938, p. 1.

123. *Automotive Industries,* April 27, 1938, p. 242.

124. *United Automobile Worker,* September 3, 1938, p. 1.

125. Membership about this time was said to have fallen to 90,000. George Douglas Blackwood, "The United Automobile Workers of America, 1935–51," unpublished Ph.D. thesis (University of Chicago, 1951), p. 110.

126. *The New York Times,* September 17, 1938, p. 5.

127. *The New York Times,* October 19, 1938, p. 3.

128. *United Automobile Worker,* February 11, 1939, p. 3.

129. Harry Bennett, *We Never Called Him Henry,* p. 109.

130. *United Automobile Worker,* October 15, 1938, p. 1. According to Martin, it was he, rather than Bennett, who initiated the interview. *The New York Times,* October 12, 1938, p. 8.

131. Keith Sward, *The Legend of Henry Ford,* p. 382.

132. Bennett, *We Never Called Him Henry,* p. 115.

133. *United Automobile Worker* (*Martin faction*), February 11, 1939, p. 1.

134. United Automobile Workers of America, *Proceedings of the Special Convention,* Cleveland, 1939, p. 16.

135. *United Automobile Worker,* January 28, 1939, p. 6.

136. AFL Executive Council Minutes (January 24–February 8, 1938), p. 211.

137. Bennett, *We Never Called Him Henry,* pp. 115–116.

138. *United Automobile Worker,* January 7, 1939, p. 5.

139. *United Automobile Worker* (Martin faction), February 11, 1939, p. 3.

140. *United Automobile Worker,* January 21, 1939, p. 1.

141. *Automotive Industries,* January 14, 1939, p. 33.

142. Fountain, *Union Guy,* pp. 97–98.

143. Report of William J. Carney, March 3, 1939 (typewritten copy in the files of Sidney Hillman).

144. *The New York Times,* March 7, 1939, p. 8.

145. AFL Executive Council Minutes (May 10–19, 1939), p. 138.

146. United Automobile Workers of America, *Proceedings of the Second Annual Convention* (1937), p. 60.

147. Fountain, *Union Guy,* p. 99.

148. Stolberg, *The CIO,* p. 163.

149. United Automobile Workers of America, *Proceedings of the Special Convention* (1939), pp. 585, 719.

150. *The New York Times,* April 3, 1939, p. 2; April 6, 1939, p. 20.

151. United Automobile Workers of America, *Proceedings of the Special Convention* (1939), pp. 102, 291.

152. Edward Levinson, *Rise of the Auto Workers,* p. 16.

153. *Automotive News* (1948 Almanac Issue), p. 74.

154. *United Automobile Worker,* June 14, 1939, p. 1.

155. *Automotive Industries,* July 1, 1939, p. 34.

156. *The New York Times,* June 23, 1939, p. 5.

157. See Fountain, *Union Guy*, chap. 10; *United Automobile Worker*, August 9, 1939, p. 1.

158. *Automotive Industries*, August 1, 1939, p. 128.

159. *United Automobile Worker*, August 23, 1939, p. 1; August 30, 1939, p. 1; September 20, 1939, p. 1.

160. *United Automobile Worker*, October 4, 1939, p. 1.

161. *Automotive Industries*, December 15, 1939, p. 650.

162. *United Automobile Worker*, December 6, 1939, p. 1.

163. *Automotive Industries*, May 1, 1940, p. 436. The AFL plants were in outlying areas: Meriden, Conn.; Norwood, Ohio; and Kansas City, Mo. All plants in Detroit, Pontiac, Flint, and Saginaw were won by the CIO.

164. Bennett, *We Never Called Him Henry*, p. 116.

165. Memorandum from Frank Winn, March 28, 1958.

166. United Automobile Workers of America, *Proceedings of the Fifth Annual Convention*, 1940, pp. 10, 384.

167. See his speech at *ibid.*, pp. 110–114, p. 428.

168. *Ibid.*, pp. 293, 297, 438.

169. *Ibid.*, p. 175.

170. See Keith Sward, *The Legend of Henry Ford*, pp. 291–306, for contrary evidence.

171. *Ibid.*, p. 374. Bennett's own account of the espionage procedure is interesting: "As the CIO's efforts to unionize the Ford Motor Company became more intense, there were accusations that I was spying on the union. The accusations were unfounded. Actually, it was a waste of time to send my men into the union to get information. There were always a certain number of men who thought the union wouldn't win out and wanted to stay in good with us. After every meeting, these men would come to us and tell us what had transpired. We were good listeners. When it seemed advisable, I would take one of these informants up to lunch with me in the executives' dining room and let him talk all he wanted." Bennett, *We Never Called Him Henry*, pp. 116–117.

172. *United Automobile Worker*, May 15, 1937, p. 1.

173. Sward, *The Legend of Henry Ford*, pp. 389–400.

174. *The New York Times*, April 8, 1937, p. 1.

175. Bennett, *We Never Called Him Henry*, p. 116.

176. Blackwood, "The United Automobile Workers, 1935–51," p. 150.

177. Sward, *The Legend of Henry Ford*, p. 348.

178. Bennett, *We Never Called Him Henry*, p. 138.

179. Sward, *The Legend of Henry Ford*, p. 348. The upper figure, which was the union estimate, was acknowledged by Harry Bennett to be "almost right." *The New York Times*, October 7, 1941, p. 18.

180. AFL Executive Council Minutes (February 10–20, 1941), p. 132.

181. *The Legend of Henry Ford*, p. 406. The quotation is from an interview in *Time*.

182. Howe and Widick, *The UAW*, p. 104.

183. *The New York Times*, April 3, 1941, p. 1. Violence was limited largely to the first day of the strike. Thereafter, the company agreed not to try to work the plant, and there were no more serious incidents.

184. Bennett, *We Never Called Him Henry*, p. 136.

185. *United Automobile Worker*, April 15, 1941, p. 1.

186. Sward, *The Legend of Henry Ford*, p. 418.

187. Computed from *Automotive News* (1948 Almanac Issue), p. 40. Ford percentage of the market for the years 1936 to 1941 was as follows:

1936 — 24.5 per cent	1938 — 22.6 per cent	1940 — 19.8 per cent
1937 — 22.3 per cent	1939 — 22.9 per cent	1941 — 20.4 per cent

188. See Bennett, *We Never Called Him Henry*, Ch. 17 and pp. 141–145 for evidence to this effect.

189. Matthew Josephson, *Sidney Hillman*, New York, 1952, p. 526.

190. Blackwood, "The United Automobile Workers 1935–51," p. 152.

191. Bennett, *We Never Called Him Henry*, p. 142.

192. *United Automobile Worker*, June 1, 1941, p. 7; July 1, 1941, p. 1.

193. Sward, *The Legend of Henry Ford*, p. 423.

194. Bennett, *We Never Called Him Henry*, p. 139.

195. *United Automobile Worker*, June 1, 1941, p. 1; June 15, 1941, p. 1.

196. *Automotive News* (1948 Almanac Issue), p. 74.

197. Levinson, *Rise of the Auto Workers*, p. 20.

198. These and subsequent facts are from Report of the Grievance Committee to the 1941 UAW convention, in United Automobile Workers of America, *Proceedings of the 1941 Convention*, pp. 243–246. See also United States Department of Labor, *Report on the Work of the National Defense Mediation Board* (Washington, 1942), pp. 156–161.

199. United Automobile Workers of America, *Proceedings of the 1941 Convention*, pp. 244, 255, 402, 403, 405, 423, 430, 433, 441.

200. See United States Department of Labor, *National Defense Mediation Board*, pp. 98–100.

201. Joel Seidman, *American Labor From Defense To Reconversion* (Chicago, 1953), p. 44.

202. Matthew Josephson, *Sidney Hillman*, pp. 538–544.

203. United Automobile Workers of America, *Proceedings of the 1941 Convention*, pp. 85, 94, 96, 303, 688, 692, 700, 701, 724.

204. Louis Stark in *The New York Times*, August 12, 1941, p. 28; August 16, 1941, p. 8.

205. See Howe and Widick, *The UAW*, pp. 108–110.

206. CIO Executive Board Minutes (March 24, 1942), p. 219.

Chapter 4   Coal Mining

1. McAlister Coleman, *Men and Coal* (New York, 1943), p. 139.

2. David J. McDonald and Edward A. Lynch, *Coal and Unionism* (1939), p. 187.

3. Glenn L. Parker, *The Coal Industry* (Washington, 1940), pp. 76, 77.

4. United Mine Workers of America, *Proceedings of the Thirty-Fourth Constitutional Convention* (Washington, D. C., January 28–February 7, 1936), p. 53.

5. The output of bituminous coal fell from 565 million tons in 1923 to 310 million tons in 1932. Between the same terminal years, employment declined from 705,000 to 406,000. Morton S. Baratz, *The Union and the Coal Industry* (New Haven, 1955), p. 40.

6. Parker, *The Coal Industry*, pp. 77–81.

7. Coleman, *Men and Coal*, p. 148.

8. The Twentieth Century Fund, *How Collective Bargaining Works* (New York, 1942), p. 270.

9. *United Mine Workers' Journal*, January 1, 1936, p. 4.

10. Parker, *The Coal Industry*, p. 82.

11. United Mine Workers of America, *Proceedings of the Thirty-Fourth Constitutional Convention*, pp. 11, 53.

12. McDonald and Lynch, *Coal and Unionism*, p. 190.

13. United Mine Workers of America, *Proceedings of the Thirty-Fourth Constitutional Convention*, p. 119.

14. *Ibid.*, p. 98; see also pages 100, 114, 122, 130.

15. Saul Alinsky, *John L. Lewis* (New York, 1949), p. 38.

16. United Mine Workers of America, *Proceedings of the Thirty-Fourth Constitutional Convention*, pp. 22, 211, 470, 471, 503.

17. Carter v. Carter Coal Company, 298 U. S. 238 (1936).

18. *United Mine Workers' Journal*, March 1, 1936, p. 24.

19. *United Mine Workers' Journal*, April 1, 1936, p. 6; May 15, 1936, p. 3.

20. *United Mine Workers' Journal*, September 1, 1936, p. 6; October 15, 1936, p. 10; February 1, 1937, p. 20.

21. 76th Congress, 1st Session, U. S. Senate, Report No. 6, Part 2 (February 13, 1939), pp. 12, 23. (This report is the La Follette Committee Report.)

22. *Ibid.*, p. 28. Sheriff Middleton refused to testify on the source of these funds on the ground of possible self-incrimination. See also *Ibid.*, pp. 31, 34, 42, 57.

23. *United Mine Workers' Journal*, February 15, 1937, p. 7.

24. La Follette Committee Report, p. 81.

25. *United Mine Workers' Journal*, June 1, 1937, p. 15.

26. United Mine Workers of America, *Proceedings of the Thirty-Fifth Constitutional Convention* (Washington, D. C., January 25–February 3, 1938), pp. 18, 22, 32.

27. In this connection, the following amusing item appeared in the official organ of the UMW: "Some malicious or irresponsible person has started a story to the effect that the new headquarters building of the United Mine Workers of America in Washington is heated with oil. That story is just an ordinary, garden-variety falsehood. We could say that any person who says our building is heated with oil is a damn liar, but we do not use that kind of language. The fact is that our building is heated with Pennsylvania anthracite, produced by Union miners who are members of the United Mine Workers of America." *United Mine Workers' Journal*, April 1, 1938, p. 9.

28. For an analysis of experience under this legislation, see Waldo E. Fisher and Charles M. James, *Minimum Price-Fixing in the Bituminous Coal Industry* (Princeton, 1955).

29. *United Mine Workers' Journal*, January 15, 1938, p. 6.

30. United Mine Workers of America, *Proceedings of the Thirty-Fifth Constitutional Convention*, pp. 72, 143, 155, 164.

31. *United Mine Workers' Journal*, March 1, 1938, p. 11.

32. United Mine Workers of America, *Proceedings of the Thirty-Fifth Constitutional Convention*, pp. 83, 125, 367.

33. Alinsky, *John L. Lewis*, p. 154.

34. This section is based largely upon Harriet D. Hudson, *The Progressive Mine Workers of America: A Study in Rival Unionism* (Urbana, 1952).

35. Hudson, *The Progressive Mine Workers*, p. 43.

36. AFL Executive Council Minutes (May 23–30, 1937), pp. 73, 103.

37. AFL Executive Council Minutes (August 22–September 2, 1938), p. 186.

38. Hudson, *The Progressive Mine Workers*, p. 71.

39. American Federation of Labor, *Report of the Proceedings of the Fifty-Eighth Annual Convention* (Houston, 1938), pp. 217, 221.

40. In the Matter of Alston Coal Company, 13 NLRB, No. 77 (1939).
41. Hudson, *The Progressive Mine Workers,* p. 75.
42. In the Matter of Stevens Coal Company, 19 NLRB No. 14 (1940).
43. American Federation of Labor, *Report of Proceedings of the Fifty-Ninth Annual Convention* (Cincinnati, 1939), p. 311.
44. Hudson, *The Progressive Mine Workers,* pp. 145, 152.
45. United Mine Workers of America, *Proceedings of the Thirty-Sixth Constitutional Convention* (Columbus, January 23–February 1, 1940), pp. 26, 27.
46. Illinois and Indiana, as well as other areas outside the Appalachian fields in Pennsylvania, Ohio, Virginia, West Virginia, Tennessee, and Kentucky, constituted the so-called outlying districts. These areas, which produced about 30 per cent of the national tonnage, generally signed on the same terms as the Appalachian agreement, but were not themselves represented in the negotiations.
47. *The New York Times,* April 15, 1939, p. 8.
48. Lewis' description of the negotiations is an amusing one: "This stupid, senseless lockout of mine workers continues. No progress has been made or is being made toward a settlement. For long periods in this conference there are no discussions. Deep silence prevails as the negotiators gaze at each other's pallid faces." *United Mine Workers' Journal,* April 15, 1939, p. 3.
49. United Mine Workers of America, *Proceedings of the Thirty-Sixth Constitutional Convention,* p. 29.
50. *Coal Age,* June 1939, p. 86.
51. United Mine Workers of America, *Proceedings of the Thirty-Sixth Constitutional Convention,* p. 30. The four states were controlled by Democratic administrations.
52. Alinsky, *John L. Lewis,* p. 165.
53. *The New York Times,* May 12, 1939, p. 1.
54. *Coal Age,* June 1939, p. 86.
55. Lewis accused Chandler of taking this action as revenge for the support which the UMW had given to Alben Barkley against Chandler in the senatorial primaries in 1938. *United Mine Workers' Journal,* June 1, 1939, p. 3.
56. *United Mine Workers' Journal,* May 15, 1939, p. 3.
57. United Mine Workers of America, *Proceedings of the Thirty-Sixth Constitutional Convention,* p. 42.
58. *Ibid.,* pp. 99, 104, 126, 136, 192, 363, 365, 366, 371, 373, 374, 378, 399.
59. See *supra,* p. 58.
60. See United Mine Workers of America, *John L. Lewis* (1952), pp. 124–131.
61. Coleman, *Men and Coal,* p. 196.
62. *United Mine Workers' Journal,* March 15, 1941, p. 3.
63. Baratz, *The Union,* pp. 100, 102. The union estimated the cost of equalization to be 3.2 cents per ton. United Mine Workers of America, *Proceedings of the Thirty-Seventh Constitutional Convention* (Cincinnati, October 6–14, 1942), p. 50.
64. *Ibid.,* p. 48. The union claimed that Charles O'Neill, chief spokesman for the operators, admitted possession of the letter and then urged that the negotiators reply to it, but that the union took the position that it was purely a private message from Knudsen to O'Neill.
65. *The New York Times,* April 7, 1941, p. 1.
66. United Mine Workers of America, *Proceedings of the Thirty-Seventh Constitutional Convention,* p. 52; *United Mine Workers' Journal,* April 15, 1941, p. 3.
67. *Ibid.,* p. 56.
68. Charles O'Neill said of this clause: "The amount of deduction from miners' gross

earnings involved in this practice has reached, in the case of three large mines in the Smokeless fields of southern West Virginia, 13 1/3 per cent of the total coal produced by these mines in 1940. . . . This coal, for which the miners were not paid, was sold in the open market by the operators." *United Mine Workers' Journal,* May 1, 1941, p. 3.

69. United Mine Workers of America, *Proceedings of the Thirty-Seventh Constitutional Convention,* p. 59. It was estimated that the northern operators represented 55 per cent of the total tonnage, the outlying districts 13 per cent, and the South the remainder.

70. *United Mine Workers' Journal.* June 1, 1941, p. 12.

71. Twentieth Century Fund, p. 308.

72. United Mine Workers of America, *Proceedings of the Thirty-Seventh Constitutional Convention,* pp. 113, 119.

73. *The New York Times,* September 26, 1941, p. 15; September 30, 1941, p. 13; October 5, 1941, p. 43; *United Mine Workers' Journal,* October 15, 1941, p. 3.

74. Benjamin F. Fairless, *It Could Only Happen in the U. S.* (United States Steel Corporation, 1957), p. 38.

75. Alinsky, *John L. Lewis,* p. 238.

76. For the text of this memorandum, see United Mine Workers of America, *Proceedings of the Thirty-Seventh Constitutional Convention,* p. 68.

77. For an account of the Currier Lumber case, to which Lewis refers in his letter, see *infra,* p. 526.

78. The antagonistic attitude of Lewis toward Hillman is well illustrated by the following editorial in the *United Mine Workers' Journal:* "Any good newspaper reporter who will follow the footsteps of this failure [of collective bargaining] will find that the pathway leads right up to the White House, where incompetent bureaucrats spill their ill advice. The Department of Labor has become a mere clerical institution for the certification of labor disputes and stoppages to the Mediation Board. The Mediation Board, in turn, has become a subservient council, reduced to fronting for the wiles and incompetency of Hillman, who never succeeded in becoming a journeyman in his own trade. Hillman admits that he is the guy who knows all, and who is responsible for all." *United Mine Workers' Journal,* November 1, 1941, p. 10; see also pp. 69, 70, 72.

79. See *The New York Times,* October 28, 1941, pp. 1, 19, for a report of these speeches.

80. Quoted in Joel Seidman, *American Labor from Defense to Reconversion* (Chicago, 1953), pp. 64–65.

81. *The New York Times,* October 30, 1941, p. 1.

82. United Mine Workers of America, *Proceedings of the Thirty-Seventh Constitutional Convention,* p. 74.

83. For the full text of the Board's opinion, see United States Department of Labor, *Report on the Work of the National Defense Mediation Board* (Washington, 1942), p. 118.

84. *The New York Times,* November 13, 1941, p. 1.

85. United Mine Workers of America, *Proceedings of the Thirty-Seventh Constitutional Convention,* pp. 75, 76.

86. *The New York Times,* November 14, 1941, p. 1.

87. United Mine Workers of America, *Proceedings of the Thirty-Seventh Constitutional Convention,* p. 77.

88. United Mine Workers of America, *Proceedings of the Thirty-Seventh Constitutional Convention,* p. 79.

89. *The New York Times,* November 17, 1941, p. 1.

90. United Mine Workers of America, *Proceedings of the Thirty-Seventh Constitutional Convention,* p. 79.

91. *United Mine Workers' Journal,* December 1, 1941, p. 3.

92. *The New York Times,* November 21, 1941, p. 1.

93. *The New York Times,* November 23, 1941, p. 1.

94. Alinsky, *John L. Lewis,* p. 247.

95. For the text of the Steelman opinion, see United Mine Workers of America, *Proceedings of the Thirty-Seventh Constitutional Convention,* p. 83.

96. CIO Executive Board Minutes (June 3–5, 1942), p. 72.

97. Alinsky, *John L. Lewis,* pp. 226–237.

98. See *supra,* p. 67.

99. CIO Executive Board Minutes (June 3–5, 1942), pp. 167, 290.

100. Alinsky, *John L. Lewis,* p. 257.

101. Alinsky, *John L. Lewis,* p. 264. Mr. Alinsky told the writer that he was a witness to this episode.

102. The vote in favor of this action was 17 to 1. Martin Wagner of District 50, who cast the only dissenting vote, resigned immediately afterwards. *United Mine Workers' Journal,* June 15, 1952, p. 3.

103. Alinsky, *John L. Lewis,* p. 271.

104. United Mine Workers of America, *Proceedings of the Thirty-Seventh Constitutional Convention,* pp. 177–188, 207, 419.

105. Coleman, *Men and Coal,* p. 218.

106. Baratz, *The Union,* p. 92.

107. Baratz, *The Union,* pp. 107, 133.

108. Bureau of Labor Statistics, *Handbook of Labor Statistics* (1948), p. 137.

109. For a good statement of this principle, see C. Lawrence Christenson, "The Theory of the Offset Factor: The Impact of Labor Disputes Upon Coal Production," *The American Economic Review* (September, 1953), p. 513.

110. Alinsky, *John L. Lewis,* p. 350.

Chapter 5 The Electrical and Radio Manufacturing Industries

1. Milton Derber, "Electrical Products," in Twentieth Century Fund, *How Collective Bargaining Works* (New York, 1942), pp. 782–783.

2. AFL Executive Council Minutes (January 23–February 1, 1934), pp. 2–3; January 29–February 14, 1935, p. 225.

3. *Ibid.,* pp. 150, 152.

4. *The Journal of Electrical Workers and Operators* (May 1936), p. 203.

5. AFL Executive Council Minutes (January 15–29, 1936), pp. 33, 36, 119.

6. *The Journal of Electrical Workers and Operators* (March 1936), p. 100.

7. *The New York Times,* February 8, 1936, p. 3; February 10, 1936, p. 13.

8. *Union News Service,* February 17, 1936.

9. *The New York Times,* February 11, 1936, p. 15.

10. *The Journal of Electrical Workers and Operators* (May 1936), p. 202.

11. AFL Executive Council Minutes (May 5–20, 1936), p. 51.

12. Committee for Industrial Organization, *Minutes of the Meeting of November 7–8, 1938* (typewritten).

13. United Electrical, Radio and Machine Workers of America, *Proceedings of the*

Second Annual Convention (Philadelphia, 1937), Afternoon Session of September 4, pp. 1–4 (mimeographed).

14. AFL Executive Council Minutes (January 15–29, 1936). p. 31.

15. *The New York Times,* February 11, 1936, p. 15; November 8, 1936, p. 2.

16. *Electrical Union News* (UE local 201), September 12, 1941, p. 1.

17. Derber, *How Collective Bargaining Works,* pp. 746–747; 791–793.

18. For an account of the strike, see *The Journal of Electrical Workers and Operators* (September 1936), p. 386.

19. Derber, *How Collective Bargaining Works,* pp. 793–796.

20. *Union News Service,* September 14, 1936.

21. United Electrical and Radio Workers, *Proceedings of the First Annual Convention* (September 4–7, 1936), p. 7.

22. United Electrical and Radio Workers of America, *Minutes of the Second Annual Convention* (Philadelphia, September 3–6, 1937), Report of the Secretary-Treasurer.

23. Derber, *How Collective Bargaining Works,* p. 747; *Union News Service,* December 21, 1936.

24. United Electrical and Radio Workers of America, *Minutes of the Second Annual Convention,* Report of the General President, p. 13.

25. Derber, *How Collective Bargaining Works,* pp. 762–764; *The New York Times,* July 11, 1937, p. 2.

26. United Electrical and Radio Workers of America, *Minutes of the Second Annual Convention,* Report of the Director of the Utilities Division, *passim.*

27. Matter of Consolidated Edison Company of New York, Inc., 4 NLRB 71 (1937).

28. Consolidated Edison Co. v. NLRB, 305 U. S. 197 (1938). Reversal was on the ground that the NLRB had failed to make the IBEW a party to the case and to give it official notice that its contracts were under attack.

29. National Labor Relations Board, *Third Annual Report,* Fiscal Year Ended June 30, 1938, p. 64.

30. United Electrical and Radio Workers, *Minutes of the Second Annual Convention,* Session of September 5, p. 2.

31. *The Journal of Electrical Workers and Operators* (October 1937), p. 438.

32. *Union News Service,* September 13, 1937.

33. United Electrical and Radio Workers of America, *Minutes of the Second Annual Convention,* Report of the General President, p. 9.

34. *Ibid.,* Report of Secretary-Treasurer, p. 5.

35. *Ibid.,* Session of September 6, 1937, p. 16.

36. United Electrical, Radio and Machine Workers of America, *Proceedings of the Third Annual Convention* (St. Louis, September 5–9, 1938), p. 1.

37. Derber, *How Collective Bargaining Works,* pp. 752–760; 787–788; *Union News Service,* June 11, 1938.

38. United Electrical, Radio and Machine Workers of America, *Proceedings of the Third Annual Convention,* pp. 226, 228.

39. *Ibid.,* pp. 117–130.

40. *Union News Service,* February 5, 1938.

41. Edward Levinson, *Labor on the March* (New York, 1938), p. 246.

42. United Electrical, Radio and Machine Workers of America, *Proceedings of the Third Annual Convention,* p. 1.

43. United Electrical, Radio and Machine Workers of America, *Proceedings of the Seventh International Convention* (Camden, September 1–5, 1941), p. 5.

44. Congress of Industrial Organizations, *Proceedings of the First Constitutional Convention* (November 14–18, 1938), p. 15.

45. *UE News,* June 17, 1939, p. 8.

46. *UE News,* January 20, 1940, p. 4. The 1937 Census of Manufactures reported that there were 389,500 wage earners in the radio, electrical machinery, refrigerator, washing machine, and business machine industries. *U. S. Biennial Census of Manufactures* (1937), Part I, p. 1082. Allowing for unemployment, this figure is close to the total given by the union for 1937.

47. United Electrical, Radio and Machine Workers of America, *Proceedings of the Fifth Convention* (Springfield, Mass., September 4–8, 1939), pp. 186, 187, 191. This was actually the fourth annual convention, but was renumbered so that the constitutional convention of 1936 could be counted as the first convention, which had not been done theretofore.

48. *UE News,* November 18, 1939, p. 1.

49. *The Journal of the Electrical Workers and Operators* (February 1940), p. 63.

50 James Carey, "We've Got the Reds on the Run," *American Magazine* (September 1948), p. 30.

51. Max M. Kampelman, *The Communist Party vs the C.I.O.* (New York, 1957), p. 122.

52. Benjamin Stolberg, *The CIO,* p. 225.

53. Kampelman, *The Communist Party,* pp. 122, 127–128.

54. Carey, *American Magazine.* There seems to be no reason to question Carey's good faith. He became president of UE at a very early age, and had had little political or trade union experience. However, for some dissenting views, see James J. Matles, *The Members Run This Union,* UE Publication No. 94 (March, 1947), and General Electric Corporation, *What To Do About Communism in Unions* (New York, 1952).

55. Kampelman, *The Communist Party,* p. 121.

56. United Electrical and Radio Workers of America, *Proceedings of the First Annual Convention* (1936), p. 41.

57. United Electrical, Radio and Machine Workers of America, *Proceedings of the Third Annual Convention,* pp. 148, 211, 214.

58. *UE News,* September 2, 1939, p. 2.

59. United Electrical, Radio and Machine Workers of America, *Proceedings of the Fifth Convention* (Springfield, Mass., September 4–8, 1939), pp. 45, 167, 176–179, 203.

60. United Electrical, Radio and Machine Workers of America, *Proceedings of the Seventh International Convention,* p. 5.

61. In the matter of Westinghouse Electric and Manufacturing Company, 22 NLRB 13 (1940).

62. Derber, *How Collective Bargaining Works,* pp. 760–761.

63. H. Z. Heinz Co. v. NLRB, 311 U. S. 514 (1941).

64. *UE News,* December 16, 1939, p. 1; June 22, 1940, p. 1.

65. *UE News,* May 11, 1940, p. 1; August 17, 1940, p. 1.

66. United Electrical, Radio and Machine Workers of America, *Proceedings of the Sixth National Convention* (Cleveland, September 2–6, 1940), pp. 13–14.

67. United Electrical, Radio and Machine Workers of America, *Proceedings of the Seventh National Convention,* p. 5.

68. *UE News,* September 30, 1939, p. 2.

69. *UE News,* February 24, 1940, p. 2; January 13, 1940, p. 8; July 27, 1940, p. 5.

70. United Electrical, Radio and Machine Workers of America, *Proceedings of the Sixth National Convention,* pp. 74, 215.

71. United Electrical, Radio and Machine Workers of America, *Proceedings of the Seventh International Convention,* p. 5.

72. *UE News,* April 5, 1941, p. 1; May 3, 1941, p. 1.

73. Kampelman, *The Communist Party*, p. 124.
74. See, for example, an article in support of the strike against North American Aviation in *UE News*, June 14, 1941, p. 3.
75. United Electrical, Radio and Machine Workers of America, *Proceedings of the Seventh International Convention*, p. 15.
76. *UE News*, October 26, 1940, p. 1. Carey, in a personal statement, urged the membership to vote for Roosevelt. *UE News*, November 2, 1940, p. 5.
77. See *UE News*, December 28, 1940, p. 4; January 25, 1941, p. 4; March 8, 1941, p. 5.
78. *UE News*, March 8, 1941, p. 5.
79. *UE News*, June 21, 1941, p. 7.
80. *UE News*, July 26, 1941, p. 4; *UE News*, September 6, 1941, p. 1.
81. *UE News*, January 18, 1941, p. 5; March 22, 1941, p. 5.
82. *UE News*, July 12, 1941, p. 5; July 26, 1941, p. 5; August 2, 1941, p. 5.
83. United Electrical, Radio and Machine Workers of America, *Proceedings of the Seventh International Convention*, pp. 25-26, 77, 81, 88, 158, 172.
84. James B. Carey, *American Magazine*.
85. United Electrical, Radio and Machine Workers of America, *Proceedings of the Seventh International Convention*, pp. 111, 137.
86. Kampelman, *The Communist Party*, p. 123.

Chapter 6 The Rubber Industry

1. John Newton Thurber, "Our History, 1935–1955," *United Rubber Worker* (September 1955), p. 6; see also p. 3.
2. Donald Anthony, "Rubber Products," *How Collective Bargaining Works* (The Twentieth Century Fund, 1942), p. 639.
3. Thurber, *United Rubber Worker*, p. 3.
4. The precise wording of the Executive Council resolution authorizing the issuance of a charter to the Rubber Workers was: "A charter to rubber workers be issued upon proper application to cover all those in that industry who are engaged in the mass production of rubber products, same not to cover or include such workers who construct buildings, manufacturing or installing of machinery, or engage in maintenance work or in work outside of the plants or factories." American Federation of Labor, *Report of Proceedings of the Fifty-Fifth Annual Convention* (1935), p. 96.
5. AFL Executive Council Minutes (April 30–May 7, 1935), p. 134.
6. Thurber, *United Rubber Worker*, p. 4.
7. United Rubber Workers of America, *Proceedings of the First Constitutional Convention* (Akron, September 12–17, 1935), pp. 15, 20, 38, 40.
8. *United Rubber Worker*, April 1936, p. 1.
9. American Federation of Labor, *Report of Proceedings of the Fifty-Fifth Annual Convention* (1935), p. 729. The resolution read as follows: "Resolved, that the Fifty-fifth convention of the American Federation of Labor formulate an Industrial Rubber Workers Union, whereby the organization shall have full jurisdiction over all employees in and around the respective factories without segregation of the employees in the Industry."
10. Thurber, *United Rubber Workers*, p. 5.
11. Harold S. Roberts, *The Rubber Workers* (New York, 1944), p. 147. I have relied heavily throughout the present chapter upon this excellent history of the rubber workers. The measure of my indebtedness to it will be obvious to anyone who is familiar with the work.

12. *United Rubber Worker,* May 1936, p. 12.

13. Letter from Sherman Dalrymple to John Brophy, dated October 7, 1936 (CIO files).

14. United Rubber Workers of America, *Proceedings of the First Convention* (September 13–21, 1936), p. 429.

15. *United Rubber Worker,* August 1936, p. 4. This estimate is in close agreement with a global industry estimate in John Dean Gaffey, *The Productivity of Labor in the Rubber Tire Manufacturing Industry* (New York, 1940), p. 60.

16. Anthony, *How Collective Bargaining Works,* p. 632.

17. The six-hour day had been instituted during the depression as a means of spreading the available work. Its maintenance was a cardinal union demand so long as unemployment prevailed.

18. Edward Levinson, *Labor on the March* (New York, 1938), pp. 143–146.

19. Committee for Industrial Organization, *Minutes of the Meeting of December 9, 1935.*

20. *The New York Times,* March 4, 1936, p. 12, quoted by Roberts, *The Rubber Workers,* p. 150.

21. Roberts, *The Rubber Workers,* p. 150. The company agreed verbally to permit the union shop committee to deal with foremen and higher management. *United Rubber Worker,* April 1936, p. 9.

22. Roberts, *The Rubber Workers,* p. 201.

23. See Thurber, *United Rubber Worker,* p. 6; Roberts, *The Rubber Workers,* p. 155, n. 69; and *United Rubber Worker,* June 1936, p. 1; July 1936, p. 2.

24. Roberts, *The Rubber Workers,* pp. 218–226.

25. Cyrus S. Ching, *Review and Reflection* (New York, 1953), p. 47.

26. *United Rubber Worker,* September 1936, p. 3. Two months later, membership was put at 35,000, of whom 25,000 were in Akron. *United Rubber Worker,* November 1936, p. 1.

27. United Rubber Workers of America, *Proceedings of the First Convention,* pp. 37, 175, 354.

28. For an account of this period, see Thurber, *United Rubber Worker,* pp. 13–14.

29. For the full text of the agreement, see *United Rubber Worker,* May 1937, p. 5.

30. *United Rubber Worker,* August 1937, p. 1; November 1937, p. 10; February 1938, p. 1.

31. See United Rubber Workers of America, *Proceedings of the Second Convention* (Akron, September 12–20, 1937), p. 63.

32. *United Rubber Worker,* March 1938, p. 2.

33. *United Rubber Worker,* April 1938, p. 4. See Roberts, *The Rubber Workers,* p. 164, for corroborative evidence.

34. Roberts, *The Rubber Workers,* p. 168.

35. *United Rubber Worker,* May 1938, p. 1; June 1938, p. 1.

36. Anthony, *How Collective Bargaining Works,* p. 654.

37. *United Rubber Worker,* September 1938, p. 1.

38. Roberts, *The Rubber Workers,* p. 233.

39. *United Rubber Worker,* June 1938, p. 6.

40. See Roberts, *The Rubber Workers,* pp. 169–171.

41. *United Rubber Worker,* June 1936, p. 6.

42. Quoted by Roberts, *The Rubber Workers,* p. 172.

43. Anthony, *How Collective Bargaining Works,* p. 657.

44. See Roberts, *The Rubber Workers,* pp. 240–245, for a detailed account of these negotiations.

45. United Rubber Workers of America, *Proceedings of the Third Convention* (Trenton, N. J., September 19–24, 1938), p. 6.

46. Anthony, *How Collective Bargaining Works*, p. 641.

47. United Rubber Workers of America, *Proceedings of the Fourth Convention* (La Crosse, Wis., September 10–15, 1939), p. 19.

48. *United Rubber Worker*, March 1939, p. 1; July 1939, p. 1.

49. Gaffey, *Productivity of Labor*, p. 171.

50. *United Rubber Worker*, April 1938, p. 1.

51. Gaffey, *Productivity of Labor*, pp. 171–173.

52. Roberts, *The Rubber Workers*, p. 342.

53. Gaffey, *Productivity of Labor*, p. 167, based on a study of A. F. Hinrichs of the U. S. Bureau of Labor Statistics.

54. Roberts, *The Rubber Workers*, pp. 343–344.

55. By 1947, Ohio tire employment had declined further to 41.6 per cent of the national total. U. S. *Census of Manufactures*, Vol. II, 1947, p. 469. In absolute terms, however, total tire employment in Ohio rose from 30,600 in 1939 to 39,000 in 1947, indicating that Akron's relative decline was largely the consequence of a tendency to invest in new facilities elsewhere, rather than to move existing facilities outside Akron.

56. Roberts, *The Rubber Workers*, p. 12.

57. In January, 1941, for example, the union printed what it asserted was an exhaustive list of 99 companies under contract with it. *United Rubber Worker*, January 1941, p. 5.

58. *United Rubber Worker*, February 1940, p. 1; July 1940, pp. 1, 3.

59. Roberts, *The Rubber Workers*, pp. 185–187.

60. United Rubber Workers of America, *Proceedings of the Fifth Convention* (Detroit, September 16–21, 1940), pp. 195–205; p. 60.

61. Roberts, *The Rubber Workers*, p. 188.

62. *United Rubber Worker*, July 1941, p. 1; October 1941, p. 1.

63. Roberts, *The Rubber Workers*, p. 188.

64. *United Rubber Worker*, August 1941, p. 2.

65. Roberts, *The Rubber Workers*, p. 320.

66. *Ibid.*, pp. 260–265, 359.

Chapter 7   The Men's Clothing Industry

1. Committee for Industrial Organization, *Minutes* (November 7 and 8, 1936), typewritten.

2. Earl D. Strong, *The Amalgamated Clothing Workers of America* (Grinnell, Iowa, 1940), p. 48.

3. Amalgamated Clothing Workers of America, *Proceedings of the Eleventh Biennial Convention* (Cleveland, May 25–30, 1936), p. 14.

4. *The Advance*, August 1935, p. 2.

5. Amalgamated Clothing Workers of America, *Proceedings of the Eleventh Biennial Convention*, p. 37.

6. Amalgamated Clothing Workers of America, *Proceedings of the Twelfth Biennial Convention* (Atlantic City, May 9–17, 1938), p. 19.

7. Twentieth Century Fund, *How Collective Bargaining Works* (New York, 1942), pp. 387–388.

8. In 1937, the officers of the UGW reported to their convention: "Without label agitation and promotion our Union Label would never have obtained any recognition through all the years since the inception of the International Union. Large sums of

money have been spent in advertising." United Garment Workers, *Proceedings of the Twenty-Second Convention* (Kansas City, August 9–13, 1937), p. 88.

9. *The Advance,* December 1936, p. 5.

10. Amalgamated Clothing Workers of America, *Proceedings of the Eleventh Biennial Convention,* p. 61.

11. Amalgamated Clothing Workers of America, *Proceedings of the Twelfth Biennial Convention,* p. 30.

12. Joel Seidman, *The Needle Trades* (New York, 1942), p. 342.

13. Amalgamated Clothing Workers of America, *Proceedings of the Eleventh Biennial Convention,* p. 56.

14. *Ibid.,* p. 50.

15. Amalgamated Clothing Workers of America, *Proceedings of the Twelfth Biennial Convention,* p. 26.

16. *The Advance,* February 1939, p. 10.

17. *The Advance,* October 1937, p. 10; Amalgamated Clothing Workers, *To Promote the General Welfare* (New York, 1950), p. 60.

18. *The Advance,* April 1939, p. 18; *The Advance,* February 1939, p. 10.

19. Amalgamated Clothing Workers of America, *Proceedings of the Twelfth Biennial Convention,* p. 36.

20. AFL Executive Council Minutes (April 25–May 5, 1938), p. 21; *ibid* (August 22–September 2, 1938), p. 38.

21. Amalgamated Clothing Workers of America, *Proceedings of the Twelfth Biennial Convention,* p. 37.

22. Some 3,000 workers in AFL Federal Local 11016, which had been organized in 1903, joined the Amalgamated in 1935. Amalgamated Clothing Workers of America, *Proceedings of the Eleventh Biennial Convention,* p. 60.

23. Amalgamated Clothing Workers of America, *Proceedings of the Twelfth Biennial Convention,* pp. 32, 161.

24. *The Advance,* December 1937, p. 2.

25. Amalgamated Clothing Workers of America, *Proceedings of the Twelfth Biennial Convention,* pp. 54, 421.

26. The data are from *The Amalgamated Today and Tomorrow,* p. 23. The wage data in the text are based upon trade union surveys. Different figures are given by the Bureau of Labor Statistics, *Handbook of Labor Statistics* (1947 edition), p. 69. Thus, for 1938, the trade union data indicate average hourly earnings of 77 cents, compared with 58.6 cents as shown by the BLS. The reasons for this difference cannot be ascertained in the absence of details regarding the compilation of the union statistics.

27. Total employment in the industry was considerably less in 1937 than in the peak production years after World War I: 158,000 in 1937 compared with 175,000 in 1919. Seidman, *The Needle Trades,* p. 340.

28. *The Advance,* September 1937, p. 2.

29. Amalgamated Clothing Workers of America, *Proceedings of the Twelfth Biennial Convention,* p. 17.

30. See *How Collective Bargaining Works,* pp. 436–439.

31. A clothing market usually comprises a city and its environs. All locals of the Amalgamated are required to be members of the joint board in their city. This body, headed by an elected "manager," is the dominant collective bargaining unit, the individual locals being required to subordinate their policies to those of the joint board. See Strong, *Amalgamated Clothing Workers,* pp. 63–68.

32. *The Advance,* May 1940, p. 13.

33. *The Advance,* November, 1939, p. 13.

34. Amalgamated Clothing Workers of America, *Proceedings of the Thirteenth Biennial Convention* (New York, May 13–24, 1940), p. 35.

35. Amalgamated Clothing Workers of America, *Proceedings of the Fourteenth Biennial Convention* (Chicago, May 15–19, 1944), pp. 139, 141.

36. *How Collective Bargaining Works*, pp. 441–444.

37. The Amalgamated itself has no doubt about the value of the plan. President Jacob Potofsky recently wrote: "Although the welfare of the worker was the principal motive underlying stabilization procedures, protection to the consumer was also a factor. By setting standards of quality and workmanship, stabilization assured the consumer of needed protection which he previously did not enjoy. Certainly, the stabilization program represents a distinct improvement over the former pattern of chaos and sweatshop production, which benefitted neither the industry, the workers, nor the consumer. The constructive implications of the stabilization program for the consumer loom large as one views it over the years." Letter to the author, March 26, 1958.

38. Amalgamated Clothing Workers of America, *Proceedings of the Thirteenth Biennial Convention*, p. 35.

39. Seidman, *The Needle Trades*, p. 70; *How Collective Bargaining Works*, p. 428; W. S. Woytinsky and Associates, *Employment and Wages in the United States* (New York, 1953), p. 586. According to BLS data, average hourly earnings in men's clothing in 1941 were 63 cents, an increase of about 6 per cent over 1935. Average hourly earnings in all manufacturing in 1941 were 72.9 cents, and in the manufacture of nondurable goods, 64 cents. The increases from 1936 to 1941 were, respectively, 33 per cent and 21 per cent. Thus, the level of hourly earnings in men's clothing in 1941 was about the same as for nondurable goods, but the gains in the former from 1935 to 1941 were much less than in the latter. Data are from Bureau of Labor Statistics, *Handbook of Labor Statistics* (1947 edition), p. 54.

40. Amalgamated Clothing Workers of America, *Proceedings of the Thirteenth Biennial Convention*, p. 69. Earnings varied from 15.7 cents per hour in Tennessee and 29 cents in Maryland to over 40 cents in New York and Pennsylvania.

41. For an account of Hillman's lobbying activities in behalf of the law, see Matthew Josephson, *Sidney Hillman* (New York, 1952), pp. 440–449.

42. Amalgamated Clothing Workers of America, *Proceedings of the Thirteenth Biennial Convention*, p. 50.

43. 1941 average hourly earnings in the manufacture of shirts, collars and nightwear were 45.5 cents; in the manufacture of underwear and neckwear, 46.7 cents. Bureau of Labor Statistics, *Handbook of Labor Statistics* (1947 edition), p. 69.

44. *To Promote the General Welfare*, p. 58.

45. Amalgamated Clothing Workers of America, *Proceedings of the Eleventh Biennial Convention*, pp. 138, 385, 400.

46. Josephson, *Sidney Hillman*, pp. 395–401.

47. *The Advance*, August 1936, p. 14. At its inception, the American Labor Party had broad labor support. George Meany, then president of the New York State Federation of Labor, participated in its formation. However, the AFL groups soon withdrew.

48. *The Advance*, December 1937, p. 6. The ALP also contributed to the selection of Democratic mayors in Buffalo, Troy, Utica, and Yonkers, all in New York State.

49. Amalgamated Clothing Workers of America, *Proceedings of the Twelfth Biennial Convention*, p. 72.

50. Amalgamated Clothing Workers of America, *Proceedings of the Thirteenth Biennial Convention*, p. 453.

51. *The Advance*, November 5, 1940, p. 3.

52. CIO Executive Board Minutes (June 13–15, 1939), p. 136.

53. CIO Executive Board Minutes (June 3–5, 1940), p. 211.
54. *The Advance*, November 12, 1940, p. 2.
55. For an account of this meeting, see *supra*, p. 60.
56. CIO Executive Board Minutes (November 15–23, 1940), p. 101.
57. Congress of Industrial Organizations, *Proceedings of the Third Constitutional Convention* (Atlantic City, 1940), p. 124.
58. Josephson, *Sidney Hillman*, pp. 182, 496.
59. *The Advance*, August 1941, p. 3.
60. *The Advance*, October 1941, p. 4. This number included 95 per cent of the clothing workers and 60 per cent of the cotton garment workers employed.

Chapter 8 The Women's Clothing Industry

1. International Ladies' Garment Workers' Union, *Report of the General Executive Board to the Twenty-Third Convention* (Atlantic City, May 3–15, 1937), p. 3.
2. The statistics are from Joel Seidman, *The Needle Trades* (New York, 1942), pp. 21–23.
3. Julius Hochman, *Industry Planning Through Collective Bargaining* (New York, 1941), p. 46.
4. Seidman, *The Needle Trades*, p. 336. The distinction between inside and contracting shops is discussed below.
5. Hochman, *Industry Planning*, pp. 10, 46.
6. Seidman, *The Needle Trades*, pp. 9–10, 40.
7. Benjamin Stolberg, *Tailor's Progress* (New York, 1944), p. 218.
8. Seidman, *The Needle Trades*, pp. 43–46.
9. Stolberg, *Tailor's Progress*, p. 216.
10. Lazare Teper, *The Women's Garment Industry* (International Ladies' Garment Workers' Union, 1937), p. 3.
11. *Justice*, February 1, 1940, p. 1.
12. Hochman, *Industrial Planning*, pp. 12, 45.
13. *Justice*, January 15, 1941, p. 16.
14. Teper, *Garment Industry*, p. 14. The prevalent piece rate system of wages facilitated the making of concessions by groups of workers, particularly since new rates had to be set on each new style.
15. Mobility of workers among firms was not typically high. See Gertrud Greig, *Seasonal Fluctuations in Employment in the Women's Clothing Industry in New York* (New York, 1949), chap. iv.
16. *Justice*, January 15, 1936, p. 6. By the term "prices" in the above quotation, the union spokesman meant wages, a common usage in the industry; that is, wage setting is usually referred to as price setting.
17. International Ladies' Garment Workers' Union, *Report of the General Executive Board to the Twenty-Third Convention*, p. 43.
18. Teper, *Garment Industry*, p. 21.
19. Seidman, *The Needle Trades*, pp. 265–266. See also *Justice*, January 15, 1936, p. 6.
20. International Ladies' Garment Workers' Union, *Report of the General Executive Board to the Twenty-Third Convention*, pp. 24, 48.
21. International Ladies' Garment Workers' Union, *Report of Proceedings of the Twenty-Third Convention*, p. 39.

22. International Ladies' Garment Workers' Union, *Report of the General Executive Board to the 24th Convention* (New York, May 27–June 8), 1940, pp. 18, 55.
23. *Justice,* December 1, 1939, p. 1; July 1, 1941, p. 16.
24. See Helen Everett Meiklejohn, "Dresses," in Walton Hamilton and Associates, *Price and Price Policies* (New York, 1938).
25. International Ladies' Garment Workers' Union, *Report and Record, Twenty-Fourth Convention* (New York, 1940), p. 295.
26. *Justice,* February 15, 1941, p. 2.
27. International Ladies' Garment Workers' Union, *Report and Record, Twenty-Fourth Convention,* pp. 67–70.
28. *Ibid.,* pp. 37, 38.
29. *Justice,* July 1, 1941, p. 16.
30. The history of this board is analyzed in detail in Dwight Edwards Robinson, *Collective Bargaining and Market Control in the New York Coat and Suit Industry* (New York, 1939). This was the only instance in which NRA machinery was preserved on a national scale.
31. Robinson, *Collective Bargaining,* p. 141.
32. The union justified its participation in such activities in the following terms: "Of equal importance with the maintenance of fair labor standards is the Recovery Board's work in connection with the enforcement of fair trade practices. It is obvious that an impoverished industry cannot uphold fair labor standards. When employers, for instance, are harassed by unjustified returns, excessive discounts, or direct or indirect forms of price pressure from large retail combinations, chain stores, and mail order houses, so that they are prevented from earning a fair return, decent labor standards are soon discarded, as past experience has shown." *Justice,* March 1, 1938, p. 15.
33. International Ladies' Garment Workers' Union, *Report and Record, Twenty-Fourth Convention,* p. 18; *ibid., Report and Record, Twenty-Fifth Convention* (Boston, 1944), p. 38.
34. "The thirty-five hour week has not solved the problem of unemployment of the cloak maker. Thousands of them are unemployed altogether or employed for incredibly short periods of time during the peak of each season. In addition, the seasons have tended to become shorter and shorter, and the periods of idleness correspondingly longer. This slack in employment must be absorbed. The only effective way of absorbing it is by establishing the thirty-hour week in that industry." International Ladies' Garment Workers' Union, *Report of Proceedings, Twenty-Third Convention,* p. 264.
35. *Justice,* August 15, 1937, p. 16.
36. International Ladies' Garment Workers' Union, *Report and Record, Twenty-Fourth Convention,* p. 46.
37. International Ladies' Garment Workers' Union, *Report and Record, Twenty-Fourth Convention,* p. 160.
38. International Ladies' Garment Workers' Union, *Financial and Statistical Report* (May 29, 1944), p. 46.
39. *Justice,* September 15, 1937, p. 16.
40. *The Position of the International Ladies' Garment Workers' Union in Relation to CIO and AFL* (New York, 1938), p. 32.
41. *Justice,* July 15, 1937, p. 3.
42. International Ladies' Garment Workers' Union, *Report and Record, Twenty-Fourth Convention,* p. 42.
43. *Justice,* January 1, 1938, p. 16.
44. *The Position of the International Ladies' Garment Workers' Union,* p. 54.

45. *Justice*, January 15, 1938, p. 2.

46. *The Position of the International Ladies' Garment Workers' Union*, p. 78.

47. International Ladies' Garment Workers' Union, *Report of Proceedings, Twenty-Third Convention*, p. 356.

48. *Justice*, August 15, 1939, p. 2.

49. *Justice*, December 1, 1939, p. 3.

50. For the text of the joint statement, see International Ladies' Garment Workers' Union, *Report and Record, Twenty-Third Convention*, p. 44.

51. AFL Executive Council Minutes (May 13–21, 1940), p. 93.

52. See *supra*, p. 63.

53. International Ladies' Garment Workers' Union, *Report and Record, Twenty-Fourth Convention*, p. 456.

54. *Justice*, December 1, 1940, p. 3.

55. International Ladies' Garment Workers' Union, *Report and Record, Twenty-Fifth Convention*, p. 11.

56. Stolberg, *Tailor's Progress*, p. 280.

57. International Ladies' Garment Workers' Union, *Report and Record, Twenty-Fifth Convention*, p. 12.

58. *Justice*, August, 15, 1937, p. 16.

59. *Supra*, p. 294.

60. Matthew Josephson, *Sidney Hillman* (New York, 1952), p. 455.

61. International Ladies' Garment Workers' Union, *Report and Record, Twenty-Fourth Convention*, p. 32.

62. *Justice*, October 15, 1940, p. 16.

63. International Ladies' Garment Workers' Union, *Report and Record, Twenty-Fifth Convention*, pp. 18, 19.

64. For the ILGWU version of these events, see *ibid.*, pp. 19–23; for the Amalgamated version, see Josephson, *Sidney Hillman*, pp. 600–606.

65. Stolberg, *Tailor's Progress*, p. 248.

66. *Justice*, May 15, 1936, p. 7.

67. *Justice*, February 15, 1938, p. 16.

68. International Ladies' Garment Workers' Union, *Report of Proceedings, Twenty-Third Convention*, p. 405.

69. Of 900 delegates to the 1944 convention, only six were communists. Stolberg, *Tailor's Progress*, p. 250.

70. *Justice*, March 15, 1937, p. 16.

71. See the debate between Hochman and Nagler in International Ladies' Garment Workers' Union, *Report of Proceedings, Twenty-Third Convention*, p. 372.

72. The author cannot refrain from including an anecdote recounted to him by an ILGWU official which illustrates the problems encountered by the leaders in their endeavor to instill a more business-like attitude toward union affairs. One of the innovations introduced in 1938 was an officers' qualification course, which was required of all aspiring paid union officials. One unsuccessful student, an older man, complained to the manager of a local about the unfairness of the course. "Could you answer questions on our contract," he was asked? "No," he admitted. "Did you pass the section on the administration of piece rates?" Again the reply was in the negative. "Well," the manager asked, "what makes you think you are qualified to act as a business agent?" The man replied: "How many other candidates can discuss the philosophy of Spinoza?"

73. Greig, *Seasonal Fluctuations*, p. 149.

74. Bureau of Labor Statistics, *Handbook of Labor Statistics* (1947 edition), p. 69.

75. International Ladies' Garment Workers' Union, *Report and Record of the Twenty-Fourth Convention* (1940), p. 91.
76. International Ladies' Garment Workers' Union, *Report and Record of the Twenty-Fifth Convention* (1944), p. 121.

Chapter 9   The Renascence of Textile Unionism

1. Herbert J. Lahne, *The Cotton Mill Worker* (New York, 1944), Ch. 13.
2. United Textile Workers of America, *The AFL Textile Workers* (1950), pp. 23–24.
3. *The AFL Textile Workers*, p. 24.
4. Committee for Industrial Organization, *Minutes of the Meeting of December 9, 1935.*
5. Textile Workers Organizing Committee, *Building a Union of Textile Workers* (Philadelphia, 1939), p. 8.
6. Lahne, *The Cotton Mill Workers*, p. 263.
7. *Building a Union of Textile Workers*, pp. 7, 8.
8. *Ibid.*, pp. 10–11.
9. *The AFL Textile Workers*, p. 26.
10. *The Advance* (April 1937), p. 4. Hillman was also motivated by a profound belief in industrial unionism, and he looked forward to the time when all the needle and textile trades would be joined into one great union.
11. *Building a Union of Textile Workers*, p. 14.
12. Matthew Josephson, *Sidney Hillman: Statesman of American Labor* (New York, 1952), pp. 419–420.
13. Even this table is very summary, and by no means reflects the full degree of product specialization and the extent of special product grouping of firms relevant to wage setting and industrial relations. The hosiery industry, for example, was divided into two distinct segments as far as collective bargaining was concerned: full-fashioned and seamless. See George W. Taylor, "Hosiery," in The Twentieth Century Fund, *How Collective Bargaining Works* (New York, 1942), p. 450.
14. Solomon Barkin, *Brief Presented on Behalf of the Textile Workers Organizing Committee in Connection with the Establishing of a Minimum Wage in the Textile Industry* (New York, 1939), p. 5.
15. Bureau of Labor Statistics, *Handbook of Labor Statistics* (1941), vol. II, p. 360.
16. *Ibid.*, and *The Advance* (October 1937), p. 4.
17. *The Advance* (November, 1937), p. 32.
18. Lahne, *The Cotton Mill Worker*, p. 92.
19. Barkin, *Brief*, p. 6B.
20. *Report on the New England Textile Industry by Committee Appointed by the Conference of New England Governors* (1952), p. 6.
21. *The AFL Textile Workers*, p. 29. It should be emphasized that the craft problem had largely been solved by the nineteen-twenties, leaving the separatist propensities of the industrial federations as the principal challenge to national union domination.
22. *Building a Union of Textile Workers*, p. 55.
23. Textile Workers Organizing Committee, *News Letter for Regional Directors*, vol. I, no. 12 (1937).
24. Textile Workers Union of America, *Proceedings of the First Constitutional Convention* (May 15–19, 1939), p. 29.
25. TWOC, *Weekly Letter for Regional Directors*, vol. I, no. 4 (1937), p. 4.

26. *Textile World* (April 1937), p. 108; (May 1937), p. 70.

27. *Building a Union of Textile Workers*, pp. 20–21; *The Advance* (September 1937), p. 6.

28. Josephson, *Sidney Hillman*, p. 421; *The Advance* (October 1937), p. 4.

29. TWOC, *News Letter for Regional Directors*, vol. I, no. 12 (1937), p. 1.

30. The data are from TWOC, *Weekly Letter for Regional Directors*, various issues, and *Building a Union of Textile Workers*, p. 24.

31. *The Advance* (July 1937), p. 6; (September 1937), p. 6; (November 1937), p. 2.

32. *Textile World* (August 1937), p. 70; *The Advance* (August 1937), p. 6.

33. *The Advance* (December 1937), p. 5.

34. *Building A Union of Textile Workers*, p. 23.

35. TWOC, *Weekly Letter for Regional Directors*, May 15, 1937; March 25, 1938.

36. TWOC, *News Letter for Regional Directors*, December 6, 1937.

37. The New Bedford Textile Council had a long history as an amalgamation of local craft unions. It was closely associated with the neighboring Fall River Textile Council. For a full account of the history and bargaining experience of these groups in what was once a major cotton textile manufacturing area, see: Martin Segal, "Interrelationship of Wages Under Joint Demand," *The Quarterly Journal of Economics* (August 1956), p. 464; Martin Segal, *The Development of Collective Bargaining in the Cotton Textile Industry of Fall River and New Bedford* (mimeographed report), Industrial Relations Library, Harvard University; Edward K. Pincus, *Development of Industrial Relations in the Cotton Textile Industry of Fall River and New Bedford Since 1938* (mimeographed report), Industrial Relations Library, Harvard University.

38. Barkin, *Brief*, p. 6B.

39. TWOC, *News Letter for Regional Directors*, May 10, 1938.

40. TWOC, *National News Letter*, June 3, 1938; October 14, 1938. The TWOC had organized only the Amsterdam plant, the Thompsonville plant having been organized independently. However, the two groups cooperated fully in the strike.

41. *Building A Union of Textile Workers*, pp. 28, 30.

42. Textile Workers Union of America, *Proceedings of the First Constitutional Convention*, p. 166.

43. *Textile Labor*, March 6, 1940, p. 1; October 1, 1940, p. 7.

44. *In the Matter of Alma Mills, Inc.*, 24 NLRB 1 (1940).

45. Lucy Randolph Mason, *To Win These Rights* (New York, 1952), pp. 98–101 and *passim*.

46. Herman Wolf, "Cotton and the Unions," *Survey Graphic* (March 1938), p. 2.

47. *New York Daily News*, July 7, 1937.

48. Textile Workers Union of America, *Proceedings of the First Constitutional Convention*, pp. 130–131.

49. Congress of Industrial Organizations, *Proceedings of the First Constitutional Convention* (Pittsburgh, November 14–18, 1938), p. 173.

50. *Textile World*, April 1939, p. 64.

51. *Textile World*, January 1939, p. 40.

52. AFL Executive Council Minutes (January 30–February 14, 1939), p. 92.

53. United Textile Workers of America, *Special Convention Proceedings* (May 8–10, 1939), pp. 5, 9; (December 1–4, 1941), p. 77.

54. United Textile Workers of America, *Special Convention Proceedings* (May 8–10, 1939), p. 21.

55. AFL Executive Council Minutes (May 10–19, 1939), p. 4.

56. *Textile Labor*, vol. I, no. 1 (February 1939), p. 1.

57. Textile Workers' Union of America, *Proceedings of the First Constitutional Con-

vention, p. 143. Some years later, there was a revision downward to 160,000 workers under contract, which seems to be more in line with the actual situation. See Textile Workers' Union of America, *Building A Textile Union* (1948), p. 22.

58. Barkin, *Brief,* p. 6B.

59. Textile Workers' Union of America, *Textile Facts,* vol. 7, no. 7 (February 15, 1941).

60. Textile Workers' Union of America, Second Biennial Convention, *Executive Council Report* (1941), pp. 16–23, 39.

61. *Textile Facts,* vol. 7, no. 4 (November 20, 1940).

62. Herbert J. Lahne, *The Cotton Mill Worker,* pp. 270–272.

63. *Textile Worker* (May, 1941), p. 1.

64. Lahne, *The Cotton Mill Worker,* p. 272.

65. Textile Workers' Union of America, Second Biennial Convention, *Executive Council Report,* pp. 46, 47.

66. There was later a downward revision of workers under contract to 215,000. Textile Workers' Union of America, *Building A Union of Textile Workers* (1948), p. 22.

67. Textile Workers' Union of America, *Proceedings of the Second Biennial Convention* (April 21–25, 1941), pp. 7, 102.

68. Textile Workers' Union of America, Second Biennial Convention, *Executive Council Report,* pp. 51–52.

69. See *Textile Labor,* vol. I, no. 22 (November 1, 1940), p. 3.

70. *The AFL Textile Workers,* p. 35.

71. United Textile Workers of America, *Special Convention Proceedings* (December 1–4, 1941), p. 52.

72. *The AFL Textile Workers,* pp. 30–31.

Chapter 10   The Meat Industry

1. Lewis Corey, *Meat and Man* (New York, 1950), pp. 259, 281, based upon the Census of Manufactures.

2. TNEC Monograph No. 35, *Concentration of Economic Power* (1940), pp. 16–17.

3. Among the major large independent meat packers are, in descending order of net worth in 1946: John Morrell, Rath Packing, George A. Hormel, Oscar Mayer, Hygrade Food Products, E. Kahn's Sons, Miller & Hart, Stahl-Meyer, Adolph Gobel, and Mickleberry's Foods. Corey, *Meat and Man,* p. 207.

4. *Ibid.,* pp. 161, 173, 193.

5. Amalgamated Meat Cutters and Butcher Workmen of North America, *Synopsis of Proceedings of the Fourteenth General Convention* (Memphis, June 8–12, 1936), p. 34.

6. Telegram from Lane to Lewis, March 3, 1936, files of the Amalgamated Meat Cutters and Butcher Workmen.

7. Telegram from Brophy to Lane, March 3, 1936, *ibid.*

8. Letter from Lane to Brophy, March 18, 1936, *ibid.*

9. Telegram from Brophy to Austin, Minnesota, *ibid.*

10. Letter from Gorman to Lewis, *ibid.,* March 15, 1937.

11. Letter from Gorman to Brophy, April 19, 1937, *ibid.*

12. Amalgamated Meat Cutters and Butcher Workmen of North America. *Minutes of Executive Board Meeting* (May 10, 1937). Lewis was obviously attempting to do with the Butcher Workmen what he had done with the Amalgamated Association of Iron, Steel, and Tin Workers (*supra,* p. 81) but Gorman was not Tighe, and the Butcher

Workmen was not a moribund organization, with no alternative but to surrender its charter.

13. Letter from Gorman to Brophy, May 12, 1937, files of the Amalgamated Meat Cutters and Butcher Workmen.

14. Letter from Gorman to Lewis, June 16, 1937, *ibid.*

15. Letter from Lewis to Gorman, June 21, 1937, *ibid.*

16. Letter to the author, February 4, 1958.

17. Corey, *Meat and Man,* p. 293.

18. Amalgamated Meat Cutters and Butcher Workmen, *Synopsis of the Proceedings of the Fourteenth General Convention,* p. 5.

19. Amalgamated Meat Cutters and Butcher Workmen, *50 Progressive Years* (Chicago, 1948).

20. Amalgamated Meat Cutters and Butcher Workmen, *Synopsis of Proceedings of the Fifteenth General Convention* (Milwaukee, 1940), p. 9.

21. Corey, *Meat and Man,* p. 172.

22. Amalgamated Meat Cutters and Butcher Workmen, *Synopsis of Proceedings of the Fourteenth General Convention,* pp. 94–97.

23. Amalgamated Meat Cutters and Butcher Workmen, *Executive Board Minutes* (January 23, 1936).

24. *The Butcher Workman,* April 1, 1937, p. 1. The conclusion that the boycott was not generally effective was derived from a reading of contemporary Amalgamated literature. However, a recent study of the industry records a somewhat different conclusion: that the profit position of Morrell in 1935–1937 was worse than that of its competitors, which is ascribed primarily to the boycott. James R. Holcomb, *The Union Policies of Meat Packers, 1929–1943* (University of Illinois, 1957), pp. 85–87.

25. Amalgamated Meat Cutters and Butcher Workmen, *Executive Board Minutes,* June 19, 1939; October 9, 1939.

26. Amalgamated Meat Cutters and Butcher Workmen, *Synopsis of Proceedings of the Fifteenth General Convention,* p. 13.

27. For the facts in this section I have relied heavily on an unpublished manuscript by Arthur Kampfert, "History of Unionism in Meat Packing Industry, 1933 to 1940," which was made available to me by the courtesy of the United Packinghouse Workers of America.

28. Kampfert, "History of Unionism," p. 18.

29. Letter from Clark to Cooney, May 5, 1937, files of the Amalgamated Meat Cutters and Butcher Workmen.

30. This section is based largely upon Kampfert, "History of Unionism," and upon an unpublished manuscript by Frank N. Schultz, "Historical Sketches of the Growth of the Packinghouse Union in Austin, Minnesota."

31. Schultz, "Historical Sketches," p. 3.

32. Schultz, "Historical Sketches," p. 5.

33. Schultz, "Historical Sketches," quoting from *The Unionist,* January 10, 1936.

34. According to the union, Jay Hormel picked Governor Olson up at the railroad station and drove him to the plant. On the way, Hormel kept pointing out to the governor the plant windows that had been broken by the strikers. "Governor Olson looked slyly at Mr. Hormel and said, 'Well, Jay, you wanted an open shop and now you've got it.' " Schultz, "Historical Sketches," p. 12.

35. Schultz, "Historical Sketches," pp. 22b, 29.

36. Kampfert, "History of Unionism," pp. 35, 37.

37. Document in the files of the United Packinghouse Workers of America.

38. Amalgamated Meat Cutters and Butcher Workmen, *Executive Board Minutes* (May 10, 1937).

39. *The Chicago American*, March 9, 1937, quoted in Kampfert, "History of Unionism," p. 62.

40. About 70 local charters had been issued by the CIO. United Packinghouse Workers of America, *20 Years with UPWA* (October, 1957), p. 6.

41. Kampfert, "History of Unionism," pp. 87–88.

42. *In the Matter of Armour & Company*, 8 NLRB 1100 (1938).

43. The Amalgamated Meat Cutters did not appear on the ballot, and had not indicated to the NLRB that it had any interest in the plant. The total vote was only about one-third of the company's payroll, the low rate of participation being due to the company's obstructive tactics. There was only one polling place at a distant location from the plant which itself extended over more than four city blocks. Voting took place only before and after work, since the company would not agree to any plan for suspension of work while balloting could take place. Company supervisors posted themselves across the street from the polling place and kept check on those who entered.

44. *CIO News, Packinghouse Workers Edition*, November 5, 1938, p. 1.

45. Kampfert, "History of Unionism," p. 125.

46. *Ibid.*, p. 4(F).

47. *CIO News, Packinghouse Workers Edition*, October 1, 1938, p. 1; October 8, 1938, p. 2; July 24, 1939, p. 1.

48. *The Butcher Workman*, September 1, 1939, p. 1.

49. Kampfert, "History of Unionism," part 3, p. 54.

50. The branch houses are warehouses and refrigeration plants from which meat products can be distributed to wholesalers and retailers. They do no slaughtering, and do not have many employees.

51. *CIO News, Packinghouse Workers Edition*, August 21, 1939, p. 1.

52. Barbara Warne Newell, unpublished manuscript on the organization of Chicago meat packing, p. 28.

53. *Ibid.*, October 2, 1939, p. 1.

54. *CIO News, Packinghouse Workers Edition*, October 30, 1939, p. 8.

55. *Ibid.*, November 27, 1939, p. 1. Kampfert, "History of Unionism," part 3, p. 63, concedes that the Amalgamated may have had no knowledge of the criminal record of Dasho.

56. *CIO News, Packinghouse Workers Edition*, February 19, 1940, p. 1; March 4, 1940, p. 1; April 1, 1940, p. 1; April 15, 1940, p. 1; August 4, 1941, p. 1.

57. The Amalgamated claimed that in making this wage adjustment, Armour followed, rather than led, the other packers. *The Butcher Workman*, September 1, 1941, p. 1.

58. *Ibid.*, August 18, 1941, p. 1.

59. Kampfert, "History of Unionism," pp. 173, 174.

60. *The Butcher Workman*, January 1, 1939, p. 4.

61. *CIO News, Packinghouse Workers Edition*, January 23, 1939, p. 1.

62. Kampfert, "History of Unionism," part 2, pp. 7–8.

63. *CIO News, Packinghouse Workers Edition*, May 13, 1940, p. 1.

64. Kampfert, "History of Unionism," p. 14.

65. *CIO News, Packinghouse Workers Edition*, February 5, 1940, p. 1.

66. Kampfert, "History of Unionism," p. 36B.

67. *CIO News, Packinghouse Workers Edition*, April 28, 1941, p. 1.

68. *CIO News, Packinghouse Workers Edition*, February 5, 1940, p. 1.

69. Wilson entered into a master agreement with the PWOC on March 27, 1943, cover-

ing five plants. Judge James D. Cooney, president of the company at the time, said in a recent interview: "Wilson would have resisted a master agreement if it had not been for the war. Such an agreement is an unsatisfactory arrangement; today or yesterday." James R. Holcomb, *Union Policies*, p. 171.

70. *In the Matter of Cudahy Packing Company*, 15 NLRB 684 (1939).

71. *CIO News, Packinghouse Workers Edition*, August 5, 1940, p. 1.

72. *CIO News, Packinghouse Workers Edition*, June 10, 1940, p. 1; May 27, 1940, p. 1; February 20, 1939, p. 1; November 10, 1941, p. 1; December 25, 1939, p. 8.

73. Corey, *Meat and Man*, p. 298.

74. Kampfert, "History of Unionism," pp. 146, 192.

75. *Ibid.*, part 2, p. 6; part 3, p. 38; part 3, p. 45; part 3, pp. 11–26, and *CIO News, Packinghouse Workers Edition*, December 12, 1938, p. 1; *ibid.*, March 20, 1939, p. 1. The Kansas City, Fort Worth, and St. Paul stockyards were also under PWOC contract by the end of 1941.

76. *The Butcher Workman*, July 1, 1937, p. 1.

77. Amalgamated Meat Cutters and Butcher Workmen, *Synopsis of Proceedings of the Fifteenth General Convention*, p. 7. Most of the Armour plants under Amalgamated contract were in the 200 to 300 employee category.

78. See *supra*, p. 356.

79. *The Butcher Workman*, October 1, 1938, p. 1; September 1. 1939, p. 1.

80. Amalgamated Meat Cutters and Butcher Workmen, *Synopsis of Proceedings of the Fifteenth General Convention*, p. 8. The 1940 figure was revised downward to 73,000 in a later publication, without explanation. Amalgamated Meat Cutters and Butcher Workmen, *50 Progressive Years*.

81. Amalgamated Meat Cutters and Butcher Workmen, *Executive Board Minutes* (October 10, 1941).

82. On leaving the PWOC in 1939, Harris was employed by the Mine, Mill and Smelter Workers Union, where he was aligned with the communist-dominated administration.

83. A. B. Held, "The CIO Packers' Convention," *The New Leader* (July 10, 1948), p. 3.

84. *CIO News, Packinghouse Workers Edition*, December 25, 1939, p. 1.

85. *The Butcher Workman*, February 1, 1940, p. 2.

86. *CIO News, Packinghouse Workers Edition*, December 9, 1940, p. 1.

87. *The Butcher Workman*, June 1, 1941, p. 4.

88. Interview with a staff member of the United Packinghouse Workers of America.

89. *CIO News, Packinghouse Workers Edition*, March 31, 1941, p. 1.

90. *The Butcher Workman*, May 1, 1941, p. 1.

91. *CIO News, Packinghouse Workers Edition*, May 12, 1941, p. 1.

92. U. S. Department of Labor, *Handbook of Labor Statistics* (1947 Edition), p. 72.

Chapter 11 The Lumber Industry

1. Quoted in National Recovery Administration, *Economic Problems of the Lumber and Timber Products Industry* (Washington, 1936), mimeographed, p. 124.

2. *Ibid.*, p. 14.

3. Advisory Commission to the Council of National Defense, *The Douglas Fir Lumber Industry* (Washington, March 1941), p. 1.

4. Vernon H. Jensen, *Lumber and Labor* (New York, 1945), p. 17. I have relied heavily upon this excellent work in the present chapter.

5. Advisory Commission to the Council of National Defense, *Lumber Industry*, p. 26;

United States Department of Labor, *Minimum Wages in the Lumber and Timber Industry* (June 1941), p. 138, mimeographed.

6. These estimates are based upon 1939 Census of Manufactures data as contained in *Minimum Wages in the Lumber and Timber Products Industry*, p. 103, and National Lumber Manufacturers Association, *Lumber Industry Facts, 1941* (Washington), p. 14.

7. *Minimum Wages in the Lumber and Timber Products Industry*, p. 25.

8. Jensen, *Lumber and Labor*, pp. 169, 185.

9. Margaret Louise Schleef," "Rival Unionism in the Lumber Industry," M. A. Thesis (University of California, 1950), p. 64.

10. *The Timberworker*, November 27, 1936, p. 4.

11. United Brotherhood of Carpenters and Joiners of America, *Proceedings of the Twenty-Third General Convention* (Lakeland, Fla., December 7–15, 1936), pp. 37, 38.

12. *Ibid.*, p. 313.

13. Jensen, *Lumber and Labor*, p. 206.

14. Federation of Woodworkers, *Proceedings of the Second Semi-Annual Convention* (Longview, Wash., February 20–22, 1937), p. 4.

15. *The Timberworker*, June 4, 1937, p. 1.

16. Jensen, *Lumber and Labor*, pp. 207, 208.

17. American Federation of Labor, *Report of the Proceedings of the Fifty-Seventh Annual Convention* (1937), p. 463.

18. *The Timberworker*, July 9, 1937, p. 4.

19. Jensen, *Lumber and Labor*, pp. 212, 213.

20. American Federation of Labor, *Report of the Proceedings of the Fifty-Seventh Annual Convention* (1937), p. 468.

21. For a detailed account of these events, see the testimony of Morris H. Jones in U. S. Senate, 76th Congress, First Session, Committee on Education and Labor, *Hearings on Proposed Amendments to the National Labor Relations Act* (1939), pp. 934ff.

22. Jensen, *Lumber and Labor*, p. 217.

23. An index of lumber employment in the Douglas Fir Region fell from a peak of 122.5 in July 1937 (1935–1939 average = 100) to 79.5 in December 1937. Advisory Commission to the Council of National Defense, *Lumber Industry*, p. 43.

24. *Hearings on Proposed Amendments to the National Labor Relations Act*, p. 1481.

25. Jensen, *Lumber and Labor*, p. 221.

26. Margaret S. Glock, *Collective Bargaining in the Pacific Northwest Lumber Industry* (Berkeley, 1958), p. 18.

27. International Woodworkers of America, *Proceedings of the First Constitutional Convention* (Portland, December 3–8, 1937), p. 8.

28. *Ibid.*, pp. 111, 145.

29. International Woodworkers of America, *Proceedings of the Third Constitutional Convention* (Klamath Falls, Oregon, October 18–22, 1939), pp. 110–112.

30. For example, Jensen notes of the outcome of a 1936 strike in Portland: "No formal agreement was entered into because an old 'Wobbly' tradition of 'no signed agreement' was strong among the men and the employers did not wish to sign an agreement either." Jensen, *Lumber and Labor*, p. 188.

31. International Woodworkers of America, *Proceedings of the First Constitutional Convention*, pp. 48–50.

32. *Ibid.*, p. 149.

33. Advisory Commission to the Council of National Defense, *Lumber Industry*, pp. 44, 48.

34. *Hearings on Proposed Amendments to the National Relations Act*, testimony of

George G. Kidwell, Director, Department of Industrial Relations, State of California, p. 874.

35. *Ibid.*, p. 1319.

36. Jensen, *Lumber and Labor,* p. 229.

37. International Woodworkers of America, *Proceedings of the Second Constitutional Convention* (Seattle, September 12–16, 1938), p. 153.

38. *Ibid.*, pp. 116, 124.

39. See *supra*, p. 390.

40. International Woodworkers, *Proceedings,* p. 256.

41. *The Timberworker,* April 29, 1939, p. 4.

42. *Ibid.*, May 13, 1939, p. 3; May 27, 1939, p. 3; June 3, 1939, p. 1.

43. International Woodworkers of America, *Proceedings of the Third Constitutional Convention* (Klamath Falls, Oregon, October 18–22, 1939), pp. 6; 300; 22; 76–77; 81–82; 94–104; 106; 127; 138.

44. Jensen, *Lumber and Labor,* p. 234.

45. International Woodworkers of America, *Proceedings of the Third Constitutional Convention,* pp. 287–88; 302–303.

46. Jensen, *Lumber and Labor,* p. 235.

47. See, for example, *The Timberworker,* June 17, 1939, p. 1; July 1, 1939, p. 4; July 29, 1939, p. 6; August 26, 1939, p. 1.

48. *The Timberworker,* February 17, 1940, p. 1; May 25, 1940, p. 1.

49. *The Timberworker,* November 2, 1940, p. 1.

50. International Woodworkers of America, *Proceedings of the Fourth Constitutional Convention* (Aberdeen, Wash., October 7–12, 1940), p. 35.

51. Jensen, *Lumber and Labor,* p. 237; *The Timberworker,* November 2, 1940, p. 1.

52. For details of this episode, involving also relationships with the AFL, see Dan Dentry Jackson, "The International Woodworkers of America," M.A. Thesis (University of California, 1953), p. 46.

53. *The Timberworker,* June 1, 1940, p. 1.

54. Jensen, *Lumber and Labor,* pp. 249–51.

55. *The Timberworker,* August 31, 1940, p. 2.

56. International Woodworkers of America, *Proceedings of the Fifth Constitutional Convention,* p. 11.

57. International Woodworkers of America, *Proceedings of the Fourth Constitutional Convention,* pp. 64, 70, 82.

58. Each delegate to the convention had one vote. Every local had at least two delegates, with an additional delegate for each 300 members up to 1000, and one additional delegate for each additional 500 members. Thus, for example, a local with 2,000 members was entitled to seven delegates, whereas one with 50 members was entitled to two. Four locals with 50 members each could outvote a large local with 2,000 members.

59. *Ibid.*, p. 229.

60. *The Timberworker,* October 19, 1940, p. 1. Germer remained on, after his dismissal, as advisor to Worth Lowery and the right-wing faction, and played a very important role in advising this group on strategy at a critical time in the history of the organization.

61. *The Timberworker,* December 21, 1940, p. 1; December 7, 1940, p. 1.

62. International Woodworkers of America, *Proceedings of the Fifth Constitutional Convention* (Everett, Wash., October 8–13, 1941), p. 12.

63. Jensen, *Lumber and Labor,* pp. 258–59.

64. *The Timberworker,* May 8, 1941, p. 1; February 1, 1941, p. 1; April 3, 1941, p. 1.

65. Jensen, *Lumber and Labor,* p. 264.

66. *The Timberworker,* June 12, 1941, p. 1.

67. Jensen, *Lumber and Labor,* pp. 264–65.

68. *The Timberworker,* August 7, 1941, p. 3; August 14, 1941, p. 1.

69. For the text of this agreement, see International Woodworkers of America, *Proceedings of the Fifth Constitutional Convention,* pp. 46, 48.

70. *The Timberworker,* September 11, 1941, p. 3; October 9, 1941, p. 3.

71. International Woodworkers of America, *Proceedings of the Fifth Constitutional Convention,* p. 11.

72. *Ibid.,* p. 109.

73. *The Timberworker,* December 11, 1941, p. 1.

74. Professor Vernon H. Jensen recently wrote of Lowery: "Lowery's leadership role needs emphasizing. He was a quiet, humble, retiring, giant of a man . . . his untimely death was a great blow to the future of the IWA and the lack of his steadying hand was felt in subsequent years." Letter to the author, February 19, 1958.

75. The communists succeeded in electing one man to the executive board — Karley Larson.

76. United Brotherhood of Carpenters and Joiners of America, *Proceedings of the Twenty-Fourth General Convention* (Lakeland, Fla., December 9–16, 1940), p. 42.

77. U. S. Department of Labor, Bureau of Labor Statistics, *Bulletin No. 840* (1945), p. 8.

78. Margaret S. Glock, *Collective Bargaining in the Pacific Northwest Lumber Industry* (Berkeley, 1955), pp. 5, 60–61.

79. *Ibid.,* p. 13.

Chapter 12   The Petroleum Industry

1. Daniel Horowitz, *Labor Relations in the Petroleum Industry* (Works Progress Administration, 1937), pp. 63–64; Harvey O'Connor, *History of the Oil Workers' International Union (CIO)* (Denver, 1950), pp. 15–28.

2. O'Connor, *History,* p. 33.

3. *Monthly Labor Review,* February 1937, p. 419.

4. Harvey O'Connor, *The Empire of Oil* (New York, 1955), p. 32.

5. O'Connor, *History,* pp. 36, 37.

6. Among the most persistent competitors were the Boilermarkers and the Teamsters. Of the latter, Harvey Fremming, president of the Oil Workers, said: "Tobin claims the men in gas stations who feed gas to autos, whom he says take the place of the stable boys who fed hay to horses." Committee for Industrial Organization, *Minutes* (December 9, 1935).

7. American Petroleum Institute, *Petroleum Facts and Figures* (1941 edition), p. 174; 174, n. 3.

8. Oil Workers' International Union, *Proceedings of the Tenth National Convention* (Hammond, Indiana, September 11–16, 1939), p. 198.

9. *Petroleum Facts and Figures,* p. 101.

10. *Oil and Gas Journal,* April 1, 1937, p. 8.

11. Horowitz, *Labor Relations,* pp. 41, 45–52.

12. Oil Workers' International Union, *Proceedings of the Eleventh Annual Convention* (Fort Worth, Texas, September 9–14, 1940), pp. 305–306.

13. Bureau of Labor Statistics, *Handbook of Labor Statistics* (1947 edition), pp. 78, 81.

14. American Petroleum Institute, *Petroleum-Industry Hearings before the Temporary National Economic Committee* (New York, 1942), p. 483.

15. Hearings Before the Temporary National Economic Committee, 76th Congress (1939), Part 16, p. 9006.

16. American Petroleum Institute, *Petroleum-Industry Hearings*, p. 486.

17. O'Connor, *The Empire of Oil*, p. 170.

18. T.N.E.C. Hearings, p. 9008.

19. Eugene V. Rostow, *A National Policy for the Oil Industry* (New Haven, 1948), p. 10.

20. The term "independent" is used for companies engaged in only one branch of the industry, as contrasted with the "integrated" companies which handle all operations, from production of crude oil to marketing of the finished product.

21. Horowitz, *Labor Relations*, pp. 74–75.

22. O'Connor, *History*, pp. 38–40.

23. In a list of CIO unions according to pro- and anticommunist leanings in 1946, the Oil Workers Union was catalogued as "uncertain and shifting." Max M. Kampelman, *The Communist Party vs. the CIO* (New York, 1951), p. 46.

24. *National Petroleum News*, February 3, 1937, p. 9.

25. *The CIO News, Oil Workers Edition*, July 9, 1938, p. 2.

26. *National Petroleum News*, April 14, 1937, p. 13.

27. *National Petroleum News*, April 28, 1937, p. 20.

28. *Oil and Gas Journal*, May 13, 1937, p. 40.

29. *National Petroleum News*, May 15, 1937, p. 9; June 23, 1937, p. 32; June 30, 1937, p. 20.

30. In a list of the fifteen largest American integrated oil companies, measured by total assets in 1938, the following places were occupied by Standard companies: Standard Oil of New Jersey, first; Socony-Vacuum Oil Company, second; Standard Oil of Indiana, third; Standard Oil of California, fifth; and Continental Oil, fifteenth. Ronald B. Schuman, *The Petroleum Industry* (Norman, Oklahoma, 1940), p. 176.

31. *National Petroleum News*, April 28, 1937, p. 20. A resolution adopted by the Metal Trades Department on April 8, 1937, explained the intent of the organization in the following terms:
"It is the purpose of the International Unions united in the Metal Trades Department to protect all their members, whether skilled craftsmen, apprentices, specialists, production workers or helpers, guaranteeing to the highly skilled workmen the right to protect the skill they have acquired, and at the same time give each subdivision of the craft a recognized voice in determining their conditions of labor, then jointly proceed to exert their combined economic power in improving wages and working conditions for all. This procedure to be followed in joint movements where more than one craft is involved, operating through Metal Trades Department and Metal Trades Councils." American Federation of Labor, Metals Trades Department, *Proceedings of the Twenty-Ninth Annual Convention* (Denver, September 27, 1937), p. 9.

32. O'Connor, *History*, p. 40. The union publicly claimed dues paying membership of over 60,000 at the time. See *National Petroleum News*, August 11, 1937, p. 19.

33. Oil Workers' International Union, *Proceedings of the Eighth Convention* (Kansas City, Mo., June 7–12, 1937), p. 31.

34. *Ibid.*, p. 54.

35. Oil Workers' International Union, *Proceedings of the Ninth National Convention* (Houston, June 6–11, 1938), pp. 63, 150.

36. *Ibid.*, Annual Report of the Executive Council, p. 11.

37. *International Oil Worker*, December 27, 1937, p. 3; January 31, 1938, p. 3.

38. *CIO News, Oil Workers Edition*, October 1, 1938, p. 1; May 7, 1938, p. 8.

39. O'Connor, *History*, p. 295; pp. 365–366; pp. 289–292.

40. *National Petroleum News,* January 4, 1939, p. 8. The president of the local union was on this blacklist.

41. Oil Workers' International Union, *Proceedings of the Tenth National Convention* (Hammond, Indiana, September 11–16, 1939), p. 69.

42. *National Petroleum News,* January 25, 1939, p. 6; *ibid.,* February 8, 1939, p. 9; *CIO News, Oil Workers Edition,* May 1, 1939, p. 1.

43. *National Petroleum News,* February 1, 1939, p. 17.

44. Oil Workers' International Union, *Proceedings of the Tenth National Convention,* p. 104.

45. O'Connor, *History,* p. 376.

46. Oil Workers' International Union, *Proceedings of the Tenth National Convention,* p. 195.

47. Oil Workers' International Union, *Proceedings of the Eleventh National Convention,* Annual Report of Executive Council, p. 25.

48. Oil Workers' International Union, *Proceedings of the Tenth National Convention,* Annual Report of the Executive Council, pp. 5, 16.

49. O'Connor, *History,* p. 42.

50. Temporary National Economic Committee, *Hearings,* p. 9004; American Petroleum Institute, *Petroleum-Industry Hearings,* p. 509.

51. *National Petroleum News,* March 27, 1940, p. 12.

52. Oil Workers' International Union, *Proceedings of the Eleventh National Convention* (Fort Worth, September 9–14, 1940), pp. 203, 283.

53. *Ibid.,* Annual Report of the Executive Council, p. 10.

54. Oil Workers' International Union, *Proceedings of the Twelfth National Convention,* Report of the Auditor (Baton Rouge, September 15–19, 1941), p. 37.

55. O'Connor, *History,* p. 377.

56. Oil Workers' International Union, *Proceedings of the Eleventh National Convention,* pp. 196, 197.

57. Oil Workers' International Union, *Proceedings of the Eleventh Annual Convention,* Annual Report of the Executive Council, p. 25.

58. Oil Workers' International Union, *Proceedings of the Eleventh Annual Convention,* p. 127.

59. *CIO News, International Oil Workers Edition,* April 7, 1941, p. 1; September 15, 1941, p. 1; July 28, 1941, p. 2.

60. Oil Workers' Union, *Proceedings of the Twelfth National Convention,* Annual Reports of the Executive Council, pp. 2, 6.

61. Oil Workers' International Union, *Proceedings of the Twelfth National Convention,* p. 290.

62. *CIO News, International Oil Workers Edition,* November 17, 1941, p. 1; O'Connor, *History,* p. 47.

63. O'Connor, *History,* p. 48.

64. *CIO News, International Oil Workers Edition,* February 2, 1942, p. 1.

65. The data are from Bureau of Labor Statistics, *Handbook of Labor Statistics* (1947 edition), pp. 78, 81.

Chapter 13   The Maritime Industry

1. In the preparation of this chapter, I have leaned heavily upon the excellent publication by Joseph P. Goldberg, *The Maritime Story* (Cambridge, 1957).

2. Goldberg, *The Maritime Story,* p. 3.

3. Maritime Labor Board, *Report to the President and to the Congress* (March 1, 1940), p. 25.

4. Goldberg, *The Maritime Story*, p. 121.

5. Wytze Gorter and George H. Hildebrand, *The Pacific Coast Maritime Shipping Industry, 1930–1948*, vol. II (Berkeley, 1954), p. 175.

6. Charles P. Larrowe, *Shape-Up and Hiring Hall* (Berkeley, 1955), pp. 15–17.

7. Quoted by Betty V. H. Schneider and Abraham Siegel, *Industrial Relations in the Pacific Coast Longshore Industry* (Berkeley, 1956), p. 10.

8. Quoted by Goldberg, *The Maritime Story*, p. 135. For a good analysis of worker objections to employer-operated hiring halls, see William S. Hopkins, "Employment Exchanges for Seamen," *American Economic Review* (June 1935), p. 250.

9. For the details of the 1934 strike, see Gorter and Hildebrand, *The Pacific Coast*, pp. 179–89. A detailed ILWU version is to be found in Mike Quin, *The Big Strike* (Olema, California, 1949).

10. See Gorter and Hildebrand, *The Pacific Coast*, pp. 188–91; Goldberg, *The Maritime Story*, pp. 139–41.

11. Gorter and Hildebrand, *The Pacific Coast*, p. 192.

12. Goldberg, *The Maritime Story*, p. 145.

13. *Seamen's Journal*, April 1, 1936, p. 136.

14. The different attitudes of the two men toward use of the job action was well illustrated at one of the first meetings of the Maritime Federation of the Pacific. Bridges submitted a resolution which defined the term "job action" as "only action taken by any union in attempting to gain from their employers, some concessions not specifically provided for in their respective agreements or awards, but shall not include action taken for demands such as increases in wages, shorter hours, etc., when such things are distinctly covered by the wording of an agreement or an award," and urged that job actions "be confined to a job such as a ship or a dock unless otherwise agreed by all unions affected." When job action might involve other organizations, "the organizations liable to be affected . . . be consulted, demands discussed and it be agreed beforehand by a majority as to what extent the job action be prosecuted and if demands are not granted when such job action will be called off. . . ." Maritime Federation of the Pacific Coast, *Minutes of the Special Convention*, November 12–22, 1935, Session of November 20, 1935, p. 15. The SUP introduced a counterresolution preserving the right of any union to use the job action when deemed necessary, "after proper consultation with other workers on the job who would be affected." *Ibid.*, Session of November 21, 1935, p. 1. In the debate, Lundeberg opposed the Bridges motion with the argument that it was impossible to define a job action in the first place.

15. Goldberg, *The Maritime Story*, pp. 148–49.

16. Gorter and Hildebrand, *The Pacific Coast*, pp. 191–97.

17. Goldberg, *The Maritime Story*, pp. 156–57.

18. Gorter and Hildebrand, *The Pacific Coast*, p. 196.

19. Robert J. Lampman, "Collective Bargaining of West Coast Sailors," unpublished manuscript (University of California, Berkeley, 1950), p. 187.

20. For a detailed description of the policies of the Marine Workers' Industrial Union, see William L. Standard, *Merchant Seamen* (New York, 1947), pp. 54–114.

21. For the details of this episode, see *Seamen's Journal*, April 1, 1936, pp. 92–94.

22. Standard, *Merchant Seamen*, p. 84.

23. Goldberg, *The Maritime Story*, pp. 150–51.

24. Goldberg, *The Maritime Story*, pp. 154–55.

25. Quoted by Goldberg, *The Maritime Story*, p. 161.

26. AFL Executive Council Minutes (February 8–19, 1937), pp. 5, 79, 125, 143, 200.

27. Elmo P. Hohman, *History of American Merchant Seamen* (Hamden, Conn., 1956), p. 69.
28. AFL Executive Council Minutes (August 21-September 2, 1937), p. 68.
29. National Maritime Union of America, *Proceedings of the First Constitutional Convention* (New York, July 19-July 30, 1937), p. 79.
30. *Ibid.*, pp. 343-44.
31. See *infra*, p. 482.
32. Lampman, "Collective Bargaining," pp. 191-194.
33. *Voice of the Federation*, November 4, 1937, p. 1.
34. Lampman, "Collective Bargaining," pp. 197-199.
35. Maritime Federation of the Pacific, *Third Annual Convention* (June 7-July 9, 1937), Session of June 14, 1937, p. 6; Session of June 28, 1937, pp. 7-8; Session of June 29, 1937, pp. 3, 5; Session of July 8, 1937, pp. 6, 8, 9.
36. Gorter and Hildebrand, *The Pacific Coast*, p. 225.
37. As an illustration of the relationship between Bridges and Lundeberg in 1937, a speech of the latter delivered at the Federation convention may be cited: "the Sailors' Union of the Pacific is a rank-and-file organization, controlled by the membership. Their delegates were elected by the membership on a coastwise basis to represent them, and I know that the membership of the Sailors' Union of the Pacific know what to do with us if we are disrupting the convention. That is their business. . . . They evidently don't believe in this attempted Moscow trial, which certain two-bit politicians make use of. There are certain politicians, certain revolutionary fakers on this coast that tend to disrupt the working classes, and as far as we are concerned all these phony politicians can all go to hell. We don't give a good god damn." Maritime Federation of the Pacific, *Third Annual Convention*, Session of June 22, 1937, p. 8.
38. This incident was described as follows in the Report of the Secretary to the 1938 Convention of the Maritime Federation: "In the meantime the 'Sea Thrush' arrived in San Francisco on April 18. In preparation for the vessel's arrival, the SUP had assembled a mass picket line around Pier 41. ILWU No. 1-10 signified its intention of working the ship and had called upon District Council No. 2 to call all groups together. The council met and adopted a resolution to submit the affair to the Maritime Federation. The SUP still refused to do so and notified all concerned they intended to carry out their plans to picket. Rumors kept coming into the office that the temper of both groups was bad and increasing and, fearing the worst, President Engstrom [of the Maritime Federation] went down to the scene to watch developments. An SUP picket line was stretched across the pier entrance, and longshoremen were standing by. . . . ILWU No. 1-10 had a sound truck with loud speaker equipment standing by and various officials asked the SUP to withdraw their men and refer the dispute to the Federation. President Engstrom pleaded with all concerned to settle the dispute around the table. The SUP (through Lundeberg) refused, and after he had stated his position the longshoremen were ordered through by Brother Bulcke, vice-president of No. 1-10. Immediately the longshoremen began surging through the picket line; a riot ensued. Who struck the first blow no one will ever know and each side blames the other. The fact remains that regardless of who was right or who was wrong we found brother slugging brother. Men who were the best of friends before, became bitter enemies later. Men who had suffered side by side and stood shoulder to shoulder on other picket lines now were battering each other down." Maritime Federation of the Pacific, *Proceedings, Fourth Annual Convention* (San Francisco, June 6-25, 1938), p. 112.
39. *Ibid.*, pp. 261-62.
40. Gorter and Hildebrand, *The Pacific Coast*, p. 253.

41. Maritime Federation of the Pacific, *Proceedings,* Fourth Annual Convention, p. 24.

42. AFL Executive Council Minutes (August 22-September 2, 1938), pp. 72, 163; *ibid.* (October 2–14, 1938), pp. 33, 48.

43. *Ibid.* (January 30-February 14, 1939), p. 104. Lundeberg later reported in more detail: "When the Seafarers' International Union entered the field, the AFL Seamen's Union was $5,000 in the hole; had less than a thousand members; no records; a few agreements that stunk, with no closed shop clause; wages and conditions were far below West Coast standards." . . . Seafarers' International Union of America, *Proceedings,* First Convention (San Francisco, March 23–28, 1942), p. 9.

44. Maritime Federation of the Pacific, *Proceedings, Seventh Annual Convention* (San Francisco, June 2–7, 1941), p. 45.

45. Gorter and Hildebrand, *The Pacific Coast,* pp. 229–31.

46. Goldberg, *The Maritime Story,* pp. 176–77.

47. National Maritime Union of America, *Proceedings of the Second National Convention* (New Orleans, July 3–14, 1939), p. 55.

48. Philip Taft, "The Unlicensed Seafaring Unions," *Industrial and Labor Relations Review* (January 1950), pp. 207, 208.

49. M. Hedley Stone, at the time director of the Great Lakes district and subsequently treasurer of the NMU, an admitted communist, answered when asked if Curran had been a Communist Party member: "No. The only time Curran was brought to a meeting by me would be when I was asked specifically to bring him to a certain place, and I believed everybody at that meeting was told and briefed how to behave themselves at the time and what subject to raise." Max M. Kampelman, *The Communist Party vs. the CIO* (New York, 1957), p. 78.

50. Kampelman, *The Communist Party,* pp. 82–90.

51. Goldberg, *The Maritime Story,* pp. 168–69.

52. National Maritime Union of America, *Proceedings of the Third National Convention* (Cleveland, July 7–14, 1941), p. 115.

53. *Ibid.,* p. 112.

54. Seafarers' International Union of North America, *Proceedings of the First Convention* (San Francisco, March 23–28, 1942), p. 25.

55. Data for four major Pacific ports show 59 such minor stoppages in 1938, 121 in 1939, 82 in 1940, and 37 in 1941. Gorter and Hildebrand, *The Pacific Coast,* p. 234.

56. Schneider and Siegel, *Industrial Relations,* pp. 21–22. It may be noted that there are still no adequate studies of longshore productivity. See Gorter and Hildebrand, *The Pacific Coast,* p. 149.

57. Goldberg, *The Maritime Story,* p. 180.

58. Lampman, "Collective Bargaining," pp. 285–86.

59. Maritime Federation of the Pacific, *Proceedings of the Sixth Annual Convention* (Astoria, Oregon, June 3–8, 1940), p. 185.

60. Kampelman, *The Communist Party,* p. 205.

61. *Ibid.,* p. 212.

62. Maritime Federation of the Pacific, *Proceedings,* Seventh Annual Convention (San Francisco, June 2–7, 1941), pp. 44, 104–108.

63. From October 1939, to November 1940, the number of jobs in the ocean-going merchant marine as a whole fell from 55,000 to 48,000. Goldberg, *The Maritime Story,* p. 200. Offshore employment on the Pacific Coast increased from 9014 in 1939 to 9382 in 1940, and again to 9757 in 1941. However, there was a decline in the number of registered longshoremen on the Pacific Coast; the figures are: 1939 — 9927; 1940 — 9245; 1941 — 9632. Gorter and Hildebrand, *The Pacific Coast,* p. 111.

64. Lampman, "Collective Bargaining," p. 288 .

65. National Maritime Union of America, *Proceedings of the Third National Convention* (Cleveland, July 7–14, 1941), pp. 115, 116.
66. Goldberg, *The Maritime Story*, pp. 202, 203.
67. Seafarers' International Union of North America, *Proceedings*, First Convention, p. 29.
68. Goldberg, *The Maritime Story*, p. 204.
69. Seafarers' International Union, *Proceedings*, First Convention, p. 29.
70. See National Maritime Union of America, *Proceedings of the Third National Convention*, pp. 358–60.
71. *Ibid.*, pp. 301–4.
72. Larrowe, *Shape-Up*, pp. 18, 22–23.
73. Goldberg, *The Maritime Story*, pp. 185–187.
74. Cosmopolitan Shipping Company, 2 NLRB 759 (1937).
75. Goldberg, *The Maritime Story*, p. 196.
76. Quoted by Lampman, "Collective Bargaining," p. 253.
77. Lampman, "Collective Bargaining," p. 259.
78. Maritime Labor Board, *Supplemental Report to the President and to the Congress* (March 1, 1942), p. 17.
79. National Maritime Union of America, *Proceedings of the Third National Convention*, p. 150.
80. Hohman, *History*, p. 82.
81. Goldberg, *The Maritime Story*, p. 193.
82. Maritime Labor Board, *Report to the President and to the Congress* (March 1, 1940).
83. Lampman, "Collective Bargaining." p. 257.
84. Goldberg, *The Maritime Story*, p. 197.
85. *Ibid.*, p. 182.
86. See, for example, National Maritime Union of America, *Proceedings of the Third National Convention*, pp. 277–90.
87. Maritime Federation of the Pacific Coast, *Second Annual Convention* (May 15–June 10, 1936), Session of May 20, 1936, p. 4.
88. Lampman, "Collective Bargaining," p. 286.
89. Total offshore employment was estimated at 8817 in 1936 and 9757 in 1941. Gorter and Hildebrand, *The Pacific Coast*, p. 111. These totals include the remaining unlicensed crafts and the licensed officers.
90. International Longshoremen's and Warehousemen's Union, *Proceedings, First Annual Convention* (Aberdeen, Washington, April 4–17, 1938), p. 104.
91. International Longshoremen's and Warehousemen's Union, *Proceedings, Third Annual Convention* (North Bend, Oregon, April 1–11, 1940), p. 120.
92. Gorter and Hildebrand, *The Pacific Coast*, p. 11.
93. International Longshoremen's and Warehousemen's Union, *The ILWU Story* (San Francisco, 1955), p. 35.
94. National Maritime Union of America, *Proceedings of the Second National Convention*, p. 225.
95. National Maritime Union of America, *Proceedings of the Fourth National Convention* (New York, July 6–12, 1943), p. 53.
96. Seafarers' International Union, *Proceedings, First Convention* (San Francisco, March 23–28, 1942), p. 9.
97. United States Census of Population (1940), vol. III, part I, p. 82.
98. See *supra*, p. 427.
99. The difference between the indices for East and West Coast seamen are due to

NOTES TO CHAPTER 13

differences in the 1935 base; after 1937, the absolute scale for the two groups was equalized, and remained identical except for very short term contract lags.

100. Goldberg, *The Maritime Story*, p. 285.
101. Gorter and Hildebrand, *The Pacific Coast*, pp. 139–141.
102. *Ibid.*, pp. 140–41.
103. Wytze Gorter and George H. Hildebrand, *The Pacific Coast Maritime Shipping Industry*, vol. I (Berkeley, 1952), p. 89.
104. Larrowe, *Shape-Up*, pp. 52, 166.
105. It should not be inferred that West Coast decasualization resulted in complete elimination of intermittent work. Annual hours worked per man fell from 1935 to 1938, rose sharply during the war period, and declined once again after the war. An examination of available employment data yielded the conclusion that "there were usually too many longshoremen to provide each with a full year's work, despite the operation of hiring halls designed to bring about a better balance between the number of longshoremen and the available jobs. In the postwar years, this surplus was especially large." Gorter and Hildebrand, vol. I, *The Pacific Coast*, p. 53.
106. Foreword to Goldberg, *The Maritime Story*, pp. viii–x.

Chapter 14 The Teamsters

1. Samuel E. Hill, *Teamsters and Transportation* (Washington, 1942), p. 78.
2. International Brotherhood of Teamsters, *Proceedings of the Thirteenth Convention* (Portland, Oregon, September 9–14, 1935), pp. 36, 59.
3. Hill, *Teamsters and Transportation*, p. 15.
4. *Official Magazine, International Brotherhood of Teamsters, Chauffeurs, Stablemen and Helpers* (March 1936), p. 9. This publication is referred to hereafter as *Official Magazine*.
5. J. B. Gillingham, *The Teamsters' Union on the West Coast* (Berkeley, 1956), pp. 8, 9.
6. Nathan P. Feinsinger, *Collective Bargaining in the Trucking Industry* (Philadelphia, 1949), p. 11.
7. *Official Magazine* (July 1937), p. 10; (April 1936), p. 15; (January 1941), p. 15.
8. Robert M. Robinson, "A History of the Teamsters in the San Francisco Bay Area, 1850–1950" (University of California, 1951), p. 473, typewritten.
9. Official Magazine (December 1940), p. 4.
10. International Brotherhood of Teamsters, *Proceedings of the Fourteenth Convention* (Washington, D. C., September 9–14, 1940), fifth day, p. 22.
11. The convention later adopted a much weaker amendment which provided that if a local union rejected an employer offer of arbitration, it could be directed to arbitrate by the General Executive Board. *Ibid.*, p. 61 (sixth day).
12. *Ibid.*, p. 27.
13. Hill, *Teamsters and Transportation*, p. 9.
14. Gillingham, *The Teamsters' Union*, pp. 35–36.
15. Hill, *Teamsters and Transportation*, pp. 38, 227.
16. Gillingham, *The Teamsters' Union*, pp. 18–19.
17. John T. Dunlop, "The Task of Contemporary Wage Theory," in George W. Taylor and Frank C. Pierson, *New Concepts in Wage Determination* (New York, 1957), p. 136.
18. See Gillingham, *The Teamsters' Union*, pp. 20, 22, 26.
19. *Official Magazine* (February 1937), p. 12; (January 1940), p. 3.

20. *Ibid.* (February 1940), p. 3; (October 1936), p. 15; (October 1940), p. 2; (January 1940), p. 3; (February 1938), p. 12; (June 1941), p. 15.

21. Hill, *Teamsters and Transportation,* p. 146.

22. Gillingham, *The Teamsters' Union,* pp. 12–13.

23. *Official Magazine* (May 1938), p. 14.

24. See, *e.g., ibid.* (January 1936), p. 7.

25. Hill, *Teamsters and Transportation,* p. 98.

26. Gillingham, *The Teamsters' Union,* p. 32.

27. AFL Executive Council Minutes (April 25-May 5, 1938), p. 32.

28. See *infra,* p. 475.

29. AFL Executive Council Minutes (January 30-February 14, 1939), p. 76.

30. *Official Magazine* (December 1941), p. 6; (March 1940), p. 5; (December 1940), p. 7.

31. Paul Jacobs, "The World of Jimmy Hoffa," *The Reporter* (February 7, 1957), p. 10.

32. *Fortune Magazine* (May 1941), p. 97.

33. *Official Magazine* (June 1941), p. 8.

34. *Official Magazine* (May 1940), p. 12; (June 1940), p. 10.

35. International Brotherhood of Teamsters, *Proceedings of the Fourteenth Convention,* fifth day, p. 119; sixth day, p. 107.

36. Harold Barger, *The Transportation Industries* (New York, 1951), pp. 225, 245.

37. Robinson, *History,* p. 473.

38. *Official Magazine* (March 1937), p. 14; (May 1938), p. 9.

39. Western Conference of Teamsters, *Report of the Proceedings of the Seventh Meeting* (Portland, Oregon, June 1–5, 1942), p. 1.

40. These were: Highway Drivers' Division, Automotive Division, Bakery Division, Beverage Division, Building and Construction Division, Chauffeurs' Division, Dairy Division, Laundry Division, Produce and Cold Storage Division, Miscellaneous Sales Drivers' Division, General Hauling Division, and General Warehouse Division.

41. Western Conference of Teamsters, *Report of Proceedings of the Seventh Meeting,* p. 14; *The Washington Teamster* (January 1940), p. 1.

42. *The Washington Teamster,* October 3, 1941, p. 1.

43. Western Conference of Teamsters, *Report of Proceedings of the Seventh Meeting,* p. 17.

44. *Fortune Magazine* (May 1941), p. 97.

45. See *supra,* pp. 288, 303.

46. *The Washington Teamster,* October 3, 1941, p. 1.

47. For the details of the Teamster role in these strikes, see Robinson, *History,* pp. 227, 254.

48. AF of L Executive Council Minutes (February 8–19, 1937), p. 150.

49. Robinson, *History,* pp. 314, 321, 326.

50. *Official Magazine* (October 1937), p. 2.

51. Robinson, *History,* pp. 334, 344, 350.

52. Gillingham, *The Teamsters' Union,* pp. 56–58.

53. Robinson, *History,* p. 397.

54. Gillingham, *The Teamsters' Union,* pp. 62–64.

55. Western Conference of Teamsters, *Report of the Proceedings of the Seventh Meeting,* pp. 284–285.

56. Another brother, William F. Dunne, became one of the top leaders of the Stalinist branch of the Communist Party.

57. For the details of the strike, see Charles R. Walker, *American City* (New York, 1937), and James P. Cannon, *The History of American Trotskyism* (New York, 1944).

58. Walker, *American City*, pp. 126, 177.

59. *The Northwest Organizer*, May 27, 1936, p. 1; April 22, 1936, p. 3.

60. AFL Executive Council Minutes (October 5–21, 1935), p. 95.

61. *The Northwest Organizer*, July 15, 1936, p. 1.

62. *The Northwest Organizer*, February 19, 1936, p. 1; July 15, 1936, p. 2; January 14, 1937, p. 1; April 15, 1937, p. 1.

63. *Ibid.*, March 31, 1938, p. 1; May 12, 1938, p. 3; May 26, 1938, p. 3.

64. *Ibid.*, August 25, 1938, p. 1; September 1, 1938, p. 1; October 19, 1939, p. 3; April 17, 1941, p. 1.

65. See Nathan P. Feinsinger, *Collective Bargaining in the Trucking Industry* (Philadelphia, 1939), p. 27.

66. *The Northwest Organizer*, April 28, 1938, p. 4.

67. *Ibid.*, September 30, 1937, p. 1; December 2, 1937, p. 1; December 23, 1937, p. 1; May 26, 1938, p. 1; October 9, 1941, p. 1.

68. *Official Magazine* (May 1941), p. 10.

69. *The Northwest Organizer*, May 29, 1941, p. 2. Those officers of Local 544 who were members of the Socialist Workers Party resigned their membership when Tobin first raised the issue. *Ibid.*, June 12, 1941, p. 4.

70. *Official Magazine* (July 1941), p. 5.

71. *The Northwest Organizer*, July 3, 1941, p. 2; September 11, 1941, p. 1.

72. *Ibid.*, June 26, 1941, p. 1, quoted from the *Minneapolis Times* of June 20, 1941. One of the huskies in the Michigan cars was identified as James R. Hoffa.

73. *Official Magazine* (November 1941), p. 14.

74. *The Northwest Organizer*, September 18, 1941, p. 1.

75. For his account of the trial, see Albert Goldman, *In Defense of Socialism* (New York).

76. The union had argued that its Defense Guard, organized in 1938, was designed merely to protect its property from the Silver Shirts and other fascist groups active in Minneapolis.

77. Dunne v. United States, 138 F. (2d) 137 (1943).

78. This section is based upon Samuel E. Hill, *Teamsters and Transportation* (Washington, 1942).

79. President Tobin as well as Secretary-Treasurer English had both come from Local 25, which had been one of the leading units in the national organization.

80. Hill, *Teamsters and Transportation*, pp. 102–103.

81. See Hill, *Teamsters and Transportation*, chap. XII, for a description of the powers and operation of this board.

82. Hill, *Teamsters and Transportation*, pp. 137, 139, 221.

83. Selig Perlman and Philip Taft, *History of Labor in the United States* (New York, 1935), pp. 362–363.

84. Gillingham, *The Teamsters' Union*, pp. 43–44.

85. AFL Executive Council Minutes (August 5–16, 1935), p. 43; (October 5–21, 1935), p. 54; (May 5–20, 1936), p. 138.

86. *Ibid.*, January 24–February 8, 1938, p. 57.

87. Gillingham, *The Teamsters' Union*, pp. 48–50.

88. AFL Executive Council Minutes (June 6–7, 1935), p. 37.

89. *Official Magazine* (June 1936), p. 10; (April 1939), p. 13.

90. AFL Executive Council Minutes (January 30–February 14, 1939), p. 238; (October 2–14, 1938), p. 66; (January 30–February 14, 1939), p. 211.

91. Obergfell v. Green, 29 F. Supp. 589 (1939).

92. American Federation of Labor, *Report of Proceedings of the Fifty-Ninth Annual Convention* (Cincinnati, 1939), pp. 564, 569.
93. AFL Executive Council Minutes (January 29–February 9, 1940), p. 76.
94. American Federation of Labor, *Report of Proceedings of the Sixty-First Annual Convention* (Seattle, 1941), p. 631.
95. Gillingham, *The Teamsters' Union*, p. 78.
96. *Official Magazine* (January 1936), p. 7; (December 1936), p. 4; (July 1937), p. 10; (January 1938), p. 8; (October 1939), p. 5; (June 1940), p. 15; (January 1941), p. 15; (October 1941), cover; (November 1939), p. 9; (January 1941), p. 15.
97. *The Washington Teamster*, December 31, 1941, p. 1.

Chapter 15   The Machinists

1. AFL Executive Council Minutes (July 8–15, 1936), p. 124.
2. *Machinists' Monthly Journal* (August 1936), p. 481.
3. International Association of Machinists, *Proceedings of the Nineteenth Convention* (Milwaukee, September 21–October 2, 1936), pp. 130–132.
4. These figures were supplied by Professor Mark Perlman, who is preparing a detailed history of the Machinists.
5. *Machinists' Monthly Journal* (January 1938), p. 33; (March 1936), p. 148.
6. For the text of the agreements, see *Machinists' Monthly Journal* (March 1936), p. 149.
7. Max M. Kampelman, *The Communist Party vs. the CIO* (1952), p. 116.
8. The IAM had members at the Ilion plant of Remington Rand before 1933. Thus, in 1931, 80 machinists employed there were IAM members.
9. These and further details of the Remington Rand strike are taken from the following sources: *In the Matter of Remington Rand,* 2 NLRB 626 (1937); Robert R. R. Brooks, *When Labor Organizes* (New Haven, 1937), chap. V; International Association of Machinists, *Proceedings of the Nineteenth Convention,* pp. 47–49.
10. *In the Matter of Remington Rand Inc.,* 2 NLRB 626, pp. 654, 657, 659, 661–662.
11. International Association of Machinists, *Proceedings of the Nineteenth Convention,* p. 188.
12. *Machinists' Monthly Journal* (May 1937), p. 316.
13. International Association of Machinists, *Proceedings of the Twentieth Convention* (Cleveland, 1940), p. 222.
14. International Association of Machinists, *Constitution* (1941), Article XIII, Sec. 2.
15. International Association of Machinists, *Minutes of the Executive Council* (February 17–26, 1936).
16. See International Association of Machinists, *Proceedings of the Nineteenth Convention,* pp. 325–329.
17. International Association of Machinists, *Minutes of the Executive Council* (July 27–July 31, 1936).
18. International Association of Machinists, *Proceedings of the Nineteenth Convention,* pp. 316–355.
19. International Association of Machinists, *Minutes of the Executive Council* (October 24–29, 1938).
20. International Association of Machinists, *Proceedings of the Twentieth Convention,* p. 434.
21. Strikes were also called against four other small shipyards which the IAM declared

were competitive with repair yards, which paid a slightly higher scale than yards producing new ships.

22. American Federation of Labor, Metal Trades Department, *Proceedings of the Thirty-Third Annual Convention* (Seattle, 1941), p. 34.

23. *Machinists' Monthly Journal* (July 1941), pp. 576–579, 603.

24. *Machinists' Monthly Journal* (August 1941), p. 645.

25. International Association of Machinists, *Executive Council Minutes* (September 13–19, 1937); *Machinists' Monthly Journal* (October 1937), p. 669.

26. See *supra,* p. 478.

27. International Association of Machinists, *Executive Council Minutes* (April 16–23, 1941).

28. *Machinists' Monthly Journal* (September 1941), p. 776.

29. The UAW sent Wyndham Mortimer and Lew Michener, the leaders of the left wing North American aviation strike, to Seattle in an endeavor to capitalize upon the disaffection there, but to no avail. See *United Automobile Worker,* June 1, 1941, p. 8.

30. In 1937, the Grand Lodge was maintaining 79 organizers on its payroll. International Association of Machinists, *Executive Council Minutes* (December 13–17, 1937). This number increased in subsequent years.

31. AFL Executive Council Minutes (May 5–20, 1936), pp. 165, 175; (August 22–September 2, 1938), p. 178.

32. *Fortune Magazine,* "Half a Million Workers" (March 1941), p. 96.

33. The Boeing local had been first organized by an AFL Federal local on an industrial basis. It was chartered by the IAM after the latter secured jurisdiction over aircraft, over the objections of the Seattle IAM lodges and the Seattle Central Labor Council, which objected to the industrial form of the local. Arthur P. Allen and Betty V. H. Schneider, *Industrial Relations in the California Aircraft Industry* (Berkeley, 1956), p. 9.

34. The IAM won an NLRB election at Consolidated in 1937. UAW organizers went into action shortly after the election, and for a year there was intense competition between the two unions. In 1938, the IAM won a decisive electoral victory, and finally managed, in April 1940, to secure a favorable agreement from the company. Allen and Schneider, *Industrial Relations,* p. 15.

35. International Association of Machinists, *Proceedings of the Twenty-First Convention* (New York, 1945), p. 34. Five years later, in April 1945, claimed aircraft membership had risen to 158,328, in 131 lodges.

36. The Twentieth Century Fund, *How Collective Bargaining Works* (New York, 1942), p. 931.

37. At North American, the UAW won recognition in March 1937, through a strike threat, but the company refused to renew the agreement in 1938. The case was taken to the NLRB, and after several years of litigation, during which the local voted to secede to the newly formed UAW-AFL, the UAW-CIO finally won an election and exclusive bargaining rights. The UAW won a contract at Ryan by virtue of a close election victory in 1940. Allen and Schneider, *Industrial Relations,* pp. 15, 16.

38. *United Automobile Worker,* February 15, 1942, p. 6.

39. See Allen and Schneider, Industrial Relations, pp. 42ff.

40. International Association of Machinists, *Proceedings of the Twenty-First Convention,* p. 36.

41. International Association of Machinists, *Executive Council Minutes* (May 6–17, 1940).

42. International Association of Machinists, *Proceedings of the Twenty-First Convention,* p. 37.

43. AFL Executive Council Minutes (January 24-February 8, 1938), p. 55; (May 10–19, 1939), p. 51; (May 13–21, 1940), p. 72.

44. *Machinists' Monthly Journal* (March 1942), pp. 198–199, 203–204.

45. For the text of the agreement, see *ibid.*, pp. 205–206, 207.

46. International Association of Machinists, *Proceedings of the Nineteenth Convention*, p. 274.

47. *Machinists' Monthly Journal* (March 1942), pp. 208, 209.

48. AFL Executive Council Minutes (May 13–21, 1940), p. 132. The carpenters were later acquitted of the charges. See *infra,* ch. 14.

49. *Machinists' Monthly Journal* (March 1940), p. 181.

50. American Federation of Labor, *Report of Proceedings of the Sixty-First Annual Convention* (Seattle, October 6–16, 1941), pp. 496ff.

51. International Association of Machinists, *Proceedings of the Twenty-First Convention,* p. 8.

52. It is interesting to note that in 1941, the Machinists suggested that the National Labor Relations Board be given authority to settle jurisdictional disputes. *Machinists' Monthly Journal* (December 1941), p. 1042.

53. Mark Perlman, *The Machinists,* to be published.

54. International Association of Machinists, *Proceedings of the Twentieth Convention,* pp. 30–37.

Chapter 16   The Building Trades

1. The unions with membership predominantly engaged in building controlled the following percentages of AFL voting strength: 1910 — 24 per cent; 1920 — 24 per cent; 1930 — 31 per cent; 1935 — 21 per cent. (Computed from annual reports of the AFL). These percentages are raised somewhat if unions such as the Teamsters, affiliated with the Building Trades Department for a portion of their membership, are included.

2. William Haber and Harold M. Levinson, *Labor Relations and Productivity in the Building Trades* (Ann Arbor, 1956), p. 30.

3. Building and Construction Trades Department, *Report of Proceedings of the Thirtieth Annual Convention* (November 1936), p. 112. These membership data are not accurate, and should be regarded only as general orders of magnitude. Each affiliated union declared its own membership to the Department, and paid per capita tax on the basis of such declaration, without any audit by the federated body. The Carpenters' Union, for example, reported 150,000 members consistently between 1936 and 1941, despite substantial growth during the period. Efforts made to induce this union to declare a more realistic membership total were unavailing. See Building and Construction Trades Department, *Report of Proceedings of the Thirty-Second Annual Convention* (September 1938), p. 95.

4. W. S. Woytinsky and Associates, *Employment and Wages in the United States* (New York, 1953), p. 678.

5. Building Trades Department, *Report of Proceedings of the Thirtieth Annual Convention* (November 1936), pp. 65–94.

6. Robert A. Christie, *Empire in Wood* (Ithaca, 1956), pp. 278–279.

7. United Brotherhood of Carpenters and Joiners of America, *Proceedings of the Twenty-Third General Convention* (Lakeland, Fla., December 7–15, 1936), p. 272.

8. See Building Trades Department, *Report of Proceedings of the Thirtieth Annual Convention,* pp. 94–95.

9. Building and Construction Trades Department, *Report of Proceedings of the Thirty-First Annual Convention* (Denver, 1937), pp. 67, 155.

10. Building and Construction Trades Department, *Report of Proceedings of the Thirty-Second Annual Convention* (Houston, 1938), p. 137.

11. William Haber, "Building Construction," in Twentieth Century Fund, *How Collective Bargaining Works* (New York, 1942), p. 203.

12. Building and Construction Trades Department, *Report of Proceedings of the Thirty-Fourth Annual Convention* (1940), p. 100.

13. Christie, *Empire in Wood*, p. 308.

14. AFL Executive Council Minutes (January 27-February 9, 1940), p. 93.

15. For the texts of the three indictments, see *The Carpenter* (January 1940), p. 12; (April 1940), p. 18.

16. *The Carpenter* (January 1940), pp. 16–18.

17. AFL Executive Council Minutes (January 27–February 9, 1940), p. 93.

18. Cited by Christie, *Empire in Wood*, p. 311.

19. Thurman Arnold, *Bottlenecks of Business* (New York, 1940), pp. 241–242, quoted by Christie, *Empire in Wood*, p. 310.

20. *The Carpenter* (October 1940), p. 2.

21. United States v. Hutcheson, 312 U. S. 219 (1941).

22. AFL Executive Council Minutes (February 10–20, 1941), p. 64.

23. United Brotherhood of Carpenters and Joiners of America, *Proceedings of the Twenty-Third General Convention* (Lakeland, Fla., 1936), p. 99. This tally predated the formation of the International Woodworkers of America as an independent union.

24. Harry C. Bates, *Bricklayers' Century of Craftsmanship* (Washington, 1955), p. 298.

25. Haber, *How Collective Bargaining Works*, p. 203.

26. Bureau of Labor Statistics, *Construction During Five Decades*, Bulletin No. 1146 (1953), pp. 26, 29.

27. For a detailed account of labor's efforts in this respect, see Bricklayers, Masons and Plasterers' International Union of America, *Tenth Biennial and Sixty-Second Report of the President and Secretary* (1938), pp. 18–28.

28. Bricklayers, Masons and Plasterers' International Union of America, *Eleventh Biennial and Sixty-Third Report of the President and Secretary* (1940), p. 40.

29. Building and Construction Trades Department, *Report of Proceedings of the Thirty-Second Annual Convention* (1938), pp. 79–81.

30. Building and Construction Trades Department, *Report of Proceedings of the Thirty-Fourth Annual Convention* (New Orleans, 1940), pp. 109–110.

31. Building and Construction Trades Department, *Report of Proceedings of the Thirty-First Annual Convention* (Denver, 1937), p. 66.

32. *Construction During Five Decades*, p. 20.

33. Taken from annual convention proceedings of the Building Trades Department. The figures are annual averages for the period July 1 to June 30 of the years indicated.

34. *The Carpenter* (January 1938), p. 30.

35. Harry C. Bates, *Bricklayers' Century*, pp. 298–299.

36. Bricklayers, Masons and Plasterers' International Union of America. *Tenth Biennial and Sixty-Second Report of the President and Secretary* (1938), p. 4.

37. International Brotherhood of Electrical Workers, *Proceedings of the Twenty-First Convention* (St. Louis, 1941), pp. 48, 67.

38. Arch A. Mercey, *The Laborers' Story* (Washington, 1955), pp. 123, 131. The rate of growth was particularly high during the defense period, for average membership in 1940 was only 183,000 (figure supplied by the union in private correspondence).

39. *CIO News,* July 31, 1939, p. 3.
40. William Green told the AFL Executive Council in October, 1940, of the following conversation with Sidney Hillman: "Mr. Hillman . . . advised Mr. Denny Lewis that he would have nothing to do with the building trades organization of the CIO; that he had opposed its organization in the first place and had requested that the CIO stay out of that field." AFL Executive Council Minutes (Meeting of September 30-October 10, 1940), p. 48.
41. CIO Executive Board Minutes (June 13–15, 1939), p. 136.
42. *CIO News,* July 15, 1940, p. 7; April 1, 1940, p. 6.
43. *United Construction Workers News,* September 15, 1940, p. 1; August 1, 1940, p. 3.
44. See *supra,* p. 483.
45. *Monthly Labor Review* (August 1937), p. 281.
46. Harry C. Bates, *Bricklayers' Century,* p. 245.
47. Bricklayers, Masons and Plasterers' International Union of America, *Eleventh Biennial and Sixty-Third Report* (1940), pp. 6–7.
48. Bricklayers, Masons and Plasterers' International Union of America, *Proceedings of the Fifteenth Biennial and Fifty-Fifth Convention* (St. Louis, 1940), pp. 77, 86.
49. Harry C. Bates, *Bricklayers' Century,* p. 245.
50. AFL Executive Council Minutes (September 30–October 10, 1940), p. 49.
51. *Ibid.*
52. See Building and Construction Trades Department, *Report of Proceedings of the Thirty-Fourth Annual Convention* (New Orleans, 1940), pp. 92–97.
53. *United Construction Workers News,* August 15, 1940, p. 1.
54. John T. Dunlop and Arthur D. Hill, *The Wage Adjustment Board* (Cambridge, 1950), p. 20. The text of this agreement may be found in this source.
55. *United Construction Workers News,* August 1, 1941, p. 1.
56. Building and Construction Trades Department, *Report of Proceedings of the Thirty-Fifth Annual Convention* (Seattle, 1941), p. 137.
57. *United Construction Workers News,* November 1, 1941, pp. 2–3, 6.
58. *The Carpenter* (December 1941), pp. 18–23.
59. *United Construction Workers News,* June 15, 1942, p. 1.
60. Their reported membership in 1929 was 322,000. Christie, *Empire in Wood.* p. 250. However, actual dues-paying membership was probably less than this. In June 1941, dues-paying membership was 382,500, and just a year later, under the spur of military construction, it had risen to 528,600. (1941 and 1942 figures are from correspondence with the union.)
61. Membership in September 1942, was 67,200, compared with 110,800 in September, 1920. Harry C. Bates, *Bricklayers' Century,* pp. 296, 299.
62. Arch A. Mercey, *The Laborers' Story,* pp. 97, 131.
63. Haber and Levinson, *Labor Relations,* pp. 30, 36.
64. United Brotherhood of Carpenters and Joiners of America, *Proceedings of the Twenty-Fourth General Convention* (Lakeland, Fla., 1940), p. 274.
65. United Brotherhood of Carpenters and Joiners of America, *Proceedings of the Twenty-Third General Convention* (Lakeland, Fla., 1936), p. 285.
66. United Brotherhood of Carpenters and Joiners of America, *Proceedings of the Twenty-Fourth General Convention* (Lakeland, Fla., 1940), p. 237.
67. Bricklayers, Masons and Plasterers' International Union of America, *Eleventh Biennial and Sixty-Third Report* (1940), p. 4.

Chapter 17 Printing and Publishing

1. In the early 1940's, some locals of mailers seceded from the International Typographical Union to form a small independent International Mailers' Union. However, mailers in the large cities generally remained in the ITU.

2. See Jacob Loft, *The Printing Trades* (New York, 1944), Ch. 12.

3. See, e.g., Seymour M. Lipset, Martin A. Trow, and James S. Coleman, *Union Democracy* (Glencoe, Ill., 1956).

4. Loft, *The Printing Trades,* pp. 145, 146. In 1940, 56 per cent of the union compositors working at their trade were employed on newspapers.

5. Robert K. Burns, "Daily Newspapers," in Twentieth Century Fund, *How Collective Bargaining Works* (New York, 1942), pp. 38–39.

6. *Monthly Labor Review* (January 1936), p. 170.

7. Loft, *The Printing Trades,* p. 203.

8. Data are computed from annual convention proceedings of the American Federation of Labor.

9. Loft, *The Printing Trades,* pp. 204, 205.

10. Burns, *How Collective Bargaining Works,* p. 46.

11. *The Typographical Journal* (August 1936), supplement, p. 15.

12. *The Typographical Journal* (August 1938), supplement, p. 6; (April 1936), p. 357; (May 1936), p. 477; (August 1936), supplement, p. 16.

13. *The Typographical Journal* (January 1937), p. 7. The benevolent society aspects of the ITU were certainly a source of weakness, rather than of strength, during this period.

14. *The Typographical Journal* (May 1938), p. 573.

15. See the discussion in International Typographical Union, *Proceedings of the Eighty-Fifth Session* (Vancouver, 1941), pp. 98–101.

16. *Ibid.,* p. 72. Flagg was the executive secretary of the Open Shop Department of the American Newspaper Publishers Association.

17. Perhaps this statement requires some qualification, at least insofar as the membership was concerned. The existence of considerable unemployment among printers, together with the policy in many cities of spreading the incidence of unemployment through share-the-work-measures, resulted in something less than a burning anxiety to organize new members on the part of many who were already in the union. The fact that many locals paid high unemployment benefits also contributed to this attitude. However, the same situation prevailed in other industries where organizing efforts proved more successful.

18. *The Typographical Journal* (July 1941), supplement, p. 6.

19. Emily Clark Brown, "Book and Job Printing," in Twentieth Century Fund, *How Collective Bargaining Works* (New York, 1942), p. 122.

20. Loft, *The Printing Trades,* p. 278; also chapter 4.

21. *Ibid.,* p. 149.

22. *The Typographical Journal* (August 1939), supplement, p. 133. The latter figure reflects a considerable amount of work sharing, imposed by local union policy in some areas.

23. Lloyd Reynolds, *The Evolution of Wage Structure* (New Haven, 1956), p. 336.

24. *The Typographical Journal* (August 1936), supplement, p. 64.

25. Lipset, Trow, and Coleman, *Union Democracy,* p. 412.

26. Loft, *The Printing Trades,* p. 209.

27. See, for example, Lipset, Trow, and Coleman, *Union Democracy,* pp. 18–25.

28. *The Typographical Journal* (April 1936), p. 355.
29. See the statement of Secretary-Treasurer Randolph in *The Typographical Journal* (September 1936), p. 236.
30. *Ibid.* (February 1937), p. 101.
31. See *supra,* p. 480.
32. *The Typographical Journal* (April 1940), p. 459.
33. International Typographical Union, *Proceedings of the Eightieth Session* (Colorado Springs, 1936), pp. 98, 101, 110.
34. International Typographical Union, *Proceedings of the Eighty-First Session* (Louisville, 1937), pp. 23, 107.
35. *The Typographical Journal* (March 1938), p. 261; (April 1938), p. 427.
36. See *The Typographical Journal* (January to June 1939), *passim.*
37. International Typographical Union, *Proceedings of the Eighty-Second Session* (Birmingham, 1938), p. 86.
38. AFL Executive Council Minutes (October 2–14, 1938), p. 17.
39. International Typographical Union, *Proceedings of the Eighty-Third Session* (Fort Worth, 1939), pp. 78, 84.
40. AFL Executive Council Minutes (January 29-February 9, 1940), p. 14.
41. *The Typographical Journal* (August 1939), supplement, pp. 29, 53.
42. *The Typographical Journal* (March 1940), p. 296; (April 1940), p. 497; (May 1940), p. 66.
43. *The Typographical Journal* (November 1940), p. 613. Baker was trying to demonstrate here that he had the support of a majority of the printers, the foreign language locals excepted.
44. AFL Executive Council Minutes (February 10–20, 1941), p. 80.
45. It would be useful, in testing this hypothesis, to compare the 1936–1942 period with periods in which one party ran the administration, e.g., 1928–1936 and 1944 to the present, and with other periods in which the executive-council was evenly divided, e.g., 1920–1924 and 1926–1928.
46. See Loft, *The Printing Trades;* Burns, *How Collective Bargaining Works;* National Labor Relations Board, *Collective Bargaining in the Newspaper Industry* (Washington, October 1938); A. R. Porter, *Job Property Rights* (New York, 1954).
47. Baker, *The Typographical Journal,* p. 120.
48. See Loft, *The Printing Trades,* p. 11, and International Typographical Union, *Proceedings of the Eightieth Session* (Colorado Springs, 1936), pp. 62ff.
49. International Typographical Union, *Proceedings of the Eighty-Fourth Session* (New Orleans, 1940), p. 105.
50. *Editor and Publisher,* December 12, 1936, p. 12.
51. Robert K. Burns, "Daily Newspapers" in Twentieth Century Fund, *How Collective Bargaining Works* (New York, 1942), p. 114.
52. National Labor Relations Board, *Collective Bargaining in the Newspaper Industry* (Washington, 1938), pp. 104–110.
53. *The Guild Reporter,* December 15, 1934, p. 9.
54. *Collective Bargaining in the Newspaper Industry,* p. 117.
55. *The Guild Reporter,* February 1, 1935, p. 3.
56. *Collective Bargaining in the Newspaper Industry,* p. 120.
57. *Editor and Publisher,* September 15, 1934, p. 24.
58. *The Guild Reporter,* December 15, 1934, p. 1; April 1, 1935, p. 3; April 15, 1935, p. 8; January 1, 1935, p. 1; February 15, 1935, p. 1; July 1, 1935, p. 1.
59. See, e.g., *ibid.,* March 15, 1935, p. 5; also July 15, 1935, p. 1; July 1, 1935, p. 2; August 1, 1935, p. 5; October 15, 1935, p. 1; November 1, 1935, p. 1; February 1, 1936,

p. 6; March 1, 1936, p. 4; September 15, 1936, p. 1; May 15, 1936, p. 10; June 15, 1936, p. 1; August 1, 1936, p. 2.

60. *Editor and Publisher*, June 6, 1936, p. 24.

61. *The Guild Reporter*, July 1, 1936, p. 3; September 1, 1936, p. 3; November 1, 1936, p. 2.

62. Charges were made that Dave Beck, who dominated the Seattle Council, was supporting the strike because the newspaper had attacked him as a labor racketeer. See *Editor and Publisher*, August 22, 1936, p. 12.

63. *The Guild Reporter*, December 1, 1936, p. 1; November 15, 1936, p. 1; December 1, 1936, p. 1; December 15, 1936, p. 1; January 15, 1937, p. 1; April 15, 1937, p. 1.

64. Associated Press v. National Labor Relations Board, 301 U. S. 103 (1937).

65. Committee for Industrial Organization, *Minutes* (August 10, 1936).

66. *The Guild Reporter*, August 15, 1936, p. 1; September 1, 1936, p. 1; June 20, 1937, pp. 2, 5.

67. *Editor and Publisher*, July 3, 1937, p. 3.

68. *Editor and Publisher*, August 21, 1937, p. 10; February 12, 1938, p. 8; *The Guild Reporter*, February 7, 1938, p. 1.

69. *Collective Bargaining in the Newspaper Industry*, p. 133.

70. *Editor and Publisher*, November 6, 1937, p. 10.

71. *The Guild Reporter*, September 13, 1937, p. 1; December 27, 1937, p. 4; November 15, 1937, p. 1; February 28, 1938, p. 1; May 30, 1938, pp. 1, 4; April 18, 1938, p. 1; June 6, 1938, pp. 5, 6; June 22, 1938, p. 6.

72. *Editor and Publisher*, April 9, 1938, p. 20; August 20, 1938, p. 11; December 10, 1938, p. 9; May 4, 1940, p. 5; September 28, 1940, p. 6; October 26, 1940, p. 46.

73. *The Guild Reporter*, August 1, 1939, p. 6; July 1, 1940, p. 1.

74. *Editor and Publisher*, June 25, 1938, p. 40.

75. American Newspaper Guild, *Proceedings of the Seventh Annual Convention* (Memphis, July 8–12, 1940), p. 13.

76. American Newspaper Guild. *Proceedings of the Eighth Annual Convention* (Detroit, June 23–27, 1941), p. 7.

77. Data for the years 1935–1940 are from American Newspaper Guild, *Proceedings of the Seventh Annual Convention*, p. 17. The figure for 1941 is from American Newspaper Guild, *Proceedings of the Eighth Annual Convention*, p. 7. It should be noted that the book membership data cited in the text are considerably in excess of membership in good standing, which was as follows:

January 1, 1939	8,520
June 1, 1940	8,290
June 1, 1941	10,958

See *The Guild Reporter*, September 1, 1941, p. 7. It was revealed that half of the increase from 1940 to 1941 resulted from reinstatement of old members rather than recruitment of new members.

78. *The Guild Reporter*, June 1, 1940, p. 3.

79. Robert K. Burns, *How Collective Bargaining Works*, p. 114.

80. *The Guild Reporter*, August 1, 1938, p. 7; August 15, 1938, p. 7.

81. *The Guild Reporter*, June 1, 1940, p. 2.

82. American Newspaper Guild, *Proceedings of the Seventh Annual Convention*, p. 146.

83. It was later charged that Max Ways, head of the Philadelphia local and leader of the anti-administration forces, had deserted under pressure from communist members in his delegation. See *Editor and Publisher*, July 20, 1940, p. 6.

84. *The Guild Reporter*, July 19, 1940, p. 1.

85. *Editor and Publisher,* December 14, 1940, p. 9; December 28, 1940, p. 42; January 25, 1941, p. 40.
86. *The Guild Reporter,* January 1, 1941, p. 5; March 1, 1941, p. 1.
87. See *supra,* p. 185.
88. American Newspaper Guild, *Proceedings of the Eighth Annual Convention,* pp. 51, 184, 278. New York contributed 34 of the 85 majority votes.
89. *Ibid.,* pp. 117, 121–122, 125, 146, 160, 161, 238.
90. *The Guild Reporter,* August 15, 1941, p. 1; October 17, 1941, p. 1.
91. Robert K. Burns, *How Collective Bargaining Works,* p. 115.

Chapter 18 Railroad Unionism

1. Texas and New Orleans Railroad Co. v. Brotherhood of Railway and Steamship Clerks, 50 Sup. Ct. 427 (1930).
2. Leonard A. Lecht, *Experience Under Railway Labor Legislation* (New York, 1955), p. 155.
3. Harry Henig, *The Brotherhood of Railway Clerks* (New York, 1937), pp. 202–204.
4. Harold Barger, *The Transportation Industries* (New York, 1951), pp. 76–77.
5. Harry D. Wolf, "Railroads," in Twentieth Century Fund, *How Collective Bargaining Works* (New York, 1942), pp. 319–321.
6. Barger, *The Transportation Industries,* pp. 96–97.
7. Henig, *Railroad Clerks,* p. 202.
8. *The Railway Clerk* (May 1937), p. 190; (October 1937), p. 424; (December 1937), p. 511.
9. Brotherhood of Railway and Steamship Clerks, *Proceedings of the Sixteenth Regular and Second Quadrennial Convention* (Toronto, 1939), p. 11. These figures imply a 1935 membership of 86,000, rather than the 72,500 reported to the AFL for that year.
10. Brotherhood of Railway and Steamship Clerks, *Report of George M. Harrison to the Sixteenth Regular Convention* (1939), p. 7.
11. Brotherhood of Railway and Steamship Clerks, *Report of George M. Harrison to the Seventeenth Regular Convention* (1943), pp. 4, 5.
12. National Mediation Board, *Seventh Annual Report* (June 30, 1941), p. 30.
13. D. W. Hertel, *History of the Brotherhood of Maintenance of Way Employees* (Washington, 1955), p. 166.
14. Data are from a preliminary study of trade union membership by Leo Wolman.
15. Railway Employees' Department, *Official Proceedings, Tenth Convention* (1951), p. 4.
16. Wolf, *How Collective Bargaining Works,* p. 340.
17. For details, see Brotherhood of Railway and Steamship Clerks, *Report of George M. Harrison to the Sixteenth Regular Convention* (1939), pp. 25–45.
18. Association of American Railroads, *The Association of American Railroads, Its Organization and Activities* (Washington, undated).
19. J. Elmer Monroe, *Railroad Men and Wages* (Washington, 1947), pp. 17, 24, 29, 58.
20. Brotherhood of Railway and Steamship Clerks, *Report of George M. Harrison to the Sixteenth Regular Convention* (1939), p. 64.
21. Wolf, *How Collective Bargaining Works,* pp. 341, 342.
22. See, e.g., *The Railway Clerk* (December 1937), p. 517.
23. Lecht, *Experience,* p. 159.
24. The board said in this respect: ". . . the level of wages of railway labor is not

high when compared with wage levels in other industries. Nor do wage trends show that railway wages have advanced proportionately greater than wages in other industries. Instead they seem to show a slight lag, though, on the other hand, they show greater resistance to decline than wages in other industries." *Report of the Emergency Board Appointed September 27, 1938*, p. 55.

25. Lecht, *Experience in Legislation*, pp. 160–161.

26. Monroe, *Railroad Men*, pp. 17, 58.

27. Brotherhood of Railway and Steamship Clerks, *Report of George M. Harrison to the Seventeenth Regular Convention* (1943), p. 38.

28. See *Report of the Emergency Board Appointed September 10, 1941*, pp. 15–20, 76.

29. Brotherhood of Railway and Steamship Clerks, *Report of George M. Harrison to the Seventeenth Regular Convention* (1943), pp. 44–47.

30. Lecht, *Experience in Legislation*, p. 166.

31. Jacob J. Kaufman, *Collective Bargaining in the Railroad Industry* (New York, 1954), pp. 154, 157.

32. Lecht, *Experience in Legislation*, pp. 121, 130.

33. *The Railway Clerk* (December 1937), p. 512.

34. Brotherhood of Railway and Steamship Clerks, *Report of George M. Harrison to the Sixteenth Regular Convention* (1939), pp. 84–85.

35. Lecht, *Experience in Legislation*, pp. 135–140.

36. The highly important 1934 amendments to the Railway Labor Act belong to a period earlier than the one we are considering.

37. *The Railway Clerk* (January 1938), p. 5.

38. See, e.g., Brotherhood of Railway and Steamship Clerks, *Report of George M. Harrison to the Sixteenth Regular Convention* (1939), p. 110.

39. Brotherhood of Railway and Steamship Clerks, *Proceedings of the Seventeenth Regular Convention*, p. 273.

40. Wolf, *How Collective Bargaining Works*, p. 374.

41. From 1936 to 1941, inclusive, total man-days lost due to labor disputes in the railroad industry amounted to 72,200. Only 2,950 workers were involved in work stoppages. Kaufman, *Collective Bargaining*, p. 79.

42. *The Railway Clerk* (May 1940), pp. 185, 186.

43. National Mediation Board, *Seventh Annual Report* (1941), pp. 28–32.

44. See, e.g., the recommendations of a six-man committee, three from labor and three from management, appointed by President Roosevelt in 1938 to consider relevant legislation, in Brotherhood of Railway and Steamship Clerks, *Report of George M. Harrison to the Sixteenth Regular Convention* (1939), pp. 126–128. Many of these recommendations were embodied in the Transportation Act of 1940.

45. *The Railway Clerk* (January 1939), p. 8.

46. Wolf, *How Collective Bargaining Works*, p. 379.

47. For an excellent treatment of this problem, see Lecht, *Experience in Legislation*, chap. XIII.

48. Henig, *The Brotherhood*, p. 186.

49. Brotherhood of Railway and Steamship Clerks, *Proceedings of the Seventeenth Regular Convention* (1943), p. 7.

Chapter 19   Some General Aspects of the Labor Movement

1. Both the mechanical and conceptual problems are discussed in Leo Wolman, *Ebb and Flow in Trade Unionism* (New York, 1936), Ch. 1; and in "Limitations of Union Membership Data," *Monthly Labor Review* (November 1955), p. 1265.

2. Congress of Industrial Organizations, *Proceedings of the Third Constitutional Convention* (Atlantic City, November 18, 1940), p. 32.

3. CIO Executive Board Minutes (November 23, 1940), p. 207.

4. See *supra,* p. 177.

5. The sources are set out in the individual chapters above.

6. CIO Executive Board Minutes (June 3–5, 1942), p. 532.

7. *Ibid.,* (June 13–15, 1939), p. 26; (March 24, 1942), p. 219; (June 3–5, 1942), p. 527.

8. *Supra,* p. 493.

9. See Mary Klemm, "Some Rivals of the AFL and CIO," unpublished manuscript (University of Wisconsin, 1943).

10. Milton Derber and Edwin Young, *Labor and the New Deal* (Madison, 1957), pp. 14, 15.

11. Leo Wolman, *Ebb and Flow in Trade Unionism* (New York, 1936), pp. 90, 130.

12. Leo Troy, *Distribution of Union Membership Among the States, 1939 and 1953* (National Bureau of Economic Research, New York, 1957).

13. Frank T. DeVyver, "The Present Status of Labor Unions in the South," *Southern Economic Journal* (April 1939), p. 485.

14. For a full discussion of these points, see F. Ray Marshall, "History of Labor Organization in the South," unpublished manuscript (University of California, Berkeley, 1955), esp. pp. 435ff.

15. Congress of Industrial Organizations, *Proceedings of the First Constitutional Convention* (Pittsburgh, November 14–18, 1938), p. 169.

16. Congress of Industrial Organizations, *Report of President John L. Lewis to the Third Constitutional Convention* (November 18, 1940), p. 10.

17. Congress of Industrial Organizations, *Proceedings of the Fourth Constitutional Convention* (Detroit, November 17–22, 1941), p. 306.

18. Marshall, *History,* p. 373.

19. Frank T. DeVyver, "The Present Status of Labor Unions in the South — 1948," *Southern Economic Journal* (July 1949), p. 1.

20. AFL Executive Council Minutes (January 24-February 8, 1938), p. 182; (April 25-May 5, 1938), p. 117.

21. *Ibid.* (September 30-October 10, 1940), p. 121; (October 5–17, 1941), p. 2.

22. American Federation of Labor, *Report of the Proceedings of the Sixty-First Annual Convention* (Seattle, 1941), p. 388.

23. Data are from annual reports of the AFL secretary-treasurer.

24. Committee for Industrial Organization, *Minutes* (November 7-8, 1936).

25. Letter from John Brophy to Sidney Hillman, April 15, 1936.

26. Report of John Brophy to the CIO Meeting, October 11, 1937 (mimeographed).

27. CIO Executive Board Minutes (June 3–5, 1942), p. 501; United Mine Workers of America, *Proceedings of the Thirty-Seventh Constitutional Convention* (Cincinnati, October 6–14, 1942), pp. 154–55.

28. CIO Executive Board Minutes (June 3–5, 1940), p. 2; (March 24, 1942), p. 242; (June 3–5, 1942), p. 374.

29. United Mine Workers of America, *Proceedings of the Thirty-Seventh Constitutional Convention,* p. 150.

30. CIO Executive Board Minutes (June 3–5, 1942), p. 374.

31. International Ladies' Garment Workers' Union, *Report and Record of the Twenty-Fourth Convention* (1940), p. 42.

32. AFL Executive Council Minutes (January 24-February 8, 1938), p. 192.

33. It should be noted in this connection that the Steel Workers' Organizing Committee repaid to the United Mine Workers by the end of 1941 a loan of $601,000 which

had been made to assist in the prosecution of the Little Steel strikes. See United Mine Workers of America, *Proceedings of the Thirty-Seventh Constitutional Convention*, p. 150.

34. Philip Taft, *The AFL in the Time of Gompers* (New York, 1957), chap. XVIII.

35. *Supra*, p. 95.

36. American Federation of Labor, *Report of Proceedings of the Fifty-Fifth Annual Convention* (Atlantic City, October 7–19, 1935), p. 759; 146; 774–775.

37. Matthew Josephson, *Sidney Hillman* (New York, 1952), pp. 394–95.

38. For a brief history of the American Labor Party, see *supra*, pp. 318–320.

39. AFL Executive Council Minutes (August 21-September 2, 1937), p. 35.

40. American Federation of Labor, *Report of the Proceedings of the Fifty-Eighth Annual Convention* (Houston, 1938), p. 405.

41. Congress of Industrial Organizations, *Proceedings of the First Constitutional Convention* (Pittsburgh, November 14–18, 1938), p. 230.

42. Congress of Industrial Organizations, *Proceedings of the Second Constitutional Convention* (October 10–13, 1939), p. 184.

43. CIO Executive Board Minutes (November 15–23, 1940), p. 14.

44. *Supra*, p. 318.

45. Congress of Industrial Organizations, *Proceedings of the Third Constitutional Convention* (November 21, 1940), p. 50.

46. AFL Executive Council Minutes (January 27-February 9, 1940), pp. 56, 118.

47. This statement may require some modification. The AFL, on occasion, had intervened in political campaigns in furtherance of its policy of punishing its enemies. In 1906, Samuel Gompers actively campaigned against Congressman Charles E. Littlefield of Maine, a bitter opponent of organized labor, and succeeded in reducing his majority. See Philip Taft, *The AFL in the Time of Gompers* (New York, 1957), p. 295. However, these attempts were quite feeble in comparison with the New Deal experience.

48. Max M. Kampelman, "Labor in Politics," in Industrial Relations Research Association, *Interpreting the Labor Movement* (1952), p. 173.

49. Harry A. Millis and Emily Clark Brown, *From the Wagner Act to Taft-Hartley* (Chicago, 1950), pp. 80, 89.

50. See American Federation of Labor, *Report of the Proceedings of the Fifty-Sixth Annual Convention* (Tampa, 1936), pp. 153–58.

51. American Federation of Labor, *Report of the Proceedings of the Fifty-Seventh Annual Convention* (Denver, 1937), p. 429.

52. AFL Executive Council Minutes (August 22-September 2, 1938), p. 6.

53. *Ibid.*, p. 96. The letter was dated August 25, 1938.

54. *Ibid.*, pp. 135, 140.

55. Congress of Industrial Organizations, *Proceedings of the Second Constitutional Convention* (October 10–13, 1939), p. 228.

56. American Federation of Labor, *Report of the Proceedings of the Fifty-Ninth Annual Convention* (Cincinnati, October 2–13, 1939), pp. 147–55.

57. American Federation of Labor, *Report of the Proceedings of the Sixty-First Annual Convention* (Seattle, October 6–16, 1941), p. 522.

58. Letter from Philip Murray to Franklin D. Roosevelt, July 30, 1941, CIO files.

59. Millis and Brown, *From the Wagner Act*, pp. 142, 148, 151, 156.

60. American Federation of Labor, *Report of the Proceedings of the Sixty-First Annual Convention* (Seattle, 1941), p. 115.

61. Congress of Industrial Organizations, *Proceedings of the Fourth Constitutional Convention* (Detroit, November 17–22, 1941), p. 81.

62. For a good discussion of this point, see Derber and Young, *Labor*, pp. 295ff.

63. Millis and Brown, *From the Wagner Act*, pp. 252–60.

64. There is a voluminous literature dealing with the effects of the NLRA upon collective bargaining and trade unionism. In addition to numerous, almost annual Congressional hearings, to endless arguments in union and employer publications, and to the previously cited summary by Millis and Brown, the interested reader is referred especially to Walter Galenson, *Rival Unionism in the United States* (New York, 1940); Charles O. Gregory, *Labor and the Law* (New York, 1946); Joseph Rosenfarb, *The National Labor Policy and How It Works* (New York, 1940).

65. See AFL Executive Council Minutes (February 8–19, 1937), p. 147; (August 21–September 2, 1937), p. 104; (October 3–16, 1937), p. 1.

66. American Federation of Labor, *Report of the Proceedings of the Fifty-Eight Annual Convention* (Houston, October 3–13, 1938), p. 154.

67. Congress of Industrial Organizations, *Proceedings of the First Constitutional Convention* (Pittsburgh, November 14–18, 1938), p. 255.

68. For a more detailed treatment of the AFL and the Fair Labor Standards Act, see Derber and Young, *Labor*, chap. 6.

69. AFL Executive Council Minutes (January 15–29, 1936), p. 132.

70. AFL Executive Council Minutes (May 5–20, 1936), p. 210.

71. AFL Executive Council Minutes (February 8–19, 1937), p. 164; (February 10–20, 1941), pp. 67, 69.

72. The AFL, for example, adopted a resolution expressing its opposition to reciprocal trade agreements "which discriminate against American workers." AFL Executive Council Minutes (April 25-May 5, 1938), p. 179.

73. AFL Executive Council Minutes (January 27-February 9, 1940), p. 148; (May 13–21, 1940).

74. See CIO Executive Board Minutes (June 3–5, 1940), p. 211.

75. See Joel Seidman, *American Labor from Defense to Reconversion* (Chicago, 1953), p. 26.

76. See *supra*, p. 525.

77. Congress of Industrial Organizations, *Daily Proceedings of the Third Constitutional Convention* (Atlantic City, November 19, 1940), p. 24.

78. Congress of Industrial Organizations, *Proceedings of the Fourth Constitutional Convention* (Detroit, November 17–22, 1941), p. 41.

79. When a resolution calling for the AFL to take the lead in setting up labor-management councils was discussed by the AFL Executive Council, the following was recorded: "Vice-President [George] Harrison stated that the railroad organizations are not all sponsoring this resolution. He stated as an observer, close to the scene of activity, he reached the conclusion that this union management cooperation plan as practiced on the railroads is nothing but a vitality sapping arrangement for the labor movement. Vice-President Harrison contended it is the function of our organizations to represent the interests of the worker and our unions grow and thrive on the opposition within the industry, and economic injustice. Vice-President Harrison stated he has never yet found an employer in the railroad industry who was willing to cooperate to do something for the good of the working man. They always claim that wages and conditions are a bargaining question and not a matter of cooperation." AFL Executive Council Minutes (February 10–20, 1941), p. 101. The resolution was not adopted.

80. Seidman, *American Labor*, pp. 28–29.

81. AFL Executive Council Minutes (February 10–20, 1941), p. 14.

82. Seidman, *American Labor*, p. 70.

83. AFL Executive Council Minutes (May 19–28, 1941), p. 121.

84. American Federation of Labor, *Report of the Proceedings of the Sixty-First Annual Convention* (Seattle, October 6–16, 1941), p. 404.

85. *Supra*, p. 225.

86. Seidman, *American Labor*, p. 72.

87. See Philip Taft, *The AFL in the Time of Gompers* (New York, 1957), pp. 234–37.

88. AFL Executive Council Minutes (January 27-February 9, 1940), p. 67.

89. John Hutchinson, "Corruption in American Trade Unions," *The Political Quarterly* (July–September, 1957), pp. 5–6.

90. Joel Seidman, *Union Rights and Union Duties* (New York, 1943), pp. 52–53.

91. AFL Executive Council Minutes (May 19–28, 1941), p. 130.

92. American Federation of Labor. *Report of the Proceedings of the Sixty-First Annual Convention* (Seattle, October 6–16, 1941), p. 572.

93. American Federation of Labor, *Report of Proceedings of the Sixtieth Annual Convention* (New Orleans, November 18–29, 1940), pp. 65, 504.

94. For background information on Fay, see Harold Seidman, *Labor Czars* (New York, 1938), pp. 162–65.

95. American Federation of Labor, *Report of the Proceedings of the Sixtieth Annual Convention* (New Orleans, November 18–29, 1940), p. 505.

96. Harold Seidman, *Labor Czars,* pp. 167–70.

97. AFL Executive Council Minutes (February 10–20, 1941), p. 53; (May 19–28, 1941), p. 113; (September 30-October 10, 1940), p. 128.

98. American Federation of Labor, *Report of the Proceedings of the Sixty-First Annual Convention* (Seattle, October 6–16, 1941), pp. 70, 543.

99. For a good analytical account of the evolution of AFL policy toward corruption, see Philip Taft, *Corruption and Racketeering in the Labor Movement* (Ithaca, New York, 1958).

100. The best treatment of this question for the period with which we are concerned is Herbert R. Northrup, *Organized Labor and the Negro* (New York, 1944).

101. Northrup, *Organized Labor,* pp. 2–5.

102. In addition to Northrup, *Organized Labor,* the reader is referred to Sterling D. Spero and Abram L. Harris, *The Black Worker* (New York, 1931); H. R. Cayton and G. S. Mitchell, *Black Workers and the New Unions* (Chapel Hill, N. C., 1939).

103. Northrup, *Organized Labor,* pp. 14–15; chapters V, VII.

104. Brailsford R. Brazeal, *The Brotherhood of Sleeping Car Porters* (New York, 1946), pp. 129–33, 138–39, 145, 149.

105. American Federation of Labor, *Report of the Proceedings of the Fifty-Fourth Annual Convention* (San Francisco, October 1–12, 1934), p. 330.

106. American Federation of Labor, *Report of the Proceedings of the Fifty-Fifth Annual Convention* (Atlantic City, October 7–19, 1935), pp. 807–809, 813–819.

107. American Federation of Labor, *Report of the Proceedings of the Fifty-Sixth Annual Convention* (Tampa, November 16–27, 1936), p. 658.

108. American Federation of Labor, *Report of the Proceedings of the Fifty-Eighth Annual Convention* (Houston, October 3–13, 1938), p. 300.

109. American Federation of Labor, *Report of the Proceedings of the Sixtieth Annual Convention* (New Orleans, November 18–29, 1940), pp. 509, 645–49.

110. Northrup, *Organized Labor,* p. 85.

111. Samuel Enders Warren, "*The Negro in the American Labor Movement,*" unpublished manuscript (University of Wisconsin, 1941), pp. 490–94.

112. Joel Seidman, *American Labor From Defense to Reconversion* (Chicago, 1953), pp. 166, 168–172.

113. American Federation of Labor, *Report of the Proceedings of the Sixty-First Annual Convention* (Seattle, October 6–16, 1941), pp. 479, 480, 482, 490.

114. See Northrup, *Organized Labor,* chap. II.

115. Northrup, *Organized Labor,* pp. 100–101.

116. This section is based largely upon Stuart Jamieson, *Labor Unionism in American Agriculture,* Bureau of Labor Statistics, Bulletin No. 836 (Washington, 1945).

117. American Federation of Labor, *Report of Proceedings of the Fifty-Fifth Annual Convention* (Atlantic City, October 7–19, 1935), p. 371.

118. American Federation of Labor, *Report of Proceedings of the Fifty-Sixth Annual Convention* (Tampa, November 16–27, 1936), pp. 583–92.

119. AFL Executive Council Minutes (May 23–30, 1937), p. 111.

120. Jamieson, *Labor Unionism,* p. 27.

121. Up to the end of 1941, the Cannery Workers received $88,000 in cash and services from the CIO. Congress of Industrial Organizations, *Executive Board Minutes* (June 3–5, 1942), p. 519.

122. American Federation of Labor, *Report of the Proceedings of the Fifty-Eighth Annual Convention* (Houston, October 3–13, 1938), p. 84.

123. Max M. Kampelman, *The Communist Party vs. the CIO* (New York, 1957), p. 173.

124. American Federation of Labor, *Report of the Proceedings of the Sixtieth Annual Convention* (New Orleans, 1940), p. 53.

125. Jamieson, *Labor Unionism,* pp. 190, 314, 323.

126. AFL Executive Council Minutes (September 30–October 10, 1940), p. 57.

127. Quoted by Jamieson, *Labor Unionism,* p. 325.

128. Alexander Morin, *The Organizability of Farm Labor in the United States* (Cambridge, Mass., 1952), p. 20.

129. Morin, *Organizability, passim.*

130. See Lewis L. Lorwin, *The International Labor Movement* (New York, 1953), chap. 10, 13.

131. American Federation of Labor, *Report of Proceedings of the Fifty-Fifth Annual Convention* (Washington, 1935), p. 717.

132. AFL Executive Council Minutes (May 5–20, 1936), p. 109; (October 8–21, 1936), p. 9; (August 21–September 2, 1937), p. 139.

133. American Federation of Labor, *Report of Proceedings of the Fifty-Seventh Annual Convention* (1937), p. 195.

134. AFL Executive Council Minutes (August 21–September 2, 1937), p. 165; (January 24–February 8, 1938), pp. 2, 25, 140.

135. Lorwin, *Labor Movement,* p. 184.

136. American Federation of Labor, *Report of the Proceedings of the Fifty-Ninth Annual Convention* (Cincinnati, 1939), p. 223.

137. AFL Executive Council Minutes (April 25–May 5, 1938), p. 71.

138. American Federation of Labor, *Report of the Proceedings of the Fifty-Ninth Annual Convention,* p. 227.

139. Congress of Industrial Organizations, *Daily Proceedings of the Second Constitutional Convention* (San Francisco, October 10–13, 1939), p. 115.

140. AFL Executive Council Minutes (May 13–21, 1940), p. 45.

141. CIO Executive Board Minutes (June 3–5, 1940), p. 178.

142. Congress of Industrial Organizations, *Daily Minutes of the Third Constitutional Convention* (Atlantic City, November 21, 1940), pp. 24, 26.

143. American Federation of Labor, *Report of Proceedings of the Sixtieth Annual Convention* (New Orleans, November 18–29, 1940), p. 202.

144. American Federation of Labor, *Report of Proceedings of the Sixty-First Annual Convention* (Seattle, October 6–16, 1941), p. 198.

145. Congress of Industrial Organizations, *Proceedings of the Fourth Constitutional Convention* (Detroit, November 17–22, 1941), p. 40.

146. Selig Perlman, "Labor and the New Deal in Historical Perspective," in Derber and Young, *Labor,* p. 369.

147. John T. Dunlop, "Structural Changes in the American Labor Movement and Industrial Relations System," *Proceedings of the Ninth Annual Meeting of the Industrial Relations Research Association* (1956), p. 14.

148. Introduction to Edward Levinson, *Labor on the March* (New York, 1956 edition), p. xiv.

Index

Addes, George, 131, 132, 151, 155, 161, 165, 171, 172, 178, 188–191

The Advance, 298, 316

Affiliated Dress Manufacturers, Inc., 305

Agar Packing and Provision Co., 372

Agricultural Workers' Industrial Union, 631

Airline Mechanics' Association, 509

Alabama Fuel and Iron Company, 195

Alabama State Federation of Labor, 14, 21

Alfange, Dean, 319

Alinsky, Saul, 214, 233, 334

Allen, Barney, 499

Allied Metal Mechanics, 496

Allis-Chalmers Company, 188, 189; local, 164, 188, 189

Alma Mills, 339

Almeda County Central Labor Council, 476

Alston Coal Company, 210

Aluminum Workers, 32, 38

Amalgamated Association of Iron, Steel and Tin Workers of North America, 16, 44, 75–84, 86, 87, 97, 114, 119, 120, 123, 328, 492, 532

Amalgamated Association of Street Railway Employees, 38

Amalgamated Clothing Workers, 3–5, 16, 32, 38, 44, 45, 52, 59, 60, 62, 63, 73, 84, 283–286, 288–290, 292–300, 302, 313, 315, 316, 318, 333, 334, 336, 347, 423, 585, 599, 606, 607; Local 300, 287, 563

Amalgamated Lithographers' Union, 530

Amalgamated Meat Cutters and Butcher Workmen of North America, 14, 349, 351–354, 357, 361, 362, 364–369, 372–375, 377, 492, 588; Local 206, 357; Armour local, 366

America First Committee, 189

American Bemberg Rayon Corporation, 347

American Civil Liberties Union, 485

American Communications Association, 32, 38, 441

American Congress of Labor, 50, 51

American Editorial Association, 558

American Federation of Government Employees, 38

American Federation of Hosiery Workers, 327, 329, 333, 343

American Federation of Labor: 1934 convention, 627; 1935 convention (Atlantic City), 3–6, 53, 77, 78, 269, 351, 606, 608, 631, 644; 1936 convention (Tampa), 9, 21, 27–31, 313, 627, 632; 1937 convention (Denver), 33, 34, 43, 56, 636; 1938 convention (Houston), 46, 47, 543, 607, 627; 1939 convention, 56, 57, 544; 1940 convention, 64, 317, 318, 597, 624, 638; 1941 convention (Seattle), 66, 629; Defense Fund, 597, 598; Executive Council, 6, 8, 10–12, 14–21, 23, 24, 26, 28–31, 35–37, 39, 43, 44, 46, 48, 49, 52, 54, 55, 63, 64, 66, 67, 70, 73, 75–82, 124–126, 130, 132, 145, 209, 240, 241, 243, 245, 267, 268, 283, 285, 287, 313, 314, 317, 318, 326, 342, 355, 382, 415, 435, 436, 441, 464, 475, 480, 488, 489–492, 495, 504, 506, 507, 510, 511, 517, 525, 542–544, 546, 553, 580, 597, 606–608, 612, 613, 616–618, 620–624, 626–628, 631–637, 644; Federal Local 17742, 287

American Federation of Radio Workers, 239

American Federation of Teachers, 21, 28

American Federation of Textile Operatives, 346

American Federationist, 595

American Iron and Steel Institute, 85

American Labor Party, 294, 312, 318–320, 606–609

American League Against War and Fascism, 251

American Merchant Marine Institute, 442

American Newspaper Guild, 21, 32, 38, 47, 319, 530, 548–565 *passim;* Boston local, 561; Los Angeles local, 562, 563; Minneapolis local, 561; New York local, 556, 559–563; Philadelphia local, 561, 563; St. Louis local, 561; San Francisco local, 559, 563; Seattle local, 563; Washington, D. C., local, 561, 563

American Newspaper Publishers' Association, 532, 548, 560